in M. Shapiro
sity of California
e

The Supreme Court
and Constitutional Rights

Readings in Constitutional Law

p - 21
P.
black
white

Library of Congress Catalog No. 67-21033

Copyright © 1967 by Scott, Foresman and Company
Printed in the United States of America
All Rights Reserved
Regional offices of Scott, Foresman and Company are located
in Atlanta, Dallas, Glenview, Palo Alto, and Oakland, N.J.

Preface

Obviously a collection of readings of this length cannot supply the comprehensive and detailed coverage of a textbook. On the other hand it is designed to be something more than a random selection of "good pieces" to be used as an addendum to a casebook. With or without a casebook, *The Supreme Court and Constitutional Rights* should provide a student, even one totally new to constitutional law, with a survey of the most important current cases, doctrines, and issues in the area of constitutional rights. While a certain amount of technical discourse is unavoidable, most of the materials included deal with important general questions of public policy. And one of the blessings of legal scholarship is that legal authors usually feel the duty of providing a brief and easily understandable survey of the background material about which the reader needs to know in order to follow the main argument. To allow greater ease of reading for the student, footnote material that is not directly relevant to the text has been omitted.

This book is substantive rather than methodological. It focuses on what the Supreme Court has done and ought to do about constitutional rights, not on what methods we ought to use to find out what the Supreme Court is doing. A brief section on research methods and problems is appended at the end.

The reader new to materials such as these should remember that legal writers are accustomed to adversary proceedings—they are likely to push their own position hard and seek to undermine their immediate or potential adversary, rather than to present a balanced view. The reader should also remember that the traditions of legal scholarship in this country are very high and that the pursuit of truth is not limited to those who wear white lab coats. Do not make the mistake of thinking that lawyers are simply engaged in cynical word games on behalf of their clients; but do not forget that the task of the lawyer is to convince you that his version of truth, and his only, is the correct one.

Martin M. Shapiro
University of California
at Irvine

Contents

Chapter I Freedom of Speech

Chapter II Freedom of Religion

Chapter III Reapportionment

Chapter IV Rights of Negroes

Chapter V Civil Rights, Expatriation, and Foreign Travel

Chapter VI The Rights of Accused Persons

Further Research 231

FREEDOM OF SPEECH

The subjects of this book are the Supreme Court and constitutional rights. The plural is used deliberately because two ranges of questions coexist here. The first concerns the desired scope of constitutional rights. For example, should Communists be allowed complete freedom of speech if they are going to urge the violent overthrow of our government? Should the indigent be provided with free legal counsel if it is going to cost taxpayers millions of dollars to defray the costs of frivolous and dilatory appeals by convicts who have nothing better to do? Should the police be held to standards of procedures so strict that they seriously hamper the suppression of dope peddling?

The second range of questions concerns the persons who should decide the first range and enforce the decisions. For instance, should the Supreme Court or Congress decide how much protection we need from Communism? Should the Supreme Court—an arm of the national government—tell the states how to operate their own criminal law machinery?

Throughout this book the reader will find a constant conflict between two schools of thought, often labeled *judicial modesty* and *judicial activism*. The judicially modest argue as follows: Congress, whose members are elected by the people, and not the Supreme Court (which is appointed for life), is the democratic branch of government. Judicial review—the power to declare acts of Congress unconstitutional—is not mentioned in the Constitution. In the very act of passing a statute, Congress declares that it is constitutional, for congressmen also take an oath to uphold the Constitution and would not pass an unconstitutional act. When the Supreme Court declares an act of Congress unconstitutional and thus void, it is simply disagreeing with Congress on a question of public policy, for constitutional decisions are largely policy decisions in disguise. In such disputes, why should the undemocratic branch of government be allowed to thwart the will of the majority as expressed by Congress, particularly when the legislature has the time and means to study questions of public policy far more thoroughly than do the courts? Thus the Supreme Court should not declare acts of Congress unconstitutional, and the Constitution, including the Bill of Rights, should be viewed as a moral admonition to Congress to do what is in the best interests of all the people. Parallel to this argument is the view that since, in a federal system, the states are to retain power over their own domestic affairs and act on the majority will of their own citizens, the Supreme Court, as both an undemocratic agency and a part of the national government, should not overrule the wishes of the states any more than is absolutely necessary to maintain the proper powers of the national government.

Judicial activists, on the other hand, argue as follows: The Constitution is the highest law of the land. When two laws are in conflict, it is a normal part of a court's business to decide which shall be upheld. Thus, when a statute and the Constitution are in conflict, naturally the Supreme Court must decide between them, and just as naturally it must always uphold the higher law, the Constitution. Although judicial review is not mentioned in the Constitution, it is implied there, for without review the Constitution is merely a scrap of paper which Congress could ignore at will. Besides, Congress is often *not* the voice of the majority but the spokesman for special interest groups. The Supreme Court may better represent the majority view or the views of those minorities, such as Negroes, who are not represented fully enough in Congress to have their rights protected there. Since the Court has the power, hallowed by long historical acceptance, to right certain wrongs in our society, it should take the responsibility for doing so, particularly when Congress or the state legislatures refuse to right those wrongs.

These two sets of issues, the scope of constitutional rights and the role of the Supreme Court, have naturally tended to become closely interconnected. If the Court constructs very strict standards of constitutionality very protective of individual rights, it is much more likely to find acts of Congress unconstitutional than if it adopts looser standards. This interconnection is particularly evident in the area of freedom of speech. In each case the justice and the outside observer must ask himself both how much freedom of speech should there be and how much should the Supreme Court do about guaranteeing the desired degree of freedom of speech.

The exchange of ideas between Laurent B. Frantz and Wallace Mendelson presented below focuses on the problem of the balancing of conflicting interests, which will recur in some of the later materials in this book. In every society there are many interests held in varying degrees by groups and individuals: e.g., the interests in, valuing of, or concern for free speech, peace and quiet, protection of private property, fair trial, national security, good highways, a decent minimum wage, and adequate free public education. When two of these interests come into conflict, is it always the duty of the government to balance them against one another, or are some interests absolutely protected by the Constitution no matter how important the interests with which they conflict?

Underlying this debate is the conflict between modesty and activism. If the Supreme Court takes the position that the First Amendment absolutely forbids any interference with freedom of speech, it will encounter many instances in which it will either have to declare a statute regulating speech unconstitutional or flatly confess that while it believes the statute to be unconstitutional, it is unwilling to interfere with the decision of the legislature. If the Court adopts the position that the Constitution allows some infringements on freedom of speech when the government has some very important interest, like national security, to balance against the infringement, then the Court can insist that it is maintaining judicial review but can find in each individual case that Congress had enough reason to regulate the speech in question to justify the infringement.

Thus the Court could maintain the facade of judicial protection for freedom of speech while never actually interfering with congressional regulation. Among the large number of distinguished proponents of judicial modesty only one, Learned Hand, has ever flatly come out in favor of totally doing away with judicial enforcement of the Bill of Rights. There is absolutely no sign of the Court's formally abandoning its powers of judicial review. Balancing of interests is, therefore, crucial to the judicially modest in insuring that the Supreme Court can, within its formally acknowledged duty to uphold the Constitution, actually allow Congress to do whatever it pleases about subversive and other obnoxious forms of speech.

Selection 1
_____

The First Amendment in the Balance

Laurent B. Frantz

The selection below and the three that follow represent a debate which is somewhat imbalanced, since it consists of two long articles by Laurent B. Frantz, a judicial activist, and two short replies by Wallace Mendelson, a proponent of judicial modesty whose views closely parallel those of the late Justice Felix Frankfurter. Those wishing to redress this difference in bulk might wish to read Mendelson's book, *Justices Black and Frankfurter: Conflict in the Court,** which triggered the exchange presented here.

Frantz believes that the courts should not employ the balancing of interests as "a substitute for an effort to find a rule or principle that can guide decision"; he does not contend, however, that the courts should *never* balance. Frantz draws a distinction between balancing as a *principle* (which is not acceptable) and balancing as the technique for choosing between alternatives that are, in principle, equally permissible (which procedure is acceptable). Mendelson comes out more strongly in favor of balancing, which he considers the essence of the judicial process—as long as it is done in the light of accepted legal principles.

"Let us consider, my Lords, that arbitrary power has seldom or never been introduced into any country at once. It must be introduced by slow degrees, and as it were step by step, lest the people should see its approach. The barriers and fences of the people's liberty must be plucked up one by one, and some plausible pretences must be found for removing or hoodwinking, one after another, those sentries who are posted by the constitution of a free country for warning the people of their danger."—Erskine, in defense of Thomas Paine, in 1792, for publication of *The Rights of Man.* WALFORD, SPEECHES OF THOMAS LORD ERSKINE 336 (1870).

The first amendment provides that "Congress shall make no law...abridging the freedom of speech...." In determining whether this provision has been violated, should a court "balance" the "competing interests" involved in the particular case?

Such an approach, for which Mr. Justice Frankfurter has been the chief spokesman, has won the support of five Justices[1] in a number of recent Supreme Court decisions, despite vehement dissent led by Mr. Justice Black. It remains obscure whether that majority regards "balancing" as applicable to all first amendment cases and, if not,

to what class of cases it applies. How other cases are to be decided is problematical and at the present writing it is not clear whether this majority has survived the retirement of Mr. Justice Whittaker and his replacement by Mr. Justice White.

The language which ultimately came to be cited as the authority for balancing originated in 1939 in *Schneider v. State,*[2] in an opinion by Justice Roberts for a majority of eight, which included Justices Black and Douglas as well as Mr. Justice Frankfurter. The problem was the constitutionality of certain city ordinances prohibiting handbill distribution. After characterizing freedom of speech and press as "fundamental personal rights and liberties" whose exercise "lies at the foundation of free government," Justice Roberts continued:[3]

"In every case, therefore, where legislative abridgment of the rights is asserted, the courts should be astute to examine the effect of the challenged leg-

"The First Amendment in the Balance" by Laurent B. Frantz, 71 *Yale Law Journal* 1424 (1962). Reprinted by permission of the Yale Law Journal Company and Fred B. Rothman & Company.

*Wallace Mendelson, *Justices Black and Frankfurter: Conflict in the Court* (Chicago: University of Chicago Press, 1961).

islation. Mere legislative preferences or beliefs respecting matters of public convenience may well support regulation directed at other personal activities, but be insufficient to justify such as diminishes the exercise of rights so vital to the maintenance of democratic institutions. And so, as cases arise, the delicate and difficult task falls upon the courts to weigh the circumstances and to appraise the substantiality of the reasons advanced in support of the regulation of the free enjoyment of the rights."

These were nondiscriminatory ordinances. Distribution by handbill was denied equally to all points of view, while all other means of dissemination remained equally accessible under the ordinance. Taken in context, the essence of the language—"weigh the circumstances and appraise the substantiality"—was that, when a means of communicating with the public is cut off, the courts will demand a more substantial justification, and give less weight to the legislative judgment, than in the case of "regulation directed at other personal activities."[4] The language was subsequently cited for the same purpose in other strongly pro-free speech decisions,[5] including one written by Mr. Justice Black.[6]

This balancing language was first turned to a different purpose in 1950 in *American Communications Ass'n v. Douds*,[7] which dealt with the constitutionality of the non-Communist affidavit provision of the Taft-Hartley Act. Unlike the problem treated in *Schneider* of nondiscriminatory elimination of a particular means of reaching the public, in *Douds* particular persons were singled out for unfavorable special treatment on the basis of their beliefs, membership, or affiliation.

Chief Justice Vinson, for the majority, began by conceding that the affidavit "necessarily" had a deterrent effect on freedom of speech and that the problem could not be disposed of merely by calling the governmental action the withholding of a privilege. He further conceded that the view expressed by Justices Brandeis and Holmes was the command of the first amendment: "Only...when force is very likely to follow an utterance before there is a chance for counter-argument to have effect may that utterance be punished or prevented."[8] But he found two reasons for not heeding this command. One was that "force may and must be met with force" and that the statute under consideration was "designed to protect the public not against what Communists and others identified therein advocate or believe, but against what Congress has concluded that they have done and are likely to do again."[9] The other was that "When the effects of a statute or ordinance upon

the exercise of First Amendment freedoms is relatively small and the public interest to be protected is substantial, it is obvious that a rigid test requiring a showing of imminent danger to the security of the nation is an absurdity."[10]

"[T]he right of the public to be protected from the evils of conduct, even though First Amendment rights of persons or groups are thereby in some manner infringed," the Chief Justice asserted, "has received frequent and consistent recognition by this Court."[11] But of the cases he cited to illustrate and prove this "frequent and consistent recognition," two did not even recognize that first amendment rights had been infringed in any manner,[12] and the remainder dealt only with conduct required[13] or prohibited[14] without reference to speech, or with regulation such as that in *Schneider*, where the government's action was neutral in its application to different points of view.[15] From this collection of cases, unlike each other and unlike the case before the Court, the Chief Justice drew the following generalization:[16]

"When particular conduct is regulated in the interest of public order, and the regulation results in an indirect, conditional, partial abridgment of speech, the duty of the courts is to determine which of these two conflicting interests demands the greater protection under the particular circumstances presented."

A year later, in *Dennis v. United States*,[17] the Court was confronted with another Communist case. But this time the statute was expressly directed at speech rather than conduct. And its impact on speech was not an "indirect, conditional, partial abridgment," merely resulting from the regulation of something else, but a direct prohibition, dealing with certain things which may not be said.

Mr. Justice Frankfurter, in a solo concurrence, announced the view that balancing is the proper approach for the Court in all free speech cases. Although he did not profess to find this in the rationale of prior cases, Mr. Justice Frankfurter took comfort in the view that it was consistent with their results. Furthermore, he regarded balancing as desirable from the standpoint of free speech, since:[18]

"Absolute rules would inevitably lead to absolute exceptions, and such exceptions would eventually corrode the rules. The demands of free speech in a democratic society as well as the interest in national security are better served by candid and informed weighing of the competing interests, within the confines of the judicial process, than by announcing dogmas too inflexible for the non-Euclidean problems to be solved."

Notwithstanding the value of judicial balancing, Mr. Justice Frankfurter placed his main reliance on the principle of judicial restraint. And, on this basis, he made it clear that he was not really advocating that the courts should do their own weighing in each case. Rather they should, except in the most extreme cases, declare the statute valid out of deference to the balancing done when it was enacted:[19]

"Free speech cases are not an exception to the principle that we are not legislators, that direct policy-making is not our province. How best to reconcile competing interests is the business of legislatures and the balance they strike is a judgment not to be displaced by ours, but to be respected unless outside the pale of fair judgment."

Chief Justice Vinson, writing for the majority, also remarked that ". . . the societal value of speech must, on occasion, be subordinated to other values and considerations."[20] But he did not undertake such a sweeping rejection of the rationale of prior decisions, nor assign to legislation so broad a power of self-validation. In the court below, Chief Judge Learned Hand had reinterpreted the "clear and present danger" test as meaning that: "In each case [courts] must ask whether the gravity of the 'evil,' discounted by its improbability, justifies such invasion of free speech as is necessary to avoid the danger."[21] This version eliminated precisely that feature of the test—the necessity of meeting words with words so long as there is time for counter-argument to have effect —which Chief Justice Vinson, only a year previously in *Douds,* had characterized not only as the Holmes-Brandeis view, but also as "the command of the First Amendment." Yet the Chief Justice now wrote of the Hand version:[22]

"We adopt this statement of the rule. . . . It takes into consideration those factors which we deem relevant, and relates their significances. More we cannot expect from words."

This "reinterpretation" of the "clear and present danger" test appears to have killed it. The *Dennis* case itself has been relied on.[23] And the Court, while resorting to the original Brandeis language, declined to use the phrase "clear and present danger," in holding that the proscription of adultery by law does not justify suppression of a motion picture merely because it teaches that adultery is not always wrong.[24] Yet the Court, in ten years which have seen many important free speech cases, has never again expressly asked itself in Hand's terms "whether the gravity of the 'evil' discounted by its improbability" justifies a particular invasion of free speech.

While "clear and present danger" has lain mouldering—or perhaps only slumbering—"balancing" has come to the fore. But it has come to the fore largely in a single type of case: that in which a compelled disclosure of membership or other association may have a deterrent effect on the exercise of first amendment freedoms, especially where private reprisals may reasonably be anticipated. Where the compelled disclosure has dealt with Communism,[25] or with attendance at a World Fellowship camp[26] by persons suspected of being subversive, the balance has been struck in favor of the government. On the other hand, when the compelled disclosure has dealt with organizations considered subversive only below the Mason-Dixon line, the balance has been struck the other way.[27]

To what cases is the Court's balancing test applicable? Judged by its origin in *Schneider,* it should apply only to regulations of the time, place, and manner of speaking which, though neutral as to the content of speech, may unduly limit the means otherwise available for communicating ideas to the public. As reformulated in *Douds,* it should apply only when the statute is construed as regulating conduct, and where the effect on speech is deemed both relatively minor and a mere incidental by-product of the conduct regulation. Other first amendment cases would presumably be tested without balancing. A somewhat similar view of its applicability has been recently stated by Mr. Justice Harlan, writing for what had by then become the familiar five-Justice majority,[28] in the 1961 *Konigsberg* case.[29]

"At the outset we reject the view that freedom of speech and association…[citation]…, as protected by the First and Fourteenth Amendments, are 'absolutes,' not only in the undoubted sense that where the constitutional protection exists it must prevail, but also in the sense that the scope of that protection must be gathered solely from a literal reading of the First Amendment. Throughout its history this Court has consistently recognized at least two ways in which constitutionally protected freedom of speech is narrower than an unlimited license to talk. On the one hand, certain forms of speech, or speech in certain contexts, has been considered outside the scope of constitutional protection…[citations]….On the other hand, general regulatory statutes, not intended to control the

content of speech but incidentally limiting its unfettered exercise, have not been regarded as the
type of law the First or Fourteenth Amendment
forbade Congress or the States to pass, when they
have been found justified by subordinating valid
governmental interests, a prerequisite to constitutionality which has necessarily involved a weighing of the governmental interest involved."

This opinion, though joined in by Mr. Justice
Frankfurter, appears to be a striking departure
from his theory. It seeks to enumerate principles
for classification of free speech cases according to
the type of regulation involved instead of assuming that only pragmatic considerations applicable
to the particular case may be employed. Moreover,
it expressly assumes that there is a "type of law"
which the first amendment forbids Congress to
pass, which could be regarded as the heart, if not
almost the whole, of the approach for which Mr.
Justice Black and the minority have all along been
vainly contending.

Yet Mr. Justice Harlan's analysis is not altogether convincing as a description of what the
Court has been doing, nor does it altogether square
with what the same majority has since said.

First, if the balancing test applies only to "general regulatory statutes, not intended to control
the content of speech but incidentally limiting its
unfettered exercise," then the Smith Act cases
would seem to be the clearest possible example
of the type of case to which it should not be applied. Surely no one could say that the Smith Act
was "not intended to control the content of speech"
or that the manner in which it limits speech is
"incidental" no matter how firmly he might believe that act to be consistent with the first amendment. Mr. Justice Harlan does indeed cite the
Smith Act cases, not as an instance of balancing,
but as an illustration of the phrase, "outside the
scope of constitutional protection." Yet *Dennis* was
decided by weighing the "gravity of the evil, discounted by its improbability," against the invasion
of free speech. Surely this is a balancing test, even
if it is not quite the same balancing test which
some more recent cases seem to employ. So the
Court has not in fact, or at least not always, used
"balancing" as narrowly as Mr. Justice Harlan
suggests.

Second, if there are categories, or "forms," of
speech which are unprotected without regard to
balancing, is it not proper to infer that there are
categories which are protected without regard to
balancing? Surely there are cases which do not
fall within either Mr. Justice Harlan's balancing
formula or his constitutionally unprotected cate-

gories. Yet the balancing Justices have not identified, or given express recognition to any unconditionally protected area. By criticizing Mr. Justice
Black, not for defining the extent of first amendment protection too broadly, but for treating it as
"absolute," they have seemed to imply that there
could be no such area.

And finally, what are we to make of the fact
that the same five Justices for whom Mr. Justice
Harlan spoke in *Konigsberg*, joined only a few
weeks later in the following statement by Mr.
Justice Frankfurter?[30]

"[W]e agree that compulsory disclosure of the
names of an organization's members may in certain
instances infringe constitutionally protected rights
of association...[citations]....But to say this much
is only to recognize one of the points of reference
from which analysis must begin. To state that individual liberties may be affected is to establish
the condition for, not to arrive at the conclusion
of, constitutional decision. Against the impediments which particular governmental regulation
causes to entire freedom of individual action, there
must be weighed the value to the public of the end
which the regulation may achieve."

Does not this say that, even where first amendment protection "exists," it need not, and often
will not, "prevail"? Yet did not the same five
Justices assure us, only a few weeks before, that it
was "undoubted" that the first amendment was an
"absolute" in a sense which would not admit of
this?[31] And the generality of the language used
suggests that the Court is talking not only about
the particular problem, but about its general method of decision. Doubtless this language does not
commit the Court to the theory, expressed in Mr.
Justice Frankfurter's opinion in *Dennis*, that the
weighing of competing interests is the method of
approach in all free speech cases, but it is certainly suggestive of that view.

Should the Court now adopt Mr. Justice Frankfurter's full theory, it would indeed be an ironic
inversion of the purpose for which "weighing the
circumstances" and "appraising the substantiality
of the reasons" was originally suggested in *Schneider*. That purpose, as we have seen, was to give
the presumption of constitutionality attending
legislative judgment *less* weight in free speech
cases, even in dealing with a regulation which
treats all points of view alike. Mr. Justice Frankfurter's version would give the legislative judgment the *same* effect it has when the validity of
economic regulation is at issue—even when Congress has undertaken to legislate against dangerous ideas or those who promote them.

It must be admitted that the Justices composing the minority—Mr. Chief Justice Warren and Justices Black, Douglas, and Brennan[32]—have also left their basic theoretical position in some obscurity. I think they have been saying that the scope properly to be accorded the first amendment is a very broad one; that whatever falls within that scope should be regarded as having an unconditionally obligatory character, not subject to be put aside by Congress, by the courts, or by both together; and that therefore the approach of the "balancer" is impermissible, as are also most of his results. Yet Mr. Justice Black, as the principal spokesman for this position, has chosen to put his argument largely in the form that the first amendment "means what it says."[33] But to treat this as a sufficient answer to questions of whether and how the first amendment applies in a particular case is to imply that its terms are self-defining, that prefabricated answers to all questions of this type can be found merely by consulting the text. This cannot be true unless the words of the amendment must be deemed to contain every proposition and require every application which can rationally be attributed to them—unless every litigant who makes a colorably rational appeal to first amendment protection must automatically win. I am quite sure this is not what Mr. Justice Black means and at times he has said that it is not what he means. Yet his failure to spell out more clearly an alternative meaning has certainly contributed to the ability of his opponents to brush his arguments aside by putting this construction upon them, as Mr. Justice Harlan does in the *Konigsberg* opinion.

The one thing which appears to emerge with reasonable clarity is that "balancing" has become the central first amendment issue. For those who have been in the majority, it is the method of decision in most recent free speech cases—and is apparently being employed with increasing frequency. For those who have been in the minority, it is the principal abuse on which their dissenting wrath is focussed. I therefore propose to "weigh" balancing—to inquire into the propriety and consequences of any such test. Since it is being vigorously asserted in some quarters that balancing is inevitable, that there is no alternative,[34] we will begin by examining this contention which, if true, forecloses discussion.

First, the inevitability of balancing is said to follow from the fact that the terms used in the first amendment are not self-defining. If the Constitution fails to tell the judge what he must do, it is argued that he has no choice but to put it aside and use his own best judgment.[35] And, in that case, what can he do but balance?

Doubtless our Constitution, being composed of general propositions, cannot, of its own unaided force, dictate answers to concrete questions. But if we therefore conclude that the text can play no part in deciding concrete questions, nothing can follow from this except the conclusion that it was an exercise in futility to write it in the first place. And this point is independent of the problems of judicial review. If the text can add no new considerations to the judiciary's deliberations, it can hardly do so for Congress, or the executive, or the people. Justice Cardozo, no naive believer in the theory that judges merely discover law and play no part in making it, did not conclude that the destruction of this myth requires the judges to live in a universe which contains nothing but *ad hoc* decisions.[36]

Second, it is maintained that balancing is still inevitable, since even the judge who undertakes to assign some meaning to the constitutional proposition contained in the first amendment must employ balancing considerations in order to decide what meaning to assign to it.[37] This proposition is true in a sense, but it errs in equating two things which are utterly unlike.

To be sure, a judge who is obliged to formulate a new rule of law must consider what its advantages and disadvantages would be and weigh them against the advantages and disadvantages of the possible alternative rules which must be adopted. For example, if the judge is asked to decide whether the first amendment protects the refusal to state one's political affiliations, he must take into consideration the possible dangers to political freedom and other values of denying such protection. And he must also consider whether protecting that refusal would strip the government of power which may be needed for legitimate, non-repressive purposes. Mr. Justice Black provided an example of this type of "balancing" when, in order to decide whether the first amendment protects a right to anonymous publication, he took into consideration the possible social values of anonymous publication as indicated by the role such publications have played in the past, and the danger of repressing controversial views if identification of the proponents were required.[38] But, though the mental process by which a judge determines what rule to adopt can be described as "balancing," this does not make it the same as balancing, independently of any rule, to determine what is the best disposition to make of a particular case. Deciding the scope to be accorded a particular constitutional freedom is different from deciding whether the interest of a particular litigant in freely expressing views which the judge may consider loathsome, dangerous, or ridiculous is outweighed by society's interest in "order," "security," or national "self-preservation."

Furthermore, once a series of cases has been decided, an additional difference emerges. The definer—the judge who undertakes to assign some distinct meaning to the constitutional proposition—has now drawn a line. It may be a wavering and uncertain line at many points. He may come up against cases which compel him to conclude that he has drawn it in the wrong place and that it should be moved. And no matter how satisfactorily the line is drawn, borderline cases can still arise which could arguably be placed on either side. Yet, despite all these difficulties, something new emerges from the mere fact that a line has been drawn. There are now cases that are not borderline: cases that are well within the line, as well as others well outside it. The definer has therefore placed limits (even though those limits are not absolutely beyond his own power to move) on his own future freedom of decision. There are cases in which (unless he is willing to change the rule or evade it with sophistries) he *must* say that freedom of speech has been unconstitutionally abridged, as well as others in which he must say it has not. The definer, in other words, must ultimately give the constitutional proposition a certain amount of content which he regards as being obligatory on the court. Consequently, in cases falling clearly within the defined area, the definer is largely relieved of responsibility for results in particular instances which he may find personally distasteful.

For the *ad hoc* balancer, the situation is quite different. For him, there can be no clearly protected area—all areas are subject to invasion whenever "competing interests" are sufficiently compelling. Furthermore, his initial assumption—without which he could never justify balancing—is that the constitutional proposition contained in the first amendment is incapable of being assigned any meaning which would not be too broad (or too narrow) for consistent application. Therefore, it must have been intended to be subject to unstated exceptions, which the court must make. And since the Constitution sheds no light on what exceptions are permissible, it is easy, if not inevitable, to fall into the assumption that the constitutional proposition is subject to any and all exceptions which the court may deem advisable. The *ad hoc* balancer's constitution is empty until the court decides what to put into it. It does not speak until the court speaks for it. It is inherently incapable of saying anything to the judge.

The third and final ground on which balancing is said to be inevitable is that to treat the first amendment as an "absolute" leads to absurd, undesirable, and self-contradictory consequences.

Although so moderate and perceptive a student of our institutions as Carl L. Becker was able to regard the provisions of the Bill of Rights as "absolutes," and to view absoluteness as the very essence of their function,[39] there has arisen a new criticism which asserts as an axiom that "there are no absolutes."[40] And this new criticism triumphantly points out that to treat the protection accorded the freedom of speech by the first amendment as "absolute" would wipe out the law on such subjects as libel, fraud, and solicitation to crime,[41] and lead to numerous other results deemed both inconvenient and absurd.

This seems no more than a *non sequitur*, based on failure to distinguish between two of the numerous meanings of the word "absolute." The premise is that the first amendment cannot be "absolute" in the sense of unlimited in scope. But the conclusion is that it cannot be "absolute" in the sense of unconditionally obligatory within its proper scope, whatever that may be.

The confidence with which it can be asserted that scope and obligation are indistinguishable is sometimes astonishing. Yet the balancing Justices have demonstrated—and in a balancing case—that they are quite capable of making this distinction:[42]

"Undeniably, the First Amendment in some circumstances protects an individual from being compelled to disclose his associational relationships. However, the protections of the First Amendment, *unlike a proper claim of the privilege against self-incrimination under the Fifth Amendment,* do not afford a witness the right to resist inquiry in all circumstances."

Is the fifth amendment self-incrimination clause an "absolute"? Certainly, it is not unlimited in scope: it does not confer the right to withhold information which is "degrading," but not "incriminating" and is subject to such limits as waiver and immunity. Nor is it self-defining; no one could ascertain with certainty, merely by consulting its text, whether it does or does not confer the right to withhold an answer which would be incriminating in a different jurisdiction, or facts which are innocent in themselves, but which might furnish leads to a possible prosecution. Yet when the question is one which the court recognizes as incriminating, when the privilege has been properly claimed, and no immunity has been conferred, the judge not only does not, but may not, base his ruling on an estimate as to whether the witness' interest in not incriminating himself is outweighed by society's need for his testimony. As Mr. Justice Harlan recognizes, the witness' interest may not be set aside even if the government is seeking his testimony in the name of "self-preservation," the "ultimate value of any society."[43]

So the fifth amendment self-incrimination clause, though neither limitless in scope nor expressed in self-defining terms, does have a hard core which, once located, does not yield to accommodate "competing interests." No amount of sloganizing against "absolutes" can explain why a hard core is possible for the fifth amendment, but not for the first.

Nor can it be said that this hard core is possible only because the fifth amendment protects a procedural right. Cases involving denial of equal protection instance treatment of a substantive right as an "absolute." In the Little Rock school case, a school district, which had attempted in good faith to carry out a desegregation plan, petitioned the district court for a postponement of desegregation on the ground that extreme public hostility had made it impossible to maintain a sound educational program with the Negro students in attendance. In granting the postponement, the district court said:[44]

"And while the Negro students at Little Rock have a personal interest in being admitted to the public schools on a nondiscriminatory basis as soon as practicable, that interest is only one factor of the equation, and must be balanced against the public interest, including the interest of all students and potential students in the district, in having a smoothly functioning educational system capable of furnishing the type of education that is necessary not only for successful living but also for the very survival of our nation and its institutions. There is also another public interest involved, namely, that of eliminating, or at least ameliorating, the unfortunate racial strife and tension which existed in Little Rock during the past year and still exists there.

When the interests involved here are balanced, it is our opinion, in view of the situation which has prevailed and will in the foreseeable future continue to prevail at Central High School under existing conditions, the personal and immediate interests of the Negro students affected, must yield temporarily to the larger interests of both races."

Admittedly, there were other issues than balancing at stake in the Little Rock school case. There was a deliberate attempt to obstruct and defeat action which the Supreme Court had held to be constitutionally obligatory. And there was the danger that permitting this attempt to achieve even partial and temporary success might encourage similar action elsewhere. Yet the Supreme Court did not suggest that the trial judge had erred by assigning too much weight to one interest or not enough to another, or by leaving out some factor which he ought to have weighed. Nor did the Supreme Court expressly restrike the balance on its own account. Instead, in an opinion announced as being that of each of the nine Justices, it resorted to "absolutist" language:[45]

"The constitutional rights of respondents are not to be sacrificed or yielded to the violence and disorder which have followed upon the actions of the Governor and Legislature. As this Court said some 41 years ago in a unanimous opinion in a case involving another aspect of racial segregation: "It is urged that this proposed segregation will promote the public peace by preventing race conflicts. Desirable as this is, and important as is the preservation of the public peace, this aim cannot be accomplished by laws or ordinances which deny rights created or protected by the Federal Constitution." *Buchanan v. Warley*, 245 U.S. 60, 81. Thus law and order are not here to be preserved by depriving the Negro children of their constitutional rights...."

But if depriving persons of equal protection is not a permissible means of preserving law and order, why should depriving them of freedom of speech be a permissible means of doing so? No amount of sloganizing against "absolutes" can explain why the right to hold and express an opinion as to what the public welfare requires cannot be made as unyielding as the rights guaranteed by the equal protection clause.

Thus *ad hoc* balancing is not unavoidable and we can meaningfully inquire whether or not it is desirable. One particularly objectionable application of balancing in some recent cases deserves note before passing to those fundamental problems which inhere in the method and are independent of the particular manner of its application.

Irrespective of the ultimate merits of balancing, it will not do to treat freedom of speech as though it were a mere private interest of the individual before the court, as the majority did in *Barenblatt*.[46] It is that, but it is also much more.[47] And it is equally unsound to equate repression with national "self-preservation" merely because government happens to be the adverse litigant.[48] This lends to the government's interest such immediacy and magnitude that any other public interest would automatically have to give way, let alone one treated as though it were merely private.

It is perfectly conceivable that the public interest—even in "security" or in national "self-preservation"—might be better served by maintaining freedom of speech than by the policies and programs to which the first amendment is asked to yield. It may be that freedom of speech is safer than repression in the long run. Not only do Justices Black and Douglas think so, but so did Justices Brandeis and Holmes, and such has been, at times, the opinion of the Court. If this is now minority doctrine, the opposite judgment cannot be deemed self-evident. And so, it is most peculiar that, in the balancing cases, the view that repression is safer than freedom does not evolve as the product of careful analysis. It appears as an unexamined initial premise. By making that assumption, the Court from the outset begs the very question which it purports to be examining. Yet without that assumption, this kind of balancing cannot begin. We cannot balance freedom against security if they both belong on the same side of the scales.

In any event, there would seem to be no justification for putting the government's objective on one side of the scales without first requiring a demonstration that it cannot be obtained by less repressive methods. Surely the end cannot justify the means unless it at least requires them. Several recent cases in which the balance has been struck against freedom of speech are conspicuously lacking in any such demonstration.[49] Yet without it, the most that can logically be put on the government's side of the scale is the convenience to the government of employing this method, rather than some other, for the pursuit of its objective.[50]

But these objectionable assumptions may not be inherent in the balancing theory—though that theory has been consistently used to sanction their adoption by the Court. Let us turn to an evaluation of the theory itself. And let us first be clear which balancing theory we are discussing. We are not discussing the theory that a judge should examine the pros and cons before defining the *scope* of a constitutional guarantee. We are not discussing whether it is proper to "weigh the circumstances and appraise the substantiality of the reasons advanced" in order to determine whether a regulation of the time, place, and manner of speaking, though neutral in its impact on various points of view, unreasonably and unnecessarily restricts the means otherwise available for communicating with the public. Nor are we discussing whether "balancing" is the proper approach when a regulation aimed not at speech but at conduct has, as an accidental and unintended by-product, some deterrent effect on the expression of opinion. We are discussing the theory that the first amendment has no hard core, that it protects not rights but "interests," that those "interests" are to be

weighed against "competing interests" on a case-to-case basis and protected only when not found to be outweighed.

This theory would seem to reduce the problem to one of expediency rather than principle since to weigh freedom of speech against considerations of mere expediency would be impossible if one could not treat the two as commensurable. One's need for a new car may be balanced against the other uses to which the same money might be put, but not against "Thou shalt not steal." But the theory, though it characterizes freedom of speech as always expendable, does not, *per se,* say anything about the position it should occupy on the value scale of expediences. Accordingly, it is conceivable that a court might apply the balancing test, yet attach so high a value to freedom of speech that the balance would nearly always be struck in its favor. It is even conceivable that a balancer who attached a very high value to freedom of speech might decide in its favor more often than a definer who applied a narrow definition. There are nevertheless objections to the balancing theory which are independent of the manner in which the competing interests are identified and characterized and the relative weight accorded them:

1. There is a fundamental logical and legal objection to "weighing" a governmental objective, however legitimate and important that objective may be, against a constitutional statement that the government may not employ a certain means for the attainment of any of its objectives. Objectives may indeed conflict and, when they do, they must be weighed against each other. Either we must decide that one is the more important or subordinate than the other, or we must arrive at some accommodation in which both are only partially achieved. But it does not follow that any objective can ever be weighed against an express limitation on the means available for its pursuit. The public interest in the suppression of crime, for example, cannot be weighed against a constitutional provision that accused persons may not be denied the right to counsel. If a constitution expressly prohibits the imposition of a particular type of tax, the government's need for revenue can be weighed against that prohibition only for the purpose of showing that it ought to be eliminated or modified by constitutional amendment. A showing of the government's need for revenue could not justify a decision that a tax of the prohibited type may be imposed, without constitutional amendment, provided it is not too large. Nor could it shed any light on the question as to whether a specific tax was or was not one of the prohibited type.

2. We have often been assured that a court's

disagreement with the policy of a statute cannot make it unconstitutional. And, when this is the point being made, we are likely to be told also that the Court's concern is with legislative "power," not with "wisdom." This would seem undoubtedly sound—but it is meaningful only if legislative power can be determined without reference to wisdom. However, the balancing doctrine rests on an undemonstrated assumption that no such determination of congressional power is possible in free speech cases independent of a decision on the "wisdom" of the balance struck by the legislature. If a court's opinion that the policy of a statute is unwise does not impair its validity, why should an opposite opinion have any tendency to confer constitutionally?

3. "One of the most fundamental social interests is that law shall be uniform and impartial. There must be nothing in its action that savors of prejudice or favor or even arbitrary whim or fitfulness."[51] Yet the balancing test, while still in its infancy, has already established that compulsory disclosure of membership lists, where likely to lead to reprisals against the members, violates the constitutional rights of members of the N.A.A.C.P.,[52] but not those of members of the Communist Party,[53] nor, apparently, those of members of the Ku Klux Klan.[54] And an officer of a local N.A.A.C.P. chapter may not be compelled to produce a list of her members,[55] but the director of a World Fellowship camp may be compelled to produce a list of his guests.[56] Perhaps a reconciliation of these results on an impartial basis can be stated,[57] but at least what can be said is that they do not look impartial, and confidence in the impartiality of the judiciary at the highest level may well be undermined. It is difficult to see how the impartiality of such judgments can be assured—much less made apparent—unless the Justices abandon *ad hoc* balancing and undertake to state a rule on this subject, by which the rights of all can be measured.

4. As treated by the balancing test, "the freedom of speech" protected by the first amendment is not affirmatively definable. It is defined only by the weight of the interests arrayed against it and it is inversely proportional to the weight accorded to those interests. When this approach is taken, there can be no floor beneath which that freedom may not be allowed to sink. No matter how low it may fall, we must always be prepared to see it fall still further if the needs of "security" increase—or if an atmosphere of fear and hysteria makes them seem to increase.

5. A balancing construction of the first amendment fails to give effective encouragement even to the amount of free speech which it theoretically recognizes. The attitude toward freedom of speech which encourages uninhibited discussion is conveyed by such popular expressions as: "You have a right to say it. This is a free country." But the assumption underlying such a statement is not that the right to speak out will probably be upheld by the Supreme Court upon a weighing of all relevant factors. Rather the assumption is that the right to speak out is so clear that there is no substantial danger that doing so might result in prosecution.

If the first amendment is subject to *ad hoc* balancing, it is inherently incapable of any such assurances. Under it, the right to speak and publish is never clear, since it is never defined. Whether one had a right to speak or publish cannot be known until after the event and depends on the unpredictable weight which a court may someday give to "competing interests." No doubt the boldest will speak anyway, but many others will be deterred merely by the pervasive and ineradicable uncertainty. Inevitably the speech so deterred will include much which, had it ever been brought before the Court, would have been held protected. The Court condemns statutes which, because of their breadth or vagueness, deter protected speech. Yet its own balancing test has a similar effect.

6. The balancing test assures us little, if any, more freedom of speech than we should have had if the first amendment had never been adopted. Rational governments do not take affirmative action without counting the costs, without having "balanced the interests" and concluded that those to be served outweigh those to be sacrificed.

Accordingly, the only difference between a balancing first amendment and none at all is that it permits the balance to be struck twice, first by Congress and then again by the courts. At first glance, this might seem a difference of great practical importance, but the more closely it is analyzed, the less likely it seems that it will prove so. The balancing of conflicting interests would seem to be inherently a legislative question for which the judicial process is very ill-adapted.[58] It requires evaluating vast arrays of facts of a kind which are not to be found in the ordinary judicial record—and which will be extremely difficult for the litigants to put there. It also involves considerations so debatable that they cannot be effectively or fairly handled by means of judicial notice. Yet the Court under the balancing theory must ask itself the very same question—is this worth what it costs?—which the Congress necessarily asked itself, and to which it gave its answer when it decided to take the action.

When these considerations are taken into account, it must be regarded as very nearly inevitable that a court which clings to the balancing test will sooner or later adopt a corollary that the balance struck by Congress is not only presumed correct, but is to be accorded extreme, almost total, judicial deference. As we have seen, Mr. Justice Frankfurter, the senior and apparently most influential advocate of balancing on the Court, adopted this corollary and gave it major stress in his initial balancing manifesto. Once such a corollary is adopted, the difference between a balancing first amendment and none at all approaches, if it does not reach, the vanishing point. No doubt the courts will save themselves some such potential check on the reins as that indicated by Mr. Justice Frankfurter's statement that courts may set aside the balance struck by Congress if it is "outside the pale of fair judgment."[59] As a practical matter, if constitutionally protected freedom of speech is to be reduced to this, then the eloquence which has been expended upon it might better have been addressed to some more significant topic. Furthermore, the courts could have saved this much without any first amendment—merely by resorting to the "liberty" aspect of the due process clause. So, if it comes to this (as, unless the balancing test is abandoned, it seems that it must), it will be difficult to say that the first amendment protects even an insignificant residue of freedom of speech which would not have been equally safe without it. Governmental power to regulate commerce in ideas will be indistinguishable, at least in principle, from governmental power to regulate commerce in goods.

7. If a balancing test is applied to the first amendment, it is hard to see why it should not be applied to the entire Constitution. If the first amendment, and only the first amendment, can be balanced away, then that amendment is assigned a status inferior to the rest of the Constitution. Thus the Court has, for the moment, achieved an ironic inversion of the old theory that the first amendment has a *preferred* status. Yet it is difficult to see how, in the long run, so strange a result can be rationalized. And, if it cannot be, it is hard to see how the courts can avoid a choice between abandoning balancing and extending it to any and all constitutional questions. The late Judge Learned Hand, if I understand him correctly, suggested such an approach to the whole of the Bill of Rights.[60] But, on what basis can one stop with the Bill of Rights? Why should these provisions be regarded as any less "absolute" than the original document, or the later amendments? If the arguments employed to justify balancing are carried to their logical conclusion, then the Constitution does not contain—and is not even capable of containing—anything whatever which

is unconditionally obligatory. Defendants in criminal cases can be tried in secret, or held incommunicado without trial, can be denied knowledge of the accusation against them, and the right to counsel, and the right to call witnesses in their own defense, and the right to trial by jury. Ex post facto laws and bills of attainder can be passed. Habeas corpus can be suspended, though there is neither rebellion nor invasion. Private property can be taken for public use without just, or any, compensation. Suffrage qualifications based on sex or race can be reinstituted. Anything which the Constitution says *cannot* be done *can* be done, if Congress thinks and the Court agrees (or is unwilling to set aside the congressional judgment) that the interests thereby served outweighed those which were sacrificed. Thus the whole idea of a government of limited powers, and of a written constitution as a device for attaining that end, is at least potentially at stake.

Finally, we must consider the argument which justifies the balancing test on grounds of "judicial restraint," albeit this seems a strange name to employ for an argument which would, on policy grounds, read a constitutional provision as meaning very nearly the opposite of what it says. The argument runs thus: if the Court does not leave Congress free to control speech so long as Congress' view is not "outside the pale of fair judgment," then the Court will be making the same mistake it made in past periods when it attempted to halt economic reform in the name of substantive "due process."

First, let us note that any constitutional limitation serves a significant function only insofar as it stands in the way of something which government thinks ought to be done. Nothing else needs to be prohibited.

But the crux of the argument is that there is no difference between the old "substantive due process" theory and a judicial attempt to treat "Congress shall make no law…" as imposing a significant limitation on Congress' freedom to make laws. Actually, there are enormous differences.

The first, of course, is that the Constitution itself treats the two problems differently.[61] A court which ignores this fact because it thinks they ought to be treated alike may be subordinating its own policy notions to those of Congress, but it is also subordinating the work of the framers to its own notions of constitutional policy. It is likewise ignoring one historically justified tradition: that a government's power to deal with mere words ought to be drastically narrower than its power to deal with acts.

For those who are unmoved by such textual

and historical arguments, there are fundamental policy reasons for treating the two problems differently. An economic mistake or injustice does not interfere with the political process and that process therefore remains open for its correction or redress if the courts refuse relief. The same cannot be said where legislation results in infringement of political rights, for the injured can hardly rely for redress on the very weapons of which they are deprived. Even Mr. Justice Frankfurter has recognized that this distinction justifies two different standards of judicial review.[62] Furthermore, economic interests are typically represented in legislative bodies—or able to obtain a hearing from them. Despised ideological minorities typically are not. In extreme situations such as those which give rise to first amendment test cases, their political influence may be less than zero, for it may be better politics for a legislator to abuse them than to listen to their grievances.

Under such circumstances, judicial deference to a legislative judgment curbing the political rights of a minority is hardly the same "judicial restraint" espoused by Justices Holmes and Brandeis, which allows considerable latitude to legislative judgments on the need for economic reform.

"Activism" in economic review narrows the range of popular choice by prescribing that there are certain legislative experiments which may not be attempted. "Activism" in libertarian review prevents a narrowing of the range of popular choice by preventing Congress from circumscribing that area of permissible discussion and advocacy which is the ultimate source of social change and legislative innovation. The historical evidence, far from suggesting that the two go together, indicates that they have always tended to be mutually exclusive.

But the advocate of "judicial restraint" will insist that where there is room for a reasonable difference of opinion between Congress and the Court as to whether certain action violates the first amendment, Congress' view should take precedence. There are excellent reasons why it should not. First of all, "Congress shall make no law…" is an obvious and express effort to restrain congressional power. If that restraint is to be effective, then Congress is the least appropriate body in the world to be accorded the final word as to what it means.[63] And, while I have no desire to re-wage the general battle for judicial review, the evidence is reasonably clear that the first amendment was proposed with the express expectation and intention that the courts would enforce it.

When a bill which is dubious on first amendment grounds is proposed in our Congress, Congress may debate its constitutionality—but it does so on the implicit, and often explicit, assumption that anything which the courts will permit is constitutional. And it appears to feel no impropriety in treating constitutionality as a mere technical obstacle which may, perhaps, be avoided by astute draftsmanship. If the statute is enacted and the courts uphold it by deferring to the legislative judgment, they are deferring to a judgment which, so far as constitutionality is concerned, has never really been exercised.[64]

Furthermore, this argument for "judicial restraint" takes no cognizance of an important feature of our system: judicial enforcement of a challenged statute is not abstention, but validation. So far as constitutional power to enact it is concerned, it is an endorsement of constitutionality by the body still recognized as having the final word on the subject. Whether that result is reached on constitutional or pragmatic grounds, or merely by deferring to the legislative judgment, it becomes a constitutional precedent which Congress can rely and enlarge upon in the future.

Perhaps Congress should take more responsibility for constitutionality. And there may be ways, even within our present system, by which that responsibility can be increased, but judicial rubber-stamping of anything which Congress at a particular moment may reasonably think desirable is not one of them.

In sum, the "balancing" test does not permit the first amendment to perform its function as a constitutional limitation. It virtually converts that amendment into its opposite. A prohibition against abridgment has become a license to abridge. And, notwithstanding that on its face this purports to be a limited license, the limitation is so narrow and, on analysis, so largely illusory, that it comes close to being an unlimited license.

The balancing test does not even permit the first amendment to serve as an effective admonition. The amendment, as construed by this doctrine, fails to tell Congress that there is anything it may not do—or even anything it ought not to do—except those things which, even without the amendment, it would have no adequate governmental motive for doing.

Not only does a "balancing" first amendment fail to protect freedom of speech, but it becomes a mechanism for rationalizing and validating the kinds of governmental action intended to be prohibited.

Such are the consequences of distorting the amendment's thunderous "Thou shalt not abridge" into a quavering "Abridge if you must, but try to keep it reasonable."[65]

Footnotes

[1]Justices Frankfurter, Clark, Harlan, Whittaker, and Stewart....
[2]308 U.S. 147.
[3]308 U.S. 147, 161.
[4]*Cf.* United States v. Carolene Products, 304 U.S. 144, 152 n.4 (1938).
[5]*E.g.,* Thornhill v. Alabama, 310 U.S. 88, 96 (1940). In Cantwell v. Connecticut, 310 U.S. 296, 307 (1940), the Court undertook to determine whether the state's interest in peace and good order had been carried to a point by a license requirement for religious solicitations where it would come into fatal collision with the overriding interest in freedom of religion and freedom of communication protected by the federal constitution (opinion by Roberts, J., for unanimous Court).
[6]Marsh v. Alabama, 326 U.S. 501, 509 (1946). Mr. Justice Black here balanced the constitutional rights of property owners against the rights of the people to freedom of press and religion, but added that "we remain mindful of the fact that the latter occupy a preferred position...." *Ibid.* Mr. Justice Black has recently urged that the balancing concept "was first accepted as a method for insuring the complete protection of First Amendment freedoms even against purely incidental or inadvertent consequences" and was later misapplied to "governmental action that is aimed at speech and depends for its application upon the content of speech." Konigsberg v. State Bar, 366 U.S. 36, 68, 70 (1961) (dissenting opinion). And he has indicated that he still approves of the type of "balancing" done in *Schneider* and *Cantwell,* but that it must not be extended to laws "directly aimed at curtailing speech and political persuasion...." Barenblatt v. United States, 360 U.S. 109, 142 (1959) (dissenting opinion).
[7]339 U.S. 382 (1950).
[8]*Id.* at 395.
[9]*Ibid.*
[10]*Id.* at 397.
[11]*Id.* at 398.
[12]Davis v. Beason, 133 U.S. 333 (1890) (denial of vote to members of society advocating polygamy upheld on ground that teaching and counseling of crime is itself a crime); *In re* Summers, 325 U.S. 561 (1945) (conscientious objector denied admission to bar).
[13]Jacobson v. Massachusetts, 197 U.S. 11 (1905) (compulsory vaccination).
[14]Reynolds v. United States, 98 U.S. 145 (1879) (bigamy). The Chief Justice also gave an "And see" citation to Giboney v. Empire Storage & Ice Co., 336 U.S. 490 (1949) (conduct in violation of state antitrust statute not immunized because carried out in part by means of speech in the form of union picketing).
[15]Kovacs v. Cooper, 336 U.S. 77 (1949) (sound trucks emitting "loud and raucous noises"); United Public Workers v. Mitchell, 330 U.S. 75 (1947) (political activity by government employees); Prince v. Massachusetts, 321 U.S. 158 (1944) (statute prohibiting child labor on street applied to sale of religious publications); Cox v. New Hampshire, 312 U.S. 569 (1941) (nondiscretionary license required for parade).
[16]American Communications Ass'n v. Douds, 339 U.S. 382, 399 (1950).
[17]341 U.S. 494 (1951).

[18]*Id.* at 524-25.
[19]*Id.* at 539-40.
[20]*Id.* at 503.
[21]United States v. Dennis, 183 F.2d 201, 212 (2d Cir. 1950).
[22]Dennis v. United States, 341 U.S. 494, 510 (1951).
[23]*E.g.,* Scales v. United States, 367 U.S. 203, 228 (1961) (holding constitutional a different clause of the statute involved in *Dennis*).
[24]Kingsley Int'l Pictures Corp. v. Regents of the Univ. of N.Y., 360 U.S. 684, 689 (1959) (opinion of Court by Stewart, J., joined only by the libertarian four who have usually found themselves in dissent in recent free speech cases but with Justices Frankfurter, Clark, Harlan, and Whittaker concurring in result).
[25]Communist Party v. Subversive Activities Control Bd., 367 U.S. 1 (1961); *In re* Anastaplo, 366 U.S. 82 (1961); Konigsberg v. State Bar, 366 U.S. 36 (1961); Braden v. United States, 365 U.S. 431 (1961); Wilkinson v. United States, 365 U.S. 399 (1961); Barenblatt v. United States, 360 U.S. 109 (1959).
[26]Uphaus v. Wyman, 360 U.S. 72 (1959).
[27]Bates v. Little Rock, 361 U.S. 516 (1960); National Ass'n for the Advancement of Colored People v. Alabama, 357 U.S. 449 (1958). See also Louisiana v. National Ass'n for the Advancement of Colored People, 366 U.S. 293 (1961).
[28]Note 1 *supra.*
[29]Konigsberg v. State Bar, 366 U.S. 36, 49-51 (1961).
[30]Communist Party v. Subversive Activities Control Bd., 367 U.S. 1, 90-91 (1961).
[31]See text accompanying note 29 *supra.* Some persons do not find this assurance in Mr. Justice Harlan's language in *Konigsberg,* but I cannot read it otherwise without first eliminating the word "undoubted." Thus I would paraphrase Mr. Justice Harlan's statement in this manner: We reject the view that freedom of speech is an "absolute" if the term "absolute" comprehends "not only" the uncontested proposition that when "the constitutional protection exists it must prevail," but also the additional proposition, which we reject, "that the scope of that protection must be gathered solely from a literal reading of the First Amendment."
[32]No implication that these four Justices share an identical position is intended. Mr. Justice Brennan has usually refrained from joining the opinions of Mr. Justice Black on this question. And even Justices Black and Douglas sometimes disagree on first amendment issues as they did in Communist Party v. Subversive Activities Control Bd., 367 U.S. 1 (1961). However, in *In re* Anastaplo, 366 U.S. 82, 110 (1961), Mr. Justice Black, in a dissenting opinion strongly rejecting the "balancing" test, spoke for all four members of the minority.
[33]Barenblatt v. United States, 360 U.S. 109, 143-44 (1959) (dissenting opinion)....
[34]Examples are Karst, *Legislative Facts in Constitutional Litigation,* 1960 Sup. Ct. Rev. 75, 79-80 (1960); Kauper, Book Review, 58 Mich. L. Rev. 619, 626 (1960). Even Prof. Charles L. Black, Jr., who sympathizes with Mr. Justice Black on the merits, has been unable to find anything more than a difference in attitude in the choice between balancing and defining. See Black, *Mr. Justice Black, The Supreme Court, and the Bill of Rights,* Harper's Magazine, Feb. 1961.
[35]The balancer's thinking processes eliminate the constitutional text so completely that he soon forgets there ever was one. Consider the following:

"Apologists for the modern version of activist Justice seem to concentrate upon its First Amendment aspects and ignore its economic implications....This permits them to rest upon—or hide behind—the hallowed generalities of democratic dogma. Even so, they do not argue that the Constitution guarantees absolute freedom of expression, or that any explicit limitation can be found in the written document. *Choice then is inevitable.* Yet we are not told why a legislative choice between competing interests here is, *a priori,* less worthy of respect than elsewhere. To put it differently, the activist position assumes that courts are somehow inherently more competent to achieve a sound balance of interests in First Amendment cases than in others." MENDELSON, JUSTICES BLACK AND FRANKFURTER: CONFLICT IN THE COURT 119-20 (1961) (italics in original).

Obviously, it would never occur to Prof. Mendelson that a court might be justified in construing two constitutional provisions differently merely because they have different histories and are expressed in radically different language. He will listen only to an *"a priori"* reason for doing so.

36"A definition of law which in effect denies the possibility of law since it denies the possibility of rules of general operation must contain within itself the seeds of fallacy and error. Analysis is useless if it destroys what it is intended to explain. Law and obedience to law are facts confirmed every day to us all in our experience of life." CARDOZO, THE NATURE OF THE JUDICIAL PROCESS 126-27 (1960 ed.).

37Kauper, Book Review, 58 MICH. L. REV. 619, 626 (1960).

38Talley v. California, 362 U.S. 60 (1960).

39"The occasions on which the sovereignty of the people can be exercised without restraint...are... constitutional conventions. In normal times the will of the majority can be effective only within those absolute limitations and through the intricately channeled procedures defined in the constitutions already established.

"The absolute limitations on governmental action are set forth in the bills of rights. Governments exist, as the Declaration of Independence has it, in order to secure the natural rights of man. But Jefferson and his contemporaries regarded some of these rights as of such fundamental importance to the individual that they should never be abolished or infringed by any government, even a republican government. In all our constitutions, accordingly, we find these rights declared to be imprescriptable, and therefore placed above and beyond the reach of legislative or administrative action. They are the so-called civil-liberties....

"[T]he purpose of thus setting them forth is to define a sphere of action that is entirely withdrawn from governmental control." BECKER, FREEDOM AND RESPONSIBILITY IN THE AMERICAN WAY OF LIFE 69-70, 72 (1945).

40Dennis v. United States, 341 U.S. 494, 508 (1951). Of course this statement, being in absolute form, is self-contradictory.

41Konigsberg v. State Bar, 366 U.S. 36, 49 n.10 (1961).

42Barenblatt v. United States, 360 U.S. 109, 126 (1959) emphasis added.

43*Id.* at 128, quoting Dennis v. United States, 341 U.S. 494, 509 (1951) (emphasis added).

44Aaron v. Cooper, 163 F. Supp. 13, 27 (E.D. Ark. 1958), *rev'd,* 257 F.2d 33 (8th Cir. 1958), *reversal aff'd,* 358 U.S. 1 (1958).

45Cooper v. Aaron, 358 U.S. 1, 16 (1958).

46Barenblatt v. United States, 360 U.S. 109, 126, 134 (1959).

47"The right of a citizen of the United States to take part, for his own or the country's benefit, in the making of federal laws, and in the conduct of the Government, necessarily includes the right to speak or write about them; to endeavor to make his own opinion concerning laws existing or contemplated prevail; and, to this end, to teach the truth as he sees it....Full and free exercise of this right by the citizen is ordinarily also his duty; for its exercise is more important to the Nation than it is to himself." Gilbert v. Minnesota, 254 U.S. 325, 337-38 (1920) (Brandeis, J., dissenting). And see Green, *The Right to Communicate,* 35 N.Y.U.L. REV. 903 (1960).

48Cahn, *The Firstness of the First Amendment,* 65 YALE L.J. 464, 479 (1956).

49Braden v. United States, 365 U.S. 431 (1961); Wilkinson v. United States, 365 U.S. 399 (1961); Barenblatt v. United States, 360 U.S. 109 (1959); Uphaus v. Wyman, 360 U.S. 72 (1959). Note also that, though a very strong case has been made that the Subversive Activities Control Act of 1950 is unnecessary—see CHAFEE, THE BLESSINGS OF LIBERTY 122–36 (1956)—Mr. Justice Frankfurter, in upholding the act by a balancing test, neither met that case nor required the government to meet it. Communist Party v. Subversive Activities Control Bd., 367 U.S. 1 (1961).

50Schneider v. State (Irvington), 308 U.S. 147, 164 (1939).

51CARDOZO, THE NATURE OF THE JUDICIAL PROCESS 112 (1960 ed.).

52Louisiana *ex rel.* Gremillion v. National Ass'n for the Advancement of Colored People, 366 U.S. 293 (1961); National Ass'n for the Advancement of Colored People v. Alabama *ex rel.* Patterson, 357 U.S. 449 (1958).

53Communist Party v. Subversive Activities Control Bd., 367 U.S. 1 (1961).

54New York *ex rel.* Bryant v. Zimmerman, 278 U.S. 63 (1928). This case is not only pre-balancing, but was decided before the incorporation of the first amendment in the fourteenth was firmly established. It held that a statute requiring oath-bound organizations to file membership lists for public record was a reasonable exercise of the police power. The deterrent effect of the listing on antisocial conduct was mentioned in order to *justify* the statute. The possibility that individuals might suffer private reprisals merely because their names were listed, and that listing might thus have a deterrent effect on mere membership, was not considered. The "nature of the organization" was referred to, not to generate a public interest to which private rights could be subordinated, but simply to show that the *exclusion* of labor unions and named fraternal orders from the statute did not result in an arbitrary classification violative of the equal protection clause.

55Bates v. City of Little Rock, 361 U.S. 516 (1960).

56Uphaus v. Wyman, 360 U.S. 72 (1959).

57The distinguishing feature is said to be "the nature of the organization regulated, and hence the danger involved in its covert operation...." Communist Party v. Subversive Activities Control Bd., 367 U.S. 1, 101 (1961). But does not a considerable element of personal approval or disapproval of the cause enter into the judicial notion of the "nature of the organization"?

58This statement may seem paradoxical, since of course the courts often balance conflicting interests.

But the interests they are accustomed to balance are much more easily and noncontroversially identifiable and operate on a much smaller scale. To decide the constitutional question involved in a case like *Barenblatt v. United States, supra* note 2, by a meaningful balancing process, it would be necessary to put into the record everything which is known about Communism, past and present, domestic and foreign. It would be necessary to make a comprehensive analysis of the international situation and forecast its future development. It would be necessary to assess the contribution to the legislative process made by the type of investigation conducted by the House Committee on Un-American Activities and the probable adequacy of other methods by which Congress might undertake to keep itself informed. There would have to be a careful estimate of how such investigations have affected freedom of expression and association, their side-effects on the national psyche, their effect on our "image" abroad, etc. And the Court would have to take into consideration the effectiveness of other anti-Communist programs and activities, including many, such as those of the F.B.I., the details of which are not readily available for judicial study. This is not the kind of "balancing" courts do to decide an equity case.

[59]Text accompanying note 19 *supra.*

[60]HAND, THE BILL OF RIGHTS 66-69 (1958). See also HAND, SPIRIT OF LIBERTY 204 (2nd ed. 1953), where Judge Hand states that the Bill of Rights is to be interpreted not as law, but merely as an "admonition to forbearance" which the judges cannot compel the legislators or the electorate to follow.

[61]This is true, at present, only with respect to the constitutional protection of freedom of speech against the federal government. The Court is currently protecting freedom of speech against the states in the name of the due process clause of the fourteenth amendment. Accordingly, in these cases, the Constitution, as currently read, does not treat the two problems differently. This is the fault of the Court majority which, in the *Slaughter House Cases,* 16 Wall. 36 (U.S. 1873), saved states' rights by construing the privileges and immunities clause of the fourteenth amendment as an essentially meaningless enactment, protecting only rights which were already protected by the supremacy clause. It is also the fault of the Court of the late 1920's and early 1930's which, in deciding to incorporate some provisions of the Bill of Rights in the fourteenth amendment, illogically resorted to the due process clause instead of reexamining *Slaughter House.* If there is one thing clear about the intent of the framers of the fourteenth amendment, it is that, if they intended incorporation of the Bill of Rights, or any part of it, it was the privileges and immunities clause, not the due process clause, which was intended to have that effect. See generally, Frantz, *Enforcement of the Fourteenth Amendment,* 9 LAW. GUILD REV. 122 (1949). Of course, if freedom of speech is protected against the states only because it is part of the "liberty" referred to in the due process clause, then the Constitution does not say that the states may not abridge it. It says that they may—provided due process is followed. And if the answer to this is that a statute which abridges liberty is "not due process," then the whole statement becomes meaningless. This is a dilemma of the Court's own making and there is no escape from it except to abandon incorporation, abandon *Slaughter House*—or ignore the difficulty.

[62]Minersville School Dist. v. Gobitis, 310 U.S. 586, 599, 600 (1940), overruled in West Virginia State Bd. of Educ. v. Barnette, 319 U.S. 624 (1943). The same distinction is suggested, but not passed upon, by Stone, J., in United States v. Carolene Products, 304 U.S. 144, 152 n.4 (1938).

[63]"We cannot, after all, make arrangement *de novo.* The Congress has traditionally decided on the merits and left the final constitutional issues to the Court. It has for a very long time enjoyed the relative freedom of decision-making which comes with such a shift of final responsibility. There is no reason to believe that Congress will give up the freedom just because the Court divests itself of the responsibility, particularly if Justices' resignation is accomplished not by a formal transfer of authority but a series of modest proposals in judicial opinions which Congress is free to ignore." Shapiro, *Judicial Modesty, Political Reality, and Preferred Position,* 47 CORNELL L.Q. 175, 194 (1962).

[64]"[T]he nature of the legislative process, combined with the nature of constitutional issues, makes it virtually impossible for Congress to make independent, unified, or responsible judgments on the constitutionality of its own statutes." Shapiro, *supra* note 63, at 193.

[65]It is beyond the scope of this article to consider how constitutionally protected freedom of speech should be defined. Any adequate discussion of that topic would require another article at least as long as this one. However, lest it be said that no definition is possible short of an "unlimited license to talk," I will indicate in skeletal form what my definition would be.

I would take as my starting point the thesis of Dr. Alexander Meiklejohn that freedom of speech is essential to self-government. See MEIKLEJOHN, POLITICAL FREEDOM: THE CONSTITUTIONAL POWERS OF THE PEOPLE (1960). And I would agree that: "Other liberties are held under governments, but liberty of opinion keeps governments themselves in due subjection to their duties." 2 LORD ERSKINE'S SPEECHES 139, 140 (1876) (speech in defense of Thomas Paine). Consideration of this function, rather than analysis of the literal words of the amendment, is the key to definition, though the words must not be ignored. As Meiklejohn points out, it is not a question of the rights of the individual, but of the constitutional powers of the people as a self-governing body.

Accordingly, I would define "the freedom of speech" as the exclusion of governmental force from the process by which public opinion is formed on public issues. Any governmental action which makes it more difficult or hazardous to take one side of a public issue than to take the other is an abridgment, whether or not this was its avowed purpose. "Public issues," for this purpose, are not limited to those on which governmental action may be taken, but include philosophy, religion, ethics, esthetics, social sciences, etc.—all those, in other words, on which an enlightened public opinion may be deemed desirable.

An act or relationship (such as a conspiracy in restraint of trade) which is itself unlawful is not immunized by the use of speech as a means. And speech employed to induce an unlawful act by another is unprotected. But the expression of a viewpoint on a public issue cannot be punished or prevented on the ground that it is likely to cause or inspire unlawful conduct, unless the Brandeis test of no-time-to-answer is met. And the "danger" that the public will be persuaded to adopt an incorrect opinion is not one which government has any right to prevent. In addition, there are narrow areas which are unprotected because no public issue is involved. Fo rexample, the speech involved in private libel cases is typically addressed to such issues as whether or not a specified private individual has committed a crime. This, if open to decision at all, is for a jury to decide, and public debate on the topic is neither necessary nor desirable.

Governmental action which tends to regulate the content of public debate, either directly, or by singling out ideological groups or tendencies for special treatment, is permissible only if it focusses narrowly on unprotected speech and has no unnecessary deterrent effect on protected speech.

The act of speaking, as distinct from the content of what is said, is always subject to regulation. But such regulations must meet three standards: (1) They must be neutral in their impact on the expression of various points of view. (2) They must avoid discretionary licensing features which would empower an official or body to use them as a means of content regulation. And (3), they must leave open reasonably adequate means — including low-cost means — of reaching the public with all points of view.

Substantial doubts in the application of any of these standards should be resolved in favor of protection.

Most, if not all, of the elements of this definition are already contained in Supreme Court opinions. Furthermore, I believe that, except for the cases in which the Court has backed away from its own principles in order to accommodate anti-Communism, there have been comparatively few decisions since 1931 which are inconsistent with this analysis.

Of course, no contention is made that this definition would eliminate the difficult borderline case. No other definition with which I am acquainted would do that —nor does balancing.

I have excluded this discussion from the text, partly because it is really extraneous to the argument, but chiefly because objections to the particular definition might otherwise distract attention from my present thesis, which is simply that definition is necessary. But if my definition does not satisfy, it does not follow that balancing is vindicated. The alternative to balancing is not my definition, but whatever definition the Supreme Court would adopt, if persuaded of the necessity of adopting one. There can be no danger that any definition which the Court could be persuaded to adopt would not be preferable to *ad hoc* balancing, if the objections to the latter are as profound as I am contending.

Selection *2*

_____

On the Meaning of the First Amendment: Absolutes in the Balance

Wallace Mendelson

"Doctrines are the most frightful tyrants to which men ever are subject, because doctrines get inside of a man's reason and betray him against himself."—W. G. Sumner[1]

In a recent article, Mr. Laurent Frantz criticizes the Supreme Court's "balancing of interests" approach in free speech cases. In the course of his argument, he also lampoons the "absolutist" approach of the dissenters, and chides its chief spokesman for putting his argument "largely in the form that the first amendment 'means what it says.'"[2] Yet in criticizing the Court, Mr. Frantz himself rests largely on what he seems to assume is a clear meaning in the "constitutional text"— and its history.[3]

In support of the Court's balancing position, I suggest that the language of the first amendment is highly ambiguous, and that this ambiguity is at best compounded by history. Professor Chaffee put it in a thimble: "The truth is, I think, that the framers had no very clear idea as to what they

meant by 'the freedom of speech or of the press.'"[4] Indeed, perhaps it is not going too far to suggest that there is no more equivocal word in the English language than "freedom." What Lincoln said of "liberty" is relevant here: "The world has never had a good definition of [it]." He also pointed out that what is freedom for the lion is death for the lamb. In short, however clear the thou-shalt-not part of the amendment may be, its chain of meaning cannot transcend the fogginess of its weakest link. Surely the framers would have communicated more clearly if they had omitted the weasel-word, and provided simply, "Congress shall pass no law abridging (or restricting) speech." This suggests, of course, that they used the word "freedom" as a limiting or qualifying, not an enlarging, term—a reference presumably to the narrow conception of free utterance that prevailed in the late eighteenth

"On the Meaning of the First Amendment: Absolutes in the Balance" by Wallace Mendelson, 50 *California Law Review* 821 (1962). Copyright 1962, California Law Review, Inc. Reprinted by permission.

century. Finally, it is noteworthy that even so stout a libertarian as Alexander Meiklejohn has chided those who insist that the words "abridging the freedom of speech or of the press" are "plain words, easily understood."[5]

Of course, as Mr. Frantz suggests, we are entitled to seek clarification in history. Doing so, he cites Jefferson's statement that "it is time enough for the rightful purposes of civil government for its officers to interfere when principles break out into overt acts against peace and good order."[6] But this is not only selective history, it is selective Jefferson. Referring to the "licentiousness" of the press that opposed him, the first of the Jeffersonians observed:

"This is a dangerous state of things, and the press ought to be restored to its credibility if possible. The restraints provided by the laws of the States are sufficient for this, if applied. And I have, therefore, long thought that a few prosecutions of the most prominent offenders would have a wholesome effect....Not a general prosecution, for that would look like persecution; but a selected one."[7]

Some of us may be excused for finding in these combined statements as much equivocation as in the first amendment itself.

Holmes presumably was one of the greatest of legal historians. Yet he gave at different times opposite interpretations of the historic meaning of the amendment. Speaking for himself and Brandeis, he observed that "History seems to me against the notion [that] the First Amendment left the common law of seditious libel in force."[8] A few years earlier he had written for the Court: "[T]he main purpose of such constitutional provisions is 'to prevent all such *previous restraints*...as had been practiced by other governments,' and they do not prevent the subsequent punishment of such as may be deemed contrary to the public welfare."[9] In this statement Holmes had the support of Cooley, who maintained that its Blackstonian outlook "has been followed by American commentators of standard authority as embodying correctly the idea incorporated in the constitutional law of the country by the provisions in the American Bill of Rights."[10] To support this proposition Cooley justifiably cites Kent, Story, and Rawle.

While Holmes' switch suggests that the historic purpose of the first amendment is something less than obvious, Mr. Frantz may find comfort in the fact that the Justice's later position was the more liberal one. Professor Chafee also seems to support the charge of vagueness, but by a switch from a generous to a more restricted view. Thus he first

asserted that the framers intended "to wipe out the common law of sedition, and make further prosecutions for criticism of the government, without any incitement to law-breaking, forever impossible."[11]

It would be ironical if Holmes reversed himself under the influence of Chafee, because Chafee later appears to have altered his own position:

"[The] argument that all the freedoms within the First Amendment are not open to any governmental restrictions...leans far too heavily on the absolute nature of its language....Especially significant is the contemporaneous evidence that the phrase "freedom of the press" was viewed against a background of familiar legal institutions which men of 1791 did not regard as objectionable, such as damage suits for libel. Many state constitutions of this time included guarantees of freedom of speech and press which have been treated as having approximately the same scope as the federal provisions. Some of these, as in Massachusetts, were absolute in terms, while others...expressly imposed responsibility for abuse of the right. The precise nature of the state constitutional language did not matter; the early interpretation was much the same. *Not only were private libel suits allowed, but also punishments for criminal libel and for contempt of court.* For instance, there were several Massachusetts convictions around 1800 for attacking the conduct of the legislature and public officials....

"The truth is, I think, that the framers had no very clear idea as to what they meant by "the freedom of speech or of the press," but we can say...with reasonable assurance....[that] the freedom which Congress was forbidden to abridge was not, for them, some absolute concept which had never existed on earth."[12]

Henry Schofield's "Freedom of the Press in the United States," which appeared in 1914, seems to be the seedbed of the modern libertarian conception of the first amendment. It begins, however, with the admission that the "nearly if not quite unanimous expressed view of our judges always has been, and is, that the constitutional declarations of liberty of the press are only declaratory of the English common-law right protected by the English courts at the time of the Revolution...."[13] Of course, it may be that Professor Schofield, writing 123 years after adoption of the amendment, had a truer insight into that history than judges and commentators who witnessed or participated in it, but surely there is room for respectful doubt.

So far, I have meant only to suggest that at best

(from the liberal point of view) history is a somewhat less than obvious key to the meaning of the first amendment. Surely, however, no such discussion can fail to mention Leonard Levy's powerful (if reluctant) case that history speaks clearly in these matters—but in a way that contradicts the libertarian position.[14]

For those who are not moved by his "textual and historical" arguments, Mr. Frantz offers three "fundamental policy reasons" for a more active judicial role in expression, than in economic, cases:

"An economic mistake or injustice [by Congress] does not interfere with the political process and that process therefore remains open for its correction or redress if the courts refuse relief. The same cannot be said where legislation results in infringement of political rights, for the injured can hardly rely for redress on the very weapons of which they are deprived."[15]

This is difficult to follow. By the Interstate Commerce Act, Congress deprives a railroad owner of his "freedom" to charge what the traffic will bear. By the Smith Act, Congress deprives a Communist of his "freedom" to teach and advocate violent overthrow of government. *Yet both the railroad owner and the Communist are perfectly free to seek political redress, i.e., repeal of the measure deemed offensive.* Both may speak freely in favor of a change in the law. Any substantial legislative interference with that kind of freedom would certainly have hard going in the Supreme Court. Even the leader of the antiactivists has made his position clear on that point.[16]

Mr. Frantz's second policy reason for giving free utterance a "preferred place" is that

"economic interests are typically represented in legislative bodies—or are able to obtain a hearing from them. Despised ideological minorities typically are not. In extreme situations such as those which give rise to first amendment test cases, their political influence may be less than zero, for it may be better politics for a legislator to abuse them than to listen to their grievances."[17]

Surely we cannot pretend that all economic interests have substantial "political influence," nor that all other interests are politically impotent. Mr. Frantz's distinction then is not between the economic and the noneconomic, but between claims which have much political leverage and those which have little or none. On this basis, some economic interests ought to enjoy a "preferred place" (including perhaps a presumption of unconstitutionality for offending legislation), just as some spiritual interests should have only a second-class status. This might entail some difficulties in application. Would the crucial test refer to absolute or relative political influence? How would such values be measured? How much political strength would be required to justify a "deferred" judicial place? Would a politically negligible religious group enjoy an advantage in the courts that would be denied to the Catholic Church? Would the latter have a "preferred place" vis-à-vis protestantism? Ideally, of course, legislators and all of us would give every "despised minority" a respectful hearing, but surely *the first amendment* does not require it.

The final policy reason presented on behalf of libertarianism on the Bench is that while "activism" in economic cases restricts the scope of "popular choice," activism in utterance cases expands it.[18] But surely a judicial veto of anticommunist legislation limits the range of popular government just as effectively as a judicial veto of minimum-wage legislation. Both say to the people these are the choices you may not make. And it is absolutely clear that democracy is poisoned by suppressing those who preach violence when all the avenues of peaceful change are open? Men of the Weimar Republic, like those of pre-1948 Czechoslovakia, might have some interesting thoughts on that question.

Having bludgeoned both the balancing and the absolutist gambits in speech cases, Mr. Frantz concludes by insisting that constitutionally protected freedom of speech ought to be "defined."[19] Yet strangely (for one who is so concerned for freedom of popular choice) he thinks this should be done not by a constitutional convention, nor by Congress, but by the Supreme Court. To insist that "freedom of speech" needs defining is to concede what I have been arguing: that it is not adequately defined either in the language of the Constitution, or by history, or by considerations of public policy so unquestionable as to be fit subjects for judicial notice.

It is largely because of the absence of defining standards, I suggest, that the Court has resorted openly to balancing in free speech cases. We have had too many opinions that hide the inevitable weighing process by pretending that decisions spring full-blown from the Constitution—a document written generations ago by men who had not the slightest conception of the world in which *we* live. "It will ever remain a mystery to me," Thomas R. Powell observed, "how intelligent jurists can make these professions of nonparticipation in the judicial process."[20] Open balancing compels a judge to take full responsibility for his decisions, and promises a particularized, rational account of how he arrives at them—more particularized and more rational at least than the familiar parade of hallowed abstractions, elastic absolutes, and selective history. Moreover, this approach should make it more difficult for judges to rest on their predispositions without ever subjecting them to the test of reason. It should also make their accounts more rationally auditable. Above all, the open balancing technique is calculated to leave "the sovereign prerogative of choice" to the people—with the least interference that is compatible with our tradition of judicial review. Absent that tradition in utterance cases, the Court might logically accept Learned Hand's view that the first amendment (like the republican-form-of-government clause) is too uncommunicative—too lacking in guidelines—to be treated as law.[21]

Those who find these thoughts offensive may recall that even modern libertarians are far from agreement on the meaning of free speech. Thus its two leading academic advocates—Chafee and Meiklejohn—are deeply divided on matters of scope and limitation. Similarly, Justices Black and Douglas have found themselves on opposite sides of utterance issues. Indeed the first amendment idea is so obscure that both of them apparently failed to see a free-expression problem in the compulsory flag salute until it was pointed out by Mr. Justice Jackson. This obscurity is also revealed in Mr. Justice Black's change of heart with respect to the validity of libel laws—and in the disagreements of Holmes and Brandeis. So too, as we have seen, Jefferson could not agree with himself on the meaning of free communication. Finally, even those two well springs of Anglo-American freedom, Milton's *Areopagitica* and Mill's *On Liberty*, are deeply at odds on the thing that they both eulogize. For surely Mill could not accept Milton's principle that only "neighboring differences, or rather indifferences" are entitled to toleration.[22]

This brings us to the anguished question that Mr. Frantz puts at least by implication: What good is the first amendment, if it is not to be given a "preferred place" by "activist" magistrates? Madison long ago gave the answer: It is futile to rely on judges and "parchment barriers"; politics is the only reliable protection for basic substantive interests.

Of course, Madison introduced and fought for the Bill of Rights—and, in so doing, referred to judicial review in support of it, as libertarians emphasize ad infinitum.[23] What they fail to mention is that this was Madison under pressure. If the "father of the Constitution" had really wanted a bill of rights, why did he not introduce and fight for one in the constitutional convention? Here is his answer:

"I have never thought the omission [of a bill of rights from the original Constitution] a material defect, nor been anxious to supply it even by *subsequent* amendment, for any other reason than that it is anxiously desired by others....

"I have not viewed it in an important light... because [among other things] experience proves [its] inefficiency on those occasions when its control is most needed....In Virginia I have seen the bill of rights violated in every instance where it has been opposed to a popular current...."[24]

Before he was pressured into supporting a bill of rights, Madison insisted the only use of a formal declaration was that "the political truths declared in that solemn manner acquire by degrees the character of fundamental maxims of free government, and as they become incorporated with the national sentiment, counteract the impulses of interest and passion."[25] If the government should act improperly, a bill of rights would be "a good ground for an appeal to the sense of the community."[26] How far this is from judicial review! And how close to Learned Hand's thought that the Bill of Rights is not law, but a moral admonition.

Madison was unenthusiastic about the Bill-of-Rights-Judicial-Review approach because he foresaw a far more reliable, and far more sophisticated, shield for civil liberty: the structure and process of politics. For him the constitutional diffusion of power and the vast expanse of the nation with its multiplicity of regional, economic, religious, and other interests were the true safeguards. Faction would resist faction; ambition would weigh against ambition. The hopes and fears of each subgroup would check and balance those of all the others. Government could act only after political compromise had found the common denominator of a host of mutually suspicious minorities. In the extended, pluralistic republic of the United States this could not be an easy, overnight venture. No program that had survived the give and take necessary to attain support by a concurrent majority of our incredibly varied factional interests could depart substantially from the Nation's moral center of gravity. No governmental system could be expected to achieve more; certainly not by idealistic fiats from the Bench that fly in the face of deeply felt community needs. In short, as Madison saw it, majority rule—given a vast empire of diffused socio-political power—was the only reliable security against governmental inhumanity.[27]

Of course, some free speech "indiscretions" might survive the sifting of the social and political processes—the Sedition Act of 1798, the Espionage Act of 1917, the Smith Act of 1940 come to mind. But these (assuming they were unjustified) would necessarily reflect such deep and widespread feelings as to defy judicial veto. The upshot is that Congress has killed thousands of bills reflecting every imaginable form of bigotry, intolerance, and demagogery; the Supreme Court has not yet struck down a national measure on the basis of any provision in the first amendment.[28] As Madison anticipated, the congressional batting average is about .999; The Court's is .000.

My point is that liberals appreciate the political process far too little, and expect far more judicial review than it has ever been able to deliver. Conservatives no longer make this mistake. They know the cost and frailty of a preferred place in court. Accordingly, since 1937, they have concentrated on legislatures, and have carried off all but a few of the prizes.

Meanwhile a select little company of libertarians—with far less social support than conservatives had in the old days—is trying to repeat all of the Old-Guard mistakes: the twisted history, the tortured parchment, the sugar-coated bias called public policy, the preferred place that can hope only to delay defeat. Sooner or later libertarians will have to face it—the real victories are won in legislatures and at the polls.[29] Man after all is a political, not a legal, animal.

Footnotes

[1]HITCHNER & HARBOLD, MODERN GOVERNMENT 509 (1962).
[2]Frantz, *The First Amendment in the Balance*, 71 YALE L.J. 1424, 1432 (1962).
[3]*Id.* at 1433–44, 1446.
[4]Chafee, Book Review, 62 HARV. L. REV. 891, 898 (1949).
[5]Meiklejohn, *The First Amendment Is an Absolute*, 1961 SUP. CT. REV. 245, 247.
[6]Frantz, *supra* note 2, at 1446.
[7]Letter from Thomas Jefferson to Thomas McKean, Feb. 19, 1803, in 8 THE WRITINGS OF THOMAS JEFFERSON 216, 218–19 (Ford ed. 1897). For extensive evidence of the restricted conception of free utterance of Jefferson, and indeed of many of the Found-

ing Fathers, see Levy, *Liberty and the First Amendment: 1790–1800,* 78 AM. HIST. REV. 22 (1962).
[8]Abrams v. United States, 250 U.S. 616, 630 (1919).
[9]Patterson v. Colorado, 215 U.S. 454, 462 (1907).
[10]COOLEY, CONSTITUTIONAL LIMITATIONS 420 (3d ed. 1874).
[11]Chafee, *Freedom of Speech in Wartime*, 32 HARV. L. REV. 932, 947 (1919).
[12]Chafee, Book Review, 62 HARV. L. REV. 891, 897–98 (1949). (Emphasis added.)
[13]Schofield, *Freedom of the Press in the United States,* in 2 ESSAYS ON CONSTITUTIONAL LAW AND EQUITY 510, 511 (1921).
[14]LEVY, LEGACY OF SUPPRESSION (1960).
[15]Frantz, *supra* note 2, at 1446.
[16]West Virginia Bd. of Educ. v. Barnette, 319 U.S. 624, 664 (1943); Minersville School Dist. v. Gobitis, 310 U.S. 586, 600 (1940).
[17]Frantz, *supra* note 2, at 1447.
[18]*Ibid.*
[19]*Id.* at 1449–50.
[20]POWELL, VAGARIES AND VARIETIES IN CONSTITUTIONAL INTERPRETATION 28 (1956).
[21]HAND, THE SPIRIT OF LIBERTY 177–78 (1st ed. 1952).
[22]THE WORKS OF JOHN MILTON 349–50 (Patterson ed. 1931).
[23]See, *e.g.,* Frantz, *supra* note 2, at 1448 n.100.
[24]Letter from James Madison to Thomas Jefferson, Oct. 17, 1788, in PADOVER, THE COMPLETE MADISON 253–55 (1953).
[25]*Id.* at 254.
[26]*Id.* at 255.
[27]Madison recognized that the sociopolitical check and balance system might not be an adequate restraint upon a state because of the relative paucity of interests at play within its boundaries. This may explain why the Supreme Court has been more willing to impose first amendment ideals upon the states than upon the Nation.
[28]Mr. Frantz criticizes the Court for not enforcing the first amendment as "absolutely" as it enforces some other Bill-of-Rights provisions. Frantz, *supra* note 2, at 1436–38. The answer is presumably that these other provisions are directed largely against judges, administrators, and police officers. It is one thing for the Supreme Court to override them; it is quite another to override the National Legislature *acting in its lawmaking capacity.* See also note 27 *supra.*
[29]Brown v. Board of Educ., 347 U.S. 483 (1954), was costly indeed, if it convinced libertarians that the judicial process is an effective tool of libertarianism. Eight years after the original decision, *all the public schools of one of the defendants* (Prince Edward County, Virginia) *remained closed.* Only .4% of the South's Negro public school pupils were in classes with whites—and they were concentrated largely in the border states. Alabama, Mississippi, and South Carolina still had no integrated public schools. What Georgia and Louisiana had achieved could not fairly be called even token integration. See generally *Is the South Really Integrating Now?*, U.S. News & World Report, Dec. 10, 1962, p. 78.

Selection 3

Is the First Amendment Law? A Reply To Professor Mendelson

Laurent B. Frantz

Professor Wallace Mendelson has recently taken me to task[1] for my criticism[2] of the Supreme Court's use of an *ad hoc* "balancing of interests" test in free speech cases. The argument over balancing tends to be one in which there is no meeting of the minds because the contending sides are arguing from opposite unspoken assumptions. Thus, I welcome Professor Mendelson's reply as tending to bring into clearer view some of the underlying questions that need to be asked and discussed, and I ask indulgence to put my rebuttal in the rather pedantic form of stating some of those questions, as they appear to me, and giving my answers to them.

First, let us attempt to define the issue under discussion. The first amendment provides that "Congress shall make no law...abridging the freedom of speech...." Should a court, to determine whether this provision has been violated, "weigh" the "conflicting interests" involved in the particular case? If the court concludes that the interests served by the governmental action outweigh the free speech "interest" (or if it feels bound to defer to what it takes to be a legislative judgment to the same effect), is this sufficient to justify holding that action constitutional?

Here is one statement of the matter in an opinion for the Court by Justice Harlan:

"Undeniably, the First Amendment in some circumstances protects an individual from being compelled to disclose his associational relationships. However, the protections of the First Amendment, unlike a proper claim of the privilege against self-incrimination under the Fifth Amendment, do not afford a witness the right to resist inquiry in all circumstances. Where First Amendment rights are asserted to bar governmental interrogation resolution of the issues always involves a balancing by the courts of the competing private and public interests at stake in the particular circumstances shown."[3]

After discussing the issue thus defined, Justice Harlan concludes "that the balance between the individual and the governmental interests here at stake must be struck in favor of the latter, and that therefore the provisions of the First Amendment have not been offended."[4]

Justice Frankfurter, in another opinion for the Court, put it this way:

"[W]e agree that compulsory disclosure of the names of an organization's members may in certain instances infringe constitutionally protected rights of association...[citations]....But to say this much is only to recognize one of the points of reference from which analysis must begin. To state that individual liberties may be affected is to establish the condition for, not to arrive at the conclusion of, constitutional decision. Against the impediments which particular governmental regulation causes to entire freedom of individual action, there must be weighed the value to the public of the ends which the regulation may achieve."[5]

It should be noted that the first of these statements is directed only to a single class of cases, those in which first amendment rights are asserted "to bar governmental interrogation." It does not say or suggest that *ad hoc* balancing is a proper approach in all free speech cases. The statement by Justice Frankfurter, however, does seem to suggest this broader view, and he has indicated elsewhere that this is his position.[6]

The Court has thus far not committed itself to the theory that balancing applies to all free speech cases. Indeed, since the balancing vogue began, it has upheld free speech claims in at least four instances without any overt resort to *ad hoc* balancing.[7] The balancing cases—or at least those in which it has been intimated that a governmental action, which would otherwise have been forbidden, may be immunized from constitutional

"Is the First Amendment Law? A Reply to Professor Mendelson" by Laurent B. Frantz, 51 *California Law Review* 729 (1963). Copyright 1963, California Law Review, Inc. Reprinted by permission.

objection by such a balancing rationale—have all dealt with freedom of association. Indeed, all but one of them[8] have dealt with the effect of a compelled disclosure of membership or other association on the freedom to associate for the advancement of causes.

Suggestions that *ad hoc* balancing is appropriate only for a particular class of cases appear in the opinions. Thus, Justice Harlan apparently regards it as applicable only to "general regulatory statutes, not intended to control the content of speech, but incidentally limiting its unfettered exercise. ..."[9] And Chief Justice Vinson had previously declared it to be the test "when particular conduct is regulated in the interest of public order, and regulation results in an indirect, conditional, partial abridgment of speech...."[10]

In this article, I am not discussing whether balancing is or is not an appropriate method for special classes of cases, such as those dealing with a non-discriminatory regulation of the time, place, and manner of speech, or those in which a statute aimed at conduct indirectly affects speech. Nor am I discussing whether the judge should examine the pros and cons before defining the *scope* of a constitutional guarantee. I am discussing the view that the first amendment does not prohibit any action that the Court (whether deferring to a legislative judgment or applying its own) finds to be justified on an *ad hoc* balancing basis. It is not my contention that the courts should *never* balance. My contention is that they should not, especially in free speech cases, employ balancing as a substitute for an effort to find a rule or principle that can guide decision. Balancing, in other words, is not acceptable as the principle. It is acceptable (and doubtless inevitable) as the technique for making a purely prudential choice between alternatives that are, in principle, equally permissible.

Though general *ad hoc* balancing has not been adopted by the Court, a discussion of it is not purely academic. It has been adopted by Justice Frankfurter[11] who, before his retirement, was the senior and apparently most influential judicial advocate of balancing. And Professor Mendelson, when he undertakes to defend balancing, does not do so on the basis of considerations peculiar to the special class of cases in which the Court has applied it. His arguments are directed to the meaning—or lack of meaning—of the freedom of speech clause and to general considerations of the proper role of courts in applying constitutional limitations. If theories justifying balancing on so broad a basis should ultimately prevail, the result could only be a first amendment devoid of any higher level judgment to which an *ad hoc* balancing judgment could be subordinated. With this in

mind let us turn to Professor Mendelson's argument and to the questions that it seems to me to raise.

IS *AD HOC* BALANCING REQUIRED BY THE AMBIGUITY OR VAGUENESS OF THE FREEDOM OF SPEECH CLAUSE?

In support of the Supreme Court's balancing position, Professor Mendelson contends "that the language of the first amendment is highly ambiguous, and that this ambiguity is at best compounded by history."[12] He apparently admits that "Congress shall make no law" is comprehensible as far as it goes, and he does not profess to be hopelessly puzzled by "abridging." But the amendment does not define "the freedom of speech," and Professor Mendelson quotes Professor Chafee[13] to the effect that "the framers had no very clear idea as to what they meant" by this phrase. Without a definition of "the freedom of speech," Professor Mendelson can make nothing of the statement as a whole, since "its chain of meaning cannot transcend the fogginess of its weakest link."[14] Accordingly, he takes the view that the courts should set the text aside as incapable of shedding any light on how specific cases should be decided, and approach free speech issues on a pragmatic case-to-case basis.[15] The constitutional text, without which courts would presumably have no authority to decide the case at all, should play no part in their decision.

Constitution writing is not a practicable undertaking if inexplicitness is to be treated as a total failure to say anything. Failure to define the key term has not proved an insuperable obstacle to applying other constitutional provisions. The Constitution prohibits "unreasonable searches and seizures" without saying what kinds are reasonable. It prohibits "excessive bail" without saying anything about the level that should not be exceeded. It guarantees "speedy" trial without telling us how to decide what delays are permissible (indeed, it is entirely possible that the framers "had no very clear idea as to what they meant" by "speedy" trial). It provides that private property shall not be "taken for public use, without just compensation" without telling us what constitutes a taking, or what uses are "public," or what standards compensation must meet in order to be called "just." Yet with all these clauses, it has been found possible to give the undefined key word *some* meaning (not necessarily "clear" meaning) and to treat that meaning as a mandatory standard for the disposition of those cases to which it is found to apply. Surely it is reading the freedom of speech clause with a scepticism verging on open hostility to say that no prohibitory content can be found in it, simply because, literally read, it may seem to prohibit *too much!*

How are the vague and undefined words of the constitution ordinarily given content? Partly by an exercise of judicial judgment, certainly, but not ordinarily by an unprincipled case-to-case pragmatic judgment, unrelated to any concept of the meaning or function of the constitutional language. Nor is it enough to inquire what applications of the language would have been thought proper at the time of its adoption. Constitutional limitations, no less than constitutional grants of power, need to be kept flexible enough to be applied to changed conditions and new problems. The starting point, in any such inquiry, should be to ascertain the *purpose* of the grant or prohibition. Once that has been done, a principled basis is generally found for deciding whether particular cases fall within the general language—as well as for extending the language to problems and conditions which the framers could not have foreseen, but which can nevertheless be recognized as within the goals we think they sought to achieve, or as examples of the evil we think they sought to guard against.

Does the freedom of speech clause have a purpose? Professor Mendelson considers the regulation of speech to be indistinguishable, both constitutionally and in principle, from the regulation of action.[16] So I suppose he must also believe that the right to say what one thinks is merely a special instance of every individual's freedom to do as he pleases—and subject to limitation for the general good on the same principles and to the same extent. If this is his standpoint, it is no wonder he finds the freedom of speech clause as incomprehensible as I should find a provision forbidding Congress to abridge "the freedom of action." It also follows, of course, that had the framers held this view, there would have been no freedom of speech clause.

If the Constitution is viewed as adopting representative government *as a device by which the people are to govern themselves,* a significant function of the freedom of speech clause is at once apparent. The device calls for reciprocal government; for the people to govern the delegated authority by which they are governed. This cannot work unless there is an independent popular concensus, protected from governmental intervention, to which the delegated authority can be held responsible. If the delegated authority is permitted to prescribe what may and may not be advocated, especially in the realm of political theory and policy, then, *pro tanto,* it is no longer responsible to a popular will independent of its own, but to a

reflection or extension of its own will. The people can still select, at the ballot box, those by whom they are to be governed, but they can no longer govern through them. The government may still be representative in form, but self-government is not its substance.

If the freedom of speech clause is conceived to serve this function, there is no difficulty about finding meaning in it. It still does not have the "clear meaning" that Professor Mendelson demands of it, but constitutional provisions seldom have "clear meaning" and I suspect that they would not prove continuously serviceable for generations and centuries if they did. Borderline cases, and mixed cases, can still be put, which may require not only an exercise of judgment, but a very difficult one. But if meaning is attributed to the freedom of speech clause, those cases will not have to be approached without reference to a principle, as Professor Mendelson apparently proposes that *all* free speech issues be approached.

Although according the freedom of speech clause a function does not do away with the difficult cases, it does, I think, create some easy ones. From this point of view, it becomes obvious that most of the cases that are supposed to confound the "absolutist"—such as the man who falsely shouts "Fire!" in the crowded theater, the man who uses speech to solicit a crime, and the man who uses speech to enrich himself by fraudulent representations—are not cases in which it has been found necessary to abridge "the freedom of speech" for the protection of some "competing interest." They are cases in which, though speech is involved, "the freedom of speech" is not. It is also obvious, I think, that mere regulations of the time, place, and manner of speech—such as protecting the citizen's ears against sound trucks making "loud and raucous noises,"[17] or protecting his privacy against unwanted doorbell pushers,[18] or prohibiting child labor on the streets whether or not engaged in the sale of religious pamphlets[19]— do not, per se, affect the "freedom" of speech. They may do so, however, if they are applied in a discriminatory manner so as to burden one point of view more than another, or if they are left open to discretionary application by officials who are empowered to use them as an instrument for regulating the content of public discourse, or if they are carried to such an extent that adequate low-cost means of reaching the public with all points of view are no longer available.

Of course, all the above determinations can be *stated* in balancing terms, because, unless a "competing interest" were present, government would have no occasion to act, even where there was no constitutional inhibition against such action. But it is not the presence or the weight of the competing interest that is determinative. It is not even the nature of the speech in which the individual desired to engage (which would require an opposite determination in the case of the child selling religious pamphlets on the streets). The crucial factor is that the *nature of the governmental action* was not such as to compromise or threaten the independence of that popular consensus to which the delegated authority must be held responsible.

It seems to me that a functional approach to the freedom of speech clause also suggests some clear cases of violation of that clause. I submit that it is not a borderline case when Communists are prosecuted, not for overt preparations for insurrection, not even for uttering or writing specific words of an insurrectionary nature, but for "conspiring" to spread a political theory and doctrine capable of inspiring insurrection on some remote hypothetical future occasion.[20] It is not a borderline case when persons are prosecuted merely for being members of an organization with knowledge that it holds such theories.[21] It is not a borderline case when a Subversive Activities Control Board is set up to try and condemn associations, not for illegal activities, but for their political coloration. And—though the framers could not have foreseen such a development—there could be no clearer violation of the intended relationship between the sovereign principal and the delegated authority than for the representatives to summon a citizen before them and demand an accounting of how he exercised his reserved powers. In fact, I cannot help wondering if perhaps Professor Mendelson's real difficulty is not so much the first amendment's ambiguity as the clarity with which it speaks to the heart of current controversy if it is permitted to mean anything.

DOES THE CASE AGAINST THE JUDICIAL "ACTIVISM" PRECLUDE TREATING THE FIRST AMENDMENT AS LAW?

In my original article, I stated that, though I did not propose to review the arguments for and against judicial review, I thought the evidence was "reasonably clear that the first amendment was proposed with the express expectation and intention that the courts would enforce it."[22] In support of this view I cited the familiar statement made by Madison in presenting the proposed Bill of Rights to the Congress:

"If they are incorporated into the Constitution, independent tribunals of justice will consider themselves in a peculiar manner the guardians of those rights; they will be an impenetrable bulwark

against every assumption of power in the Legislative or Executive; they will be naturally led to resist every encroachment upon rights expressly stipulated for in the Constitution by the declaration of rights."[23]

But, says Professor Mendelson, this was "Madison under pressure." This was not what he really thought. What he really thought was that the omission of a Bill of Rights from the original document was not "a material defect" and that supplying one would do little good because "experience proves" its "inefficiency on those occasions when its controul is most needed." Madison, Professor Mendelson tells us, "was unenthusiastic about the Bill-of-Rights-Judicial-Review approach because he foresaw a far more reliable, and far more sophisticated, shield for civil liberty: the structure and process of politics."[24]

Madison also wrote:

"[I]n a representative republic, where the executive magistracy is carefully limited; both in the extent and the duration of its power; and where the legislative power is exercised by an assembly, which is inspired, by a supposed influence over the people, with an intrepid confidence in its own strength; which is sufficiently numerous to feel all the passions which actuate a multitude, yet not so numerous as to be incapable of pursuing the objects of its passions, by means which reason prescribes; it is against the enterprising ambition of this department that the people ought to indulge all their jealousy and exhaust all their precautions."[25]

It is hard to believe that the author of these lines was an early prophet of the view that there should be no limits to the powers of the Congress except those automatically imposed by "the structure and process of politics."

And if he was, what of it? The issue is not what Madison really thought, but how the first amendment was presented to those who voted for its enactment. If Madison thought that the document he proposed was not really needed and would prove ineffective, then the Congress that adopted his proposal, and the states that ratified it, overruled him in that respect and his true opinion can no longer be put into effect, except by further recourse to the amending process.

Professor Mendelson notes that I criticized the Court "for not enforcing the first amendment as 'absolutely' as it enforces some other Bill-of-Rights provisions." To this he responds:

"The answer is presumably that these other provisions are directed largely against judges, administrators, and police officers. It is one thing for the Supreme Court to override them; it is quite another to override the National Legislature *acting in its lawmaking capacity.*"[26]

So it seems to be contended that the first amendment ought to be assigned a constitutional status *inferior* to the rest of the Bill of Rights. A provision that undertakes to limit the powers of the national legislature is more unwise than one which merely addresses itself to the powers of judges, administrators, and police officers. It *ought* to be accorded less enforcement. It is indeed a serious matter to limit the powers of Congress "acting in its lawmaking capacity." It might, however, be even more serious for the power of Congress, especially in this area, to be subject to no limits except those under its own control. The framers may well have been aware of the seriousness of both when they wrote "Congress shall make no law...."

And, while it is not necessary to my present argument to contend that the courts should discriminate for or against any constitutional provision, surely it is obvious that, if such a discrimination were to be made, the opposite discrimination would be far more justifiable than that which Professor Mendelson suggests. The question of the proper relationship and division of competence between representative government and the people represented goes to the fundamental nature and purpose of the constitutional plan and is thus of a higher level of importance than even such matters as the fundamentals of fair trial. Furthermore, it would be far more tolerable to give Congress the last word on what the Constitution means when it puts restraints on judges, administrators, and police officers than to give Congress the last word on the constitutional limits of its *own* powers.

Professor Mendelson persistently reminds us of the "activists" of the old Court, who read essentially economic judgments into the Constitution by means of "substantive due process" and "liberty of contract." Present-day libertarian "activists," such as Justice Black, are, he insists, making the same mistake.[27] He insists that judicial enforcement of the first amendment is not distinguishable from "substantive due process" because, in both cases, the judgment of individual justices must intervene between the constitutional generalization and the particular result. But the matter cannot be reduced to presence or absence of judgment. There is also a consideration of how much judgment, what kind of judgment, and the degree to which the judgment is related to the constitutional text and to a defensible concept of its probable purpose.

The due process clause reads "No person shall be...deprived of life, liberty, or property, without due process of law." A judge who decides that an economic regulation is "not due process" because it abridges a liberty he thinks ought not to be abridged, has not construed the key term "due process." He has read it out. He has made the amendment read: "no person shall be deprived of [this kind of] liberty [by any process whatsoever]." Purely as a matter of judicial "activism" or "restraint," and leaving out all other considerations, this is an entirely different type of judgment than one that occurs when a court draws from the language of the freedom of speech clause an inference that, though the language may not make it inescapable, is nevertheless *within* the language, related to a defensible concept of its probable purpose, and which is inescapably the *kind* of inference that the court *must* make if it is to give the language *any* effect.

Professor Mendelson writes that "surely a judicial veto of anti-communist legislation limits the range of popular choice just as effectively as a judicial veto of minimum wage legislation. Both say to the people these are choices you may not make."[28] It is difficult to see why a process for amending the Constitution was thought necessary, unless it was conceived that there were some choices that might not be made, *except by that process.* However, these two kinds of "judicial veto" are not at all comparable in terms of their effect on "popular choice." The "judicial veto" of wage legislation says to the people: "Your present opinion may not be implemented because it is wrong." The "judicial veto" of anti-communist legislation says to the people: "Your present opinion may be implemented in many ways, but it may not be put beyond the possibility of criticism and reconsideration. Your freedom to choose is very broad. But the choice of abolishing your own future freedom of choice is one that you may not make, except by constitutional amendment."

If a judgment made by a majority of both Houses of Congress and concurred in by the President is entitled to great judicial deference, then is not some deference also due to a judgment made by two-thirds of both Houses and ratified by three-fourths of the states? If my contention that the first amendment was adopted with the expectation and intention that it would be enforced by the courts is conceded, then (whether or not its adoption was a mistake) any "judicial activism" inherent in giving effect to that intention is merely the carrying out of a role that the Court has been assigned by constitutional processes.

Furthermore, if the premise be conceded, it is literally impossible for the Court to escape from that role to a less "activist" one. If it is "activist" for the judge to mediate between the general proposition written into the Constitution and the specific problem presented by the particular case, it cannot be *less* "activist" for him to deny the drafters and ratifiers *any* voice in the matter by putting the text aside so that the Court can determine, on a pragmatic case-to-case basis uninhibited by constitutional principles, what the particular results should be. The only third alternative is to decide not to decide. But that (if my premise be conceded) is the most "activist" choice of all. If it is "activist" to put a statute aside on the ground that it is contrary to what the Court conceives to be the meaning of the Constitution, surely it cannot be "restraint" to put a constitutional provision aside on the ground that it is contrary to what the Court conceives to be sound political theory.

And while we are remembering the "activism" of the old Court, let us not forget what happened when President Franklin D. Roosevelt tried to find an institutional remedy for it. The Congressmen found that their mail from home ran heavily against the proposal, though it was one which fell far short of stripping the Court of its powers. So the best indication that we have of the popular will with regard to judicial review is that the people would rather risk temporary frustration of their will by myopic decisions than risk a government that no longer has to submit its actions to an independent determination of their constitutional validity. And this choice was made at a moment when the Court was not only overruling an overwhelmingly popular program on exceedingly questionable constitutional grounds, but also making it difficult for the nation to find effective remedies for the great depression.

So it would seem that the Court has no popular mandate, formal or informal, to behave in the way Professor Mendelson thinks it ought to behave. A constitutional amendment leaving the first amendment in force as an admonition to Congress, but denying the courts the power to enforce it by declaring acts of Congress unconstitutional, would not be difficult to draft. Those who think this is the right arrangement should draft such an amendment and submit it to the ratification process. Let us not, in the name of "judicial restraint," attempt to convince the judges that the present constitutional arrangement is wrong and *they* should therefore change it by refusing to discharge the function assigned them, or by reading an amendment beginning "Congress shall make no law" as imposing no significant limitation on Congress's freedom to make laws.

Professor Mendelson's contentions seem to go far beyond even this, if I understand him correctly. In answer to the "anguished question" which he thinks I put, at least by implication—what good is the first amendment if it is construed as the balancing test construes it?—he observes: "Madison long ago gave the answer: It is futile to rely on judges and 'parchment barriers'; politics is the only reliable protection for basic substantive interests.[29] And he continues, paraphrasing Madison:

"For him the constitutional diffusion of power and the vast expanse of the nation with its multiplicity of regional, economic, religious, and other interests were the true safeguards....Government could act only after political compromise had found the common denominator of a host of mutually suspicious minorities....No program that had survived the give and take necessary to obtain support by a concurrent majority of our incredibly varied factional interests could depart substantially from the Nation's moral center of gravity. No governmental system could be expected to achieve more; certainly not by idealistic fiats from the Bench that fly in the face of deeply felt community needs. In short, as Madison saw it, majority rule—given a vast empire of diffused socio-political power—was the only reliable safeguard against governmental inhumanity."[30]

Whether this was Madison's answer or not, any contention that it is a sufficient answer goes far beyond the issue of first amendment balancing, and even far beyond the issue of judicial review. It amounts to saying that the whole idea of a government of limited powers, deriving its powers from a written constitution and holding them subject to limitations prescribed in that charter, is simply wrong.

I am aware, if course, that the British enjoy considerable freedom under a system of legislative supremacy, and without legally enforceable limits on the powers of Parliament. Yet it seems to me that all that needs to be said about the British system in this connection is: we cannot possibly get to it from where we are. The special virtues of the British system cannot be achieved merely by absence of a written constitution, or refusal to apply one. Renouncing our whole constitutional heritage as merely a set of futile "parchment barriers," and announcing that henceforth there are to be no limits except such as "politics" itself may set, will not give us the special virtues of the British system—it will merely destroy the special virtues of our own without giving us anything to take their place.

In any case, if some of us are now convinced that legislative supremacy is the true principle, surely that view ought to be presented to Congress and the people as the basis for a new constitutional convention. This is not an argument to be presented to the justices as the proper theory for them to apply in construing a Constitution not based upon it. Let us not, in the name of "judicial restraint," ask the judges to carry out a major constitutional revolution without consulting the people.

DOES THE CASE AGAINST JUDICIAL REVIEW JUSTIFY *AD HOC* BALANCING?

Professor Mendelson's argument that the judges ought not to decide seems to me curiously at odds with the doctrine he set out to defend. If his whole argument were accepted, the most that could follow would be that the Court should declare: "Whether this is consistent with the first amendment is not for us to say. The fact that Congress has passed it implies a congressional judgment that it is. From that judgment there is no appeal, except to the electorate." I have already indicated my reasons for finding this unacceptable. But, acceptable or not, it is a far cry from the balancing test, which says: "If this action is needed, then the mere fact of that need makes it constitutional. This Court [still the Constitution's authoritative spokesman] so holds." There is a vast difference between these two statements, and I submit that the latter is far more unfavorable to freedom of speech than the former. Under the balancing test, Congress gets whatever power it wants, but is expressly relieved of constitutional responsibility. The Court takes the responsibility, but without any basis for exercising an independent judgment. Congress can say to the voters: "We not only chastised the heretic and discouraged the heresy, but we did it without violating the first amendment. We have a certificate from the Constitution's authoritative spokesman that this is the case. And this certificate is also a precedent which establishes that whenever we think it necessary to take other similar actions in the future, it will be constitutionally right and permissible for us to do so."

Even Professor Mendelson, following Learned Hand, appears to concede that the first amendment ought to stand as an admonition to Congress.[31] But the amendment, as read by the balancing test, tells Congress only: "Don't abridge freedom of speech, unless you think it needs to be abridged." This merely amounts to: "Don't abridge freedom of speech any more than you would have thought proper if the Constitution had made no provision on the subject." Where is the admonition?

Professor Mendelson tells us, with apparent approval, that Madison

"insisted that the only use of a formal declaration [of rights] was that 'the political truths declared in that solemn manner acquire by degrees the character of fundamental maxims of free government, and as they become incorporated with the national sentiment, counteract the impulses of interest and passion.' If the government should act improperly, a bill of rights would be 'a good ground for an appeal to the sense of the community.' "[32]

Is "don't abridge freedom of speech except when it needs to be abridged" one of the "fundamental maxims of free government"? If *this* version of the first amendment's meaning becomes "incorporated with the national sentiment," will it "counteract the impulses of interest and passion"? Will it not, rather, explicitly invite "interest and passion" to do their will?

I tend to agree with Professor Mendelson that relatively too much of the libertarian effort in this country has been and is focused on the constitutional struggle in the courts, and that the proportion of that effort that has gone into educating the people on the meaning and value of their constitutional heritage has been far too small. But that does not mean that a choice must be made between the two methods. Both can be used simultaneously and each can stimulate and reinforce the other.

What Professor Mendelson's argument completely ignores is that the Court's official declaration that a controversial action is or is not constitutional necessarily injects into the legislative process and the political process a judgment that will be accorded enormous moral weight and will greatly affect the outcome of these processes. His failure to see this is shown by his statement that the School Segregation decision[33] was "costly indeed, if it convinced libertarians that the judicial process is an effective tool of libertarianism."[34] And, in support of this judgment, he cites statistics showing that the percentage of compliance with the decision is still low.[35]

Yet would anyone deny that both the Negro demand for full equality and white acceptance of that demand have risen further and faster since that decision than at any time since Reconstruction? Would anyone deny that a considerable, though not measurable, part of that tempo was due to the impetus provided by the Supreme Court's decision that this country had a constitutional commitment to racial equality and that segregation was in violation of that commitment? Suppose the Court had reaffirmed *Plessy v. Ferguson*[36] and held that compulsory segregation *is* constitutional whenever "equal" facilities are provided. Can anyone doubt that such a decision would have been a grievous blow to the fight for racial equality, not just in the courts, but also in the legislative halls, at the ballot box, and at every conceivable level?

This powerful role of the judicial judgment in political process itself cannot be eliminated by "judicial restraint." It can be eliminated only if the Court's function of construing the Constitution is expressly and openly abolished, so that no failure to say "This is unconstitutional" can be construed as a judgment to the contrary. The type of "judicial restraint" represented by the balancing test injects into the political process an authoritative declaration from the Constitution's official spokesman, saying, in effect: "This country has no constitutional commitment to freedom of dissent. True, we ordinarily permit it—but that is only because ordinarily there is no sufficient reason not to. Whenever such a reason arises, it is perfectly constitutional to set that freedom aside."

No argument that the courts ought *not* to decide, and that libertarians should take their case to the people instead of to the courts, can justify *this* result.

DOES *AD HOC* BALANCING GIVE
A BETTER ACCOUNT
OF HOW THE DECISION WAS REACHED?

Professor Mendelson writes:

"Open balancing compels a judge to take full responsibility for his decisions, and promises a particularized, rational account of how he arrives at them—more particularized and more rational at least than the familiar parade of hallowed abstractions, elastic absolutes and selective history. Moreover, this approach should make it more difficult for judges to rest on their predispositions without ever subjecting them to the test of reason. It should also make their accounts more rationally auditable."[37]

He does not tell us how or why "open balancing" will have these results. He just asserts that it will. I am not convinced.

Let us take a balancing case. The House Committee on Un-American Activities has heard testimony from a Mr. Crowley that Mr. Barenblatt, during a period ending some four years previously, had been a Communist while he was a student and teaching fellow at the state university. The Committee summons Mr. Barenblatt, demands to know whether he is or has ever been a Communist,

and he refuses to answer.[38] What are the "interests" on either side that the Court must "balance"?

On the government's side, it might be the Committee's interest in verifying Mr. Crowley's testimony, or its desire for more sources of information, or its desire to put any one of several possible messages before the public, or its desire for unobstructed freedom in determining what it ought to investigate, or its desire to punish a contumacious witness, or to discourage contumacy in future witnesses, or to vindicate its own authority, or that of the Congress, or the individual's public obligation to give testimony. Or it might be the interest of Congress in being fully informed when it legislates, or the public interest in having legislation based on full information, or the national interest in being fully informed on the nature and extent of communist activities, or the nation's (or democracy's, or humanity's) interest in the fight against communism (or against tyranny in general). Or it might be "national self-preservation."

Mr. Barenblatt's interest in remaining silent might be his desire to withhold the information, or to protect his reputation and employability, or to protect the friends whom the Committee will require him to identify if he testifies fully, or his own right to choose his ideas and associates without governmental supervision, or to behave as his conscience dictates, or to vindicate the first amendment, or freedom of speech and association, or freedom in general. Or it might be the public or national interest in freedom of discussion and association, or in maintaining the effectiveness of the first amendment, or of constitutional limitations in general, or in discouraging arbitrary assaults on individual freedom. Or (on the theory that political freedom is safer than repression in the long run) "national self-preservation" might belong on Mr. Barenblatt's side.

Which "interest" is the judge to balance against which? It is obvious that if he balances Mr. Barenblatt's personal interests against "national self-preservation" he will get one result. If he balances the Committee's desire to verify Mr. Crowley's testimony against freedom of speech, and also assumes that an important public interest is at stake in the latter, he will get another. So it appears to be very difficult for him to identify the "interests" without predetermining the result. The difficulty is emphasized by the ease with which Justice Black, while continuing to protest "balancing," demonstrates that, for him, it would produce an opposite result.[39] He simply trims the asserted governmental interest to more moderate size, puts a more generalized (and therefore weightier) free speech interest on the other side of the scales, and there you are. Anyone can do it. And anyone can reverse it just as easily by the opposite process.

How is the judge to convert balancing into something that does not merely give him back whatever answer he feeds into it? Presumably, he should generalize one interest exactly as much as the other, but how can he be sure he has done so? He might take a particularized view of the interests on both sides. Surely he will not, in that case, do justice to the interests on either side. There is a great deal more at stake on both sides than the desire of the particular litigants to obtain a particular result. Yet how can he state what more is involved without assuming, in some form or other, that a *principle* is at stake? If he does that, he is back in the very situation from which "balancing" was supposed to extricate him—except that he can choose his principles as he pleases, without reference to the Constitution.

Suppose the judge has solved this conundrum, or managed not to see it. He has now identified the "interests." He next has to "weigh" them. But they are not quantitative and therefore they cannot, except in a vague metaphorical sense, be "weighed" at all. What does the metaphor mean? If the judge determines merely the intensity with which the particular litigant desires the particular result, he is once more ignoring the fact that there is really more at stake than that. And obviously, both litigants desire the result with considerable vigor, or they would not be in the Supreme Court. Yet on what basis is it possible to say that one interest "weighs" more or less than the intensity with which it is desired—unless the judge can refer to some principle that tells him that some claims are more legitimate, or more important, than others? If there is such a principle, would not the judge give us a better account of his process of decision if he told us what he conceives the principle to be, and how it relates to the Constitution, and why he thinks the facts present it—instead of using it as an unstated premise for regarding one "interest" as "weightier" than another?

As soon as he finishes measuring the unmeasurable, the judge's next job is to compare the incomparable. Even if he has succeeded in stating the interests quantitatively (or thinks he has), they are still interests of different kinds and therefore they can no more be compared quantitatively than sheep can be subtracted from goats. It is literally impossible for him to compare them unless he has some standard independent of both to which they can be referred. What is that standard to be? Is it to be the Constitution? If so, what did the judge gain by abandoning the Constitution for a long process of reasoning that merely led him back

to it? And, if not the Constitution, then what is to it be?

I cannot join Professor Mendelson in finding in this process any promise that the real basis of decision will be more fully disclosed. On the contrary, it seems to me to make the real basis of the decision more difficult to identify than the economic "activists" of the old Court, at their worst, ever made it. Nor do I find in the cases that purport to have been decided by this process anything that will enable a lawyer to advise his client of his rights.

Does such a process make it "more difficult for judges to rest on their predispositions without ever subjecting them to the test of reason"? That *ad hoc* balancing does just the opposite seems to me so painfully obvious that I am almost at a loss how to argue it. What is there that can assure, or even promote, impartiality of results, if there is no rule that can be impartially applied? I do not understand how impartiality can even be conceived without assuming the existence of such a rule. Even if we assume that "balancing" is capable of giving impartial results (which seems to me very unlikely), how can the losing litigant look at balancing language and feel any assurance that the judge succeeded in keeping his personal preferences out of his "scales"? How can the public do so? How can the judge himself do so?

DOES THE CRITICISM OF "ABSOLUTES" JUSTIFY *AD HOC* BALANCING?

As anyone can verify by consulting the nearest dictionary, the word "absolute" has several quite different recognized meanings. Accordingly, putting the issue in the form, "is the freedom of speech absolute?" or "is the first amendment an absolute?" is unlikely to result in anything but confusion and failure to communicate unless some further effort is made to specify precisely what is meant by the question. Confusion and failure to communicate are, in my opinion, what we have chiefly been having in this area.

"Absolute" might mean: without limits. And some people seem seriously to regard the first amendment "absolutists" as guilty of some inconsistency because they do not insist that first amendment protection is infinite in scope. A legal rule that was "absolute" in this sense would control all possible cases. No case, however remote, could be excluded from it without giving the rule a limit and thereby destroying it "absoluteness." Such a rule would eliminate the possibility of having any other rule. It would also be meaningless, since we could not give it meaning without defining it and to define is to set limits. It is not difficult to demonstrate that the first amendment is not "absolute" in this sense, but to do so is to knock down a straw man. No one contends, or ever has contended, that it is.

"Absolute" might mean: not open to exceptions. This seems to be approximately what most of the "anti-absolutists" have in mind—though I have yet to find one who specifies clearly what he does have in mind. The argument that takes this form requires that it be either expressly or tacitly assumed that "the freedom of speech" means each individual's right to say anything he pleases, on any subject, at any time, in any manner he pleases, and regardless of the circumstances. The next step is to show instances in which the "freedom" thus defined would have to be abridged. This is taken to demonstrate that "the freedom of speech" is "not absolute." Accordingly, when the government undertakes to regulate the content of public debate, it is insisted that, since "the freedom of speech" is not "absolute," the first amendment cannot be regarded as containing any "dogmatic" assertion that the government has no such power. There is thus nothing to do but to "balance," to determine on an *ad hoc* pragmatic basis whether the particular regulation seems justified under the particular circumstances.

Even if this meaning of "the freedom of speech" is accepted, arguendo, it is simply a non-sequitur to argue that "balancing" is therefore inescapable. If a legal rule has been stated too broadly and unstated exceptions must therefore be read into it, it does not necessarily follow that it is therefore open to any and all exceptions that the decision-maker wants to make, without regard to whether they are consistent or inconsistent with the function and purpose of the main rule.

Government can and must exercise a great deal of control over radio, yet no one supposes that it necessarily follows that there would be no impropriety in a regulation allowing Democrats to broadcast, but not Republicans, or leaving the airways open to those who wish to praise government policy, but not to those who wish to criticize. The chairman of a meeting, if business is to be transacted, must exercise considerable control over "the freedom of speech" of those present, so I suppose it must be conceded that that "freedom" is not "absolute." It does not follow that the chairman would not be abusing his powers if he permitted speech in favor of the motion, but not speech against it, or vice versa. I am not suggesting, of course, that the proper reading of the first amendment could be derived from either of these very imprecise analogies. The point is simply that, from "some regulation is inescapable," it just does not follow that "therefore no regulation of any

particular kind can be regarded as in principle impermissible." It is this non-sequitur that the sloganizing against first amendment "absolutes" serves to conceal.

Furthermore, the whole argument falls without the initial premise that "the freedom of speech" means, as Justice Harlan put it, "an unlimited license to talk."[40] It is only on the basis of this premise that the "freedom" has been shown to be "not absolute." So the whole argument proves nothing unless it can first be demonstrated that the freedom of speech clause is not capable of any meaning that could be consistently applied. The first amendment non-absolutists have not undertaken any such demonstration. They have not even bothered to explore what other meanings are possible. It is much too convenient to rest on "the first amendment is not an absolute," without any close inquiry as to what such a statement might mean, thus leaving the way open to put first amendment freedoms aside whenever we think they should be put aside—or, to put it bluntly, whenever we want to do so.

So the statement that the first amendment is "not an absolute" (though I would agree that it is true, not merely in one sense, but in several of its possible senses) does not seem to me capable, at least without further analysis, of shedding much light on the problem to which it purports to be addressed. For a further demonstration of this, let us experiment with putting the same question in a different form. Instead of asking, "Is the first amendment an absolute?" let us ask, "Are there any limits to the powers of our national legislature, assuming that it has been democratically elected and that its efforts have majority support?" Now it is Justice Black who is saying that those powers are very broad indeed, but they are not absolute, since the Constitution sets limits. Now it is Professor Mendelson who is insisting that the principle of "majority rule" admits of neither limits nor exceptions—and comforting us with the thought that, in view of the clash of infinitely varied interests across our vast expanse of territory, it will never have need of either limits or exceptions. Who is the "absolutist" now? If the Justice is open to a charge of employing "absolutes," his critic is no less so—he simply employs a different one. It might even be thought that Professor Mendelson's "absolute" is a good deal broader and more sweeping than Justice Black's—that absolute limits on power, even if sometimes inconvenient, are rather less to be feared than absolute power, even if the latter is founded on the premise of majority will. In any case, there must be some better way of choosing between these points of view than labeling the Justice's position "absolutist," thus subjecting it to a purely verbal criticism that can be turned the other way merely by inverting the form of the question.

"Absolute" might mean: mandatory. It might, in other words, be a judgment addressed, not to the meaning and scope of the constitutional proposition, but simply to its obligatory character once that meaning and scope have been determined.

Much of what is frequently decried as a demand for "absolutes" seems to me nothing more than a demand that the Court should ask itself *first*, "Is this the type of governmental action that the first amendment forbids?" And, if it thinks that question requires an affirmative answer, it should say: "We cannot give more deference to a legislative judgment that this is needed (whether or not we agree) than we give to a constitutional judgment, reached by a more solemn and binding process, that the power to do it is a dangerous one which the government ought not to have. The exact content of the latter judgment is not always certain, but it is there and we must apply it as best we can. Whatever it forbids can be authorized only by the same process by which it was forbidden, *i.e.*, by constitutional amendment." If this is employing "absolutes," then it is also employing "absolutes" for a court to choose between two possible constructions of a statute and then say: "If this is what the legislature meant, as we think it is, then our judgment as to whether it is desirable is beside the point. Our job is to apply the statute, not to reach an *ad hoc* result based on the same considerations we might have applied had it never been written."

If either of these is employing "absolutes," then "absolutes" are the day to day stuff of adjudication. Indeed, if it is impossible or impermissible for a court to apply such "absolutes," then it would seem that Professor Mendelson's candidates for supremacy, the statute-writers, are, no less than the constitution-makers, engaged in a very fruitless occupation.

Much of what is phrased in the form of a demand for the rejection of "absolutes" seems to me a demand that the question "Is this desirable?" should not only be asked *first*, but should be the sole determinative factor in the final result. Only *after* the decision has been made is the first amendment to be called in and required to give its constitutional blessing, willy nilly, to a decision in which it played no part. If this is what the demand for a rejection of "absolutes" means, it is simply a demand that the first amendment should not be treated as a constitutional limitation.

Nor do I think that the philosophical proposition that "there are not absolutes,"[41] whatever it may mean, justifies treating the first amendment as though it were something like a folding chair, subject to be collapsed at will whenever it might otherwise be in the way. John Stuart Mill long ago observed that repressing any opinion is always an assumption of infallibility.[42] This seems to me a wise observation. An assumption of infallibility is a strange result to justify on the basis of a philosophical observation that all things are relative. If we wish to apply the philosophical observation to the free speech issue, I would suggest we begin with the proposition that our present normative judgments about how society ought to be organized, and what is correct political theory, and what governmental policy ought to be, are "not absolute"—and therefore we should keep them open, as "absolutely" as we can, to continuous criticism and re-examination.

IS THE AMERICAN CITIZEN "A POLITICAL, NOT LEGAL, ANIMAL?"

Professor Mendelson concludes his article with the observation:

"Sooner or later libertarians will have to face it—the real victories are won in legislatures and at the polls. Man after all is a political, not a legal, animal."[43]

I cannot agree. It seems to me that if you look at any society, even the most primitive, you will find some kind of law. It may be traditional, unwritten, and attributed to supernatural sources, but it is law nonetheless. So it seems probable that law is about as old as society. Politics is, by comparison, quite a recent invention.

Furthermore, most of the specimens with which I am acquainted do not show the primacy of the political impulse that Professor Mendelson attributes to the species. Indeed, I had thought it was one of the most serious problems of our form of government that it seems to need a citizen who has somehow been trained or inspired to be much more political than he has any innate inclination to be. Most of my friends and neighbors resort to politics only sporadically and reluctantly. When the crisis or election is over, they relapse into political inactivity with an ease and naturalness that suggests that the latter is their more natural mode of existence. Yet I think they demand law—and moral standards capable of identifying something more than a mere conflict of interests in the choices to be made—as the limiting framework and guidelines of everyday living, because without them life in society would be intolerable. I do not think they will willingly settle for the view that justice is the interest of the stronger—even if stronger means politically stronger.

Finally, the American citizen is heir to a British struggle to set limits on governmental power which goes back to the "Glorious Revolution" of 1689, to the Puritan Revolution which preceded it, and even to that episode, seven and a half centuries ago, when the barons wrung from King John promises that he would not use power in certain ways, promises that came to be called the Magna Charta. And the American citizen's own immediate forebears on this side of the ocean have spent the better part of two centuries trying to translate the British "the king is under law" into "the goverment is under the Constitution and the Constitution is law." It is a bit breathtaking to be told, in effect, that this was all a mistake, that it is only the government's will that should be limited, not its powers, and that even its will should not be limited by anything other than the difficulty of finding a majority consensus among a myriad of conflicting interests.

The problem of "rights" is, after all, just the reverse side of the problem of power. And the meaning of the doctrine that there are no rights, but only "interests," is that power has no limits.

Footnotes

[1]Mendelson, *On the Meaning of the First Amendment: Absolutes in the Balance*, 50 CALIF. L. REV. 821 (1962).
[2]Frantz, *The First Amendment in the Balance*, 71 YALE L.J. 1424 (1962).
[3]Barenblatt v. United States, 360 U.S. 109, 126 (1959).
[4]*Id.* at 134.
[5]Communist Party v. Subversive Activities Control Bd,. 367 U.S. 1, 90–91 (1961)....
[6]Dennis v. United States, 341 U.S. 494, 517–46 (1951) (Frankfurter, J., concurring).
[7]Edwards v. South Carolina, 372 U.S. 229 (1963); Wood v. Georgia, 370 U.S. 375 (1962); Tally v. California, 362 U.S. 60 (1960); Kingsley Int'l Pictures Corp. v. Regents of the Univ. of N.Y., 360 U.S. 684 (1959).

[8]N.A.A.C.P. v. Button, 371 U.S. 415 (1963).
[9]Konigsberg v. State Bar, 366 U.S. 36, 50 (1961). This statement fails to take account of the *de facto* balancing done in Dennis v. United States, 341 U.S. 494, 510 (1951), in which the statute was not of the character to which Justice Harlan refers.
[10]American Communications Ass'n v. Douds, 339 U.S. 382, 399 (1950).
[11]Dennis v. United States, 341 U.S. 494, 517–46 (1951) (Frankfurter, J., concurring).
[12]Mendelson, *supra* note 1, at 821.
[13]*Id.* at 821, 823.
[14]*Id.* at 821.
[15]*Id.* at 825–26.
[16]Mendelson, *supra* note 1, at 824–25.
[17]Kovacs v. Cooper, 336 U.S. 77 (1949).
[18]Breard v. Alexandria, 341 U.S. 622 (1951).
[19]Prince v. Massachusetts, 321 U.S. 158 (1944).
[20]Dennis v. United States, 341 U.S. 494 (1951).
[21]Scales v. United States, 367 U.S. 203 (1961).
[22]Frantz, *supra* note 2, at 1448.
[23]1 ANNALS OF CONGRESS 457 (1789).
[24]Mendelson, *supra* note 1, at 827.
[25]THE FEDERALIST No. 48, at 339–40 (Dunne ed. 1901) (Madison).
[26]Mendelson, *supra* note 1, at 828 n.38 (Italics in original).
[27]Mendelson, *supra* note 1, at 824–28....
[28]Mendelson, *supra* note 1, at 825.
[29]Mendelson, *supra* note 1, at 826. Professor Mendelson's version of my "anguished question" is: "What good is the first amendment, if it is not to be given a 'preferred place' by 'activist' magistrates?" Since the question is attributed to me, I have taken the liberty of rephrasing it.
[30]*Id.* at 827–28.
[31]*Id.* at 827.
[32]*Ibid.*
[33]Brown v. Bd. of Education, 347 U.S. 483 (1954).
[34]Mendelson, *supra* note 1, at 828 n.39.
[35]This argument, of course, ignores the fact that *any* integration in the South, even "token" integration, is an enormous step forward. In fact, it is quite possibly the largest single step along the whole road—and the one hardest to take.
[36]163 U.S. 537 (1896).
[37]Mendelson, *supra* note 1, at 825–26.
[38]Barenblatt v. United States, 360 U.S. 109 (1959).
[39]Lathrop v. Donohue, 367 U.S. 820, 874 (1961) (dissenting opinion); Konigsberg v. State Bar, 366 U.S. 36, 71 (1961) (dissenting opinion); Barenblatt v. United States, 360 U.S. 109, 144 (1959) (dissenting opinion).
[40]Konigsberg v. State Bar, 366 U.S. 36, 49–50 (1961).
[41]Dennis v. United States, 341 U.S. 494, 508 (1951).
[42]MILL, ON LIBERTY 21–22 (Library of Liberal Arts ed. 1956).
[43]Mendelson, *supra* note 1, at 828.

Selection *4*

The First Amendment and the Judicial Process: A Reply to Mr. Frantz

Wallace Mendelson

In a wide-ranging debate, Mr. Laurent Frantz and I have singled out two key issues on which we—and perhaps activists and anti-activists generally—are divided.[1] One concerns the meaning of the first amendment; the other the "balancing of interests" in free utterance cases.

THE MEANING OF THE FIRST AMENDMENT

To come at once to the heart of the problem: Mr. Frantz assumes that the first amendment incorporates Meiklejohn's book, *Political Freedom*.[2] This wise little study suggests that

"When men govern themselves, it is they—and no one else—who must pass judgment upon unwisdom and unfairness and danger....Just so far as, at any point, the citizens who are to decide an issue are denied acquaintance with information or opinion or doubt or disbelief or criticism which is relevant to that issue, just so far the result must be ill-considered, ill-balanced planning for the general good. *It is that mutilation of the thinking process of the community against which the First Amendment...is directed.*"[3]

Surely no one dedicated to democracy and human decency could fail to find inspiration in these words. But philosophy is one thing, and history another. Dean Levy and others have shown that at best (in the libertarian view) the historic meaning of free utterance is found in Blackstone. In short it permitted prosecution for seditious libel. This view stands unrefuted; even Chafee ultimately accepted it.[4] Mr. Justice Iredell—appointed to the Supreme Court by President Washington—gave the gist of the matter in charging a grand jury with respect to the Sedition Act of 1798:

"That objection is, that the act is in violation of this amendment of the Constitution.

" 'Congress shall make no law respecting an establishment of religion, or prohibiting the free exercise thereof; or abridging the freedom of speech, or of the press, or the right of the people peaceably to assemble, and to petition the government for a redress of grievances.'

"The question then is, whether this law has abridged the freedom of the press?

"Here is a remarkable difference in expressions as to the different objects in the same clause. They are to make no law *respecting* an establishment of religion, or prohibiting the free exercise thereof, or *abridging* the freedom of speech, or of the press. When, as to one object, they entirely prohibit any act whatever, and, as to another object, only limit the exercise of the power, they must, in reason, be supposed to mean different things. I presume, therefore, that Congress may make a law *respecting* the press, provided the law be such as not to *abridge its freedom*. What might be deemed the freedom of the press, if it had been a new subject, and never before in discussion, might indeed admit of some controversy. But, so far as precedent, habit, laws, and practices are concerned, there can scarcely be a more definite meaning than that which all these have affixed to the term in question."[5]

....

"It is believed that, in every State in the Union, the common law principles concerning libels apply; and in some of the States words similar to the words of the Amendment are used in the Constitution itself, or a contemporary Bill of Rights, of equal authority, without ever being supposed to exclude any law being passed on the subject. So that there is the strongest proof that can be of a universal concurrence in America on this point, that the freedom of the press does not require that libellers shall be protected from punishment."[6]

"The First Amendment and the Judicial Process: A Reply to Mr. Frantz" by Wallace Mendelson. Copyright 1964, by the Vanderbilt University School of Law; this material was originally printed in Volume 17, Number 4, of the *Vanderbilt Law Review*, and is used by permission.

Of course, we are not inevitably obliged to honor the purposes of those who gave us the Bill of Rights. What then of judicial precedent? I suggest that in first amendment cases pure and simple no decision of the Supreme Court goes beyond Blackstone (though perhaps some of its language does). Indeed, no act of Congress has ever been held invalid on first amendment grounds.

What kind of law is it that was never enacted by the political processes, nor adopted by the judges? By what authority does Mr. Frantz get Mr. Meiklejohn into the First Amendment? Both history and judicial precedent (federal and state) are overwhelmingly against him—to say nothing of the other agencies of government. And surely he can claim no social support remotely comparable to the forces that put Herbert Spencer's *Social Statics* into the fourteenth amendment. Law cannot support itself by its own bootstraps, or thrive on the dreams of a few idealists. Moreover, even so ardent a libertarian—and so competent a lawyer —as Chafee found Meiklejohn's approach judicially unworkable.[7]

Of course, on his *philosophic* premise much of what Mr. Frantz says would have to be accepted. And only on that premise can he ask such paradoxical questions as "Is the First Amendment Law?," and why does the Court not enforce it?[8] The answer is that the amendment *is* law, and (insofar as it goes) *is* judicially enforced. It is Meiklejohn's book that is not law and not enforced.

In effect Mr. Frantz is chiding the Court for not legislating Meiklejohn into, and something else out of, the Constitution. This, perhaps, a court may do when it "feels behind it the weight of such general acceptance as will give sanction to its pretension to unquestioned dictation."[9] Meanwhile, "it must be content to lag behind the best inspiration of its time"—as reflected in men like Alexander Meiklejohn.[10]

BALANCING AND FREEDOM

Mr. Frantz rejects the "balancing of interests" as a general approach in utterance cases. He let go of the cat when he confessed about Meiklejohn. I now confess that (except perhaps in simple cases which seldom reach the Supreme Court) balancing seems to me the essence of the judicial process —the nexus between abstract law and concrete life. Lawmakers cannot anticipate all the combinations and permutations of circumstance. What Cardozo called "the great generalities of the Constitution" are no more amenable to mechanistic application by liberals than they were by Mr. Justice Roberts in his famous squaring analogy.

Moreover, balancing would seem to be implicit in an adversary system which inevitably contemplates at least two sides to every case—the lopsided ones being weeded out in law offices and the lower courts. As T. R. Powell observed long ago, "It will ever remain a mystery to me how intelligent jurists can make...professions of nonparticipation in the judicial process.[11] Surely the choice is simply this: shall the balancing be done "intuitively" or rationally; covertly or out in the open? Of course, it should always be done in the light of accepted legal principles[12]—and obviously the light of Meiklejohn is quite different from that of Blackstone.

Di Santo v. Pennsylvania[13] is a classic example of covert, and probably "intuitive," balancing. There the old Court held invalid a state regulation of commerce as a "direct burden"—and that is virtually all there was in the opinion. No observer could tell what interests were weighed against what. Ostensibly the Court merely applied a well-known rule of law. But who outside the court could know, and thus appraise, the decisive considerations that marked the burden in question as "direct" rather than "indirect"? Mr. Justice Stone, joined by Holmes and Brandeis, observed in dissent:

"In this case the traditional test of the limit of state action by inquiring whether the interference with commerce is direct or indirect seems to me to be too mechanical, too uncertain in its application, and too remote from actualities, to be of value. In thus making use of the expressions, "direct" and "indirect interference" with commerce, we are doing little more than using labels to describe a result rather than any trustworthy formula by which it is reached."[14]

What a world of difference between the Court's approach in *Di Santo*, and its approach in *Southern Pacific Co. v. Arizona*![15] There Stone gave the positive side of his earlier dissent, revealing in detail factors considered on each side of the judicial scale. Appraisal of the process could then proceed rationally. Perhaps even more important, the open balancing operation itself tends to focus the attention of all concerned on actualities and away from the never-never land of private, and perhaps unconscious, preconceptions.

It seems a fair guess that if in *Di Santo* the Court had felt compelled to reveal the ingredients of its decision, there would have been less Herbert Spencer in the scales, and more of the real-life considerations mentioned in the Brandeis dissent.

In short, the Court might have been compelled either to reach a different result, or reveal for all to see a vulnerable exercise in the accommodation of law and life.

Mr. Frantz does not like the balancing that occurred in *Barenblatt*.[16] The Court could easily have reached the same result via the *Di Santo* route. But in balancing openly, it gave Mr. Frantz an opportunity for *reasoned* criticism of the proffered weighing process. The *Di Santo* technique hides the inevitable balancing behind a verbal, and often Platonic, barrier. Strictly followed, it means a Mr. Frantz must argue that the burden on commerce "'taint," while the Court holds "'tis," direct (whatever that means). Our debt to Holmes, Brandeis, and Stone is that they cut through the net of formality, and encouraged us to "think things, not words." This, I believe, is the crux of the open balancing approach. It is not foolproof and certainly will not make a great judge of a little man. But it offers hope of progress for inquiring minds. What Walter Lippmann said in another context is relevant here: "When men act on the principle of intelligence, they go out to find the facts....When they ignore it, they go inside themselves and find only what is there. They elaborate their prejudice instead of increasing their knowledge."

Dean Griswold has suggested that the balancing approach is misnamed, that it might better be called the "comprehensive" or "integral" approach.

"Instead of focusing on a few words, and ignoring all else, including the effect and meaning of those words, as distinguished from their apparent impact when isolated from everything else...the comprehensive or integral approach accepts the task of the judge as one which involves the effect of all the provisions of the Constitution, not merely in a narrow literal sense, but in a living, organic sense, including the elaborate and complex governmental structure which the Constitution, through its words, has erected.[17]

In any event, the essence of balancing is realism —a repudiation of the modern activists' rhetorical, or magic phrase, technique. The latter characteristically begins with an honored phrase or doctrine —the clear and present danger rule, for example; knocks the brains out of it, by stretching it so broadly as to deprive it of any ascertainable meaning; and then uses it in talismanic fashion to "resolve" all manner of difficulties—from non-utterance by moppets in their classrooms[18] to trial by newspaper,[19] to a struggle between lunatic fringe hate groups for what Hitler called "the conquest of the streets."[20] Paul Freund gave the epitaph for this cycle of activist word-play when he wrote

"No matter how rapidly we utter the phrase 'clear and present danger,' or how closely we hyphenate the words, they are not a substitute for the weighing of values. They tend to convey a delusion of certitude when what is most certain is the complexity of the strands in the web of freedom which the judge must disentangle."[21]

Or, as Mr. Justice Jackson observed in the *Terminiello* case (after his conversion at Nuremberg), the activists reverse

"this conviction by reiterating generalized approbations of freedom of speech with which, in the abstract, no one will disagree. Doubts as to their applicability are lulled ·by avoidance of more than passing reference to the circumstances of Terminiello's speech and judging it as if he had spoken to persons as dispassionate as empty benches, or like a modern Demosthenes practicing his Philippics on a lonely seashore.[22]

Cut loose from its foundation in the distinction between discussion and incitement, the clear and present danger test lost its rational meaning and became a cloak for "vague but fervent transcendentalism." In short, the activists destroyed it as an intelligible guide to decision—and then abandoned it about a dozen years ago. Meanwhile they have tried, and apparently discarded, one "new" verbalism after another. The latest is Mr. Justice Black's absolutist concentration on two untroubled words in the first amendment: "no law." This gambit—"no law means no law"—again begs all the difficulties simply by ignoring them. As Dean Griswold has suggested, it reminds one of the fundamentalist church sign which proclaimed, "God said it. We believe it. That's all there is to it."[23]

CONCLUSION

The need for judicial balancing, I suggest, results from the imperfection of mundane law. In a better world, no doubt, clear and precise legal rules would anticipate all possible contingencies. No wonder, then, that idealists are impatient with the balancing process. Mr. Frantz' solution has a familiar ring. He suggests that law precedes, and apparently even transcends, politics.[24] Here is our old friend "the brooding omnipresence"—"the higher law"—that Holmes and Brandeis among others fought so hard to kill. Surely *in a democracy* law is a creature of the political processes, constitutional and legislative. Judges, of course, cannot avoid legislating in some degree, but to repeat

Holmes' much quoted phrase they must do so only interstitially—lest they rather than the people govern. For judges now to treat Meiklejohn's book as "higher law" seems at least as far from mere gap-filling as was their predecessors' treatment of Herbert Spencer.

If libertarians are convinced that the Court is wrong, and that Meiklejohn's views reflect the community consensus, surely a constitutional amendment would be a feasible and proper remedy. If there is no such consensus, how could we justify imposing a minority view upon the people? The old Court tried that in the 1930s and destroyed itself. Obviously most of the "nine old men" and their supporters were just as certain as libertarians are today that their values were "fundamental" and indeed indispensable to freedom—as well as inherent in "higher law." Holmes' answer was that "certitude is not the test of certainty."[25] Another response was the Brandeis brief with its invitation to open balancing as a substitute for word-play and Platonic abstraction in court opinions.

I end where I began, amused yet troubled by the continuing activist-idealist pretense that all answers to all problems are in (or above) the Constitution—and that the judicial process for extracting them is largely mechanical or automatic.

Editor's note: In 1965 the Supreme Court for the first time in its history struck down a federal statute as inconsistent with the First Amendment [*Lamont* v. *Postmaster General*, 381 U.S. 301 (1965)]. In the same year, in *Freedman* v. *Maryland* [380 U.S. 51 (1965)] the Court for the first time laid down guidelines for a constitutionally permissible system of prior restraint (i.e., advanced licensing) of motion pictures, which are regarded by the Court as a form of artistic expression protected by the First Amendment. Thus the Court continues to break new ground in the controversy outlined by Frantz and Mendelson.

Footnotes

[1]Frantz, *The First Amendment in the Balance,* 71 YALE L.J. 1424 (1962); Mendelson, *On the Meaning of the First Amendment: Absolutes in the Balance,* 50 CALIF. L. REV. 821 (1962); Frantz, *Is the First Amendment Law?—A Reply to Professor Mendelson,* 51 CALIF. L. REV. 729 (1963).

[2]*Id.* at 735. See also Emerson, *Toward a General Theory of the First Amendment,* 72 YALE L.J. 877, 878, 916 (1963).

[3]MEIKLEJOHN, POLITICAL FREEDOM 27 (1960).

[4]Chafee, Book Review, 62 HARV. L. REV. 891 (1949).

[5]See WHARTON, STATE TRIALS OF THE UNITED STATES DURING THE ADMINISTRATION OF WASHINGTON AND ADAMS 477–78 (1849). For a similar view see the Report of a House Committee, 38 ANNALS OF CONG., 5th Cong., 3d Sess. 2985–93. (1799).

[6]WHARTON, *op. cit. supra* note 5, at 479.

[7]Chafee, Book Review, 62 HARV. L. REV. 891 (1949).

[8]FRANTZ, *supra* note 1, 51 CALIF. L. REV. at 738.

[9]HAND, THE SPIRIT OF LIBERTY 15–16 (2d ed. Dilliard 1953).

[10]*Id.* at 15.

[11]POWELL, VAGARIES AND VARIETIES IN CONSTITUTIONAL INTERPRETATION 28 (1956).

[12]How much weight should be given to congressional judgment is another matter. Apparently modern, overt balancers find that the step from a general and ancient constitutional precept to the problems of modern life is largely legislative. Hence, presumably, their special deference (via the reasonable man approach) for legislative policy. Learned Hand put it briefly: "If a court be really candid, it can only say: 'We find that this measure will have this result; it will injure this group in such and such ways, and benefit that group in these other ways. We declare it invalid, because after every conceivable allowance for differences of outlook, we cannot see how a fair person can honestly believe that the benefits balance the losses.'" HAND, THE SPIRIT OF LIBERTY 179 (2d ed. Dilliard 1953).

[13]273 U.S. 34 (1927).

[14]*Id.* at 44.

[15]325 U.S. 761 (1945).

[16]Barenblatt v. United States, 360 U.S. 109 (1959); Frantz, *supra* note 1, 51 CALIF. L. REV. at 746.

[17]Griswold, *Absolute Is in the Dark,* 8 UTAH L. REV. 167, 172 (1963).

[18]West Virginia Bd. of Educ. v. Barnette, 319 U.S. 624 (1943).

[19]Bridges v. California, 314 U.S. 252 (1941).

[20]Terminiello v. Chicago, 337 U.S. 1 (1949).

[21]FREUND, ON UNDERSTANDING THE SUPREME COURT 27–28 (1949).

[22]337 U.S. at 13.

[23]Griswold, *supra* note 17, at 172.

[24]Frantz, *supra* note 1, 51 CALIF. L. REV. at 754.

[25]HOLMES, *Natural Law,* in COLLECTED LEGAL PAPERS 310, 311 (1920).

Selection 5

Obscenity Censorship:
The Core Constitutional Issue — What Is Obscene?
William B. Lockhart and Robert C. McClure

Obscene literature raises one of the basic questions underlying all First Amendment debate. The stated purpose of most obscenity legislation is to prevent citizens from having the prurient thoughts that allegedly result from reading or viewing pornography. Should the government try to control the thought of its citizens, deciding for them which thoughts are permissible and which are not? When the question is stated so baldly, most of us would reply, "Obviously not." Although most Americans probably are opposed to the peddling of pornography, they are also opposed to the government or anyone else telling them what they can or cannot read and think. Yet the traditional and continued presence of obscenity laws in nearly every federal, state, and local jurisdiction has the effect of imposing government "thought control" on citizens, at least in the area of sex. It is this dilemma with which the Supreme Court grapples.

The Supreme Court has carefully excluded obscenity from First Amendment protection so that it cannot fall under an absolutist or a clear-and-present-danger doctrine of freedom of speech and press. Under either, of course, all obscenity laws would be unconstitutional, since obscenity laws *do* restrict speech and there is no real evidence that obscene expression has ever created a clear and present danger of evil action. What much of the Court's maneuvering on this question boils down to is that it wishes to give expression dealing with sex a great deal of constitutional protection; but if it ruled that *all* such expression fell under the First Amendment, it would have to declare a lot more statutes unconstitutional than it wishes.

The article below, by the two leading American commentators on obscenity law, summarizes their two earlier, long and definitive articles which have been cited innumerable times both by other academic commentators and by the courts themselves.* Indeed, the views of William Lockart and Robert McClure have been one of the most important influences on the evolution of American obscenity law.

In this article Lockhart and McClure made two major points: that the Court had not framed one doctrine of obscenity but had adopted *in toto* all the previous and contradictory doctrines; and that the Court ought to adopt a "hard-core pornography" standard. The Court has subsequently supported both these positions by keeping all the previous doctrines and adopting the hard-core pornography standard as well, thus creating even more contradiction and confusion

"Obscenity Censorship: The Core Constitutional Issue—What Is Obscene?" by William B. Lockhart and Robert C. McClure, 7 *Utah Law Review* 289 (1961). Reprinted by permission.
*See "The Law of Obscenity and the Constitution," 38 *Minnesota Law Review* 295 (1954); and "Censorship of Obscenity. The Developing Constitutional Standards," 45 *Minnesota Law Review* 5 (1960).

than ever. Indeed, it has apparently added not one but two or three hard-core pornography standards. In addition, it has failed to agree on a uniform approach to even the simplest problems of the old doctrine. For instance, some of the justices feel that in applying a community standard test the national community ought to be employed, while others use the local community in which the prosecution arose. The Court displays all these confusions and contradictions in *Jacobellis* v. *Ohio* [378 U.S. 184 (1964)]. Indeed, it has now adopted yet another test earlier suggested by Chief Justice Warren. The seller of obscene works may now sometimes be successfully prosecuted on the basis of his promotion and selling techniques if they suggest "dirt for dirt's sake," even if the material sold is not itself necessarily obscene under the other current constitutional tests. (See *Ginzburg* v. *United States* [383 U.S. 463 (1966)].) About all that is certain is that in terms of the actual works that the Court has found not obscene, the justices have continued the trend toward liberalization, the first stages of which are described in the article that follows.

INTRODUCTION

In 1948 the United States Supreme Court considered for the first time the claim that literature attacked as obscene is entitled to constitutional protection. The occasion was an appeal from New York's censorship of Edmond Wilson's *Memoirs of Hecate County*—a work of high literary quality by a distinguished author and critic. But after what must have been a most interesting debate in conference the Court wrote no opinion and gave us no guidance, because it was equally divided. And the *Memoirs* remained censored in New York.

In 1954 my colleague, Professor Robert McClure, and I explored this unresolved problem in an article published in the *Minnesota Law Review*. We recognized that not all material posing as literature or art is entitled to constitutional protection for freedom of expression. But we took the position that literature attacked as "obscene" should be judged by constitutional standards that would give appropriate weight to social and literary values and adequate protection to the basic rights of free expression and freedom to read.

Three years later in 1957 the Supreme Court, with Justices Black and Douglas dissenting, upheld the constitutionality of federal and state obscenity laws in the *Roth* case, declaring that obscenity is "not within the area of constitutionally protected speech and press." The exponents of censorship hailed the decision, apparently seeing in it an end to this foolishness about constitutional protection for material relating to sex.

Yet in 1960 and 1961 we find *Memoirs of Hecate County* published without apparent fear of censorship, of all places in Boston, long a stronghold of censorship forces. And we find *Lady Chatterley's Lover*, unexpurgated, published freely in competing editions, after the Department of Justice declined to appeal to the Supreme Court a Court of Appeals ruling that the Postmaster General could not constitutionally censor *Lady Chatterley* as obscene.

The explanation for this turn of events is found in careful analysis of the *Roth* opinion and six other Supreme Court decisions between 1957 and 1960—in three of which no opinions were written. Professor McClure and I have just published a second article in the November 1960 *Minnesota Law Review* in which we analyze the developing constitutional requirements for censorship of obscenity as reflected in these decisions, and point out how we believe these standards should evolve in the future.

My objective...is not to summarize the essence of all Professor McClure and I have written in two long articles. Instead, I will only seek to provide some understanding of the direction that constitutional developments have taken thus far, and to present my views on the key problem in obscenity censorship under a constitution that protects freedom of expression.

It is quite apparent that the *Roth* decision in 1957 and its progeny in 1958-1960 have resulted in a high degree of constitutional protection for literature and other materials of a type frequently censored under obscenity laws in the 1930's and 40's and 50's. Since 1957 state and federal courts have been increasingly reluctant to enforce censorship. Even the prosecuting authorities have recognized that they must have much stronger cases than formerly. Primarily they are now concentrating on hard-core pornography and material bordering on pornography—pure trash or worse.

The initial explanation for this marked shift narrowing the scope of censorship can be found in portions of the *Roth* opinion that were over-looked at first by the proponents of censorship. What they noted and hailed was the ruling that obscenity statutes are not unconstitutional, that "obscenity is not within the area of constitutionally protected speech or press" because "obscenity" is "utterly without redeeming social importance." What they overlooked—at first—was the more important statement in the majority opinion that "sex and obscenity are not synonymous" and that the "portrayal of sex, e.g., in art, literature and scientific works" is entitled to constitutional protection, so long as it falls short of "obscenity." Indeed, the opinion stressed the importance of sex as a "subject of absorbing interest to mankind through the ages" and one of the "vital problems of human interest and concern." In the Court's view, it was, therefore "vital" that the "standards for judging obscenity safeguard the protection of freedom of speech and press for material which does not treat sex in a manner appealing to the prurient interest."

Just what does this mean? What the Court seems to have said in *Roth* is that "obscenity" is *not* entitled to constitutional protection, but treatment of sex in literature and art *is* entitled to constitutional protection if it is not obscene. In other words, some treatments of sex are constitutionally protected from censorship and others are not, and the court attaches the label "obscene" to material that it finds not entitled to constitutional protection. Then the Court sought in *Roth* to state a standard for determining what is "obscene" and hence outside the constitutional protection for freedom of expression. Obscene material, the Court said, "is material that deals with sex in a manner appealing to the prurient interest." Material is subject to censorship if "to the average person, applying contemporary community standards, the dominant theme of the material taken as a whole appeals to prurient interest." And in the opinion, the Court equates "average person" with "normal person."

This formula, announced in *Roth* as the standard for judging obscenity for constitutional purposes, has been repeated over and over again by the lower courts since 1957—with precious little effort to probe its true meaning and its ambiguities. It has been affirmatively useful in protecting freedom of expression by giving constitutional status to the average or normal person requirement and to the requirement that material be judged as a whole, not by its isolated parts. It has raised some difficult problems by its ambiguous reference to "contemporary community standards." Professor McClure and I consider these and other collateral problems in our recent article. But the formula

provides no real guidance to the solution of the core problem of obscenity—the determination of what is "obscene" under the constitutional ruling in *Roth* that portrayal of sex is constitutionally protected except when "obscene."

[In this article] I address myself only to that core problem.

THE CORE PROBLEM: WHAT IS "OBSCENE"

What the Court has said

I suggest, first, that the Court's definition of obscenity as "material that deals with sex in a manner appealing to the prurient interest" gets us nowhere. It simply pushes the core question back one notch and makes us inquire: what is the appeal to the prurient interest that makes sexual matter obscene?

"Appeal to the prurient interest" does not have an established meaning in law. The expression was rare in obscenity law until *Roth,* and though it has frequently been repeated by the lower courts since *Roth,* the repetition has not added to its meaning or our understanding of it. Even the word "prurient" is not in common usage, and when used is ordinarily used to describe a type of abnormal person, a meaning inconsistent with the Court's ruling that material is to be judged by its effect upon the normal person.

The Court borrowed the phrase "appeal to the prurient interest" from a tentative draft of the American Law Institute's Model Penal Code, but the Court and the Institute did not agree upon what the phrase meant. The Institute, which most of us know as the ALI, resorted to the phrase in its model obscenity statute in an effort to escape the prevailing unsatisfactory tests for obscenity. It rejected the test of "tendency to arouse lustful thoughts or desires because it is unduly broad for a society that plainly tolerates a great deal of erotic interest in literature, in advertising, and art." And it rejected the test of "tendency to corrupt or deprave" because of the lack of evidence of any connection between obscenity and misconduct. Instead, the ALI used the expression "appeal to the prurient interest" to focus on the nature of the appeal of the material — "the kind of appetite to which the purveyor is pandering." This, ALI pointed out, is "quite different from an inquiry as to the effect of a book upon the reader's thoughts, desire, or action." And the Institute defined prurient interest as a "shameful or morbid interest in nudity, sex, or excretion" — as "an exacerbated, morbid, or perverted interest growing out of the conflict between the universal sexual drive of the individual and equally universal social controls of sexual activity."

That ALI standard might be hard to apply, but the Court spared us the necessity of applying it for constitutional law. For while the Court borrowed the ALI expression — "appeal to the prurient interest" — it did not accept the limited meaning ALI gave that phrase. For in *Roth* the Court said that "material which deals with sex in a manner appealing to the prurient interest" *is* "material having a tendency to excite lustful thoughts" and went on to say, "we perceive no significant difference between the meaning of obscenity developed in the case law and the definition of the ALI Model Penal Code." At this point the Court cited the very page where ALI explicitly rejected the prevailing case law tests for obscenity — including the test of "tendency to excite lustful thoughts" — and where it differentiated its "prurient interest" test from all the others. And in a separate concurring opinion in *Roth* Mr. Justice Harlan pointed out this contradiction between the ALI explanation of its prurient interest test and the use of that expression in the *Roth* majority opinion. In *Roth* the Court could not have failed to be fully aware that it was not accepting as a *constitutional* test for obscenity the ALI approach to obscenity. Instead, when the Court said it saw no "significant difference" between the definitions of obscenity prevailing in the case law and the ALI definition, it must have meant that their differences were without *constitutional* significance.

So what the Court really said in *Roth* was that in the constitutional sense "obscenity" is "material that deals with sex in a manner appealing to the prurient interest," but that this *includes* the prevailing tests in the case law — the "tendency to arouse lustful thoughts or desires" and the "tendency to corrupt and deprave" as well as the ALI test of "appeal to the prurient interest" in the sense of a "shameful or morbid interest" as spelled out in more detail in the ALI notes. This really means that the nicely turned phrases that the lower courts are now quoting as the verbal formula for testing obscenity for constitutional purposes is not a single formula at all but one that embraces all the current definitions of obscenity, including the ALI definition. Any one of these verbal formulas may be constitutionally acceptable as a *definition* of obscenity, provided it meets the other requirements that the material be judged as a whole instead of by its parts, and by its appeal to or effect upon the normal person, instead of the weak and susceptible — and provided the definition is only *applied* to material that the Court considers obscene. For what really counts is not definitions or verbal formulas but the kind of material the Court views as obscene.

Perhaps I should not have taken so long to arrive nowhere, for we end up with the conclusion that as a constitutional test for obscenity "appeal to the prurient interest" really adds nothing by way of guidance to what the Court is willing to classify as "obscene" and hence censorable. Yet because of the repeated reference to this formula, both in judicial decisions and in commentaries, it seemed necessary to point out that it does lead precisely nowhere. So we must look elsewhere for guidance on the core problem—what is "obscene" in the constitutional sense.

What the Court has done

The most dependable guide to the Court's thinking is to be found in what the Court has actually *done,* not what it has *said.* Just because the verbal formula gives us little or no guidance does not mean that the Justices are without any personal concept of obscenity. On several occasions since *Roth* the Justices have ruled, either as a Court or in separate opinions, that certain material is not obscene and hence not censorable, but with no explanation of how they reached that result.

In three per curiam decisions in the term immediately following *Roth* the Court unanimously reversed without opinion three U.S. Court of Appeals decisions that had upheld censorship of material found "obscene" by the trial court. It did not send the cases back for a new trial or for reconsideration. It flatly "reversed" the judgment, citing *Roth* for authority, and ended the censorship then and there. The record in these cases, and the issues raised on appeal, make it reasonably clear that the only ground upon which the reversal could have been based was the Court's conclusion that the material censored was not "obscene" under the constitutional requirements. Also, in 1959, Justices Harlan, Frankfurter and Whittaker in a separate concurring opinion gave as one reason for reversing New York's censorship of the motion picture version of *Lady Chatterley's Lover* their unexplained conclusion that the picture was not "obscene."

These per curiam and unexplained conclusions that the material under attack was not obscene are significant on two scores. First, they support by actual decision the statement in *Roth* that the constitutional right to free expression protects material attacked as obscene because of its treatment of sex —so long as the Court finds it is not "obscene" for constitutional purposes. Second, they give us some light on the kind of material that the Court considers *not* obscene, which is perhaps as important as knowing what the Court considers obscene.

In our recent article Professor McClure and I have described the nature of the material in the three per curiam decisions. It is sufficient for present purposes to note that the material held not obscene—but without opinion—included the following:

(1) The first was a French motion picture, "The Game of Love," which starts with an episode in which a sixteen-year-old boy is shown completely nude on a bathing beach in the presence of a group of younger girls as a result of a boating accident, and proceeds to depict a series of illicit sexual relations, both with an older woman and a girl of his own age. The Court of Appeals, in finding the picture obscene, concluded: "The narrative is graphically pictured with nothing omitted except those sexual consummations which are plainly suggested but meaningfully omitted and thus, by the very fact of omission, emphasized."

(2) The second was a magazine for homosexuals entitled *One-The Homosexual Magazine,* which was definitely not a scientific or critical magazine, but appears to have been written to appeal to the tastes and interests of homosexuals.

(3) The third was *Sunshine and Health,* a nudist magazine that the lower court had found obscene because of photographs showing quite distinctly male and female genital organs and pubic areas.

In each of these cases the lower court found the material obscene and the Supreme Court reversed on the authority of *Roth,* thus terminating the censorship proceedings apparently on the ground that these materials were not "obscene" within the constitutional requirements for censorship.

Similarly in 1959 when the Court reversed New York's censorship of the motion picture *Lady Chatterley's Lover* on the ground that New York could not make it unlawful to portray acts of sexual immorality as "desirable, acceptable or proper patterns of behavior," Justices Harlan, Frankfurter and Whittaker wrote a separate concurring opinion in which they concluded that the New York decision was based also upon "actual scenes of a suggestive and obscene nature." Included were scenes which showed the gamekeeper-lover help Lady Chatterley unbutton her blouse and unzip her dress, reach with his hand under her dress to note that she had come to him with no undergarments and caress her buttocks, and which showed them lying in bed in an apparent state of undress before and after consummation of their love. The three Justices concluded that the motion picture was not obscene and hence not censorable, but

did not explain their conclusion, or make any attempt to spell out their concept of obscenity.

I am not sure what kind of conclusions we can draw from these unexplained decisions except that the Supreme Court's concept of obscenity is a very narrow one. Is it significant that the two motion pictures stop short of depicting sexual intercourse itself? Is it significant that the Lady Chatterley motion picture had something important to say about the social order? Is it significant that the publishers of the nudist magazine and the homosexual magazine both purported to be seeking to create an understanding of a way of life, unorthodox though it be? These questions I leave for you to ponder as we move on to consider another basis for understanding what the Court's concept of obscenity may be.

Before doing so, I would like to say that I think the Court was wise in not seeking to explain its decisions in these early cases. The Court has just now moved into an area in which no court yet has satisfactorily explained the basis for its obscenity decisions. It is charting a new course in a very difficult and treacherous area. It is more likely to chart a true course that will avoid dangerous shoals in the future if it gains substantial experience in dealing with difficult cases before it makes an effort to verbalize its standards for determining what is obscene. In time it must do so in order to provide adequate guidance to lower courts—and to publishers—but presently I think it has been wise to limit its explanations to problems on the periphery and simply to *decide* without explanation when it has faced the core problem of what is obscene.

But while the Court is wisely and discretely silent, commentators need be neither discrete nor wise, and perhaps plunging in where the Court sensibly holds back may provide some aid to the Court and to others dealing with these problems.

What the Court probably conceives of as obscene

We have noted a few judicial applications of whatever may be the Justices' concept of obscenity. But these applications only tell us what in the Justices' view obscenity is *not;* they do not tell us what they think obscenity *is.* Do we have any basis for judgment as to what the Justices consider obscene in the constitutional sense? I think we do. I believe the underlying concept of obscenity held by the members of the Court is "hard-core pornography," though I doubt that even the Justices know whether they will stop there.

On what do I base that belief? First, on the type of thing the Court has held *not* to be obscene

—which we have already noted indicates a very narrow scope for obscenity, far narrower than most courts have viewed obscenity in the past. Second, there is good reason to believe that when the Court in *Roth* held "obscenity" wholly outside the area of constitutionally protected speech and press, so as not to require appraisal under the usual clear and present danger test, the Justices had "hard-core pornography" uppermost in their minds. Let me explain the reason for this belief.

In *Roth* the question was not whether any particular material could be censored or was obscene. As presented to the Court, the sole question was whether the federal and state obscenity statutes were constitutional in the abstract, independent of any particular application. In this posture the United States Solicitor General contended that the federal statute was essential to prevent the country from being flooded with hard-core pornography, which constituted ninety per cent of the material caught by the statute. He urged that the validity of the statute must be judged "by this mass of 'hard-core' pornography, which…is its main objective and its major catch." He described hard-core pornography as erotic objects, photographs, books, and movies, all depicting men and women in "every conceivable kind of normal and abnormal sexual relations" and "excesses." He pointed out that such material is produced solely for and solely produces erotic effect, that the only "idea in hard-core pornography is that there is pleasure in sexual gratification, whatever the means," and explicitly noted that "the social value of such notions is, of course nil." Then, apparently to make sure that the Court understood the nature of hard-core pornography, the Solicitor General sent to the Court a carton containing numerous samples of hard-core pornography and in an accompanying letter pointed out their "extremely repulsive nature," again reminding the Court that at least ninety per cent of the convictions under the federal statute were for this kind of material.

In voting to hold obscenity statutes constitutional, the Justices could not fail to have had material of this kind in mind, for hard-core pornography, particularly in pictorial form, is so blatantly shocking and revolting that it would have been impossible for the Justices to put it out of mind. To give free circulation to such repulsive and totally worthless material in the name of constitutional freedom of expression was unthinkable. In this setting—none of which is apparent in the opinion itself—the Court's rejection of obscenity as "utterly without redeeming social importance" takes on new and significant meaning. And in this setting it seems probable that the Court's concept of "ob-scenity" as material "utterly without redeeming social importance" centered on hard-core pornography. But due to the abstract nature of the issue in *Roth* the Court had no reason to consider the underlying nature of pornography, or to consider whether some types of material may constitutionally be held "obscene" though not pornographic.

A COMMENTATOR'S ANALYSIS OF THE CORE PROBLEM: WHAT IS OBSCENE?

Considering the true nature of pornography, it is my view that the only material that should be considered constitutionally "obscene," and hence free from the usual constitutional protection for freedom of expression, is material *treated as hard-core pornography* by the manner in which and the primary audience to which it is sold. Censorship of material outside that category would have to be judged by the same standards that apply to other interferences with free expression, including the requirement that there be a clear and present danger of harmful consequences that the state has the right to prevent.

To explain this position, I will try briefly to make clear to you the true nature of pornography as I understand it, the purpose of limiting this to "hard-core," and what I mean by material "treated as hard-core pornography."

The nature of hard-core pornography

The term "hard-core pornography" is used freely by many with no attempt to explain what it means, apparently on the assumption that everyone knows just what "hard-core pornography" is. Certainly, much hard-core pornography can be recognized for what it is without a sophisticated understanding of its true nature. But an understanding of the true nature of pornography is, I believe, essential to a reasoned effort to determine what is "obscene" in the constitutional sense.

Dr. Margaret Mead, the noted anthropologist, gives us one of the best explanations of pornography. She says that pornography is "calculated to stimulate sex feelings independent of the presence of another loved and chosen human being." Its "essential element" is "the daydream as distinct from reality." According to Dr. Mead:

"The material of true pornography is compounded of daydreams themselves, composed without regard for any given reader or looker, to stimulate and titillate. It bears the signature of nonparticipation—of the dreaming adolescent, the frightened, the impotent, the bored and sated, the senile, desperately concentrating on unusualness, on drawing that which is not usually drawn, writing words on a plaster wall, shifting scenes and actors about, to evoke and feed an impulse that has no object: no object either because the adolescent is not yet old enough to seek sexual partners or because the recipient of pornography has lost the precious power of spontaneous sexual feeling."

Margaret Mead's conception of pornography as daydream material calculated to feed the auto-erotic desires of the immature and perverted and senile is supported by the Kronhausens' detailed analysis of pornographic books. They found in pornographic books the same sexual fantasy that Dr. Mead emphasized. Pornographic books are made up of a succession of increasingly erotic scenes without distracting non-erotic passages. The purpose is to stimulate erotic response, never to describe or deal with the basic realities of life.

Many other scholars have noted in pornography its essential daydream quality, designed to feed the erotic fantasies of the sexually immature. D. W. Abse says that pornography "simply encourages people to luxuriate in morbid, regressive, sexual-sadistic phantasy." W. G. Eliasberg speaks of the appeal of pornography to "immature sexuality" which is "the non-genital, not individualized, not-loving, amorphous interest in sex." London and Caprio note that those who are morbidly interested in or collect pornography "have a libido that is fixated at the paraphiliac level" meaning "psychic auto-eroticism." Benjamin Karpman calls indulgence in pornography a form of psychic masturbation.

In their extensive study on pornography and the law, the Kronhausens describe the various types of erotic scenes characteristic of pornography. These are commonly scenes of willing, even anxious seduction, of sadistic defloration in mass orgies, of incestuous relations consummated with little or no sense of guilt, of super-permissive parent figures who initiate and participate in the sexual activities of their children, of super-sexed males and females, of Negroes and Asiatics as sex symbols, of male and particularly female homosexuality, and of flagellation, all described in taboo words. I have given you only the briefest summary; the Kronhausens develop these characteristic types of pornography in much greater detail. While no list of typical pornography could ever be complete, the Kronhausen study provides a guide that helps to give concreteness to the theoretical analysis of pornography as daydream material nourishing erotic fantasies.

One characteristic of pornography is that it appeals only to the sexually abnormal or immature person, because it feeds his craving for erotic stimulation and fantasy. To the normal, sexually mature person pornography is repulsive, not attractive. The normal person may look at it once out of curiosity, but its effect on him is not erotic stimulation; instead he is repelled by it.

So analyzed, pornography as a concept assumes manageable form: Pornography is daydream material, divorced from reality, whose main function is to nourish erotic fantasies of the sexually immature, or as the psychiatrists say, to nourish auto-eroticism. This concept of pornography provides a reasonably satisfactory and workable tool for distinguishing pornographic material from the non-pornographic.

But in order to make pornography a usable tool for testing obscenity we must exclude a type of widely accepted non-literary material that might be thought to nourish erotic fantasies of a sort. I have in mind the type of material illustrated by the pin-up girl, scantily clad but sculpturally perfect, who may appeal to the artistic in some of us but may also provide a dream world of sorts for others, with possibly some minor element of erotic stimulation. Such pictures are accepted fare in our society, never attacked as obscene or pornographic. To except such material, we must add the qualification "black market" or "hard-core" to "pornographic" in order to indicate that to be "obscene" in the constitutional sense, non-literary material must not only nourish erotic fantasies but be grossly shocking as well. So limited, hard-core pornography becomes a useful tool for drawing the line between the constitutionally obscene and non-obscene.

But note I said a "tool," not a test of the litmus paper variety, for hard-core pornography as I have described it necessarily leaves much room for judgment in making the application—judgment that must be influenced by considerations relating to social value, or lack of social value, of the materials in question, and the importance to society of free expression. For, after all, we must not forget that the most basic freedom in a democracy is at stake in these adjudications, and the reason for ruling that the right to freedom of expression does not protect "obscenity" from censorship is that obscenity is "utterly without social importance." Necessarily, then, the social value of the material in question will influence a close judgment on whether it is obscene.

Material treated as hard-core pornography.

You will recall that just before describing hard-core pornography I stated that in my judgment the "obscenity" that is free from constitutional protection should be limited to material *treated* as hard-core pornography. Why did I put it that way, rather than to say simply that obscenity should be limited to hard-core pornography?

Because in my judgment censorship should not depend upon the intrinsic nature of the material independent of its audience and method of marketing. Instead, it should depend upon the manner in which it is marketed and the primary audience to which it is sold. In this way constitutional protection can be given to the occasional legitimate distribution of hard-core pornography for scientific purposes, while at the same time censorship of material that is *not* intrinsically hard-core pornography can be permitted when the manner of marketing and the primary audience to which it is marketed indicate that it is being treated as hard-core pornography—that its function in that setting is to nourish erotic fantasies of the sexually immature. For these reasons I believe that obscenity should be a variable concept, depending upon the manner of marketing—the appeal in the marketing —and the nature of the primary audience to which the appeal is made.

Let me illustrate. In rare instances hard-core pornography is sold to social scientists or psychiatrists engaged in the study of pornography and its addicts. For example, the Kinsey Institute imported some hard-core pornography for scientific study and a federal district court ruled it was not obscene when marketed in this manner to this class of purchaser. In the *Kinsey* case, hard-core pornography was not *treated* as pornography—it was neither marketed nor bought for its appeal to erotic fantasies. In a constitutional sense, it was not "obscene" when sold to the Institute for scientific study because, as the District Court ruled, it did not "appeal to the prurient interest" of the special audience to which it was marketed.

To the other extreme, I would not be surprised to see a case arise in which a news stand near a high school purchases a huge supply of the un-expurgated edition of *Lady Chatterley's Lover*, and through posters and otherwise makes a special sales pitch to high school students, not emphasizing the novel's high literary quality and its social message but its sexual passages. I am confident that Lawrence's great novel is not obscene when marketed in the normal way to the public at large; this was the unanimous conclusion of the U.S. Court of Appeals, Second Circuit, and the Department of Justice apparently agreed, for it did not appeal. But if *Lady Chatterley's Lover* is *treated* as pornography by the manner of marketing and response of the primary audience of sexually immature youngsters to whom it is sold, then as to

that seller and that primary audience of buyers the material *is* hard-core pornography and should be classified as "obscene." Constitutional freedom of expression requires that Lawrence's novel be free from censorship when sold to a primary audience made up of the public at large, consisting largely of mature, adult buyers. But when it is marketed in such a manner as to appeal to a primary audience of sexually immature kids to nourish their craving for erotic fantasy, then the reason for constitutional protection is not present and there is reason for censorship.

In my opinion this approach—making the finding of "obscenity" depend upon whether the material in question is treated as hard-core pornography by its primary audience, rather than using a constant standard of obscenity without regard to its audience—serves a triply useful purpose. It permits material needed for scientific purposes to be freely distributed to scientific audiences, regardless of its intrinsic pornographic nature. It takes a narrow view of what is obscene when distribution is to a primary audience of sexually mature adults, thereby protecting the basic freedom both of the artist and the audience. But it gives much wider protection against "obscenity" when the primary audience is made up of the sexually immature, whether adolescents or abnormal adults, and permits control over material marketed to such audiences to nourish their craving for erotic fantasies. In my judgment, this approach would permit control over most, if not all, of the material that could reasonably be thought harmful to youth when marketed to such an audience.

It is, of course, true that when the primary audience is made up of mature adults, an occasional purchase may be made by an adolescent or by a sexually immature adult, who will find nourishment for erotic fantasies in material that is not hard-core pornography nor treated as such by its primary audience—*Lady Chatterley's Lover*, for example. But this is one of the prices we must pay in order to avoid limiting adult reading fare to that fit for children. The Supreme Court so ruled in the *Butler* case in 1957 shortly before the *Roth* decision, and again in the *Roth* decision when the Court ruled that obscenity must be tested by the average or normal adult, not the susceptible or immature.

This variable obscenity approach requires that in each instance the finding of obscenity be based upon the nature of the primary audience to which the sales appeal is made and the nature of the material's appeal to that audience. In each instance the question should be: With respect to this *primary audience* is the material treated as hard-core pornography—to satisfy or nourish erotic fantasies of the sexually immature? This requires that any *peripheral audience* be disregarded. The Supreme Court has already ruled that this is so when the primary audience is made up of mature adults: the fact that a few children may gain access to the material through this channel cannot justify banning its sale, at least to adults. Similarly, when a hole in the wall specializing in erotica, with a specialized primary audience of the sexually immature, stocks *Lady Chatterley's Lover,* it is a reasonable conclusion that the novel is offered and sold to such an audience, not for its literary and social values, but as a stimulant to their erotic fantasies. When sold to such a primary audience, *Lady Chatterley* would be treated as pornography and could reasonably be held obscene, even though an occasional normal, mature adult in the peripheral audience might accidentally see the novel in the window and buy it for its true values.

As I suggested earlier, one advantage of this approach is to permit the judgment on obscenity to be made on the basis of the appeal to the young, the susceptible or the sexually immature when they constitute the primary audience. One of the criticisms aimed at the Supreme Court's handling of this problem thus far is that in *Butler* and in *Roth* it seems to say that material must be judged by its appeal to the normal adult, and harmful impact upon the immature cannot be considered. I have adequately indicated my opinion that this position by the Court is sound when applied to sales to a primary audience of sexually mature adults. But when the primary audience is made up of the sexually immature, there is no reason to give constitutional protection to material *treated* by that audience as hard-core pornography, even though it would not be obscene when offered to an audience of mature adults. To the immature audience, resorting to the material for satisfaction of their hunger for erotic fantasy, the material is treated as pornography and should be subject to the same controls.

Those who have read the *Roth* opinions might well object to my suggestion that "obscenity" and hence censorship should depend upon the appeal to the sexually immature when they constitute the primary audience. You may ask, "Didn't the Court say in *Roth* that it was rejecting a test of obscenity based upon the young and susceptible and that obscenity must be judged on the basis of its appeal to the average or normal man?" It is true; the Court did say that. But to this question I have two answers.

First, a test based upon the prurient appeal to the normal sexually mature adult would, if applied rigidly, exclude all control over hard-core pornography. For hard-core pornography has no appeal to the normal, sexually mature adult. As I have indicated, it is repulsive and revolting to him. Hard-core pornography has its appeal only to the sexually immature—the sexually abnormal adult and some youngsters who have not reached sexual maturity. If, to be obscene, material must appeal to the prurient interest—whatever that means—of the normal, sexually mature adult, then hard-core pornography would never be obscene, although it is the one class of material that most certainly is obscene and is not entitled to constitutional protection. Obviously, something is wrong with such a test.

Second, when the Court rejected the test of the effect upon children in *Butler* it was dealing with the case of a sale to an adult and there was no suggestion that the seller was appealing to a primary audience of adolescents. And when the Court stated in *Roth* that material must be judged on the basis of its appeal to normal adults, it was rejecting the old *Hicklin* doctrine that had come to stand for the proposition that sales to all audiences must be judged by the possible harmful impact on the young and susceptible.

In my judgment the Court's formula in *Roth* used the positive as a means of stating the negative. In this light, the statement that material is to be judged by its effects on or appeal to the average or normal person is simply a way of stating that material disseminated to the public generally must not be judged by its effects on or appeal to the weak or susceptible, for as Mr. Justice Frankfurter said in the *Butler* case that would be to "burn the house to roast the pig." That reasoning is sound applied to the general situation before the Court in the two cases, but it has no application to the situation in which a seller is directing his sales pitch at a susceptible audience of the sexually immature. In such a case, I think the Constitution and the Supreme Court will permit controls reasonably designed to protect that susceptible audience so long as the constitutional right to sell to a primary audience of sexually mature is not infringed.

And this interpretation makes sense in dealing with hard-core pornography, which is the principal if not the sole occupant of the category "obscene." For it permits control over hard-core pornography, or anything treated as such, without the fiction of pretending that such stuff appeals to the prurient interest of the normal adult in order to make it fit the verbal formula announced in *Roth.*

I wish to suggest two possible exceptions to my proposal that obscenity censorship should be limited to material treated as hard-core pornography by the manner in which and the primary audience to which it is sold.

The first is not really an exception, but needs explanation to avoid misunderstanding. I would not give constitutional protection to the sale of intrinsically hard-core pornography to a buyer who is apparently a sexually mature adult, absent some showing that he was buying it for scientific study. This is not really an exception to my proposed test, for since hard-core pornography has no appeal to the sexually mature adult, it is never marketed to a primary audience of normal, sexually mature adults, apart from the small special audience of scientific students exemplified by the *Kinsey Institute* case. Hard-core pornography is under-the-counter stuff, sold clandestinely, usually in out-of-the-way shops that cater to those whose interests are erotic. Therefore, while a normal adult might pick up such material once out of curiosity, he would belong to a small peripheral audience that would not give immunity to the dealer whose primary audience is made up of the sexually immature.

The second is a true exception that might arise in the case of a statute that explicitly forbids the sale of matter that is obscene to adolescents. A problem would arise under that statute if a book dealer catering to a primary audience of normal, sexually mature adults sold to a youngster a book that was not "obscene" for adults but whose only appeal to youngsters was an appeal to erotic fantasy. *Lady Chatterley's Lover* is probably, again, a good illustration. Conceivably the Court might hold that despite the primary audience of adults, a different standard must be applied in the case of a sale to a child. But there are serious questions of practicality here, for the difficulty of guarding against sales to children might well result in the bookseller reducing his entire inventory of books offered to his primary audience in order to avoid any difficulty over sales to children. In that case, the evil the Court sought to avoid in the *Butler* case would be upon us again in a different form. The ultimate validity of such an "adults only" requirement for part of the stock of a bookseller catering primarily to an adult audience may well depend upon pragmatic experience with efforts to comply with such statutes designed to protect children but to leave adults free to buy sophisticated books.

Though I have already exhausted my audience, I have not exhausted the problems and questions that could be raised concerning the proposal that obscenity in the constitutional sense be limited to material treated as hard-core pornography by its primary audience. For further discussion of such matters, such as the feasibility of this proposal from the standpoint of enforcement officials, I must refer you to the recent Lockhart-McClure article.

At this point I can only take time to add one final argument in support of my proposal. Some may say that my proposal limiting the constitutionally "obscene" to material treated as hard-core pornography will not adequately protect youth. They may believe that certain materials are harmful in their effect upon children, even though they are not treated as hard-core pornography—that is, are not used to nourish erotic fantasies. My answer is that such non-pornographic materials are subject to the same constitutional protection for freedom of expression accorded all other communications. That freedom of expression is not absolute. Distribution of "non-obscene"—non-pornographic—material thought harmful to youngsters can still be prohibited if the Court is satisfied that there is a "clear and present danger" of a harm the government has the right to prevent. I will not try to expand on "clear and present danger" except to refer you to the 1954 Lockhart-McClure article, and to add that under this approach the Court would weigh the social value of the material under attack, and the importance of free expression with respect to such material, against the seriousness of the harm sought to be prevented and the probability that reading or viewing the material in question will cause much harm.

But my concern [here] is not with such issues. My discussion...is limited to consideration of where the line should be drawn on material that the Court says is not even subject to the freedom of expression protections—as to which we do not even get to the "clear and present danger" issues because the material is labeled "obscene." And my proposition is that that line should be drawn at material *treated* as hard-core pornography by the *primary audience* to which it is directed.

CONCLUSION

In conclusion, let me say just a word about the Supreme Court's function in the developing constitutional law relating to censorship of obscenity. You may gather from my discussion of the core problem, "What is obscene," that the Court has provided very little guidance, and that the guidance it has provided needs much refinement. I suppose the Justices themselves would be the first to admit this. But remember the point I made earlier. The Court will do a better job long-range, if it feels its way now in this brand new field of constitutional adjudication, decides only what it has to decide, and says very little while it gets the feel of the problem. Remember that people like McClure and me have spent a large share of time for several years, off and on, studying this problem, whereas the Justices can devote very little time, actually, to resolving each case.

But while the Court has not provided much direction—yet—on the core problem of obscenity, it has made a great deal of progress and some very significant law on the collateral problems involved in the administration of obscenity laws. It has established the constitutional requirement that material must be judged by the dominant theme of the material as a whole, not by its isolated parts. It has established the requirement that a bookseller must be chargeable with knowledge of the alleged obscenity in order to be convicted criminally. It has made it clear that the constitutional guarantee protects the right to advocate unconventional ideas and behavior "immoral" by current standards, and do so in effective and dramatic ways, so long as the manner of conveying the ideas is not "obscene." And it is becoming increasingly apparent that the Court will not permit a finding of "obscenity" by an administrator or lower court to conclude the matter; independent judicial review of the finding of obscenity seems assured, with review of enough cases in the Supreme Court to keep the other appellate courts in line.

These collateral protections still require refinement, but that will come as appropriate cases arise to permit these refinements to be hammered out in concrete settings. So long as we have independent judicial review, I am satisfied that in the long run freedom of expression will be adequately protected. The Court will occasionally make mistakes—as I think it did when late in January upheld five to four the power to require a censor approval of motion pictures in advance of show ing, despite the powerful dissenting opinion k Chief Justice Warren showing the serious abuse of such power, to which commercial interests w often bow as a practical matter rather than cha lenge the particular abuse as they could do su cessfully if they appealed to the Courts. But th problem of prior restraint is outside the scope this discussion. I would only add that independe judicial review of particular exercises of the ce sor's power in the last year or two has reduce substantially the extent of movie censorship. Th impact of the decisions to date has been felt all forms of communication, where there is muc greater freedom of expression than before 195 I, for one, am satisfied that under the direction the Supreme Court our state and federal cour will protect freedom of expression and at the sam time permit society to protect the immatu against the evils of pornography.

FREEDOM OF RELIGION

ost of the problems to which the reader was introduced in the speech and scenity areas recur in the other great area of First Amendment interpretation, ligion. Is freedom of religion absolute, or should the religious rights or inter- ts of some citizens be balanced against the religious and other interests of the st? Just how and to what extent are the religious guarantees of the First nendment incorporated into the Fourteenth and thus binding on the states?*) what extent has the Court succeeded in reconciling later decisions with rlier, and in stating principles that will allow us to anticipate with some cer- inty its future rulings?

The religious freedom aspects of the First Amendment are complicated by o factors that do not arise in freedom of speech cases. First, there are two auses dealing with religion rather than one. The Constitution declares that ingress shall make no law (1) respecting an establishment of religion or) prohibiting the free exercise thereof. As we shall see shortly, not only is there nsiderable difficulty about what these clauses mean—as there is with the eech clauses—but the two can be read sometimes as in harmony and some- nes as in conflict with each other. Quite different results may follow depending)on which is used as the starting point for any line of reasoning about religious)erty. Second, the religion cases almost always arise in conjunction with the iblic schools, which are the most widely accepted but also the most peculiar pect of American governmental activity. No other activity seeks so directly shape the ideas, values, and conduct of the citizenry.

If Americans were asked to name the most coercive and potentially totali- rian aspect of American government, few would choose the public schools. ideed, Americans rarely think of schools as part of government at all. Yet the ee public school and compulsory school attendance laws impinge more upon e individual's privacy and intellectual freedom than does any other aspect of)vernment. It forces him to surrender his children, at the most impressionable id critical period of their intellectual development, to an institution designed to inculcate in them not the private beliefs of the parent but the public ideology

---

*The Fourteenth Amendment states, "No State shall make or enforce any law which shall abridge the privileges or immunities of citizens of the United States; nor shall any State deprive any person of life, liberty, or property, without due process of law;..." In *Gitlow* v. *New York* [268 U.S. 652 (1925)], the Supreme Court held that the guarantees of the First Amendment were "incorporated" into the due process clause of the Fourteenth Amendment. While *Gitlow* involved freedom of speech, not religion, a series of later decisions does seem to incorporate the entire First Amendment into the Fourteenth.

dictated by the majority of citizens. And each day more and more of the private duties and privileges of the parent, from proper nutrition to sex instruction, are being transferred from the family to the school. The availability of private schools is a comforting but largely illusory escape hatch from such coercion. Relatively few parents who now send their children to public schools could afford to send them to private schools, and fewer yet would be willing to incur the great expense involved in doing so in order to gain some indefinite increment in intellectual freedom. In a great many American communities and for a great many American parents, there is really no practical alternative to the public schools.

When religious differences are injected into this, our peculiarly public institution, the winds of controversy are likely to blow hot. Yet with the increasing disintegration of our faith in the capacity of the family, or indeed in any non-governmental institution, to perform adequately most of the crucial tasks of society, the pressure mounts on the schools to inculcate our children with a belief in God, as well as all the other values and beliefs we find socially desirable. Thus, although the "free exercise" and "no establishment" clauses might touch upon many aspects of American life, the latest and greatest furor about them has been at the nexus of religion and education, and it is upon these matters that we concentrate here.

The First Amendment permits us to carry on a public controversy about religion in the abstract vocabulary of constitutional rhetoric and thus allows us to avoid the kind of direct, cards-on-the-table debate that would be extremely dangerous in a multireligious society. This great dividend yielded by constitutional phrase-making, however, should not be allowed to distract the individual student of the problem from plumbing the basic reasons why he personally chooses one side or the other in the debate. For many Jews, religion in the schools means Christianity in the schools. It may be painful for them to say that they do not want to contribute either their children or their tax money to an institution that teaches that a Jewish carpenter was God, especially when the adherents of that particular persuasion have been persecuting them for two thousand years. For many Protestants and nonbelievers it is easier to talk about "no establishment of religion" than it is to say openly that they do not want public funds spent on supporting parochial schools that inculcate a religion that they believe to be compounded of superstitious mumbo jumbo and rigorously enforced orthodoxy essentially inimical to their own intellectual and religious liberty.

Anyone who seeks to assess honestly his own or anyone else's response to the coolly legal words of Paul Kauper and Louis Pollak that follow must take such viewpoints, true or false, into account. This is not to say that men of good will but differing religious convictions cannot carry on a rational debate and even reach a mutually acceptable agreement within the conventional bounds of constitutional argumentation. But it does mean that in the end such an agreement will depend upon finding an acceptable compromise between conflicting religious interests, not on discovering the magic meaning of a few phrases in the Constitution or, for that matter, in Madison's or Jefferson's voluminous and often contradictory writings. Kauper believes such a compromise may best be found by putting some religion in the schools, Pollak by keeping it out. Although this author personally agrees with Pollak, that is hardly important; what is important is the realization that religion in the schools is a complex and potentially explosive problem, not an exercise in legal logic.

One final note about politics. The constant ghost at the feast of legal, historical, and psychological arguments in the freedom of religion cases is federal aid to parochial schools. The reader will, for instance, find a great deal of discussion about whether the school prayer cases ought to have been decided under the "no establishment of religion" or the "free exercise" clause. Behind much of this discussion lies the fact that decisions emphasizing free exercise would have no adverse effect on possible parochial school aid because no religious minority is coerced in parochial schools. On the other hand, "no establishment" decisions, stressing the principle that the government may neither help nor hinder any religion, are obviously inimical to such aid. Indeed, the reader will find in the Pollak selection two opinions by Justice Douglas that have almost nothing to do with the prayer in public school cases in which they were issued but were largely calculated to prepare a strongly fortified position from which aid to Catholic schools could be struck down when and if it reached the Court. Study of the school prayer cases is as good an introduction as any to the political aspects of constitutional law.

Selection 6

Prayer, Public Schools and the Supreme Court
Paul G. Kauper

Kauper's article focuses on the decision in *Engel* v. *Vitale*. At the start the reader will be faced with the names of other cases that obviously are important but are not immediately explained. Everything will become clear in due course, however, for Kauper, taking each issue in turn, fully canvasses the legal arguments and precedents. Early in the selection he also mentions some cases that were still pending at the time he wrote. His story is continued by Pollak.

Kauper spends some time on one issue that lawyers find endlessly fascinating but outsiders often dismiss as "technical," that of *standing* (i.e., the rendering of decisions as to who has been sufficiently injured by a governmental action to have a right to sue the government in court). Behind the standing problem lies an important issue of Court power. The Supreme Court may not issue advisory opinions. It may only decide genuine cases and controversies between two parties, one of whom has been sufficiently injured or affected by the actions of the other to warrant legal action. Obviously, the more rigorous the Court's rules on standing, the more difficult it is for the Court to intervene on constitutional grounds against the actions of other parts of government. Under the most rigorous rules of standing, for instance, the Court might never be able to declare federal aid to parochial schools unconstitutional even if the justices thought it was, for no individual may be injured by such a program, even if it is unconstitutional, except to the infinitesimal degree that his tax dollars are spent on it—and that is rarely enough to gain standing in a federal court.

The reader should be aware that Kauper's article is itself a piece of political campaigning. If a legal scholar wishes the Supreme Court to adopt a certain

"Prayer, Public Schools and the Supreme Court" by Paul G. Kauper, 61 *Michigan Law Review* 1031 (1963). Reprinted by permission of The Michigan Law Review Association.

position in the future and senses that the Court's last decision was heading in a contrary direction, his best bet is to criticize the last decision in such a way as to show the Court the undesirable consequences of continuing in that direction and the ways in which the proper outcome can be achieved in the future without unduly disturbing past precedents. Kauper, writing after the decision in *Engel*, skillfully shows the Court what he finds good and bad about the decision and how, in the pending cases, the Court might do much better without seeming to deviate abruptly from its previous stand.

Public reaction to the Supreme Court's decision in *Engel* v. *Vitale*,[1] decided in June 1962 and holding invalid a non-sectarian prayer prescribed for use in the public schools of the State of New York, made clear that the decision had touched a vital and sensitive spot in the national life. Unfavorable response to the holding ranged from intemperate and abusive denunciation of the Court as Godless to more thoughtful and reflective criticism that was directed to various considerations such as that the Court in interpreting the first amendment had failed to give due weight to the place of religion in American tradition and life, had misinterpreted the original meaning and purpose of this amendment, had conferred a constitutional blessing upon secularism as the official American orthodoxy, and had unduly subordinated the majority will and the community consensus to the sentiments and wishes of a small minority. Some, while not disturbed by the result reached with respect to the problem immediately before the Court, saw large and portentous implications in the decision. Did it mean that the Constitution forbade not only religious practices in the public schools but also any consideration of religion in public school programs? And did it mean that all acknowledgments of Deity on official occasions was forbidden?

Not all of the immediate reaction to *Engel* was critical. Secularists and strict separationists hailed the decision as adding strength to the wall of separation between church and state, while others applauded the decision as a further contribution to religious freedom. Moreover, much of the initial criticism was dissipated when the Court's full opinion was read and understood. A substantial part of the press and a number of religious leaders and groups announced their support of the decision as one which, by restricting the state's power to intervene in the sensitive area of prayer, thereby advanced and protected the liberty of both the believer and the non-believer. Also, some who supported the holding asserted that it did not outlaw all recognition of religion in the public schools and had nothing to say whatever about acknowledgment of Deity in public pronouncements and on official occasions. The decision did not make God

an outlaw so far as the national life was concerned. Likewise, any larger implications of the case with respect to the use of public funds or property to aid religious activities were attributable not to the majority opinion but to Mr. Justice Douglas' concurring opinion.

A more complete understanding of the case, while doing much to temper the initial outburst of disapproval, did not by any means dispel all criticism of the decision or allay all the apprehensions aroused by it. Believing that the Supreme Court's opinion was premised on a fundamentally erroneous interpretation of the establishment clause of the first amendment, Bishop James A. Pike headed a movement to amend the Constitution so as to restore what he regarded as the true and intended meaning of its pertinent language. In the meantime, the Supreme Court has agreed to review and has heard argument on cases dealing with the constitutionality of Bible reading and recitation of the Lord's Prayer in public schools.[2] The decisions in these cases may be expected to result in resumption of the public debate sparked by *Engel*.

THE NEW YORK TRIAL COURT'S OPINION

The facts of the *Engel* case are simply stated. A local public school board, acting on the recommendation of the New York Board of Regents, adopted a resolution directing the daily recitation of the following prayer which the Board had composed for this purpose:

"Almighty God, we acknowledge our dependence upon Thee, and we beg Thy blessings upon us, our parents, our teachers and our country."

The prayer was to be recited at the beginning of the school day, following the pledge of allegiance to the flag. The school board's regulation made no allowance for students who objected to participation, but the board did provide in an instruction that was not incorporated in its resolution or otherwise publicized that no child was to be required or encouraged to join in the prayer against his or her wishes. Only one request that a child be excused from saying the prayer was received in the schools of the district, which request was respected; and no child had directly asked to be excused from joining in the prayer, nor had either a parent or a child sought permission for a child to leave the classroom during the saying of the prayer. The petitioners, who were taxpayers of the school district and parents of children in the schools of the district and whose group included Jews, Unitarians, members of the Society of Ethical Culture and one non-believer, after an unsuccessful demand upon the school board that the daily prayer practice be terminated, brought a proceeding in a New York court for a mandatory order directing that the prayer practice be discontinued. Asserting that the use of this official prayer in the public schools was contrary to the beliefs, religions, or religious practices of both themselves and their children, they contended that the state's action, both in authorizing the use of this prayer and in ordering its daily recitation by children in public school classrooms, was unconstitutional. Reliance was placed upon the first and fourteenth amendments to the Constitution of the United States and upon the provisions of the New York constitution guaranteeing the free exercise and enjoyment of religious profession and worship, without discrimination or preference, and forbidding public aid to a school in which any denominational tenet or doctrine is taught.

It is unfortunate that all the attention riveted on the final opinion in the case by the United States Supreme Court has served to obscure the opinion by Justice Meyer of the New York trial court.[3] It was an extraordinarily able, thorough and scholarly opinion which did more to illuminate the problems and issues of the case than any other opinions at further stages of the litigation. The gist of the trial court's holding may be briefly stated before we take a closer look at the judge's opinion. He held that the prayer exercise did not violate that clause of the first amendment protecting the free exercise of religion so long as the school board established procedures designed to assure voluntariness of participation in the prayer practice by protecting those who objected to saying the prayer, and found also that it did not constitute an establishment of religion as forbidden by the first amendment. He further found that the prayer practice was not "denominational" within the meaning of the New York constitution and emphasized that this was a prayer *exercise* and not religious instruction in any real sense of the word. While he denied the petitioners the relief they had requested, he did direct the school board to adopt

and publicize regulations stating the rules to be observed with respect to the rights of non-participants. He recommended for this purpose the regulation adopted by the New York City Board of Education, which made clear that neither teachers nor any school authority could comment on participation or non-participation in the exercise or suggest or require any particular posture, language, or dress in connection with recitation of the prayer. Non-participation could take the form either of remaining silent during the exercise, or, if the parent or child so desired, of being excused altogether from the exercise. He recommended that the regulations provide that prayer participants could proceed to a common assembly while non-participants attended other rooms, or that non-participants would be permitted to arrive at school a few minutes late or attend separate opening exercises, or authorize any other procedure which assured equal freedom for both participants and non-participants.

The heart of the trial court's extensive and well-documented opinion dealt with the issues raised under the first amendment as made applicable to the states by means of the fourteenth amendment. Stating as a fundamental rule of interpretation that the meaning of a constitutional amendment is to be determined by the "sense of the nation" at the time of its adoption, Justice Meyer, after reviewing historical practices and pointing out that prayer and Bible reading in public schools have been common American practices, concluded that prayer recitation in public schools did not violate the fourteenth amendment as construed by the sense of the nation when this amendment was adopted in 1868. Recognizing, however, that the Supreme Court had held that the first amendment applies to the states by means of the fourteenth amendment, the trial court found no violation of the free exercise clause so long as the right of objectors not to participate in the prayer exercise was adequately protected. So far as the establishment clause was concerned, the court again relied upon historical practice and understanding to demonstrate the sense of the nation that recitation of prayers in public life was not "an establishment of religion" in the sense used in the Constitution or as understood by men such as Jefferson or Madison. Nor did the trial court find that the Supreme Court's opinions interpreting the establishment language required a different result. In the end it placed chief reliance upon the holding and opinion in the *Zorach*[4] case in concluding that some form of prayer would fall within the realm of permissible accommodation of the public school system to the religious needs of the nation.[5]

In weighing the reasons for including this kind of prayer exercise in the public school program, the trial court concluded that it could not be justified on the ground that this was a means of familiarizing students with the religious nature of our heritage since there are other equally effective and constitutionally uninhibited means of achieving that end. Moreover, it could not be justified on the ground that the state could prescribe exercises designed to inculcate in pupils a love of God or teach "spiritual values," since an exercise directed to such purposes would constitute religious instruction in violation of the establishment clause and in violation of the parents' right to control the education of his child. However, the court concluded that the recognition of prayer as an integral part of our national heritage was demonstrated by practices widely accepted at the time of the adoption of the first and the fourteenth amendments and that, therefore, these constitutional provisions could not have been intended to prohibit prayer in public schools any more than in other aspects of public life.[6]

In summary, the trial court concluded that, since the first and fourteenth amendments should be construed with reference to the "sense of the nation" at the time of their adoption and since recognition of prayer was an integral part of our national heritage, prayer in public schools did not constitute an establishment of religion and did not violate religious freedom so long as the regulations made clear that student participation in the prayer exercise was a voluntary matter and adequate provision was made for those children desiring not to participate.

The trial court's decision was affirmed on appeal by the New York appellate courts.[7] Their opinions rested on substantially the same grounds as those stated more extensively in the trial court's opinion. Judges Dye and Fuld of the New York Court of Appeals dissented on the ground that the prayer exercise violated the establishment clause as interpreted by the Supreme Court in *Everson*[8] and *McCollum*.[9]

THE SUPREME COURT'S OPINIONS

The Supreme Court of the United States on review of the case reversed the decision of the New York Court of Appeals and found the prayer practice unconstitutional because it constituted an establishment of religion in violation of the first and fourteenth amendments.[10] The case was decided by a seven-man court, Justices Frankfurter and White not participating in the decision. The majority opinion written by Mr. Justice Black

received the support of Mr. Chief Justice Warren and Justices Brennan, Clark and Harlan. Mr. Justice Douglas concurred in a separate opinion and Mr. Justice Stewart wrote a dissenting opinion.

At the outset, Mr. Justice Black stated the Court's conclusion that New York "by using its school system to encourage recitation of the Regents' prayer…has adopted a practice wholly inconsistent with the Establishment Clause."[11] In passages of the opinion that followed he stated that there was no doubt that the New York program of daily classroom invocation of God's blessings was a religious activity, that counsel was correct in asserting that the use of prayer to further religious beliefs breached the constitutional wall of separation between church and state, and that the constitutional prohibition "must at least mean that in this country it is no part of the business of government to compose official prayers for any group of American people to recite as a part of a religious program carried on by government."[12]

In building up his case on the significance of the first amendment's establishment clause in its application to the prayer situation, Mr. Justice Black drew upon the history of practices in England whereby Parliament, in asserting control over the established Church of England and over the Church's Book of Common Prayer, determined what prayers should be included in this book. Objections to this practice led some people to come to this country to find religious freedom, and in England the control by Parliament over prayer led to competition of various groups to secure approval of their particular form of prayer. Mr. Justice Black then stated that many of those who came to this country to find religious freedom in turn established their official religions and were equally intolerant and oppressive. Nevertheless, intensive opposition to the practice of establishing religion by law followed in the wake of the Revolutionary War. This movement crystallized rapidly into an effective opposition that eventually led to the enactment of the famous "Virginia Bill of Religious Liberty," by which all religious groups were placed on an equal footing so far as the state was concerned. By the time, then, that the Constitution was adopted there was widespread awareness among many Americans of the danger of a union of church and state—the danger to the freedom of the individual to worship in his own way when government places its stamp of approval on one particular kind of prayer, and the bitter strife that comes when zealous religious groups struggle to obtain the government's approval from each ruler that may temporarily come to power. The first amendment to the Constitution was added as a guarantee that neither the power nor the prestige of the federal government would be used to control, support or influence the kinds of prayer the American people can say.

Mr. Justice Black then stated there could be no doubt that the New York school prayer program officially established the religious beliefs embodied in the Regents' prayer and so violated the establishment clause of the first amendment which is operative against the states also "by virtue of the fourteenth amendment."[13] It was immaterial that the prayer was "non-denominational" or that the observance of prayer practice by students was voluntary. Voluntarism might free the prayer from objections under the free exercise clause but not from the establishment clause. The two clauses, even though they overlap, forbid two quite different kinds of "encroachment upon religious freedom."[14] The establishment clause does not depend upon any showing of direct governmental compulsion and is violated by the enactment of laws which establish an official religion, whether these laws operate directly to coerce non-observing individuals or not. But at this point Mr. Justice Black saw fit to inject that this is not

"to say, of course, that laws officially prescribing a particular form of religious worship do not involve coercion of individuals. When the power, prestige and financial support of government is placed behind a particular religious belief, the indirect coercive pressure upon religious minorities to conform to the prevailing officially approved religion is plain."[15]

But, continued Mr. Justice Black, the purposes underlying the establishment clause go much farther than that. Its first and most immediate purpose is grounded on the belief that a union of government and religion tends to destroy government and to degrade religion. Another purpose rests upon an awareness of the fact that governmentally established religion and religious persecution go hand in hand.

Denying that this application of the Constitution to prohibit state laws respecting an establishment of religious services in public schools indicated a hostility to religion or toward prayer, Mr. Justice Black, noting that the history of man is inseparable from the history of religion and also that men of faith in the power of prayer led the fight for adoption of the Constitution and the Bill of Rights, concluded:

"It is neither sacrilegious nor antireligious to say that each separate government in this country should stay out of the business of writing or sanctioning official prayers and leave that purely religious function to the people themselves and to those the people choose to look to for religious guidance."[16]

Referring to the argument that the Regents' prayer did not amount to a total establishment of one particular religion and that governmental endorsement of this prayer was relatively insignificant when compared with the governmental encroachments upon religions which were commonplace two hundred years ago, Mr. Justice Black quoted the following words from James Madison, whom he described as "the author of the first amendment":

"It is proper to take alarm at the first experiment on our liberties....Who does not see that the same authority which can establish Christianity, in exclusion of all other Religions, may establish with the same ease any particular sect of Christians, in exclusion of all other Sects? That the same authority which can force a citizen to contribute three pence only of his property for the support of any one establishment, may force him to conform to any other establishment in all cases whatsoever?"[17]

Mr. Justice Douglas concurred in a separate opinion in which he premised his whole case on the argument that government cannot constitutionally finance a religious exercise. He made clear that in his opinion there was no element of compulsion or coercion involved in the New York prayer practice. But he condemned New York's action because it financed a religious exercise and went on to state his opinion that all practices (and in a footnote he referred to numerous ones), whereby a public official on a public payroll performs or conducts a religious exercise in a governmental institution, fall within the same category. While he could not say that to authorize this prayer was to establish religion in "the strictly historic meaning"[18] of those words, yet once government finances a religious exercise it inserts a divisive influence into our communities. The first amendment leaves the government in a position not of hostility to religion but of neutrality. If government interferes in matters spiritual, it will act as a divisive force. "The First Amendment teaches that a government neutral in the field of religion better serves all religious interests."[19]

Mr. Justice Stewart dissented. Emphasizing that it could not be argued that New York had interfered with the free exercise of anybody's religion, he rejected the idea that letting those who wanted to say this prayer say it thereby established "an official religion." On the contrary, he viewed the prayer practice as an opportunity for children to share in the nation's spiritual heritage. Unimpressed by the review in the majority's opinion of the history of an established church in England or in eighteenth century America, he found much more relevant, as an aid to interpretation of the first amendment, "the history of the religious traditions of our people, reflected in countless practices of the institutions and officials of our government."[20] He pointed to the prayers used in opening the Supreme Court's daily session and the daily sessions of both houses of Congress, the prayer found in the third stanza of the National Anthem, the motto "In God We Trust" impressed on our coins, and the inclusion of the phrase "under God" in the pledge of allegiance to the flag. He stated that it was all summed up in the Court's opinion in *Zorach* when it said, "We are a religious people whose institutions presuppose a Supreme Being."[21] What New York had done, as well as the Court, the Congress and the President, had been "to recognize and to follow the deeply entrenched and highly cherished spiritual traditions of our Nation."[22]

THE SCOPE OF THE HOLDING

What then is the significance of the *Engel* case? Viewed with reference to its facts, the case can be limited to a narrow holding, namely, that a state may not prescribe the daily recitation by children under the teacher's supervision of an officially composed prayer in a public school classroom as part of the school's regular program. All of these elements become significant. Not only was the state sanctioning a particular prayer but was using the public school system's machinery to make it an official prayer, and by requiring it as a part of the regular school program conducted by the teacher—the symbol of classroom authority—it was encouraging children to participate. Indeed, in view of all the circumstances, and with due recognition of the psychology of the classroom, objecting children, though free not to participate, were subject to a subtle pressure to conform.

The *Engel* decision reaches only the official prescription of an officially approved prayer for daily recitation in a public school classroom. Of course, it does not outlaw prayer in the public schools. Pupils and teachers are free to engage in silent prayer, and it is consistent with the decision to permit a period for silent prayer. Moreover, it is important to note that the case deals with an officially approved prayer which the teacher is *required* by order of the school board to conduct. The case does not deal with the situation where those in charge of the classroom have a discretionary authority to permit opportunity for children voluntarily to express their individual prayers. Nor does the case deal with the question whether ministers may offer prayers in connection with public school programs. In neither of these situations are public officers or employees charged with a duty of conducting in a public school a religious program centered on a state-approved prayer. It was the degree of the state's involvement in this particular prayer, infusing it with the force and compulsive character of state-sanctioned action, which peculiarly identifies the problem of the *Engel* case and also suggests the limits on the holding.

Even less does the holding in *Engel* suggest that the public schools must display a studied indifference to religion or exclude from their programs a consideration and appreciation of religion in the nation's life or deny opportunity for children, individually or collectively, to engage in exercises that reflect belief in God or acknowledge the nation's dependence upon Him. The following passage taken from a footnote to the majority opinion is of special interest in this connection:

"There is of course nothing in the decision reached here that is inconsistent with the fact that school children and others are officially encouraged to express love for our country by reciting historical documents such as the Declaration of Independence which contain references to the Deity or by singing officially espoused anthems which include the composer's professions of faith in a Supreme Being, or with the fact that there are many manifestations in our public life of belief in God."[23]

This important statement is a concession by the Court which in a very significant way limits the holding and rationale of the case. Even though the Court goes on to say that "such patriotic or ceremonial occasions bear no true resemblance to the unquestioned religious exercise that the State of New York has sponsored in this instance," the fact remains that whether children sing or recite a prayer and whether the prayer is identified with expressions of patriotic sentiment or not, the school program is being used to encourage an expression of religious faith in accordance with the dominant national and community *ethos*. The distinction is made by the Court that such patriotic exercises are not distinctively religious in character. How solid a basis this is for distinction is questionable. The non-sectarian prayer in its invocation of God's blessing upon "our country" also fosters love of country. Moreover, since the prayer followed the pledge of allegiance to the flag, it could be viewed as part of a total program in which patriotic and religious sentiments were commingled. The Court in the footnote passage referred to did not expressly mention the pledge of allegiance, which now contains the phrase "under God." But if the national anthem, including its third stanza which is distinctively a prayer, can appropriately be sung in the public schools, it should follow also that recitation of the pledge of allegiance is permitted.

Whether a distinction drawn in legal terms between school exercises which are primarily religious in character, even though they include an underlying patriotic sentiment and can be said to be directed to patriotic ends, and those which are primarily patriotic in character and yet are also infused with a religious sentiment and consciousness, is a substantial and tenable one is open to question. At most it is a distinction of degree, and under such a test some form of prayer would be permissible. It seems to the writer that the element which adds substance to the distinction drawn by the Court is that the religious beliefs and sentiments expressed in national historical documents and utterances and in the National Anthem have been an established part of the national tradition as compared with a prayer specially composed by state authorities for official use and lacking the sanction established by common and nationwide historical usage. This at once raises the question whether the fact that the non-sectarian prayer was an officially *composed* as well as an officially approved prayer was an important element in the decision. The language in the body of the opinion as well as the distinction made in the footnote discussed above suggest that this was a critical factor. But should it be? On the surface it should be immaterial whether public school authorities themselves compose a prayer prescribed for recitation in public schools or adopt for official use a prayer composed by some other person or persons or regularly used by one or more religious bodies. In either case the government is putting its stamp of approval upon a particular prayer. But if, as suggested above, a distinction can be made between the historic expressions of religious faith that have evolved out of the national life and have become a part of the common national heritage and those not similarly sanctioned by history, the fact that a prayer actually originates with public officials does assume special significance. This question assumes a critical importance in cases which are presently before the Court and which raise the issue whether recitation of the Lord's

Prayer in the public schools comes under the ban of the *Engel* decision.[24] Here is a prayer sanctioned by historical usage and one, reflecting the common religious heritage of a majority of Americans. It cannot be attributed to the government. On its face the Lord's Prayer is non-sectarian but it is subject to special attack on the ground that it is distinctively the prayer of Christians and that hence the state in presenting or authorizing its use is preferring one religion over another. In this situation it appears likely that the Court, faced with the choice of either approving the recitation of the Lord's Prayer on the ground that it is not officially composed but has its own special sanction in history or holding it invalid as sectarian and preferential in character, will follow the latter course. If this proves to be the case, the element of official composition loses its significance, and officially recognized prayers and acknowledgments of Deity may be prescribed for daily ritualistic use in public schools only if incorporated in an exercise of recitation or song which in its totality is characterized as patriotic in character.

The cases[25] before the Court this term also involve state laws which require or authorize the reading without comment of a chapter of the Bible or a certain number of biblical verses at the beginning of the school day. Here the considerations are somewhat different. Students are not asked to recite something as an expression of their own religious belief. The religious and moral ideas of the Bible carry their own spiritual authority, unlike religious ideas stamped as authoritative because they are composed and approved by public officials. In relation to religion, morality and culture, the Bible as a book assumes a prominent place in the world's literature. No one can seriously argue that exposure to or study of the Bible is out of place in the public schools. But the Bible can also be characterized as a sectarian book. For Christians, the Bible is the book of historic revelation on which their faith is founded. The Jewish religious community looks to the Old Testament for its sacred scripture. Any use of the New Testament in the public schools to promote the Christian faith is offensive to persons of the Jewish faith. And in turn Catholics object to the use of biblical translations which they regard as distinctively Protestant in character. Objections may be made by other persons of varying beliefs to any use of the Bible which carries the connotation that it is officially regarded and accepted as revelation of divine truth. Despite these considerations, it should be permissible to read and study the Bible in the public schools both because of its historical and literary features and because it is a source of religious and moral ideas that have influenced our culture and civilization. But to use it in the public schools as a means of religious indoctrination or for the cultivation of religious faith is objectionable. The difficulty with a prescribed daily reading of the Bible without comment is that, rather than a meaningful program of study, it becomes more like a religiously ritualistic exercise, premised on the assumption that the Bible's teachings are inspired and authoritative, and subject to the charge that the state is thereby giving a preference to the religious groups that regard the Bible as their sacred scripture. But to state these considerations is to recognize that Bible reading in the public schools does raise considerations not present in the prayer case. State courts have disagreed on whether Bible reading is a forbidden form of sectarian instruction.[26] In the light of the long history of this practice, its widespread prevalence at present, its sanctioning by a number of state courts, and doubts that the Court may entertain as to whether Bible reading is as distinctively a religious exercise as the recitation of a prayer and whether such reading serves a valid educational purpose, the way is open to the Supreme Court, if it so chooses, to hold that *Engel* does not require the invalidation of Bible-reading practices.

With respect to other aspects of the general problem respecting religion and the public schools, the *Engel* decision makes no directly relevant contribution. The majority opinion does not cite the released-time cases, and the case has no immediate bearing upon the continued validity of the distinction drawn by the Court between released time on the school premises[27] and released time off the school premises.[28] While the *Engel* opinion is premised on the ground that the school program cannot be used to promote religious exercises and religious indoctrination, thereby suggesting that all forms of released time are invalid, a distinction can clearly be observed between the state's promotion of religious faith by means of an officially adopted prayer prescribed for daily recitation under the supervision of a publicly paid teacher, and the state's willingness to excuse children for one hour of the week from the public school's regular program in order to permit opportunity for religious instruction at the hands of teachers furnished by the churches. What the state can do to sanction a state-sponsored religious exercise as part of a public school's daily program and what it can do to accommodate its public school program to a felt need for religious instruction furnished by the churches, thereby acting to implement religious freedom, are two different questions. In both situations it may be claimed that the state is establishing religion, but in the released-time situation there is a stronger basis for asserting that the establishment limitation should yield to the competing free exercise principle. Even Mr. Justice Douglas, in his far-reaching and, for the most part, gratuitous opinion, in which he stressed that public funds or property cannot be used to finance religious exercises conducted by public officials, gave no indication that he now regards the *Zorach* decision as an incorrect one.

Finally, in appraising the reach of *Engel,* it is clear that it has little if any relevancy in respect to prayers or acknowledgment of Deity in phases of public life apart from the public school situation. Thanksgiving proclamations and declaration of a day of prayer by the President, prayers by ministers on public occasions, the use of chaplains to open sessions of Congress, the inscription of "In God We Trust" on our coins—all involving a recognition of the place of prayer and of the religious consciousness in our national life—are distinguishable. In none of these cases is government prescribing an official form of prayer or an official expression of religious belief for the public's own use. Moreover, the situation is totally unlike that of the problem presented in the classroom, where immature and impressionable children are susceptible to a pressure to conform and to participate in the expression of religious beliefs that carry the sanction and compulsion of the state's authority.

The conclusion that *Engel* does not admit of the wide interpretation given to it, particularly in the immediate response to the decision, is supported by the unusual extra-judicial statement by Mr. Justice Clark who, in the course of a public address and with reference to the criticism directed at the school prayer decision, said that it was a misinterpretation of the decision to say that it barred all religious observances in the public schools or other public places. Nor, according to him, did the Court hold that "there could be no official recognition of a Divine Being...or public acknowledgment that we are a religious nation." All the Court did, Mr. Justice Clark continued, was to rule unconstitutional "a state-written prayer circulated to state-employed teachers with instructions to have their pupils recite it in unison at the beginning of each school day."

CONSTITUTIONAL THEORY

The attempt has been made up to this point to examine the reach of the *Engel* decision. We turn now to an analysis of the *Engel* holding and opinion in terms of basic constitutional theory respecting the first and fourteenth amendments on which the Court relied.

The establishment clause of the first amendment

The Court found that the state action involved in the *Engel* situation violated the first amendment as made applicable to the states by the fourteenth amendment. More particularly, the prayer practice prescribed under authority of New York law violated the provision of the first amendment prohibiting laws respecting an establishment of religion. It is important to note that the Court expressly stated that it was not resting its case on the free exercise clause of the first amendment, although it did observe that it was plain that objecting children were placed under implied pressure to conform by participating in the prayer. The Court interpreted the establishment clause as stating an independent limitation which may overlap the free exercise clause in part but which also reaches wider objectives. The officially prescribed New York prayer was held invalid because it established the religious beliefs expressed in the prayer and thereby became a law respecting an establishment of religion.

In commenting on these propositions, it should be pointed out, first of all, that the majority opinion did not cite a single case in support of the conclusions reached by it. Indeed, the decision is unique in its failure to cite, much less discuss, earlier opinions dealing with the interpretation of the establishment limitation. This is all the more remarkable since the Court in the celebrated *Everson* opinion[29] had laid down broad statements on the meaning of this limitation, and in its *McCollum* decision[30] had invalidated a program of released time on public school premises on the ground that this constituted a use of the publicly owned and operated school system to enlist students for religious instruction in violation of the ideas first advanced in *Everson*. In the well-known dicta of his *Everson* opinion, Mr. Justice Black had stated that the effect of the first amendment's twin phrasing was to establish a principle of separation of church and state, and he had referred to Jefferson's letter in which he characterized the Constitution as establishing a wall of separation between church and state. He had further stated that the effect of the first amendment's establishment clause was not only to forbid an established church or to forbid giving a preference to one or more religions, but that it went farther and forbade aid to all religions, whether preferential or not, and that tax monies could not be spent to support any religious activities or institutions. Thus, the *Everson* opinion had read into the first amendments a theory of strict separation of church and state going far beyond the notion of an established church in the historic sense of the word.

The simplest explanation of the Court's failure to cite any precedent is that the earlier cases, dealing with use of public funds to provide for the transportation of children to parochial schools, with programs of released time for religious instruction furnished by the churches—whether on or off the school premises—and with Sunday closing laws, were not directly in point. The closest analogy was furnished by the *McCollum* decision, where the Court had invalidated a program of released time for religious instruction conducted on the school's premises by teachers who were furnished by the churches. This case supported the broad proposition that no part of the public school program could be used in the furtherance of religious instruction or exercises on the school premises. But *McCollum* involved a close working relation between the schools and the churches and a substantial use of public school property for religious instruction. Neither factor was present in *Engel*. Apart, however, from reliance on the precedent furnished by the *McCollum* decision, Mr. Justice Black could have found much in the language he used in his prior opinions for the Court in *Everson* and *McCollum* to support the ideas relied upon in *Engel*. He had stated in *Everson* that government cannot pass laws "which aid one religion, aid all religions, or prefer one religion over another."[31] In the *McCollum* opinion he had cited this language with approval. The prescribed non-sectarian prayer could easily be characterized either as an aid to all religions or as a preference for the particular religious beliefs embodied in this prayer. Why Mr. Justice Black chose to disregard his opinions in *Everson* and *McCollum* is a matter for speculation. In view of the statement by Mr. Justice Douglas in his concurring opinion, that he now regards the actual decision in *Everson* as incorrect,[32] it may be that Mr. Justice Black's failure to cite *Everson* assumes substantial significance. His failure to cite *McCollum* is perhaps more readily explained, since any reference to *McCollum* would have been incomplete without citing *Zorach* as well. Not only did *Zorach* limit *McCollum* by holding that a program of released time for religious instruction was valid if conducted off the school premises, but Mr. Justice Douglas' opinion had indicated a substantial retreat in the interpretation of the establishment clause from that enunciated in the *Everson* opinion. He had stated there that the first amendment did not establish an over-all principle of separation of church and state, that the state could take account of the religious interests of its people and that it could accommodate its public school program to these interests. The *Zorach* opinion thus undermined the absolutism expressed in *Everson* and *McCollum* and appeared to recognize that the establishment limitation must at times be balanced against the free exercise principle and that the legislature may in appropriate instances, in the interest of neutrality, choose to advance the free exercise of religion at some expense to the establishment prohibition. It is for these reasons that *Zorach* was generally regarded as substantially limiting, if not undermining, much of what was said in *Everson* and *McCollum*—a view that seemed to be shared by the four Justices, including Mr. Justice Black, who dissented so vigorously in *Zorach*. It is understandable, therefore, that Mr. Justice Black in writing the opinion in *Engel* wished to avoid any discussion of precedents that might involve his approval of *Zorach* and the views stated there. Finally, it is open to speculation also that differences within the Court in interpreting and reconciling the prior cases and the supporting opinions made it prudent for Mr. Justice Black, in writing an opinion that would command the support of at least four other Justices, to avoid all discussion of prior cases. But Mr. Justice Black's opinion, although it does not rely on prior cases, does appear to restore the broad and absolutist interpretation of the establishment clause first stated in the *Everson* opinion.[33]

Whether the *Everson* opinion, postulating a broad no-aid-to-religion idea, correctly stated the meaning of this clause is open to serious question.[34] As Mr. Justice Douglas frankly recognized in his concurring opinion in *Engel*, the prescription of a school prayer for voluntary participation by students is not an establishment of religion within the historic meaning of this language. In *Everson*, Mr. Justice Black relied in large part on the views of James Madison and Thomas Jefferson in giving the establishment language its broad construction. Madison and Jefferson viewed this language as furnishing protection for freedom of conscience and protection against ecclesiastical domination of political affairs by imposing a barrier to any kind of governmental sanction or support of religious activities. In their view the establishment language served as a counterweight to the free exercise clause. But there is no evidence that the committee that approved the text of the first amendment and the Congress that submitted the amendment and the state legislatures that approved it supposed that the establishment language carried the wide connotations attributed to it by Madison. There is, however, some evidence to support the conclusion that those responsible for the final wording used in the first amendment —and this included persons besides Madison—did have in mind something more than an officially established church and something more than giving

a preference to one or more religions. Fragmentary evidence supports the idea that this language was intended to keep Congress "from establishing articles of faith or a mode of worship."[35] It does not appear to be a distortion of words to say that prescription of an official prayer for recitation in public schools is the establishment of an official mode of worship and is, therefore, forbidden. But, as a practical matter, even this interpretation in its application to prayer in schools is open to question when consideration is given to the practical construction afforded by the whole course of American history. Here the opinion of the New York trial court is particularly illuminating in showing that public recognition of prayer and of Deity reflected the "sense of the nation" at the time of the adoption of the first and fourteenth amendments and should be taken into account in the process of constitutional interpretation. It is indeed remarkable that Mr. Justice Black in his opinion in *Engel* completely disregarded the long history with respect to prayers in public life and in schools.

Mr. Justice Black did refer to history—the control of the Book of Common Prayer by Parliament and the evils resulting from it and the concern that eventually developed in this country that there should be no union of church and state, since such a union tended to degrade religion and to subject the state to risk of ecclesiastical domination. But, as Mr. Justice Stewart pointed out in his dissenting opinion, it is a far cry from control of prayer in an officially established church to a public school program that gives opportunity for voluntary participation in common prayer. Insofar as the Court relied on history in *Engel*, it followed a highly selective process in determining what history was relevant. The Court's selection of history in determining what it will read into the establishment clause is in itself a highly subjective process. But in this respect *Engel* again demonstrates that the Constitution is what the judges say it is.

It seems clear that, if the no-aid-to-religion principle is a valid interpretation of the establishment language, the Court reached a correct result in the *Engel* case. In *Everson*[36] the Court upheld the expenditure of public funds to reimburse parents for the cost of transporting children to parochial schools. The Court recognized that this resulted in aid to parochial school education but said that this result was incidental to the valid secular purpose of promoting the safe transportation of children to school. In the Sunday closing law cases[37] the Court held that the validity of Sunday laws as proper exercises of the police power to promote the general welfare was not impaired by the fact that they had the incidental effect of favoring the Christian day of worship. Thus, the Court, in the cases where it has purported to follow an absolutist interpretation of the establishment language, has, nevertheless, permitted aid to religion as an incident to a lawful secular purpose. But in the *Engel* case the prayer practice was seen to be directed to wholly religious ends and the aid to religion was primary and not incidental. The opposing argument that the prayer exercise was intended to serve a patriotic purpose by creating an awareness and appreciation of prayer as part of the American heritage proved too much and if accepted would have undermined the whole no-aid idea. Nevertheless, the Court itself came perilously close to this idea and created difficulties for itself when it recognized that school children may properly be encouraged to recite patriotic passages containing references to Deity and to sing the National Anthem which in its third verse incorporates a prayer that expresses some of the same sentiments found in the New York Regents' prayer. As pointed out earlier, this is justified on the ground that such activities are not distinctively religious exercises. To put the matter in another way, schools may engage in religious exercises if they are incident to patriotic purposes. All of this suggests that the no-aid principle is not so absolute as it sounds and is not a very viable principle for solving problems with respect to the interrelationship of government and religion. Moreover, the whole course of American governmental practices, not only in giving recognition to the nation's religious heritage and consciousness but also in sanctioning various forms of direct and indirect assistance for religious activities, is a repudiation of the extreme Madisonian view and lends no support to the kind of absolutism that appears on the surface in the *Engel* opinion.[38]

Reference may be made at this point to alternative theories on the construction of the free exercise and establishment clauses of the first amendment. Mr. Justice Douglas in speaking for the majority in *Zorach*[39] stated that government must be neutral between sects, and in his concurring opinion in *Engel*[40] stated that government must be neutral in the field of religion. Professor Katz has advanced the idea that the primary thrust of the first amendment's religious clauses is to protect religious liberty, that this objective is best attained when government remains neutral in respect to religious matters, but that government must abandon neutrality in some situations where adherence to the establishment limitation would result in an interference with the free exercise of religion.[41] Professor Kurland proposes the thesis

that the first amendment requires the government to be neutral in the sense that it can do nothing to hinder or promote religion as such, that a religion or religious activities cannot be the basis for classification.[42] The difference between the Douglas and Katz view, on the one hand, and the Kurland view, on the other, is that the former is addressed to the problem of neutrality within the framework of a first amendment view that recognizes the free exercise and establishment principles as independent, sometimes overlapping, and sometimes competing principles, whereas the Kurland thesis accepts these principles as mutually exclusive of each other. It is fair to say that the Supreme Court's opinions on the whole reflect the view that the two religion clauses of the first amendment state independent limitations, and that the problem of neutrality may be approached on this basis.

It is clear that government must be neutral as between competing religious claims. It may not prefer one religion over another. But to say that government must be neutral as between religion and non-religion raises more questions. If this means that government can do nothing which in fact aids religion, this may in some situations mean that government must discriminate against religion and thereby violate the free exercise clause. The Constitution does not require this. On the contrary, any meaningful concept of neutrality must permit government some discretion in striking a balance between the establishment and the free exercise principles since they may conflict. If neutrality means that government must be indifferent to religion, and must base its policies, actions and programs on the theory that religion is irrelevant to life, it means that government is committed to a philosophy of secularism, and then the question must be raised whether secularism as an officially established orthodoxy is any more consistent with the first amendment than a religious orthodoxy. But such a concept of neutrality is inconsistent with the unbroken tradition of American life in giving expression to the religious habits and consciousness of the American people, a tradition supporting the Court's assertion in *Zorach* that "we are a religious people whose institutions presuppose a Supreme Being."[43] Indeed, if the public schools disregard the religious factors in the educational process, they are not neutral. Neutrality is a two-edged sword and its application in a given situation invites study of a variety of considerations.

The decision in *Engel* may be measured by the standard of neutrality. Clearly the state's action in sanctioning a particular prayer was an expression of governmental preference for the religious beliefs embodied in that prayer, and to this extent it discriminated against persons who did not accept these principles or who preferred to pray in another way. The state, then, was not being neutral in the narrower sense of the term. But did the Court in denying the state the power to prescribe an official prayer for recitation in public schools thereby compel the state to discriminate on the basis of religion or to interfere with religious freedom? Although the argument was made before the Court that the prayer exercise implemented the religious freedom of children who wanted to participate, the proposition that the right to recite prayers in public schools is *essential* to religious freedom is hardly convincing. The general right of prayer is not affected by the decision and, as previously noted, some form of prayer in the classroom is consistent with the *Engel* decision. Nor can it be said that a prohibition of officially sanctioned prayer in public school classrooms violates neutrality by forcing the state to use its schools to promote secularism as the officially established orthodoxy. Consistent with the decision the schools and government may still follow practices and educational programs that reflect a sympathetic awareness of religion and its relevancy to the life of the individual and the community. The state, then, was supporting a practice which sanctioned and gave a preferred position to the expression of religious ideas even though it was not constitutionally required to do so in the interests of either religious freedom or strict neutrality. This leaves the basic question of whether the Constitution does require a strict or absolute neutrality in regard to religious matters, or whether, in at least a limited way, government may in its institutional life and programs express a preference for the expression of religious ideas that are in accord with the national tradition and reflect the beliefs shared by a preponderant element of the community.

Numerous governmental practices at all levels make clear that government has never been absolutely neutral in religious matters. Moreover, the Court's opinion in *Engel* in sanctioning public school exercises which are viewed as primarily patriotic in character but also have religious significance seems to make clear that the public schools are not required in the interest of a strict neutrality to abandon exercises that invite student participation in expressions of religious faith. What seems to be really important is not that government be strictly or abstractly neutral but that government in its policies and programs does not trespass in any significant way upon the rights of minorities. To criticize *Engel* on the ground that it permits a minority to exercise a commanding influence in determining public school policies is itself a pointless argument since a major purpose of a constitutional system is to place a check on the will of the majority in the interest of protecting minority rights. There can be no quarrel with the Court's overruling the majority will in *Engel* if it may be assumed that minority rights were involved.

Personal rights and the standing question

This leads to a consideration of a major difficulty raised by *Engel*. The Court did not rest its decision on the ground that the prayer practice subjected objecting children to an implied pressure to participate and thereby offended freedom of religion or a personal freedom of conscience. Instead, the Court made it clear that it was resting its case on the establishment clause, and that this clause, while designed in part to protect individual freedom, was also designed to prevent a union of government and religion. But insofar as the establishment clause is invocable by individuals, must it not be shown that a practice alleged to constitute an establishment of religion infringes on constitutionally recognized freedoms or interests? At this point it is useful to inquire whether the prohibition of laws respecting an establishment of religion can be translated into a protection of some kind of fundamental freedom. For Madison and Jefferson it assumed significance as a protection for freedom of belief and conscience which transcends the more limited concept of freedom of religion. This view finds support in the following statement taken from Mr. Justice Roberts' opinion for the Court in *Cantwell v. Connecticut:*

"The constitutional inhibition of legislation on the subject of religion has a double aspect. On the one hand, it forestalls compulsion by law of the acceptance of any creed or the practice of any form of worship. Freedom of conscience and freedom to adhere to such religious organization or form of worship as the individual may choose cannot be restricted by law. On the other hand, it safeguards the free exercise of the chosen form of religion. Thus the Amendment embraces two concepts—freedom to believe and freedom to act."[44]

Mr. Justice Roberts went to the heart of the matter when he interpreted the establishment clause to protect freedom of belief by forestalling *compulsion by law* of the acceptance of any creed or the practice of any form of worship. This freedom is violated when a person is forced to profess a belief whether or not contrary to conviction, is denied a right or privilege because of refusal to profess an officially sanctioned belief, or is forced to pay taxes in support of a church or religious practices. Unless the New York prayer practice, though voluntary in form, had the effect of indirectly coercing objectors who did not care to participate, it is difficult to see what rights were violated. It can hardly be claimed that taxpayers were subjected to any additional burden because of the use of school facilities or personnel in connection with the prayer exercise.

Moreover, apart from the question of whether an individual in order to claim the protection of the establishment clause must show that his freedom of conscience is violated, the requirement of proper standing as a party in interest to raise constitutional questions must still be considered. What standing did the petitioners have in this case? They brought this suit as parents and the theory of the trial court, relying on the *Zorach* decision, was that the petitioners were asserting their rights to control the education of their children and the right to be free from a religious practice in the public schools which was contrary to their own beliefs or unbeliefs and those of their children.[45] The Supreme Court did not even discuss the question of standing. It seems proper to infer then that the standing requisite to maintain the suit in the state court carried forward as a basis for standing before the Supreme Court. Since the Supreme Court has not disavowed the party in interest requirement, since it accepted a standing premised originally on a claim of violation of the petitioners' rights, and since it stated that it had agreed to review the case because it involved "rights protected by the First and Fourteenth Amendments,"[46] it appears to be implicit in the decision that some substantial legal interests of the petitioners were at stake in the case. Admittedly, however, the Court's express statement that it was not basing its holding on the ground that the prayer exercise was a violation of religious freedom and its failure to discuss the standing question emerge as puzzling aspects of the decision.

Whatever questions are raised respecting the rights and the standing of the petitioners under the first amendment become even more acute when the restrictions of this amendment are translated into fourteenth amendment limitations. There is a danger of forgetting that the first amendment was not directly involved in the *Engel* case, since by its terms it is a limitation only on Congress. It becomes involved only on the theory that the fourteenth amendment operates in some way to make the first amendment applicable as a limitation on the states. On this question Mr. Justice Black's opinion is extraordinarily interest-

ing. All that he found it necessary to say is that the first amendment's provisions "are operative against the States by virtue of the Fourteenth Amendment."[47] What language of the fourteenth amendment has this effect? On this point, Mr. Justice Black's opinion is eloquently and discreetly silent. But the fourteenth amendment is not an abstraction or some mysterious event in history achieving constitutional change without resort to words. Is it not pertinent to ask what language of the fourteenth amendment has the effect of making the first amendment applicable?

Any thorough exploration of the questions with respect to the interrelationship of the first and fourteenth amendments would unduly extend the scope of this article. But some basic theories of interpretation should be stated. Three lines of thought may be identified:

(1) The main line of interpretation of the fourteenth amendment, as a basis for protecting substantive and procedural rights against state impairment, has turned on the clause of its first section which states, "nor shall any State deprive any person of life, liberty or property, without due process of law." The classic theory expressed in the judicial gloss on this language is that the "liberty" clause serves to protect those freedoms which are ranked as fundamental and that there is no necessary relationship between these and the Bill of Rights. In the application of this theory the *freedoms* of the first amendment came to be recognized as fundamental. Thus, in the *Cantwell* decision Mr. Justice Roberts stated that "the fundamental concept of liberty embodied in [the fourteenth amendment] embraces the liberties guaranteed by the First Amendment."[48] Whether the language used is that first amendment freedoms are ranked as fundamental or that they are absorbed or selectively incorporated into the due process clause, the result is the same, namely, the first amendment freedoms are a part of the liberty protected under the due process clause.

(2) A variant of the fundamental rights theory is that when liberties specified in the Bill of Rights are recognized as fundamental they have the same dimensions and quality, when incorporated into the due process clause, as they have in their original setting in the Bill of Rights and are subject only to the limitations there recognized. This may be characterized for purpose of convenience as the Brennan theory, since Mr. Justice Brennan has most clearly articulated this idea in recent cases.[49] This theory of interpretation becomes a means of enlarging the fundamental freedoms as limitations on state action since it by-passes the usual due process consideration that the fundamental liberties may be restricted so long as the

state is acting reasonably to achieve legitimate governmental purposes. But this theory is still centered on the protection of fundamental freedoms.

(3) A third view, the one advanced by Mr. Justice Black and supported by Mr. Justice Douglas, which may be referred to as the Black theory, is that the effect of the fourteenth amendment was to make the entire Bill of Rights apply to the states. Mr. Justice Black persists in this theory which he bases on an interpretation of historical intent despite its being discredited by legal historians. The significance of this view is that its subjects the states to the Bill of Rights, without reference to the fundamental freedoms concept and without regard to usual due process considerations.

The relevancy of these three approaches to the first amendment question is apparent. Under all three views, the first amendment is recognized to have a special significance with respect to the states. But the "fundamental rights" interpretation and the Brennan theory place emphasis upon the freedoms of the first amendment, as part of the liberty protected under the due process clause, whereas under the Black view all of the first amendment is applicable to the states and hence it is not necessary to inquire whether a question of fundamental freedoms is involved. The practical effect of his theory is that by judicial act the first amendment is amended to read, "Neither Congress *nor the States* shall make any law respecting an establishment of religion...." Thus, he could rest his opinion in *Engel* on the establishment clause without finding that the petitioners' freedoms were violated. Moreover, since the first amendment's language is absolute, there is no place in Mr. Justice Black's thinking for an inquiry into whether the state had acted in an arbitrary or unreasonable way in impinging upon the petitioners' interests.

The interpretation of the first amendment's establishment clause as a limitation on the states without regard to the usual due process considerations was already foreshadowed in the *Everson* and *McCollum* decisions. But *Everson* turned on the right of a taxpayer not to have out-of-pocket expenditures of tax funds made in support of religious activities, and *McCollum* could be interpreted to turn on the right of a person who was both taxpayer and parent not to have school property used, in a substantial way for religious instruction and not to have her child's freedom impaired by a public school attendance requirement imposed only on those who did not attend the religious education classes. The *Engel* opinion, however, is unique in that it finds a state practice invalid as an establishment of religion without regard to whether it offended any rights or interests of the petitioners.

It is not surprising that Mr. Justice Black in his *Engel* opinion saw the problem as wholly a first amendment establishment question, unrelated to the due process clause and the deprivation of liberty, since he has committed himself to this view. What is surprising is that some other members of the Court who supported the majority opinion appeared *sub silentio* to endorse a view of the first and fourteenth amendment interrelationship which rests on a spurious interpretation of history, disregards the main line of fourteenth amendment interpretation, and marks a bold high in the long history of judicial free-wheeling in the construction of this amendment.

Whatever significance may attach to the surface of the opinion in *Engel,* some aspects of the case do suggest that the decision finds its ultimate justification on the ground that the prayer practice carried a compulsive force notwithstanding its apparent voluntary character, and that it therefore resulted in violation of freedom of conscience. Why should the Court otherwise have emphasized all the elements of the exercise that give it such an official nature? Indeed, Mr. Justice Black stated that the "indirect coercive pressure upon religious minorities to conform to the prevailing officially approved religion is plain."[50]

Regardless of its underlying theory, the *Engel* decision does suggest substantial problems with respect to protection of minority rights. How far may the dominant sentiment of the community be given expression in the public schools, or for that matter in public life generally, where the expression of this sentiment is offensive to minority groups? The answers to these questions, inherent in our pluralistic society, are not easy. Must all practices offensive to minority groups be barred, or is it enough that they be free not to participate? We may put alongside the problem of *Engel* the question presented in *West Virginia State Bd. of Educ. v. Barnette,*[51] when the Court held that a Jehovah's Witness could not be denied the privilege of attending a public school because of his refusal to stand up and salute the flag at a school exercise held at the beginning of the day. For the Jehovah's Witnesses a salute to the flag is an obeisance which is idolatrous and, therefore, offensive to their religious beliefs. Mr. Justice Jackson, delivering the opinion of the Court, did not rest the case on the ground of religious freedom but significantly on the broader ground of freedom of thought. In the well-known passage from his opinion, he said:

"If there is any fixed star in our constitutional constellation, it is that no official, high or petty, can prescribe what shall be orthodox in politics, nationalism, religion, or other matters of opinion or force citizens to confess by word or act their faith therein."[52]

But there was no indication that the school board was under a duty to eliminate the flag-salute exercise in order to protect the Jehovah's Witnesses against the embarrassment and pressures arising from their non-participation. It was enough that the Jehovah's Witness could not be compelled to take part. What distinguishes this case from *Engel* where the Court finds that the prayer exercise must be discontinued? Superficially, the distinction suggests itself that in the flag-salute case the state is promoting a proper secular purpose—cultivation of patriotic sentiments. Even if this distinction is tenable, it does indicate that the extent to which public schools may engage in practices that are offensive to conscience is a question of degree. But actually the distinction is not as convincing as it seems. Mr. Justice Jackson's opinion in *Barnette* rested on the ground that the state may not prescribe any orthodoxy or force citizens to confess their faith therein. In other words, quite apart from the specific prohibition on the establishment of religion, the state may not officially establish any faith—political or religious. At this point it should also be noted that Mr. Justice Black said in *Torcaso v. Watkins*[53] that religious freedom under the Constitution extends to such non-theistic religions as Ethical Culture and Secular Humanism. Putting *Barnette* and *Torcaso* together, it may be said, then, that the Constitution forbids the establishment of either theistic or non-theistic orthodoxies. If this is so, then it may be questioned whether in the interest of protecting the non-conformist a distinction should be observed between the state's promoting a non-theistic political orthodoxy which offends a minority religious group and its action in promoting a theistic orthodoxy which offends a minority of believers and non-believers. If the protection afforded in the name of religious freedom against a state-prescribed non-theistic orthodoxy is that a person cannot be compelled to participate, whereas the protection afforded in the name of the establishment clause is that a person may demand that any exercise promoting theistic belief be completely eliminated, the result is that the freedom protected by the establishment clause is regarded as having a higher value than the freedom protected by the free exercise clause. Perhaps the simplest explanation of this situation is that the Jehovah's Witnesses have not demanded that the flag salute exercise be completely eliminated in order to avoid an implied coercion on their children to participate, but to point up this problem is to indicate that the degree of protec-

tion accorded non-conformists who object to public practices they find offensive is a matter requiring further careful probing.

To state the problem in this way is to recognize that the first amendment's explicit clause respecting an establishment of religion, as well as its implied prohibition of the establishment of any kind of orthodoxy, as recognized in *Barnette,* cannot be given an absolute construction but must be balanced against a variety of competing factors, including considerations of community interest that are legitimated by American life and experience. In construing the freedoms expressly safeguarded by the first amendment—freedom of religion, freedom of speech and freedom of press—the Court has recognized that these freedoms, whether as first amendment freedoms, or as absorbed into the liberty protected by the fourteenth amendment, are not absolute, but may be restricted by legislation directed to the protection of appropriate public interests as defined by the legislature. Why the establishment limitation and the liberties implicit in it should be elevated to a higher place than these freedoms has not been made clear. James Madison's "three pence" argument, if valid to support an absolutist interpretation of the establishment principle, should be equally valid to support the absolutist interpretation which the Court has rejected in its interpretation of the first amendment freedoms generally.

Is it the effect of the *Engel* decision to bar the recitation of prayers by public school children in the situation where no parents voice an objection? Conceivably there are communities in the United States where all parents are ready and willing to have their children participate in such a practice. If the *Engel* case rests on an abstract and absolute non-establishment limitation, unrelated to infringement upon personal liberty, all school boards are in principle bound thereby, even though in the absence of objecting parents a serious standing problem would be presented as regards the bringing of a lawsuit to compel the school board to comply with the law as established by the *Engel* decision. If, as has been suggested, the *Engel* case finds its real justification in the consideration that the officially prescribed prayer subjected all children to a compulsion to participate and thereby impaired the liberty of children and their parents, then *Engel* has no relevancy where all parents are willing to have their children participate. In a country as large as the United States, with great variations in the communities so far as religious elements are concerned, there is no compelling reason why the Constitution should be interpreted to require a uniform rule prohibiting all prayer exercises, without regard to the elements of coercion, impairment of rights of objectors and the effect of the exercises in promoting community divisiveness.

CONCLUSIONS

Viewed with respect to the precise problem before the Court, the decision in *Engel* is not a disturbing one, when evaluated in terms of underlying policy considerations. Prayer, religious faith, and the freedom of religion are not damaged by the Court's holding. On the contrary, the decision maintains the dignity and religious significance of prayer by keeping it free from state compulsion and interference, and, by the same token, it preserves the freedom of both the believer and the non-believer in respect to prayer. Nor should it be of consequence that the prayer was "non-sectarian." Even such a prayer can be productive of religious divisiveness, not only because it is objectionable to non-believers or non-theistic religionists, but also because theistic believers may find it an offense to conscience to engage in prayer except in accordance with the tenets of their own religion. Moreover, religionists can have little enthusiasm for an officially sanctioned non-sectarian expression of religious belief which at most reflects a vague and generalized religiosity. Any usefulness of a prayer practice in public schools as symbolic of the religious tradition in our national life, of the values of religion to our society, and of religious ideas shared in common, must be weighed against the peril that the official promotion of common-denominator religious practices, conspicuous by their vagueness and syncretistic character, will contribute to the furtherance and establishment of an official folk or culture religion which many competent observers regard as a serious threat to the vitality and distinctive witness of the historic faiths.

The decision makes sense in terms of constitutional considerations if the case is confined to the fact emphasized by the Court and if the constitutional rights of objecting parents and children are viewed as vital to the result. It is, however, the Court's broad and absolutist interpretation of the first amendment, its disregard of the sanctions furnished by history for religious practices in the public schools, its indifference to the problem of standing, its failure to relate the establishment limitation to meaningful considerations of personal liberty—a failure all the more conspicuous when the relevancy of the fourteenth amendment is taken into account—and its failure to come to grips with the delicate problem of the rights of nonconformists in a community that recognizes a common religious heritage that present the constitutional problems and difficulties. A decision resting on the narrower ground of freedom of religion or of conscience, explaining why the considerations advanced in support of the prayer practice were outweighed by the rights of the objectors, and why under the circumstances the feature of voluntary participation did not sufficiently protect the interests of objectors, would have been much more satisfactory. The Court's reliance instead on a broad and abstract ground of establishment warrants Reinhold Niebuhr's criticism that the Court used a meat-axe when it should have used a scalpel.[54]

The issue raised in *Engel* is symptomatic of the problem we face in a religiously pluralistic society. Protestantism can no longer claim a dominating position in shaping the American *ethos*. It is understandable that practices such as prayers and Bible reading in public schools, which had their origin in days of Protestant domination, should come under fresh scrutiny as the Court exercises its role of accommodating constitutional interpretation to the changing social scene, although it would be refreshing to have the Court acknowledge its creative and policy-making function in this respect instead of making it appear that the result is required either on the basis of a literal textual exegesis or by reference to the intent of the Founding Fathers. The larger question, however, is whether and to what extent the government and its institutions may reflect a dominant religious consciousness of the community that has its roots in the nation's history and tradition. Due regard for our religious pluralism as well as for the larger pluralism that takes account of non-theistic ideologies and non-belief requires that government, in any recognition it gives to the dominant religious consciousness, carefully abstain from practices that in any significant way coerce conscience or otherwise impair minority rights. On the other hand, it is equally clear that the Constitution, in establishing a secular state that cannot prescribe any official belief or creed for its citizens, whether theistic or non-theistic and whether religious or political, does not require and, indeed, does not permit government to establish secularism or secular humanism as the nation's orthodoxy.

Religionists have ground for complaint if the public schools by studied indifference teach that belief in God is irrelevant to life. The *Engel* decision does not require such indifference. Consistent with it the schools may follow practices and teaching programs that help to create awareness, appreciation and understanding of the religious factor in the life of the nation and its citizens. They may create respect for the moral values which reflect the community consensus and which illuminate the purposes and processes of our democratic society. But it is not their responsibility or function to cultivate an official faith or ideology, whether religious or humanistic in character, or to indoctrinate students in any system of beliefs and values that rests on a claim of insight into ultimate truth with respect to the meaning and purpose of life. Parents who desire religious instruction for their children as part of a school program have the option of sending them to parochial schools. One effect of the school prayer decision is to highlight the importance of private schools and of the parents' freedom of choice in our free and pluralistic society that does not recognize governmental monopoly of the educational process. But the majority of Americans who are concerned with the relevancy of religious teaching to the total educational program do not see the parochial school as the answer to the problem. Their interest may lie in the further development of dismissed- or released-time programs in connection with the operation of the public school systems. Moreover, in view of the present impasse with respect to the parochial school situation, it may well be that the shared-time plan offers the greatest promise for reconciling the felt needs for religious instruction with the secular limitations placed on the public school systems. All proposals of this kind deserve careful study. Needless to say, any constructive solution to the problem will require a generous measure of sympathetic understanding, good will and tolerance on the part of all concerned elements of the community.

Whatever the merits of plans for accommodating the educational system to programs of formal religious instruction, they should not serve to obscure the fundamental consideration that the cultivation of religious faith is the responsibility of home and church. If secularism triumphs as the dominant American ideology, it will not be because of the Constitution or the Supreme Court or because the public schools have failed in their limited tasks, but because meaningful and vital religious faith has lost its place in the hearts and lives of the people. The *Engel* decision is a forceful reminder to parents and the churches that theirs is the task and responsibility of making prayer, worship and religious instruction rich and meaningful in the lives of their children.

Footnotes

[1]370 U.S. 421 (1962).
[2]The cases under review are Murray v. Curlett, 228 Md. 239, 179 A.2d 695 *cert. granted*, 371 U.S. 809 (1962), in which the Maryland Court of Appeals had sustained the constitutionality of the Maryland school commissioner's rule requiring the daily reading of a

chapter of the Bible and/or daily recital of the Lord's Prayer in public school and Schempp v. School Dist., 201 F Supp. 815 (E.D. Pa.), a decision of a three-judge court holding unconstitutional a Pennsylvania statute requiring ten verses of the Bible to be read daily in public schools and also the school district's practice of mass recitation of the Lord's Prayer. Argument on these cases was heard on February 28 and March 1, 1963.
[3]Engel v. Vitale, 18 Misc. 2d 659, 191 N.Y.S.2d 453 (Sup. Ct. 1959).
[4]Zorach v. Clauson, 343 U.S. 306 (1952).
[5]Engel v. Vitale, 18 Misc. 2d 659, 693-94, 191 N.Y.S.2d 453, 490-91 (Sup. Ct. 1959).
[6]*Id.* at 673, 191 N.Y.S.2d at 470.
[7]Engel v. Vitale, 11 App. Div. 2d 340, 206 N.Y.S.2d 183 (1960), *aff'd*, 10 N.Y.2d 174, 176 N.E.2d 579, 218 N.Y.S.2d 659 (1961).
[8]Everson v. Board of Educ., 330 U.S. 1 (1947).
[9]McCollum v. Board of Educ., 333 U.S. 203 (1948).
[10]Engle v. Vitale, 370 U.S. 421 (1962).
[11]*Id.* at 424.
[12]*Id.* at 425.
[13]*Id.* at 430.
[14]*Ibid.*
[15]*Id.* at 430-31.
[16]*Id.* at 435.
[17]*Id.* at 436.
[18]*Id.* at 442.
[19]*Id.* at 443.
[20]*Id.* at 446.
[21]343 U.S. at 313.
[22]Engel v. Vitale, 370 U.S. at 450.
[23]*Id.* at 435 n.21.
[24]Schempp v. School Dist., 201 F. Supp. 815 (E.D. Pa.), *prob. juris. noted*, 371 U.S. 307 (1962); Murray v. Curlett, 228 Md. 239, 179 A.2d 698, *cert. granted*, 371 U.S. 809 (1962).
[25]Cases cited in note 24 *supra*.
[26]The majority of state courts that have dealt with the problem have upheld Bible-reading practices....
[27]McCollum v. Board of Educ., 333 U.S. 203 (1948).
[28]Zorach v. Clauson, 343 U.S. 306 (1952).
[29]Everson v. Board of Educ., 330 U.S. 1 (1947).
[30]McCollum v. Board of Educ., 333 U.S. 203 (1948).
[31]330 U.S. at 15.
[32]370 U.S. at 443.
[33]Mr. Justice Douglas' views may have a vital impact on the course of the Court's future decisions in this area. Opinions expressed by him in dissent in the Sunday closing law cases [See, *e.g.*, McGowan v. Maryland, 366 U.S. 420, 563-64 (1961).], together with his emphasis in his separate opinion in *Engel* on the idea that no public funds or properties can be used to finance religious exercises and his express questioning of the result reached in *Everson*, raise the question whether Mr. Justice Douglas still adheres to the ideas he expressed in *Zorach*. On the other hand, his failure in his separate opinion in *Engel* to repudiate the result in *Zorach*, all the more conspicuous because of doubts he expressed as to the holding in *Everson*, may indicate that he continues to draw the line between use of public funds, property and personnel in aid of religious instruction and exercises and "accommodation" of the public school program to religious instruction given under church auspices off the school premises....
[34]For varying interpretations of the intended meaning of the establishment language, see PARSONS, THE

First Freedom (1948); 1 Stokes, Church and State in the United States 538-61 (1950); Katz, *Freedom of Religion and State Neutrality*, 20 U. Chi. L. Rev. 426 (1953); Pfeffer, *Church and State: Something Less Than Separation*, 19 U. Chi. L. Rev. (1951).

[35]1 Stokes, *op. cit. supra* note 34, at 546; Katz, *supra* note 34, at 434. See also Smylie, *The First Amendment and Bishop Pike*, The Christian Century, Oct. 31, 1962, pp. 1316-18.

[36]Everson v. Board of Educ., 330 U.S. 1 (1947).

[37]McGowan v. Maryland, 366 U.S. 420 (1961); Two Guys from Harrison-Allentown, Inc. v. McGinley, 366 U.S. 582 (1961); Braunfeld v. Brown, 366 U.S. 599 (1961); Gallagher v. Crown Kosher Super Mkt., 366 U.S. 617 (1961).

[38]See examples cited in Engel v. Vitale, 370 U.S. 421, 437 n.1 (1962) (Douglas, J., concurring). Fellman, The Limits of Freedom 40–41 (1959); Kauper, Civil Liberties and the Constitution 35–39 (1962)....

[39]343 U.S. at 314.

[40]370 U.S. at 443.

[41]Katz, *supra* note 34, at 428.

[42]Kurland, Religion and the Law 17-18, 111-12 (1962). The *Engel* decision is clearly in accord with Professor Kurland's thesis since, by prescribing a religious exercise, the state was acting on the basis of a classification that promoted religious activity as such. For his analysis and comments on *Engel*, see Kurland,

The Regents' Prayer Case: "Full of Sound and Fury, Signifying...", 1962 Supreme Court Rev. 1.

[43]343 U.S. at 313.

[44]310 U.S. 296, 303 (1940). See also Madison's statement, when the first amendment was pending in Congress in substantially its final form, that "he apprehended the meaning of the words to be, that Congress should not establish a religion, and enforce the legal observation of it by law, nor compel men to worship God in any manner contrary to their conscience." 1 Annals of Cong. 730 (1834) [1789-1791]. This statement is quoted by Mr. Justice Reed in his dissenting opinion in McCollum v. Board of Educ., 333 U.S. 203, 244 (1948).

[45]Engel v. Vitale, 18 Misc. 2d 659, 666-67, 191 N.Y.S.2d 453, 464-65 (Sup. Ct. 1959).

[46]370 U.S. at 424.

[47]370 U.S. at 430.

[48]310 U.S. at 303.

[49]See, *e.g.*, Ohio *ex rel.* Eaton v. Price, 364 U.S. 263, *rehearing denied*, 364 U.S. 855 (1960).

[50]370 U.S. at 431.

[51]319 U.S. 624 (1943).

[52]*Id.* at 642. It should be noted, however, that Justices Black, Douglas, and Murphy in their concurring opinions laid stress on the religious freedom argument.

[53]367 U.S. 488, 495 n.11 (1961).

[54]Niebuhr, *The Court and the Prayer: A Dissenting Opinion*, The New Leader, July 9, 1962, p. 3.

Selection 7

Public Prayers in Public Schools

Louis H. Pollak

Pollak's article continues the story begun by Kauper. The reader will note that while this selection has the same dispassionate and lawyer-like approach, it differs in tone and in its view of a proper policy.

Pollak concentrates on *Abington Township* v. *Schempp*, which is the immediate sequel to *Engel*. Another case decided in the same term, *Sherbert* v. *Verner* [374 U.S. 398 (1963)], bears on the Sunday Law Cases to which both authors refer and gives us additional clues to the Court's general attitude toward state intervention in religious affairs—an attitude which will surely affect future decisions in the education field. In the Sunday Law Cases the Court approved various "blue laws" preventing businesses from operating on Sunday on the grounds that such "day-of-rest" statutes were basically economic regulations only incidentally resulting in some secondary religious effects (even though they seriously disadvantaged Orthodox Jews). In *Sherbert* the Court indicated that the Sunday Law Cases should not be read too permissively by the states.

To quote from the Court's opinion:

"Appellant, a member of the Seventh-day Adventist Church, was discharged by her South Carolina employer because she would not work on Saturday, the

"The Supreme Court, 1962 Term, Foreword: Public Prayers in Public Schools" by Louis H. Pollak, 77 *Harvard Law Review* 62 (1963). Copyright © 1963 by The Harvard Law Review Association. Reprinted by permission.

Sabbath Day of her faith. When she was unable to obtain other employment because from conscientious scruples she would not take Saturday work, she filed a claim for unemployment compensation benefits under the South Carolina Unemployment Compensation Act. That law provides that, to be eligible for benefits, a claimant must be 'able to work and…is available for work'; and further, that a claimant is ineligible for benefits '[i]f…he has failed, without good cause,…to accept available work when offered him by the employment office or the employer….' The appellee Employment Security Commission, in administrative proceedings under the statute, found that appellant's restriction upon her availability for Saturday work brought her within the provision disqualifying for benefits insured workers who fail, without good cause, to accept 'suitable work when offered…by the employment office or the employer….'"

The Court held that such state action imposed a burden on the free exercise of religion that was not justified by any compelling state interest and thus was unconstitutional. The Court then rested on the free exercise clause and a form of balancing of interests. But the dissenters argued that the majority had itself violated the no establishment clause by providing a special exception to a general statute for one particular religious group. The majority replied:

"In holding as we do, plainly we are not fostering the "establishment" of the Seventh-day Adventist religion in South Carolina, for the extension of unemployment benefits to Sabbatarians in common with Sunday worshipers reflects nothing more than the governmental obligation of neutrality in the face of religious differences, and does not represent that involvement of religious with secular institutions which it is the object of the Establishment Clause to forestall."

Justices Douglas and Stewart, in concurring, argued that this decision deviated from those in the Sunday Law Cases; they applauded the deviation, since they had dissented in the earlier cases. Justices Harlan and White also noted this deviation in their dissent, in which they argued that the state ought to be free to use its own judgment in either providing or not providing a special exception to its unemployment rules for those who refuse work because of their religious scruples.

The difficulties of the religion cases indicate that the free exercise and no establishment clauses should remain an active area of Supreme Court concern for some time to come.

Operating, as has recently been its wont, on a not-with-a-whimper-but-a-bang theory of judicial timing, the Supreme Court, in June 1962, closed out its 1961 Term by announcing that recitation of the New York Regents' Prayer—"Almighty God, we acknowledge our dependence upon Thee, and we beg Thy blessings upon us, our parents, our teachers, and our country"—as a regular part of the daily opening exercises of a public school was unconstitutional.[1] Since the prayer, as the Court viewed it, was an official establishment of religion, the fact that participation was not required could not operate to validate it. One year after *Engel v.*

Vitale[2] dispatched the Regents' Prayer, the Court, in *School Dist. v. Schempp*,[3] wound up the 1962 Term by administering a similar *coup de grâce* to recitations of the Lord's Prayer and of Bible passages, which were part of the opening exercises in certain Pennsylvania and Maryland public schools.

The clamorous public hostility[4] which greeted *Engel* could hardly have come as a great surprise to the Justices. They surely knew that in entering the lists against officially sponsored professions of religious faith they were pitting the Court's authority against a vastly powerful adversary—an adversary which commands strong and widespread popular support, as segregation does among white southerners, and which is championed by potent interest groups, as is malapportionment of state legislatures. Moreover, in this combat the Court could not realistically have expected to enlist major allies; the nonsouthern national consensus has upheld the Court's stand against segregation, but massive popular opposition to official prayer is nowhere to be found. Likewise, there are many substantial interest groups which have a stake in the democratic rationalization of our legislatures, but few major interest groups are deeply committed antagonists of official prayer.

To turn aside from enforcement of the Constitution because enforcement is unpopular would be wholly antithetic to one of the Court's chief responsibilities. But the obvious hazards of the prayer issue, taken together with the Court's need to husband the judicial authority already taxed so heavily, might quite plausibly have led the Justices, two years ago, to give thoughtful attention to avoiding the problem by denying certiorari in *Engel.* And the disposition to deny certiorari might have been strengthened by a feeling that New York's attempt to write a prayer had produced such a pathetically vacuous assertion of piety as hardly to rise to the dignity of a religious exercise. The Court might very reasonably have decided to save its scarce ammunition for a prayer that soared, rather than squander it on New York's clay-footed pigeon.

The decision was otherwise. Just why the Justices—or, to be precise, a minimum of four of the Justices—voted to grant certiorari in *Engel,* can only be conjectured. But perhaps (assuming the Justices' vote to grant certiorari was accompanied by an expectation that on the merits they would vote the prayer down) the explanation is as follows: First, the Court knew that denial of certiorari would merely delay, not avoid, the prayer question; *Schempp,* which the Court had already remanded for appraisal of an amendment to the Pennsylvania statute, would almost certainly return on appeal, no matter how the three-judge district court disposed of it. Second, the Court may have sensed that invalidation of the Regents' Prayer would compel a like disposition of a Lord's-Prayer-and-Bible-reading case; as Justice Goldberg was to put the matter in a concurring opinion in *Schempp,* "That...[the state] has selected, rather than written, a particular devotional liturgy seems ...without constitutional import."[5] Third, possibly the Court anticipated that the public outcry sure to be engendered by a seeming judicial assault on the Lord's Prayer and the Bible might in some degree be mitigated by the prior decision of a kindred but less unsettling case—a sort of judicial

inoculation calculated to give the public a partial immunity to the affliction which was to ensue.

Perhaps none of this was planned. But it is nevertheless true that *Schempp* provoked far less furor than *Engel.* This is not to say that many school systems will adhere to *Schempp* with alacrity. Indeed it may well be that a substantial number will make no move to comply until they find themselves the direct targets of court decrees, and it is entirely possible that in many communities there will be no decrees because there are no willing plaintiffs. (This in turn may well depend on who one must be to be a plaintiff. In *Schempp* the plaintiffs were schoolchildren and their parents. But, since the issue turns out to be one of state establishment of religion rather than restraint of individual rights of freedom of worship, a fair case can be made for the proposition that any member of the affected community, whether or not he is or has a child in school, has a litigable interest in the matter. To the extent that the Court, in viewing the issue as a problem of establishment and thereby obviating proof of individual constraint, was desirous of relieving particular children of the burden of proving their differentness, the reasons for adopting more generous criteria of standing become weightier.)

The rationality of *Engel* and *Schempp* is of no concern to those who denounce them out of hand. But, for most Americans, and in the long flux of time, the vitality of these Supreme Court decisions, as with others of great moment, must depend upon their intrinsic persuasiveness. Therefore it becomes relevant to turn from the judgments in *Engel* and *Schempp* to the opinions: to consider, that is, what the Justices have said in explanation of the new injunction they have placed upon their countrymen.

I

In *Engel,* the opinion of the Court was written by Justice Black. The senior Justice had written for the Court in *Everson,*[6] which back in 1947 sustained, by a vote of five to four, a New Jersey school board's program of paying the bus fares of parochial school children. He had also written for the Court a year later, in *McCollum,*[7] which invalidated, by a vote of eight to one, the Champaign program of optional religious instruction on school premises during school hours. In 1952, he had dissented, as had Justices Frankfurter and Jackson, from the decision in *Zorach v. Clauson,*[8] which upheld New York City's "released time" program of optional religious instruction during school hours but off school premises. In *Engel*—joined by the Chief Justice and Justices Clark, Harlan, and Brennan—Justice Black condemned the Regents' Prayer in the following terms:

"There can be no doubt that New York's state prayer program officially establishes the religious beliefs embodied in the Regents' prayer....Neither the fact that the prayer may be denominationally neutral nor the fact that its observance on the part of the students is voluntary can serve to free it from the limitations of the Establishment Clause, as it might from the Free Exercise Clause, of the First Amendment, both of which are operative against the States by virtue of the Fourteenth Amendment. Although these clauses may in certain instances overlap, they forbid two quite different kinds of governmental encroachment upon religious freedom. The Establishment Clause, unlike the Free Exercise Clause, does not depend upon any showing of direct governmental compulsion and is violated by the enactment of laws which establish an official religion whether those laws operate directly to coerce nonobserving individuals or not."[9]

To buttress his holding, Justice Black turned not to the recent cases construing the establishment clause but to the seventeenth- and eighteenth-century history which was its predicate—especially the calamitous efforts, culminating in the Act of Uniformity, to make the Book of Common Prayer the standard of English religious observance, and the spillover of that unhappy enterprise in the American colonies. "It was in large part," wrote Justice Black, "to get completely away from this sort of systematic religious persecution that the Founders brought into being our Nation, our Constitution, and our Bill of Rights with its prohibition against any governmental establishment of religion."[10]

Justice Stewart—the sole dissenter in *Engel*, as he was to be in *Schempp*—felt that the Court had looked to the wrong history. What was really relevant, he thought, was "the history of the religious traditions of our people, reflected in countless practices of the institutions and officials of our government"[11]—for example, the invocation of the Deity at the inauguration of every President, and at the commencement of each working day of Congress and the Supreme Court "[T]o deny the wish of these schoolchildren to join in reciting this prayer is to deny them the opportunity of sharing in the spiritual heritage of our Nation."[12]

Justice Douglas concurred in the Court's judgment in *Engel*, but he traveled a very different route. For him the constitutional difficulty was that "the teacher who leads in prayer is on the public payroll."[13] Granted that the fraction of the teacher's time thus spent was "minuscule," any official subvention of religion is foreclosed by the establishment clause. In reaching this conclusion the Justice acknowledged that *Everson*—the New Jersey school bus opinion written by Justice Black and joined in by Justice Douglas—was erroneous. But Justice Douglas, who had written the Court's opinion in *Zorach*—the New York "released time" decision, from which Justice Black had dissented—could not agree that, apart from the element of subvention, history supported the Court's holding in *Engel*: "I cannot say that to authorize this prayer is to establish a religion in the strictly historic meaning of those words. A religion is not established in the usual sense merely by letting those who choose to do so say the prayer that the public school teacher leads."[14] Indeed, it does seem that the history relied on by Justice Black was somewhat overdrawn. As Professor Arthur Sutherland observed, writing in the pages of this *Review* a year ago, "A skeptical man might doubt that if the Regents' Prayer had been promulgated for optional use in Stuart days it would have sent the Pilgrims to a stern and rockbound coast."[15] Justice Black seems to have recognized that the historical analogy was far from complete for he acknowledged that the Regents' optional and nondenominational recital "seems relatively insignificant when compared to the governmental encroachments upon religion which were commonplace 200 years ago."[16] Nevertheless, he and the four Justices joining him felt, with Madison, that " 'it is proper to take alarm at the first experiment on our liberties.' "[17]

Madison's admonition, however, simply furnishes an approach to constitutional adjudication. It does not conclude the process. The very question in *Engel* was whether the Regents' Prayer constituted "a first experiment on our liberties." If, as the Court's silence seemed to indicate, little help could be gotten from the tangled doctrinal skein linking *Everson* and *McCollum* and *Zorach*, reference to history was surely appropriate. But when such reference only suggests that the danger now scotched is "relatively insignificant" in contrast with the dangers once apprehended, it seems uncertain that the Regents' Prayer was really "a first experiment," heavy with hazard, rather than a last and inconsequential gasp of a once weighty threat. History, as used in *Engel*, offers no persuasive guide for distinguishing the unconstitutional menace of the schoolchild's "Almighty God, we acknowledge our dependence upon Thee," from the ceremonial platitude of the Supreme Court Marshal's "God save the United States and this Honorable Court." And for the Court to say, as it did say in *Engel*, that the many patriotic and ceremonial "manifestations in our public life of belief in God ...bear no true resemblance to the unquestioned religious exercise that the State...has sponsored in this instance,"[18] merely announces a demarcation without indicating how either history or law serves to place a challenged observance in one category rather than another.

In *Schempp*, the Court tried out a different method of constitutional adjudication. Speaking through Justice Clark, the eight members of the majority eschewed history for earlier cases—or, to be more precise, the language of earlier cases. And from its own prior language the Court distilled a principle of governmental "neutrality" with respect to religion which led—ineluctably, it appeared—to the demise of the Lord's Prayer and Bible reading in public schools:

"As we have indicated, the Establishment Clause has been directly considered by this Court eight times in the past score of years and, with only one Justice dissenting on the point, it has consistently held that the clause withdrew all legislative power respecting religious belief or the expression thereof. The test may be stated as follows: what are the purpose and the primary effect of the enactment? If either is the advancement or inhibition of religion then the enactment exceeds the scope of legislative power as circumscribed by the Constitution. That is to say that to withstand the strictures of the Establishment Clause there must be a secular legislative purpose and a primary effect that neither advances nor inhibits religion."[19]

The Court discussed the free exercise clause as well, but clearly emphasized the establishment clause in resolving the issue at bar. The "test" announced was thus of central importance, but all that emerges clearly from it is that recitation of the Lord's Prayer and reading of the Bible are not permissible ingredients of exercises commencing the public school day. How does the "released time" program sustained in *Zorach v. Clauson* meet the test? The Court dutifully distinguished "released time" on the grounds that there the actual religious instruction took place outside of school and was not conducted by public school teachers. But could it have been said in *Zorach* that there was a "secular legislative purpose"? And could it also have been said in *Zorach* that the "primary effect" of the program "neither advances nor inhibits religion"? If the answer to either of these questions is in the affirmative, then the application of the test would appear to require a sophistication and a dexterity which have not been fully explicated. Nor is *Zorach* the only case for

which the test seems ill-suited. How, for example, does one gauge the "primary effect"—not to mention the underlying "legislative purpose"—of a Sunday Closing Law? Moreover, assuming judges can in due course learn how to measure "primary effect," why should they also be urged to venture into the quicksands of "legislative purpose"? If, on inspection, a "primary effect" either "advances" or "inhibits religion," the lawmakers' impelling purpose is of no constitutional import. But, conversely, if a legislature heavy with nonsecular legislative purpose was simply incompetent to produce a result that had a perceptible impact on religion one way or another, why should a court be thought to have any supervisory responsibility in the premises?

And if the Court's test of an establishment poses more problems than it answers, what of the apparent breadth of the Court's constitutional premises? The Court asserts that the establishment clause "withdrew all legislative power" in the domain of religious belief and expression. But does not such an assertion tend to muddy, however inadvertently, the remote and currently placid constitutional waters in which ministers are exempt from the draft, donors can deduct their tithes, and churches are exempt from tax and other regulatory laws? Citation of these isolated examples serves as a reminder of what the whole course of American constitutional history regularly confirms: to characterize constitutional limitations as inflexible imperatives is an unproductive form of judicial activity.

With respect to the class of constitutional problems presented in *Schempp* and *Engel*, it is instructive to recall the style of the Court's opinion in *Zorach*, sustaining New York's "released time" program: "There cannot be the slightest doubt that the First Amendment reflects the philosophy that Church and State should be separated....The First Amendment, however, does not say that in every and all respects there shall be a separation of Church and State. Rather, it studiously defines the manner, the specific ways, in which there shall be no concert or union or dependency one on the other. That is the common sense of the matter."[20]

What made *Zorach* wholly unintelligible in its retreat from *McCollum*, the case in which the Court invalidated the Champaign program of religious instruction, is precisely that it depended upon the first amendment alone to "studiously" define "the manner, the specific ways" in which church and state are required to stay apart. There is no "common sense of the matter" to be distilled from the words "free exercise" and "establishment" unless a disciplined appraisal is made of the role of religion in public education, an appraisal in turn geared to a thoughtful review of the first amend-ment's history and its "line of ... growth."[21]

So, too, with respect to school prayers. Neither *Engel's* abbreviated history, nor *Schempp's* glossy inventory of the Court's case-hardened rhetoric, nor even a combination of the two, seems suitably comprehensive.

II

Frequently, it falls to an individual Justice to place in sharper focus both what is right and what is wrong about the limited generalities upon which majorities can agree. Thus, in retrospect, Justice Frankfurter's concurrence in *McCullom* seems more and more to have been the weightiest state-ment of the case. And—especially now that Justice Douglas has disavowed the holding in *Everson*— Justice Rutledge's dissent in *Everson* today ap-pears the most influential appraisal of the problem there presented. Regrettably, with respect to the school prayer problem, that office was not per-formed in *Engel* by the one concurring opinion filed—that of Justice Douglas. Nor was it per-formed in *Schempp* by Justice Douglas' concur-ring opinion. In both cases the Justice stressed what seems a peripheral aspect of the cases, the issue of public expenditures in aid of religion. The sums involved were so minute—whether or not they surmounted what might be termed the Plim-soll line of *de minimis*—that to have made decision turn on them would have tended to demean the larger issues. Justice Douglas' opinions in *Engel* and *Schempp* foretell deep constitutional trouble for proposals to appropriate federal funds to aid church-related schools.[22] But programs of this kind were not before the Court in *Engel* and *Schempp*.

Justice Goldberg's concurring opinion in *Schempp*, in which Justice Harlan joined, did not purport to attempt an independent examination of the legal and historical issues involved. Justice Goldberg was primarily concerned with empha-sizing, first, the common purpose of the free exer-cise and establishment clauses; second, the limited nature of the Court's holding—*e.g.*, "it seems clear ... that the Court would recognize the propriety ... of the teaching *about* religion, as distinguished from the teaching *of* religion, in the public schools;"[23] and, third, the capacity of courts to distinguish ceremonial exercises which have a re-ligious flavor but no real moment from practices which "involve the state so significantly and di-rectly in the realm of the sectarian as to give rise to those very divisive influences and inhibitions of freedom which both religion clauses of the First Amendment preclude."[24]

Justice Brennan's concurrence was the one opinion which attempted a comprehensive survey both of the history of prayer in American educa-tion and of the developing impact of the first amendment on American public schools. He made the sensible, but not necessarily obvious, point that "whatever Jefferson or Madison would have thought of Bible reading or the recital of the Lord's Prayer in what few public schools existed in their day, our use of the history of their time must limit itself to broad purposes, not specific practices."[25] American public education is, of course, a form of government activity which has mainly developed since their time; these state schools, serving a re-ligiously diverse constituency, have managed to avoid "the evils the Framers meant the Establish-ment Clause to forestall" because they have con-centrated on "the training of American citizens in an atmosphere free of parochial, divisive, or sepa-ratist influences of any sort...."[26] The first amend-ment, in Justice Brennan's view, guarantees the American parent a choice between this form of public education and private education oriented to any religious belief the parent may elect.

"The relationship of the Establishment Clause of the First Amendment to the public school system is preeminently that of reserving such a choice to the individual parent, rather than vesting it in the majority of voters of each State or school district. The choice which is thus preserved is between a public secular education with its uniquely demo-cratic values, and some form of private or sectarian education, which offers values of its own.... The choice between these very different forms of edu-cation is one—very much like the choice whether or not to worship—which our Constitution leaves to the individual parent. It is no proper function of the state or local government to influence or restrict that election. The lesson of history—drawn more from the experiences of other countries than from our own—is that a system of free public edu-cation forfeits its unique contribution to the growth of democratic citizenship when that choice ceases to be freely available to each parent."[27]

Of the four members of the *Schempp* majority who filed opinions, Justice Brennan, in the lan-guage just quoted, came much the closest to pro-viding a constitutional framework adequate to the problems before the Court. The chief difficulty with Justice Brennan's opinion (apart from its failure fully to meet Justice Stewart's free-exercise counterargument, discussed below) is that he sought to do too many other things. For example, he sought to accommodate the Court's leading past decisions, including the intractable *Zorach*, to his construct. Also he went beyond his establishment clause analysis to decide that the prayer programs contravened the free exercise clause. This was so, notwithstanding the fact that participation in the prayers was not required, because many children, dissenters at heart but anxious to conform to group mores, would fear to avail themselves of the option of nonparticipation.

Justice Brennan's secondary holding reflects a widely shared and very plausible view of the actual impact of a school prayer program. In a speech given between *Engel* and *Schempp*, Professor Paul Freund argued just this position. But he argued it as a position to be taken in preference, not in addition, to a holding anchored in the establishment clause—as a position which would enable the Court "to put to one side all the problems of state aid on which feelings are now running high, and to limit the decision to the context of the school room." However, to have pitched the decision of *Engel* and *Schempp* on the free exercise clause would have seriously undercut the likelihood of their effective implementation in other school districts. For such a holding would presumably have meant that the prayer programs were constitutionally unobjectionable unless and until challenged, and, therefore, that school boards would have been under no discernible legal obligation, as assuredly they now are, to suspend ongoing prayer programs on their own initiative. Moreover, unless the holding carried with it a radical revision of accepted notions of standing, challenges could only have been forthcoming from schoolchildren and/or their parents, a limitation which would not seem so compelling when the case is made on establishment grounds. Indeed, the hypothetical schoolchild plaintiff, whose free exercise rights would thus be enforced, would have to be a child with the gumption not only to disassociate himself from the prayer program but to prefer litigation to the relatively expeditious exit procedure contemplated by the excusal proviso. To have tailored the holdings in *Engel* and *Schempp* to the undoubted sensitivities of schoolchildren would not have significantly eased their burdens.

Moreover, for the Court to have held that prayer programs infringe only the rights of dissenting children would not merely have left untouched the programs conducted in the many school districts where litigation might not arise. Such a holding might well have been widely understood as legitimizing such programs, absent vocalized dissent. In short, the Court would have risked conveying the impression that, notwithstanding the establishment clause, an American public school might properly spend official energies in religious indoctrination—provided only that the entire school community was so minded, or at least that doubters remained discreetly mute. That the Court did not accept this equivocal position—that in fact it placed *Engel* and *Schempp* firmly on establishment grounds—evidenced a high order of judicial responsibility. Once the Court made its initial decision, reflected in the grant of certiorari in *Engel*, to come to grips with the school prayer issue, it assumed a heavy obligation to decide the issue in full—to vote prayer programs up or down—not to leave so controversial and widespread a governmental undertaking gasping for breath in the thin atmosphere of quasi-constitutionality.

III

Twenty years ago, in its handling of the flag salute controversy, the Court thought that it faced a somewhat similar issue of doctrinal choice. At that time it eschewed a free exercise holding for one of apparently broader compass. It is arguable that this was error. And this in turn might seem to confirm the view that the Court in *Engel* and *Schempp* should have elected the narrower doctrinal alternative. The plaintiffs in *West Virginia State Bd. of Educ. v. Barnette*[28] were Jehovah's Witnesses whose children could not, compatibly with their religious faith, salute the American flag. They sought injunctive relief to protect their children from having to participate in the required exercise. The Court held for the plaintiffs, but (as Justice Brennan noted in *Schempp*[29]) Justice Jackson's opinion for the Court traveled beyond the free exercise rights of the plaintiffs' children and others similarly situated:

"Nor does the issue as we see it turn on one's possession of particular religious views or the sincerity with which they are held. While religion supplies appellees' motive for enduring the discomforts of making the issue in this case, many citizens who do not share these religious views hold such a compulsory rite to infringe constitutional liberty of the individual. It is not necessary to inquire whether non-conformist beliefs will exempt from the duty to salute unless we first find power to make the salute a legal duty."[30]

And thereafter the Court's opinion concluded that the state had no such power. It seems that Justice Jackson wrote as he did for essentially instrumental reasons; that he sought a ground for reopening the prior holding in *Minersville School Dist. v. Gobitis,* a case in which Justice Frankfurter, writing for the Court, had started from the proposition, "that the flag-salute is an allowable portion of a school program for those who do not invoke conscientious scruples is surely not debatable."[31] Justice Jackson proceeded to debate what Justice Frankfurter had said was "not debatable," with the end in view of showing that *Gobitis* was wrong in its initial assumption that, as Justice Jackson put it, "power exists in the State to impose the flag salute discipline upon school children in general."[32]

In achieving his instrumental objective the Justice laid claim to broader constitutional ground than the Court has ever seriously attempted, or justly could attempt, to occupy. He was not merely making the easy point that the first amendment should be read to protect from forced participation in the salute those who had political or philosophic, as well as religious, reservations. He was not even pointing out that once a moral scruple is asserted, it is inappropriate for a court to evaluate whether a "genuine" morality is being applied. He was denying in general the existence of governmental power to require the salute of schoolchildren, and thereby vesting in each schoolchild a "constitutional liberty" to decline to participate quite apart from any rights which the child might have had to protect "non-conformist beliefs." In short, Justice Jackson read into the Constitution a curtailment of state power broader than was necessary to protect either the freedom of worship or the freedom of speech and belief aspects of the "liberty" enshrined in the fourteenth amendment.

This is, certainly, an unconventional view of the constitutional limitations imposed upon the states. The states, after all, are the repositories of general governmental power. And—questions of federal supremacy aside—this means that for the most part the Constitution limits state authority only insofar as particular exertions of the state's general governmental power impinge on the several federal rights specified in the fourteenth amendment and other limiting provisions of the Constitution. Surely what Justice Frankfurter meant, when he said in *Gobitis* that West Virginia's power to include a flag salute in the school program was "not debatable," was that—apart from the question of the state's power to require the salute of those who asserted particularized federal liberties—West Virginia had as much authority to require a flag salute as to make each schoolchild learn the national anthem or take courses in the history of West Virginia and the United States.

There would appear to be only two qualifications of the broad proposition that the states may,

apart from the particularized federal liberties, exert their general governmental powers as they will. One qualification, which has thus far substantially defied judicial enforcement, is that the states must maintain a republican form of government. Another is that the states must refrain from undertaking programs "respecting an establishment of religion." The flag salute was not regarded as an establishment of religion by Justice Jackson or those Justices who joined his opinion. Nor should it have been so regarded, for it was not a religious exercise. It was simply an exercise which impinged on the religious, and perhaps other, first amendment scruples of some schoolchildren. Moreover, if the flag salute had been an establishment of religion, this would not have meant merely that the schools of West Virginia could not require participation in the exercise; it would have meant that the schools of West Virginia could not sponsor such an exercise at all.

Justice Jackson failed, in *Barnette,* to recognize the difference between the protections accorded religious beliefs and those accorded secular scruples. As Justice Rutledge put the matter, "the sphere of religious activity, as distinguished from the secular intellectual liberties, has been given... two-fold protection and, as the state cannot forbid, neither can it perform or aid in performing the religious function. The dual prohibition makes that function altogether private."[33] *Barnette* was a case in which government used its schools to foster an idea—namely, allegiance to the state—which lies in the "secular intellectual" realm. This is the sort of thing government does all the time, and is fully entitled to do, provided that it does not infringe the individual's right of intellectual nonconformity, religious or otherwise. By contrast, *Engel* and *Schempp* are cases in which government used its schools to foster "religious activity." Their holdings deny the legitimacy of such a government program and thereby they operate, in Justice Rutledge's phrase, to keep "the religious function... altogether private." The two decisions complement Brandeis' insistence on privacy by fortifying "as against the Government, the right to be let alone —the most comprehensive of rights, and the right most valued by civilized men."[34] As such, the decisions occupy rightfully, and successfully, an even broader constitutional ground than that which *Barnette* sought, and failed, to usurp. They are not small arms hanging over the fireplaces of the stalwart, ready for use against official intruders ranging beyond their lawful authority. They are weapons of heavier caliber which ring every home, keeping government permanently at its constitutionally prescribed distance and thereby guarding that core of individuality the Constitution makes "altogether private."

IV

Justice Stewart, dissenting in *Schempp*, argued that the appropriate disposition of the two cases before the Court was to remand for further proceedings. With respect to the claim under the establishment clause, Justice Stewart felt that no issue was presented if, as he supposed to be the fact, the prayer programs were actually so administered as not to be confined to "a particular religious book and a denominational prayer," but rather in such a fashion as would make "the variety and content of the exercises, as well as a choice as to their implementation, matters which ultimately reflect the consensus of each local school community."[35] But since Justice Stewart felt that the records before the Court were insufficient to justify a confident finding one way or another as to the way in which the programs were administered, he favored sending the cases back to elicit further information. Underlying his bid to amplify the records was Justice Stewart's legal conclusion that "religious exercises are not constitutionally invalid if they simply reflect differences which exist in the society from which the school draws its pupils. They become constitutionally invalid only if their administration places the sanction of secular authority behind one or more particular religious or irreligious beliefs."[36] Passing the practical questions of how, under Justice Stewart's formula, a school board would establish a community consensus, what its visible and audible manifestations would be, and how those manifestations would avoid the official connotation that religion is better than irreligion, it is apparent that the Justice simply does not subscribe, as his brethren of the majority do, to Justice Rutledge's conclusion that "the state...neither can...perform or aid in performing the religious function."[37]

There is an aspect of Justice Stewart's dissent in *Schempp* which—because it is not fully met by the Court's opinion or by any of the three concurrences—demands more extended consideration. In *Engel*, it will be recalled, Justice Stewart expressed concern at denying "the wish of these school children to join in reciting this prayer" and thereby denying "them the opportunity of sharing in the spiritual heritage of our Nation."[38] In *Schempp* the Justice's concern blossomed into a full-blown constitutional argument—apparently intended to show that, even assuming remand would disclose a prayer program constituting an establishment, the

free exercise claims of children seeking to pray would furnish a "constitutional justification" of that establishment:

"[T]here is involved in these cases a substantial free exercise claim on the part of those who affirmatively desire to have their children's school day open with the reading of passages from the Bible.

"It has become accepted that the decision in *Pierce* v. *Society of Sisters*, 268 U.S. 510, upholding the right of parents to send their children to nonpublic schools, was ultimately based upon the recognition of the validity of the free exercise claim involved in that situation. It might be argued here that parents who wanted their children to be exposed to religious influences in school could, under *Pierce*, send their children to private or parochial schools. But the consideration which renders this contention too facile to be determinative has already been recognized by the Court: "Freedom of speech, freedom of the press, freedom of religion are available to all, not merely to those who can pay their own way." *Murdock* v. *Pennsylvania*, 319 U.S. 105, 111.

"It might also be argued that parents who want their children exposed to religious influences can adequately fulfill that wish off school property and outside school time. With all its surface persuasiveness, however, this argument seriously misconceives the basic constitutional justification for permitting the exercises at issue in these cases. For a compulsory state educational system so structures a child's life that if religious exercises are held to be an impermissible activity in schools, religion is placed at an artificial and state-created disadvantage. Viewed in this light, permission of such exercises for those who want them is necessary if the schools are truly to be neutral in the matter of religion. And a refusal to permit religious exercises thus is seen...as the establishment of a religion of secularism, or, at the least, as government support of the beliefs of those who think that religious exercises should be conducted only in private.[39]

It is at once apparent that Justice Stewart and Justice Brennan have a common point of constitutional departure. They both acknowledge that the first amendment gives parents a choice between public and private, including church-related, schools.[40] For Justice Brennan, the first amendment choice of schools sufficiently protects the parent's interest in his child's religious instruction. Justice Stewart disagrees, and on grounds which cannot be lightly brushed off in a democratic society. Most parents cannot afford to send their children to private schools. And freedom of religion is not just a privilege of the well-to-do. Justice

Brennan does not really come to grips with Justice Stewart's demurrer, so it behooves us to look at the matter further. Justice Stewart's argument seems to suggest in part that those who cannot afford to go to religious schools of their choice are entitled by that fact alone to require the state to furnish an equivalent religious experience in the public schools. Such an argument proves too much. It suggests that whether or not the state were to operate a public school system, and whether or not its public school system were compulsory, the state would remain under an affirmative duty to provide religious education to those children whose parents could not afford to send them to private schools. Moreover, the logic of the argument would seem to compel insistence on state sponsorship of the full panoply of denominational instruction available in private schools to the well-to-do. Random tidbits of religious activity, such as those involved in *Engel* and *Schempp*, would not seem adequate to fulfill this conception of the first amendment's mandate. But let us accept that Justice Stewart would find decisive exactly the fact that Pennsylvania and Maryland, like all other states of the Union, maintain public schools and require attendance either at them or at accredited private schools. Justice Stewart's constitutional concern then narrows to this: the child who cannot afford a private school which reflects his religious or antireligious choice is forced to spend a large measure of his day in state-fashioned, secular surroundings.

Yet a constitutional question could arise only if the schooling that the child was compelled to undergo operated to disparage religion. And that, at bottom, is Justice Stewart's argument. As he sees it, "the basic constitutional justification for permitting the exercises at issue in these cases" is that "a compulsory state educational system so structures a child's life that if religious exercises are held to be an impermissible activity in schools, religion is placed at an artificial and state-created disadvantage."[41]

This assertion appears to relate to two different claims. The first is that of the child who merely desires to pray aloud or as part of a group, and who is told that he must take the initiative of doing so before or after school, and with groups of his own formation—a displacement which by itself hardly seems to present a real constitutional problem. The second claim is that the absence of a religious exercise at the commencement of school operates to suffuse the balance of the school day with an antireligious, perhaps even "secularist" bias.[42] It seems highly doubtful that such an evaluation—be it proffered as a finding of fact or conclusion of law—is a generally valid description of

American public education. But, assuming that as to some identifiable students in some identifiable schools the evaluation is meaningful, it becomes relevant to inquire into the propositional function which this evaluation serves.

It is, in the words of Justice Stewart, the "basic constitutional justification" of the school prayer programs. This appears to suggest that, unless the characterization is true, the challenged programs would be without "constitutional justification"— would be what at least Justice Stewart's brethren would regard as an establishment of religion. This means, of course, that proof of the "constitutional justification" is an essential ingredient of the case for school prayers. There is no middle ground such as Justice Stewart tried to find later in his opinion: "strictly speaking, what is at issue here is a privilege rather than a right. In other words, the question presented is not whether exercises such as those at issue here are constitutionally compelled, but rather whether they are constitutionally invalid. And that issue, in my view, turns on the question of coercion."[43] For if the child too poor to attend a private school does not require school prayers to sustain his freedom of worship—if, in short, the asserted "constitutional justification" of the prayer program is not demonstrable—then the program is not a permissible enterprise; it is invalid.[44] Conversely, if a prayer program is demonstrably necessary to protect the religious freedom of some public schoolchildren, this would seem to mean that, where requested, the prayer program is "constitutionally compelled." Moreover, that a prayer program involves coercion of a few dissenting schoolchildren seems hardly decisive if the program is necessary to the maintenance of religious freedom of other children, for in that case, children's beliefs are being coerced whether or not the program is present.

Behind Justice Stewart's "constitutional justification" for school prayers apparently lies the idea that a prayerless compulsory school, like a chaplain-less draft army, is an institution in which the free exercise and establishment clauses inevitably collide. But, assuming that it is constitutionally permissible for the United States to employ army chaplains, the "constitutional justification" for this government program is that otherwise the draftee would have no effective opportunity whatsoever to satisfy his religious needs, a situation which does not, of course, obtain for the schoolchild. Moreover, the availability of the chaplain to a religiously oriented draftee need not, and presumably does not, operate to suffuse the army experience of all draftees with an officially sponsored program of religious activity. But a school prayer program, whether or not participation is characterized as voluntary, operates through and on the pupil group and each of its members. If as to a particular schoolchild a particular prayerless public school really operates to restrain his religious faith, this surely suggests not that such a religious establishment should be tolerated, but that the child would be constitutionally exempt from compliance with the compulsory school laws.

v

What was sorely needed in *Engel* and *Schempp* was the kind of analysis Justice Frankfurter made in his *McCollum* concurrence—an analysis culminating in language which, with minor changes, could have been transposed to the school prayer problem:

"Separation is a requirement to abstain from fusing functions of Government and of religious sects, not merely to treat them all equally. That a child is offered an alternative may reduce the constraint; it does not eliminate the operation of influence by the school in matters sacred to conscience and outside the school's domain.... The children belonging to...non-participating sects will thus have inculcated in them a feeling of separatism when the school should be the training ground for habits of community, or they will have religious instruction in a faith which is not that of their parents.... These are consequences not amenable to statistics. But they are precisely the consequences against which the Constitution was directed when it prohibited the Government common to all from becoming embroiled, however innocently, in the destructive religious conflicts of which the history of even this country records some dark pages.
..."In no activity of the State is it more vital to keep out divisive forces than in its schools, to avoid confusing, not to say fusing, what the Constitution sought to keep strictly apart."[45]

Such an analysis would have operated, as Professor Freund argued that a free exercise holding would have operated, "to limit the decision to the context of the school room." It would have recognized that the public school presents a distinctive situation, that analogies from army posts, state tax policy, government ceremonies, and even the administration of state unemployment compensation programs[46] are of limited relevance. And, to the ~~ent that~~ ~~...~~ ~~...~~ould th~~...~~ ~~...~~ed t~~ the schoolroom and its position of unique responsibility in American society, the prayer cases could serve not merely to free the schools of a function that cannot justify, but to encourage them in those activities which only they can perform. It may well

be that most American schools do very little to enlarge student awareness of the role of religion in a democratic society. To the extent that this is so, it is a salient item in a more general indictment —that American public schools do a woefully poor job of fostering citizen understanding of the nature of American freedoms and of the institutions charged with protecting those freedoms. Classroom study of the *Engel* and *Schempp* cases might be an excellent beginning point for such understanding. Many lessons might emerge from such a study. One would be a sense of the sanctity of religion. Another would be a sense of the high place of nonconformity. Still another would be a sense of the subtlety of the responsibilities Americans impose upon their legislatures and their courts. But perhaps the final lesson would be a recognition that these institutions are, in the last analysis, only secondary architects of the American experience. As Justice Frankfurter observed in *McCollum,* "The public school is at once the symbol of our democracy and the most pervasive means for promoting our common destiny."[47]

Footnotes

[1]Engel v. Vitale, 370 U.S. 421 (1962). A year earlier, the Court had also utilized the last day of the Term to announce a first-magnitude constitutional decision. The case was Mapp v. Ohio, 367 U.S. 643 (1961), holding that evidence seized by state officers in the course of an unreasonable search is inadmissible in a state criminal trial, and overruling Wolf v. Colorado, 338 U.S. 25 (1949), a decision announced on the last day of the 1948 Term.
[2]370 U.S. 421 (1962).
[3]**374 U.S. 203 (1963).**
[4]See Pollak, *W.B.R.: Some Reflections,* 71 YALE L.J. 1451, 1455-56 n.17 (1962).
[5]374 U.S. at 307. (Justice Harlan joined in Justice Goldberg's opinion.) Of course, Justice Goldberg was not on the Court when *Engel* was decided, let alone when certiorari was granted. His statement is quoted merely to suggest that the likeness of *Engel* and *Schempp* which he and Justice Harlan expressly articulated when *Schempp* was decided may well have been in the forefront of the Court's thinking when the petition for certiorari in *Engel* was under consideration.
[6]Everson v. Board of Educ., 330 U.S. 1 (1947).
[7]Illinois *ex rel.* McCollum v. Board of Educ., 333 U.S. 203 (1948).
[8]343 U.S. 306 (1952).
[9]370 U.S. at 430.
[10]*Id.* at 433.
[11]*Id.* at 446.
[12]~~Id~~ ~~...~~ ~~45. J~~ ~~...~~ ., pre ~~...~~ *Engel* ~~...~~ when the case was decided, did not participate. Neither did Justice White, who was appointed to the Court after *Engel* was argued.
[13]*Id.* at 441.
[14]*Id.* at 442. (Footnote omitted.)
[15]Sutherland, *Establishment According to Engel,* 76 HARV. L. REV. 25, 35–36 (1962).

[16]370 U.S. at 436.

[17]*Ibid.*

[18]*Id.* at 435 n.21.

[19]374 U.S. at 222.

[20]343 U.S. at 312.

[21]*Cf.* Holmes, J., in Gompers v. United States, 233 U.S. 604, 610 (1914).

[22]See Pollak, *supra* note 4, at 1455–58. *Cf.* Justice Douglas' discussion in *Schempp* of "appeals by church groups for public funds to finance their religious schools." 374 U.S. at 229.

[23]*Id.* at 306.

[24]*Id.* at 307. See also *id.* at 308.

[25]*Id.* at 241.

[26]*Id.* at 241–42.

[27]*Id.* at 242.

[28]319 U.S. 624 (1943).

[29]374 U.S. at 252.

[30]319 U.S. at 634–35.

[31]310 U.S. at 586, 599 (1940).

[32]319 U.S. at 635.

[33]Everson v. Board of Educ., 330 U.S. 1, 52 (1947) (dissenting opinion). Justice Clark, in *Schempp*, quoted Justice Rutledge's views. 374 U.S. at 218–19.

[34]Olmstead v. United States, 277 U.S. 438, 478 (1928) (dissenting opinion).

[35]374 U.S. at 315–16.

[36]*Id.* at 317–18.

[37]See note 33 *supra*. Presumably Justice Stewart also felt that remand was required to get the factual data necessary to dispose of the free exercise claim. But it is hard to be certain of this because Justice Stewart did not, in his opinion, expressly differentiate the free exercise and establishment claims. It is not clear, therefore, whether the Justice sees the same issue of "coercion" as dispositive of both claims. Consider, for example, the following sentences:

"In the absence of coercion upon those who do not wish to participate—because they hold less strong beliefs, other beliefs, or no beliefs at all—such provisions [*i.e.,* provisions requiring the religious exercises to reflect a community consensus] cannot, in my view, represent the type of support of religion barred by the Establishment Clause. For the only support which such rules provide for religion is the withholding of state hostility—a simple acknowledgment on the part of secular authorities that the Constitution does not require extirpation of all expression of religious belief." 374 U.S. at 316.

[38]370 U.S. at 445. See text accompanying note 12 *supra*.

[39]374 U.S. at 312–13.

[40]*Pierce,* cited by Justice Stewart, is the only instance in which the Court actually confronted a state law which sought to channel all children into public schools. And that case, as Justice Brennan was careful to observe, "obviously decided no First Amendment question but recognized only the constitutional right to establish and patronize private schools—including parochial

schools—which meet the state's reasonable minimum curricular requirements." 374 U.S. at 248. Justice Stewart's intimation that *Pierce* has acquired its first amendment status after the event is entirely proper. *Pierce* has undergone a sort of constitutional seachange. It is one of the decisions which links the Constitution's past emphasis on economic liberty and its present emphasis on personal liberty. The single note of caution worth mentioning here is that, if *Pierce* had never been decided and the issue were to arise afresh today, it is by no means certain that the Court would hold the states powerless to require all children to attend the same schools. Yet, in view of the gloss on *Pierce,* and, even more important, in view of the extreme unlikelihood that any state legislature would today attempt to curtail parental option, present discussion may as well proceed on the assumption, jointly postulated by Justices Stewart and Brennan, that the choice of public or private schooling is indeed grounded in the first amendment.

[41]*Id.* at 313.

[42]The Court has elsewhere denied, in effect, that every public school curriculum which lacks a prayer program is ipso facto antisectarian. In *McCollum* Justice Black observed, in a passage quoted by Justice Stewart in *Schempp, id.* at 311, that "to hold that a state cannot…utilize its school system to aid any or all religious faiths or sects in the dissemination of their doctrines and ideals does not…manifest a governmental hostility to religion or religious teachings." Illinois *ex rel.* McCollum v. Board of Educ., 333 U.S. 203, 211 (1948).

[43]*Id.* at 316.

[44]Compare Justice Brennan's apparent view that the federal government may, but is not required to, provide chaplains to cater to the religious needs of prisoners and of military personnel who would otherwise have no effective opportunity to exercise their freedom of worship. *Id.* at 299. (In his dissent in *McCollum,* in 1947, Justice Reed noted that West Point cadets and Annapolis midshipmen were required to attend church services. 333 U.S. at 254. This practice, if it still obtains, seems plainly insupportable. The issue is of course distinguishable from that presented in Hamilton v. Regents of the Univ. of Cal., 293 U.S. 245 (1934), which sustained a state university's requirement of military training even as to students of pacifist religious persuasion. *Cf. Barnette.*) Compare Sherbert v. Verner, 374 U.S. 398 (1963), decided the same day as *Schempp,…* Justice Stewart, concurring sharply, argued that the Court's holding was inconsistent with what he felt to be the "not only insensitive, but positively wooden" view of the establishment clause reflected in *Engel* and *Schempp.* 374 U.S. at 414.…

[45]Illinois *ex rel.* McCollum v. Board of Educ., 333 U.S. 203, 227–28, 231 (1948) (concurring opinion).

[46]See Sherbert v. Verner, 374 U.S. 398 (1963).

[47]333 U.S. at 231.

Chapter III

REAPPORTIONMENT

From the Court-packing fight of the late 1930's to the end of the 1950's, the Supreme Court passed through a period of relative eclipse, contributing little to American politics. In more recent years, however, it has rendered the two most significant and far-reaching decisions of domestic public policy to be reached by any agency of government in the postwar period. The Reapportionment Cases constitute one, the Segregation Cases (which will be taken up in the next chapter) the other.

In most states there has been a movement of population from rural areas into the cities and suburbs. Legislative district boundaries set many years ago often remained the same no matter how many people moved out of rural districts and into urban. (District lines do not change automatically as population moves but only when new laws are passed providing such changes.) In many instances this meant that an urban or suburban district containing 500,000 people and a rural district containing 50,000 each elected only one representative to the state legislature. In this way, old rural districts often dominated their legislatures long after the majority of the state's population—as a result of changing patterns of population growth—had moved into urban or suburban areas. State legislatures or conventions could have changed the district boundaries, but in many instances this would have required that the members of the legislature vote themselves out of their own seats. Rural legislators were understandably reluctant to transfer seats from rural to urban areas to correspond with shifts in relative population when it was their own seats that would have to be transferred. Moreover, in each state many groups and individuals found that the existing composition of the legislature, no matter how inequitable, favored their interests. The dominant political parties in some states were able on occasion to deliberately malapportion electoral districts to reduce the strength of the minority party. The various political forces favoring existing inequalities grounded themselves on the solid foundations of incumbent legislators' reluctance to give up their own seats and were frequently able to block reforms. Malapportionment existed not only in the two houses of the state legislatures—although it was frequently argued that state upper houses might equitably be chosen on some other basis than population, as is the U.S. Senate—but also in the districting for the U.S. House of Representatives, which is provided for in state statutes.

The Supreme Court has now forced the states to institute reforms. Particularly in the most heavily populated and industrialized states, reapportionment of both houses of the legislature on a "one man, one vote" basis (equal numbers of voters electing equal numbers of representatives) will upset the balance of power between urban and rural, liberal and conservative forces which malapportionment had maintained for many years. These decisions, therefore, will inevitably contribute to major changes in state politics—although changes in public policy may in many instances be gradual and quiet ones. The decisions are made and, short of a highly unlikely constitutional amendment, cannot be changed. There is not much point now in debating whether the Court should have made them or left the states to clean their own houses. Yet it should be noted that the Court did not act until the states had consistently demonstrated their own inability or unwillingness to eliminate very high levels of voting inequality, which few Americans would care to defend under any theory of democracy.

Baker v. *Carr* and the later Reapportionment Cases are history; yet the basic problem of democratic theory that underlies those decisions has not been solved, and an appreciation of that problem must precede any sound evaluation of those decisions or of future arrangements made to bring state electoral laws into conformity with them. At the simplest level, democracy means rule by the people. Most commentators would add to this definition the corollary of political equality for each individual. Thus democracy becomes equal rule by each citizen. Let us say that the citizens of a community, one hundred in number, unanimously vote in favor of some government decision that benefits them all equally. Here we have the ideal type of democracy—all the citizens participated equally in making a political decision that benefited them all equally. Now let us suppose a vote that was not unanimous. Sixty citizens wanted policy X, which benefited them. Forty wanted policy Y, which benefited *them*. We normally solve such a problem by resorting to majority rule. But majority rule is a practical expedient for handling disagreements and is only partially compatible with the basic principles of a democracy. We may argue that equality was maintained because each man cast one vote. But there was not equality in making the governmental decision. The sixty made the decision; the forty did not. Nor was there equality of benefits from the decision. The sixty got something they wanted; the forty got nothing. In short, it is easy to talk glibly about majority rule and government by the "people"; but the person who always casts his one equal vote, and always finds himself in the minority, and never gets anything he wants, may not think of himself as quite equal to the person whose vote is always in the majority and who always gets what he wants.

The problem of permanent minorities is sometimes expressed in the language of groups. When we look at democracy as it actually operates, we often see groups of persons united by some common interest. California tuna fishermen as a group want a ban on imports of cheap Japanese tuna. Mississippi Negroes want to be able to vote in Mississippi. Indeed, in an increasingly large and complex society, the "person" is not likely to be heard by the "people" unless he speaks through some group. Thus, perhaps equality should mean that each group is equal to every other group. But of course this is not possible, for some groups' demands directly conflict with those of others. Consumers as a group want cheap tuna fish and do not care whether fishermen are rich or not. Mississippi whites do not want Mississippi Negroes to vote. All groups can be equal in the formal sense that each is allowed to participate in making government decisions, but again some must be more equal than others, for all cannot equally get everything they want.

Two factors help to alleviate these problems. First, most people will find that their vote has been cast sometimes with the majority and sometimes with the minority. Since they win a few and lose a few under majority rule, they feel a rough equality with their fellow citizens who do the same. Second, most individuals belong formally or informally to many groups, since they have many different interests. At any given moment, some of the groups to which they belong will win and others will lose. The tuna fisherman may not get his tariff from the federal government, but San Diego may get a new superhighway, built with federal funds, on which the fisherman can drive to his boat from his home. The tuna fishermen, as a group, lost and the citizens of San Diego won. Furthermore, each group sometimes wins and sometimes loses. So each person finds some of his groups winning at any given moment and each of his groups winning sometimes and again feels a rough equality at the group level.

The problem of democratic equality is to prevent any given individual or group from always losing. This is not only a moral problem; if any individual or group always finds itself in the minority under the democratic rules, it is likely to resort to the gun rather than the ballot box to get what it wants. Simply parroting the slogan "one man, one vote," therefore, is not going to create democratic equality. In California, for instance, in what sense will a farmer in Alpine County be equal to an industrial worker in Los Angeles County under a "one man, one vote" system in which the urban, industrial area of Los Angeles alone controls nearly half the votes in the state legislature? In many instances, "one man, one vote" representation increases democratic equality by insuring that certain minorities cannot always block certain majorities. In others, it contributes to isolating certain individuals and socioeconomic groups as permanent minorities.

Although we cannot easily afford permanent minorities, it is also true that if we so arrange our electoral districts that a minority of voters controls a majority of the legislators, we substitute minority rule for majority rule. Similarly, if a minority is allowed to block the policy desires of the majority, as it can for instance if it controls one house of a two-house legislature, we have minority rule—at least in those areas where the majority wants change and the minority wants the status quo. The real trick of successful democratic politics is to give minorities sufficient strength to force certain concessions and compromises out of majorities as the cost of finally allowing the basic features of the majority's program to become law, without giving them so much strength that the majority is unable to pass the legislation it desires. The majoritarian will argue that any such arrangement is a betrayal of democracy because any "concession" to a minority is in fact a substitution of what the minority wanted for what the majority wanted no matter what nice language you dress it up in; but the preceding paragraphs have, hopefully, shown that majoritarianism is not synonymous with democracy and a betrayal of majoritarianism not necessarily a betrayal of democracy.

The Supreme Court's decisions on reapportionment prevent us from giving certain minorities an extra margin of representation that would insure their real participation in policy-making. As a result, these decisions have deprived us of one means of overcoming the dilemmas that arise when we realize that rule by the majority is not the same as rule by the people. Other means are available, and, in most states, previously overrepresented areas will still remain powerful enough to bargain relatively effectively—particularly when, as is very often true, the "majority" areas cannot put up a united front. Most questions of politics are questions of degree. The reapportionment decisions do not suddenly change ours from a minoritarian to a majoritarian political system; but they do change the balance of power between minorities and majorities and contribute to the general historical tendency of American government to become increasingly majoritarian.

The Reapportionment Case

Robert G. McCloskey

Robert G. McCloskey's article, written immediately after *Baker* v. *Carr*, traces the historical and legal problems underlying the 1962 decision. At that time it was impossible to determine exactly what the decision meant; from the actual wording of the opinions the Court might have been adopting any standard from a strict "one man, one vote" to an approach that would find any apportionment constitutionally valid for which the state legislatures could provide a rationale.

In the light of this uncertainty, McCloskey speculates on various standards short of "one man, one vote" and suggests one that he feels would be best. The later Court opinions go all the way in adopting a "one man, one vote" standard, but McCloskey's analysis is interesting because it points out the essential weakness in the Court's position. *Baker* v. *Carr* in effect eliminated the huge inequalities in districting for which there was no excuse in democratic theory. But the later decisions requiring "one man, one vote" create the problems of permanent minorities that we have just examined, particularly in making it impossible for the states to give added weight to rural areas in one of their houses. Indeed, as McCloskey points out, the majority cannot even choose to give a special position to isolated minorities through new state constitutional provisions.

If, subsequent to *Baker*, the Court had adopted some solution similar to that suggested by McCloskey, it could have both eliminated the unjustifiable inequalities and left sufficient flexibility in the state electoral systems to allow them to be used to insure some level of equality for the persons and groups who may otherwise fall into permanent minorities. The Supreme Court got rid of one kind of inequality in the electoral system by freezing another kind into it, although the Court could have eliminated existing inequalities *and* provided a means of handling future ones as well.

FOREWORD: THE REAPPORTIONMENT CASE

On March 26, 1962, the Supreme Court startled the nation with the announcement of its long-awaited decision in *Baker* v. *Carr*,[1] the *Reapportionment Case*. The alarums and excursions that ensued in the legal-political world exceeded anything evoked by a Supreme Court decision since 1954, and memory would have to reach back a good many years more to find another adequate comparison. Indeed, if we did not know better we might suspect the Justices of a conscious taste for the dramatic. For the decision came after several months of a term that had been, constitutionally speaking, rather uneventful; and the watchers in the stalls might have begun to feel that the author-players would coast for this term after the very considerable exertions of the last. This seemed a

"The Supreme Court, 1961 Term, Foreword: The Reapportionment Case" by Robert G. McCloskey, 76 *Harvard Law Review* 54 (1962). Copyright © 1962 by the Harvard Law Review Association. Reprinted by permission.

reasonable possibility, and a cautious spirit might have chosen it. But it is the ability to transcend the obvious and confound our expectations in such a moment that marks the authentic dramatist.

The judgment was attended by six separate opinions, including three concurrences and two dissents in addition to the opinion of the Court. This forest of prose will be explored more fully a little later. But it is well to have some of the main features of Mr. Justice Brennan's majority opinion before us at the outset.

The case involved an action under the Civil Rights Acts[2] brought by certain Tennessee voters on their own behalf and on behalf of others similarly situated and alleging that the present apportionment of the state legislature deprived them of their federal constitutional right to equal protection of the laws. A district court was asked for a declaratory judgment invalidating the 1901 state legislation on which the apportionment was based, for an injunction restraining the defendant election officials from holding an election under the existing system, and for a decree reapportioning the legislature, or in the alternative, for an order that the next election be held at large.[3] The argument, as ultimately presented by the complainants and by the United States, appearing as amicus curiae, was in essence that, although the Tennessee constitution provided for decennial apportionment of representatives and senators among counties and districts according to their respective numbers, the legislature had failed to make such a reapportionment since 1901; that because of population changes in the past sixty years the votes of the appellants had been unconstitutionally debased, since the equal protection clause forbids arbitrary and unreasonable apportionment of legislative seats. The starting point, it was said, for measuring an apportionment against this prohibition is *"per capita* equality of representation,"[4] and departures from that standard must rest on a rational foundation. The action had been dismissed by the district court on the grounds that the court lacked jurisdiction of the subject matter and that the complaint failed to state a claim upon which relief could be granted. These stated grounds reflected the district court's understanding of the "federal rule, as enunciated...by the Supreme Court...that the federal courts, whether from a lack of jurisdiction or from the inappropriateness of the subject matter for judicial consideration, will not intervene in cases of this type to compel legislative reapportionment."[5]

The Supreme Court held that the dismissal was error. The federal courts do possess jurisdiction of the subject matter; the appellants have stated a justiciable cause of action upon which they "would be entitled to appropriate relief"; and they do have standing to challenge the statute.[6] The issue presented is not, as the district court thought, a "political question" immune from judicial control. *Colegrove v. Green* and other supposed precedents have been misread on that point.[7] And the claim does not involve any of the characteristics that have caused the Court in the past to label a question "political" and deny jurisdiction. The cause was therefore remanded for trial and decision. It is perhaps worth emphasizing at this point that the Supreme Court offered the lower court no standards by which the decision should be reached and no hints about the remedy that might be appropriate if the plaintiffs prevailed. "Judicial standards under the Equal Protection clause," Justice Brennan said, "are well developed and familiar"[8] and it would be "improper now to consider what remedy would be most appropriate...."[9]

I

History can be an intractable wench, going her own way without regard to the paths we have envisioned for her, and one who writes contemporaneously about a Supreme Court term is uneasily aware of her capriciousness. There is no assurance that posterity will see the term as the present sees it, will concur with us in singling out the events that are noteworthy. Some little-observed horseshoe nail may have dropped by the way in the spring of 1962, and the future, with its advantage of hindsight, may decide that this was the really consequential incident of the season.

But with these concessions to an uncertain world duly registered, it must still be guessed that 1962 will appear to historians of the Supreme Court as the Year of the *Reapportionment Case.* By almost any criterion for assaying such matters this seems a fair conjecture. For one thing, no development since the *Segregation Cases*[10] has so focused the public eye on the doings of the Court. The publicity and popular interest evoked by a court decision may be among the less dependable of indices for evaluating its importance, but they cannot be left altogether out of the account. Those who will wear the boot are not perhaps the only judges of whether it will pinch when it is broken in, but their judgment commands our attention. Especially does this seem so when we reflect that a court decision can become, in a sense, what the public thinks it is. The public version of the Chief Justice's opinion in *Dred Scott*[11] was a very different thing from the opinion that he wrote, but it was the public version that helped to kindle the Civil War.

For another thing, it is hard to recall a decision in modern history which has had such an immediate and significant effect on the practical course of events, or—again excepting the *Segregation Cases* —which seems to contain such a potential for influencing that course in the future. The short-term response has been nothing short of astonishing. It has been as if the decision catalyzed a new political synthesis that was already straining, so to speak, to come into being. Not only federal judges, but state judges as well, have taken the inch or so of encouragement offered by the Supreme Court and stretched it out to a mile. Legislatures all over the country have been bidden to redistrict or to face the prospect of having the judiciary do the job for them. Under this spur, and sometimes in anticipation of it, a number of them have set going their laborious machinery of conflict and compromise. The shape of the apportionment plans that will emerge from this strange confluence of judicial and legislative power remains to be seen, but there can be no doubt that the American political world is stirring.

The long-term results are, of course, even more speculative, but the immediate reaction just described may cast a few shadows ahead. As we know, court decisions have not always generated such a ready—almost over-ready—spirit of compliance. When a decision fails to strike a responsive chord in the public breast, the tendency is at best to abide by its minimum compulsions grudgingly interpreted. The tendency suggested by early reactions to the reapportionment decision seems very different from this, and it may warrant the conjecture that the Court here happened to hit upon what the students of public opinion might call a latent consensus. It is quite true, as Justice Frankfurter reminds us,[12] that neither our past nor our present political institutions have treated numbers as the "basic" principle of representation. But institutions sometimes lag behind opinion, and it may be that most Americans have come to think of some version of the majority principle as at least the presumptive democratic standard. If so, the implied ratification of the standard in the *Reapportionment Case* may have struck them, in Jefferson's terms, as "the common sense of the subject," commanding their assent as "an expression of the American mind."[13] And the decision, even without further adumbration, may precipitate a train of events that will alter profoundly the nature of representation in American politics.

But this is speculation, not premonition, much less confident prophecy. For the present, there is no way of being sure about these and other possibly enduring effects—which political party will gain and which lose; whether the increment of electoral strength will be greater for suburbia or for central cities; whether the vitality of state government will be augmented or diminished; whether the cause of racial equality will be significantly advanced. The nature and scale of such repercussions will depend on imponderables and unforeseeables—including the substantial question whether and how the Supreme Court itself will elaborate the jurisdictional potential this decision created. The one thing that seems fairly certain is that seismic events will be continuing for some years to come.

II

The decision is also important to those who ply the lonely, slighted trade of tracing and unravelling the strands of Supreme Court doctrines, for it writes a new and salient chapter in the history of the timeworn doctrine of "political questions." In fact, although it would be too much to say that the chapter closes the book, we may legitimately wonder whether the doctrine it treats will now have a very lively future, for its viability as an aid to a policy of judicial self-restraint would seem to have diminished considerably.

This brings us back to Justice Brennan's majority opinion and to some of the dissents and concurrences that flanked it. The opening question for the Court was, of course, whether federal courts were barred altogether from entertaining such a suit, either at the threshold because of lack of jurisdiction of the subject matter or lack of standing, or just beyond the threshold because no judicially determinable duty had been asserted or no judicial protection for the claimed right could be devised. The first of these possible grounds for forbearance raised issues of constitutional and statutory authorization and of standing. The second plunged the Court explicitly into the issue of whether this cause, in the light of the Court's precedents and traditions, should be regarded as a "political question"; and that becomes the crux of the dialogue between the majority and the dissenters.

Justice Brennan's reading of the political question tradition contains a mystery or two, but it seems to run somewhat as follows. To begin with, he tells us, the record shows that a question has been recognized as political and therefore nonjusticiable only when it involved the problem of separation of powers—"the relationship between the judiciary and the co-ordinate branches of the Federal Government"[14]—or when there is "a lack of judicially discoverable and manageable standards for resolving it."[15] Indeed, some of his language might suggest that the applicability of the doctrine is strictly limited to causes which concern the power of the federal judiciary as against the power of the President or Congress; that the relationship between the federal judiciary and the state governments cannot raise a political question. But this can hardly be what is meant, for he elsewhere speaks of the possible lack of judicially discoverable standards as a factor to be considered in *Baker v. Carr* itself,[16] which concerned, of course, no coordinate branch of the federal government. So it must be that this is an independent factor: the absence of such standards could cause the Supreme Court to stamp a question as "political" no matter what branch of government—state or federal—was involved.

Nevertheless it seems fairly clear that for Justice Brennan "the lack of judicially discoverable and manageable standards" is the *only* reason that might cause the Court to call a question involving state governmental arrangements a political question. He is at pains to emphasize that claims do not become nonjusticiable simply because they touch upon matters of state governmental organization.[17] And the "formulations" he lists that may describe a political question seem all—again with the exception of the unmanageable standards item —concerned with intrafederal relationships, as are the precedents he examines in such fields as foreign affairs, the duration of hostilities, "validity of enactments," and the status of Indian tribes. The precedents treating the claim that state governmental forms violated the guaranty of a republican form of government might seem to point in the other direction, for such claims have been uniformly held nonjusticiable.[18] But the reason for this, as Justice Brennan sees it, has been that guaranty clause claims "involve those elements which define a 'political question.' "[19] These are, as elsewhere explained, unmanageable standards or the problem of intrafederal relationships (*i.e.*, the Court has withheld its hand out of a feeling that the guaranty clause was for Congress to enforce and not out of a feeling that matters of state governmental organization were intrinsically unfit for judicial control).

If the Court's analysis means what it appears to mean, the scope of the political question doctrine has been significantly narrowed. Admitting that the contours of the doctrine have been desperately hard to ascertain with confidence, three underlying ideas have seemed to run through it: the idea that the courts should not intervene in areas which, either by their nature or by constitutional language, are peculiarly committed to the President or Congress; or in which "standards meet for judi-

cial judgment" cannot be framed; or in which the "framework and political character" of government, (state or national) are called in question. No doubt the three have sometimes tended to run together— *e.g.*, the reluctance to interfere with the framework of government or to challenge Congress in a particular field is influenced by the uncertainty about standards to implement a policy of judicial supervision. But at the same time each of them has been thought to have a measure of independent force—the policy of letting "the people and their political representatives"[20] decide the root questions of the political framework has mirrored the feeling that these matters are too "high,"[21] too nakedly power-oriented, and perhaps too explosive for judicial control, quite apart from whether armchair ingenuity could devise standards that sounded plausibly applicable. It amounts to respect, either prudential or normative in origin, for the arrangements the political process has worked out for shaping the political process. It now appears that this respect will henceforth operate as a separate determinant only when the federal courts confront their peers—the President and the Congress—not when they confront the states.

No doubt this amputation will make the analytic problem somewhat simpler, for the idea just discussed has always been elusive and impalpable. The Court has taken jurisdiction in the past in a number of cases involving apportionment and other problems of state governmental organization, and though many of these are arguably distinguishable as Justice Frankfurter, dissenting, shows, their cumulative effect has been to weaken the premise that such problems are judicially ungovernable. Moreover the Court has from time to time plunged into maelstroms at least as "political" and turbulent as questions of state governmental organization are likely to be. Of course the conception has been that there is a subtle difference between the sense in which questions of national power to regulate commerce are "political" and the sense in which questions of apportionment are "political." Justice Frankfurter would presumably concede the Court's historic power to entertain the former questions, but would insist on drawing the line against judicial intrusion into "those large contests of policy...by which governments and the actions of governments are made and unmade."[22] But he himself admits that these are differences of degree and that "within a certain range of cases on a continuum, no standard of distinction can be found to tell between them."[23] They are differences that depend on "feel," on intuitions, and those who do not sense them cannot be persuaded of their meaningful existence. It is simpler to say that the mere fact of involvement in state governmental arrangements is irrelevant to the political question doctrine and go on to the residual inquiries: whether the matter under consideration involves a possible conflict with other branches of the federal government, or whether appropriate judicial standards are lacking. The former query answers itself with respect to the present case: *Baker v. Carr* does not present a "question decided, or to be decided, by a political branch of government coequal with this Court."[24] So the sole and determinative issue remaining is that of "judicially discoverable and manageable standards."[25]

But that issue, *mirabile dictu*, is not treated at all in the opinion of the Court. One sentence suffices to dismiss it:

"Judicial standards under the Equal Protection Clause are well developed and familiar, and it has been open to courts since the enactment of the Fourteenth Amendment to determine, if on the particular facts they must, that a discrimination reflects *no* policy, but simply arbitrary and capricious action."[26]

This is the moment toward which the whole course of the analysis has been directed. The cases have been reviewed, the citations have been multiplied so that other possible factors in the judgment can be cleared away and this factor can stand forth as the only one that need be considered. And then it is not considered. The very question on which the whole judgment has been made to hang is whether standards *are* "well developed and familiar" in this field; and now that question is answered by a simple and wonderfully pregnant "yes."

However, whether this keystone sentence quite carries the argumentative burden that falls on it or not, its implications for the future of the "political question" doctrine are sufficiently devastating. If the problem of state governmental organization as such no longer calls that doctrine into being, and if the problem of judicially manageable standards is obviated by an incantatory reference to terms like "equal protection," there is not a great deal left. Presumably it may survive in connection with the relationship of the federal courts to the President and Congress—in foreign relations for example. And for Justice Brennan at least, the guaranty clause is still confided to the care of Congress. But even this inference is somewhat clouded if we press the logic of *Baker v. Carr*, for if the guaranty clause intrinsically raises political questions, this cannot be because it "is not a repository of judicially manageable standards."[27] Its standards are not any more nebulous than those of the equal protection clause in this context. Indeed, as Justice Frankfurter says, the republican form of government issue and the equal protection issue are inextricably related halves of the same question, because the Court must decide what is the basic republican norm before deciding whether departures from it are unreasonable. So what exempts guaranty clause claims from judicial reach must be the possibility of conflict with "a political branch of government coequal with this Court"[28] and nothing else, since that is the only political question criterion not undermined by the opinion. While that criterion lasts the doctrine of political questions may retain some remnants of vitality, but its status as a major doctrine of our constitutional jurisprudence seems to be impaired beyond recovery.

With all respect to its age and ancestry, this may not be altogether a bad thing. The political question doctrine has been used in the past as a talismanic phrase to signal the fact that a subject was thought, for a variety of reasons, to be inappropriate for judicial control. It has been, that is, a kind of verbal redundancy in a general theory of judicial self-restraint, much as the old doctrine of "business affected with a public interest" was merely another way of saying that a price regulation was deemed "reasonable" under the due process clause. Such fictions designed to "beautify what is disagreeable to the sufferers,"[29] may once have been useful in that they allowed the Court to express an intuitive conclusion to abstain without explaining it. But as *Baker v. Carr* shows, they are two-edged, because they also permit a court to intervene, equally without explanation. Their mischief is, in short, that they may encourage those who live by them to bypass the thought process that is supposed to underlie them. In *Baker,* the focus on whether apportionment presented a "political question" enabled the Court to talk about everything but the real issue—which was whether the courts *ought* to enter this thicket. It is hard to mourn the enfeeblement of a doctrine that has served this obscurantist purpose.

III

That brings us to the final reason for regarding *Baker v. Carr* as a momentous occasion in constitutional history: its relevance to the developing contemporary debate over the proper scope of judicial review. In a sense, of course, that debate has been continuous since 1789, but in earlier days it has often been hampered by the insistence of the Court and many of its defenders that there was no choice, that the range and nature of judicial power were simply determined by the inescapable imperatives of the Constitution. A discussion can hardly proceed when the participants thus challenge the very premise of its existence. However, in the twentieth century this hindrance was at least partially eroded by scholarly skepticism, much of it from the Justices themselves. After Holmes and Brandeis and Stone, to mention only the dead, it was difficult to contend that the sovereign prerogative of choice between self-restraint and intervention was nonexistent. Although there might still be room to argue about the extent of the leeway the Court enjoyed, the way was open for fruitful consideration of how it ought to use the leeway it plainly had. The need for such considerations was all the more pressing after 1937 when it became evident that the Court, having abandoned most of its old authority in the economic field, was proceeding to stake out a substantial dominion in the area of civil rights. New tasks in a new historical context made it desirable to think anew the question of the Court's role in relation to the other branches of government.

Even so, the dialogue was slow to get going. From the Court itself Justice Stone and Justice Frankfurter gave it a promising start in the first *Flag Salute Case*,[30] but thereafter in that forum it developed fitfully and not very productively. Perhaps the Court is not the best place to carry on such a discussion, partly because the mystique of this venerable institution sometimes still inhibits plain talk, and partly because the adversary relationship between concurrers and dissenters encourages each side to argue as if the rightness of its own view is almost too obvious for discussion. At any rate, instead of proceeding as a dialogue should, in the direction of increased understanding and ultimate synthesis, this dispute has carried the participants farther apart to a point where competing assertions take the place of discussion. Justice Frankfurter has tried to join the issue more determinedly than most of the others, and his opinion in *Baker* is, as far as it goes, brilliant argumentation. But it is noteworthy that even he stops short of really explaining why courts should not tamper with legislative apportionment, why the standards devisable in this field are not "meet for judicial judgment." The evaluation evidently rests on his heavily documented insistence that history argues for a policy of judicial restraint and on his educated revulsion against such meddling with the stuff of politics. But the Court in recent times has shown little disposition to, bear the yoke of history against its own inclinations, and even one who respects the past may not be willing to surrender his judgment to it. And revulsion is often incommunicable to those who do not already share it.

Outside the Court, the dialogue was at length propelled into its present, active phase by Judge Learned Hand. He was uniquely well-cast for the part: as one of the most respected of American jurists, he was sure to be heeded when he declared that the Court has a choice, that the question of "when a court should intervene"[31] merits discussion; yet, not being himself on the Supreme Court, he could speak his mind freely. The most widely noticed rejoinder to Judge Hand came from Professor Wechsler.[32] He tried in a sense to cut the discussion off before it was well begun by arguing that both the duty and the limits of judicial intervention were predetermined by organic law; even the apparent discretion to abstain implied in the doctrine of political questions is, he said, illusory; the only justifiable basis for invoking that doctrine is that the constitutional text commits the subject to the political branches. But as Professor Bickel has remarked, the political question doctrine cannot be "domesticated" in this manner,[33] and neither can the broad issue of "when a court should intervene." It would set the understanding of constitutional law back several decades to contend that courts really do act, or fail to act, in response to inescapable external commands; and it is not likely that Professor Wechsler was offering this as an empirical observation. Rather he seemed to be saying that courts *ought* to proceed only in these terms. This is an interesting proposition, but it is doubtful that a tribunal so constrained could have played the Supreme Court's historical part; and it is equally doubtful that any future Court would bridle itself in such a fashion.

Nevertheless Wechsler, whatever his intentions, further animated the dialogue Hand had begun, because he went on to urge that the Court, when it does intervene, should make its judgments on the basis of "neutral principles." For him of course this prescription is logically related to his belief that the Court's jurisdiction is ordained rather than moulded, but the relationship is not necessarily inevitable. For the demand for "neutral principles" is a special way of saying that the Court should work only with "standards meet for judicial judgment" and the question whether such standards are discernible is, as *Baker v. Carr* shows, a major factor in the question of "when a court should intervene." It may be legitimate for the Court to base a decision to abstain on the inarticulable hunches that often define "prudence."[34] But the decision to intervene must rest on a predetermination that the subject will turn out to be judicially manageable. In short one can believe that the

Court has substantial discretion in defining the areas it will supervise and can still believe that its discretion should confine it to those areas where appropriate judicial criteria can be contrived.

IV

The question is then—to get back to the case at hand—whether the Court embarked in *Baker v. Carr* on a course in which such criteria are lacking. But an answer to this would depend in turn on the answer to two other questions: how is it decided whether a standard is meet for judgment by the Supreme Court of the United States; and, what *is* the course of development that *Baker* portends?

Surely the starting-point for an answer to the first of these questions is a conception that might be called "differentiation of function." In Justice Frankfurter's words: "The Court's authority—possessed neither of the purse nor the sword—ultimately rests on sustained public confidence in its moral sanction."[35] This confidence itself depends heavily on the idea that what judicial review adds to the governmental process is significantly different from what the political branches contribute. We need not pause now to inquire whether or to what degree this idea may be delusion; delusion or not, the idea is vital to the Court's position as "the ultimate organ of 'the supreme Law of the Land.' "[36] If the public should ever become convinced that the Court is merely another legislature, that judicial review is only a euphemism for an additional layer in the legislative process, the Court's future as a constitutional tribunal would be cast in grave doubt.

Nor need we decide here what all the factors are that contribute to this idea of the Court's differentness. For present purposes the relevant point is the supposition that the Court works with decision standards that are really, not just rhetorically, distinguishable from those a legislature characteristically applies. The distinction is elusive, and no single word can quite express it. "Impartial," "disinterested," "impersonal," "general"—which Mr. Wechsler tells us he considered[37]—will not quite serve. Nor will "neutral," which was his final choice; nor "detached,"[38] nor "objective."[39] Wechsler himself comes closer to the crux of the matter when he says that judicial criteria should be capable of being "framed and tested as an exercise of reason and not merely as an act of willfulness or will."[40] But even this formulation must be taken with the understanding that it involves "a matter of degree."[41] Legislators are not always strangers to the reasoning process; judges cannot always eliminate all quality of fiat from their decisions.[42] Perhaps the most we can say is that judges should

be thought of as striving more determinedly to reduce the element of fiat, that they must be more reluctant to reach the point where will alone rules.

The nature of this misty ideal may be clarified a little by a brief revisit to a decision that has probably received more nearly unanimous criticism than any other in the twentieth century—*Lochner v. New York*.[43] What, after all, was so bad about it apart from the fact that it reflected an economic theory later generations find distasteful? Two of its vices, apposite to our present problem, stand out. In the first place, it promulgated a constitutional value for which there was little or no detectable constitutional warrant: the value of freedom of contract, of *laissez faire*. Neither the language nor the intent of the Constitution supported this interpretation of its meaning. Indeed it was arguable that the kind of restraint it imposed was alien to the spirit in which the Constitution was framed. This objection is summarized aphoristically in two famous sentences of Justice Holmes' dissent: "The Fourteenth Amendment does not enact Mr. Herbert Spencer's Social Statics" and "...a constitution is not intended to embody a particular economic theory, whether of paternalism and the organic relation of the citizen to the State or of *laissez faire*."[44]

The second fault of *Lochner* was that it propounded a rule that could not be applied as "an exercise of reason." The Court did not lay it down that working hours were entirely exempt from state control; that would have been a palpable enough standard all right, but not even Justice Peckham could think it feasible. Under the "rule" announced, hours regulation was valid if the Court thought it reasonable and invalid if the Court thought it unreasonable; and no guidance whatever was provided for objectifying this discrimination. The only standard was the Court's value-loaded intuition that "the limit of the police power has been reached and passed...."[45]

The point is that the judgment criteria here employed are indistinguishable, even in degree, from those that characterize the legislative process. The ideal of "standards meet for judicial judgment" is that they possess the qualities the *Lochner* standards did not—that they be somehow plausibly rooted in constitutional language or intent, and that their application can be to some significant degree an "exercise of reason."

It would be idle to pretend that the Court has always adhered to this ideal, though to be sure many of the apparent departures from it can be extenuated. A specific intent to forbid racial segregation in public education cannot be wrung from the language or history of the fourteenth amendment, but history does suggest a general purpose hostile to legally enforced racial distinctions, and it further suggests that the differentiation in function between the Court and Congress in the implementation of this purpose was left to posterity for decision.[46] In the light of the nature of American constitutional history it is reasonable to assume that the Court was expected to play a part in effectuating this purpose. And the Court's fiat, if it is one, is more warrantable in such a field. Similar considerations may be relevant to the Court's disposition of controversies between states in a case like *Nebraska v. Wyoming*,[47] which Justice Douglas cites in support of his contention that "adjudication is often perplexing and complicated."[48] For these cases there is often no other means of resolution; deference to the political processes is not feasible. Here the Justices can fairly say that they act "not by authority of our competence but by force of our commissions."[49] It might even be contended that long-standing judicial custom can also have a bearing on the issue. The criteria historically employed to judge state laws impinging on interstate commerce—the "direct" or "undue" burden concepts for example[50]—are hardly amenable to precise, reasoned application. As an original question, it might be doubted whether judges were uniquely qualified to make such evaluations, but their assumption of authority to do so is more than a century old;[51] the passage of years may validate a power that would be hard to justify on other grounds.

Nevertheless there have, of course, been salient occasions in constitutional history when the Court has, without the benefit of such extenuating considerations, imposed on the other branches a standard which was neither inferable from the constitutional text, nor capable of objective, "reasoned" application. *Lochner* itself and its relatives in the field of substantive due process provide us with one such example. Another, more congenial to the post-1937 judicial generation, is the line of cases in which freedom of speech has been protected, particularly against state actions. It cannot be said that freedom of speech is any more clearly embodied in the mandatory language of the due process clause than was freedom of contract; and the intent of the framers about such matters is, at best, ambiguous.[52] Moreover, the balancing formula, which now enjoys ascendancy as the guiding standard in the field, is no more amenable to precise, reasoned application than were the old formulations like "business affected with a public interest."[53] The process of decision based on it is not easy to distinguish in principle from the legislative process.

The Court then has, it must be admitted, sometimes broken the ideal here described. This can serve to remind us that an institution of such vitality and of such historic antecedents will never be entirely cribbed and confined by any prescriptions we write for it. When the men who hold these lofty commissions see an evil that they believe imperatively calls for redress, they will on occasion strike out, with little regard for consistency or caution. So it is; and so it has been; and if history can validate their other prerogatives, it may validate this one as well. But even here a few qualifying points can still be made. For one thing, it is noteworthy that the modern Court has seemed a little uneasy about its jurisdiction in the free speech field. The balancing formula has been used primarily to uphold governmental authority.[54] In its free speech decisions invalidating governmental action the Court has often sought and found criteria that seemed more ponderable, more historical, more "judicial": the well-worn idea of federal preemption;[55] procedural concepts like vagueness;[56] familiar-sounding legal terms like "prior restraint."[57] Even Justice Black's insistence on "absolutes" in this area[58] is a left-handed acknowledgment that it is somehow inappropriate for the judiciary to operate free from the restrictions of concrete standards. And for another thing, it must be urged that a price is paid for each judicial venture into uncharted and unchartable seas, whether or not an analogue can be found in past or present judicial behavior. Each such venture tarnishes a little more the idea that the judicial process and the legislative process are distinguishable, and this idea, as has been said, is indispensable to judicial review. The idea can survive—has survived—a certain amount of this treatment, but there is no reason to think that it is ineradicable. A prudent court will seek always to minimize doctrinal developments that cut so close to the very fulcrum of judicial power.

v

As for the implications of *Baker*, they are for the moment almost completely uncertain. Strictly speaking, as Justice Stewart emphasizes in his concurrence,[59] the Court decided only that the appellants were entitled to present their claim that the equal protection clause was violated by the Tennessee apportionment: the federal courts were not barred from hearing it by the political question doctrine. Even the idea that the clause will be held to limit the states in some way is an inference —though an almost unavoidable one unless this whole elaborate structure of argument and counterargument is to be thought of as an adventure in futility. If we can trust common sense we must conclude that the Court will sooner or later declare what standards will be imposed to implement the jurisdiction it has now embraced. The possibilities seem to fall in two broad categories.

First there is a set of considerations that are, broadly speaking, "procedural" in character, *i.e.*, they relate to the question of how the decision was reached to apportion in the challenged manner. Here, as the situation in Tennessee itself suggests, the heart of the inquiry might be whether the ultimate constituent power was being allowed an adequate opportunity to express itself. It is certainly untrue that "one man, one vote" was regarded by the framers as an imperative basic principle for carrying on the day-to-day, year-to-year process of government; and it is at least dubious that any such principle became embodied in our constitutional tradition in the years that followed.[60] But it is beyond doubt that the framers acknowledged popular consent as the indispensable basis for setting up that process of government in the first place. Though the government might take various forms and possess various powers, those characteristics were *derived* from the consent of the governed. If this central principle, so plain in the Declaration, was not expressed in the explicit language of the Constitution, it is because after 1776 it was taken for granted. Its claim to be a fundamental principle of the Constitution is about as solid as any claim could well be.

All this is relevant to the Tennessee-case facts as alleged. There is, it seems, no provision for popular initiative in Tennessee.[61] The procedure for inaugurating a constitutional amendment is locked in the hands of the legislature chosen under the existing apportionment system. This might itself raise a question as to whether the channels of popular consent were being kept open; but in this case the doubt is compounded by the fact that the present apportionment, ordained by the legislature in 1901, is grossly at odds with the standard set by that last expression of the popular will. The constituent power is not only being thwarted from re-expressing itself; it is being flouted.

It seems possible then that the standards ultimately established under the fourteenth amendment could be focused on matters like these. If there has been a significant passage of time since the last constituent decision on apportionment, and if population shifts in the interval have substantially altered the distribution of legislative seats, and if the channels of popular access to the issue are obstructed—the present apportionment might be held to violate the fourteenth amendment. But no constitutional question could be raised as to the actual, substantive nature of the apportionment, if the popular will had expressed itself or possessed adequate means for doing so.

The second possibility is that the courts might go behind these procedural considerations and undertake to approve or disapprove the actual distribution of legislative seats. They might start, as has been suggested, from a presumption in favor of per capita equality of representation and might then proceed to evaluate departures from that norm. Such departures would be required, however, to be "reasonable" both in basis and in degree. "[G]eography, economics, urban-rural conflict"[62] and various other nonlegal bases can make some claim to historical support and might conceivably be allowable within limits. But it would be the responsibility of the courts to decide *how much* departure from the norm of equality would be "rational"; and at what point such variations would become "arbitrary and capricious."

Either of these courses of judicial action is at least imaginable on the basis of the opinions in *Baker v. Carr*. Justice Brennan's majority opinion, as has been said, leaves the issue wide open. His only reference to the question of criteria is the statement that judicial standards under the equal protection clause are "well developed and familiar," but he goes on to remark that "it has been open to courts since the enactment of the Fourteenth Amendment to determine...that a discrimination reflects *no* policy, but simply arbitrary and capricious action."[63] The italics are his, and they may be significant. They could mean that an apportionment will still be presumed valid if it reflects *some* policy determination by the state, and that the Court will not undertake to judge the determination on substantive grounds. Even if this is too much to squeeze from a single italicized word, the fact remains that the Brennan opinion commits the Court to no particular kind of criteria in future cases. This is also true of Justice Stewart's opinion. And Justice Clark, though he embarks on a daring arithmetical enterprise in substantive standard-setting, plainly says that he would not do so if the people of the state had been given any other means for obtaining the apportionment they might want.[64] If he had put the horse before the cart, he would have had no need to reach the substantive question at all—an apportionment system's validity would depend on whether it had been established, or could be altered, by the popular will. Only Justice Douglas, among the majority, appears to have no hesitation at all about plunging into the question of substantive standards. The dissenters, Justices Frankfurter and Harlan, would, of course, prefer that the Court stay out of the apportionment quagmire altogether, but their strictures against the majority holding lean heavily on the conviction that courts are unequipped to weigh the substantive factors that enter into the question of political districting.

VI

Assuming then that the question of standards is open and yet assuming further that some standards will be adumbrated in pursuance of the doctrinal swerve in *Baker v. Carr*, what should those standards be? Should the Court undertake a *Lochner*esque responsibility for defining the substantive constitutional norm (*e.g.*, "one man, one vote") and for determining whether each departure from the norm is "rational" or "capricious"? Or might it better restrict itself to the "procedural" considerations outlined above—chiefly the question whether the constituent power had expressed itself or had been given fair opportunity to do so? Suppose, to be concrete about it, that an organic apportionment principle has recently been ratified by popular vote, or that adequate procedures for initiating such a principle are available if "an aroused popular conscience"[65] should develop. Or suppose, as in the Tennessee case, that the legislature is ignoring the constitutional mandate that does exist, but that there is, as there is not in Tennessee, a provision for direct popular legislation. Should the courts go beyond these assurances that the principle of popular consent is unthwarted, and judge the rationality of the apportionment system itself?

The reasons for believing they should not are weighty. The standards for such a judgment are not inferable from the constitutional language or purpose, nor is the judicial authority to prescribe them vindicated by custom. We must assume, as the majority of the Court seems to assume, that they might make room for some consideration of geography, of insular minorities, of economics and of other historically familiar factors in establishing a noninvidious distribution of voting strength. It is hard to see how the process of balancing these complexities and subtleties could be reduced to anything even resembling "an exercise of reason," how it could reflect anything more than a subjective ipse dixit. It is equally hard to see how the judicial process thus conceived could differ from the legislative process unless it would be by virtue of an abstract moralism that ignored reality. If the courts are to invade the center of this thicket, they must be prepared to grapple with the problems that inhabit it; and if they do, they are acting as legislators. As has been suggested above, the judiciary may sometimes feel constrained to act this part in pursuit of an ideal it regards as transcendent. But it should do so as seldom as a sober conscience will permit and only when a more "judicial," more restrained alternative is unavailable.

Here there is such an alternative. A rule that focused only on the opening up of the procedures of popular consent would not be above criticism. It would be novel in its application to this subject, but then the subject itself is novel. It would pose ticklish problems of remedy; but the basic decision that the subject is justiciable is responsible for that; and at least this kind of rule would not thrust the judiciary into the anomalous task of remapping election districts on its own account.[66]

On the other hand such an approach would rest on an arguably valid constitutional base; and it would provide the judiciary with palpable, fathomable criteria of decision. Questions of degree would still arise as they always must in the law: the judgment process would not become automatic. But the range of factors to be considered would be channeled; the evaluation of them would be communicable. There is a vast difference between the question whether the constituent power has had a fair opportunity to make a decision and the question whether the decision itself was substantively fair. It is comparable to the difference between asking whether a man had a fair hearing before he was hanged and asking whether it was just to hang him at all. The one question is the kind that courts can handle as well, and sometimes better, than the "political" agencies of government. The second question carries the judiciary into an uncircumscribed realm of moral and practical choices that is indistinguishable from the legislative realm and in which judicial competence to judge wisely is something less than self-evident.

There is a further, final reason for believing that the Court should content itself with this approach to its newly assumed task. It has to do with an observation made in the opening paragraphs of this commentary: that the *Reapportionment Case* seems to have generated an astonishing spirit of compliance and that this may indicate that the decision has activated a latent consensus in American opinion. It must be pleasant for the Justices, who have been vilified so much in recent years, to find a major decision so kindly received. The preceptor is always gratified by willing students. But before they proceed to the next lesson, they would be well advised to speculate about the precise nature of this consensus they seem to have aroused. Speculation it must be, for there are few certainties about such matters. But if the past is any guide, we can guess that the agreement consists, not of dogmas about how government should be organized, but of the underlying dogma that the people should be free to establish the governmental forms they want. Insofar as the reapportionment decision implied an affirmation of that dogma, its reception is not surprising. But if the judiciary should go beyond the premise of popular consent and should attempt to prescribe "from its own bosom"[67] what the populace may consent to, the climate might alter drastically. Then indeed it might turn out that this new development, which began with such bright promise, had impaired "the Court's position as the ultimate organ of the 'Supreme Law of the Land.'"[68]

Footnotes

[1]369 U.S. 186 (1962).
[2]Rev. Stat. §§ 722, 1979 (1875), 42 U.S.C. §§ 1988, 1983 (1958).
[3]Brief for the United States as Amicus Curiae on Reargument, pp. 2–6, Baker v. Carr, 369 U.S. 186 (1962).
[4]*Id.* at 26.
[5]Baker v. Carr, 179 F. Supp. 824, 826 (M.D. Tenn. 1959).
[6]369 U.S. at 197–98.
[7]*Id.* at 232–34.
[8]*Id.* at 226.
[9]*Id.* at 198.
[10]Brown v. Board of Educ., 347 U.S. 483 (1954); Bolling v. Sharpe, 347 U.S. 497 (1954).
[11]Scott v. Sandford, 60 U.S. (19 How.) 393 (1857).
[12]369 U.S. at 301 (dissenting opinion).
[13]Becker, The Declaration of Independence 25–26 (2d ed. 1958), quoting from 7 The Writings of Thomas Jefferson 304 (1869).
[14]369 U.S. at 210.
[15]*Id.* at 217.
[16]*Id.* at 226.
[17]See especially *id.* at 218.
[18]See cases cited 369 U.S. at 218–26.
[19]*Id.* at 218.
[20]Luther v. Borden, 48 U.S. (7 How.) I, 51 (1849) (dissenting opinion of Woodbury, J.), quoted in Baker v. Carr, 369 U.S. at 296 (dissenting opinion of Frankfurter, J.).
[21]McCloskey, *The McCarran Act and the Doctrine of Arbitrary Power*, 4 Public Policy 228, 244-45 (Friedrich & Galbraith ed. 1953); Finkelstein, *Judicial Self-Limitation*, 37 Harv. L. Rev. 338, 345 (1924).
[22]369 U.S. at 287 (dissenting opinion).
[23]*Id.* at 283.
[24]*Id.* at 226.
[25]*Id.* at 217.
[26]*Id.* at 226.
[27]*Id.* at 223.
[28]369 U.S. at 226.
[29]Tyson & Bro. v. Banton, 273 U.S. 418, 446 (1927) (dissenting opinion of Holmes, J.).
[30]Minersville School Dist. v. Gobitis, 310 U.S. 586, 601 (1940) (Frankfurter, J., for the Court, Stone, J., in dissent), overruled by West Virginia State Bd. of Educ. v. Barnette, 319 U.S. 624 (1943).

[31]Hand, The Bill of Rights I (1958).
[32]Wechsler, *Toward Neutral Principles of Constitutional Law*, 73 Harv. L. Rev. I (1959).
[33]Bickel, *Foreword: The Passive Virtues, The Supreme Court, 1960 Term*, 75 Harv. L. Rev. 40, 46 (1961).
[34]Bickel, *supra* note 33, at 46.
[35]369 U.S. at 267 (dissenting opinion).
[36]*Ibid.*
[37]Wechsler, Principles, Politics and Fundamental Law at xiii (1961).
[38]369 U.S. at 267 (dissenting opinion of Frankfurter, J.). His word is "detachment."
[39]Braden, *The Search for Objectivity in Constitutional Law*, 57 Yale L. J. 571 (1948).
[40]Wechsler, *supra* note 32, at II.
[41]369 U.S. at 283 (dissenting opinion of Frankfurter, J.).
[42]Fuller, *Reason and Fiat in Case Law*, 59 Harv. L. Rev. 376 (1946).
[43]198 U.S. 45 (1905).
[44]*Id.* at 75.
[45]*Id.* at 58.
[46]Bickel, *The Original Understanding and the Segregation Decision*, 69 Harv. L. Rev. I (1955).
[47]325 U.S. 589 (1945).
[48]369 U.S. at 245 (concurring opinion).
[49]West Virginia State Bd. of Educ. v. Barnette, 319 U.S. 624, 640 (1943).
[50]Stern, *The Problems of Yesteryear—Commerce and Due Process* in Essays in Constitutional Law 150 (McCloskey ed. 1957).
[51]Wilson v. Black Bird Creek Marsh Co., 27 U.S. (2 Pet.) 245 (1829); Cooley v. Board of Wardens, 53 U.S. (12 How.) 299 (1851).
[52]Fairman, *Does the Fourteenth Amendment Incorporate the Bill of Rights? The Original Understanding*, 2 Stan. L. Rev. 5 (1949).
[53]Munn v. Illinois, 94 U.S. 113 (1877); Tyson & Bro. v. Banton, 273 U.S. 418 (1927).
[54]*E.g.*, Braden v. United States, 365 U.S. 431 (1961); Wilkinson v. United States, 365 U.S. 399 (1961); Barenblatt v. United States, 360 U.S. 109 (1959); Uphaus v. Wyman, 360 U.S. 72 (1959); American Communications Ass'n v. Douds, 339 U.S. 382 (1950).
[55]Pennsylvania v. Nelson, 350 U.S. 497 (1956).
[56]Winters v. New York, 333 U.S. 507 (1948); Joseph Burstyn, Inc. v. Wilson, *supra* note 56.
[57]Near v. Minnesota, 283 U.S. 697 (1931); Joseph Burstyn, Inc. v. Wilson, *supra* note 56.
[58]Black, *The Bill of Rights*, 35 N.Y.U.L. Rev. 865 (1960).
[59]369 U.S. at 265.
[60]*Id.* at 301–24 (dissenting opinion of Frankfurter, J.).
[61]369 U.S. at 193, n.14.
[62]369 U.S. at 269 (dissenting opinion of Frankfurter, J.).
[63]*Id.* at 226.
[64]*Id.* at 258–59.
[65]*Id.* at 270 (dissenting opinion of Frankfurter, J.).
[66]In the case of a state with a present apportionment grossly at variance with the standard set by the last expression of the constituent power, as in Tennessee, the court might give the legislature reasonable time to conform with those standards, under threat of an alternative of holding the next election at large. If, because of population changes and shifts, there was reason to believe that the state constitutional standards might themselves be superannuated, and if the electorate had no access to a remedy, the court might require that the machinery of popular reconsideration

be set in motion within a reasonable time, again under the threat that an election would otherwise be held at large. In the perhaps unlikely event that the legislature failed to act in response to that threat, the election would have to be held at large. But then the apportionment plan voted by a legislature so elected might itself be held to be a sufficiently reliable reflection of the popular will on the question. Drastic as the remedy of election at large is from the viewpoint of the state, its virtue from the judicial point of view is that it would spare the courts the inappropriate and burdensome task of acting as apportionment boards for the nation.

[67]Hand, *The Contribution of an Independent Judiciary to Civilization*, in THE SPIRIT OF LIBERTY 125 (1959).

[68]369 U.S. at 267 (dissenting opinion of Frankfurter, J.).

Selection **9**

Some Comments on the Reapportionment Cases

Paul G. Kauper

As the title of Paul G. Kauper's article indicates, it is not a full-scale study, but rather a series of reflections on the course of the reapportionment decisions written after "one man, one vote" had become clearly established as the rule for all such cases. It is particularly valuable for its description of the cases between *Baker* v. *Carr* and the Reapportionment Cases discussed in Robert G. Dixon's article, which appears later in this chapter.

Any appraisal of the Supreme Court's decisions in the legislative reapportionment cases must necessarily distinguish between the basic policy ingredients and social consequences of the decisions on the one hand, and the question whether the results were reached by a proper exercise of judicial power on the other. Respecting the first of these considerations, I have no difficulty identifying the social advantages accruing from these decisions. Because of the stress on the population principle, the decisions will afford a greater voice to urban interests, will make the legislative process more responsive to current needs of particular concern to urban dwellers, will force the states to adhere more faithfully to standards that, in part at least, they have already set for themselves, and, in vitalizing the processes of state government, hopefully will contribute to the strength and integrity of our federal system. These plus considerations must be weighed against the risk that the kind of apportionment now required by judicial mandate will subject various kinds of minority interests to the overriding concerns of well-organized majorities and against the further consideration that the adoption of a single rule of apportionment, frozen into the Constitution by judicial interpretation, may preclude consideration of other and varied schemes that are responsive to the extensive, expert thinking that has gone into the subject. At this point, however, it may be conceded that the immediately discernible social advantages accruing from the decisions outweigh the more speculative disadvantages.

But whether these results were appropriately achieved through the exercise of judicial power is another matter, and it is to this question that my comments are addressed. The Court's decisions deal with a problem that is essentially political: namely, what are the proper standards for legislative representation. Admittedly, the decisions are revolutionary in character, and here I speak particularly of the recent state legislative reapportionment cases. These decisions, lacking support in judicial precedent, force the states to depart from legislative apportionment patterns that have had the sanction of history and from schemes that have been approved by the electors of the states through their own constitutional processes. Moreover, the implementation of the Court's decisions has had the effect of giving federal and state courts a field day in using their equity powers with an almost cavalier disregard of the legislative power and of the orderly processes of government. We are being treated to an unprecedented assertion of judicial

"Some Comments on the Reapportionment Cases" by Paul G. Kauper, 63 *Michigan Law Review* 243 (1964). Reprinted by permission of the Michigan Law Review Association.

supremacy. These consequences give ground for pause before standing up to give three cheers for the decisions.

EVOLUTION OF THE ONE MAN-ONE VOTE RULE

Baker v. Carr[1] opened this new chapter of judicial adventurism. That decision was understandable: I have no basic quarrel with the proposition that a state apportionment scheme is subject to judicial examination under the Constitution. The situation in Tennessee presented a particularly appealing case, since the state legislature had failed to act in accordance with the mandate of the state constitution and the state constitutional system provided no effective opportunity for redress through the processes of popular referendum or initiative.

The real difficulty presented by *Baker*, it appears to me, was the Court's reliance upon the equal protection clause as the basis for judicial examination. It is difficult to avoid Mr. Justice Frankfurter's conclusion, stated in his dissent, that the Court, in the name of equal protection, was in effect opening up the question of what constitutes a republican form of government for judicial examination.[2] This is the central issue in these cases —what form of apportionment is compatible with a representative form of government—and the guarantee of a republican form of government is the explicit constitutional provision relevant to the problem. But, the emphasis on equal protection and its subsequent development in terms of a discriminatory impairment of the right to vote paved the way for a judicial treatment that centered upon what I regard as a specious conception of personal right rather than upon the institutional aspect of the problem. This was not a necessary consequence, however, since the equal protection standard was broad and flexible enough to permit an inquiry directed to the question whether a state apportionment scheme was unreasonable or arbitrary when measured by a general standard of what is essential to the processes and institutions of representative government.

The later decision of *Gray v. Sanders*,[3] holding invalid the county unit system employed in Georgia to count votes cast for state officers in a statewide election, understandably rested upon an equal protection ground. Once a state has determined the boundaries of a voting district (for the purpose of this election the state was the district) it is difficult to defend the rationality of a subclassification that deliberately weights the votes cast on a county basis, thereby giving to some electors a disproportionate voting power in the choice

of state officers. Mr. Justice Douglas stated that "the conception of political equality from the Declaration of Independence, to Lincoln's Gettysburg Address, to the Fifteenth, Seventeenth and Nineteenth Amendments can mean only one thing —one person, one vote."[4] *Gray* dealt with a very special question that did not go to the heart of the legislative apportionment problem. Thus, the holding in *Gray* could be kept within narrow limits. But the broad statement by Mr. Justice Douglas was expansible and capable of being forged into a principle premised upon personal right, which, if carried far enough, would furnish an almost automatic answer to the legislative apportionment problem.

Next in progression was *Wesberry v. Sanders*,[5] wherein the Court committed itself to the one man-one vote principle (whatever this may mean in this context), so far as apportionment of the House of Representatives of the Congress of the United States is concerned. This decision was based upon interpretation of article I of the Constitution, which provides that Representatives shall be elected by the people of the several states. Starting with this constitutional requirement, the Court leaps to the dubious conclusion that districts set up under state law must, as far as practicable, be equal in population. Mr. Justice Black found support for this conclusion in the proceedings of the Constitutional Convention and in the views of prominent figures in the early history of the country. Mr. Justice Harlan, in his dissent, does an effective job in demolishing Mr. Justice Black's historical argument by establishing that those historical facts prove nothing more than that it was intended that representation of a state in the lower house of Congress should be determined on a population basis as distinguished from the Senate where each state was to have two representatives regardless of population. Moreover, as Mr. Justice Harlan points out, article I of the Constitution commits to Congress the ultimate authority to legislate with respect to congressional districting. Congress did expressly exercise this power for some years and did require voting districts to be approximately equal. But, it later repealed this legislation and thereby left the fixing of congressional districts to the discretion of state legislatures. There is much strength in Mr. Justice Harlan's argument that Congress, with ultimate authority in this matter, has made a decision within the sphere of its constitutional competence, that this determines the status of the question as a "political question," and that there is, therefore, no room at this point for judicial intervention. It should be kept in mind, in this connection, that the Court in its earlier opinion in *Baker* had said that it was the relationship between the judiciary and the coordinate branches of the federal government that had given rise to the political question concept, thereby strongly intimating that the Court would not impose its will in an area committed by the Constitution to congressional discretion. Yet this aspect of *Baker* is promptly disregarded in *Wesberry*, which dealt with a question committed to a coordinate branch of the federal government. *Wesberry* can possibly be interpreted to mean that the standard stated by the Court is the one to be followed by the states in the absence of standards stated by Congress. Since the Constitution requires representation of the states in the House of Representatives to be based upon population, it is not unreasonable for the Court to say that equality of districts in terms of voting population should be the general rule unless different or more flexible standards are prescribed by Congress. This, however, is a strained interpretation of the *Wesberry* opinion, which, on its face, quite clearly demonstrates that the Court has now fixed a single constitutional standard for congressional districting and that there is no room for congressional legislation that would permit deviation from this standard. Given this latter, more realistic construction, *Wesberry* does represent a substantial judicial intrusion upon congressional power and a judicial decision on a "political question" as the Court defined that concept in *Baker v. Carr*.

A feature of the *Wesberry* case that deserves special attention is the emphasis in the latter part of Mr. Justice Black's opinion on the right to vote.[6] He there points out that the right to vote for federal offices is a constitutionally created right under article I, and he makes it clear that, in his opinion, this right to vote is unconstitutionally abridged or restricted unless congressional seats in a state are equally apportioned on a population basis. From the right to vote, he deduced the one man-one vote principle, which in turn is the key to equality in representation. There is a gap in this reasoning. No one was contending in this case that qualified voters were denied a right to vote for congressmen, and it was equally clear that every qualified voter had one vote. The right that the Court relied upon was not the right to vote, but rather a personal right to a numerically determined proportionate share of political influence. But the Constitution does not speak of such a right. Of course, there is a constitutionally created right to vote for federal officers, and Congress may act to protect this right by punishing fraud, corruption, and intimidation at the polls; the cases cited by Mr. Justice Black prove no more than this. It is another thing to say that this right to vote fur-

nishes the key to legislative apportionment problems.

It is also easy to see that, if the right to vote, expanded into a right to equal representation based on numbers, furnishes the basic premise in these cases, the Court has equipped itself with a simple answer to the apportionment problem. By assuming this question-begging premise, the Court's conclusion is clearly indicated. This became evident when the Court handed down its decisions in the batch of state legislative reapportionment cases at the end of the recent term.[7] According to these cases, only one general standard—the population standard—is constitutionally permitted in apportioning both houses of a state legislature. This in turn means that population must be apportioned to the several voting districts on an equal basis, so far as practicable, and that any deviation therefrom will be permitted only when a rational necessity for the deviation is shown. With one blow the Court struck at the heart of the well-established, traditional bicameral system of state government. Even more surprising was the Court's decision in the Colorado case, setting aside a legislative apportionment scheme that had been submitted to and approved by the electors in a free and open election. The Court felt it necessary to assume a guardian's role in order to protect the voters against themselves and in order to establish the Court's own predilection as to the kind of political system that our Constitution should sanction, even though this frustrated the expression of the popular will.

PROBLEMS OF ANALYSIS AND APPLICATION

As stressed earlier, the basic issue in these cases is what kind of representation processes and institutions are required to assure a government that rests upon the will of the people. This issue opens up a large and complex area involving many theories and modes of representation. Although the Constitution does not provide express answers for the states, the Court devised a single and simple solution: all representation must be based upon population alone, and population must be equally apportioned to the several districts.

My basic criticism is that the Court, by judicial fiat, is projecting a simple, but absolute, solution to a complex problem. I find nothing in history or political theories of representation to support the idea that representation on the basis of population equally apportioned is the only system consistent with either republican or democratic ideas of government. If effectuation of majority rule is the premise underlying this exclusive theory of representation, then why not carry through to the logical conclusion and require state-wide election of all legislators? Or, if effective counting of each man's vote is the objective, then why not say that the Constitution requires a system of proportionate voting and representation? To raise these questions is to suggest the complexity of the problem and the range of possible solutions. The basic scheme of representation goes to the heart of a state's political processes: how political strength and influence shall be distributed and diffused. This is a matter that should be left to the people of the state to determine through their own constitutional processes, subject to a judicial check to determine whether the system chosen employs standards that are constitutionally objectionable, such as race or religion, or is otherwise so arbitrary or capricious that it cannot fit into any rational scheme of representation. Population, geography, the political organization of the state, the nature and variety of economic interests, and the diffusion or concentration of voting strength are all factors that are relevant in determining whether a state by its apportionment scheme has worked out a fair and balanced scheme of representation responsive to the state's own characteristics. The fact that the people of a state in an open election have by majority vote adopted a scheme that they deem responsive to the state's needs and characteristics is also a consideration that should carry substantial weight in any judicial determination of the issue. And surely history should not be lightly disregarded. One may cheerfully concede that the pattern established for the Congress of the United States does not in itself prove the validity of any particular apportionment scheme adopted by the states; yet, the long established state bicameral legislative scheme, which gives effect to varying theories of representation as between the two houses, affords persuasive evidence of what we heretofore have understood the republican form of government to include.

The Court uses the equal protection clause as the formal vehicle for condemning apportionment schemes that do not satisfy the population standard. Its conclusion is that a system that does not afford equal representation to voters results in discriminatory denial of the right to vote. The right to vote emerges, then, as a critical element. This raises interesting questions. For example, what is the constitutional source of the right to vote? Article I assures the right to vote for federal officers. The right to vote for state officers must have its source elsewhere. The Court refers to it as a fundamental right.[8] As a fundamental right, it must have its source either in the substantive rights interpretation of the due process clause or in the guarantee of a republican form of government.

Actually, in applying the equal protection clause, it is not necessary to show that there is a discriminatory denial of a *fundamental* right. It is enough to show that a person is denied the equal enjoyment of a right, privilege, or immunity by reference to an *irrational classification*. But, the Court chose to rely upon its characterization of the right to vote as fundamental in constructing its theory under the equal protection clause: The more fundamental the right, the more important it is that the Court inject its theory as to the kinds of classifications that may be used to restrict this right; an apportionment system that does not rest upon equal apportionment of population dilutes and debases the fundamental right to vote and, hence, results in discriminatory treatment. It dilutes and debases the right because it does not afford equal representation.

Here again, the right to vote gets tangled up with the Court's theory of proper representation. There can be no quarrel with the proposition that the Court should look carefully at classifications that determine a person's right to vote; however, what is really involved in these cases is not a discriminatory denial of the right to vote, but rather a violation of the judicially created right to a system that recognizes numbers as the only basis for representation. That the right to vote drops out of the picture at this point is evidenced by the fact that the Court, in speaking of population as the proper standard, does not speak of voting population but instead speaks of the total population of a given district.

By reading all that it does into the right to vote, the Court automatically reaches its conclusion under the equal protection argument. For, if the right to vote carries with it a personal right to a proportionate share of political influence determined only upon the basis of numbers by the ratio of one man's vote to the total population in the state, then, of course, any system of apportionment not based upon equal apportionment of population must necessarily fail. The right that the Court creates leaves no room for a judicial inquiry into whether a legislative apportionment scheme can be fitted into a rational scheme of representation by reference to the characteristics and problems of a particular state. The Court, by the premise it postulates on the nature of the right, assumes the conclusion respecting the equal protection argument. Indeed, by positing this right the equal protection argument becomes merely a facade that embellishes the conclusion. Thus, the decisions turn less upon equal protection than upon a new conception of fundamental right or upon the Court's implied understanding of what constitutes a republican form of government.

Ample precedent supports the idea that legislative classification meets equal protection demands if it rests upon a rational basis by reference to the purpose of the legislation. According to the established theory of equal protection, a voter's right to equal treatment is satisfied if he is treated equally with other voters within a class established pursuant to a rational theory of legislative representation. As Mr. Justice Stewart pointed out, a wide variety of considerations may be taken into account by the legislature or by the people themselves in determining the basis of representation.[9] In deciding that the Constitution permits only representation based upon population equally apportioned, the Court makes a policy decision and expresses its preference for one exclusive theory of apportionment.

It may be argued that, once the Court had embarked upon the process of examining apportionment schemes, it had a bear by the tail and had no choice in the end except to adopt a population standard, since any inquiry into the rationality of an apportionment scheme would have required the Court to articulate and weigh the factors determining rationality, whereas the population factor furnishes a clear-cut and simple standard. This simple solution to complex problems by the invocation of absolutes has its appeal, whether in politics or in law. As Dean Griswold has pointed out, reliance upon absolutes avoids the necessity of the kind of judgment that appraises all of the relevant considerations.[10] Yet, it is this kind of judgment that goes to the heart of the judicial process. Surely the Court has the resourcefulness to conduct a meaningful review of state apportionment schemes, based upon the wide thinking and literature on the subject, without having to make a radical break with the system and theories that find ample support in American experience and practice.

Justices Stewart and Clark demonstrated in their opinions that the Court could have made an inquiry into legislative apportionment schemes without setting up any single, judicially formulated standard and that such an inquiry would have been meaningful and would not have meant a judicial rubber-stamping of just any apportionment scheme or practice.[11] According to Mr. Justice Stewart, the equal protection clause demands but two basic attributes of any plan for state legislative apportionment. "First, it demands that in the light of the state's own characteristics and needs, the plan must be a rational one. Secondly, it demands that the plan must be such as not to

permit the systematic frustration of the will of a majority of the electorate of the state. I think it is apparent that any plan of legislative apportionment which could be shown to reflect no policy, but simply arbitrary and capricious action or inaction, and that any plan which could be shown systematically to prevent ultimate effective majority rule, would be invalid under accepted Equal Protection Clause standards."[12]

Mr. Justice Stewart's pragmatic approach makes much sense. It suggests a meaningful judicial inquiry that is empirical because it examines actual data to see what are the problems of representation faced by a state; it recognizes the variety of interests that may be appropriately considered by a state in its apportionment scheme; it preserves the primacy of the states in making choices in an area where the Constitution does not dictate a single formula; and it sets an outer limit on choice by reference to a concept of "ultimate effective majority rule." I find it regrettable that the majority saw fit instead to impose a single standard that incorporates "their own notions of wise political theory."[13] It strains credulity to suggest that this result is required by the Constitution.

Any comments upon the Court's decisions must take account also of the extraordinary authority assumed by some lower federal courts and some state courts in dealing with apportionment issues. Never before has the country witnessed such a spectacle of judicial power run riot. Courts have issued ultimata to legislatures and, in a few instances, have themselves undertaken to prescribe proper apportionment plans. This bold intrusion of the judiciary into the apportionment struggle invites the risk that the courts, wittingly or unwittingly, may become involved in the process of political gerrymandering. Moreover, in this election year, courts, in a scramble to implement the Supreme Court's decisions, have displayed a reckless impatience and imprudence in forcing adoption of new schemes without opportunity for careful consideration and at the expense of orderly election processes. For this chaotic state of affairs the Supreme Court must assume some responsibility. Its failure to establish standards in *Baker* created a situation that led lower courts to shift for themselves. What is more important, the Court could have firmly and effectively directed the lower courts to proceed in an orderly and deliberate way in implementing the new constitutional principle.

SOME CONCLUDING OBSERVATIONS

The reapportionment cases again reveal the dilemma of judicial review in a democratic society. As long as a court is vested with the power to review legislation, the temptation is present to use judicial power as a means of creating constitutional policy in accordance with the Court's conception of the ideals served by the Constitution or in accordance with what the Court regards to be wise policy as determined by its own predilections and preferences. To adapt constitutionally stated policy to new conditions is one thing; to create new constitutional policy in the guise of judicial interpretation is another.

It may well be that the new constitutional principle forged by the Court is a good one. As stated at the outset, the total consequences are likely to be salutary. Perhaps we should say that representation based upon equal apportionment of population affords the only permissible basis of representation in a system that rests upon the will of the people. It may be that the idea of a bicameral legislature is obsolete. But, I am not prepared to accept the idea that these conclusions should be forced upon the people by the judiciary, absent a clear-cut mandate to this effect in the Constitution. The notion that the Court, by creating new constitutional principles, should push the nation forward to the achievement of what the Court regards as the national ideal is not without its advocates. As stated by Mr. Justice Harlan in his dissenting opinion in *Reynolds v. Sims*, the view exists in some quarters that "every major social ill in this country can find its cure in some constitutional 'principle,' and that this Court should 'take the lead' in promoting reform when other branches of government fail to act."[14] It may be that we shall make greater advances in our national life if basic policy questions are decided for us by what Professor Burgess described as the "aristocracy of the robe,"[15] or by what Judge Learned Hand more bluntly characterized as a "bevy of Platonic Guardians."[16] Any court, however, that aspires to a constitutional policy-making role creates for itself the risks and hazards to which political organs are subject. I would prefer that the Court take a more modest view of its role and authority, if for no other reason than that it is important for the Court to retain the popular respect earned by it over the years as a judicial tribunal interpreting and applying the principles expressed in the Constitution. Fortunately, as our history amply demonstrates, public opinion and the reaction of the coordinate branches of the government operate with a salutary force in restraining the Court when it ventures too far in imposing its will in areas that belong primarily in the domain of legislative discretion or the popular will. I expect this to be the case with respect to the new wave of judicial activism we are now experiencing.

The Court had a function to perform in rescuing the state legislative process from systems of apportionment that could not be fitted into a rational scheme and that, in a number of instances, did not conform to the standard prescribed by state law itself. Indeed, if the Court had contented itself with the responsibility of requiring the states to bring their legislative apportionment up to date in order to conform with the plan of representation provided for in their own constitutions, it would have rendered a valuable service. But, in condemning all plans that do not conform to the Court's conception of wise apportionment policy— a policy buttressed by reference to a synthetic right forged from question-begging premises—and in reaching its sweeping conclusions in disregard of history and accepted principles of constitutional interpretation, the Court has gone far beyond the necessities of the case.

Footnotes

[1] 369 U.S. 186 (1962).
[2] *Id.* at 297.
[3] 372 U.S. 368 (1963).
[4] *Id.* at 381.
[5] 376 U.S. 1 (1964).
[6] *Id.* at 17–18.
[7] Lucas v. 44th Gen. Assembly of Colo., 377 U.S. 713 (1964) (Colorado); Roman v. Sincock, 377 U.S. 695 (1964) (Delaware); Davis v. Mann, 377 U.S. 678 (1964) (Virginia); Maryland Comm. for Fair Representation v. Tawes, 377 U.S. 656 (1964) (Maryland); WMCA, Inc. v. Lomenzo, 377 U.S. 633 (1964) (New York); Reynolds v. Sims, 377 U.S. 533 (1964) (Alabama).
[8] Reynolds v. Sims, *supra* note 7, at 561-62.
[9] "What constitutes a rational plan reasonably designed to achieve this objective will vary from State to State, since each State is unique, in terms of topography, geography, demography, history, heterogeneity and concentration of population, variety of social and economic interests, and in the operation and interrelation of its political institutions. But so long as a State's apportionment plan reasonably achieves, in the light of the State's own characteristics, effective and balanced representation of all substantial interests, without sacrificing the principle of effective majority rule, that plan cannot be considered irrational." Lucas v. 44th Gen. Assembly of Colo., 377 U.S. 713, 751 (1964).
[10] Griswold, *Absolutes in the Dark*, 8 UTAH L. REV. 167, 171-75 (1963).
[11] Both concurred in the holdings in the cases dealing with the legislative apportionment plans in Alabama, Virginia, and Delaware. Mr. Justice Clark concurred in the result in the Maryland case, whereas Mr. Justice Stewart voted to vacate the judgment and to remand the case to the Maryland Court of Appeals for consideration of the question whether the Maryland apportionment "could be shown systematically to prevent ultimate effective majority rule." Both dissented in the New York and Colorado cases. Their basic views are set forth in their dissenting opinions in Lucas v. 44th Gen. Assembly of Colo., 377 U.S. 713, at 741 and 744 (1964). Mr. Justice Clark, while writing a short

opinion of his own, also joined Mr. Justice Stewart's opinion.

Mr. Justice Harlan, it should be noted, dissented from the decisions in all the recent state legislative apportionment cases. His dissenting opinion, applicable to all the cases, is found in Reynolds v. Sims, 377 U.S. 533, at 589 (1964). His dissent, in accordance with his views expressed in dissent in *Baker, Gray,* and *Wesberry,* is based on the central proposition that questions of legislative apportionment are political questions not appropriate for judicial determination. [12]Lucas v. 44th Gen. Assembly of Colo., *supra* note

11, at 753-54. According to Mr. Justice Clark, "if one house is fairly apportioned by population . . . then the people should have some latitude in providing, on a rational basis, for representation in the other house." *Id.* at p. 742.
[13]*Id.* at 748. Mr. Justice Stewart dissenting in Lucas v. Forty-Fourth Gen. Assembly of State of Colorado.
[14]Reynolds v. Sims, 377 U.S. 533, 624 (1964).
[15]1 Burgess, Political Science and Constitutional Law 365 (1891).
[16]L. Hand, The Bill of Rights 73 (1958).

Selection 10

Reapportionment in the Supreme Court and Congress: Constitutional Struggle for Fair Representation
Robert G. Dixon, Jr.

Dixon takes up the story where Kauper leaves off and examines the second round of Reapportionment Cases. He too is much concerned with the varieties of inequality that remain below the surface of (and are, indeed, often caused by) the "one man, one vote" rule. His remarks also indicate that the complexity of state electoral systems is so great and the alternatives under the "one man, one vote" rule so many that the reapportionment question will be with us yet for some time to come.

Perhaps the most intriguing question facing the Court is whether, having brushed aside all other considerations but sheer numbers, it will be prepared to accept any reapportionment scheme that maintains the proper mathematics no matter how wildly it is manipulated to favor certain political, geographic, or economic interests over others. For instance, even with districts of exactly equal size, it is possible to give a party with 55 per cent of the popular vote only 25 per cent of the seats in the legislature by carefully drawing the district lines. Having struck at malapportionment (the improper manipulation of the size of districts), will the Court next attack gerrymandering (the improper manipulation of the shape of districts)?

"Legislators represent people, not trees or acres. Legislators are elected by voters, not farms or cities or economic interests."—Chief Justice Warren, *Reynolds v. Sims*

"But legislators do not represent faceless numbers. They represent people, or more accurately, a majority of the voters in their districts—people with identifiable needs and interests."—Justice Stewart, *Lucas v. 44th General Assembly, Colorado*

The Supreme Court's *Reapportionment Decisions*[1] of June 15, 1964, rank as one of the most far-reaching series of decisions in the history of

American constitutionalism. Under the new equal population district standard, at least one house of the legislature in virtually every state, and in most instances both houses, are putatively unconstitutional, whether or not formally so declared.

The pathway to these decisions, which seem destined to re-make the political map of America, was opened in the spring of 1962 by *Baker v. Carr,*[2] the Tennessee state legislative reapportion-

"Reapportionment in the Supreme Court and Congress: Constitutional Struggle for Fair Representation" by Robert G. Dixon, Jr., 63 *Michigan Law Review* 209 (1964). Reprinted by permission of The Michigan Law Review Association.

ment case, in which the Supreme Court overturned well-established precedent and authorized federal court review under the fourteenth amendment of the apportionments and districts that determine the composition of state legislatures. For decades, reapportionment, like Pandora's box, was felt to be so full of intricate political factors that courts, particularly federal courts, should sit on the lid and never look inside. As Mr. Justice Frankfurter had said in an early congressional districting suit, courts should not enter the "political thicket" because it is "hostile to a democratic system to involve the judiciary in the politics of the people."[3] In a series of cases this thought had become the touchstone also for state legislative apportionment. But the Frankfurter touchstone is now an epitaph. Courts not only have entered the thicket, they occupy it.

Fair representation is the ultimate goal. At the time of the *Reapportionment Decisions,* much change was overdue in some states, and at least some change was overdue in most states. We are a democratic people and our institutions presuppose according population a dominant role in formulas of representation. However, by its exclusive focus on bare numbers, the Court may have transformed one of the most intricate, fascinating, and elusive problems of democracy into a simple exercise of applying elementary arithmetic to census data. In so doing, the Court may have disabled itself from effectively considering the more subtle issues of representation. Reapportionment is a political power struggle, but one looks in vain in the controlling opinions in the *Reapportionment Decisions* for an awareness and concern regarding the group dynamics of American politics.

THE DECISIONS AND THEIR IMPLICATIONS

Unlike *Baker v. Carr,* whose extensive opinions called for and merited intensive analysis, the series of opinions in the *Reapportionment Decisions* proceed from simple premises and can be summarized rather readily. The principal opinion of the Court was delivered by Mr. Chief Justice Warren in the Alabama case, with brief but consistent elaborations in separate opinions in the other five cases. As a basic test, the Court espoused an equal population district system for both houses of a bicameral legislature. This was variously expressed in such phrases as "substantial equality of population among the various districts"[4] and "as nearly of equal population as is practicable."[5] The Court added, as a secondary test (perhaps to garner the votes of Justices Clark and Stewart for some of the cases), a prohibition on "crazy quilts, completely lacking in rationality."[6]

There were two interesting and potentially inconsistent statements in the Chief Justice's principal opinion that will bear watching in the future. He spoke forcefully of the need for "fair and effective representation of all citizens,"[7] which could point in the direction of representing people and viewpoints in proportion to their strength in the state as a whole. But later he turned about and seemed to reject the group dynamics of American politics by saying that neither "economic or other sorts of group interests" are relevant factors in devising a representation system.[8]

Mr. Justice Stewart, who produced the principal dissent, was the only Justice to try to come to grips with the philosophic and practical complexity of the concept of representation in a large, polycentric society. Not willing to have the Court try to do everything, but not wanting the Court to do nothing, he agreed with the *decision* in three of the six cases (Alabama, Delaware and Virginia), but with the *rationale* in none. He would have remanded the Maryland case and would have approved the existing apportionments in the Colorado and New York cases. His vote to remand the Maryland case explains well his two guiding principles. His narrower principle, and the easier to apply, is that crazy quilts, *i.e.,* patterns of apportionment defying rational explanation, are bad. Because the Maryland Senate was based on a fairly consistent political subdivision principle, it passed muster for Mr. Justice Stewart under this crazy-quilt test. But, because of a lack of sufficient data, the constitutionality of the Maryland Senate was not then determinable under Mr. Justice Stewart's broader and more difficult principle; *i.e.,* apportionments that systematically "prevent ultimate effective majority rule"[9] are unconstitutional. It may be noted in passing that both of these tests find their juristic home more naturally under the due process clause than under the equal protection clause, which has come to dominate and confuse the Court's handling of apportionment matters.

Mr. Justice Harlan wrote a fitting epilogue to Mr. Justice Frankfurter's monumental dissenting opinion in *Baker* and would go back to pre-*Baker* times by dismissing all of the cases as "an experiment in venturesome constitutionalism."[10] His historical and textual argument is overpowering, all the more so because not rebutted by Mr. Chief Justice Warren's opinions for the Court. But, like the history he used, his opinion seems destined to become history, unless it has some influence in the current discussions of constitutional amendments either to take federal courts out of the reapportionment business or specifically to authorize use of non-population factors in reapportioning one house of the legislature. Mr. Justice Clark, beyond joining in the basic opinion of Mr. Justice Stewart in the New York and Colorado cases, adhered to his "crazy-quilt" theory as expressed in his *Baker* opinion. He would accept non-population factors in one house if the other were based substantially on population. Therefore, in terms of basic rationale, the Court split six-two-one. There were six for a tight equal population district system; two, Justices Stewart and Clark, for more flexible standards, with preservation of majority rule and avoidance of crazy-quilts as outer boundaries; and one, Mr. Justice Harlan, for a complete hands-off approach.

The Colorado case has attracted special attention and raises deeper philosophic issues than any of the others in the packet of fifteen reapportionment cases decided last June. It presented an apportionment plan placing one house on a straight population basis and the other on a modified population basis, which had been approved by every county in Colorado in a popular referendum, 305,700 to 172,725. In the same "one man-one vote" statewide referendum, an alternative plan placing both houses on a straight population basis had been resoundingly rejected, 149,892 to 311,-749. None of the other five cases decided on June 15 – Alabama, Delaware, Maryland, New York, Virginia—nor the nine additional apportionment cases disposed of briefly a week later, involved this popular referendum feature.

How did we get ourselves so quickly to these decisions? Why is it that the important questions about representation that should engage our attention are not treated in the opinions and now stand unresolved—or resolved *sub silentio* upon inadequate premises? Why, with so much on the record in the law reviews,[11] did so little show up in oral argument and in the opinions of the Court? In these *Reapportionment Decisions*, Justices Stewart and Clark, who dissented from the Court's results in some of the cases and from the Court's reasoning in all of the cases, have strong foundation in the law review analyses of the problem. But the Court majority has strong foundation in the oral argument.

To those who sat through the Supreme Court oral arguments in all of the cases, as I did, the imbalance in the oral argument was at first annoying, then frightening, and finally, just pathetic. The imbalance was caused not so much by the admitted competence of the plaintiffs and the Solicitor General of the United States as "co-counsel," but by the inadequacy on the defendants' side— the inadequacy, to be precise, in the way many state attorneys general's offices handled these cases. Too many of the defendants' counsel wasted many of their precious hours of oral argument. They dwelt on the varied topography and geography of their states, sounding like a misplaced chamber of commerce commercial; or, they stressed history, which, to a Court that had decided the desegregation case[12] on broad principles of developing constitutionalism, was like trying to get Bertrand Russell to take Holy Communion; or, they simply fell into the trap Mr. Justice Clark had constructed more neatly than he knew in *Baker*,[13] by trying to establish how *every* inter-district population disparity could be shown to be the result of some clear and "rational" formula, which is almost always an impossibility.

The representation issue

Few of the counsel and none of the opinions, except Mr. Justice Stewart's, showed an adequate awareness of the complexity of representative government—the complexity involved in trying to achieve *fair* representation in a multi-membered body chosen from geographic districts of the many interests and groupings and shades of opinion in our pluralistic society. As Mr. Justice Stewart has said: "[L]egislators do not represent faceless numbers. They represent people, or, more accurately, *a majority of the voters in their districts...*"[14] The phrase "*majority* of the voters" is crucial, with stress on the word "majority." As Mr. Justice Stewart also pointed out, even with districts of equal population, twenty-six per cent of the electorate (a bare majority of the voters in a bare majority of the districts) can, using the same kind of theoretical mathematics that the Court majority used in these cases, elect a majority of the legislators.

For the majority of the Justices in these cases, two kinds of mathematical data seemed to be crucial. One was the "population-variance-ratio," computed by comparing the population of the smallest district and the largest district, disregarding the possible atypicality of the largest and the smallest district and the possibility that much of a state's population may be in districts having a population reasonably close to the average. On this basis, ratios ranging from a two-to-one disparity up to ten-to-one, or twenty-to-one, or even higher can be obtained. The other measure was a commonly used scale device, sometimes called the Dauer-Kelsay Scale, to indicate the minimum population that theoretically could control a majority of seats in the respective houses of the legislature. The percentage figure is obtained by ranking the legislative districts in order of population and then accumulating population from the least populous districts upward until a majority of legislative seats has been reached. The actual division of the population along political party lines is ignored. It is important to note that on this scale a perfect score for any one house of a legislature is not one hundred per cent, but fifty per cent. Also, in a large legislature, even with relatively equal population districts, the minimum population that could control a majority of seats under this theoretical measure is only about thirty-seven and one-half per cent if a twenty-five per cent deviation from strict equality is allowed in arranging districts, and about forty-three and seven-tenths per cent if the allowable deviation is reduced to fifteen per cent.[15] And yet, the scale figures of the percentage of the population that theoretically could control the legislatures in some of the cases decided last June were close to or above thirty-eight per cent. For example:

State	Senate	House
Virginia	41.1%	40.5%
New York	41.8	34.7
Colorado	33.2	45.1
Ohio	41.0	30.3

(Note: See more complete table in Appendix *infra*.)

What scale figures such as these prove is uncertain. These computations treat each district as a unified entity, whereas in real life all districts are split internally by various partisan and interest alignments.

Traditionally, American legislators have been elected, not under a statewide party list system or a proportional representation system, but instead from geographic districts, either single-member or multi-member. And yet, our real concerns, our partisanship and our interests, are not spread evenly through these geographic districts. Nor are they grouped in balanced fashion in competing sets of districts. Herein lies the crux of the apportionment-districting problem—the true challenge to constitution-making. Casually drawn districts or carefully drawn districts, whether of equal population or not, may seriously under-represent or seriously over-represent identifiable interests such as political parties, organized labor, farmers, etc.

Actual examples of the complexity of representation and the insufficiency of a simple "equal population" formula are not hard to find. For example, a few days after the equal population rule for congressional districts was announced in the *Wesberry*[16] case last February, Maryland's old-line legislative leaders, acting under judicial pressure, provoked howls of shock and anguish by unveiling a plan for new, arithmetically equal districts that actually would have worsened the position of the under-represented suburbs that had brought the redistricting suit.[17] The plan, subsequently passed

by one house of the legislature but defeated in the second, carved and regrouped the populous counties without regard to community of interest in order to yield equal population districts that fully preserved the preexisting power structure.

As another example, we can assume a populous urban-suburban area into which we are to put ten single-member districts. If the larger political party had a fifty-five to forty-five per cent edge over the smaller party and party strength were fairly evenly spread, it would be a simple matter to draw mathematically equal districts under which the party with forty-five per cent support would never elect a single man.[18] And, it would not even be necessary to engage in gerrymandering in the sense of odd-shaped districts. The inequities in these examples are caused by what can be designated as the "wild card" factor of party member location, plus some gerrymandering.

But there are other possible causes of gross inequities, even under an equal population standard. A second cause is the familiar balance of power factor. A significant interest group over-representation can occur when a minority religious, racial, or dogmatic interest group holds the balance of power in a series of districts. The Prohibitionists proved this by going all the way and even obtaining a constitutional amendment. Fear of this balance of power factor may be one explanation for the Colorado popular referendum in 1962. The voters there *rejected* a straight equal population principle for both houses and *approved* a plan placing one house on something less than an equal population principle. Why? One reasonably plausible explanation would be that some urban and suburban voters may have voted for under-representation in one house in order to better protect interests they shared with others in the state—*and* which may be dominant interests when the state is taken as a whole. But, a majority of the United States Supreme Court Justices, without discussing this point, were singularly unimpressed with the referendum and nullified the voter-selected apportionment plan in last June's packet of reapportionment cases.[19]

A third cause of gross inequities, even under an equal population standard, may be the possible operation of multi-member districts. The populous urban-suburban centers in the South provide interesting examples of this in regard to two minorities—the Republicans and the Negroes. If single-member districts are used, the housing patterns in some populous areas will produce some Republican seats and some Negro seats. But, if the legislators are chosen in large, plural-member districts, the Negroes and the Republicans will be swamped despite their substantial numbers. These are the kinds of things that can happen if courts simply flush uncontrolled action out of the political thicket. In short, a one man-one vote principle guarantees change; taken alone, it may not always guarantee fair representation, which should be the ultimate goal.

Numbers are easy to play with so long as they remain mere numbers. If, as Aristotle said, "Law is reason unaffected by desire," the reapportionment opinions of Mr. Chief Justice Warren show up well as an ideal prescription for a theoretical society. But if what the Founding Fathers called "factionalism" rears its ugly head, and if, as Justice Holmes said, "The life of the law has not been logic; it has been experience," then the Warren opinions are inadequate.

Why are all these interesting, perplexing, realistic, and troublesome matters simply swept under the rug in the majority opinions in the reapportionment cases? The answer may be found in the way the Court has characterized the basic nature of a reapportionment case. The Court views all these cases as simply being civil rights cases, involving the personalized right of the individual voter to cast a vote that will have "equal weight" with the votes of all other voters. (And the Court does this even though the basic data used is population data, not voting pattern data.)[20] In one sense, of course, these cases do involve voting. But, by this exclusive characterization, the Court ignores the crucial point that in apportionment cases the personal civil right of the voter is intertwined with large, overriding questions concerning representation—*i.e.*, concerning political philosophies and practices of representation in a dynamically democratic public order, in which groups are as relevant as individuals. Indeed, groups and parties are the building blocks of political power. Because apportionment involves the creation and control of political power, the group dynamics of American politics cannot be ignored forever in reapportionment litigation, although it has received little attention in this "first round" of reapportionment cases.

Moreover, even as a civil rights case, the Court's formulation of an arithmetic absolute of equal population districts is a marked departure from previous constructions of the equal protection clause. Except in regard to race, where we have sought to erect—and I think properly—a concept of a color-blind Constitution, judicial interpretations of the equal protection clause have stressed respect for legislative discretion and a flexible approach toward legislative classifications. *McGowan v. Maryland*[21] and the other Sunday closing cases illustrate this well.

Further, if the goal, however arrived at in terms of constitutional source, be to weigh each voter's vote equally and thereby to give each voter an equally effective vote, this is a deceptive concept, impossible to achieve in practice, as the previous illustrations demonstrate. In any election in any district system, there is a minority that is weighted at zero and a majority who elects its man or its slate and so is weighted, at least until the next election, at one hundred per cent. Some vote weighting necessarily is involved in any system for the election of a multi-membered body from separate districts. How these one hundred per cent majorities and zero minorities add up across a state is the important issue in assessing the fairness of the system and its effectiveness in representing the various organized and unorganized interests that make up the body politic. Semantics have helped to impede clarity of thought in this field. For example, "equal population" is an objective term with clear meaning; but, the terms "equal representation" and "equal vote-weighting," which are sometimes used as substitutes, are subjective terms that have no clear meaning. These latter terms describe problems; they do not label anything. Judicial creation of equal population districts, without more, cannot be counted on to produce either "equally weighted" votes or "equally effective" votes.

Implications of "One Man-One Vote"

Let us now take the goal of "one man-one vote" or "equal vote weighting" at face value and inquire into its implications. If we are serious about "one man-one vote," we will want to maximize the prospects for it being an *effective* vote. The question then naturally arises whether the one man-one vote principle includes a right to have a large area divided into single-member districts, so that a sizable cluster of like-minded people will not be submerged as a permanent minority in a large multi-member district. Mr. Chief Justice Warren, in what I think was a rather casual dictum since the point was not before him, intimated in his opinion for the Court in the Alabama case, *Reynolds v. Sims*,[22] that a state could elect to use single-member districts, multi-member districts, or floterial districts,[23] as long as there was substantial equality of population among the various districts. In regard to multi-member districts, he did suggest some practical problems, such as length of ballot and burden on the voter, but he gave no hint of constitutional restraint.

Two lower federal courts, however, already have suggested that the equal protection clause may require breaking up multi-member districts into single-member districts. Under a statute voided by a federal district court in Georgia last March,[24] some voters had their own state senator in a single-member district. Other voters who were located in populous counties having more than one senator were under a system whereby each senator was chosen at large in the county even though assigned, for representation purposes, to a subdistrict in the county where he also had to have his residence. The court held that there was unconstitutional discrimination between the single-member district voters, who "owned their man" so to speak, and the voters in the sub-districts in the plural member counties, who might be represented by a man elected by the county at large but disfavored by the very sub-district he represented. It doesn't take much imagination to see that this system could operate, and perhaps was designed to operate, to overcome sub-district majorities that vote contrary to the county-wide majority.

In Pennsylvania, a federal district court last April held that both political philosophy and constitutional law prohibited the use of multi-member districts along with single-member districts.[25] The court said "one man-one vote" means that each voter must vote for the same number of legislators. Otherwise, some voters would have only one legislator looking out for their interest; others would have two, three, or four, although, of course, their districts might be two, three, or four times larger. The court added the more respectable rationale that "minority groups living in particular localities may well be submerged in elections at large but can often make their voting power much more effective in the smaller single-member district in which they may live."[26]

I am not prepared to say that the Georgia decision, or even the Pennsylvania decision, is wholly wrong, despite the Warren dictum. Indeed, if "fair representation" is the true, but unarticulated, goal in all of these apportionment matters, then I rather like these decisions. But I would find it highly amusing—if it were not so indicative of how little we have thought through this critical problem—to compare these lower federal court decisions, which suggest that equal protection requires the formation of single-member voting districts, with comments by both Justices Stewart[27] and Harlan[28] in the recent reapportionment cases that state-wide election at large of all legislators could be the ultimate outcome of the one man-one vote principle espoused by the Court majority. Lately we have heard much of the merit of "neutral principles," *i.e.*, precise and consistent principles, for constitutional adjudication. Apparently, the one man-one vote principle is better than a mere neutral principle; it is a chameleon principle which can yield opposite conclusions.

If in the next year or two the Supreme Court should act on a case of this sort, I would expect the plea for a constitutional right to sub-districting to receive respectful consideration. Indeed, if the first case were one brought by a racial minority, I would be inclined to expect the Court to require sub-districting as a further offshoot of equal protection. As I see it, the New York City congressional districts case, *Wright v. Rockefeller,*[29] which the plaintiffs lost, is a different case and would not stand in the way. And, if the Court ordered sub-districting for an impacted and unrepresented racial minority, I do not see how they could refuse to do so for an impacted political party minority. The basic democratic interest in each case would be the same—to achieve at least some representation of a particular viewpoint in a multi-membered deliberative body.

One more very recent case on the "frontier of equal protection" should be noted. In South Carolina, as in a few other states, there is a requirement that, in at-large voting in plural member districts, each voter, in order to have his votes counted, must vote for *all* offices even though his own party has nominated only one or two men. In a case filed last June before a federal district court in South Carolina,[30] it is being contended that this provision is unconstitutional under the equal protection clause as applied to the election of ten members of the state legislature from Richland County. The Democrats nominated a full slate of ten men, but the Republicans nominated only two men. The gist of the complaint is that this system can be mathematically shown to endanger and possibly frustrate equal vote-weighting and majority rule. For example, let us assume, as in South Carolina, that with ten men to be elected at large in a county to a given class of office such as state legislator, Party A puts up only two men and Party B puts up a full slate of ten. If the per cent of total voters who favor Party A's two men are a majority and if they cast their "other" votes for the same B Party men, then this group of voters will elect *all* its choices (2A, 8B). However, if this same majority of total voters who favor Party A's two men should happen to evenly spread their "other" votes over the full ten-man slate of Party B, then the men nominated by Party A will lose unless they have the support of more than seventy-two per cent of the total number of voters. Between these two mathematical extremes lie the actual voting patterns. But, the crucial point is that, even with support of a majority of the voters, Party A's two men may lose if their supporters spread their remaining votes at random over the Party B slate. To this extent, the South Carolina law leaves majority rule to chance, which seems contrary both to the spirit and to the language of the majority opinions in the Reapportionment Decisions.

Reapportionment and the Vigor of State Government

Seeing in *Baker v. Carr* the "death knell of minority state government,"[31] many commentators have predicted that reapportionment would lead to a great resurgence of state government, a heightened concern for urban problems at state capitals, and a lessened need for direct federal-local relations to solve urban problems. These thoughts have been common in social science and popular literature for decades. The Kestnbaum Commission on intergovernmental relations highlighted these same thoughts in its 1955 report.[32] They are repeated in a report on apportionment issued by the United States Advisory Commission on Intergovernmental Relations.[33]

There undoubtedly is some foundation for these observations, although there is precious little proof of actual minority rule. However, data compiled by the U.S. Advisory Commission on Intergovernmental Relations in another study provides some sobering statistics.[34] The study surveys the relatively dismal record of attempts in the years 1950-1961 to achieve city-consolidation or other major governmental integration in eighteen metropolitan areas. Enhanced ability to serve urban needs was a major purpose of the plans. But ten of the eighteen failed to pass the popular referendum hurdle, even though the vote was not state-wide, but rather was confined to the metropolitan area. In almost every instance, the specter of higher taxes, whether real or fancied, was a major argument of the opponents and presumably a major factor in the defeats. The commentators on the St. Louis experience said: "Taxpayers are strangely immune to arguments [explaining tax provisions] and many voters were convinced that adoption of the district would mean a substantial tax increase."[35] Another major difficulty was voter *apathy*—people are not concerned enough to favor increased local action on metropolitan problems.

Looking to the future, whatever reapportionment may accomplish, it does not seem to be well-adapted as a remedy for voter apathy and tax fears. In order to bring state government into its place in the sun as a major vehicle for solving urban problems and restraining the power flow to Washington, reapportioned legislatures are going to have to vote higher taxes. The needs for service and control in such matters as transportation and transit, housing, slum clearance and renewal, health, welfare, employment, and the like are ex-

pensive. Even under reapportionment, continued reliance upon federal programs and funds may seem to be the path of political wisdom for state and local politicians. Census Bureau and Budget Bureau reports on state and local government finances reveal a fairly heavy reliance upon federal funds.[36]

Another common idea that was seriously questioned by the Advisory Commission study of "metro plan" defeats is that reorganization plans carry in urban areas but fail to get a concurrent majority —where that is also required—in the outer reaches of the proposed new district. "Of the 18 proposals surveyed," according to the report, "only 2 of the 10 which failed of adoption owed their defeat directly to the demand for concurrent majorities. ..."[37] Two that passed would have failed if a concurrent majority had been required. The Commission also noted that, in twelve of the eighteen, "pluralities ran parallel in the central and the outlying parts of the area concerned, favorably in six instances and unfavorably in the other six."[38]

The tiny handful of empirical studies of urban-rural conflict in the actual operation of state legislatures likewise provides no basis for supposing that reapportionment will be a panacea for the ills of urbanized society. Separate studies of the Illinois and Missouri legislatures conducted a few years ago by Professors George D. Young and David R. Derge indicated that "the city's bitterest opponents in the legislature are political enemies from within its own walls, and those camped in the adjoining suburban areas." The research supported these findings:[39]

"1. Non-metropolitan legislators seldom vote together with high cohesion against metropolitan legislators.

"2. Metropolitan legislators usually do not vote together with high cohesion.

"3. Metropolitan legislators are usually on the prevailing side when they do vote together with high cohesion."

A separate study by Professors Steiner and Gove of the effects of the 1955 reapportionment on the Illinois legislature concluded that there were "no profound changes," but that Republican suburban politics had become more competitive.[40]

Remaining problems

Characterization. Looking to the future, I see a number of remaining problems and a number of creative possibilities. The first need, I think, is to characterize correctly what these cases are all about and the effect the court orders unavoidably will have. In reapportionment cases, courts sit in judgment on the structure of political power; they even effect a judicial transfer of political power. Thus, to speak in terms of distribution of political power is to talk not of legislative acts and not of judicial acts in the previously accepted concept of judicial review, but rather to talk of *constitutive* acts. Reapportionment re-structures government at the core. In taking on this task, the courts have assumed the function of a state constitutional convention. To an extent, of course, such a function is implicit in much judicial review under the federal supremacy principle that is derived from the supreme law of the land clause. But the task is especially grave in a reapportionment case because of the delicacy and intricacy of the policy issues involved and the superficiality of all "quickie" formulas.

Significantly, of all the vital compromises at the Constitutional Convention of 1787, only the one concerning the basis of representation is entitled to be called the Great Compromise. Apportionment and districting decisions are determinative of the quality of representative democracy. From popular suffrage derives the majoritarian principle of democracy. From apportionment and districting derive the representation features that temper majoritarianism with requirements of deliberation and consensus.

Perception of the true nature of reapportionment litigation should help clear up the semantical bog of "one man-one vote" and "equal representation." It should eliminate the misconception that the cases involve only a sharply pin-pointed issue of civil rights. It also should open the way to a fresh dialogue—long overdue—about the character and function of representation in a twentieth century mass democracy.

Political data. Although the judiciary is well launched on a stormy sea of reapportionment litigation, there is not nearly enough information available for intelligent decision-making. Apart from the overt act of casting a ballot, little is known about the manner in which political feelings are translated into action, the actual effect of malapportionment, or the identity of the beneficiaries of reapportionment. One recent study of the lower house of Congress, in which congressmen's votes on four issues were weighted by the population of their districts and recomputed, rather surprisingly suggests that the "liberals" benefit from such congressional maldistricting as now exists.[41] A weighted vote recomputation of all roll call votes in the current session of Congress (lower house) that I have under way so far shows little

change in the totals. A study of twenty-two roll call votes in two sessions of the Texas legislature, using this same technique of recomputing legislators' votes according to the population of their districts, indicates that the outcome would have differed on only one measure.[42] This then is an area where political science, unfortunately, has let us down rather badly. We know very little about the actual operation of legislatures and the relationships between legislators and their constituencies.

Effective representation. The matter of standards will need perpetual refinement as legislators develop new patterns of apportionment under which some identifiable group is disproportionately represented. It is demonstrably impossible to arrange districts of equal population under which no groups or political parties are specially advantaged or disadvantaged. The problem I speak of here is far more delicate, and probably far more important, than the abstract one of ascertaining how much district inequality may be tolerated under the Court's mandate for "an honest and good faith effort" to achieve districts "as nearly of equal population as is practicable." That could be a meaningless fight over percentage points. The more critical problem is to put real meaning into the language found in another part of Mr. Chief Justice Warren's opinion, where he characterized the goal as being "full and effective participation by all citizens in state government."[43] A few lines farther on he stated even more clearly that "fair and effective representation for all citizens is concededly the basic aim of legislative apportionment."[44]

To achieve this goal, I suggest that the Court will have to move forward in two directions beyond the equal population principle. In one direction, it will have to join Mr. Justice Stewart in his concern for "ultimate effective majority rule."[45] It will have to be disposed to act against gerrymander devices, whereby a political party spreads its voters over enough districts to control a majority of seats, even though it is a minority party in the state as a whole. In the opposite direction, it should be disposed to act against gross and continued under-representation of a minority party or group that finds itself so distributed and "locked into" a district system that its votes, though substantial, always achieve zero representation.

Hearing from the minority. I would venture the prediction that, as we move into a new era of equal population districts, we will see a renewed interest in various governmental devices to "hear from the minority." Students of government have known for years that the single-member district system has a strong tendency to over-represent the majority party. I think this well-known tendency may be enhanced, rather than lessened, by the equal population requirement. Indeed, one of the few respectable functions of the old "rotten borough system" was occasionally to give the minority party exaggerated representation from some districts in order to offset their total loss in other areas where they were a sizable, but perpetually submerged, minority. If this hunch is correct, we soon may see a renewed interest in such "hear from the minority" devices as proportional representation,[46] cumulative voting (which has been practiced in Illinois for years),[47] and limited voting. For example, a limited voting system was recently put into effect in New York City in order to improve political party balance in the city council. Its constitutionality was sustained in state litigation, and the United States Supreme Court denied review.[48]

Remedies. Lastly, I would like to add a word concerning remedies, about which the Court said little in the recent decisions. There has been much loose talk about the device of an election at large, including statements to the effect that it squarely accords with the one man-one vote principle. In a literal sense, the at-large election does yield one man-one vote. But, in a functional sense, it does not provide fair representation, yielding instead only a winner-take-all majoritarianism. The battle cry has been "one man-one vote," but what the plaintiffs really have been complaining about is lack of weight in the legislature commensurate with their numbers. An election at large, therefore, is not a *remedy* in the sense of being an alternative and better representation system. From the standpoint of representation, it creates more problems than it solves. Rather, it is a *sanction* to compel change, and, hopefully, improvement in the representation system.

A judicial order in the nature of an actual reapportionment would be an ultimate remedy in the true sense of the term. At least three of the handful of examples so far of direct judicial reapportionment have involved judicial choice and designation from among prefabricated proposals originating in the legislature, as in Alabama;[49] or from plans emanating from a state-sponsored research bureau, as in Oklahoma;[50] or from a special legislative apportionment commission, as in Michigan.[51] To ensure that the court will have available this kind of advice and assistance, both at the remedies stage and earlier, it would be advisable to develop a practice of intervention by political party chairmen in reapportionment suits, as was allowed in Con-

necticut.[52] When courts must act politically, they at least should not act blindly.

In devising remedies, the courts also should guard against undue haste, because they are dealing with eggs that, once scrambled, cannot be put back in the shell. How anomalous it is to contrast the "hell-bent for election" speed with which some courts approach reapportionment with the lengthy delay and procrastination in desegregation of public education. Desegregation is conceptually far more simple than legislative apportionment and, unlike reapportionment, is almost exclusively a matter of vindicating a personalized civil right. And yet, in desegregation we have had "all deliberate speed" over a ten-year period, whereas in reapportionment we have been treated to the spectacle of courts pressuring and threatening legislators and fixing exact deadlines measured in months, or even weeks.

The initial order entered by the federal district court in Connecticut seemed to be an unprecedented example of judicial regulation of the political process.[53] In that order the court set up a timetable for three special elections within a ten-month period and called for an immediate special session of the legislature to set up the mechanics for a constitutional convention. It also said that the legislature elected under the old apportionment formula in November 1964 should conduct no public business other than implementing constitutional changes made by the constitutional convention. At this point the Governor remonstrated and the court accepted a modified, but still speedy, plan. Under it, a special session of the legislature was to meet on September 10, 1964, to perform the two-fold task of itself reapportioning the state in time for the November 1964 election and arranging for a constitutional convention to make a permanent apportionment. When the special session failed to reapportion the districts in accordance with directions, the court cancelled the November elections for a new legislature. It then ruled that the 1963 legislature can continue to legislate provided it reapportions within ninety days. The court will appoint a special master to operate concurrently with a new special legislative session. He will hold public hearings and will be empowered to use electronic computers to establish a new apportionment. If the legislature fails to create a reapportionment schedule by January 30, 1965, the special master's plan will be imposed on the state.[54] Judicial pressure to force an immediate reapportionment on the eve of the November 1964 election (*e.g.*, Michigan, Oklahoma), or to limit the life or powers of the legislatures to be elected in November 1964 under unmodified apportionment plans (*e.g.*, Vermont), or to schedule special elections (*e.g.*, New York) has been common in many states.

Conclusion

In reapportionment there are no "easy outs." I cannot reject *Baker v. Carr* out of hand and join Mr. Justice Harlan on the Olympian heights of judicial detachment, even though I must admit that his opinions are challenging. On his side he has constitutional text, history, and logic.

There seem to be times, however, despite the instinctive preference for "neutral principles," when judicial *review* becomes judicial *prescription.* Such times must be rare, else there can be no judicial "review." But, when they do occur, perhaps the best one can do is to revert to these lines of Mr. Chief Justice John Marshall—so wonderfully useful because so semantically meaningless: "We must never forget that it is a constitution we are expounding." The highest commitment is to the viability of the system and to the maintenance of popular faith in it. With political avenues for redress of malapportionment blocked in many states and with protest mounting, the Court has concluded that some judicial participation in the politics of the people is a pre-condition to there *being* any effective politics of the people. However, at the same time I fear that the Court, having entered the fray, will find its simple one man-one vote standard to be more like a set of Emperor's clothes than a shining suit of democratic armor.

The questions raised in this paper do not demonstrate the invalidity of the equal population district principle. They may demonstrate its insufficiency as an exclusive guide to *fair representation.* A representative democracy may be sufficiently majoritarian to guarantee majority, rather than minority, rule; but, an excess of the majoritarian principle may rob the system of its representative character and may yield action without accommodation.

Footnotes

[1]The cases decided with full opinions after oral argument were the Alabama cases, Reynolds v. Sims, Vann v. Baggett, McConnell v. Baggett, 377 U.S. 533 (1964); the New York case, WMCA, Inc. v. Lomenzo, 377 U.S. 633 (1964); the Maryland case, Maryland Comm. for Fair Representation v. Tawes, 377 U.S. 656 (1964); the Virginia case, Davis v. Mann, 377 U.S. 678 (1964); the Delaware case, Roman v. Sincock, 377 U.S. 695 (1964); and the Colorado case, Lucas v. 44th Gen. Assembly of Colo., 377 U.S. 713 (1964). The following week the Court, using the same principles, disposed of reapportionment cases from the following states in memorandum decisions: The

Michigan cases, Beadle v. Scholle, 377 U.S. 990 (1964), and Marshall v. Hare, 378 U.S. 561 (1964); the Washington case, Meyers v. Thigpen, 378 U.S. 554 (1964); the Oklahoma case, Williams v. Moss, 378 U.S. 558 (1964); the Illinois case, Germano v. Kerner, 378 U.S. 560 (1964); the Idaho case, Hearne v. Smylie, 378 U.S. 563 (1964); the Connecticut case, Pinney v. Butterworth, 378 U.S. 564 (1964); the Florida case, Swann v. Adams, 378 U.S. 553 (1964); the Ohio case, Nolan v. Rhodes, 378 U.S. 556 (1964); the Iowa case, Hill v. Davis, 378 U.S. 565 (1964).
[2]369 U.S. 186 (1962).
[3]Colegrove v. Green, 328 U.S. 549, 553-54 (1946).
[4]Reynolds v. Sims, 377 U.S. 533, 579 (1964).
[5]*Id.* at 577.
[6]*Id.* at 568. Because one's past always rises to haunt him, it was to be expected that the Chief Justice would be reminded in the public press and on the floor of Congress of this statement he made as Governor of California in 1958: "Many California counties are far more important in the life of the State than their population of the State. It is for this reason that I have never been in favor of restricting the representation in the senate to a strictly population basis." U.S. News and World Report, June 6, 1964, p. 34; 110 CONG. REC. 15516 (daily ed. July 8, 1964).
[7]377 U.S. at 565.
[8]*Id.* at 579-80.
[9]Maryland Comm. for Fair Representation v. Tawes, 377 U.S. 656, 677 (1964).
[10]Reynolds v. Sims, 377 U.S. 533, 625 (1964).
[11]See references cited note 4 *supra.*
[12]Brown v. Board of Educ., 347 U.S. 483 (1954), in which Mr. Chief Justice Warren had written: "In approaching this problem, we cannot turn the clock back to 1868 when the Amendment was adopted.... We must consider public education in the light of its full development and its present place in American life throughout the Nation." *Id.* at 492-93. This was one of the decisions that invoked Professor Wechsler's, *Toward Neutral Principles of Constitutional Law,* 73 HARV. L. REV. 1 (1959), and Professor Pollak's rebuttal, *Racial Discrimination and Judicial Integrity: A Reply to Professor Wechsler,* 108 U. PA. L. REV. 1 (1959).
[13]Baker v. Carr, 369 U.S. 186, 254-58 (1962).
[14]Lucas v. 44th Assembly of Colo., 377 U.S. 713, 750 (1964). (Emphasis added.)
[15]These figures are obtained by assuming a state legislative house of one hundred single-member districts, each of which would have a population of ten thousand under "ideal" districting. A twenty-five percent deviation would yield fifty districts of 12,500 population and fifty districts of 7,500 population. The latter fifty districts, plus one of the larger districts, yield the minimum population that theoretically could elect a majority of the senators. The figure is 387,500 or 38.75% of the total state population.

Of course, if there were a tiny legislature based only on four single-member districts, each of which would have ten thousand population under "ideal" districting, the percentage computations would be radically different.
[16]Wesberry v. Sanders, 376 U.S. 1 (1964).
[17]N.Y. Times, March 8, 1964, p. 86, col. 4. In the case that impelled the action, the federal district court subsequently voided the original districts but allowed their use for the 1964 election. Maryland Citizens Comm. for Fair Congressional Redistricting

v. Tawes, 226 F. Supp. 80, 228 F. Supp. 956 (D. Md. 1964).

[18]For another example, consider the following diagram:

Party X	Party Y	Total Population	Seats Before"Equalizing" Reapportionment	Seats After "Equalizing" Reapportionment
County A	5,000	20,000	25,000	1	1
County B	55,000	45,000	100,000	1	4

Before reapportionment: Each party, one seat. Party votes split 60,000 to 65,000.
After reapportionment: Party X, 60,000 votes, four seats;
Party Y, 65,000 votes, one seat.

Source: This chart is taken from Dixon, *Representation Goals,* 52 NAT'L CIV. REV. 545 (1963).

[19]Lucas v. 44th Gen. Assembly of Colo., 377 U.S. 713 (1964).

[20]Some persons have suggested that the proper data to examine in apportionment-malapportionment studies is not population data but data on the number of potential voters, or of registered voters, or of actual voters. Wholly apart from the question of theoretical merit, attempts to use indices more refined than the readily available census data, or to work out a political participation index as an apportionment factor, have normally been rejected because of the additional effort involved. See Silva, *Legislative Representation— With Special Reference to New York,* 27 LAW & CONTEMP. PROB. 408 (1962); Silva, *Making Votes Count,* 52 NAT'L CIV. REV. 489 (1963).

[21]366 U.S. 420, 426 (1961). In this case, Mr. Chief Justice Warren said: "A statutory discrimination will not be set aside if any state of facts reasonably may be conceived to justify it." *Id.* at 426.

[22]377 U.S. 533 (1964).

[23]377 U.S. at 577-83, 686 n.2. A "floterial district" is one that includes within its boundaries several separate districts or political subdivisions that independently would not be entitled to additional representation but whose conglomerate population entitles the entire area to another seat in the particular legislative body being apportioned.

[24]Dorsey v. Fortson, 228 F. Supp. 259 (N.D. Ga.), *prob. juris. noted,* 33 U.S.L. WEEK 3127 (U.S. Oct. 5, 1964).

[25]Drew v. Scranton, 229 F. Supp. 310 (M.D. Pa. 1964), *appeal docketed,* 32 U.S.L. WEEK 3449 (U.S. June 19, 1964) (No. 1237); for subsequent history, see asterisk footnote on page 242.

[26]*Id.* at 327. (

[27]377 U.S. 713, 731 n.21 (1964).

[28]377 U.S. 533, 622 n.82 (1964).

[29]376 U.S. 52 (1964).

[30]Boineau v. Thornton, Civ. No. AC-1465, E.D.S.C., Aug. 10, 1964 (complaint dismissed), *aff'd per curiam,* 33 U.S.L. WEEK 3141 (U.S. Oct. 19, 1964), petition for rehearing filed, Oct. 30, 1964.

The petition for rehearing filed in the Supreme Court in Boineau, *supra,* stresses very properly the anomaly of the Court's action in affirming the South Carolina case without oral argument at a time when oral argument had been scheduled in the Georgia case, *Fortson v. Dorsey* (see note 24 *supra*), and a request for review and oral argument was pending in the Pennsylvania case, *Drew v. Scranton* (see note 25

supra). All three of these cases raise interrelated aspects of one central problem, *i.e.,* the relation of the new "one man-one vote" philosophy to multi-member district systems, to the subtleties of gerrymandering which may be associated with such systems, and to voting arrangements within multi-member districts.

For the Court to stop now, or to continue to make major reapportionment decisions on the basis of inadequate briefs and argument, would be most unfortunate. If well handled, full dress argument in *Dorsey, Drew,* and *Boineau* could illuminate, for the first time, the political realities and deeper philosophic issues of representation that have been ignored so far in most reapportionment litigation.

[31]Address by Charles Rhyne, past president of the American Bar Association, general counsel of the National Institute of Municipal Law Officers, and one of the counsel in *Baker v. Carr,* delivered before the New York University Alumni Association a few months after *Baker v. Carr.*

[32]COMMISSION ON INTERGOVERNMENTAL RELATIONS (KESTNBAUM COMMISSION), REPORT TO THE PRESIDENT (1955).

[33]U.S. ADVISORY COMMISSION ON INTERGOVERNMENTAL RELATIONS, APPORTIONMENT OF STATE LEGISLATURES (1962).

[34]U.S. ADVISORY COMMISSION ON INTERGOVERNMENTAL RELATIONS, FACTORS AFFECTING VOTER REACTIONS TO GOVERNMENTAL REORGANIZATION IN METROPOLITAN AREAS (1962).

[35]*Id.* at 21.

[36]Annual federal grants-in-aid to state and local governments have risen from three billion to 7.5 billion dollars in the period from 1955 to 1962, and the trend continues. Bureau of the Budget figures, reported in U.S. ADVISORY COMMISSION, PERIODIC CONGRESSIONAL REASSESSMENT OF FEDERAL GRANTS-IN-AID TO STATE AND LOCAL GOVERNMENTS 67 (1961). Although federal payments *directly* to local governments provided less than two per cent of local general revenues in 1960, new federal legislation in 1961 is expected to increase these amounts significantly during the next several years. Bureau of the Census figures, reported in U.S. ADVISORY COMMISSION, LOCAL NON-PROPERTY TAXES AND THE COORDINATING ROLE OF THE STATE 18 (1961).

[37]U.S. ADVISORY COMMISSION ON INTERGOVERNMENTAL RELATIONS, *op. cit. supra* note 35, at 27.

[38]*Ibid.*

[39]Derge, *Metropolitan and Outside Alignments in Illinois and Missouri Legislative Delegations,* 52 AM. POL. SCI. REV. 1065 (1958), incorporating findings of George D. Young, The 1958 Special Session of the Missouri General Assembly, Missouri Political Science Association Newsletter, No. 3 (1958).

[40]STEINER & GOVE, LEGISLATIVE POLITICS IN ILLINOIS 132 (1960).

[41]HACKER, CONGRESSIONAL DISTRICTING 90 (1963).

[42]McDonald, Legislative Malapportionment and Roll Call Voting in Texas: 1960–1963, M.A. Thesis, Univ. of Tex., 1964. Studies of this sort necessarily ignore the differences in nominations, campaigns, and elections that might have resulted from reapportionment or redistricting.

The technique of weighting each legislator's vote by the actual popular population of his district has also been suggested as a species of *remedy* for malapportionment. The New Mexico Legislature, under strong judicial pressure to reapportion, approved in

1963 a weighted vote system as a way of achieving "one man-one vote" apportionment. The plan was nullified by a state court because it was thought to be inconsistent with state constitutional clauses providing that for various purposes various percentages of "members" shall cast votes. Cargo v. Campbell, Santa Fe County Dist. Ct., N.M., Jan. 8, 1964. The Court did not discuss the possible overriding force of the fourteenth amendment. Documents and press clippings concerning the "weighted voting" battle in New Mexico are collected in Irion, Apportionment of the New Mexico Legislature, Univ. of N.M. Dep't of Gov't Research Report, 1964.

This past July a district court in Washington, after declaring the existing legislature invalid, suggested a weighted voting scheme as the most appropriate form of relief. Thigpen v. Meyers, 231 F. Supp. 938 (W.D. Wash. 1964). However, because all parties felt the plan was unworkable, *e.g.*, committee assignments, the court reconsidered and deleted this relief in its October 5 decree and allowed continued use of the "invalid" districts for one year.

[43]377 U.S. 533, 565 (1944).

[44]*Ibid.*

[45]Maryland Comm. for Fair Representation v. Tawes, 377 U.S. 656, 677 (1964).

[46]Under proportional representation no single-member districts are used. All candidates run at large, and all voters rank the candidates in order of their preferences or vote for party lists. The aim is to have each group represented in the legislature in direct proportion to its numerical strength. In this country, much opposition to proportional representation stems from the fear that it would encourage each minority to run a few candidates, and thus break down the two-party system and lead to unstable, coalition governments. See HERMENS, DEMOCRACY OR ANARCHY? A STUDY OF PROPORTIONAL REPRESENTATION (1941); LAKEMAN, VOTING IN DEMOCRACIES: A STUDY OF MAJORITY AND PROPORTIONAL ELECTORAL SYSTEMS (1955); Laughlin, *Proportional Representation: It Can Cure Our Apportionment Ills,* 49 A.B.A.J. 1065 (1963).

[47]The Illinois cumulative voting system, which is not being used this year because of the special election at large, has in the past ensured minority party representation in the lower house of the Illinois legislature. Representatives are elected from plural member districts each having three legislators; each voter has three votes which he can allocate all to one man, divide between two men, or spread evenly among three candidates. See ILL. CONST. art. 4, § 7; Snowden v. Hughes, 321 U.S. 1 (1944); LAKEMAN, *op. cit. supra* note 41. See also BLAIR, CUMULATIVE VOTING: AN EFFECTIVE ELECTORAL DEVICE IN ILLINOIS POLITICS (1960); Blair, *The Case for Cumulative Voting in Illinois,* 47 Nw. U.L. REV. 344 (1952).

[48]Some minority party representation is guaranteed in New York's City Council by the new provision that enlarges the Council by adding two members at large for each borough, but that allows each party to nominate only one at-large candidate in each borough and each voter to cast only one vote for the office. The provision was sustained in Blaikie v. Power, 13 N.Y.2d 134, 243, N.Y.S. 2d 185, 193 N.E.2d 55 (1963), *appeal dismissed,* 375 U.S. 439 (1964). See MACKENZIE, FREE ELECTIONS 55-56 (1958).

[49]Sims v. Frink, 208 F. Supp. 431 (M.D. Ala. 1962), *aff'd sub nom.* Reynolds v. Sims, 377 U.S. 533 (1964).

[50]Moss v. Burkhart, 220 F. Supp. 149 (N.D. Okla. 1963), *aff'd sub nom.* Williams v. Moss, 378 U.S. 558 (1964).

[51]*In re* Apportionment of Legislature, 372 Mich. 418, 126 N.W.2d 731 (1964) and subsequent opinions and order filed June 22 and 24, 1964. Contrast State v. Zimmerman, 22 Wis. 2d 544, 126 N.W.2d 551 and 128 N.W.2d 16 (Wis. 1964).

[52]Butterworth v. Dempsey, 229 F. Supp. 754 (D. Conn. 1964), *aff'd sub nom.* Pinney v. Butterworth, 378 U.S. 564 (1964). In this case, and in a later filed suit concerning Connecticut congressional districts, both the Republican and Democratic state chairmen intervened. N.Y. Times, Feb. 23, 1964, p. 49, col. 1; *id.* March 8, 1964, p. 75, cols. 2-4.

[56]N.Y. Times, July 24, 1964, p. 28, col. 3; *id.* July 28, 1964, p. 30, col. 3.

Following the failure of the special legislative session to agree on an acceptable redistricting plan, the district court took the apparently unprecedented step of cancelling the Nov. 3, 1964, election and requesting counsel to draw up a new timetable to include an early special election, a special legislative session to reapportion temporarily, and a constitutional convention to reapportion the state permanently. N.Y. Times, Sept. 25, 1964, p. 1, cols. 7-8.

[54]*Id.,* Oct. 30, 1964, p. 26, col. 8.

Chapter IV

RIGHTS OF NEGROES

Brown v. *Board of Education*, the School Segregation Case, is now beginning to seem like ancient history. It is, however, surely the most important Supreme Court decision of the twentieth century—not only in its effects on education, but also as a catalyst for all sorts of civil rights movements. The segregation decisions were one of the principal elements triggering the great campaigns by and for Negro interests that have been waged in both South and North during recent years. Although organizations like the NAACP had long been at work, the Supreme Court gave them their first great victory.

When the School Segregation decisions were handed down in 1954, they were subjected to two major criticisms (aside, of course, from the attacks of those who wished to preserve segregation). The first criticism was that the Court should have moved more slowly rather than attempting to desegregate all levels and varieties of public schools simultaneously. The Court had originally held in *Plessy* v. *Ferguson* [163 U.S. 537 (1896)] that the equal protection clause of the Fourteenth Amendment was satisfied by "separate but equal" facilities; thus it refused to interfere with the institution of segregation. In a series of decisions stretching across several years, the Court had more recently held that (1) each state must either provide a law school for Negroes equal to that for whites or admit Negroes to the white school [*Missouri* v. *Canada*, 305 U.S. 337 (1938), *Sipuel* v. *University of Oklahoma*, 332 U.S. 631 (1948)]; (2) once admitted to a white graduate school, Negro students might not be segregated within it [*McLaurin* v. *Oklahoma State Regents*, 339 U.S. 637 (1950)]; and (3) the state might segregate law students only if the Negro law school were in every way equal to the white, considering "intangible" as well as "tangible" factors [*Sweatt* v. *Painter*, 339 U.S. 629 (1950)]. Since the intangible factors to be considered included the status of alumni, the prestige of the institution, and the opportunity to associate with one's future colleagues at the bar, the Court made it patently impossible for any southern state to meet the separate but equal requirement, at least for law schools. It thus appeared that the Court was whittling away at segregation from the top; by manipulating the "intangibles" requirement, it could gradually strike down more and more educational segregation, particularly at the university and vocational school levels where the unequal benefits of white and Negro schools in terms of prestige and alumni were most obvious.

Brown v. *Board of Education*, while solidly grounded on these earlier decisions, particularly on the "intangibles" argument, abandoned this gradual approach for an abrupt and comprehensive attack on all school segregation. Under the *Brown* decision, actual progress in desegregating schools has been slow, but it surely would have been no faster if the Court had adopted a more gradual approach. More important, a gradual approach would have deprived the Negro of the dramatic symbol that *Brown* became in awakening both whites and Negroes to the outrage of segregation in twentieth-century American society.

The second major criticism of *Brown* was presented in a well-known series of lectures by Herbert Wechsler, published under the title of "Toward Neutral Principles of Constitutional Law"* and reprinted in *Principles, Politics, and Fundamental Law: Selected Essays,*† which is referred to throughout this book. Wechsler had two major purposes. The first was to refute the arguments of Learned Hand and others of the judicially modest viewpoint by showing that the court had the right and duty to exercise its powers of judicial review. One argument of the modest viewpoint had been that judicial review simply meant that the Court imposed its policy views over those of Congress. To this Wechsler replied with his second major point, that the Court should make its constitutional judgments not according to the justices' feelings about what the best public policy would be, or which of the litigants is the "good guy" and which the bad, but according to "neutral principles" of constitutional law. He required a

"principled decision...one that rests on reasons with respect to all the issues in the case, reasons that in their generality and then neutrality transcend any immediate result that is involved. When no sufficient reasons of this kind can be assigned for overturning value choices of the other branches of the Government or of a state, those choices must of course, survive."‡

Wechsler did not find in the equal protection clause, (No state shall...deny to any person...the equal protection of the laws....") any principle outlawing segregation and in effect accused the Supreme Court of simply disliking segregation and striking it down without adequate constitutional justification. For Wechsler, the real constitutional right involved in segregation was not equal protection but freedom of association. Viewed in this light there seems to be, as Wechsler himself suggested, almost no solution to the problem. Segregation violates the Negro's freedom of association by preventing him from associating with those whites with whom he wishes to associate. Integration, on the other hand, violates the white's freedom of association by forcing him to associate with Negroes with whom he does not wish to associate. Here again, as in the religion cases, the peculiarly coercive nature of the public schools sharpens the more general problem. The school law must force either segregation or integration. It cannot stand neutral, because it forces every child to go to school—i.e., it forces him to associate in one way or the other.

The principal and "principled" reply to Wechsler is surely that segregation *is* a matter of equal protection and that his argument really boils down to the old one in *Plessy* that segregation is not inherently unequal because the whites are just as separated from the Negroes as the Negroes are from the whites. No matter how much this neat little piece of logic may appeal to the lawyer's mind, the notion that segregation as practiced in the United States does not reek of

---

*73 *Harvard Law Review* 1 (1959).
†Harvard University Press (1961).
‡73 *Harvard Law Review* 1,4 (1959).

inequality is such sheer nonsense that no court could reach a truly principled decision based on such a position. That, in fact, has been the main point of several distinguished lawyers who have replied to Wechsler. One such reply, that of Charles L. Black, Jr., is presented in this chapter.§

Another aspect of Segregation Cases, however, has drawn almost universal criticism. The *Brown* decision itself emphasized that segregation in education was inherently unequal because it deprived Negro children of the incentive to learn. It was not the segregation itself but the unequal educational opportunities resulting from educational segregation that were unconstitutional. Thus the reasons the Court gave for striking down segregation in *Brown* could only justify striking down segregation in *education*. For instance, segregation of public bathing beaches does not, presumably, interfere with Negroes' ability to swim or to enjoy the sun and sand just as much as white persons on the next beach. Yet in a series of decisions following Brown, the Court made it clear that *all* segregation of state facilities was unconstitutional, without offering any reason for its decisions other than a citation to *Brown*—as if *Brown* gave such reasons, when clearly it does not.

The segregation decisions illustrate a tactic that the Court has frequently used in recent years. In controversial areas it first issues a narrowly limited opinion which is relatively easy to defend because it *is* limited. Then, after the attackers have exhausted themselves and the initial public clamor has died, it issues its second and far more sweeping opinion. This latter opinion, if issued in the first place, would have caused so much opposition that it might have been swept away. Now, the enemy's fire having been drawn by the first foray while the Court stayed partially under cover, and the public having had time to calm down and get used to the new exercise of Court power, the second opinion causes far less stir than did the first. By dividing the opposition between two opinions and moving two small steps instead of one big one, the Court dampens the public sentiment that might have led either to a constitutional amendment reversing its position or to massive resistance to its decrees. The Supreme Court first issued a desegregation decision limited to schools and then struck down the segregation of all public facilities. It first condemned the use of a school prayer composed by state officials and only later said that it meant *all* prayers, not just officially composed ones. It first said that some apportionments, particularly those that are totally irrational, are probably unconstitutional and much later insisted that what it really intended all along was that all elected officers must be chosen on a strictly "one man, one vote" basis. Such tactics are politically clever and have worked for the Court so far. It remains to be seen, however, whether such an approach will not undermine the public's confidence in Supreme Court opinions so that they will take any opinion, no matter how narrowly delimited, and assume that it really means the most extreme and wide-ranging exercise of judicial power that it could later be used to cover.

In defense of the Court it must be said that the justices acted in both the reapportionment and segregation areas only after the legislatures had proven themselves incapable of doing so. Negroes are badly underrepresented in Congress. This fact, together with the strong grip Southerners have on many key positions of power in Congress, made it impossible for many years to pass civil rights legislation. The Court finally started the ball rolling. The School Segregation decisions opened two possible lines for keeping it rolling. The first line of action was for the Court itself to expand the concept of state action far beyond

§See also: Louis H. Pollak, "Racial Discrimination and Judicial Integrity: A Reply to Professor Wechsler," 108 *University of Pennsylvania Law Review* 1 (1959).

the area of state-owned facilities like schools so that more and more discrimination could be declared unconstitutional. Obviously, when a school official
discriminates in admitting students, that is discriminatory state action. There
are, however, many situations in which it is not clear whether state action is
involved or merely private discrimination, which is not prohibited by the
Fourteenth Amendment. For instance, if a privately owned bank chartered and
regulated by the state discriminates or if a state court enforces a contract
between two private individuals that binds them to discriminate, are these state
discriminatory actions? How far the Supreme Court enlarges the scope of the
state action concept will in part determine the extent to which Negroes achieve
full equality.

The second route to substantial equality is for Congress to react to invig-
orated Negro demands by passing federal statutes making more and more
segregation illegal. Thomas P. Lewis' article, reprinted below, explores these two
alternative lines of action and finds action by Congress the more effective of the
two. Subsequent to Lewis' article, Congress passed a series of statutes striking
down discrimination in such public facilities as restaurants and hotels, as well
as in voting, thus making it unnecessary for the Court to move on the constitutional front against these particular problems. Similarly the President, by
executive order, is eliminating discrimination in programs aided by federal
funds. Nevertheless, many areas of discrimination are not now covered by
statute, and thus the Supreme Court may yet choose to expand the area of its
concern through further use of the state action concept. Even in education, for
instance, it is unclear whether northern *de facto* school segregation based on
residential segregation will meet the tests of constitutionality.

The evolution of constitutional rights for Negroes has been and will probably continue to be a process of interaction between Congress and the Supreme
Court, with each agency's actions either stimulating, forestalling, or supple-
menting the other's, depending on the circumstances. In spite of the historical
irreversibility of *Brown* v. *Board* and the success of the new Civil Rights Acts
passed by Congress, this remains a rapidly developing field in which the Supreme
Court will encounter new problems in delimiting the scope of "state action," in
dealing with *de facto* segregation, and in testing the constitutionality of new
federal and state statutes concerned with Negro rights.

Selection 11
_____

The Lawfulness of the Segregation Decisions
Charles L. Black, Jr.

Black's article is brief and consistently strikes a common-sense note. The reader
should pay particular attention to Black's final footnote, which concerns itself
with the Court's treatment of the social effects of discrimination. There was
much criticism of *Brown* for its resort to "sociology," apparently because in a
footnote to its holding that segregation created a sense of inferiority, the Court
cited three well-known works on segregation by sociologists. The criticism stems

"The Lawfulness of the Segregation Decisions" by Charles L. Black, Jr., 69 *Yale Law Journal* 421 (1960). Reprinted by permission of the author.

in part from the old—and patently incorrect—notion that courts should concern themselves exclusively with purely legal problems. There is also the fear that sociology is so inexact a science that once a judge enters the sociological thicket he will find confusing and conflicting evidence supporting both sides of the question. Of course, he will find confusion and conflict no matter *what* thicket he enters. The job of courts is to untangle conflicting evidence; they deal with complex and conflicting medical, engineering, and other sorts of scientific evidence as a routine part of personal injury, patent, and other sorts of cases every day.*

The Court's real problem seems to have arisen out of its intention in *Brown* to write an opinion that would strike down segregation only in education while leaving other varieties for the moment intact, for reasons we have already examined. To do this, the Court put together a chain of sociological and psychological causes and effects—that segregation causes feelings of inferiority, that these feelings of inferiority cause negative attitudes toward learning, and that these negative attitudes actually interfere with the student's ability to learn and so result in unequal educational opportunities. As Black suggests, if the Court had said what it really quite obviously meant—that any fool could plainly see that segregation was designed to maintain the inferior position of the Negro— it might have avoided all the byplay about sociology. The Court need not be blind to what everyone knows; and surely everyone knows the precise purpose of segregation, although not everyone may care to admit it.

If the cases outlawing segregation[1] were wrongly decided, then they ought to be overruled. One can go further: if dominant professional opinion ever forms and settles on the belief that they were wrongly decided, then they will be overruled, slowly or all at once, openly or silently. The insignificant error, however palpable, can stand, because the convenience of settlement outweighs the discomfort of error. But the hugely consequential error cannot stand and does not stand.

There is pragmatic meaning then, there is call for action, in the suggestion that the segregation cases cannot be justified. In the long run, as a corollary, there is practical and not merely intellectual significance in the question whether these cases were rightly decided. I think they were rightly decided, by overwhelming weight of reason, and I intend here to say why I hold this belief.

My liminal difficulty is rhetorical—or, perhaps more accurately, one of fashion. Simplicity is out of fashion, and the basic scheme of reasoning on which these cases can be justified is awkwardly simple. First, the equal protection clause of the fourteenth amendment should be read as saying that the Negro race, as such, is not to be significantly disadvantaged by the laws of the states. Secondly, segregation is a massive intentional disadvantaging of the Negro race, as such, by state law. No subtlety at all. Yet I cannot disabuse myself of the idea that that is really all there is to the segregation cases. If both these propositions can be supported by the preponderance of argument, the

cases were rightly decided. If they cannot be so supported, the cases are in perilous condition.

As a general thing, the first of these propositions has so far as I know never been controverted in a holding of the Supreme Court. I rest here on the sólid sense of *The Slaughterhouse Cases*[2] and of *Strauder v. West Virginia*,[3] where Mr. Justice Strong said of the fourteenth amendment:

"It ordains that no State shall make or enforce any laws which shall abridge the privileges or immunities of citizens of the United States (evidently referring to the newly made citizens, who, being citizens of the United States, are declared to be also citizens of the State in which they reside). It ordains that no State shall deprive any person of life, liberty, or property, without due process of law, or deny to any person within its jurisdiction the equal protection of the laws. What is this but declaring that the law in the States shall be the same for the black as for the white; that all persons, whether colored or white, shall stand equal before the laws of the States, and, in regard to the colored race, for whose protection the amendment was primarily designed, that no discrimination shall be made against them by law because of their color? The words of the amendment, it is true, are prohibitory, but they contain

---

*See the materials collected in Carl A. Auerbach, Lloyd K. Garrison, Willard Hurst, and Samuel Mermin, *The Legal Process* (San Francisco: Chandler Publishing Company, 1961), pp. 99-137.

a necessary implication of a positive immunity, or right, most valuable to the colored race,—the right to exemption from unfriendly legislation against them distinctively as colored,—exemption from legal discriminations, implying inferiority in civil society, lessening the security of their enjoyment of the rights which others enjoy, and discriminations which are steps toward reducing them to the condition of a subject race."[4]

If *Plessy v. Ferguson*[5] be thought a faltering from this principle, I step back to the principle itself. But the *Plessy* Court clearly conceived it to be its task to show that segregation did not really disadvantage the Negro, except through his own choice.[6] There is in this no denial of the *Slaughterhouse* and *Strauder* principle; the fault of *Plessy* is in the psychology and sociology of its minor premise.

The lurking difficulty lies not in "racial" cases but in the total philosophy of "equal protection" in the wide sense. "Equal protection," as it applies to the whole of state law, must be consistent with the imposition of disadvantage on some, for all law imposes disadvantage on some; to give driver's licences only to good drivers is to disadvantage bad drivers. Thus the word "reasonable" necessarily finds its way into "equal protection," in the application of the latter concept to law in general. And it is inevitable, and right, that "reasonable," in this broader context, should be given its older sense of "supportable by reasoned considerations."[7] "Equal" thereby comes to mean not really "equal," but "equal unless a fairly tenable reason exists for inequality."

But the whole tragic background of the fourteenth amendment forbids the feedback infection of its central purpose with the necessary qualifications that have attached themselves to its broader and so largely accidental radiations. It may have been intended that "equal protection" go forth into wider fields than the racial. But history puts it entirely out of doubt that the chief and all-dominating purpose was to ensure equal protection for the Negro. And this intent can hardly be given the self-defeating qualification that necessity has written on equal protection as applied to carbonic gas. If it is, then "equal protection" for the Negro means "equality until a tenable reason for inequality is proferred." On this view, Negroes may hold property, sign wills, marry, testify in court, walk the streets, go to (even segregated) school, ride public transportation, and so on, only in the event that no reason, not clearly untenable, can be assigned by a state legislature for their not being permitted to do these things. That cannot have been what all the noise was about in 1866.

What the fourteenth amendment, in its historical setting, must be read to say is that the Negro is to enjoy equal protection of the laws, and that the fact of his being a Negro is not to be taken to be a good enough reason for denying him this equality, however "reasonable" that might seem to some people. All possible arguments, however convincing, for discriminating against the Negro, were finally rejected by the fourteenth amendment.

It is sometimes urged that a special qualification was written on the concept of "equality" by the history of the adoption of the amendment—that an intent can be made out to exclude segregation from those legal discriminations invalidated by the requirement of equality, whether or not it actually works inequality. This point has been discussed and documented by Professor Alexander Bickel,[8] who, though he finds convincing arguments for the conclusion that school segregation was not among the evils the framers of the amendment intended for immediate correction,[9] suggests that they intended at the same time to set up a general concept for later concrete application.[10] Other recent writers take somewhat similar views. The data brought forward by Professor Bickel do not seem to me as persuasive, on his first point, as they do to him. But in supporting his second point he develops a line of thought tending to establish that the legislative history does not render the segregation decisions improper, and I am glad to join him in that practical conclusion. I would add only one point: The question of the "intent" of the men of 1866 on segregation *as we know it* calls for a far chancier guess than is commonly supposed, for they were unacquainted with the institution as it prevails in the American South today. To guess their verdict upon the institution as it functions in the midtwentieth century supposes an imaginary hypothesis which grows more preposterous as it is sought to be made more vivid. They can in the nature of the case have bequeathed us only their generalities; the specifics lay unborn as they disbanded. I do not understand Professor Bickel to hold a crucially different view.

Then does segregation offend against equality? Equality, like all general concepts, has marginal areas where philosophic difficulties are encountered. But if a whole race of people finds itself confined within a system which is set up and continued for the very purpose of keeping it in an inferior station, and if the question is then solemnly propounded whether such a race is being treated "equally," I think we ought to exercise one of the sovereign prerogatives of philosophers—that of laughter. The only question remaining (after we get our laughter under control) is whether the segregation system answers to this description.

Here I must confess to a tendency to start laughing all over again. I was raised in the South, in a Texas city where the pattern of segregation was firmly fixed. I am sure it never occurred to anyone, white or colored, to question its meaning. The fiction of "equality" is just about on a level with the fiction of "finding" in the action of trover. I think few candid southerners deny this. Northern people may be misled by the entirely sincere protestations of many southerners that segregation is "better" for the Negroes, is not intended to hurt them. But I think a little probing would demonstrate that what is meant is that it is better for the Negroes to accept a position of inferiority, at least for the indefinite future.

But the subjectively obvious, if queried, must be backed up by more public materials. What public materials assure me that my reading of the social meaning of segregation is not a mere idiosyncrasy?

First, of course, is history. Segregation in the South comes down in apostolic succession from slavery and the *Dred Scott* case. The South fought to keep slavery, and lost. Then it tried the Black Codes, and lost. Then it looked around for something else and found segregation. The movement for segregation was an integral part of the movement to maintain and further "white supremacy"; its triumph (as Professor Woodward has shown) represented a triumph of extreme racialist over moderate sentiment about the Negro.[11] It is now defended very largely on the ground that the Negro as such is not fit to associate with the white.

History, too, tells us that segregation was imposed on one race by the other race; consent was not invited or required. Segregation in the South grew up and is kept going because and only because the white race has wanted it that way—an incontrovertible fact which in itself hardly consorts with equality. This fact perhaps more than any other confirms the picture which a casual or deep observer is likely to form of the life of a southern community—a picture not of mutual separation of whites and Negroes, but of one in-group enjoying full normal communal life and one out-group that is barred from this life and forced into an inferior life of its own. When a white southern writer refers to the woes of "the South," do you not know, does not context commonly make it clear, that he means "white southerners"? When you are in Leeville and hear someone say "Leeville High," you know he has reference to the white high school; the Negro school will be called something else—Carver High, perhaps, or Lincoln High to our shame. That is what you would expect when one race forces a segregated position on another, and that is what you get.

Segregation is historically and contemporaneously associated in a functioning complex with practices which are indisputably and grossly discriminatory. I have in mind especially the long-continued and still largely effective exclusion of Negroes from voting. Here we have two things. First, a certain group of people is "segregated." Secondly, at about the same time, the very same group of people, down to the last man and woman, is barred, or sought to be barred, from the common political life of the community—from all political power. Then we are solemnly told that segregation is not intended to harm the segregated race, or to stamp it with the mark of inferiority. How long must we keep a straight face?

Here it may be added that, generally speaking, segregation is the pattern of law in communities where the extralegal patterns of discrimination against Negroes are the tightest, where Negroes are subjected to the strictest codes of "unwritten law" as to job opportunities, social intercourse, patterns of housing, going to the back door, being called by the first name, saying "Sir," and all the rest of the whole sorry business. Of course these things, in themselves, need not and usually do not involve "state action," and hence the fourteenth amendment cannot apply to them. But they can assist us in understanding the meaning and assessing the impact of state action.

"Separate but equal" facilities are almost never really equal. Sometimes this concerns small things —if the "white" men's room has mixing hot and cold taps, the "colored" men's room will likely have separate taps; it is always the back of the bus for the Negroes; "Lincoln Beach" will rarely if ever be as good as the regular beach. Sometimes it concerns the most vital matters—through the whole history of segregation, colored schools have been so disgracefully inferior to white schools that only ignorance can excuse those who have remained acquiescent members of a community that lived the Molochian child-destroying lie that put them forward as "equal."

Attention is usually focused on these inequalities as things in themselves, correctible by detailed decrees. I am more interested in their very clear character as *evidence* of what segregation means to the people who impose it and to the people who are subjected to it. This evidentiary character cannot be erased by one-step-ahead-of-the-marshal correction. Can a system which, in all that can be measured, has practiced the grossest inequality, actually have been "equal" in intent, in total social meaning and impact? "Thy speech maketh thee manifest..."; segregation, in all visible things, speaks only haltingly any dialect but that of inequality.

Further arguments could be piled on top of one another, for we have here to do with the most conspicuous characteristic of a whole regional culture. It is actionable defamation in the South to call a white man a Negro. A small proportion of Negro "blood" puts one in the inferior race for segregation purposes; this is the way in which one deals with a taint, such as a carcinogen in cranberries.

The various items I have mentioned differ in weight; not every one would suffice in itself to establish the character of segregation. Taken together they are of irrefragable strength. The society that has just lost the Negro as a slave, that has just lost out in an attempt to put him under quasi-servile "Codes," the society that views his blood as a contamination and his name as an insult, the society that extralegally imposes on him every humiliating mark of low caste and that until yesterday kept him in line by lynching—this society, careless of his consent, moves by law, first to exclude him from voting, and secondly to cut him off from mixing in the general public life of the community. The Court that refused to see inequality in this cutting off would be making the only kind of law that can be warranted outrageous in advance—law based on self-induced blindness, on flagrant contradiction of known fact.

I have stated all these points shortly because they are matters of common notoriety, matters not so much for judicial notice as for the background knowledge of educated men who live in the world. A court may advise itself of them as it advises itself of the facts that we are a "religious people," that the country is more industrialized than in Jefferson's day, that children are the natural objects of fathers' bounty, that criminal sanctions are commonly thought to deter, that steel is a basic commodity in our economy, that the imputation of unchastity is harmful to a woman. Such judgments, made on such a basis, are in the foundations of all law, decisional as well as statutory; it would be the most unneutral of principles, improvised *ad hoc*, to require that a court faced with the present problem refuse to note a plain fact about the society of the United States—the fact that the social meaning of segregation is the putting of the Negro in a position of walled-off inferiority—or the other equally plain fact that such treatment is hurtful to human beings. Southern courts, on the basis of just such a judgment, have held that the placing of a white person in a Negro railroad car is an actionable humiliation; must a court pretend not to know that the Negro's situation there is humiliating?

I think that some of the artificial mist of puzzlement called into being around this question originates in a single fundamental mistake. The issue is seen in terms of what might be called the metaphysics of sociology: "Must Segregation Amount to Discrimination?" That is an interesting question; someday the methods of sociology may be adequate to answering it. But it is not our question. Our question is whether discrimination inheres in that segregation which is imposed by law in the twentieth century in certain specific states in the American Union. And that question has meaning and can find an answer only on the ground of history and of common knowledge about the facts of life in the times and places aforesaid.

Now I need not and do not maintain that the evidence is all one way; it never is on issues of burning, fighting concern. Let us not question here the good faith of those who assert that segregation represents no more than an attempt to furnish a wholesome opportunity for parallel development of the races; let us rejoice at the few scattered instances they can bring forward to support their view of the matter. But let us then ask which balance-pan flies upward.

The case seems so onesided that it is hard to make out what is being protested against when it is asked, rhetorically, how the Court can possibly advise itself of the real character of the segregation system. It seems that what is being said is that, while no actual doubt exists as to what segregation is for and what kind of societal pattern it supports and implements, there is no ritually sanctioned way in which the Court, as a Court, can permissibly learn what is obvious to everybody else and to the Justices as individuals. But surely, confronted with such a problem, legal acumen has only one proper task—that of developing ways to make it permissible for the Court to use what it knows; any other counsel is of despair. And, equally surely, the fact that the Court has assumed as true a matter of common knowledge in regard to broad societal patterns, is (to say the very least) pretty far down the list of things to protest against.

I conclude, then, that the Court had the soundest reasons for judging that segregation violates the fourteenth amendment. These reasons make up the simple syllogism with which I began: The fourteenth amendment commands equality, and segregation as we know it is inequality.

Let me take up a few peripheral points. It is true that the specifically hurtful character of segregation, as a net matter in the life of each segregated individual, may be hard to establish. It seems enough to say of this,...that no such demand is made as to other constitutional rights. To have a confession beaten out of one might in some particular case be the beginning of a new and better life. To be subjected to a racially differentiated curfew might be the best thing in the world for some individual boy. A man might ten years later go back to thank the policeman who made him get off the platform and stop making a fool of himself. Religious persecution proverbially strengthens faith. We do not ordinarily go that far, or look so narrowly into the matter. That a practice, on massive historical evidence and in common sense, has the designed and generally apprehended effect of putting its victims at a disadvantage, is enough for law. At least it always has been enough.

I can heartily concur in the judgment that segregation harms the white as much as it does the Negro. Sadism rots the policeman; the suppressor of thought loses light; the community that forms into a mob, and goes down and dominates a trial, may wound itself beyond healing. Can this reciprocity of hurt, this fated mutuality that inheres in all inflicted wrong, serve to validate the wrong itself?

Finally it is doubtless true that the *School Segregation Cases*, and perhaps others of the cases on segregation, represented a choice between two kinds of freedom of association. Freedom from the massive wrong of segregation entails a corresponding loss of freedom on the part of the whites who must now associate with Negroes on public occasions, as we all must on such occasions associate with many persons we had rather not associate with. It is possible to state the competing claims in symmetry, and to ask whether there are constitutional reasons for preferring the Negroes' desire for merged participation in public life to the white man's desire to live a public life without Negroes in proximity.

The question must be answered, but I would approach it in a way which seems to me more normal—the way in which we more usually approach comparable symmetries that might be stated as to all other asserted rights. The fourteenth amendment forbids inequality, forbids the disadvantaging of the Negro race by law. It was surely anticipated that the following of this directive would entail some disagreeableness for some white southerners. The disagreeableness might take many forms; the white man, for example, might dislike having a Negro neighbor in the exercise of the latter's equal right to own a home, or dislike serving on a jury with a Negro, or dislike having Negroes on the streets with him after ten o'clock. When the directive of equality cannot be followed without displeasing the white, then something that can be called a "freedom" of the white must be impaired. If the fourteenth amendment commands equality, and if segregation violates equality, then the status of the reciprocal "freedom" is automatically settled.

I find reinforcement here, at least as a matter of spirit, in the fourteenth amendment command that Negroes shall be "citizens" of their States. It is hard for me to imagine in what operative sense a man could be a "citizen" without his fellow citizens' once in a while having to associate with him. If, for example, his "citizenship" results in his election to the School Board, the white members may (as recently in Houston) put him off to one side of the room, but there is still some impairment of their freedom "not to associate." That freedom, in fact, exists only at home; in public, we have to associate with anybody who has a right to be there. The question of our right not to associate with him is concluded when we decide whether he has a right to be there.

I am not really apologetic for the simplicity of my ideas on the segregation cases. The decisions call for mighty diastrophic change. We ought to call for such change only in the name of a solid reasoned simplicity that takes law out of artfulness into art. Only such grounds can support the nation in its resolve to uphold the law declared by its Court; only such grounds can reconcile the white South to what must be. *Elegantia juris* and conceptual algebra have here no place. Without pretending either to completeness or to definitiveness of statement, I have tried here to show reasons for believing that we as lawyers can without fake or apology present to the lay community, and to ourselves, a rationale of the segregation decisions that rises to the height of the great argument.

These judgments, like all judgments, must rest on the rightness of their law and the truth of their fact. Their law is right if the equal protection clause in the fourteenth amendment is to be taken as stating, without arbitrary exceptions, a broad principle of practical equality for the Negro race, inconsistent with any device that in fact relegates the Negro race to a position of inferiority. Their facts are true if it is true that the segregation system is actually conceived and does actually function as a means of keeping the Negro in a status of inferiority. I dare say at this time that in the end the decisions will be accepted by the profession on just that basis. Opinions composed under painful stresses may leave much to be desired;[12] it may be that the per curiam device has been unwisely used. But the judgments, in law and in fact, are as right and true as any that ever was uttered.

Footnotes

[1]Brown v. Board of Educ. (The School Segregation Cases, 347 U.S. 483 (1954); Bolling v. Sharpe, 347 U.S. 497 (1954); New Orleans' City Park Improvement Ass'n v. Detiege, 358 U.S. 54 (1959); Gayle v.

Browder, 352 U.S. 903 (1956); Holmes v. Atlanta, 350 U.S. 879 (1955); Mayor & City Council v. Dawson, 350 U.S. 877 (1955); Muir v. Louisville Park Theatrical Ass'n, 347 U.S. 971 (1954).
[2]83 U.S. (16 Wall.) 36 (1873).
[3]100 U.S. 303 (1880).
[4]*Id.* at 307-08.
[5]163 U.S. 537 (1896).
[6]"We consider the underlying fallacy of the plaintiff's argument to consist in the assumption that enforced separation of the two races stamps the colored race with a badge of inferiority. *If this be so, it is not by reason of anything found in the act, but solely because the colored race chooses to put that construction upon it." Id.* at 551. (Emphasis added.) The curves of callousness and stupidity intersect at their respective maxima.
[7]See Lindsley v. Natural Carbonic Gas Co., 220 U.S. 61 (1911).
[8]Bickel, *The Original Understanding and the Segregation Decision,* 69 HARV. L. REV. 1 (1955).
[9]*Id.* at 58.

[10]*Id.* at 61-65.
[11]WOODWARD, THE STRANGE CAREER OF JIM CROW ch. II *Capitulation to Racism,* at 49-95 (1957).
[12]I do not mean here to join the hue and cry against the *Brown* opinion. The charge that it is "sociological" is either a truism or a canard—a truism if it means that the Court, precisely like the *Plessy* Court, and like innumerable other courts facing innumerable other issues of law, had to resolve and did resolve a question about social fact; a canard if it means that anything like principal reliance was placed on the formally "scientific" authorities, which are relegated to a footnote and treated as merely corroboratory of common sense. It seems to me that the venial fault of the opinion consists in its not spelling out that segregation, for reasons of the kind I have brought forward in this Article, is perceptibly a means of ghettoizing the imputedly inferior race. (I would conjecture that the motive for this omission was reluctance to go into the distasteful details of the southern caste system.) That such treatment is generally not good for children needs less talk than the Court gives it.

Selection *12*

The Sit-In Cases: Great Expectations

Thomas P. Lewis

Following the School Segregation decisions, Negroes sought to integrate other kinds of facilities. They hit upon the tactic of sitting in at courtrooms, libraries, lunch counters, restaurants, and other places that denied them service or segregated them. Then by being prosecuted for trespassing and disturbing the peace, they hoped to bring their constitutional claims before the courts and to direct public attention to these denials of equal treatment.

Lewis uses the resulting Sit-in Cases as a jumping-off point for a discussion of the larger problem of "state action," i.e., where to draw the line between discrimination by the state, which is unconstitutional, and discrimination by private persons, which presumably is not subject to constitutional limitation. The sit-in tactic, however, also raises other important issues. Sit-ins frequently involve trespass, i.e., entry onto another's property without his permission. Is the individual entitled to violate someone else's right—his right to personal property—in order to pursue what he believes to be his own rights? Laws against trespass are universally acknowledged to be constitutional. Does the individual have a right, constitutional or moral, to violate a valid law because he believes he is doing so in defense of his constitutional and moral rights?

The Supreme Court has thus far avoided creating a constitutional right to trespass in a good cause. But it has come close. The first Sit-in Cases came to the Court when Negro lunch-counter demonstrators were convicted of disturbing the peace. The Supreme Court simply found that there was no evidence that the peace had been disturbed [*Garner* v. *Louisiana,* 368 U.S. 157 (1961)]. Subsequently, in the cases discussed by Lewis, the convictions were for trespass, but the Court found that the property owners had not invoked the trespass laws because they personally wished Negroes off their property but because state law or custom required segregation. Thus those who "sat in" had violated not the private property rights of the store owners but state segregation practices which were themselves unconstitutional.

Since Lewis wrote this article, there has been a third round of Sit-in Cases, this time involving demonstrators convicted of trespass in privately owned restaurants and other "public facilities" after state laws requiring segregation had been invalidated or repealed and before the new Civil Rights Acts requiring equal services in such facilities had been enacted. Here, finally, was a private property owner asserting his rights in a purely private capacity and a Negro infringing on those rights in pursuit of his own right to be treated equally. Some may see this as a clash between an economic or property right and a personal or moral right and automatically side with the Negro. Before doing so, the reader might pause to remember that it is his property rights that would prevent policemen from breaking in and searching his house at any hour of the day or night, and the government from seizing his house, car, and money because it did not like his politics.

In any event, the Supreme Court managed to avoid the choice. It argued that soon after these trespasses occurred the new Civil Rights Act came into effect and forbade restaurant owners and other such proprietors from refusing service to Negroes. As a result, if the same prosecutions for trespass were to occur now, they would be quashed because trespass exists only when the individual has no legal right to be on the property of another. The Civil Rights Act gave the Negro a legal right to enter and be served on the property of the restaurant owners. The Court then resorted to an old legal doctrine that in effect says that when an individual is convicted of violating a law and, before his conviction becomes final the law is changed so that his action would no longer be a crime, his conviction may be reversed [*Bell* v. *Maryland,* 378 U.S. 226 (1964)]. Thus the Court has not officially declared a constitutional right to sit in, but in every instance it has managed to reverse the convictions of those who have been arrested for such activities.

Sit-ins, of course, involve not only equal protection but freedom of speech as well, for sit-in demonstrators often claim that their demonstrations are in effect proclamations of what they believe to be true and attempts to convince others of that truth just as a public speech or political rally would be. Here again, the question is whether the individual may exercise his right to speech by invading someone else's right to property.

Justice Black, who has campaigned long and hard for freedom of speech, reminds us that breaking the law and violating the legal rights of others cannot so easily be constitutionally or morally excused by waving the flag of freedom as some enthusiasts believe.

"Their argument comes down to this: that...they had a perfect constitutional right to assemble and remain in the restaurant, over the owner's continuing objections, for the purpose of expressing themselves by language and 'demonstrations' bespeaking their hostility to [the owner's] refusal to serve Negroes.... Unquestionably petitioners had a constitutional right to express these views wherever they had an unquestioned legal right to be. But there is the rub....

The right to freedom of expression is a right to express views—not a right to force other people to supply a platform or a pulpit....

A great purpose of freedom of speech and press is to provide a forum for settlement of acrimonious disputes peaceably, without resort to intimidation, force, or violence. The experience of the ages points to the inexorable fact that people are frequently stirred to violence when property which the law recognizes as theirs is forcibly invaded or occupied by others. Trespass laws are born of this experience. They have been, and doubtless still are, important features of any government dedicated, as this country is, to rule of law....The Constitution does not confer upon any group the right to substitute rule by force for rule by law. Force leads to violence, violence to mob conflicts, and these to rule by the strongest groups with the control of the most deadly weapons....At times the rule of law seems too slow to some for the settlement of their grievances. But it is the plan our Nation has chosen to preserve both 'Liberty' and equality for all. On that plan we have put our trust and staked our future. This constitutional rule of law has served us well."*

In reflecting upon Justice Black's words, the reader should bear in mind that invading a man's property, disrupting his business, and physically preventing him from carrying on his lawful occupation are precisely the kinds of force that Justice Black condemns, whether they are undertaken by truncheon-wielding storm troopers or by "nonviolent" crusaders for civil rights.

Mr. Justice Black's view has prevailed by a very slim margin in the recent case of *Adderley v. Florida* [87 S. Ct. 242 (1966)] in which the Supreme Court held that trespass laws may be enforced against demonstrators in order "to preserve the property under [the owner's] control for the use to which it is lawfully dedicated." The five to four vote in this case, and the many marginal situations which may arise, suggest that this is not the last time the Court will deal with this problem.

In the *Sit-in Cases*[1] decided last Term the Supreme Court inched closer to a confrontation with perhaps the most interesting, most discussed—perhaps most crucial—issue since the decision of the *School Segregation Cases*.[2] In some respects the resolution of this issue, whether the Fourteenth Amendment provides the Negro with a self-executing federal right to equal treatment by the proprietors of private establishments catering to all the public except Negroes, may have more far-reaching implications and greater consequences than even the *School Segregation Cases*.[3] For in addition to the increasingly important social and legal problems embodied in the issue, there are involved equally important questions about the role the Court should play in the solution of this and similar problems in which the interests of private groups conflict. The Court has shown an understandable and wise reluctance boldly to seize and dispose of the broader issues concerning the scope of the Fourteenth Amendment's protections, though counsel have tendered them more than

once. In a series of recent cases, beginning with *Boynton v. Virginia*[4] and culminating, temporarily, in the *Sit-in Cases,* the Court has ruled consistently in favor of Negroes seeking service in places of public accommodation, or about to suffer penalties for having sought service. But it has rested its decisions on a variety of grounds concerned with the peculiar facts of the various cases, all of which are too narrow to support conclusions about the larger issue.

Important limitations on the power of managers of places open to the public to discriminate against Negroes had been established even before the petitions for certiorari were granted in the *Sit-in Cases*. Places of public accommodation operated by a state or its agents cannot constitutionally exclude patrons because of race.[5] Nor may the state avoid this result by leasing the property for operation by a "private" lessee.[6] Indeed, it is probably safe to conclude that the lessee of any identifiable

---

Bell v. Maryland 84 S.Ct. 1814, 1878-79 (1964).

state property, using it for a business that caters to the public, may not refuse to serve patrons because of their race.[7] The proprietor of a restaurant operated as an integral part of an interstate carrier's terminal is required under the Interstate Commerce Act to serve the carrier's passengers without regard to their race.[8] The state cannot require a private establishment to segregate its customers; the mere presence of a Negro in an establishment traditionally refusing service to Negroes or segregating them cannot constitute a criminal offense.[9] It follows from this that a police officer cannot on his own initiative lawfully order a Negro to leave a segregated establishment and the state cannot base a criminal charge on the refusal to obey.[10] The choice of discrimination is foreclosed to the state. If discrimination in a private establishment catering to the white public is legally permissible under the Constitution, the Court has made it clear that it can survive only where it is established that the state has not coerced or unduly influenced the choice. This is the teaching of *Garner,* but it is more emphatically and pervasively the teaching of the *Sit-in Cases.*

The *Sit-in Cases* came to the Court in typical fashion. Negro defendants (there was one white defendant in *Lombard*) sought review of their convictions under trespass or criminal mischief statutes for having refused to leave "white" lunch counters in privately owned department stores. The principal opinion was handed down in *Peterson v. City of Greenville.*[11] This case, as well as the others, could have been analyzed as presenting the question whether the Constitution permits a lunch counter proprietor to refuse integrated service to Negroes, or whether it permits the state to enforce such private discrimination. But the City of Greenville had an ordinance making it "unlawful for any person...managing...any hotel, restaurant, cafe, eating house...to furnish meals to white persons and colored persons in the same room...."[12] And there was testimony in the record that the store manager had asked the Negroes seeking service to leave "because integrated service was 'contrary to local customs'...and in violation of the...City ordinance...."[13] Thus, a court might have found that the choice to discriminate was not private at all; rather, that it was dictated by the city and merely obeyed by the manager. The conviction of the defendants, turning on the dictation of discrimination by the city, would clearly violate the Fourteenth Amendment. But Chief Justice Warren, writing for the majority in *Peterson,* chose a broader explanation for the reversal of the convictions. He said that the city had removed the decision to discriminate from the sphere of private choice. The store management, in excluding Negroes, acted precisely as the city had directed. Building from these observations, Chief Justice Warren found irrelevant a contention that the store manager might have made his choice to exclude Negroes without regard to the city ordinance:[14]

"[T]hese convictions cannot stand, even assuming, as respondent contends, that the manager would have acted as he did independently of the existence of the ordinance. The State will not be heard to make this contention in support of the convictions....When a state agency passes a law compelling persons to discriminate against other persons because of race, and the State's criminal processes are employed in a way which enforces the discrimination mandated by that law, such a palpable violation of the Fourteenth Amendment cannot be saved by attempting to separate the mental urges of the discriminators."

Having removed the need to inquire into the actual effect on the proprietors of the existence of ordinances requiring segregation, the Court, relying on its statement of the *Peterson* case, reversed the convictions in *Gober v. City of Birmingham,* vacated the judgment and remanded *Avent v. North Carolina,* and reversed the judgment in *Lombard v. Louisiana.* There were special complications in *Lombard.* Neither the state nor the city of New Orleans has a law forbidding desegregation of the races in restaurant facilities. But shortly prior to the activity for which the defendants in *Lombard* were arrested, both the chief of police and the mayor of New Orleans had issued public statements to the effect that sit-in demonstrations were not in the public interest and would not be permitted. There was some evidence that the store manager who asked the demonstrators in *Lombard* to leave felt bound by the pronouncements of the city officials to do so. The Court treated the city "exactly as if it had an ordinance prohibiting"[15] the demonstrations, and rested its decision to reverse the convictions squarely on the *Peterson* rule. In none of the cases did the Court's conclusions depend upon a finding that the ordinances or pronouncements actually affected the conduct of the store managers.

This prompted Mr. Justice Harlan to dissent in part in *Lombard, Gober,* and *Avent.* He balked at the effectual creation by the majority of an irrebuttable presumption of obedience to the ordinances and pronouncements by the private managers. He noted that laws requiring segregation "have already found their just constitutional deserts in the decisions of this Court," and may have a purely formal existence in some localities. While he recognized that their existence might well have a significant effect on private decision-making, he believed "the question in each case, if the right of the individual to make his own decisions is to remain viable, must be: was the discriminatory exclusion in fact influenced by the law?" He continued: "The inexorable rule which the Court lays down reflects insufficient reckoning with the demands of history."[16]

The logic of the matter appears to be with Mr. Justice Harlan. But the position of the majority may be supportable exactly because there is behind Chief Justice Warren's conclusions an attempt to reckon "with the demands of history." The positions of both the majority and dissent are meaningful only if they are compatible with the momentary assumption that a purely private choice to discriminate at department store lunch counters is not reached by the Fourteenth Amendment; that use of state courts to enforce this private choice is permissible. To hold, as Mr. Justice Harlan does, that a discriminatory choice compelled by the state is prohibited is not incompatible with the assumption. On the other hand, there would seem to be nothing wrong with a private choice made without reference to—perhaps without knowledge of—an ordinance directing the choice. Since the momentary hypothesis is that private choice in the absence of an ordinance is legal, why is not private choice legal that is completely uninfluenced by an ordinance? And though the result of the majority is not without a degree of poetic justice, its tendency to make a segregation law operate as an antidiscrimination law is at least superficially curious and at war with the basic assumption momentarily posited. It may be sufficient answer to this to say that the civil trespass remedy, self-help, and refusal to serve are still open to the private establishment—unless, of course, the majority would broaden its rule to close these doors. It did not close them by its language in these cases. Indeed, the majority seemed to emphasize the unseemliness of the state's insistence in a criminal prosecution that choice was private in spite of city law directing the same choice. To the extent, then, that private choice is still possible, either because the repeal of the segregation laws will remove the state intrusion or because other means of preserving the choice than a criminal trespass action are available to a private agency, the majority's refusal to inquire into the effect of the segregation laws is not incompatible with the assumption that private discrimination is beyond the reach of the Constitution.

Still, there is a strong current of constitutional doctrine that excludes from the consideration of the Court laws that do not rise from the dead words of the statute books. Certainly in some contexts it can be said that an unenforced law or the unauthorized direction of a public official is not law. In *Poe v. Ullman*,[17] for example, the Court dismissed suits brought by a physician, a married couple, and married women challenging the validity of Connecticut's anticontraceptive law. Looking to a long history of nonenforcement of the law, the Court held the parties failed to show they had sustained or were immediately in danger of sustaining a direct injury. Mr. Justice Frankfurter, writing for himself and three other Justices, said, " 'Deeply embedded traditional ways of carrying out state policy...'—or not carrying it out—'are often tougher and truer law than the dead words of the written text.' "[18] This idea, that action speaks louder than words, could cut either way in the sit-in context. Even though the segregation laws are clearly unconstitutional and in this sense dead-letter, enforcement action based upon the laws could have a seriously harassing effect on proprietors, influencing their action. On the other hand, the laws might be ignored and forgotten by enforcement officials. Only through factual inquiry of the sort made in *Poe* can the status and effect of such laws within a community be determined.

There is a close analytical similarity between *Poe* and the *Sit-in Cases*. Paul and Pauline Poe, husband and wife, alleged that the pregnancy of Mrs. Poe would jeopardize the physical and mental health of both because of a history of congenital abnormalities in previous children born to them. Because their doctor, an eminent gynecologist, allegedly feared prosecution under Connecticut law, he could not provide advice in methods of preventing conception. The Poes suffered from the law not because of threats of its enforcement directly against them but because it affected their relationship with another who feared prosecution. In the *Sit-in Cases*, the segregation laws affected the Negro defendants, if at all, through their effect on the relationship between the Negroes and the private proprietors who may have felt the pressure of the laws. In *Poe*, the Court refused jurisdiction in spite of allegations of Dr. Buxton's fear of prosecution; in the *Sit-in Cases*, the Court considered the actual effect of the laws to be irrelevant. Several cases establish the doctrine that A may complain of a law's effect on B who, because of the law, will not enter into a relationship with A. *Truax v. Raich*[19] and *Pierce v. Society of Sisters*[20] come to mind and were cited in *Poe*. But they were distinguished on the ground that a real fear of prosecution existed in the mind of B in each of those cases, while Dr. Buxton's fear of the Connecticut laws could only be "chimerical." This distinction points up the importance and relevance of the actual effect of the laws which are questioned.

In a case decided last Term, the Court dealt with a similar problem. In *Bantam Books, Inc. v. Sullivan*,[21] the Court, at the instance of a publisher, condemned the action of a state agency that systematically gave advice to book distributors concerning the obscene nature of the publisher's books and magazines. While the agency had no enforcement powers, it did couple its advice with the threat of prosecution by other officials if the advice to remove the books was not followed. The standard applied by the agency to determine obscenity was broad: the Rhode Island Attorney General admitted in argument that the agency's application exceeded the constitutionally permissible. Moreover, Rhode Island law condemned only the sale to minors of certain types of publications, while the agency advised removal of the publications from the shelves of sellers in order to avoid prosecution. The private distributor could have ignored many of the threats of prosecution with a reasonable degree of safety, at least if he were willing to fight each attempt to the United States Supreme Court. But when he acted on the threats by collecting and returning to the publisher all the objectionable publications, this was proof enough that his fear of prosecution and harassment was real. The case is analogous to the *Sit-in Cases* in that action by a private individual, presumably constitutional viewed as private action, formed the basis of a constitutional attack by the publisher against the state agency because the latter influenced the private distributor's decision. But again, the Court relied upon a finding that the distributor's decisions were in fact caused by the agency action, a finding that is irrelevant under the rule of the *Sit-in Cases*.

There is, however, an important difference between these cases and the *Sit-in Cases*. In each of the cases cited the party challenging the state law or state action was the initiator of the suit. Absent proof of a causal relationship between threats of enforcement of the law and an injurious effect upon the plaintiff, no adversary case could be made out. Justiciability was needed and this could be supplied only by a real quarrel between plaintiff and officials. In the *Sit-in Cases*, defendants challenged the segregation laws, and since they were fighting convictions, the Court had "cases." The question was one not of justiciability but of the scope of review. Generally even the defendant can challenge the constitutionality only of laws applied to him, and the segregation laws could have application only through their proved influence on the proprietors or through direct enforce-

ment. But there is a line of cases that, by analogy, may provide an adequate foundation for the Court's statement of the dispositive rule.

Without articulating a clear doctrine, the Court has in many cases struck down laws for vagueness or overbroadness. Usually the assertion of void-for-vagueness has come from a defendant prosecuted for violation of the law. While the Court often speaks of the need to protect that defendant's right to be warned of the conduct that will violate the law, recent scholarship in this area has presented persuasive evidence that the plight of the defendant before the Court is only one factor. Suggested as more important factors are the need to protect other persons from deprivation *sub silentio* of constitutional rights, and the need to preserve the efficacy of federal judicial machinery established for the protection of constitutional rights.[22] Persons of unknown numbers and identity may lose rights by submitting, because of fear of prosecution, to broadly worded legislation that restricts protected as well as punishable conduct. And since the broadness of the law creates an unclear, variable standard of guilt for the fact-finder, or permits an unduly broad discretion in the administrator, the possibilities of an even-handed application of law and of effective judicial review are substantially decreased.

These observations suggest analogies on which the sit-in rule might rest. If the Court had been concerned only for the defendants of the cases, the actual effect of the segregation laws on the specific private proprietors would have been highly relevant. The Court, however, was equally concerned with persons unknown and unknowable who might be affected by the cumulative pressure of such laws on a variety of proprietors in a variety of environments. In addition, a different rule would require proof in each specific case tending to "separate the mental urges of the discriminators." When only the proprietor can know what his "mental urges" are, and when even he might find difficulty in separating them, judicial review will be more effective for the mass of cases that might be presented if the Court by the announcement of its rule makes it as certain as it can that proprietors and officials alike appreciate the precise status of segregation laws. In explanation of the void-for-vagueness doctrine, Professor Amsterdam said:[23]

"Because of the Court's limited power to reexamine fact on a cold record, what appears to be going on in the administration of the law must be forced, by restrictive procedures, to reflect what is really going on; and because of the impossibility, through sheer volume of cases, of the Court's effectively policing law administration case by case, those procedures must be framed to assure, as well as procedures can assure, a certain overall *probability* of regularity."

The *Sit-in Cases* may reflect the decision of the Court that an over-all "probability of regularity" can best be assured by a rule that will wipe the books clean of segregation laws. The pattern of segregation in the South is well known. It has been observed that state and local Jim Crow laws share responsibility for the ingrained habits of the people.[24] The enactment of these laws probably reflected the unchecked desires of a dominant group, but it is clear that the customs of the people and their laws have reinforced each other and that they have a chicken-and-egg relationship.[25] A group of North Carolinians observed recently that the existence of segregation laws on the statute books:[26]

"...is an invitation to misunderstanding, confusion and violence. They should be repealed. It is not that a Negro is about to be prosecuted for using white facilities....Rather, the danger is that so long as these compulsory statutes are on the books, some private citizens are more than likely to take it upon themselves to try to enforce segregation. ...Neither private citizens, nor law enforcement officers ought to be misled by these dead letters."

The laws probably erect other barriers to untrammeled private choice. There was evidence in the *Peterson* case that both the proprietor and the police relied upon Greenville's segregation law. The people affected by the laws may tend to utilize them even if they may feel no real obligation to abide by them. New Orleans has no law commanding segregation in restaurants, but there is a city ordinance that prohibits the mixing of races in places where liquor is sold.[27] Conversation with a law enforcement official in New Orleans indicates that while restaurants are being desegregated, liquor-serving places are not, and several "pure" restaurants have applied for liquor licenses "in an effort to prevent service to Negroes under the city ordinance." Thus private proprietors may feel compelled to obey segregation laws or they may use them as a shield or crutch. While it is adequate generally to invalidate laws held unconstitutional on a case-by-case basis, there is a peculiar need, arising out of the assumed distinction between private and official choice, for the obliteration of state choice expressed in written law. The rule of the *Sit-in Cases* is designed to serve

this need, just as the invalidation of a law for vagueness serves purposes other than the protection of the specific defendant in the case. If private choice in the sit-in context is left untouched by the Fourteenth Amendment, the Court is justified in taking those steps procedurally available to it to insure that the choice preserved is as private as it can be. In light of the history of discrimination in the South, buttressed by a multitude of reminders in the form of Jim Crow laws, the Court was probably more justified in "playing 'Hamlet' without Hamlet" in the *Sit-in Cases* than it was in *Winters v. New York*.[28]

The formula adopted by the Court in the *Sit-in Cases* does invite the serious objection that it may render temporarily unenforceable truly private choices. But the context of such a result should not be ignored. The sit-in disputes are essentially suits to try title. Private proprietors did not lose suits for actual damages; their interests were not sacrificed: the larger issue of their ability to select patrons on the basis of race remains to be decided. At the same time the cases in which the Court has avoided answering the fundamental titular question are no less important because of the avoidance. In the process of avoidance, during which the Court has followed its practice of deciding the narrowest constitutional question presented, all-important time has been gained. If the Court eventually finds a duty of service to all in the Equal Protection Clause (or a state duty to insure equal service or to refrain from assisting in any way a private refusal of service), the people likely will find it a more acceptable ruling than they would have even a year ago. The Negroes themselves have been utilizing the time to educate whites in the justice of their claim and in the importance they attach to it. The tenor of the Court's opinions and of Mr. Justice Douglas' concurring opinions in *Garner* and *Lombard,* coupled with the results of the leading state-action cases, has laid a foundation for ultimate decision in favor of the Negroes. If the ultimate decision leaves private choice unfettered, the interim decisions' contribution will be even more significant for having helped to create an atmosphere in which the choice can be as private as law reasonably can make it. Cases in which the Court may write more definitive opinions are already before it.[29] Others are on their way up. Further clarification of the manner in which private choice may be supported by the state may result. Now as never before, however, the attention of the people is focused on the broader question of the nature of the limitations on the scope of the Fourteenth Amendment, the so-called state-action concept.

BEYOND THE SIT-IN CASES

The subject has been pretty thoroughly canvassed, but its amenability to a variety of analyses invites further discussion. To comment on the concept of state action is to venture into the process, described by Professor Freund, of attempting "to prove the unknown by means of the more unknown—what the logicians call *ignotum per ignotius.*"[30] The frontier cases like *Shelley v. Kraemer*[31] create more questions than they answer. In seeking answers, we must recognize that the vagueness of the Fourteenth Amendment permits an analysis that concludes that there is no requirement, properly described as state action, in the Amendment. Here, as everywhere, much depends upon the postulates on which analysis rests. Problems of racial discrimination, especially discrimination in places of public accommodation, have caused the concept of state action to be scrutinized more closely than ever before. The strong feeling that the Fourteenth Amendment should and does deny to the states the power to countenance such discrimination is perhaps the primary reason many persons have questioned the validity of a concept that, as conventionally understood, seems to stand in the way. Some have accepted the verbal concept of state action and devised theories that in certain situations will ascribe private discrimination to the state.[32] Others have urged a more sophisticated approach based on recognition of the fact that there is "state action" at least in any situation in which the state has the power to act and has had an opportunity to do so through its courts. The decision whether a state acted as it should have in each case is for the Supreme Court.[33] Of course, if state action is ever-present, the phrase as a verbalized shorthand description of a division of powers within a federal structure ceases to have meaning. This division of power is recognized by a third analysis.[34] Finally, it is suggested that while the problem of racial discrimination in places of public accommodation does not readily answer to any of the lines of development traced out as significant state involvement, neither does its solution require a radical departure by the Court from its traditional role of judicial review of state action.[35] The special nature of the problem renders it amenable to the Fourteenth Amendment interpreted by the accepted judicial method of analogical reasoning, a process the Court has apparently used in all of the leading state-action cases.

THE MECHANICS OF STATE ACTION

Some of the most popular theories for subjecting private proprietors to the Equal Protection Clause of the Fourteenth Amendment, or for denying them the aid of state courts in their discrimination, are traceable to language in the classically enigmatic *Civil Rights Cases.*[36] In announcing that the Amendment was directed to "State action of a particular character" and that individual "invasion of individual rights is not the subject matter of the amendment," Mr. Justice Bradley also described immune private acts as the acts of "a mere individual," and said the "civil rights, such as are guaranteed by the Constitution against State aggression, cannot be impaired by the wrongful acts of individuals, unsupported by State authority in the shape of laws, customs, or judicial or executive proceedings."[37] Mr. Justice Harlan, dissenting, urged, *inter alia,* the licensing connection between the state and private establishments such as restaurants and theaters as the basis for application of the Amendment to the private establishment.

From this language have grown theories that private "rights" of discrimination cannot be recognized or enforced by state courts because they are then supported by state law; that a state may not use its licensing power to legitimize a business that discriminates; and that action conforming to well-established custom is not private in the sense of the Amendment. The arguments based on these theories generally link the state to private discrimination, then call upon existing precedents condemning discrimination by the state. The illusion that a court has nothing to do but mechanically to apply precedent is thereby created. The weakness of these theories, so used, is that they cannot adequately explain or advance one toward the decision of the real issue. They are not acceptable principles of state action because they are not principles. Their application must be limited, but there is no clue within the terms of the theories of the limiting considerations. A court's enforcement or recognition of private discrimination is obviously not sufficient reason in every case or even most cases to attribute the discrimination to the state, and it is natural to ask in which cases the theory should apply and why it should apply. If factors outside the mere fact of court enforcement must be called upon to draw lines, it is questionable whether the theory adds anything but confusion. An analysis may be developed that pinpoints state responsibility for certain private discrimination at the juncture where the aid of state courts is sought to enforce the private discrimination. But this is a different approach; it recognizes the need to call into play other vital considerations. If the Court decides the Equal Protection Clause calls for nondiscrimination in places of public accommodation, it might begin (and end) by nullifying state court proceedings recognizing or enforcing the discrimination. Thus, while the involvement of the state through its courts may have important consequences, it is not acceptable analysis simply to urge that a state court cannot enforce private choices that its legislature cannot make.

Similar objections must be made to the licensing theory. "Licenses" are usually tax receipts, health permits, or permits to sell alcoholic beverages. Building permits might as well be included. It is apparent that all the enterprises so "licensed" will not be subject to all or some of the limitations imposed on the states by the Fourteenth Amendment. Such licenses are issued for activities ranging from the erection of a private home, through the operation of a private club, down to the operation of a restaurant. The licenses are not traditionally considered as grants from government to supply some service that government requires but serve as a means of regulation. The licensing theory can hardly mean that all such regulated phases of private activity must meet the requirements of the Fourteenth Amendment, and if the theory were so all-encompassing it would be logical to ask why only the regulated, as contrasted with activity that *might* be regulated, should be singled out. The theory might emphasize "privilege" as the incident of licensing or taxation, but many privileges, including home ownership, are taxed or regulated. Licensing just will not do service in a mechanical fashion as an aid to judicial interpretations of the Fourteenth Amendment. The activity that is licensed must be considered and, once considered, it is questionable whether the fact of licensing adds anything. Repeal of a licensing system after restaurants were opened to all the public because of the system would not change any really significant fact. With or without a licensing scheme the factors that are of importance to the victims of discrimination remain unchanged in importance. Why attempt to disguise them with a superficial gloss? Should control of public accommodations by government be extended to forbid racial discrimination, an existing licensing scheme would provide a convenient control mechanism. Forfeiture or suspension of licenses as a penalty for repeated noncompliance with an antidiscrimination mandate should prove effective. But the license is a means of control, not the reason for the control.

A mechanical theory of custom fares little better. Custom and law cannot be thoroughly equated for the purposes of the Fourteenth Amendment. The equation again proves too much. But an argument based on custom can advance further than an argument based on licensing, for custom goes to the merits of the real social and legal problems involved. Absent a widespread custom of discrimination in public accommodations, the problem would be of small proportion. A well-established custom tends to have the effect of law because of its nearly universal observance and the consequent pressure of obedience that it places on the individual. But serious problems are encountered when too heavy reliance is placed on custom to explain the Supreme Court's function. The same custom that generates discrimination in one sphere of life generates it pervasively through almost all spheres. Pressures generated by customs are felt in realms of activity beyond those involving racial discrimination. Unless custom is to be equated with law wherever it is found, and this on analysis will prove to be not only unwise but, fortunately, impossible, other factors once more must mediate between that conduct which will be permitted and that which will not. For example, federal law protects the right of the worker to refuse to participate in concerted activity with his fellow workers. But few would conceive as a denial of that guaranteed choice the custom that exerts powerful pressures on the worker and makes the strike and picket line powerful tools of restraint.

Customs "having the force of law" must be distinguished from custom that derives its power from the human desire to conform to a pattern of conduct. The former was apparently operating in *Garner,* where police officers on their own initiative arrested Negroes simply for sitting at a lunch counter reserved by the management for whites. It was obviously operating in *Baldwin v. Morgan,*[38] where policemen, acting on instructions from their superiors, assured segregated waiting rooms in a railroad terminal. The statements of the chief of police and mayor of New Orleans in *Lombard,* as interpreted by the Court, could be taken by proprietors to articulate custom having the force of law. Discriminating actions of a state official are subject to the Fourteenth Amendment, unless they occur in his purely private capacity, whether they are authorized, unauthorized, or positively forbidden by the written law of a state.

The possibilities for a more refined theory of custom, and an analysis that emphasizes the customary treatment of whites instead of the customary treatment of Negroes, are discussed below.

THE DEEPER SEARCH FOR A SOLUTION

Competing Constitutional Rights

A mechanical or conceptual approach to state action touches either too much or too little. It either prevents decisions such as *Shelley v. Kraemer* or extends its coverage to ludicrous extremes. And, to quote half of a sentence of Professor Henkin's, "one feels that *Shelley v. Kraemer* is 'correct.'..."[39] With this the threshold of inquiry into the meaning of *Shelley* and cases like *Marsh v. Alabama*[40] and *Smith v. Allwright*[41] is approached. But further progress is difficult because of the scope of the Fourteenth Amendment.

A recurring question used to test the meaning of *Shelley* is the status of a householder seeking the aid of a court against a trespasser because of his race. There is a much wider reef along which a given rationalization of state action may run aground. A finding that X is subject to standards applicable to the state for purposes of racial discrimination invites questions about the relevance to X of standards governing an individual's rights of privacy, speech, religion, and property as against the state. It may seem proper to hold X to the standards of the state or deny him the aid of a state court on the one score, while it would seem nonsensical to subject him to other restrictions applicable to the state. At the same time, a nonconceptual approach to the state-action problem, limited to the equal protection guarantee, would put many issues beyond the reach of the Court and cast doubt upon cases like *Marsh v. Alabama* and *Smith v. Allwright*. A few illustrations point up the problem. The public building in which the coffee shop in the *Burton* case was located also contained a jewelry shop and a bookstore leased under the same circumstances as the coffee shop. What does the holding that the coffee shop must not discriminate in its service mean with respect to freedom of the press limitations on the bookstore's operation, or equal protection obligations of the jewelry shop in its employment policies? A similar problem is contained demoniacally in a case in which a religious organization leasing an auditorium for a temporary period from a city insisted on seating Negroes in rear seats.[42] The Court in *Burton* subjected a lessee of state property to the Fourteenth Amendment. But a broad rule that the lessee of state property is an agent of the state would probably prevent the leasing of property by a state to a religious organization. The creation of a flat prohibition of this sort is not likely, but this means a lessee is sometimes subject to the Amendment, sometimes not. It is apparent from existing precedents that the Court will take a particularistic approach to the state-action problem, an approach difficult if not impossible to capture in a meaningful rule or principle. Most commentators urge such an approach because of the sheer volume and variety of not-so-hypothetical situations that invite judicial solution. Suppose a

corporation discharges an employee because of his political views; a labor organization refuses to admit Negroes, or to represent Negro members of the bargaining unit fairly; a medical society refuses to admit persons because of race; a religious organization effectively bans the showing of a motion picture in a community. The unending combination of variables that seems possible has led many to the conclusion that any concept of state action is too sticky and unwieldy. A rule developed to reach any given problem may reach too far.

A solution that is becoming increasingly popular in the journals might be described as a "balancing of interests" or "competing constitutional rights" analysis. The first step necessary to the adoption of this alternative is recognition that law, and in our system this means primarily state law, is allpervading. Potentially all actions and personal relationships are subject to the regulation of law; the law must choose constantly between competing assertions of rights and privileges. In a suit between an ex-employee and the employer who fired him because of his political views, a state court must rule in favor of one or the other. Since the state will have acted through its courts in any event, its decision under the "balancing of interests" approach should be subject to review by the Supreme Court to see if the state denied due process.[43] As one writer has said of the case in which a seller discriminates on the basis of race or religion in the sale of his home:[44]

"The issue is not whether there is state action at all. Rather, the issue is to be resolved by the balancing of the constitutional right against racial or religious discrimination on the one hand, with the freedom of the private citizen to engage in his personal discrimination as he wishes."

In our employee-employer case, interests to be weighed would be the corporation's right to manage its property and, perhaps, freedom to contract and the employee's freedom of speech. Discrimination in places of public accommodation according to this analysis simply presents an instance of competing constitutional rights, not distinguishable in its constitutional dimension from a case such as *Saia v. New York*,[45] where regulation of the use of loudspeakers was in issue and the Court had to balance interests of two private groups to ascertain the validity of the regulation.

At least three factors make this analysis attractive: (1) the problems to be solved are enormously complex and delicate: any state-action requirement will be too insensitive to the problems; (2) the many problems seem to demand solution more quickly than nonjudicial agencies are able or willing to solve them, and a sense of greater security attaches to the ability of an aggrieved party to take his grievance to a court; (3) the advocates of the analysis generally can easily strike a balance of the competing interests in a way that will solve the most pressing problems, *i.e.*, those presenting serious and blatant racial discrimination.

One of the most thorough presentations of a "competing constitutional rights" analysis in which "state action" is debunked and cast aside is Professor Henkin's. His analysis is directed especially to the competition between a claim under the Due Process Clause and a claim under the Equal Protection Clause. It is not clear whether Professor Henkin would limit the analysis to cases presenting this clash—primarily racial and religious discrimination cases—or expand it to cover cases presenting, say, a claim of freedom of speech against a claim of property or contract. Others would apply the analysis without special limitation to racial and religious discrimination.

Professor Henkin's point of departure is *Shelley v. Kraemer*. Noting that a state might be held responsible for discrimination that it encourages or sanctions, Henkin argues that the state is responsible for discrimination that its courts render effective. The question is not whether there is state action in such a case—there obviously is—but whether the choice that the state court makes between competing private claims is constitutionally permissible. Normally, he continues, the Equal Protection Clause prohibits the state from giving effect to racial or religious discrimination, but in each case, the competing claim, in *Shelley* the claimed right of Kraemer to choose his neighbors and to contract for that purpose, must be appraised. If this competing interest "outweighs" the claim of equal protection, the state may, perhaps must, choose to give it effect; otherwise it must choose in favor of equal protection by refusing to give effect to private discrimination. Henkin sums up the meaning of *Shelley* as follows:[46]

"If the competing claims of liberty and the possibility that they may sometimes prevail are recognized, *Shelley v. Kraemer* must be given a more limited reading, and new qualifications must be made to discussions of state responsibility for discrimination. *Shelley*, we would say, holds that generally a state may not enforce discrimination which it could not itself require or perpetrate. Such enforcement is state action, makes the state responsible for a denial of equal protection. But there are circumstances where the discriminator can invoke a protected liberty which is not constitutionally inferior to the claim of equal protec-

tion. There the Constitution requires or permits the state to favor the right to discriminate over the victim's claim to equal protection; the state, then, is not in violation of the fourteenth amendment when it legislates or affords a remedy in support of the discrimination. This may perhaps be viewed as a form of 'reasonable classification,' the traditional basis for permissible discrimination under the equal protection clause. It may, instead, be viewed as the result of the inevitable need to choose between competing constitutional rights; when the equal protection clause and the due process clause conflict, the equal protection clause prevails except in that small area where liberty has its special claim."

Professor Henkin frankly admits that his analysis "entails important changes in the jurisprudence of the Fourteenth Amendment"[47] and has "implications for cases which do not involve racial and religious discrimination."[48] The analysis does, indeed, have broad and important implications resulting from a subtle but crucial shift in the role of the Supreme Court. For the analysis greatly increases the bulk of constitutional litigation in which substantial questions are presented by changing the nature of the issues presented.

Gordon v. Gordon,[49] where a discriminatory provision in a will was given effect in Massachusetts over Fourteenth Amendment objections, provides a convenient illustration. A legatee who lost part of his bequest because he married outside the Jewish faith in contravention of a condition in the will claimed violation by the state of the Equal Protection Clause. This claim, under the suggested analysis, "competed" with the rights of testators arbitrarily to dispose of their property. Since the state in such a case unquestionably is involved in the administration of estates, we may put the state aside and think in terms of competing private constitutional rights. Since these "rights" collide, and since they are, by force of the analysis, "constitutional" rights, one must prevail over the other and the Supreme Court must have the final say, unless it rejects the case by denial of the petition for certiorari. The state has the first choice in making a rule to govern the conflict, but is subject to reversal by the Supreme Court because the choice is between constitutional rights. And in reviewing the state choice, the Supreme Court cannot inquire simply whether the state court acted arbitrarily or unreasonably in the conventional sense of those tests. The same question may be asked, but the test of reasonableness will be whether the state chose to uphold the proper constitutional right. It is true that this process is not greatly different in description from that employed

by the Court when it balances interests to determine if a particular state legislative choice is
constitutionally permissible. But in the *Gordon v.
Gordon* context, a legislative choice typically subject to constitutional review would either direct
a particular form of discrimination or forbid it. In
either event, this kind of affirmative choice by the
state would be tested by weighing the police
power of the state against the effects of the legislation on individuals. The contest would be between the state and the individual in the fullest
sense. If the state won, the result would be that it
may so regulate individuals, not that it *must* so
regulate them. In *Gordon v. Gordon*, the problem
essentially was one of nonregulation—the testator
was not forced by state law either to discriminate
or to refrain from discrimination. The effect of the
"competing constitutional rights" analysis, fully accepted, is not only to force the state to make a
regulatory choice but to transfer to the Supreme
Court as a matter of its routine function the power
to decide which choice must be made. Had
Gordon v. Gordon been decided by the Supreme
Court under the Henkin analysis, it seems the
result would have to be either that a testator must
be allowed to invoke religious discrimination in the
circumstances or he must not be allowed to. While
the Court presently can permit a state to allow
such discrimination through nonregulation, it being open to the state to attempt later to regulate
against the discrimination, the Court would face
a very different question if the result of permitting
nonregulation by the state were tantamount to
elevating the individual's power to discriminate to
the status of a constitutional right. The analysis, in
its theory, provides a formula for "instant" total
regulation, ameliorated by the inability of the
Court to decide more than a few important questions each year.

Professor Henkin anticipated this objection by
reminding the reader that the Constitution may
"permit" state nonregulation in given instances
without requiring it. But if the ultimate prevalence
of one of two competing constitutional rights is not
inevitable, the thrust of the analysis is in this direction. It appears throughout his discussion. The
state can enforce discrimination where, "against
the claim of equality, important countervailing
rights of liberty and privacy that enjoy substantial
constitutional protection exist."[50] "The state, we
suggest, may 'give effect' to such private discrimination, as it gives effect to other traditional rights
of private property for which, too, the state is
'responsible,' in the sense that under the Constitution the state could not freely deprive the individual of these property rights."[51] "The special
cases, we suggest, are rather those few where the

state supports that basic liberty, privacy, autonomy, which outweighs even the equal protection of
the laws."[52] "In the few instances in which the
right to discriminate is protected or preferred by
the Constitution, the state may enforce it."[53] "The
proposed formula puts responsibility on the states
when they have power, not when that power is
denied them."[54] "It may be urged that the formula
provides that the state may enforce a discrimination only where it must enforce it, that it leaves no
area of state neutrality—no discretion for states to
experiment and differ. If this is accepted as the
consequence, it may yet be justified: what we are
doing is carving a limited area of exception to the
generality of *Shelley v. Kraemer*....This is the
consequence of the preferred weight which the
Constitution gives to equality. In fact, of course,
the result suggested would not necessarily follow
from the formula."[55]

Is there in these words evidence of some uneasi-
ness concerning the methodology of the Justices
under the proposed formula? What is needed is an
accounting for the case in which the Court accepts
nonregulation by the state without finding a constitutional right of individuals to be free from
regulation. If emphasis is taken away from the use
of *"competing constitutional rights"* terminology
and placed on the idea that a state, in leaving a
segment of private conduct unregulated, is making
a choice between private interests—a choice that
might be regarded as an unreasonable one—the
three alternatives open to the Supreme Court
emerge more clearly. The Court might forbid state
effectuation of given private discrimination; it
might allow it because the freedom of the individual to discriminate or not to discriminate is
itself constitutionally protected; or it might permit
it because nonregulation of the private relationship
by the state is not unreasonable, though not constitutionally required. What is inescapable under
the analysis, however, is that any of the three solutions can be adjudged only after a careful application of the Constitution to the specific facts of each
case. Where the Court now can find that the Constitution is not addressed to certain problems created by a state's failure to regulate, under the
proposed formula it could reach the same result
only by finding the failure to regulate a constitutionally proper or permissible solution after carefully weighing all the interests involved.

It is true, as Professor Henkin maintains, that
the Court, following his analysis, would bring to
bear on the cases "a standard depending on degree, like that of due process." He continues:
"That standard in fact is the one which the Court
would apply if the state legislated to regulate these
same rights of liberty or property; it is the standard

by which the Court would test legislation to outlaw discrimination in a particular context."[56] But this comparison may inadequately reflect the distinctions between conventional constitutional questions and new ones the Court would face. In equal protection cases, a limitation of the Clause to state imposed discrimination erects as the standard of equality the legal status of the majority or favored class. Absent a reasonable basis for classification, all persons must be treated equally by the state and provided with equal legal rights and capacities. If the Clause is not limited to state action or cases of "significant state involvement," affirmative duties to create greater factual equality for persons in private relationships may be required of the state. What affirmative action would be required would be decided by the Supreme Court and Congress. Inasmuch as Congress probably suffers no serious lack of power whatever the fate of the state-action concept, the real problem concerns the role of the Court. The proposed analysis provides power and a standard like that of due process for the Court in an area where power otherwise is lacking in direct proportion to the "absoluteness" with which the Court defines needed state action. In cases in which private interests that would be referred to the Due Process Clause collide—for example, the case in which a discharged employee claims he was discharged because of his political views—the Court again would work with the established language of constitutional law, but in a new and harder setting. In the conventional case of constitutional review, the Court evaluates the complaints of individuals against various forms of state regulation. In the new cases that would come to the Court, evaluation of one individual's interest in having the state regulate another individual for the protection of the complainant would take place. For example, after the Court decides an individual has a right to be free of state censorship, it will have further decisions to make concerning an individual's right to have a forum where his views may be expounded. The Court decided in *Thornhill v. Alabama*[57] that picketing is a form of expression entitled to a degree of protection from state prohibition by the Constitution. Conflict between private constitutional rights is presented only when the problem of *Thornhill* is extended by an employee's complaint that he was discharged because of his picketing activity. The guidance that the Constitution provides for a conflict between individual and state is largely missing for the conflict between individuals.

Nonregulation by the state of private relationships, where the power to regulate exists, does in a sense represent a choice by the state. And state responsibility can thus be isolated and made subject to the Constitution as other state action is. But this cannot be done without a basic shift in the federal structure as it has been understood in the past. Paradoxically, but not uniquely, by emphasizing state responsibility in this way, a large portion of responsibility is transferred to the Supreme Court.

Even within the framework of a due process versus equal protection competition, to which Henkin's discussion is limited, many difficult cases not generally thought to involve constitutional questions would become, without some limiting device, grist for the Court's mill. The case of the discriminatory will and all the various contexts in which racial, religious, or some other form of discrimination occurs in private relations bring to mind the many hard choices the Court would be called upon to make. When the constitutional arena is enlarged to include all the conceivable conflicts between private parties (which can be described currently as unregulated) that could present claims of deprivation of "constitutional rights," once the Fourteenth Amendment is interpreted to be addressed effectually to private parties, the enormity of the task that the Court would have to face or evade becomes apparent. There is reason to question whether the cause of civil liberties would be advanced or set back if the Court entered the arena as a primary source of law. The burden of cases raises one question. The effects that an assumption by the Court of this broadened responsibility might have on state courts, legislatures, and Congress raise another serious question. Conjecture here is not parallel to the conjecture that the Court's power to invalidate legislation creates an irresponsible attitude among the legislators. Rather, new arguments against corrective legislation would be created. If, for example, the Court ruled on the *Gordon* problem that state nonregulation is constitutionally permissible, there would be a tendency by the people to accept nonregulation as the "right" solution. (The mental processes in which the Justices would engage in deciding this question according to the proposed formula must be borne in mind.) The atmospheric conditions created by the original announcement of the "separate but equal" doctrine are worth considering in this connection. Additionally, the persons aggrieved by private conduct might tend to shift pressure from the legislatures to the Court if they felt this easier avenue for relief held promise. To the extent the Court acted upon the proposed formula, uniformity would replace the flexibility that the fifty states bring to difficult problems. This would have advantages as well as disadvantages. The emphasis of the formula, and the word "emphasis" is carefully chosen, would be to make of the Supreme Court an appellate common-law court for the nation. The Justices would be more nearly big brothers than "elder cousins once removed."[58] The very frequency of resort to the Constitution, especially for the solution of many problems for which the document was not designed, might well undermine the solid respect that most people still feel for it.

Significant State Involvement

If there is merit in the suggestions that a purely conceptual use of the state action limitation is unrealistic, and that the balancing of interests formula would shift too large a workload to the Supreme Court, there remains the need to suggest a further alternative. An alternative is available, one which places a factor called "significant state involvement," for want of a better phrase, in the balance. This alternative analysis is based on recognition of the apparent design of constitutional restraints as restraints on government, and on the belief that there is value in marking off a large area of private relationships for which the state, or Congress acting pursuant to delegated powers, has primary responsibility. The analysis begins with repetition of the statement that the Fourteenth Amendment is addressed to the state, not to individuals, and the assertion that state support of private choices, in which the state is neutral in the sense that it does not command or attempt to influence the choice, generally is permissible. It is generally permissible because the Constitution in its general design leaves the decision whether to fill the blank of nonregulation with regulation to the states and Congress. Given a society in which legal procedures are made available for the peaceful settlement of private disputes, private choices and the freedom they imply are possible only with such state support. From this beginning, the analysis could be developed so as to apply the Constitution only to those choices made by the state agencies or officials and directing or forbidding specific private conduct. On the other hand, this development of the analysis may be qualified by recognition that realistically a hard and fast bright line cannot be drawn between state action and private action. This the Court has wisely done and the product is represented by cases such as *Shelley, Marsh,* and *Allwright.*

The weight of state involvement is easily felt by contrasting a religious organization's boycott of some literature with official state censorship, or arbitrary discrimination exercised by a private club with the same discrimination commanded by the state, or the pressures of custom on an individual to exhibit a belief in religion with a scheme of rewards and penalties created by the state to foster religious belief. In matters of religion particularly, the complexion of a problem changes entirely when a private choice is substituted for a state source of action. The results of *Shelley, Marsh,* and *Allwright* at the lower court levels, if created by statutes zoning property, outlawing religious proselyting on city sidewalks, and denying the vote to Negroes, would be too clearly condemned by the Constitution to merit debate. A state's delegation to private parties of the power to "zone" property, "govern" communities, and set voter qualifications similarly should be condemned or coupled with the duty to see that basic civil liberties are not denied by arbitrary private exercises of the power. Discrimination by the seller of a house, the insistence of a homeowner on a wall of privacy between him and the Jehovah's Witness, the exclusion of persons because of race or religion from a private club that may exercise considerable political power because of the local influence of its members, all pursuant to powers existing because the state has not acted to regulate their exercise, present questions different in degree, perhaps in kind, from those thus far resolved by the Court. These questions are representative of a host of others. When a state chooses to leave such private conflicts unregulated, it often does so because of a lack of assurance that the creation of a remedy will constitute a net gain for satisfactory human relationships. Failure to regulate does not necessarily involve governmental approval of the specific uses of resulting private power. To leave parties to their own devices is significantly different from the imposition of a choice upon private parties. And so long as a requirement of state action or state involvement exists, failure of the Court to review, or review resulting in a decision that the Constitution does not govern the conflict, leaves the merits of the controversy untouched. But the state choice of nonregulation will not always survive. The leading cases that establish the current frontiers of "significant state involvement" prove this.

In each of these cases, however, the Court has been able to renew allegiance to a distinction between state and private action—an allegiance not robbed of meaning by the results of the cases. Of course the Court has balanced interests. But the Constitution informs the Court that a private individual has less interest in institutionalizing his values than he has in the ability to pursue his own values individually. The Constitution informs the Court that the individual has no interest as an individual or as a member of a private power bloc in imposing his values on governmental functions, or in controlling the electoral process so as to effectively to deny the Negro the right to vote. It tells the Court in these and similar situations that there is constitutional warrant for intervention. The Court is reminded of limits on its function by the language of the Fourteenth Amendment, which is addressed to the state. This language also reminds the Court of the need to explain case by case, where "private" action is reached directly or indirectly, the significant involvement of the state that warrants a finding of state responsibility for the results of given nonregulation.

The challenge presented by an analysis that seeks to account for a state-action requirement while divesting it of its conceptual armor is the resulting need to supply a protective definition. If the requirement was met in *Shelley* and *Marsh,* it may be argued the sophisticated judge can supply it in any case by emphasizing a number of contacts between the individual and state that will always be present. And since interests must be weighed in the absence of a concept to serve as a mechanical aid to decision, can a straight-out balancing of underlying private interests really be avoided? First, it should be said that the difference between the balancing-of-interests approach and an approach that balances interests but also seeks to account for state action or involvement is one of emphasis. The difference between verbal descriptions of the two analyses is light and subtle. But it is suggested that the differences in operation and effect of the analyses, in the acceptableness of the decisions reached through their use and in the responses of the various organs making up the federal totality to results of the two analyses, may be marked. Under one analysis the parties go to the Court with claims described as constitutional, the dispute being over whose constitutional right should prevail. Under the other analysis, a party goes to the Court to determine if his grievance is referable to the Constitution. Under the first analysis, the Constitution would provide the source of power for the Supreme Court over the controversy without providing much guidance concerning the solution. Under the second analysis, the factors that tend to justify Court intervention on the basis of significant state involvement will also add clarity to the directions toward solution that the Constitution provides. The major difference between the two approaches, then, is one primarily of emphasis; review of the merits is the rule for the first analysis, and the explained exception to the rule for the second.

The critical phase of the state involvement analysis in a case before the Court is the phase in which it is determined whether the complainant's claim is referable to the Constitution. If this is determined simply by inquiring whether the complainant's interest is more important than the other private party's, state involvement will be no more than a cover or disguise for the balancing-of-interests method. *Significant* state involvement must mean something considerably more than state responsibility grounded merely on the state's power to act, else the phrase is meaningless. If the Court in this phase of a case attempts to reconcile its role of judicial review with the postulates of a healthy federalism, and the primary value of the state involvement analysis is that it calls upon the Court to do just this, the success of the attempt over a period of time can be judged. It will be judged not alone by the results reached, but by the pattern of power distribution that a series of cases defines, keeping in mind that the purpose of the analysis is to preserve a responsible role for the states and Congress as primary lawmakers and to prevent an unhealthy reliance upon the Constitution and the Court as the producers of a panacea.

In filling in the content of "significant state involvement," the Court has already established several lines of development. "Governmental function" is a suitable tag for one line and is represented by *Smith v. Allwright* and *Marsh v. Alabama* and perhaps *Shelley v. Kraemer.* "Governmental assistance" is another and is represented by *Kerr v. Enoch Pratt Free Library*[59] at the Court of Appeals level and possibly *Burton v. Wilmington Parking Authority* at the Supreme Court level. The latter case has something to say, too, about a possible line called "state-owned property use." *Dorsey v. Stuyvesant Town Corp.,*[60] today, could easily be decided in favor of Negro renters without doing violence to a state-action or state-involvement analysis. "Extraordinary private power" is another line of development which is in the offing. All these words and phrases are nebulous when put against concrete situations. But if they fail to explain a lot, they nevertheless have something to say if they are used to explain why limitations applicable to government should, in rare instances, be applied to exercises of apparently private power. The facts of the cases from which the phrases are derived must be borne in mind. The considerations that underlie the use of the phrases offer the possibility that meaningful acceptable applications of constitutional commands can be achieved that are at once consistent with our democratic principles and cognizant of the complexity of modern society in which the state and the individual are not always entirely separable.

The pull of Professor Wechsler's "neutral principles"[61] will provide a check on the Court's tracing-out of the lines of development even if the phrase means no more "than that the conflict of values should be frankly articulated and that the

Court should not simply be guided by its preference in the case before it, but by consistency of reasoning."[62] One of the important values in conflict is that of the function of the Court in relation to the other agencies of government; this value will have to be articulated with consistency of reasoning. For example, if the Court should seize upon tax exemption accorded various charities as the state involvement in a racial discrimination case, it could not fail to recognize that the decision would lay the foundation for the withdrawal of exemption for churches or create a need for explanation of a distinguishable effect for their exemption. It would be important to consider why tax exemption is the type of involvement that should carry obligations similar, if not identical, to those placed on the states. Emphasis would surely be placed on the element of government assistance. And if this factor is strong enough in this context to carry Fourteenth Amendment obligations, it would seem strong enough to provide a serious First Amendment establishment problem. This is not to say that significant state involvement, once found, should be equivalent for all purposes to conventional state action. When the state is immediately involved in regulation that is challenged under the Constitution, the results are far from automatic. The balancing of interests that is necessary to determine whether a state has violated the Constitution would be just as necessary to determine whether the state could tolerate specific policies of exempt organizations, if exemption were held to constitute the significant state involvement necessary to present a constitutional question. And the presence of agencies or individuals in the case, private in nature to some degree, would place additional interests on the scales. In rejecting tax exemption as significant state involvement, the Court might notice the broad base on which exemption is placed, with a resulting lack of identification between the government and the specific goals of the exempted organizations. The values of relatively unrestricted private philanthropy weighed against the effects and uses of consolidations of wealth would also be important. Not the least important consideration would be whether the Court ought to become involved in the broad range of problems that would be opened.

State involvement that is considered significant should carry some weight; it should suggest an answer to the question: Should X private person or agency be subjected in Y circumstances to the Fourteenth Amendment, bearing in mind that the Amendment is addressed to the state? It is submitted that the power permitted private parties by the state in *Marsh, Allwright,* and *Shelley,* appraised in light of pertinent constitutional provisions, does suggest the answers the Court supplied. Licensing by the state in the form of health permits and tax receipts is a kind of involvement that carries little or no weight by itself. It does not suggest an answer to the question. The power exercised by licensed private agencies does not differ in any way because of the licenses. The licenses do not serve to magnify or consolidate private power. The effects of the exercised power are not changed in any way. The same cannot be said of the monopoly-granting franchise.

If the Court does evolve applications of the Constitution along lines of significant state involvement, where will this leave the public accommodations problem? It is doubtful whether the problem falls clearly into the path of any of the lines so far tentatively projected. Governmental function, state assistance, extraordinary private power, in the sense in which they were involved in the principal peripheral cases, are absent. If the private power is extraordinary, it is not because of a formal institutional nature that it enjoys, such as is found in large corporations, labor unions, or enforced restrictive covenant schemes, but because it is a power used to deny extraordinarily important interests of a class of citizens. In the South, there is, or has been, an extraordinarily uniform exercise of private power by otherwise diverse individuals and companies. And the custom that explains the uniformity of discriminatory practices is in part at least traceable to laws in many states and communities that direct discrimination. Custom that has been generated, or at least supported, by law possibly presents a case of significant state involvement. An analogy between the widespread, uniform results that such a custom creates and the control over property exercised through covenants can be drawn. The "deep-seated pattern of segregation of the races"[63] existing in parts of the South has doubtless been nurtured by ubiquitous Jim Crow laws dating back to the nineteenth century. The laws are unconstitutional, but simply invalidating them, or even wiping them off the books, without more, leaves the pattern of discrimination substantially intact though legally unenforceable. The question is whether the inertial force that continues after the forward thrust of state action has been checked provides an adequate basis for judicial intervention. Active encouragement, even a stated preference by the state for discrimination in private relationships, will be met by reversal of state court proceedings supporting the discrimination. The *Sit-in Cases* establish this. The use of a law-generated custom theory beyond this kind of application is more questionable. Isolated as the significant state involvement, custom would push the Court in many directions. In the sphere of racial discrimination, Jim Crow laws have not kept pace with all forms of actual discrimination, but they have not been far behind. The Court could cope with this problem by considering the varying interests that would be involved in the way Professor Henkin suggested as an across-the-board approach. Segregation laws have been aimed at fraternal organizations as well as public establishments, and the Court would surely hesitate to interfere with discriminatory practices in fraternal organizations. But the Negroes' interest in protection from this kind of discrimination would be much slighter and the members' associational interest greater than the respective interests involved in public accommodation discrimination.

More serious questions remain. To use custom as the basis for direct application of the Equal Protection Clause to private establishments, or for finding a state duty to secure equal treatment, would imply that, absent custom, the private choice would be immune from the Clause. Is it unduly technical to suggest that a decision to this effect would carry its own death wound? For the result of the opinion would immediately begin to undercut its own foundation. How widely practiced must conduct be to be considered customary? Furthermore, the theory would dictate different constitutional rights for Negroes in different parts of the country, perhaps in different parts of a state. This has pragmatic appeal, since the theory seems to provide protection where it is most needed, but the resistance a decision would meet that draws this kind of distinction between South and North might also be considered. If the Court were to rely on the present or recent existence of segregation laws, constitutional rights would depend upon the varying patterns created by the laws. If the Court emphasized custom, instead of the laws that have supposedly generated it, the Court might find itself mired in an unseemly bog of psychoanalysis. There is no reason to believe that the persons restricted by decisions based on custom would readily accept the restrictions. Every effort would be made by some of these persons to turn the rationale of the decisions against the Court as the period of transition that has already begun in the South relieves the custom of discrimination. More important, however, should not freedom from discrimination in places of public accommodation be broadly principled so as to apply in every corner of the country? The Negro's complaint is grounded on the affront to his dignity as an individual resulting from discrimination as well as the personal inconvenience and hardship he suffers. The affront will occur wherever he is rejected. Finally, time and events, the latter including especially Negro demonstrations, Supreme Court decisions, and in-

stances of state and federal government policy enforcement, are rapidly removing the psychological basis for a custom theory. With the removal of the crutch of the law, and the shattering of state-wide customs of segregation in most states, it is becoming increasingly difficult to attribute the discrimination of particular proprietors to custom expressing the policy of the state, or having the force of effects of law. The other side of the phenomenon of custom, the customary treatment at public accommodations of the accepted classes, may provide a firmer base from which to project the application of the Equal Protection Clause.

THE SPECIAL NATURE OF THE PUBLIC
ACCOMMODATIONS PROBLEM

Preoccupation with the state-action concept as traced from the *Civil Rights Cases* has obscured or tended to oust fresh analysis of the precise nature of the problem of discrimination in places of public accommodation, assuming a conventional interpretation of the Equal Protection Clause. The solution of the problem lies within the reach of the Clause when it is interpreted by the well-established judicial method of analogical reasoning. To see this, it will first be necessary to sketch very briefly the original misunderstanding of the framers of the Fourteenth Amendment.

Study of the debates in Congress concerning the Fourteenth Amendment shows that the members of Congress, including those who drafted the provisions, did not carefully consider just how the language of the Amendment was to be applied to accomplish all the specific objectives that came to their minds or to leave untouched certain areas of conduct seemingly affected. It is unquestionable that the primary aim of the Amendment was to make the Negro a citizen equal before the law with other citizens. But whether the Amendment was to have a larger content, in terms of equalizing the Negro's status, was not carefully analyzed. The question of the scope or measure of equality is similar to the question of content for the Privileges and Immunities Clause of the Amendment. That language was borrowed from Article IV, Section 2, of the Constitution, but there was evident misunderstanding of the meaning of this section based on the misleading early case of *Corfield v. Coryell*.[64] In that case, Mr. Justice Washington said that the privileges and immunities of one state's citizen while in another state are those privileges and immunities which belong of right to citizens of all free governments, a natural-law theory that would give the Supreme Court the final word as to content. From this, many in Congress derived the notion that the phrase "privileges and immunities" conveyed a content of its own, unaware that the phrase as used in Article IV should take its measure from the privileges and immunities a state accords its own citizens. The Equal Protection Clause was the subject of similar confusion. It is apparent from the debates that the bulk of, if not the total, content of the phrase was to be measured by the legal status of the favored class within a state. The Negro, or member of any other race, was to have the same legal rights and capacities a state provided for the favored race. The Civil Rights Act of 1866,[65] which prompted the drive for a constitutional amendment to make its provisions more permanent, provided that citizens of every race and color should have the same rights in every state to make contracts, sue, buy and sell property, inherit, serve as witnesses, and be protected in person and property by the law.

The Equal Protection Clause is admirably designed to secure equal legal rights and capacities for all persons in a state, but the design is the source of the limiting state-action concept. Legal rights and capacities are defined by the states, and implemented by state administration. While the protection guaranteed is a federal protection, the scope of protection is measured by the bundle of rights, privileges, and immunities created by a majority within a state for their own protection and enjoyment. State action as well as state inaction may run afoul of the Clause because discrimination may occur through a state's action taking away from one race rights provided for other races, or by the failure of state officers to enforce laws to protect members of one race while enforcing the same laws for the protection of other races. The standard of equal protection comes with the theory of interpretation. The limitations of the interpretation become acute as soon as serious inequalities in fact develop that are based not on law but on attitudes expressed in private relationships. If no one has a legal right to enter and be served in a restaurant, equation of rights calls for the same status—no legal right—for the Negro. If equal protection means more, for example, that the state has duties to see that all races enjoy a degree of equality in their private relationships, the question of degree is immediately presented. Congress and the Supreme Court would have to define the state duties; a clear standard is no longer available in the Equal Protection Clause itself. If the Equal Protection Clause were so interpreted, its application could go forward broadly and intelligently only by a balancing-of-interests approach as suggested by Professor Henkin. A shift of power from the states to the federal government would take place, and this was recognized as one of the problems of interpretation in the *Civil Rights Cases*.[66] It is less than clear that the framers intended this consequence.

The Privileges and Immunities Clause, once separated from its moorings in Article IV, had a sufficiently undefined content that it could have provided the source of power for Congress to combat factual inequality among the races. But this was not the course of development. The Court in the *Slaughter-House Cases*[67] limited the Privileges and Immunities Clause as a source of affirmative rights just as it limited the Equal Protection Clause in the *Civil Rights Cases*, and for much the same reason. The Privileges and Immunities Clause does not embody a clear standard, and to turn definition over to the Court or Congress would tend to shift the power to govern personal relationships from the states to the federal government. At least in part to avoid interpretations that might have this effect, the Court refused to give substantial content to the Privileges and Immunities Clause and suggested that the standard for the Equal Protection Clause is the status under state law of the favored class of citizens.

Standing between the Negro and a right to service in places of public accommodation, then, is the gap created by the absence of a "legal right" to such service in any person. Absent remedial legislation, the restaurateur may refuse to serve anyone and for any reason no matter how arbitrary. Under the traditional interpretation of the Equal Protection Clause, the Negro would have to be provided a right to service by public accommodations if any persons were. Analysis of the white's real status vis-à-vis places of public accommodation may contribute to a solution of this problem of inequality.

There is probably no expectation, with or without a legal basis, that is more firmly established than the expectation of the average person that he will be served in places of public accommodations. The expectation is cemented in the private enterprise system that created the accommodations. They exist to serve; it would be absurd in the extreme to imagine that a place built and designed to serve the people would be used in a way inconsistent with the purpose for which it was built and inconsistent with the use that will allow it to survive and prosper. "The customer is always right" is not entered on any statute book, but it has an authority no less powerful than the law. And high or low, rich or poor, beautiful or homely or nondescript, the customer is always The Customer. Mr. Justice McLean once spoke of "usages...which have become a kind of common law, and regulate the rights and duties of those who act within their respective limits."[68] What usage has a stronger claim to status as a "kind of common law" than one that is so thoroughly established that formal law likely will never come into being to replace it? Neither patrons nor proprietors generally think of their relationships as commanded by law, and there is a certain lack of reality in describing service and accommodations for the majority in terms of legal rights and duties. But we suggest the lack of reality stems precisely from the fact that the relationship is built upon a foundation deeper, stronger, and more natural than law. The expectation of service has become a piece of the fabric of society. It is not possible to separate the expectation of service from the system that has been privately created to provide it. And so it is difficult to imagine circumstances in which the need to establish legal rights to service for the generality of customers could arise. The certainty that law would respond to the need if it arose persists nevertheless. In an age when most of us lack the rudimentary knowledge necessary to survival if limited to our own resources, we have come vitally to depend upon the rendition of services and the sale of products by establishments created for that purpose. More, our system has developed a broad range of establishments that cater to all without arbitrary classifications, except that of race. Of the realities that govern the lives of most of us, which is the more meaningful: the absence of a legal right, the existence of a slogan, "We reserve the right to refuse service to anyone," or the expectation that service will not be refused? The slogan simply has no relevance for the well-behaved majority. The assumption of the average white person that he will be accommodated by places that were designed to serve that function and that have accommodated the public as a matter of course is so firm and automatic that he is hardly conscious of it. Few if any assumptions we make are more strongly warranted by experience.

Might the Court or Congress act upon this customary treatment of whites as a standard for equality that is fully as relevant in the unique context of public accommodations as a legal right, an admittedly valid standard? The gap between this custom and law is so small as to be barely visible. And *Shelley, Marsh,* and *Allwright* bridged gaps. History provides some support for the analogy between the expectation of service and a legal right to service. The common-law duty of carriers and innkeepers did not go unnoticed by the framers and it was believed the Equal Protection Clause would insure the extension of the obligation to all. Was this result to depend upon the accident of a state's adoption or rejection of the common-law obligation? Or was it projected on the basis of the considerations that had brought the common-law

rule into existence? It was assumed by more than a few members of Congress that theaters and places of amusement would be or could be opened to all as a result either of the Equal Protection Clause or the Privileges and Immunities Clause. Why would the framers believe this? Some mentioned the law's regulation of such enterprises, but this is not enough. Some other standard must delineate between the regulated who must offer equal treatment and those who need not. Whites did not have a legal right to demand admittance to the above-mentioned enterprises, but they were admitted. Perhaps this observed conduct was confused with required conduct, just as the observed status of the citizens of all free governments—the governments that Washington, J., could observe—was mistaken for inherent rights to the status. The important point is that the framers, or some of them, believed the Amendment would open places of public accommodation, and study of the debates reveals this belief to be the observed expectations of the majority, tantamount in practice to legal rights. The passage by Congress of the Civil Rights Act of 1875, which was challenged in the *Civil Rights Cases,* is evidence of Congress' belief that the Fourteenth Amendment could be applied to public accommodations. Mr. Justice Harlan, dissenting in the *Civil Rights Cases,* and addressing himself to the relationship of the citizen to places of public amusement, as well as to inns and carriers, repeatedly speaks of "rights" of accommodation. The purpose of the Amendment, he observed, was to secure equality of rights for all races, and to secure those rights for the Negro that inhere in the freeman and citizen. These rights, to him, clearly included the right to patronize places of public amusement. He seems to have made an equation between "rights" and usages for purposes of establishing the content of the Amendment.[69]

If the Court were governed by this observed customary acceptance of all but Negroes, would there be widespread sincere feeling that the Justices had simply imposed their own preferences on the parties? The standard is quite as visible as the standard of legal right. The common-sense inclusion of this standard would do no more violence than the common-sense exclusion of defamation and obscenity from the protection of the First and Fourteenth Amendments. Custom will identify the "public accommodations" against whose discrimination the Negro is entitled to state protection. Included would be those establishments that accept whites without question and from which the white customer has come to expect service without any question of arbitrary limitations. The expectations of the white customer, objectively warranted by the established practices of a given enterprise, would be the measure. Private clubs fall outside the standard because the white has no reasonable expectation of unquestioned acceptance. While a club of white members will not reject a white applicant because of race, they may reject him for any number of arbitrary reasons. Arbitrariness is expected and a value because in questions of association "reasonable" standards will not adequately categorize welcome and unwelcome associates. Expected arbitrariness might include arbitrary factors such as race or religion—at least until legislative action forbids it in particular circumstances. The sale and rental of housing, private schools, and "Mrs. Murphy's boardinghouse" are of a different class. Whatever may be said about these spheres of private activity, public accommodation is not involved in the sense that service or exchange of property occurs without question or previous negotiation. The expectations of the parties are not of a kind with those experienced by the patron of the typical restaurant, hotel, or amusement park. If a white person believes he can simply present himself and his rent and expect lodging and board at Mrs. Murphy's, he simply does not know Mrs. Murphy. His subjective expectations are not relevant. If he can truly expect these services, if his inference is firmly grounded in provable past practices, it is a case of mistaken identification—he is at Mrs. Smith's public accommodation, not Mrs. Murphy's boarding house. Application of the standard may present some close questions; application in the bulk of the cases will be obviously appropriate or inappropriate.

Use of the standard would be responsive to the problem of discrimination in places of public accommodations. Because all whites use such accommodations without arbitrary limitations, discrimination is particularly humiliating to the Negro. The purpose of the accommodations indicates the felt need of the favored class for their services, a need that is equally felt by all races. The broad acceptance of the public in the establishments defined indicates that the interest in freedom of association is slight. The standard will maintain a balance between the interests in accommodation and the interests in association. The phenomenon of unlimited acceptance of whites in the establishments and the serious, observable inequality that results from refusal to serve Negroes surely account for the persistent feeling that the state is abusing a licensing power when it issues health permits to the establishments, and that the analogy between public utilities and places of public accommodation is strong. Use of the standard would put court enforcement of particular private discrimination in its proper place: outlawed because it

leaves fully intact the white expectation while denying it to the Negro. The standard explains particular inequality and the Fourteenth Amendment's relation to it in a way that carries force for the layman and the lawyer, and in a way that will have application across the land.

Application of the standard lies within the reach of conventional constitutional analysis. The result would hardly be described as routine, but no basic shift in the Court's function would occur. The result would naturally create questions about possibilities for further extensions, but its justification would rest on the unique character of the public accommodations defined by the standard. The bridge erected by analogy would be as sturdy as the bridge built of *de facto* status which crosses an occasional gap left by an absent *de jure* status. It would be less fictional than the treatment of the corporation as a citizen for the purposes of diversity jurisdiction. Judgment would be required —a judgment which only those charged with the ultimate responsibility of judging can make. If the analogy were adjudged a proper one, it would be anchored in the realities of life, establishing a principle of constitutionally appropriate generality.

CONCLUSION

The insensitiveness of other organs of government to minority needs has resulted in tremendous pressures on the Supreme Court. The rights of minorities are logically referable in large measure to constitutional protections, and it is hardly surprising to find increasing resort to the Court for their vindication. But there are limitations on the Court's function found in the language of the Constitution and the philosophy of government it embodies. The recommendation that the Court greatly expand its function by a basic reinterpretation of the limiting language in the Fourteenth Amendment is unwise. There is a degree of flexibility in the language that creates a large area that must yet be subjected to rigorous judgment without any fundamental shift in the function of the Court. The problem of discrimination in places of public accommodation lies within this area. A judgment in favor of the victims of discrimination could be readily justified in the light of the history and philosophy of the Equal Protection Clause. There are other factors, however, that will place strain on the Court if it faces the broad issue. Congress may pass the bill now pending with the provisions that will open most places of public accommodation to all persons. The possibility reflects the developments of the past few months, heartening in the sense that other organs of government have been energized to begin to share a burden too often shunted to the

Court in the past. But the same pressures that will force legislative representatives across the land at last to take a position are generating an emotional charge that may envelop the constitutional issues if they should be left to the Court without benefit of prior positive congressional action. The constitutional issue of discrimination in places of public accommodation seems more firmly settled by existing precedents than it is. The atmosphere created by *Plessy v. Ferguson*[70] made it virtually impossible to challenge seriously the results, much less the radiations, of the *Civil Rights Cases* until 1955. New consideration of the constitutional issue is now in order, but the Court, if it should decide in favor of the minority, can hardly avoid the impression that it is overturning firmly established doctrine. Such a decision, if it is rendered against a background of massive racial demonstrations, will be misunderstood by many people willing to try to understand the Court's work.

While this article has dealt at some length with constitutional issues relevant primarily to the Supreme Court, it does not seem inappropriate to conclude with a prayer that the Congress will discharge the responsibility charged to it by the last section of the Fourteenth Amendment so as to alleviate the strain increasingly being placed on the Court as an institution. The analysis of the problem contained in this paper has relevance for the Congress as well as the Court. While there is no serious question of Congress' power to regulate the mass of public accommodations, questions have been raised concerning the scope of its power to enforce the Fourteenth Amendment. And so long as legislative power is referred to the Commerce Clause, the problem of drawing lines is acute, for that Clause provides few clues as to what lines should be drawn. The expectations of the majority, where they are clear enough to support an analogy between them and legal rights, provide a theory for implementing the commands of the Fourteenth Amendment and establish a line between those enterprises that should be regulated and those which may be left alone. Congress can act on the analysis much more readily than can the Court. For while the gap that analogy would close is a narrow one in theory, the practical consequences flowing from the gap have radiated far and wide. Congressional action can provide a firmer and broader base from which to project enforcement efforts tailored to the nature of the enforcement problem.

Footnotes

[1]The principal "sit-in" case is Peterson v. City of Greenville, 373 U.S. 244 (1963). Also included in the

style, *Sit-in Cases*, are Lombard v. Louisiana, 373 U.S. 267 (1963); Avent v. North Carolina, 373 U.S. 375 (1963) (per curiam); and Gober v. City of Birmingham, 373 U.S. 374 (1963) (per curiam). Shuttlesworth v. City of Birmingham, 373 U.S. 262 (1963), is a related case. Mr. Justice Harlan's opinion concurring in *Peterson* and dissenting in whole or in part in the remaining cases appears at 373 U.S. 248. Griffin v. Maryland, 225 Md. 422 (1961), *cert. granted*, 370 U.S. 935 (1962), was argued last Term, but was restored to the calendar for re-argument, 373 U.S. 920 (1963).

[2]Brown v. Board of Education, 347 U.S. 483 (1954).

[3]The issue can be phrased in different ways according to the analysis of the person stating it. For example, one who emphasizes state court action as state action that is prohibited by the Equal Protection Clause will not speak of a right to service, but of rights as against given state court action. Probably the most that the Fourteenth Amendment can do is impose duties of protection upon the states. The issue stated in the text is broadly stated for convenience and, it is submitted, is not misleading in light of the analysis that will be offered; the lesser issues will be discussed in the course of the article.

[4]364 U.S. 454 (1960).

[5]Watson v. City of Memphis, 373 U.S. 526 (1963); New Orleans City Park Improvement Ass'n v. Detiege, 358 U.S. 54 (1958) (per curiam); Mayor and City Council of Baltimore v. Dawson, 350 U.S. 877 (1955) (per curiam); Holmes v. City of Atlanta, 350 U.S. 879 (1955) (per curiam).

[6]Muir v. Louisville Park Theatrical Ass'n, 347 U.S. 971 (1954) (per curiam); Derrington v. Plummer, 240 F.2d 922 (5th Cir. 1956), *cert. denied*, 353 U.S. 924 (1957).

[7]See Burton v. Wilmington Parking Authority, 365 U.S. 715 (1961). The central facts in *Burton* showed the operation of a coffee shop in a parking building erected by the parking authority. The lessee of the space had outfitted it as a coffee shop at his expense and could have used the space for any legitimate purpose. The Court held the coffee shop must be open to Negroes, but cautioned that its decision was based on all the facts, which were detailed at length....

[8]Boynton v. Virginia, 364 U.S. 454 (1960).

[9]Garner v. Louisiana, 368 U.S. 157 (1961).

[10]*Ibid.* See also Wright v. Georgia, 373 U.S. 284 (1963).

[11]373 U.S. 244 (1963).

[12]*Id.* at 246.

[13]*Ibid.* There was also evidence in the record indicating the police had arrested defendants on their own initiative and to enforce the city ordinance. Brief for Petitioners, pp. 7–8.

[14]373 U.S. at 248. Whether the city had removed the decision to discriminate from the sphere of private choice should be a question of fact. It is possible that proof directed to the issue would have shown one or more of the ordinances had no such effect. The lunch counters involved in *Lombard* and *Avent* were integrated as a result of private negotiation before the cases were argued in the Supreme Court. New York Times, Nov. 6, 1962, p. 14, cols. 4 and 5. This fact throws light on the status of the Durham city ordinance and the official pronouncements made in New Orleans, but does not prove what the mental attitudes of the proprietors were at the time service was first refused.

[15]373 U.S. at 273.
[16]*Id.* at 252, 253.
[17]367 U.S. 497 (1961); see also Standard Computing Scale Co. v. Farrell, 249 U.S. 571 (1919) (Brandeis, J.).
[18]367 U.S. at 502, quoting Nashville, C. & St. L. R.R. v. Browning, 310 U.S. 362, 369 (1940).
[19]239 U.S. 33 (1915).
[20]268 U.S. 510 (1925).
[21]372 U.S. 58 (1963).
[22]Amsterdam, *The Void-for-Vagueness Doctrine in the Supreme Court*, 109 U. PA. L. REV. 67, 81 (1960). See also Freund, *The Supreme Court and Civil Liberties*, 4 VAND. L. REV. 533, 539–41 (1951).
[23]Amsterdam, *supra* note 22, at 89.
[24]See WOODWARD, THE STRANGE CAREER OF JIM CROW 80–92 (1955).
[25]*Id.* at 65–87.
[26]EQUAL PROTECTION OF THE LAWS IN NORTH CAROLINA, REPORT OF THE NORTH CAROLINA ADVISORY COMMITTEE TO THE UNITED STATES COMMISSION ON CIVIL RIGHTS 227 (1962).
[27]New York Times, July 13, 1963, p. 7, col. 1.
[28]333 U.S. 507 (1948)....
[29]*E.g.,* Griffin v. Maryland, 225 Md. 422 (1961), *cert. granted,* 370 U.S. 935 (1962) (amusement park); Bell v. Maryland, 227 Md. 302 (1962), *cert. granted,* 374 U.S. 805 (1963) (restaurant).
[30]FREUND, THE SUPREME COURT OF THE UNITED STATES, ITS BUSINESS, PURPOSES, AND PERFORMANCE 73 (1961).
[31]334 U.S. 1 (1948).
[32]See text *infra,* at notes 36 & 37.
[33]See text *infra,* at notes 39–58.
[34]See text *infra,* at notes 59–63.
[35]See text *infra,* at notes 64–69.
[36]109 U.S. 3 (1883).
[37]*Id.* at 11, 24, and 17.
[38]287 F.2d 750 (5th Cir. 1961). See also Wright v. Georgia, 373 U.S. 284 (1963).
[39]Henkin, *Shelley v. Kraemer, Notes for a Revised Opinion,* 110 U. PA. L. REV. 473, 479 (1962).
[40]326 U.S. 501 (1946).
[41]321 U.S. 649 (1944).
[42]Ford v. Tennessee, 355 S.W.2d 102 (Tenn. 1962),

petition for *cert.* filed, September 1, 1962, 31 U.S.L. Week 3094 (1962).
[43]See generally, GELLHORN, American Rights 182–190 (1960), at ch. 9; Henkin, *supra* note 39; Horowitz, *The Misleading Search for State Action under the Fourteenth Amendment*, 30 SO. CAL. L. REV. 208 (1957); Williams, *The Twilight of State Action*, 41 TEX. L. REV. 347 (1963); *cf.* Lewis, *The Meaning of State Action*, 60 COLUM. L. REV. 1083 (1960).
[44]Williams, *supra* note 43, at 372.
[45]334 U.S. 558 (1948).
[46]Henkin, *supra* note 39, at 490.
[47]*Id.* at 502.
[48]*Id.* at 503.
[49]332 Mass. 197 (1955), *cert. denied,* 349 U.S. 947 (1955). See also United States Nat'l Bank v. Snodgrass, 202 Ore. 530 (1954).
[50]Henkin, *supra* note 39, at 487.
[51]*Id.* at 491.
[52]*Ibid.*
[53]*Id.* at 496.
[54]*Id.* at 502.
[55]*Id.* at 503.
[56]*Id.* at 502.
[57]310 U.S. 88 (1940).
[58]See Freund, *Individual and Commonwealth in the Thought of Mr. Justice Jackson,* 8 STAN. L. REV. 9, 10 (1955).
[59]149 F.2d 212 (4th Cir. 1945), *cert. denied,* 326 U.S. 721 (1945).
[60]299 N.Y. 512 (1949), *cert. denied,* 339 U.S. 981 (1950).
[61]Wechsler, *Toward Neutral Principles of Constitutional Law,* 73 HARV. L. REV. 1 (1959).
[62]FRIEDMANN, LAW IN A CHANGING SOCIETY 48 (1959).
[63]Douglas, J., concurring, in Garner v. Louisiana, 368 U.S. 157, 179 (1961).
[64]6 Fed. Cas. 546, No. 3230 (C.C.E.D. Pa. 1823).
[65]14 STAT. 27 (1866).
[66]109 U.S. 3 (1883)....
[67]16 Wall. 36 (1872).
[68]United States v. Macdaniel, 7 Pet. 1, 14 (1833).
[69]109 U.S. at 48–62.
[70]163 U.S. 537 (1896).

Selection **13**

Congressional Power to Enforce the Fourteenth Amendment Against Private Acts

Laurent B. Frantz

Lewis shows that the Supreme Court and Congress generally have been assumed to be bound by the state action concept (i.e., the theory that the Fourteenth Amendment can be applied only to discrimination by the state, not by

---

"Congressional Power to Enforce the Fourteenth Amendment Against Private Acts" by Laurent B. Frantz, 73 *Yale Law Journal* 1353 (1964). Reprinted by permission of the Yale Law Journal Company and Fred B. Rothman & Company.

private persons). For this reason the expansion of the limits of state action discussed by Lewis has seemed crucial to many legal scholars. For the same reason Congress has based much of its new civil rights legislation not on the Fourteenth Amendment but on the Interstate Commerce Clause ("The Congress shall have power...to regulate commerce...among the several states"). If, however, it were now found that Congress was constitutionally empowered to enforce the Fourteenth Amendment directly on private citizens, the way might be cleared and a further stimulant provided for even more congressional action against discrimination in the future. Laurent B. Frantz' article, the last in this chapter, deal with this possibility. Of course, ultimately both the Supreme Court and Congress would have to make constitutional judgments on these issues.

Fourteenth Amendment

Sec. 1. All persons born or naturalized in the United States, and subject to the jurisdiction thereof, are citizens of the United States and of the State wherein they reside. No State shall make or enforce any law which shall abridge the privileges or immunities of citizens of the United States; nor shall any State deprive any person of life, liberty, or property, without due process of law; nor deny to any person within its jurisdiction the equal protection of the laws.

❖   ❖   ❖

Sec. 5. The Congress shall have power to enforce, by appropriate legislation, the provisions of this article.

It is generally believed that the subject of this article does not exist, since Congress cannot enforce the fourteenth amendment against private acts, but only against "state action." This is supposed to have been the constitutional result of the Supreme Court decisions of the 1870's and 1880's invalidating much of the civil rights legislation of the Reconstruction period. In particular, the *Cruikshank*,[1] *Harris*,[2] and *Civil Rights*[3] cases are supposed to have laid down the unqualified rule that if federal civil rights legislation is directed at merely "private acts" it must be denounced as unauthorized by the fourteenth amendment, and hence as unconstitutional unless some alternative constitutional authority for it can be established. Yet the consensus is almost as general that, whatever the original understanding may have been[4] as to the new legislative powers being conferred on the Congress, it certainly did not correspond to this state-action-only formula. Even those who have defended the formula have generally been content to do so on policy grounds without venturing to claim that it is an accurate, or even tenable, reading of the original intent. The latter position would be a difficult one to defend, in the light of the historical context.

As the Supreme Court has itself pointed out[5] one of the most significant clues to the original

understanding is the situation which the amendment was designed to remedy. That situation is described at length and in detail in the testimony on conditions in the South taken by the Joint Committee on Reconstruction,[6] the committee which drafted the fourteenth amendment and proposed it to the Congress. This testimony does refer here and there to instances of discriminatory state legislation, actual or threatened, and more frequently to abuse of power by state officials. But it requires no more than a glance at the testimony in order to see that "state action" in this sense, while it may have had some effect on the flavor of the stew, is very far from being its principal ingredient. The principal ingredient is a pervasive pattern of private wrongs, motivated by popular prejudice and hostility, directed against Negroes primarily and to a lesser, but significant, degree against Northern whites and against those Southern whites who had been disloyal to their states by being loyal to the Union. If the orthodox theory of the fourteenth amendment is correct, then the committee which studied the situation and attempted to draft a constitutional remedy for it came up with a solution which wholly failed to relate to the main body of the problem. When the testimony is examined more closely, it becomes apparent that the great bulk of it deals with injustices which are not only "private acts," but acts which would violate any state's ordinary laws against homicide and assault and battery. And the aspect of the matter which justifies bringing it to national attention, and which is felt as requiring a national remedy, is not the nature, severity, nor even the frequency of these acts, but the fact that the ex-Confederate states, though they have laws against homicide and assault and battery, and though they enforce those laws in general, cannot or will not enforce them in this particular connection. The situation is summed up in the testimony of a Freedmen's Bureau Agent:

"Of the thousand cases of murder, robbery, and maltreatment of freedmen that have come before me, and of the very many cases of similar treatment of Union citizens in North Carolina, I have never yet known a single case in which the local authorities or police or citizens made any attempt or exhibited any inclination to redress any of these wrongs or to protect such persons....That seems to me the worst indication of the state of society there—worse than the fact that these things take place."[7]

The evidence taken by the Joint Committee, together with its report and recommendations, was printed in 150,000 copies for distribution by Congress, and excerpts from it, as it was given from day to day, were published and commented upon in the Northern press. Thus, when the Republican Party presented itself to the electorate in 1866 with the fourteenth amendment and the Civil Rights Bill as its platform, it was with the testimony taken by the Joint Committee as the factual basis to explain and justify those pieces of legislation. This being the case, it is reasonable to infer that not only in the Congress, but in the ratifying legislatures and amongst the voters who elected the ratifying legislatures, the fourteenth amendment was widely thought of as something which would empower the Congress to deal effectively with the situation depicted in the testimony.

Furthermore, the framers and backers of the fourteenth amendment were primarily interested in enlarging the powers of the Congress, not those of the federal judiciary, which was looked upon with considerable distrust. It is almost impossible to imagine that a group motivated by this objective would have considered acceptable, as a definition of the new powers to be conferred, one couched in terms only of acts of *state* aggression. They could not have thought that it would often be appropriate to restrain a state's legislative or judicial acts otherwise than by an appeal to the federal judiciary. A "state action" concept of congressional enforcement power is almost automatically limited to punishing abuses of power by state officials; even here, it can operate only in very extreme instances, since it could seldom be appropriate, or even practical, for Congress to prescribe in detail the duties and functions of state officials. So the traditional "state action" interpretation pulls inevitably toward producing an amendment which confers new power primarily on the federal judiciary, while granting only minimal power to the Congress. A proposal with this built-in tendency (which would have been apparent at the time had contemporaries read the language as it is now usually read) would certainly not have been satisfactory to the framers and backers of the fourteenth amendment. Furthermore, the central problem with which they were

attempting to deal—a pervasive pattern of private wrongs sheltered by state *inaction*—is one which congressional power cannot reach at all, unless Congress can deal with the private acts directly. For Congress to command the states to give better and more even-handed enforcement to their homicide and assault and battery laws, and to punish the states if they failed to do so, would be a most cumbersome mode of operating.

And indeed for the first seven years after the fourteenth amendment was ratified, Congress believed it possessed, and actually exercised a power to protect the newly-freed Negro from private aggression, as well as from "state action." During this period it enacted three statutes intended in whole or in part to enforce the amendment. The first two undertook, among other things, to punish conspiracies by two or more persons to prevent any citizen from enjoying any right or privilege granted or secured to him by the federal Constitution or laws[8] or to deprive any person or class of persons of the equal protection of the laws.[9] The third prohibited racial discrimination in access to inns, public conveyances, and places of public amusement.[10] The three implementing statutes were sponsored and enacted by the same group in Congress, and to a large extent by the same individuals, as the amendment itself. They therefore amount to an almost contemporaneous construction of the amendment by its authors.

Finally, the framers wrote in the light of apparently settled constitutional doctrine that the mere recognition of a right in the federal Constitution gives Congress implied power to protect it from interference by private acts,[11] but does not give Congress implied power to exercise any control over a state's officers and agencies.[12] It was also settled constitutional doctrine that a guarantee contained in the federal Constitution is not binding on the states unless explicitly made so.[13] Many of the framers also seem to have believed, though with less basis in reported judicial opinions, that the federal government, in return for the allegiance of its citizens, has some duty to protect them in the enjoyment of their fundamental rights, even within the states. When this background of greater congressional power over individuals than over the states is taken into account, one can better understand how the framers may have supposed that a constitutional provision recognizing certain persons as United States citizens, forbidding the states to abridge their rights as such or deny them equal protection, and empowering Congress to enforce this by appropriate legislation, would result in a congressional enforcement power which would extend not only to private acts but *even* to "state action."

Flack's summary of the debates on the enforcement legislation indicates that Congress supposed it could reach private acts on either of two theories. First there was the power of the national government to secure to United States citizens the full and unhindered enjoyment of any right inherent in national citizenship.[14] Second was the equal protection clause, which was read as equivalent to a guarantee that persons shall enjoy equality of protection. Congress thought that with power given to Congress by section five it could supply such equal protection whenever a state failed to do so. The first of these theoretical bases the courts have, as an abstract proposition, never denied. Its practical effect, however, was defeated by the narrow concept of the rights appurtenant to national citizenship developed in the *Slaughterhouse* cases.[15] The problem to which this article is addressed is: what happened to the second of these propositions, the one on which members of Congress most frequently and consistently relied?[16]

During the debates on the Ku Klux Act of 1871,[17] three major views on this question emerged. At one extreme, according to Prof. Harris, were those who

"embraced a construction of the amendment which sustained almost unlimited congressional power to protect constitutional rights against both official and private action, to the point of displacing state authority altogether without awaiting abridgments of constitutional rights."

At the other extreme were those who argued "that congressional power was limited to the elimination of unequal laws and the correction of official or state action alone...." The latter view, though it is the one now considered orthodox, was in 1871 "advanced by a minority consisting almost exclusively of Democrats,"[18] the same faction which had originally opposed the fourteenth amendment on the ground, among others, that it would bring about such a vast expansion of congressional power as to wipe out the states. There was, however, a moderate view standing between these two extremes, to the effect that "Congress had the responsibility to protect constitutional rights in the event of failure of the states to do so, but only after the states had failed or refused to do their duty."[19] This moderate view was best expressed by president-to-be James A. Garfield, then a Representative from Ohio:

"But the chief complaint is not that the laws of the State are unequal, but that even where the laws are just and equal on their face, yet, by a systematic maladministration of them, or a neglect or refusal to enforce their provisions, a portion of the people are denied equal protection under them. Whenever such a state of facts is clearly made out, I believe the last clause of the first section [of the fourteenth amendment] empowers Congress to step in and provide for doing justice to those persons who are thus denied equal protection.

Now if the...pending bill can be so amended that it...shall employ no terms which assert the power of Congress to take jurisdiction of the subject until such denial be clearly made, and shall not in any way assume the original jurisdiction of the rights of private persons and of property within the states—with these conditions clearly expressed ...I shall give it my hearty support."[20]

According to the traditional interpretation, the Supreme Court, when the Reconstruction legislation came before it, adopted the extreme view which, in Congress, had been expressed by the fundamentally anti-fourteenth amendment minority. This article will attempt to show that it did not; that it adopted instead the middle view of the moderate Republicans for whom Representative Garfield spoke. The theory is a subtle and complex one which is far less limiting in its effect on congressional enforcement power than the "state action" theory. It may be summarized as follows:

1. The fourteenth amendment places the primary responsibility for enforcing equality of civil rights on the states, but lodges in Congress adequate power to insure that the state's failure to discharge this responsibility shall not result in leaving these rights unprotected.

2. Where a racial group is discriminated against through a cultural pattern in which private acts play a part, the *constitutional* wrong, under the fourteenth amendment, is not the act of the individual, but the failure of the state to take adequate steps to prevent it, or to afford redress.

3. Congress, however, is not limited to striking directly at the constitutional wrong. It may also offset it by providing the protection which the state has failed to provide. But this power exists only when the state fails to do its duty.

4. Congress may provide in advance for a possible violation. But, if it does so, such legislation must be made conditional on the state's failure to act.

5. Congressional legislation which impinges directly on the conduct of private individuals *and which operates uniformly regardless of the role played by the state* is unconstitutional. But this is not because "private acts" are beyond the limits of congressional power. Rather, it is because: (a) Congress may not presume that states will fail to discharge their constitutional duties; (b) Congress

may not deprive the states, in advance of any default on their part, of the very function the amendment commands them to perform.

The theory, of course, has never been directly tested since no federal civil rights legislation, limited in this fashion, has ever been enacted. The investigation will therefore require a somewhat painstaking analysis of the *ipsissima verba* of the decided cases to uncover relevant dicta and to disclose the constitutional theory underlying the decisions. It also requires an investigation of what went before, both on and off the Court, since the context of the opinions gives them a significance which a mere reading does not disclose.

THE CONTEXT OF THE 1883 DECISIONS

The Reese approach to statutory construction

The initial cases on legislation under the fourteenth amendment must be understood in the context of the rather unusual approach to the question of the constitutionality of an overly broad statute which the Supreme Court adopted for the first time in the *Reese* case,[21] and which seems to have been uniformly applied in other decisions involving the validity of federal civil rights legislation until it was finally rejected in 1960.[22] The *Reese* decision was handed down on March 27, 1876, the same day the *Cruikshank* case was decided. The question in *Reese* was the validity of an indictment charging that the defendant, a state election official, had refused, because of race or color, to accept and count the vote of a qualified Negro citizen. However, the indictment was brought under a statute which, as the Court construed it, was broad enough to punish any unlawful interference with the right of franchise, whether or not based on race or color, at any election.

The Court begins by reasoning that, though the fifteenth amendment does not directly confer the right of suffrage on anyone, nevertheless it has given United States citizens the right not to be discriminated against with respect to suffrage because of race, color, or previous condition of servitude, and it has given Congress the power to enforce that right.[23] Since the election involved was a state election, it is only because of the fifteenth amendment that Congress may act, and that amendment gives the power of enforcement only if the right to suffrage has been denied because of race. The statute is unconstitutional, therefore, since it may extend to denials of suffrage on other than racial grounds.

But if the situation before the Court is within the fifteenth amendment, what occasion is there for the Court to inquire whether the statute might be construed to reach situations which are outside it? Chief Justice Waite replies that penal statutes must be so construed that the citizen may know whether or not he is violating the law. It might be possible to save the constitutionality of the statute, to disregard some of its language, but the court may not write into the statute words of limitation that are not there.[24]

The decisions on the Civil Rights Act of 1875 follow the *Reese* pattern. The original decision[25] holding that statute unauthorized by either the thirteenth or fourteenth amendments disposed of a group of cases, one of which involved segregation of an interstate railroad passenger. Yet the Court, over the express protest of Justice Harlan,[26] stated:

"And whether Congress, in the exercise of its power to regulate commerce amongst the several States, might or might not pass a law regulating rights in public conveyances passing from one State to another, is also a question which is not now before us, as the sections in question are not conceived in any such view."[27]

In 1913, in *Butts v. Merchants & Miners Transp. Co.*,[28] a Negro woman who had been segregated on a steamer passage between Boston and Norfolk brought suit to recover the penalties provided by Sections One and Two of the Civil Rights Act of 1875.[29] Her lawyer did not challenge the decision in the *Civil Rights Cases*, but he contended that it decided only that the act could not take effect within the territorial jurisdiction of the states. The Court held unanimously that the law was not separable, that it could not make a law for the territories, the District of Columbia, and the high seas out of one which Congress had intended to apply to the whole nation.

Since the Court seems never to have suggested that a federal civil rights statute could be treated as valid in one application and invalid in another, all the cases on this legislation must be read with a basic caveat constantly in view: the fact that the Court held a particular statute unconstitutional does not necessarily mean that a valid statute could not have been framed to reach the same conduct.

The early judicial reaction

In view of the reliance placed by the Supreme Court in later times on the allegedly contemporary construction of the fourteenth amendment by judges personally familiar with the circumstances of its framing and adoption, it is interesting to note the chronology of the cases from which we have derived our modern ideas about the effect of the amendment on congressional power. The Supreme Court decisions on this point begin with *Reese*[30] and *Cruikshank*[31] in 1876, and culminate with *Harris*[32] and the *Civil Rights Cases*[33] in 1883. In 1876 the structure of Reconstruction was already crumbling and its impending defeat was evident. In 1883 its defeat was a fact which the North had accepted and acquiesced in for six years. On the other hand, the earliest judicial reaction to fourteenth amendment enforcement legislation which I have been able to find parallels very closely the congressional theory. This is the case of *United States v. Hall*,[34] decided on circuit in 1871, when the tide of Reconstruction was still running high. The opinion is by Circuit Judge W. B. Woods, who was later to be elevated to the supreme bench, and who was still later to deliver the Supreme Court's opinion in the *Harris* case.

The *Hall* case was decided on a demurrer to an indictment and, consequently, the opinion tells us very little about the facts. The indictment, drafted under Section Six of the Enforcement Act of 1870,[35] charged that the defendants had conspired to injure, oppress, etc. certain citizens of the United States to prevent their free exercise and enjoyment of the rights of freedom of speech and freedom of assembly. It was contended on demurrer that these were not rights "granted or secured...by the Constitution or laws of the United States," and hence the indictment failed to charge a violation of the statute. The court overruled the demurrer.

Unlike most later tribunals, Judge Woods begins his analysis of the fourteenth amendment with the first sentence declaring native born persons (with exceptions not relevant here) to be American citizens. This clause, he remarks, has the effect of making national citizenship define state citizenship whereas formerly the reverse had been true. Judge Woods then quotes the privileges or immunities clause of the amendment and defines such privileges and immunities as all those which are "fundamental," including all those singled out in the Bill of Rights. These rights are now secured against the states by the fourteenth amendment. Ignoring the due process clause, Woods next quotes the equal protection clause and notes that Congress is given an express grant of enforcement power:

"From these provisions it follows clearly, as it seems to us, that Congress has the power, by appropriate legislation, to protect the fundamental rights of citizens of the United States against unfriendly or insufficient state legislation, for the fourteenth amendment not only prohibits the mak-ing or enforcing of laws which shall abridge the privileges of the citizens, but prohibits the states from denying to all persons within its jurisdiction the equal protection of the laws. Denying includes inaction as well as action, and denying the equal protection of the laws includes the omission to protect, as well as the omission to pass laws for protection. The citizen of the United States is entitled to the enforcement of the laws for the protection of his fundamental rights, as well as the enactment of such laws. Therefore, to guard against the invasion of the citizen's fundamental rights, and to secure their adequate protection, as well against state legislation as state inaction, or incompetency, the amendment gives congress the power to enforce its provisions by appropriate legislation. And as it would be unseemly for congress to interfere directly with state enactments, and as it cannot compel the activity of state officials, the only appropriate legislation it can make is that which will operate directly on offenders and offenses, and protect the rights which the amendment secures. The extent to which congress shall exercise this power must depend on its discretion in view of the circumstances of each case. If the exercise of it in any case should seem to interfere with the domestic affairs of a state, it must be remembered that it is for the purpose of protecting federal rights, and these must be protected even though it interfere with state laws or the administration of state laws."[36]

Two years after *Hall*, Supreme Court Justice Strong, who was later to write the Court's opinions in a very important group of fourteenth amendment cases,[37] handed down an opinion in circuit, *United States v. Given*,[38] dealing with congressional enforcement power under the fifteenth amendment. Congress, in the 1870 act,[39] had undertaken to make it an offense to refuse, on grounds of race, color, or previous condition of servitude, to permit any citizen to perform any act necessary to become qualified to vote. Upholding an indictment under this provision, Justice Strong argued that the "primary object" of the Reconstruction amendments was to enlarge the rights of private persons. It does not necessarily follow that because the fifteenth amendment is worded as a prohibition upon the states and the federal government private persons did not gain rights because of it, or that Congress cannot enforce those rights. The fact that a mere recognition in the original Constitution of a master's right to reclaim a fugitive slave,[40] even without any express provision for congressional enforcement, had been held to authorize Congress to enact a comprehensive statutory scheme to make the right fully effective, including legislation impinging directly on private individuals,[41] led Justice Strong to conclude:

"[T]he rights secured, recognized, and guaranteed by the thirteenth, fourteenth, and fifteenth amendments [are] objects of legitimate protection by the law-making power of the federal government. Those amendments have left nothing to the comity of the states affecting the subjects of their provisions. They manifestly intended to secure the right guaranteed by them against infringement from any quarter.... It was well known when it [the fifteenth amendment] was adopted that in many quarters it was regarded with great disfavor. It might well have been anticipated that it would meet with evasion and hindrances, not from state legislatures, for their affirmative action was rendered powerless by it, or not from a state's judiciary, for their judgments denying the rights were reviewable by federal courts, but by private persons and ministerial officers.... It was not intended to leave the right without full and adequate protection. Earlier prohibitions to the states were left without any express power of interference by congress; but these later, encountering as they did so much popular prejudice and working changes so radical, were fortified by grants to congress of power to carry them into full effect—that is, to enact any laws appropriate to give reality to the rights declared."[42]

Thus, "It is ... an exploded heresy that the national government cannot reach all individuals in the states."[43] Seven years after the fourteenth amendment was proposed, five years after its ratification, the notion that congressional enforcement power under the fourteenth and fifteenth amendments cannot reach "private acts" was so far from Justice Strong's mind that, even in dealing with the case of a state official charged with making racially discriminatory use of his official powers, the Justice did not even bother to stress the "state action" aspects of the case before him.

The Bradley Theory: Cruikshank in Circuit

The first Supreme Court case involving congressional legislation passed to enforce the fourteenth amendment was *United States v. Cruikshank*.[44] The case grew out of a bloody incident known as the "Colfax massacre." In Louisiana two groups, one Democrat and one Republican, claimed to have won the 1872 election, and the federal government recognized the Republican faction. In the little town of Colfax, the Republican sheriff summoned a Negro posse and took over the building which was used as a court house. On April 13,

1873, a white mob surrounded the improvised court house, set it afire, and shot the Negroes to death as they emerged from the burning building. An investigation by the Department of Justice resulted in indictments under the Enforcement Act,[45] charging that the defendants had "banded together" and "conspired" to injure, oppress, etc. their victims, citizens of the United States of African descent, in order to deprive them of: freedom of assembly, the right to bear arms, their lives and liberty without due process, the full benefit of all laws and proceedings, etc. enjoyed by white citizens, their rights, privileges and immunities, as citizens of the United States and of Louisiana, on account of race or color, the right to vote in future elections, and all rights and privileges secured to them in common with other citizens. The defendants were also charged with conspiring to injure their victims because they had voted in the election of 1872, and with murdering them in executing the conspiracies charged.

The defense persuaded Justice Bradley of the Supreme Court, who was believed to doubt the constitutionality of the Enforcement Act, to sit with Judge W. B. Woods at the trial in Circuit Court. The defendants were acquitted on the murder counts, but convicted of the conspiracy charges. On motion in arrest of judgment, the judges were disagreed. Justice Bradley delivered an opinion[46] holding the entire indictment void and the case was certified to the Supreme Court.

Parts of Justice Bradley's opinion have been quoted with approval by the Supreme Court, and none of it seems ever to have been expressly disavowed. Apart from its value as a precedent, however, it is a clue both to the early stages of the Supreme Court's thinking about the enforcement legislation and to the interpretation of the language used by Justice Bradley nine years later in his opinion for the Court in the *Civil Rights Cases*.[47]

"The main ground of objection," Justice Bradley begins,

"is that the act is municipal in its character, operating directly on the conduct of individuals, and taking the place of ordinary state legislation; and that there is no constitutional authority for such an act, inasmuch as the state laws furnish adequate remedy for the alleged wrongs committed."[48]

So it is to be noted that the defendants themselves, as reported by Justice Bradley, did not contend that congressional enforcement power can never operate "directly on the conduct of individuals." They contended merely that, where "state laws furnish adequate remedy," Congress is not authorized to pass legislation so operating which is "municipal in its character" and takes "the place of ordinary state legislation."

In adopting this argument Justice Bradley does not intend to reach the conclusion that no implied powers over individuals are given to Congress by the fourteenth amendment since the words of the amendment are directed only at states. Rather, using a quotation from *Prigg v. Pennsylvania*,[49] he denounces such narrow constitutional construction and contends that recognition of a right in the federal Constitution necessarily implies congressional power to do anything necessary to make it fully effective. Justice Bradley then observes that the constitutionally appropriate method of enforcement will depend on the character of the right, and a method applicable to one may not be applicable to another. As to those rights which form a part of the citizen's "political inheritance,... vindicated by centuries of stubborn resistance to arbitrary power,"

"they belong to him as his birthright, and it is the duty of the particular state of which he is a citizen to protect and enforce them, and to do naught to deprive him of their full enjoyment. When any of these rights and privileges are secured in the constitution of the United States only by a declaration that the state or the United States shall not violate or abridge them, it is at once understood that they are not created or conferred by the constitution, but that the constitution only guaranties that they shall not be impaired by the state, or the United States, as the case may be. The fulfillment of this guaranty by the United States is the only duty with which that government is charged. The affirmative enforcement of the rights and privileges themselves, unless something more is expressed, does not devolve upon it, but belongs to the state government as a part of its residuary sovereignty. ... The enforcement of the guaranty does not require or authorize congress *to perform the duty which the guaranty itself supposes it to be the duty of the state to perform,* and which it requires the state to perform. The duty and power of enforcement *take their inception from the moment that the state fails to comply with the duty enjoined,* or violates the prohibition imposed."[50]

The fourteenth amendment is not here conceived as consisting exclusively of restraints upon the states. It is conceived as also requiring the states to perform positive duties. Congressional enforcement power may take its inception from failure to perform the duty, as well as from violation of the prohibition. And when it does, there is not a word to suggest that Congress has only the

obviously impractical power to command the state to act.

Applying these observations to the three Reconstruction amendments, Justice Bradley first discusses the thirteenth.[51] He views it as not merely a negative prohibition of slavery, but a positive bestowal of liberty on the former slaves, to which Congress has the power to give full effect. Since disability to be a citizen and to enjoy equal rights was deemed one form or badge of servitude, Congress had power to place the other races on the same plane of privilege as that occupied by the white race. This being the case, it necessarily had also the power

"to go further and to enforce its declaration by laws for the prosecution and punishment of those who should deprive, or attempt to deprive, any person of the rights thus conferred upon him. Without having this power, congress could not enforce the amendment."[52]

This, however, is not a power to punish ordinary, non-racially motivated crimes against the Negro where the state has not been guilty of any failure to protect him.

"All ordinary murders, robberies, assaults, thefts, and offenses whatsoever are cognizable only in the state courts, unless, indeed, the state should deny to the class of persons referred to the equal protection of the laws. Then, of course, congress could provide remedies for their security and protection."[53]

The fifteenth amendment, according to Justice Bradley, though negative in form, confers a positive right. That right, however, is not a right to vote, but merely a right not to be excluded from voting for the prohibited reasons.[54] As to how this new right is to be enforced:

"When the right of citizens of the United States to vote is denied or abridged by a state on account of their race, color, or previous condition of servitude, either by withholding the right itself *or the remedies which are given to other citizens to enforce it,* then, undoubtedly, congress has the power to pass laws *to directly enforce the right and punish individuals for its violation,* because that would be the only appropriate and efficient mode of enforcing the amendment. Congress cannot, with any propriety, or to any good purpose, pass laws forbidding the state legislature to deny or abridge the right, nor declaring void any state legislation adopted for that end. The prohibition is already in the constitutional amendment, and laws in violation of it are absolutely void by virtue of that prohibition. So far as relates to rendering null and void the obnoxious law, it is done already; but that does not help the person entitled to vote. By the supposition the state law gives him no remedy and no redress. It is clear, therefore, that *the only practical way congress can enforce the amendment is by itself giving a remedy* and giving redress."[55]

Where the state laws are in harmony with the amendment, or at least contain nothing repugnant thereto, Justice Bradley sees no impropriety in having Congress pass laws to enforce the right concurrently with the state. The citizen owes a dual allegiance to state and nation, and the same act may offend the laws of both.

"The real difficulty in the present case is to determine whether the amendment has given to congress any power to legislate except to furnish redress in cases where the states violate the amendment. Considering, as before intimated, that the amendment, notwithstanding its negative form, substantially guaranties the equal right to vote to citizens of every race and color, I am inclined to the opinion that Congress has the power to secure that right not only as against the unfriendly operation of state laws, but against outrage, violence, and combinations on the part of individuals, irrespective of state laws. Such was the opinion of congress itself in passing the law at a time when many of its members were the same who had consulted upon the original form of the amendment in proposing it to the states. And as such construction of the amendment is admissible, and the question is one at least of grave doubt, it would be assuming a great deal for this court to decide the law, to the extent indicated, unconstitutional."[56]

The limitations of the amendment, Justice Bradley hastens to add, must be kept in mind. Private interference with the right to vote is not within congressional power merely because the victims are Negroes, but only where such interference is racially motivated.

Summing up his views on the effect of the thirteenth and fifteenth amendments, Justice Bradley states:

"The war of race, whether it assumes the dimensions of civil strife or domestic violence, whether carried on in a guerilla or predatory form, or by private combinations, or even by private outrage or intimidation, is subject to the jurisdiction of the government of the United States; and when any atrocity is committed which may be assigned to this cause it may be punished by the laws and in the courts of the United States; but any outrages, atrocities, or conspiracies, whether against the colored race or the white race, which do not flow from this cause, but spring from the ordinary felonious or criminal intent which prompts to such unlawful acts, are not within the jurisdiction of the United States, but within the sole jurisdiction of the states, unless, indeed, the state, by its laws, denies to any particular race equality of rights, in which case the government of the United States may furnish remedy and redress to the fullest extent and in the most direct manner. Unless this distinction be made we are driven to one of two extremes—either that congress can never interfere where the state laws are unobjectionable; *however remiss the state authorities may be in executing them,* and, *however much a proscribed race may be oppressed;* or that congress may pass an entire body of municipal law for the protection of person and property within the states, to operate concurrently with the state laws, for the protection and benefit of a particular class of the community. This fundamental principle, I think, applies to both the 13th and 15th amendments."[57]

Justice Bradley concludes with a few observations on the effect of the fourteenth amendment, in which he deals only with the privileges or immunities clause. He rejects the argument that this clause empowers Congress "to pass laws for directly enforcing all privileges and immunities of citizens of the United States...." By the rationale of the recent *Slaughterhouse* decision he should have answered this argument by saying that the rights of which the defendants' victims were deprived were conferred on them by the state of Louisiana and were quite unconnected with their United States citizenship. But Justice Bradley, evidently still clinging to his *Slaughterhouse* dissent, answers the argument in a quite different way:

"If the power to enforce the amendment were equivalent to the power to legislate generally on the subject matter of the privileges and immunities referred to, this would be a legitimate conclusion. But, as before intimated, that subject matter may consist of rights and privileges not derived from the grants of the constitution, but from those inherited privileges which belong to every citizen, as his birthright, or from that body of natural rights which are recognized and regarded as sacred in all free governments; and the only manner in which the constitution recognizes them may be in a prohibition against the government of the United States, or the state governments, interfering with them. It is obvious, therefore, that the manner of enforcing the provisions of this amendment will depend upon the character of the privilege or immunity in question. If simply prohibitory of governmental action there will be nothing to enforce until such action is undertaken. How can a prohibition, in the nature of things, be enforced until it is violated? Laws may be passed in advance to meet the contingency of a violation, but they can have no application until it occurs."[58]

This prelude does not lead Justice Bradley to the conclusion that congressional enforcement, even under the privileges and immunities clause, can never reach "private acts." Instead:

"If these views are correct, there can be no constitutional legislation of congress for directly enforcing the privileges and immunities of citizens of the United States by original proceedings in the courts of the United States, where the only constitutional guaranty of such privileges and immunities is, that no state shall pass any law to abridge them, and where the state has passed no laws adverse to them, but, on the contrary, *has passed laws to sustain and enforce them.*"[59]

Justice Bradley, then, believed that racially motivated private acts, designed to deprive Negroes of equality of rights, might be reached by Congress under the thirteenth amendment, regardless of the role played by the state. They can also be reached under the fifteenth, where racial equality in suffrage is the right attacked. Private conduct which is not racially motivated is not within congressional power merely because the victims are Negroes. But legislation *is* within congressional power when the state "denies to any particular race equality of rights," either because state laws are objectionable or because "state authorities" are "remiss...in executing" state laws. Whether this power to provide congressional protection against private acts when state protection fails is attributed to the thirteenth amendment, to the equal protection clause of the fourteenth, or both is not entirely clear. The matter is adverted to as part of the thirteenth amendment discussion, but the language of equal protection is used. There is no separate discussion of the equal protection clause. It is clear that, when state protection fails, Congress is not limited to exhorting the state to act, and to punishing lax officials. Instead, "the government of the United States may furnish remedy and redress to the fullest extent and in the most direct manner."

If the power to extend national protection where state protection fails is attributed solely to the thirteenth amendment, then there is no explicit statement as to the full extent of congressional power to reach "private acts" under the fourteenth amendment. It is said, however, that under the fourteenth amendment Congress has no power to move against private acts where the state has in no way failed in its duty. But the reason for this is not that congressional enforcement power can reach only acts which the amendment itself forbids, a rationale which would contradict Justice Bradley's own reading of the fifteenth amendment, as well as the *Prigg v. Pennsylvania* approach to construction, which he took as his starting point. The reason is that Congress would then be taking over the very duty which amendment "requires the state to perform," without affording the state any opportunity to perform it.

It seems clear that the theory which Justice Bradley in the end adopts is the same as that which, in the beginning, he stated as the defendants' contention. But it is not a theory that "private acts," as such, are beyond the reach of congressional enforcement power. It is rather a theory that, where "the state laws furnish adequate remedy" Congress is not authorized to assume the initial and primary responsibility for regulating private acts by means of legislation which is "municipal in its character" and takes "the place of ordinary state legislation."

Cruikshank in the Supreme Court

In the Supreme Court, Justice Bradley's judgment quashing the indictment was affirmed in an opinion[60] which was substantially unanimous, although Justice Clifford, concurring on procedural grounds, found it unnecessary to discuss any constitutional questions.

Chief Justice Waite, delivering the opinion of the Court, is not nearly so luminous as Bradley. He restates the *Slaughterhouse* distinction in sweeping generalities. Each citizen of the United States who resides in a state has two allegiances and two citizenships. His rights under one may not be the same as his rights under the other. Each of the two governments has a duty to protect him, but only within the limits of its powers.

The right of free assembly is both too ancient and too fundamental to have anything to do with national citizenship.

"The government of the United States, when established, found it in existence, with the obligation on the part of the states to afford it protection. As no direct power over it was granted to Congress, it remains...subject to state jurisdiction."[61]

It is very difficult to say what this means. The right of free assembly "remains subject to state jurisdiction." There is nothing necessarily inconsistent with Bradley about that. The state is not assigned merely a negative disability to invade the right, but an affirmative "obligation to afford it protection." But that obligation does not spring from the fourteenth amendment, or even from the Constitution; it was in the bosom of the natural law when the United States was established. But to whom is the obligation owed? Is it merely the state's obligations to its citizens, or has the fourteenth amendment made the affirmative protection of citizens in the enjoyment of their rights an obligation which the state owes to the United States? If the latter, is Congress' power limited to trying to coerce an unwilling state to take affirmative action—the complete impracticality of which is pointed out in the opinion which the Chief Justice is reviewing—or is there some point at which the failure of the state to discharge its obligations would give Congress power to assume the function? "No *direct* power" over the subject has been granted to Congress. But what is the nature of that indirect power in Congress, the possibility of which is not excluded?

Chief Justice Waite simply leaves these questions unanswered. But, significantly, he leaves Justice Bradley's theories unchallenged, in spite of the fact that he is reviewing and affirming the Circuit Court decision which will be cited for any proposition which the Supreme Court fails to disavow. If the majority of the Supreme Court were clearly of the opinion that Bradley's approach was unsound, it would seem that a few well-placed dicta in the majority opinion would be in order. Significantly, too, Justice Bradley silently concurs. If he understood the majority opinion to reject his views, though agreeing with his disposition of the case, there seems to be no reason why he should not repeat his views in a special concurrence. It is conceivable, of course, that Justice Bradley, even in this short interval, may have changed his views, but we have no indication that he did.

Chief Justice Waite found that the right of free assembly was not, in general, a privilege of United States citizenship, but he qualified this view:

"The right of the people peaceably to assemble for the purpose of petitioning Congress for a redress of grievances, or for anything else connected with the powers or the duties of the National Government, is an attribute of National Citizenship and, as such, under the protection of and guaranteed by, the United States.... If it had been alleged in these counts that the object of the defendants was to prevent a meeting for such a purpose, the case would have been within the statute and within the scope of the sovereignty of the United States."[62]

Here, there is a slight suggestion that Chief Justice Waite may be seeking a different compromise from the one Justice Bradley suggested between the two extremes which he had pointed out. Instead of letting Congress act on individuals when the state has failed to discharge its constitutional obligations, let Congress act on individuals when the right at stake is one which the nation, as such, has an interest in preserving. But this distinction is not brought forward as an interpretation of the fourteenth amendment or any other specific clause of the Constitution. Rather:

"The very idea of a government, republican in form, implies a right on the part of its citizens to meet peaceably for consultation in respect to public affairs and to petition for a redress of grievances."[63]

It almost seems that the Chief Justice prefers not to get his constitutional law too closely entangled with the text of the document. But it is clear that, if he does intend to substitute this new distinction for the one suggested by Justice Bradley, he does not do so in the name of the new amendments. So the essential question—what are Congress' *new* powers, and upon whom may they be exercised— remains unanswered.

The Chief Justice also expressly takes the position that whatever may be the rights which belong to a United States citizen as such, those rights Congress may protect against individual acts of aggression. He finds that the counts on right to assemble and right to bear arms fail, because these rights are not guaranteed against individual invasion, and the count on the deprivation of life and liberty also fails, because the due process clause "adds nothing to the rights of one citizen as against another." But to reach a similar conclusion regarding the count for depriving the victims of "the full benefit of all laws and proceedings," he finds it necessary to observe that there is "no allegation that this was done because of the race or color of the persons conspired against." He also points out that because this allegation was omitted, no question arises under the Civil Rights Act of 1866. So it seems that, though the equal protection clause also does not "add anything to the rights which one citizen has under the Constitution against another," it is impliedly admitted that Congress might be able to add something to the rights of one individual against another, at least when a race motive is involved.

The implications of Waite's opinion, then, are that private conduct *not racially motivated* does not constitute a violation of the due process clause or the equal protection clause. Therefore, when a federal statute makes it a crime for individuals to conspire to deprive citizens of their constitutional rights, an allegation that defendants conspired to deprive citizens of their lives and liberty without due process, or to deny them equal protection, is not sufficient to charge a violation of this statute. Further, the privileges or immunities of national citizenship may be protected against private aggression. But these rights do not include a general right of freedom of assembly, though they do include the right to assemble to discuss national issues. There is nothing here inconsistent with *Bradley*, except the view that the privileges or immunities clause does not protect fundamental rights. This difference does not touch Bradley's theory, since he, forewarned by *Slaughterhouse*, worked out his whole approach without relying on that clause.

The 1880 cases

On the whole, the judicial history of the Reconstruction civil rights legislation is one of the progressive dismantling by the courts of most of what Congress had attempted. But there was one sharp interruption of this process in 1880 with a group of five decisions,[64] predominantly nationalistic in tone, two of them dealing directly with the powers of Congress under the fourteenth amendment. In each, Justices Clifford and Field in dissent maintained that the police jurisdiction of the states is a sacred area in which Congress, even in the exercise of an express power, may not meddle. In each, the majority refused to consider the tenth amendment, or the nature of the federal system, as implying any limitations on the exercise of an express federal power.

In *Ex parte Virginia*[65] the Court upheld, in the first such holding, and the only one prior to 1945,[66] a federal criminal statute passed under the authority of the fourteenth amendment. The measure involved was section four of the Civil Rights Act of 1875,[67] which made it a crime to exclude any citizen, on grounds of race or color, from a state or federal jury. The Supreme Court upheld an indictment charging a state judge with having excluded Negroes in the selection of a state jury. It pronounced the act "fully authorized by the Constitution." Justice Field, dissenting, argued with respect to all three of the Reconstruction amendments that:

"The provision authorizing Congress to enforce them by appropriate legislation does not enlarge their scope, nor confer any authority which would not have existed independently of it. No legislation would be appropriate which should contravene the express prohibitions upon Congress. ...[T]he implied prohibitions...are as obligatory as the express prohibitions. The Constitution... contemplates the existence and independence of the States in all their reserved powers....Legislation could not, therefore, be appropriate which, under pretence of prohibiting a State from doing certain things, should tend to destroy it, or any of its essential attributes. To every State, as understood in the American sense, there must be, with reference to the subjects over which it has jurisdiction, absolute freedom from all external interference in the exercise of its legislative, judicial, and executive authority."[68]

From the presence of the due process clause in the fourteenth amendment, Justice Field argues that congressional enforcement was never intended. He maintains that congressional power to enforce such a clause would result in authority to prescribe the conditions on which property can be acquired and held, the means by which the liberty of the citizen should be protected, and a code of criminal procedure for the states. Hence:

"The existence of this clause in the Amendment is to me a persuasive argument that those who framed it, and the Legislatures of the States which adopted it never contemplated that the prohibition was to be enforced in any other way than through the judicial tribunals, as previous prohibitions upon the States had always been enforced."[69]

Justice Strong, speaking for the majority, replied to Justice Field's latter argument by calling attention to the congressional enforcement clause which appears at the end of each of the Reconstruction amendments:

"All of the Amendments derive much of their force from this latter provision. It is not said that the *judicial power* of the general government shall extend to enforcing the prohibitions and to protecting the rights and immunities guaranteed.... *It is the power of Congress which has been enlarged.*...Whatever legislation is appropriate, that is, adapted to carry out the objects the Amendments have in view, whatever tends to enforce submission to the prohibitions they contain, and to secure to all persons the enjoyment of perfect equality of civil rights and the equal protection of the laws against state denial or invasion, if not prohibited, is brought within the domain of congressional power."[70]

To Justice Field's argument from the independence of a state, "as understood in the American sense," Strong responded:

"Nor does it make any difference that such legislation is restrictive of what the State might have done before the constitutional amendment was adopted....[A] state cannot...deny to the general government the right to exercise all its granted powers, though they may interfere with the full exercise and enjoyment of rights she would have had if those powers had not been thus granted. Indeed, every addition of power to the general government involves a corresponding diminution of the governmental powers of the States. It is carved out of them...."

*   *   *

"Such legislation must act upon persons, not upon the abstract thing denominated a State, but upon the persons who are the agents of the State in the denial of the rights which were intended to be secured."[71]

The last remark must be read in the context of the particular case. The issue between Field and the majority is whether Congress, to enforce the amendment, can go *so far* as to control one of the state's own instrumentalities. "Persons who are the agents of the State" are contrasted not with private individuals but with "the abstract thing denominated a State."

The case does not involve and the opinions do not consider whether circumstances can ever arise in which congressional enforcement power may impinge directly on the conduct of private individuals toward each other. But the statements that it is congressional power, not judicial power, which has been enlarged, and that Congress, in the absence of a prohibition, can do anything adapted to carry out the objects of the amendments "and to secure to all persons the enjoyment of perfect equality of civil rights," suggest a very broad doctrine indeed. The latter phrase may or may not be read as limited by the expression "against state denial or invasion." But, if it is, state "denial," which is contrasted to "invasion," would seem to refer to a failure to afford affirmative protection.

In the scope of congressional power which its language would seem to imply, Justice Strong's opinion in *Strauder v. West Virginia*[72] is even broader. There a Negro had been indicted in the state court for murder. A state statute, enacted after the Reconstruction amendments, limited jury service to whites. Under these circumstances, the Court held that Section 641 of the Revised Statutes, providing for the removal of proceedings by defendants unable to enforce in a local tribunal rights granted them by the Civil Rights Bill, authorized the removal to federal court of the trial of this purely state offense. The Court held also that the statute, as thus construed, was a very appropriate one for the enforcement of the fourteenth amendment. Justice Strong for the Court argued that the common purpose of the thirteenth, fourteenth, and fifteenth amendments is to secure *all* civil rights to the Negro and that they must be interpreted in the light of that purpose. The fourteenth makes no attempt to enumerate the rights it protects, but uses language designedly general to make its coverage as comprehensive as possible. And, although its language is prohibitory, every prohibition implies rights and immunities, prominent among which is immunity from inequality of legal protection, either for life, liberty, or property. Here, again, the question of congressional legislation impinging on private individuals is not before the Court and is not discussed. But the theoretical approach is that the amendment creates affirmative rights in individuals, not merely restraints upon the states. And the Court expressly takes the view, of the utmost importance for this question, that the *form* and *manner* of the protection to be provided are questions of legislative discretion for Congress.

The juxtaposition of this case with *Virginia v. Rives*[73] provides an interesting clue to the direction of the Court's thinking at this point. As in the *Strauder* case, the defendant was charged with murder and sought to remove his case to the federal court. His petition for removal alleged that, although Negroes were eligible for jury service by state law, no Negroes had ever been chosen for jury services in the state; that all members of the venire were white; that he had moved to have a venire composed one-third of Negroes selected, and this motion had been refused; that he was charged with the murder of a white man, and that feeling in the community was so high that a trial by an all-white jury could not be fair and impartial. The Court decided that all of this did not add up to a case for removal under the statute. It limited the statute to cases in which the defendant could not secure his rights because the state law itself was unfavorable. The statute left other cases of denials of equal rights by state courts to the revisory power of the Supreme Court.

This is expressly a construction of the removal statute, not of the Constitution. The Court points out that the reach of the statute is not as broad as that of the amendment and finds it unnecessary to consider whether a removal statute broad enough to remove a case merely because of a state court's discriminatory application of the law would be constitutional.

The aspect of the case which relates it to *Strauder* is this statement:

"But when a subordinate officer of the State, in violation of State law, undertakes to deprive an accused party of a right which state law accords him...it ought to be presumed the court will redress the wrong."[74]

The idea that it must be presumed that the state will discharge its obligations reappears frequently in the cases. Thus, in *Neal v. Delaware*[75] the state statute, enacted in 1848, confined jury service to electors, and the state constitution, adopted in 1831, confined the suffrage to whites. But it was held that this did not make a case within the rule that there is a right of removal where the discrimination is on the face of the law. The state constitution must be understood as having been automatically amended by the effect of the fifteenth amendment in striking the word "white" from its suffrage sections. The Court remarked:

"The presumption should be indulged, in the first instance, that the State recognizes, as is its plain duty, an amendment of the Federal Constitution, from the time of its adoption, as binding on all its citizens and every department of its government, and to be enforced, within its limits, without reference to any inconsistent provisions in its own Constitution or statutes."[76]

By the presumption in *Neal* and *Rives*, it is clear that removal in the *Strauder* case was available only because the state statute had been passed after the amendment. Thus the advance presumption that state will always obey the federal Constitution had been rebutted in what is perhaps the only way such a presumption could be rebutted: the state had officially announced its advance intentions in incontrovertible form.

In *Ex parte Siebold*,[77] which was decided contemporaneously with the *Virginia*, *Rives*, and *Strauder* cases, the fourteenth amendment was not involved, but the case shows the same general pattern of thinking, with Clifford and Field in dissent and the majority refusing to divide state and federal functions into watertight compartments. Congress had passed a statute imposing federal criminal penalties on state election officials for failure to discharge, at a federal election, duties imposed upon them by state law. The majority in an opinion by Justice Bradley held this valid under the constitutional power of Congress to "make or alter" the regulations in federal elections:

"The objection that the laws and regulations, the violation of which is made punishable by the acts of Congress, are State laws and have not been adopted by Congress, is no sufficient answer to the power of Congress to impose punishment....The State laws which Congress sees no occasion to alter, but which it allows to stand, are in effect adopted by Congress. It simply demands their fulfillment. Content to leave the laws as they are, it is not content with the means provided for their enforcement. It provides additional means for that purpose; and we think it is entirely within its constitutional power to do so....[T]he duties devolved on the officers of election are duties they owe to the United States as well as to the State...."[78]

It would, perhaps, be pressing this argument too far to suggest that where the state law on its face gives adequate protection to civil rights, Congress might adopt it and add further means for its enforcement. The fourteenth amendment does not contain the "make or alter" language which is under consideration here. But at least it establishes that the nature and structure of the federal system do not preclude the possibility that enforcement of state laws by state officers may become a federal function.

THE HARRIS AND CIVIL RIGHTS CASES

Two cases decided in 1883, *United States v. Harris*[79] and the *Civil Rights Cases*,[80] are customarily cited as having established the doctrine, already said to have been announced in *Cruikshank*, that the power conferred on Congress by the fourteenth amendment can never extend to private acts, but only to the states and the agents by which states act. The precedents for *Harris* and the *Civil Rights* cases, however, do not approach stating this doctrine. The nearest thing to an authority for it is the *Cruikshank* case.[81] But the *Cruikshank* case decides nothing on Congress' fourteenth amendment enforcement power. It decides merely that the fourteenth amendment does not, of its own force, without congressional action, impose constitutional obligations on private individuals. Hence, when Congress provides in general terms that it shall be a crime to conspire to deprive a citizen of his rights under the federal Constitution and laws, a mere private wrong not sanctioned in any way by the state, is not within that statute. It does not say, nor does it clearly imply that Congress has no power to impose new duties on private individuals. It contains a rather strong implication that Congress does have such a power, at least where private wrongs are racially motivated.

United States v. Harris[82] was an indictment of Harris and nineteen others for lynching four persons, who were in the custody of a deputy sheriff. The indictment was framed under Section 5519 of the Revised Statutes, which had been part of section two of the Ku Klux Act of 1871.[83] The section made it a crime to conspire to deprive any person of equal protection or to prevent or hinder the authorities of any state or territory from giving equal protection. The Court held the statute unconstitutional, Justice Harlan dissenting without opinion. The Court's opinion is by Justice Woods, who, as circuit judge twelve years before, had expounded the congressional theory of the fourteenth amendment in *United States v. Hall.*

After citing *Slaughterhouse* to establish the constitutional irrelevance of the fact that the deceased were citizens of the United States, Justice Woods relies on three authorities: Justice Bradley's opinion in circuit in *Cruikshank,* Chief Justice Waite's opinion in the same case, and *Virginia v. Rives.* But, as we have seen, the Bradley opinion is expressly in favor of a congressional power to reach private action, but only where the act is racially motivated and where the state's protection has been withheld. Waite's opinion says only that an outrage by private persons, not affirmatively alleged to be motivated by racial antagonism, cannot, independently and of its own force, amount to a violation of the fourteenth amendment. Most interesting of all, *Virginia v. Rives* does not touch the private action problem. It deals with action which was admittedly that of the state—with the presumption that a state will not fail to redress a wrong which is a violation of its own laws.

Referring to these cases, Justice Woods declares:

"These authorities show conclusively that the legislation under consideration finds no warrant for its enactment in the Fourteenth Amendment. The language of the amendment does not leave the subject in doubt. When the State has been guilty of no violation of its provisions,...when, on the contrary, the laws of the State, as enacted by its legislative, and construed by its judicial, and administered by its executive departments, *recognize and protect the rights of all persons,* the amendment imposes no duty and confers no power upon Congress."[84]

Observe the expansive conditions which must be met before the statement "the Amendment...confers no power upon Congress" takes effect. Legislatively, judicially, and administratively, the state must not merely recognize but protect the rights of all persons.

"Section 5519 of the Revised Statutes is not limited to take effect only in case the State shall abridge the privileges or immunities of citizens of the United States, or deprive any person of life, liberty, or property without due process of law, nor deny to any person the equal protection of the laws. It applies, no matter how well the State may have performed its duty."[85]

If the rule were that the power of Congress under the amendment cannot reach private acts, all this discussion would be quite meaningless and unnecessary. It would be sufficient to point out that the statute on which indictment was based was one penalizing purely private acts, and that would dispose of the whole case. There is a clear negative inference here that Congress' power can reach private individuals, but only when the state has somehow failed in its duty.

"As, therefore, the section of the law under consideration is directed *exclusively* against the action of private persons, *without reference* to the laws of the State *or their administration* by her officers, we are clear in the opinion that it is not warranted by any clause in the Fourteenth Amendment."[86]

This is the same criticism which Representative Garfield had made of the statute when it was before the Congress. And in holding the statute unconstitutional, Justice Woods, who wrote the *Hall* opinion and who voted to uphold the *Cruikshank* indictment, is not adopting the extreme view that congressional enforcement power never extends to "private acts." He is adopting the view of Garfield and the moderates that it does not extend to such acts in the absence of some showing that state protection has failed or has been withheld. And he is applying the latter view in the light of the presumptions, established in *Virginia v. Rives* and *Neal v. Delaware,* that the state will perform its constitutional duties and will enforce its own laws.

Did the Court, after expressing the moderate view in *Harris,* shift to the extreme states-rights view a few months later in the *Civil Rights Cases?*[87] In the latter case, the Court held unconstitutional those sections of the Civil Rights Act of 1875[88] which had attempted to prohibit racial discrimination in the enjoyment of the facilities of inns, public conveyances, and places of public amusement. Justice Bradley stated that:

"The first section of the Fourteenth Amendment (which is the one relied on), after declaring who shall be citizens of the United States, and of the several States, is prohibitory in its character, and prohibitory upon the States....[T]he last section of the amendment invests Congress with power to enforce it by appropriate legislation. To enforce what? To enforce the prohibition. To adopt appropriate legislation for correcting the effects of such prohibited State laws and State acts, and thus to render them effectually null, void and innocuous. This is the legislative power conferred upon Congress, and this is the whole of it. It does not invest Congress with power to legislate upon subjects which are within the domain of State legislation; but to provide modes of relief against State legislation, or State action, of the kind referred to. It does not authorize Congress to create a code of municipal law for the regulation of private rights; but to provide modes of redress against the operation of State laws, and the action of State officers executive or judicial, when these are subversive of the fundamental rights specified in the amendment. Positive rights and privileges are undoubtedly secured by the Fourteenth Amendment; but they are secured by way of prohibition against State laws and State proceedings affecting those rights and privileges, and by power given to Congress to legislate for the purpose of carrying such prohibition into effect: and such legislation must, necessarily, be predicated upon such supposed State laws or State proceedings, and be directed to the correction of their operation and effect. A quite full discussion of this aspect of the amendment may be found in *United States v. Cruikshank ...Virginia v. Rives...* and *Ex parte Virginia....*"[89]

This language, taken by itself, is certainly open to the construction that congressional enforcement power cannot deal with private acts. Yet it does not clearly and unequivocally say this. It says merely that enforcement legislation must be "predicated upon some supposed state law or state proceedings, and be directed to the correction of their operation and effect." Though it may be a little awkward to think of a state failure to protect as constituting a "law" or "proceeding," the notion that congressional protection against private acts may be extended where state protection fails or is withheld is not explicitly excluded. Furthermore, here, as in *Harris,* the nature of the authorities cited throws light on what is intended by the language used. *Cruikshank* held merely that the amendment does not, of its own force, give one private individual rights against another (not that congressional enforcement legislation may not do so). *Ex parte Virginia* expresses a very broad view of congressional enforcement power and holds that it extends *even to* (but not necessarily only to) control of the state's own instrumentalities. Here, as in *Harris,* if one assumes that the Court is distinguishing between state and private action, then it is impossible to account for the invocation of *Virginia v. Rives,* which dealt with action admittedly that of the state. If the Court were now saying that under no circumstances can congressional enforcement power forbid something which is not "state action," then this would be new doctrine, going considerably beyond anything the Court had previously held. Surely in that case Justice Bradley would not have said that a "quite full discussion" of this new point was to be found in three cases which in fact do not discuss it at all.

Had Justice Bradley stopped here, this view of his opinion might be deemed tenuous and uncertain. However, he did not stop. Instead, as Justice Woods had done in *Harris,* he went on to develop an argument which, if congressional power were wholly limited to dealing with "state action," would have been entirely superfluous:

"An inspection of the law shows that it makes *no reference whatever to any supposed or apprehended violation* of the Fourteenth Amendment on the part of the States. It is not predicated on any such view. It proceeds *ex directo* to declare that certain acts committed by individuals shall be deemed offences, and shall be prosecuted and punished by proceedings in the courts of the United States. It does not profess to be *corrective of any constitutional wrong* committed by the States; it does not *make its operation to depend upon* any such wrong committed. It applies equally to cases arising in States *which have the justest laws* respecting the personal rights of citizens, and *whose authorities are ever ready to enforce such laws,* as to those which arise in States which may have violated the prohibition of the amendment. In other words, it steps into the domain of local jurisprudence, and lays down rules for the conduct of individuals in society towards each other, and imposes sanctions for the enforcement of those rules, *without referring in any manner to any supposed action of the State or its authorities.*"[90]

If the statute were void because prevention of private acts of discrimination is beyond congressional power, then the fact that the state has "the justest laws" to protect civil rights and that its authorities are ever ready to enforce such laws could not make it any the more void. It seems plain enough that this is Justice Bradley's old theory that congressional enforcement power takes its "inception from the moment that the state fails to comply with the duty enjoined" and that, absent such failure, Congress is not authorized "to perform the duty which the guaranty itself supposes it to be the duty of the state to perform, and which it requires the state to perform." Or rather, we are back to the version of that theory, as merged with presumptions that the state will perform its constitutional duties and enforce its own laws, which the Court had already adopted in the *Harris* case.

CONCLUSIONS

Whatever one may think of its application in the particular cases, the underlying theory of the early cases construing congressional power under the fourteenth amendment is not very far from what some recent pro-civil rights commentators have concluded the theory should be. Nor is it very far from some recent interpretations of the original understanding with which the fourteenth amendment was enacted.[91] The theory that congressional power to enforce the fourteenth amendment can deal only with "state action" will not stand up. It is obviously at odds with the original understanding. Even if we are not certain precisely what the original understanding was, we know that it could not have been this. The theory leaves still unsolved —and still incapable of any national solution—the principal problem which the amendment was designed to remedy. The cases which are believed to have established this theory do not do so.

It is difficult to say whether the more moderate and complex theory which the cases actually express (if I read them correctly) can still be exhumed after generations have grown accustomed to a contrary reading. It is still more difficult to say just how useful, if useful at all, that theory might prove to be if its rescue and revitalization are still possible. Admittedly, adoption of this theory would leave many difficult problems unresolved.

Some may doubt, too, whether decisions such as those in the *Cruikshank, Harris,* and *Civil Rights Cases* are now of anything more than historical interest. Those cases, whether read one way or the other, are expressions of a judicial attitude vastly different from that which now obtains. Surely the present Court, if compelled to choose between following those cases (as they have generally been understood) or overruling them, would choose the latter. Yet, unless we are willing to attribute to Congress vast and undefined powers which might alter the federal-state balance more than we wish or need to alter it, overruling those cases would not solve the problem, but merely restate it: if "state action" is not the limit of congressional power to enforce the fourteenth amendment, then what is that limit? Perhaps the Garfield-Bradley-Woods theory might furnish an acceptable answer to that question.

Very little fourteenth amendment enforcement, either judicial or legislative, had received judicial approval by 1883. The growth of the judicial decisions under the fourteenth did not fairly begin until after that date. Thereafter, the power of the courts under the fourteenth evolved greatly while the power of Congress under the same amendment was left to wither on the vine. Yet this did not happen because the courts had given Congress a fourteenth amendment power só restricted that no further experiments would have been justified. It happened because, by the time its first efforts had been judicially rejected, Congress was no longer interested in making another try. The Hayes-Tilden Compromise had been accepted, and Congress had gone out of the civil rights business, which it was not to attempt to re-enter for more than half a century. Indeed, by 1883 some Congressmen may have been only too anxious to give the decisions their modern reading as an excuse for taking no further action. In any case, once that restrictive reading was established, there was no way in which it could be judicially re-examined unless Congress made the challenge by enacting a statute which goes beyond that narrow concept of its powers. We may nevertheless be pardoned for suspecting that the framers of the fourteenth amendment—and even the justices of the 1883 Court—would have been far more astonished by the powers later exercised by the judiciary under the fourteenth amendment than by an assertion that that amendment empowers Congress to enact a public accommodations bill, or a statute to punish racially-motivated acts of private intimidation.

In the end, civil rights were largely nationalized after all—and the process of their nationalization is still continuing. Yet this nationalization has taken place in a peculiarly one-sided manner, with the judiciary obliged, at least until the recent legislation, to assume the whole responsibility of defining the new consensus and almost the whole responsibility of enforcing it. The fourteenth amendment was adopted in part to give Congress power to deal with a racial crisis. Yet, in the current racial crisis, there is, according to present theories, almost nothing of major importance which Congress can do—except where it can find power to act in the commerce clause, or some other source independent of the fourteenth amendment.

In view of the fact that an enlargement of federal legislative, rather than judicial, power seems to have been the primary intent, this is an ironic and upside down result. It is also, in my view, an unfortunate one. Piecemeal litigation is hardly an ideal method for the accomplishment of sweeping social reforms. And the civil rights crisis which has precipitated the current legislation certainly indicates that, if further proliferation of lawsuits was ever an adequate answer, it is so no longer. Furthermore, a readjustment of the social, economic, and legal structure so profound that it is being widely referred to as a "revolution" is hardly a process over which the courts should be expected to preside alone and largely unaided, except for an occasional show of force when a court order is openly defied.

Moreover, the presently orthodox theory in effect informs the die-hard white supremacists that, so long as they resist through the forms of law, "state action" is sure to be found, and they remain within the actual or potential orbit of federal power. At the same time, it assures them that, if they act outside the law, then the Constitution commands the federal government to keep hands off and leave them to such sanctions as their friends and sympathizers in state and municipal governments can be persuaded to apply. Thus the orthodox theory is an open invitation to vigilantism. At the same time, the apparent impotence of the national government to define and enforce the newly emerging consensus gives rise, on the other side, to a sense of frustration which can find outlet only in direct action.

Should Congress ever be minded to enforce the fourteenth amendment by appropriate legislation rather than approaching the problem through the commerce clause, it will be venturing into almost wholly unexplored territory. That territory has not been judicially charted—but neither has it been judicially interdicted. The Congress need not conceive its fourteenth amendment enforcement powers in terms of a narrow and pessimistic reading of a handful of nineteenth century cases—especially since that reading seems only a misreading after all.

Footnotes

[1]United States v. Cruikshank, 92 U.S. 542 (1876).
[2]United States v. Harris, 106 U.S. 629 (1883).
[3]Civil Rights Cases, 109 U.S. 3 (1883).
[4]No detailed review of the original understanding will be attempted here. It is believed that none is necessary, since this is oft-plowed ground. See, for example: FLACK, THE ADOPTION OF THE FOURTEENTH AMENDMENT (1908); KENDRICK, JOURNAL OF THE JOINT COMMITTEE OF FIFTEEN ON RECONSTRUCTION (1914); TENBROEK, THE ANTISLAVERY ORIGINS OF THE FOURTEENTH AMENDMENT (1951); JAMES, THE FRAMING OF THE FOURTEENTH AMENDMENT (1956); HARRIS, THE QUEST FOR EQUALITY (1960); 2 CROSSKEY, POLITICS AND THE CONSTITUTION 1083-1118 (1953); Boudin, *Truth and Fiction about the Fourteenth Amendment*, 16 N.Y.U. L.Q. 19 (1938); Graham, *The "Conspiracy Theory" of the Fourteenth Amendment*, 47 YALE L.J. 371, 48 YALE L.J. 171 (1938); Fairman, *Does the Fourteenth Amendment Incorporate the Bill of Rights? The Original Understanding*, 2 STAN. L. REV. 5 (1949); Frank & Munro, *The Original Understanding of "Equal Protection of the Laws"*, 50 COLUM. L. REV. 131 (1950); Graham, *The Early Antislavery Background of the Fourteenth Amendment*, 1950 WIS. L. REV. 479 & 610 (1950); Crosskey, *Charles Fairman, "Legislative History," and the Constitutional Limitations on State Authority*, 22 U. CHI. L. REV. 1 (1954); Fairman, *A Reply to Professor Crosskey*, 22 U. CHI. L. REV. 144 (1954); Graham, *Our "Declaratory" Fourteenth Amendment*, 7 STAN. L. REV. (1954); Bickel, *The Original Understanding and the Segregation Decision*, 69 HARV. L. REV. 1 (1955).
[5]Maxwell v. Dow, 176 U.S. 581, 601-02 (1900).

[6]REPORT OF THE JOINT COMMITTEE ON RECONSTRUCTION (Gov't Printing Office, 1886).
[7]*Id.*, pt. II at 209.
[8]16 Stat. 140 (1870).
[9]17 Stat. 13 (1871).
[10]18 Stat. 335 (1875).
[11]Prigg v. Pennsylvania, 41 U.S. (16 Pet.) 539 (1842); Ableman v. Booth, 62 U.S. (21 How.) 506 (1859).
[12]Kentucky v. Dennison, 65 U.S. (24 How.) 66, 107 (1861). This case, like the two cited in note 11 *supra*, grew out of an aspect of the fugitive slave problem. All three cases must therefore have been quite familiar to abolitionists.
[13]Barron v. Mayor of Baltimore, 32 U.S. (7 Pet.) 242 (1833).
[14]FLACK, *op. cit. supra* note 4, at 210-77.
[15]83 U.S. (16 Wall.) 36 (1873).
[16]FLACK, *op. cit. supra* note 4, at 210-77.
[17]17 Stat. 13 (1871), 42 U.S.C. § 1983 (1958).
[18]HARRIS, *op. cit. supra* note 4, at 45.
[19]*Ibid.*
[20]CONGRESSIONAL GLOBE, 42d Cong., 1st Sess. 153 (Appendix) (1871).
[21]United States v. Reese, 92 U.S. 214 (1876).
[22]United States v. Raines, 362 U.S. 17 (1960).
[23]United States v. Reese, 92 U.S. 214 (1876).
[24]*Id.* at 221. For analogous holdings, see also Baldwin v. Franks, 120 U.S. 678 (1887); and James v. Bowman, 190 U.S. 127 (1903).
[25]Civil Rights Cases, 109 U.S. 3 (1883).
[26]*Id.* at 60-61 (dissenting opinion).
[27]*Id.* at 19.
[28]230 U.S. 126 (1913).
[29]18 Stat. 336 (1875).
[30]United States v. Reese, 92 U.S. 214 (1876).
[31]United States v. Cruikshank, 92 U.S. 542 (1876).
[32]United States v. Harris, 106 U.S. 629 (1883).
[33]109 U.S. 3 (1883).
[34]26 Fed. Cas. 79 (No. 15,282) (C.C.S.D. Ala. 1871).
[35]16 Stat. 141 (1870).
[36]*Id.* at 81-82.
[37]Tennessee v. Davis, 100 U.S. 257 (1880); Strauder v. West Virginia, 100 U.S. 303 (1880); Virginia v. Rives, 100 U.S. 313 (1880); *Ex parte* Virginia, 100 U.S. 339 (1880).
[38]25 Fed. Cas. 1324 (No. 15,210) (C.C.D. Del. 1873). The Court gave no statement of facts other than that the defendant was found guilty and moved in arrest of judgment on the grounds of the unconstitutionality of the act.
[39]16 Stat. 140 (1870).
[40]U.S. CONST. art. IV, § 2, cl. 3.
[41]Prigg v. Pennsylvania, 41 U.S. (16 Pet.) 345 (1842); Ableman v. Booth, 62 U.S. (21 How.) 506 (1859).
[42]25 Fed. Cas. at 1326-27.
[43]*Id.* at 1328.
[44]92 U.S. 542 (1876).
[45]16 Stat. 140 (1870).
[46]United States v. Cruikshank, 1 Woods 308, 25 Fed. Cas. 707 (No. 14,897) (1874).
[47]109 U.S. 3 (1883).
[48]25 Fed. Cas. at 708-09.
[49]*Id.* at 709-10; Prigg v. Pennsylvania, 41 U.S. (16 Pet.) 539 (1842).
[50]*Id.* at 710 (emphasis added).
[51]*Id.* at 711-12.
[52]*Id.* at 711.
[53]*Id.* at 711-12.

[54]*Id.* at 712.
[55]*Id.* at 713 (emphasis added).
[56]*Ibid.*
[57]*Id.* at 714 (emphasis added).
[58]*Ibid.*
[59]*Ibid.*
[60]United States v. Cruikshank, 92 U.S. 542 (1876).
[61]*Id.* at 551.
[62]92 U.S. at 552-53.
[63]*Id.* at 552.
[64]Tennessee v. Davis, 100 U.S. 257 (1879); Strauder v. West Virginia, 100 U.S. 303 (1879); Virginia v. Rives, 100 U.S. 313 (1879); *Ex parte* Virginia, 100 U.S. 339 (1879); *Ex parte* Siebold, 100 U.S. 371 (1879).
[65]100 U.S. 339.
[66]Screws v. United States, 325 U.S. 91 (1945).
[67]18 Stat. 335 (1875).
[68]100 U.S. 339, 361-62.
[69]*Id.* at 366.
[70]*Id.* at 345-46 (emphasis added).
[71]*Id.* at 346-47.
[72]100 U.S. 303 (1879).
[73]100 U.S. 313 (1879).
[74]*Id.* at 321-22.
[75]103 U.S. 370 (1881).
[76]*Id.* at 389-90.
[77]100 U.S. 371 (1879).
[78]*Id.* at 388-89.
[79]106 U.S. 629 (1883).
[80]109 U.S. 3 (1883).
[81]92 U.S. 542 (1876).
[82]106 U.S. 629 (1883).
[83]17 Stat. 13 (1871).

[84]106 U.S. at 639 (emphasis added).
[85]*Ibid.*
[86]*Id.* at 640 (emphasis added).
[87]109 U.S. 3 (1883).
[88]18 Stat. 335 (1875)
[89]109 U.S. at 10-12.
[90]*Id.* at 14 (emphasis added).
[91]"[D]espite differences of opinion concerning the scope of congressional power under the amendment, a majority of the members of the Thirty-ninth, Forty-second, and Forty-third Congresses, some of whom were members of all three and of the Committee of Fifteen on Reconstruction, believed that the equal protection clause did more than condemn official or state action. They believed that it vested Congress at the very least with a primary power to set aside unequal state laws and a secondary power to afford protection to all persons in their enjoyment of constitutional rights when the states failed in their primary responsibility to do so either by neglecting to enact laws or by refusal or impotence to enforce them." Harris, The Quest for Equality 53 (1960).

"If the abolitionist origins of the Fourteenth Amendment are accepted, . . . the states are forbidden to fail to carry out their primary duty of protection; and, when carrying it out, are forbidden to fail to adhere to the standard of equality. Congress is authorized to enforce this provision, that is to say, is authorized to supply the protection of the laws when the states do not, and to correct deviations by the states from the prescribed standard of equality." tenBroek, The Antislavery Origins of the Fourteenth Amendment 98 (1951).

Chapter V

CIVIL RIGHTS, EXPATRIATION, AND FOREIGN TRAVEL

Since 1937 the Supreme Court has only very rarely declared a congressional statute unconstitutional. In recent years, however, the Court has waged a campaign to declare unconstitutional various federal laws providing for deprivation of citizenship. The Court is not of one mind on this question. Some of the justices believe that loss of citizenship under any circumstances is a cruel and unusual punishment forbidden by the Constitution. Others believe that Congress may impose loss of citizenship when it is "reasonably calculated to achieve... the avoidance of embarrassment in the conduct of our foreign relations..." [*Perez* v. *Brownell*, 356 U.S. 44, 61 (1958)]. If it is not so calculated, they believe that loss of citizenship is a violation of the due process clause of the Fifth Amendment. Here again is the conflict between those who propose an absolute right to citizenship and those who wish to balance that right against another interest—in this instance, the successful conduct of our foreign policy.

John P. Roche examines the leading expatriation cases in the selection below. Since this article appeared, the Supreme Court has struck down yet another such statute, this one denaturalizing naturalized citizens who return to and live in their native country for three years [*Schneider* v. *Rusk*, 377 U.S. 163 (1964)]. Justice Douglas' opinion indicates that some of the justices still believe in an absolute right to citizenship but that a majority could be formed only through an alliance of the absolutists with those justices who, in this case, struck the balance against Congress' interest in a successful foreign policy and in favor of the individual's interest in freedom of travel. Justices Harlan, White, and Clark, in dissent, found the balance to be on the side of Congress.

Another area in which the foreign relations powers of Congress and the President collide with individual freedom is that of travel. Does the government have the constitutional power to deprive the individual of a passport and thus prevent him from traveling abroad? In recent years the Supreme Court has been creating a constitutional right to travel. This right was introduced in *Kent* v. *Dulles* [357 U.S. 116 (1958)] and affirmed in *Aptheker* v. *Secretary of State* [378 U.S. 500 (1964)] as part of the liberty guaranteed by the due process clause. Of course it is also intimately tied to the freedoms of speech and association, since passports have generally been withheld from those whose political activities are suspect. The majority, however, has been careful not to assert an absolute right to travel. In *Kent* the Court found that the Secretary of State, in withholding the passports of certain persons, was exercising a power that Congress had not given him. In *Aptheker*, the statute that prohibited the issuance of a passport to a member of a Communist organization was found to be overly broad and vague, because the statute allowed too extensive an invasion of liberty in the course of achieving a congressional purpose that might have been achieved just as well by a narrowly drawn statute providing less opportunity for arbitrary infringements on individual rights. Apparently, then, Congress may regulate travel—but only to the degree that the Court finds reasonably necessary to the conduct of our foreign policy.*

These first cases in which foreign policy and civil rights came into conflict are likely to assume greater importance in the future. The conduct of foreign policy has become a more and more important power of the national government and the success of that policy more and more vital to us all. The temptation thus increases to sacrifice individual rights to international success. So far this temptation has affected only a few areas, such as passports and expatriation, and these areas touch only a few of our citizens. But some proposed international covenants might well limit our freedom of speech and association. Further, it is not hard to imagine a situation where, in order to reduce international tensions, it might seem reasonable to conclude treaties that provide that the press of each signatory nation should not be permitted to criticize other signatories. It has never been clear to what extent the grants of power over foreign policy in the Constitution would allow Congress and the President to do things that would be unconstitutional if concerned with strictly domestic affairs.† The Supreme Court has spoken of the inherent powers of the President in foreign affairs, and the Constitution grants Congress the powers necessary and proper to carry out its responsibilities in foreign affairs and defense matters. The argument can be constructed that if the national government is responsible for foreign policy, it has the power to do whatever is necessary to pursue a successful foreign policy. It is not far from this to the proposition that the government may do anything necessary to make our foreign policy a success. The Expatriation Cases, and others in the same area, thus introduce a new problem in civil liberties that will require the alert attention of legislatures, courts, and citizens for some time to come.

Selection 14

The Expatriation Cases: "Breathes There the Man, with Soul So Dead...?"

John P. Roche

On Feburary 18, 1963, in the cases of Francisco Mendoza-Martinez and Joseph Henry Cort[1] the Supreme Court struck down as unconstitutional a provision of the Nationality Act providing that "[D]eparting from or remaining outside of the jurisdiction of the United States in time of war or ...national emergency for the purpose of evading or avoiding training and service in the military, air, or naval forces of the United States"[2] created in effect, an irrebuttable presumption of a voluntary decision to expatriate, *i.e.*, to surrender American nationality. The reader who winces at this convoluted formulation should brace himself: worse is yet to come. For it is hard to discover an area

of American public law in which the premises and logic of action have been more absurdly attenuated or the historical record so flagrantly distorted.

The crucial difficulty derives from the fact that a set of improvisations, formulated over a century and a half, were promoted into an ideology in 1940. Since all good ideologies must have historical

"The Expatriation Cases: 'Breathes There the Man, with Soul So Dead...?'" by John P. Roche, reprinted from page 325 of *Supreme Court Review*, ed. Philip B. Kurland, by permission of The University of Chicago Press. Copyright © 1963 by The University of Chicago Press.
*See *Zemel* v. *Rusk*, 381 U.S. 1 (1965).
†See *Missouri* v. *Holland*, 252 U.S. 416 (1920).

foundations, there was a hasty movement to the archives and, with appropriate selectivity, a "history" was concocted. Opponents of the expatriation formula, of course, needed a history of their own, or, let us call it, an "anti-history." These two versions of the development of expatriation in the United States have appeared inseparably in all subsequent litigation. The Government has maintained that deprivation of citizenship is not a "penalty" but merely a formalization of voluntary individual action; its opponents have asserted that deprivation of nationality, except on a clearly voluntary basis, is an unconstitutional innovation, a break with all the traditions of the past.

The subject is suffering, in short, from an acute case of hardening of the categories. The time has come to attempt a dispassionate explication of the history and logic of expatriation. This does not imply that I have no opinions on the validity or wisdom of the expatriation statutes,[3] but rather that they will be, to the best of my ability, stated rather than guised as "historic truths." The historian, unlike the brief-writer, can never proceed on the assumption that history unfolds backward in neat legal categories; his task, whatever his opinions on the merits of contemporary policies, is to analyze the past on its own terms. But I shall confine myself here to the major problems presented by the *Mendoza-Martinez* and *Cort* cases.

HISTORICAL BACKGROUND

There is an ancient Talmudic caveat that the existence of a question does not necessarily require the existence of an answer. Yet when the Supreme Court faces the issue of the constitutionality of a statute written in 1940 or 1952, it must assume that there is an answer concealed in the corpus of American constitutional history, that there is a "logic of constitutionality" that makes it possible for events in 1963 to be squared with the intentions of 1787. There is, in short, an assumption of equivalence that serves as the rationale of judicial review, and this juridical fiction in turn activates the brief-writers in their desperate quest for history and anti-history. It would hardly do for the Supreme Court, asked how the framers would feel about expatriation, property rights in space, or the obligation of commitments to the United Nations, to stand silent—though it might be the course recommended by sophisticated intelligence. Instead, an elaborate *Gestalt* is promulgated with the key question: How *would* the framers have reacted to the issues of 1963 *if* they had been given the opportunity? It need hardly be noted that in practice the views of the framers thus construed bear a striking resemblance to those of the Justices writing the opinions.

The practical outcome of this role-playing is, I suspect, that Justice Black knows a good deal more about what James Madison had in mind when he introduced the First Amendment into the House of Representatives than James Madison did at the time. And all legal practitioners are surely aware of the esoteric divination that often goes into the construction of statutes, a technique that achieved something of a high point in the *Cort* case in 1962 when the Supreme Court gave the McCarran-Walter Immigration and Nationality Act of 1952 a "liberal" construction![4] What must be emphasized is that the history of expatriation in the United States does not fall into anybody's *post hoc* categories. Our ancestors were neither "liberal" nor "conservative" by contemporary standards. Confronted by issues of citizenship, they dealt with them extemporaneously in terms of their value systems. In fact, before the Civil War there was a conspiracy among the political leadership to avoid a clear definition of United States citizenship. This was not perversity, but was founded on a recognition that the status of the Negro, notably of the free Negro, was a great source of conflict between North and South and, in the interests of political harmony, had best be left "unclarified."

If citizenship was juridically obscure, what can one expect with respect to loss of citizenship? The United States was a nation of immigrants and it is in this context that one must understand the significance of the "natural right of expatriation." In the international forum, it was American policy to deny the doctrine of indefeasible allegiance. When our spokesmen talked of the right of expatriation, they were not concerned with loss of American citizenship; they were combating in specific situations, *e.g.*, the British impressment of British-born, naturalized Americans from our ships, the traditional doctrine that a citizen could not shift his allegiance without the consent of his sovereign. Yet in the municipal forum the United States, like the British, endorsed the doctrine of indefeasible allegiance. In other words, we claimed the right to naturalize immigrants but denied Americans the right to give up their American nationality, a classic nationalist posture.

In *Shanks v. Dupont*[5] the Supreme Court gave its conclusions on the subject. Justice Story said: "The general doctrine [governing American law] is that, no person can, by any act of their own, without the consent of the government, put off their allegiance, and become aliens."[6] And Chancellor James Kent in his *Commentaries* concluded a discussion of expatriation thus:[7]

"From this historical review...the better opinion would seem to be, that a citizen cannot renounce his allegiance to the United States without the permission of government, to be declared by law; and that, as there is no existing legislative regulation on the case, the [perpetual allegiance] rule of the English common law remains unaltered."

Only Congress could legitimate expatriation for Americans, but after several abortive efforts, the last in 1818, the legislature dropped the topic. Living as we do in the shadow of the Fourteenth Amendment, it is difficult for us to appreciate the disruptive force of state-rights doctrines in the ante-bellum period. A legislative examination of the problem of citizenship and its loss automatically opened a bitter debate on the nature of sovereignty. Those who argued that national citizenship derived from state citizenship insisted that provision for expatriation lay within state jurisdiction. The Abolitionists, who were urging the primacy of national citizenship, assigned the expatriation authority to Congress. Those interested in peace and quiet simply kept the dilemma off the floor. This may seem quaintly abstract, but it should be recalled that the heart of the *Dred Scott* decision[8] was the theoretical question of Scott's citizenship in Missouri, *i.e.*, his standing to bring action for trespass in the federal forum under the diversity clause of Article III of the Constitution.

According to the standard mythology, the right of expatriation for Americans was finally established in 1868 when Congress passed an "expatriation act." This statute began strongly enough by asserting that:[9]

"Whereas the right of expatriation is a natural and inherent right of all people, indispensable to the enjoyment of the rights of life, liberty, and the pursuit of happiness...."

But a persistent reader, one who continued beyond this rhetorical flourish, would get a different sense of legislative intent, one consonant with the title of the statute, an "Act concerning the Rights of American Citizens in Foreign States." The statute continued:

"...and whereas in the recognition of this principle this Government has freely received emigrants from all nations, and invested them with the rights of citizenship; and whereas it is claimed that such American citizens, with their descendants, are subjects of foreign states, owing allegiance to the governments thereof; and whereas it is necessary to the maintenance of public peace that this claim of foreign allegiance should be promptly and finally disavowed: Therefore any declaration, instruction, opinion, order, or decision of any officer of the United States which denies, restricts, impairs, or questions the right of expatriation, is declared inconsistent with the fundamental principles of the Republic."

In other words, the "expatriation act" of 1868 was merely another affirmation of the rights of foreign nationals to expatriate, *i.e.*, to become naturalized American citizens, and an announcement to the world at large that the United States considered these adopted citizens fully within its protection.

During the remainder of the nineteenth century, the President, the Secretary of State, and the courts engaged in desultory excursions into the question whether Congress had intended the right of expatriation to extend to Americans. The preponderant opinion was that Congress had so intended. But it was not a subject of heated debate. Many problems did arise in connection with the marriage of American women to aliens and an ingenious improvisation, too illogically delightful to pass over, was employed to dispose of the question. The citizenship of an American woman married to an alien went into a specially designed limbo. While living abroad her American citizenship was "in abeyance" or "inactive" for the duration of foreign residence and coverture, but she could regain it by "returning to and dwelling in the country of her maiden allegiance." This was a halfway station between two contending legal traditions: the first asserting the rule of perpetual allegiance and the second maintaining the primacy of the husband's status.

In 1906 and 1907, Congress finally took official notice of the legal problems created by nonstatutory denaturalization and expatriation and passed two statutes that, for the first time, systematized immigration and nationality procedures. The Expatriation Act of 1907,[10] which alone is relevant here, essentially gave statutory validity to the administrative law of expatriation that had been developed in the preceding years. An American who became a naturalized citizen of a foreign state, or who took an oath of allegiance to another sovereign; a naturalized American who returned to his native land or took up permanent residence in another foreign state; an American woman who married an alien—all were held to have voluntarily given up their American citizenship. This is an oversimplification—naturalization, for example, established an irrebuttable presumption of expatriation, whereas foreign residence by a naturalized citizen created a rebuttable presumption (and the citizenship of women was put into the limbo described earlier)—but the important point is that

Congress adopted the basic propositions that have governed expatriation legislation ever since: (1) Expatriation must be voluntary. (2) The United States can establish the outward and visible standards of such volition and compel an individual to accept the consequences of his freely willed decision.

At the same time, it should be carefully noted that the expatriation categories of the 1907 statute were all related to a putative transfer of allegiance. That is, they established criteria for determining when an American had taken up a new nationality (or reverted to his original status). The proviso on women had, indeed, a quaintly arrogant ring: "[A]ny American woman who marries a foreigner shall take the nationality of her husband."[11] In other words, the 1907 enactment was not designed to penalize Americans for their sins; it may have had that impact in marginal cases, but its main purpose was to regularize the arrangements by which the United States took notice that an American national had *sua sponte* abandoned his citizenship. The Supreme Court viewed the matter in this light: after stipulating that "It may be conceded that a change of citizenship cannot be arbitrarily imposed, that is, imposed without the concurrence of the citizen,"[12] the Court held the statute to be part of the "inherent power of sovereignty":[13]

"As a government, the United States is invested with all the attributes of sovereignty. As it has the character of nationality, it has the powers of nationality, especially those which concern its relations and intercourse with other countries."

Thus, there developed a firm category of expatriates: those who, by their actions, indicated that they voluntarily abandoned American nationality in favor of citizenship of, or at least allegiance to, a foreign sovereign. In 1940 this category was expanded to include one who took service in a foreign army, if "he has or acquires the nationality of such foreign state";[14] one who accepted or performed "the duties of, any office, post, or employment under the government of a foreign state or political subdivision thereof for which only nationals of such state are eligible";[15] and one who voted in a political election in a foreign state.[16] The 1952 statute retained these provisions with slight modifications.[17]

LOSS OF CITIZENSHIP AS PUNISHMENT: MORE HISTORY

Beginning in 1940 the Congress added several new provisions to the section setting forth standards of voluntary expatriation that were qualitatively distinct from those described above. They were not recognitions of a transfer of allegiance except in the most abstract ideological sense; they were punishments for sins against the sovereign. An American was held to have expatriated himself by committing treason;[18] by deserting from the armed forces in wartime;[19] by leaving the country or remaining outside the country to avoid military service;[20] and by attempting, conspiring, etc., to teach and advocate the overthrow of the United States government by force or violence.[21] Conviction for treason, desertion, sedition thus carried with it automatic denationalization; the proviso on draft-dodging, involved in the *Cort* and *Mendoza-Martinez* cases, was not triggered in this fashion: it was not feasible to convict absentees in criminal actions. Indeed, only when an individual, like Mendoza-Martinez, returned to the United States and was apprehended for draft evasion could a trial take place. In *Cort's* instance, for example, an indictment had been returned against him in federal court and a warrant was out for his arrest for draft-dodging, but until he returned to the jurisdiction no further action was possible. The decision that an individual had departed from or remained outside of the United States to avoid military service was thus left in the hands of the administrative authorities. The Immigration and Naturalization Service could exclude an individual from the United States on the ground that he had expatriated himself by evading military service. The Department of State could withdraw an individual's passport and inform him of his loss of nationality under this clause. It was not an easy provision to administer, but Congress in 1952 stepped in with a helpful presumption: "[F]ailure to comply with any provision of any compulsory service laws...shall [in the instance of an American abroad] raise the presumption that the departure from or absence from the United States was for the purpose of evading or avoiding training...."[22]

Admittedly, I have taken for granted the very issue that was *sub judice* in *Trop v. Dulles*,[23] *Rusk v. Cort*, and *Kennedy v. Mendoza-Martinez* (and was evaded on technical grounds in *Perez v. Brownell*),[24] namely, that deprivation of nationality under these rubrics was in fact a punishment, a criminal sanction, rather than a mere recognition of transfer of allegiance, an official government *imprimatur* on a private, voluntary act of expatriation. The Solicitor General labored mightily in *Cort* and *Mendoza-Martinez* to demonstrate that "punishment" was not involved, but this was obviously done in an effort to distinguish those cases from *Trop*, where the Court had invalidated the desertion provision, and to fit them into the mold of *Perez,* where the Court sustained the voting in a foreign election category. The historian, fortunately, is not bound by the deductive requirements of pleading and can confidently call a spade a spade.

Had it not been for the eccentricities of precedent, one and all would surely have admitted what is patent on the face of the legislation: that it is essentially penal in character. Indeed, both historically and contemporaneously denationalization has been widely employed as a punishment for "bad" behavior. At this moment one may be deprived of his Nicaraguan citizenship for "expounding political doctrine running counter to the ideal of the Fatherland, affecting its national sovereignty or tending to destroy the republican system of government."[25] In Albania and Yugoslavia it is sufficient to refuse "to do one's duty";[26] in Brazil, to engage in activities "against the public interest";[27] and in a number of states one is thus penalized for indications of disloyalty, disaffection, or a mentality contrary to the national spirit.[28]

The United States, happily isolated and isolationist, had no statutes of this kind on its books in the nineteenth century. Having no external politics of any consequence, no peacetime conscription, and little competitive nationalism, it had no need for such sanctions. There was one early effort in this direction that suggests that it was the lack of sufficient motivation rather than the lack of contrary principles that prevented denationalization from being used punitively: the proposed Thirteenth Amendment. Introduced in 1810, this measure provided that:[29]

"If any citizen of the United States shall accept, claim, receive, or retain any title of nobility or honor, or shall, without the consent of Congress, accept and retain any present, pension, office, or emolument of any kind whatever, from any Emperor, king, prince, or foreign power, such person shall cease to be a citizen of the United States, and shall be incapable of holding any office of trust or profit under them or either of them."

As originally introduced, the Amendment also penalized intermarriage with a person of royal blood![30] (It may seem strange that this was done in the form of a constitutional amendment, but the dominant Jeffersonian view held that citizenship was within the jurisdiction of the states; a statute would thus have been a federal usurpation of state power.) The proposal received the necessary two-thirds vote in the House of Representatives without debate, and with only slight changes in the Senate, and fell but one state short of the three-quarters necessary for adoption.[31]

The statutory ancestor of the punitive provisions of the Nationality Act of 1940 was not this obscure enterprise but a Civil War measure aimed at draft-dodgers and deserters. In 1865, an amendment was added to the Enrollment Act that provided that draft-dodgers and deserters who did not return to military service within sixty days of the passage of the Act were "deemed to have voluntarily relinquished and forfeited their rights of citizenship."[32] There has been some argument in recent years over whether this statute deprived deserters of their citizenship or merely of their civil rights (right to vote, hold office, etc.). No one can read the minds of the dead with certainty, but in the context of the measure it seems that when Congress said "rights of citizenship," it meant precisely that; the Chairman of the House Military Affairs Committee, who guided the bill through that chamber, presented this section as a disfranchisement. But even if, improbably, Congress meant to deprive deserters of their nationality, there is no escaping the fact that this was a punitive sanction. It was so treated after the close of World War I when President Calvin Coolidge, on March 5, 1924, issued a "Proclamation of Amnesty" in which he granted "amnesty and pardon to all persons who have heretofore [been convicted of desertion in wartime] to the extent that there shall be... fully remitted as to such persons any relinquishment or forfeiture of their rights of citizenship."[33]

In 1940 the desertion provision served as a model for the sections of the Nationality Acts that "expatriated" (to convert an intransitive verb into the active mood) traitors, and later those who left or stayed out of the United States to evade military service, and still later those convicted under the Smith Act. The "rights of citizenship" employed in the old law was quietly converted to "citizenship"; when queried on this change in the Hearings on the 1940 Act, State Department Counsellor Richard Flournoy stated that the Department had always construed the Act of 1865 as depriving Americans of their nationality, and that seemed to settle the question.[34]

Thus in the present nationality code, in addition to the category examined earlier providing loss of American citizenship for those who concretely evidenced a shift of allegiance to a foreign sovereign, there is a second category based on the proposition that "Bad Americans" should be deprived of their nationality. The first category had a rational foundation in international law; the second operates purely in the municipal forum to create stateless persons. It provides a mode of punishment additional to those provided by the criminal law for certain heinous offenses against sovereignty. Admittedly one can conjure up abstract arguments that a traitor has opted for another allegiance, but in fact he is merely a technically stateless inmate of a federal penitentiary. Again one can claim that Communists convicted under the Smith Act have indicated by their own free will their superior loyalty to the Soviet Union, but then what does one do with convicted Trotskyites, who can at best be described as would-be nationals of a non-existent foreign power? And most deserters from the armed forces, far from evidencing a superior loyalty to the enemy, are simply interested in a quiet life away from gunfire and the rigors of military existence. Perhaps, as will appear from the case of Mendoza-Martinez, special provisions could be formulated to deal with the problems created by dual nationals who evade military service by moving to the state of their alternative citizenship. But, generally speaking, as in Cort's instance, draft-evaders have violated the national service laws without any concomitant indication of allegiance to another sovereign.

THE CONSTITUTIONAL ISSUES

When the Supreme Court was confronted with the question of the constitutionality of these two expatriation categories, it had singularly few guidelines to follow. History provided no answer or, perhaps, too many conflicting answers. The founders of the nation were no help because they were concerned with a different question: was admission to the community a state or a national prerogative? The burden of evidence indicates to me that national citizenship was originally viewed as derivative from state citizenship, and all early discussions of loss of nationality came to grief on the reef of states' rights. The Fourteenth Amendment settled this issue and presumably vested any jurisdiction over expatriation in the national government. But still there was no authoritative doctrine on the reach of the expatriation power. The states in the revolutionary period had deprived Tories of their state citizenship, and the working definition of "Tory" was often pretty loose. But aside from the abortive "Thirteenth Amendment" of 1810 and the Wade-Davis Bill there were no later examples of efforts to employ expatriation in a punitive fashion. The 1865 desertion statute left only a wake of conflicting interpretations. There was, to that point, no "theory" of expatriation because the problem simply was not important enough to warrant serious jurisprudential effort.

In the twentieth century, after the passage of the 1907 statute, the federal courts had been confronted with a number of problems, but all of these arose from litigation in the first category, *i.e.*, they were concerned with issues of transfer of allegiance. The provisions of the 1907 law on loss by marriage to an alien husband were, for example, sustained as a legitimate exercise of congressional authority over international relations.[35] In *Perkins v. Elg*,[36] the leading modern case, the Supreme Court overruled the administrative authorities by holding that the American-born child of naturalized American parents who subsequently reverted to their former nationality and took her with them to Sweden had not lost her citizenship. In the course of the opinion, Chief Justice Hughes provided the widely cited rationale:[37]

"Expatriation is the voluntary renunciation or abandonment of nationality and allegiance. It has no application to the removal from this country of a native citizen during minority. In such a case the voluntary action which is of the essence of the right of expatriation is lacking."

Hughes, however, did not invoke constitutional grounds; indeed, he was careful to state the basis of the decision narrowly:[38]

"As at birth she became a citizen of the United States, that citizenship must be deemed to continue unless she has been deprived of it through the operation of a treaty or congressional enactment or by her voluntary action in conformity with applicable legal principles."

This still left the judiciary with no constitutional bearings on loss of nationality imposed by law or by treaty—and it might be added that a number of treaties dating from the Bancroft Treaty of 1868 with the North German Confederation[39] did, in effect, impose loss of American citizenship upon naturalized citizens who returned to North Germany or other former sovereignties for two years or more.

Thus the Supreme Court, when it turned to the problem of loss of nationality by desertion, voting in foreign political elections, or leaving the nation to evade military service, was really writing on a blank constitutional slate. All previous decisions tended to support the proposition that the United States could "expatriate" its nationals as an inherent coefficient of sovereignty, but in no previous holding had a punitive provision (in the sense described above) been under litigation. History was useless, and the existing body of harum-scarum administrative and judicial improvisations provided no base, no logical line of development. (Indeed, it was not unknown for the Department of State to take one position and the Department of Labor, which then had jurisdiction over the Immigration

and Naturalization Service, to take the opposite.)
There was a loose tradition that expatriation had
to be "voluntary," but this word had been given a
peculiar, disembodied gloss. An individual did not
have the option of deciding whether he wanted to
lose his citizenship; one merely had the freedom to
decide whether or not to undertake a commitment
that carried with it denationalization, *e.g.,* marriage to an alien husband. Consequently voluntary
marriage could, and did, lead to involuntary expatriation, *i.e.,* to a loss of citizenship that was in
subjective terms unwanted. Curiously this technique had been anticipated by Representative
Lowndes of South Carolina in 1818. Opposing a
bill to enounce the "right of expatriation," Lowndes
told the House: "If you pass this bill, you have
only one step further to go, and say that such and
such acts shall be considered as presumption of
intention of the citizen to expatriate, and thus take
from him the privileges of a citizen."[40]

The legal fall-out from the Nationality Act of
1940 began to drift into the Supreme Court chambers in the early 1950's. The early cases were concerned with the special problems of Japanese-
Americans, dual nationals caught in Japan at the
outbreak of war, and are of little relevance here
except as they reinforced the maxim that expatriation must be voluntary. This was again emphasized
in 1952 by Justice Jackson with respect to an
Italian-American dual national, though four members of the Court dissented from what they
took to be "an existential definition of duress."[41]
Jackson seemed to assume in his short opinion
that the fact that a dual national had been con-
scripted into the armed service of his alternative
sovereign was in itself a conclusive demonstration
of "duress," *i.e.,* of involuntary action. The constitutional issues were studiously avoided by the
extended definition of duress.

Then in 1958 the Court reached to the heart of
the matter in three decisions that left the issues as
obscured as ever. The simplest of the three decisions was *Nishikawa v. Dulles,*[42] which turned on
the duress issue. Seven Justices agreed that the
decision of the Court of Appeals should be reversed because the United States had not demonstrated that Nishikawa's service in the Japanese
army was "voluntary" by "clear, convincing, and
unequivocal evidence." Beyond this, the Court
fragmented. Justices Black and Douglas went to
the constitutional merits;[43] Justices Frankfurter
and Burton concurred in the result but rested on
narrower grounds than those set forth in the
opinion of the Court;[44] Justices Harlan and Clark
dissented.[45]

In *Perez v. Brownell,*[46] in which the constitutionality of two expatriation provisions was at

issue, the Court achieved the remarkable feat of
dividing 5½ to 3½. Perez was a dual national of the
United States and Mexico who had both voted in a
Mexican election and remained in Mexico to avoid
American military service. After a number of desultory encounters with the Immigration and Naturalization Service, he brought suit in 1954 for
a declaratory judgment that he was an American
national. There was no plea of duress; Perez
simply asserted that the expatriation provisions
were unconstitutional, a contention rejected at
both the district and intermediate appellate levels.
In essence he challenged the whole proposition
that the United States can apply a doctrine of
"constructive volition," that it can on the basis of
certain overt acts extrapolate an inner decision to
abandon American nationality.

Justice Frankfurter refused, as one might have
anticipated, to be drawn into the wider arena.
After a skillful summary of the history of the voting provision, he sustained expatriation on this
ground as a necessary facet of congressional power
to regulate the foreign relations of the United
States. On the specific connection between loss of
citizenship and voting he stated:[47]

"Is the means, withdrawal of citizenship, reasonably calculated to effect the end that is within the
power of Congress to achieve, the avoidance of
embarrassment in the conduct of our foreign relations attributable to voting by American citizens
in foreign political elections?...The critical connection between this conduct and loss of citizenship is the fact that it is possession of American
citizenship by a person committing the act that
makes the act potentially embarrassing to the
American Government and pregnant with the possibility of embroiling this country in disputes with
other nations. The termination of citizenship termi-
nates the problem. *Moreover, the fact is not without significance that Congress has interpreted this
conduct, not irrationally, as importing not only
something less than complete and unswerving allegiance to the United States but also elements of an
allegiance to another country in some measure, at
least, inconsistent with American citizenship.*"

This murky sentence has been emphasized because
it was the closest Justice Frankfurter came to the
traditional rationale of expatriation: the voluntary
transfer of allegiance to another sovereign. If his
opinion meant anything in this context, it was that
there had to be a rational nexus between individual acts and denationalization at the institutional,
not the personal, level. The logic of congressional
decision was decisive; the logic of individual action
(absent duress) irrelevant. Having sustained the

first count against Perez, Frankfurter naturally refused to examine the validity of the second, which involved remaining out of the country to avoid military service in wartime.

It was a busy day for the dissenters. Chief Justice Warren, joined by Justices Black and Douglas, rejected Justice Frankfurter's disembodied institutional framework for one which emphasized the logic of individual action. The key section of the Warren opinion argued that:[48]

"There might well be circumstances where an American shown to have voted at the behest of a foreign government to advance its territorial interests would compromise his native allegiance.

...The fatal defect in the statute before us is that its application is not limited to those situations that may rationally be said to constitute an abandonment of citizenship."

Justice Douglas, joined by Black, penned a further dissent. He interpreted the Court's decision as a capitulation to the "British scheme" of legislative supremacy and an exaltation of procedural due process; he did not like this at all.[49] Justice Whittaker, peculiarly, accepted the opinion of the Court, but not the result;[50] his remarks suggest that he did not understand Frankfurter's *ratio decidendi*.

The third decision, *Trop v. Dulles*,[51] saw a reversal occasioned by Justice Brennan's switch from Frankfurter's position to Warren's, or—to put it more precisely—to agreement with the Chief Justice's conclusion though not his constitutional formulation. Here the Court came to grips for the first time with punitive expatriation: Trop had been deprived of his American nationality for wartime desertion. The Chief Justice, joined by Justices Black, Douglas, and Whittaker, announced the judgment of the Court and delivered a plurality opinion that denationalization for desertion was an unconstitutional violation of the Eighth Amendment's ban on cruel and unusual punishments. One may speculate as to the basis for this esoteric holding: it would seem to have been an effort to put punitive expatriation under absolute constitutional interdict, thus forestalling efforts to "exalt" procedural due process (*pace* Justice Douglas' dissent in *Perez*).[52] No matter how much due process an individual received, the Chief Justice suggested, he could not be stripped of his birthright by this "penal law."

Indeed, a moment's reflection will indicate that it is not easy to find an explicit constitutional peg on which to hang a decision that punitive expatriation is completely forbidden. Since this problem has plagued the Court in its subsequent holdings,

it might be well to canvass the alternatives. First, one could take the Douglas-Black line that involves standing the Fourteenth Amendment on its head, *i.e.*, arguing that the provision that "all persons born in the United States and subject to the jurisdiction thereof are citizens of the United States" is legally irreversible except by individual option, individually exercised. But this runs into rough historical water: the same legislators who drew up the Fourteenth Amendment had earlier passed by overwhelming majority the Wade-Davis Bill that deprived all top-echelon Confederates of their citizenship.[53] Lincoln pocket-vetoed the measure, but it still suffices to destroy the notion that the men who drafted the Fourteenth Amendment felt that citizenship was an "absolute." Second, one could advance the position, as did the Chief Justice, that punitive expatriation falls into the category of cruel and unusual punishments. What this lacks in precedental weight, and the Eighth Amendment is an underdeveloped area, is certainly balanced by its ingenuity. It marks, receiving as it did the support of four Justices, the major modern effort to give this constitutional provision a meaning transcending distaste for sheer physical cruelty and in a sense harkens back to Justice Field's dissent in *O'Neil v. Vermont*.[54] This view runs into some difficulty, of course, when one realizes that a wartime deserter can be executed. But the Chief Justice took a hasty detour around the subject of the death penalty[55] and the commonsense presumption that a convicted deserter would consider the firing squad's function a good deal more cruel and unusual than a message from the Secretary of State that he was expatriated.

Third, one can develop the argument, as did Justice Brennan in providing the crucial fifth vote in *Trop v. Dulles*,[56] that expatriation for desertion (and by implication all punitive expatriation) rests upon an unconstitutional extension of congressional power, in this instance the war power. As Brennan put it with stark simplicity:[57]

"I can only conclude that the requisite rational relation between this statute and the war power does not appear—for in this relation the statute is not 'really calculated to effect any of the objects entrusted to the government...,' *M'Culloch* v. *Maryland*...and therefore...[it] falls beyond the domain of Congress."

This position had a truly Marshallian flavor; it avoided all the problems of history and anti-history, of precedents and anti-precedents (Harlan's only cited precedent was *McCulloch v. Maryland!*) in favor of a logically unassailable line of defense. True, it lacked the luster of absolutism. Had Brennan's analysis of the facts indicated to him that there was a "rational relation" between the war power and denationalization, he would presumably have voted to sustain the statute. Indeed, he had voted to uphold expatriation for voting in a foreign election as a legitimate exercise of the power over foreign relations.

The coalition of these three viewpoints triumphed in *Trop v. Dulles*, and, predictably, Justice Frankfurter wrote a somewhat testy dissent.[58] Perhaps because the Justice was confused by the uncertain target presented by the various majority positions, his opinion was logically diffuse. Had he remained on the high ground he assumed in *Perez* and simply argued that there was in fact a rational nexus between the war power and denationalization of deserters, no one could raise any logical objections. But he went beyond this to argue not only that such expatriation was not a cruel and unusual punishment, but that it was not even punishment "in any valid constitutional sense."[59] Whatever one may think of the latter judgment— and I think it is nonsense—this issue had no relevance to the structure of his argument in *Perez*, namely, that it is the institutional logic rather than the impact on individuals that is decisive. In other words, if Congress could reasonably believe that the threat of expatriation would deter wartime desertion, the question whether or not it was a "punishment" should, in Justice Frankfurter's eyes, have been wholly immaterial.

MENDOZA-MARTINEZ AND CORT

The 1958 decisions, despite the cross-currents they occasioned among the Justices, arose from simple situations. For the next five years, perhaps because it had exhausted its judicial ingenuity, the Court shunned another confrontation with expatriation. Then in the 1962 Term, with two new appointees, it undertook to unravel two cases of enormous complexity: *Kennedy v. Mendoza-Martinez* and *Rusk v. Cort*. The underlying issue in both was simple: the constitutionality of that provision of the Nationality Act depriving Americans of their citizenship for leaving, or remaining outside of, the United States to evade military service. But each case was encumbered by intricate ancillary issues: a three-judge court and a collateral estoppel question in *Mendoza-Martinez*; the validity of declaratory judgment procedure and the legitimacy of a statutory presumption in *Cort*.

Francisco Mendoza-Martinez was born in the United States on March 3, 1922, of Mexican parents. He was thus by birth a dual national, and in 1942 he left the United States and went to Mexico where he sat out the war. Returning in 1946, he was arrested and convicted in June, 1947, on a charge of draft-evasion; he pleaded guilty and served a year and a day in federal penitentiary. In 1953, he was arrested for deportation. In the administrative proceedings, he argued fruitlessly that he was a citizen of the United States. In October, 1953, the Board of Immigration Appeals held that he had expatriated himself by remaining in Mexico after September 27, 1944 (the effective date of § 401 (j) of the Nationality Act), to evade service in the armed forces of the United States. Mendoza-Martinez then went into the federal courts in California, but received no succor. The district judge sustained the administrative determination; the Ninth Circuit affirmed.[60]

Mendoza-Martinez appealed to the Supreme Court, which at that time had the *Perez* case, involving in part the constitutionality of § 401 (j), *sub judice*. The Court, however, did not reach the merits of § 401 (j). But a week after the *Perez* and *Trop* decisions it issued a per curiam order in *Mendoza-Martinez* vacating the judgment of the Court of Appeals and remanding the cause to the district court "for determination in light of *Trop v. Dulles*."[61] This was clearly telegraphing a punch— the *Trop* majority was obviously ready to drop the trap on § 401 (j) as it had on § 401 (g)—and Gilbert H. Jertberg, D.J., got the message. He declared § 401 (j) to be an unconstitutional extension of the war power, adopting the position taken by Justice Brennan in *Trop*. In April, 1960, the Supreme Court again remanded in order that the question of collateral estoppel could be adjudicated.[62] Judge Jertberg ruled that the criminal conviction for draft-evasion did not necessarily, or in actual fact, involve any determination that he was a citizen because the conscription laws were applicable to resident aliens as well as to citizens. He reaffirmed his holding that § 401 (j) was unconstitutional and added a second ground: that § 401 (j) was a penal law that was implemented in violation of the Fifth Amendment's guarantees of due process of law. The case was argued at the 1961 Term of Court, but was put over to the 1962 Term for reargument.

The determination that Mendoza-Martinez was not a citizen was in the first instance made by the Immigration and Naturalization Service. Joseph Henry Cort's case emerged from a different administrative tribunal, the Passport Board of Review in the Department of State. Cort, a research physician, went to Great Britain in 1951 on a research fellowship, having previously registered both for the regular and for the "Doctor's" draft. Later that year the American Embassy in London told him to turn in his passport so that it could be validated only for return to the United States. He ignored these requests. But in 1952, while still in Britain, he accepted a teaching position at Harvard Medical School and seemingly prepared to return to the United States. At this point, however, he was informed that the position at Harvard did not carry with it draft deferment and this led to a change in plans. As he put it to the Chairman of the Physiology Department at Harvard Medical School: "I am reluctant to take a decision that may prove to be foolish or premature."[63] In an earlier letter to his draft board asking for exemption, Cort announced blandly that he had "applied for deferment from Selective Service from the sincere belief that my present, and particularly my future, civilian function is and shall be far more essential to my country than military service."[64] This sentiment echoes, of course, the inner convictions of draftees since time immemorial, but Cort proceeded to implement it: he turned down the Harvard position[65] and subsequently refused to respond to demands from his draft board that he report for physical examination. Moreover, he suddenly realized that if he returned to the United States, he would become a victim of McCarthyism (he had once been a member of the Communist Party).[66]

American officials in Britain apparently brought pressure on the Home Office to cancel Cort's residence permit.[67] In 1954, with the left-wing press in full cry at this denial of asylum, he went to Czechoslovakia where he accepted a research position in Prague. Meanwhile, back in Massachusetts, Cort was indicted by a grand jury for violation of the Selective Service laws. From 1954 to 1959, the situation remained unchanged, but then Cort began a campaign with the administrative authorities to obtain an American passport. In October, 1959, he was informed by the Department of State that he had expatriated himself by remaining abroad to evade military service.[68] The statute invoked here was the successor to § 401 (j), § 349 (a)(10) of the Immigration and Nationality Act of 1952.[69] The 1952 measure went beyond the 1944 provision; it included an addition that "failure to comply with any compulsory service laws of the United States shall raise the presumption that the departure from or absence from the United States was for the purpose of evading or avoiding training and service in the...forces of the United States."

At this point the legal battle began. Cort, through counsel, brought suit in the District of Columbia for a declaratory judgment that he was a citizen of the United States, alleging that § 349 (a)(10) was unconstitutional. A three-judge court was convened pursuant to statute and ruled that the *Trop* decision governed and the statute was invalid. Before this matter could go any further, however, a complicated jurisdictional question had to be solved. The Nationality Act of 1940, § 503, had established a suit for declaratory judgment as the judicial remedy for those held expatriated by the administrative authorities. No differentiation was made between claimants in the United States or abroad.[70] Section 360 of the Act of 1952 seemed to establish some differentiation between those in the United States and those abroad. It continued *expressis verbis* the declaratory judgment procedure for those in the United States, unless "the issue of such person's status as a national of the United States (1) arose by reason of, or in connection with any exclusion proceeding..., or (2) is an issue in any such exclusion proceeding."[71] Section 360 (b), however, provided that a person not within the United States who claimed that the administrative authorities had illegally deprived him of his nationality "may make application to a diplomatic or consular officer...for a certificate of identity for the purpose of traveling to a port of entry in the United States and applying for admission."[72] The issuance of this certificate was made discretionary with the Secretary of State. Section 360 (c) stated that those to whom certificates were granted under § 360 (b) would be processed as aliens at the port of entry and added: "A final determination by the Attorney General that any such person is not entitled to admission to the United States shall be subject to review by any court of competent jurisdiction in habeas corpus proceedings and not otherwise."[73]

Now it is common knowledge that the McCarran-Walter Act was, in purely technical terms, a legislative monstrosity, a measure of such convoluted intricacy that the Immigration and Naturalization Service had to run a special two-month course for its officers to acquaint them with the bizarre details. The measure was a sort of bouillabaisse into which everyone involved in immigration and nationality affairs tossed a few ingredients. In personal terms, it represented the views of Senator McCarran and Congressman Walter, occasionally mitigated by those of Congressman Celler. In practical terms, it was a triumph for restrictionism tempered with unintelligibility. The precise problem before the Supreme Court was whether §§ 360 (b) and (c) established the exclusive judicial remedy for one who, like Cort, was outside the United States. Or whether § 360 (b) was merely an enlargement of the remedy provided in § 360 (a) which would make it possible for one in Cort's position not only to bring suit, by counsel, in the United States, but also to travel to the United

States and bring his action personally. In precise terms, did the District Court have jurisdiction to adjudicate Cort's claim? Or did the latter have to obtain a certificate of identity, travel to a port of entry, be excluded as an expatriate, and then raise the issue in habeas corpus proceedings?

Contemporary understanding was that § 360 was designed to limit the judicial remedies open to expatriates abroad. If one cuts through the muddy phraseology of § 360, it comes down to a simple proposition: declaratory relief is reserved for those claimants in the United States. All others, whether abroad or at ports of entry, which technically are not in the United States, shall be handled as aliens with habeas corpus as the only legal remedy. The travel document stipulated in § 360 (b) was thus designed to give one access to exclusion proceedings. It was on the basis of this understanding of the purpose that § 360 was opposed vigorously by those concerned with the maintenance of liberal provisions of judicial review.

The Supreme Court, through Justice Stewart, however, held that the purpose of § 360 was to liberalize the existing law.[74] Capitalizing on the foggy draftsmanship in the bill and drawing selectively from the measure's legislative history, the Court ruled that declaratory judgment procedure was still appropriate for those outside of the United States. Pointing out that unless a statute specifically precluded review in explicit terms, § 10 of the Administrative Procedure Act remained in force, and that the McCarran-Walter Act contained no express exemption, Justice Stewart sustained the jurisdiction of the district court. Justice Harlan's dissent, joined by Justices Frankfurter and Clark,[75] contained a more compelling summary of legislative intent, but trailed off on the technical point of exemption from the provisions of the Administrative Procedure Act. The great masters of technicalities, the Immigration and Naturalization Service and the Passport Division of the Department of State, were thus, ironically, frustrated on a technicality. The *Cort* case was scheduled for argument on the merits.

On February 18, 1963, Mr. Justice Goldberg delivered the opinion of the Court in the two companion cases.[76] First of all, he disposed of the two marginal issues in the *Mendoza-Martinez* litigation: the problem of collateral estoppel and the three-judge court question. Holding that Mendoza-Martinez's 1946 conviction did not estop later administrative action to deny his citizenship and that the circumstances of the case did not require the convening of a three-judge district court, Justice Goldberg moved rapidly to the constitutional issues presented by §§ 401 (j) and 349 (a) (10). In-

stead of arguing that punitive expatriation was a cruel and unusual punishment absolutely forbidden by the Eighth Amendment, however, Goldberg invoked what might be described as the "relativist" position that the provisions under adjudication fell afoul of the Fifth and Sixth Amendments. Buttressed by an elaborate historical survey, he announced that denationalization for draft-evasion was penal in character and that the statutory provisions were unconstitutional inasmuch as they did not provide the required procedural safeguards. This opinion was joined by Justices Douglas, Black, Warren, and Brennan. Justice Douglas wrote a one-paragraph concurrence for himself and Justice Black in which they affirmed their absolutist conviction that Congress has no power to deprive a citizen of his nationality. Justice Brennan wrote a separate concurrence which went beyond Justice Goldberg's rationale to argue that even if expatriation for draft-evasion were surrounded with procedural safeguards, he would still consider it beyond the legitimate reach of congressional power. And he spent a good deal of time laboring with the inadequacies, as he saw them, of the dissenting opinions. But at least there was a majority agreed on one *ratio decidendi*.

It was an interesting majority, because it is clear that four of its five members felt that the goal of the legislation was unconstitutional: Black and Douglas so stipulated, as did Brennan (on different grounds), and we can presume that Chief Justice Warren's notion of punitive expatriation as cruel and unusual punishment had not been abandoned by him. Goldberg thus became the swing vote and his maximum position determined the posture of the majority. Looked at from another angle, the voting in this litigation indicated that the *Trop* majority was undercut by the appointments of Justices White and Goldberg. In fact the alignment raised some curious hypothetical questions about how the Court would today rule on *Trop*, where loss of citizenship was conditioned upon conviction by court-martial and the approval of the President. Or, to shift from the military sector, where admittedly due process is a bit eccentric, one may speculate on how the present Court would divide on the remaining punitive provision in the nationality statute expatriating those convicted of treason or sedition, since it can take place only with the full panoply of procedural safeguards guaranteed by the Fifth and Sixth Amendments.

In other words, if we tally the four dissenters in *Mendoza-Martinez* and *Cort* who believed that expatriation was not a punishment, with Justice Goldberg who insisted it was penal but seemed to feel that it was a legitimate penalty if procedural safeguards were provided, we would appear to be confronted by a five-Justice bloc that might permit denationalization for treason or sedition, or, for that matter, for leaving the country to evade military service if the statute were rewritten to include expatriation as part of the sentence in a criminal conviction.

A word should perhaps be said about the two dissents in these cases. Justices Stewart and White argued at length that the provisions were not punitive, that they were legitimately founded on the war powers of Congress, and that it was "hardly an improvident exercise of constitutional power for Congress to disown those who have disowned this Nation in time of ultimate need." These two Justices, however, held that the presumption included in § 349 (a) (10) was arbitrary and constitutionally invalid because, in a formulation drawn from the *Tot* case,[77] there was insufficient "rational connection between the fact proved and the ultimate fact presumed."[78] They therefore endorsed the expatriation of Mendoza-Martinez, but voted to vacate the decision of the district court and remand the *Cort* case in order that a new hearing could be held by the Department of State "free of the evidentiary presumption of Section 349 (a) (10)."[79] Justices Harlan and Clark dissented across the board, but devoted their opinion largely to disputing the presumption question with Stewart and White.

Curiously no one in the minority raised the matter of Mendoza-Martinez' dual nationality, which would seem to provide an obvious common-sense basis for differentiating between his situation and Cort's. Could one not argue, within the framework of *Perez*, that a dual national who takes refuge from American military service in his alternative homeland falls into a different category than an individual like Cort, a native-born citizen without dual allegiance who simply takes up residence in a foreign state? Such a provision for dual nationals could logically be defended under the foreign relations power and, further, as supplying a reasonable evidential standard of voluntary abandonment of American citizenship for an alternative status. It would in no sense be on all fours with the *Cort* situation where expatriation was clearly penal.

CONCLUSION

It is perhaps too easy to be critical of the Supreme Court's handling of expatriation issues. As Justice Jackson, with his usual insight, remarked: "[I]t would be as easy as it would be unrewarding to point out conflict in precept and confusion in practice on this side of the Atlantic, where ideas of nationality and expatriation were in ferment during the whole Nineteenth Century."[80] Practice simply outran theory. Because the whole problem of loss of nationality was so trivial, and so marginal to the main concerns of public policy, a legal tradition developed on the basis of pragmatic accretion. A special problem was met by an *ad hoc* remedy, and the *ad hoc* remedies, in aggregate, constituted the law on the subject. Nobody worried about the constitutionality of the Bancroft treaties, any more than the congressmen who passed the Wade-Davis Bill tossed in their beds wondering what constitutional power bulwarked § 14. If there had to be a constitutional justification, the Attorney General could doubtless conjure one up, or find a professor of constitutional law to do the job for him.

In the past half-century, however, nationality matters have moved to the center of public policy. There has been continuing dispute over immigration issues, a tightening-up of standards for naturalization, and finally, in the last twenty-five years, two major campaigns for codification and rationalization of nationality practices. The first resulted in the Nationality Act of 1940 and the second in the Immigration and Nationality Act of 1952. A mass of earlier statutes and administrative regulations were codified into the section regulating loss of nationality, § 401, of the Nationality Act of 1940. And a few new provisions were added, with no furor, that were allegedly patterned on existing provisos, for example, desertion. Here the old Civil War statute was assimilated. But where the 1865 enactment deprived deserters (and draft-evaders) of their "rights of citizenship," the 1940 revision forfeited "citizenship." Then, on the model of the desertion provision, a similar proviso denationalized traitors, and was extended in 1954 to include those convicted under the Smith Act. Had someone proposed that Americans convicted of gambling or traffic violations be denationalized, there would undoubtedly have been a heated controversy. But no congressman could get very interested in the problems of traitors, deserters, draft-dodgers, or sedition-mongers. These provisions had to be constitutional; the precedent, after all, was an act of 1865. Moreover, it was not really a punishment; like denaturalization,[81] deportation,[82] or, later, depriving those deported on security grounds of their Social Security benefits.[83] It was merely a civil action that small-minded litigants persisted in branding punitive.

The federal courts had the perplexing burden of making constitutional sense out of this corpus of improvisation. And it was not a simple task. To borrow a classic instance from the area of naturalization law, when the Supreme Court was confronted with the problem of *res judicata* involved in a denaturalization suit under the 1906 statute, it sustained the reopening of an earlier naturalization judgment on the ground that before 1906 naturalization had been an *ex parte* matter which though "conducted in a court of record...[was] not in any sense an adversary proceeding...[but] was closely analogous to a public grant of land...."[84] Or, to put the matter differently, Justice Pitney declared that a naturalization judgment had, for a century or more, not been a "case or controversy"! This remarkable announcement raised a few judicial eyebrows, but Justice Brandeis explained in a later case that the commotion on the subject was unfounded: "If the proceedings were not a case or controversy within the meaning of Article III, § 2," he said, "this delegation of power upon the courts would have been invalid."[85] This masterly injection of circular logic put an end to the argument.

When the courts came to grips with expatriation legislation, they found themselves dealing with a mixed bag. As was suggested at an earlier point in this analysis, they discovered two fundamentally different types of expatriation provisions, the first relating to transfers of loyalty, the second concerned with betrayals of allegiance. Yet the two were interwoven in one statute and alleged to be founded on the same constitutional foundation: the right of an American citizen voluntarily to abandon his nationality. Moreover, the Constitution and early precedents were totally useless on the subject. What then is perhaps surprising is that the Court has, in its own fashion, so closely approximated the objectives of a rational expatriation policy: one that treats denationalization as a dimension of foreign relations rather than of the penal code, one that minimizes the creation of stateless persons, one that recognizes that depriving an American of his citizenship is not a casual legal undertaking that can be left in the hands of virtually invisible administrative bodies.

Editor's note: In *Afroyim* v. *Rusk*, decided on May 29, 1967, the Supreme Court by a five to four vote reversing earlier decisions, found that the Congress lacks the constitutional power to pass laws depriving an American citizen of his nationality without his consent.

Footnotes

[1]Kennedy v. Mendoza-Martinez, 372 U.S. 144 (1963).
[2]58 Stat. 746 (1944), as amended by 66 Stat. 163 (1952), 8 U.S.C. § 1481(10) (1958).
[3]In the forlorn hope of quashing in advance charges of inconsistency, let me set out my position on judicial

review in constitutional cases: (1) On the theoretical plane I do not consider Supreme Court review of policy matters to be democratic in character. See ROCHE, COURTS AND RIGHTS 93–105 (1961). (2) As a participant in American society in 1963—somewhat removed from the abstract world of democratic political theory—I am delighted when the Supreme Court takes action against "bad" policy on whatever constitutional basis it can establish or invent. In short, I accept Aristotle's dictum that the essence of political tragedy is for the good to be opposed in the name of the perfect. Thus, while I wish with Professors Wechsler and Kurland, *inter alios,* that Supreme Court Justices could proceed on the same principles as British judges, it does not unsettle or irritate me when they behave like Americans. Had I been a member of the Court in 1954, I would unhesitatingly have supported the constitutional death-sentence on racial segregation, even though it seems to me that in a properly ordered democratic society this should be a task for the legislature. To paraphrase St. Augustine, in this world one must take his breaks where he finds them. (3) Finally, I insist that the task of the historian (Professors Black and Cahn to the contrary notwithstanding) is not to fortify useful myths, but to attempt to plumb the realities of the past.
[4]Rusk v. Cort, 369 U.S. 367 (1962).
[5]3 Pet. 242 (1830)....
[6]3 Pet. at 246.
[7]2 KENT, COMMENTARIES 49-50 (1827).
[8]Scott v. Sandford, 19 How. 393 (1857).
[9]25 Rev. Stat. § 1999 (1875). It is perhaps worth recalling the proposition that preambles have no legal force. Jacobson v. Massachusetts, 197 U.S. 11 (1905).
[10]34 Stat. 1228 (1907). The companion legislation dealt with naturalization. 34 Stat. 596 (1906).
[11]34 Stat. 1228–29 (1907).
[12]MacKenzie v. Hare, 239 U.S. 299, 311 (1915).
[13]*Ibid.*
[14]54 Stat. 1169 (1940).
[15]*Ibid.*
[16]*Ibid.* There was also a special provision for renunciation of American nationality designed for use by dual nationals living abroad. See § 401(a).
[17]66 Stat. 267 (1952), 8 U.S.C. § 1481 (1958). There were some additions and changes. Service in the armed forces of a foreign state was held to expatriate without regard to the stipulation of the 1940 act quoted in the text. Accepting service for a foreign government cost one his nationality if (*a*) he had or acquired the nationality of such state, or (*b*) if he were required to declare allegiance to such foreign power as a prerequisite for employment.
[18]54 Stat. 1169 (1940).
[19]*Ibid.*
[20]58 Stat. 746 (1944).
[21]68 Stat. 1146 (1954).
[22]66 Stat. 268, 8 U.S.C. § 1481(a)(10) (1958).
[23]356 U.S. 86 (1958).
[24]356 U.S. 44 (1958).
[25]See summary of various provisions for denationalization in U.N. General Assembly Doc. A/CN.4/66, § 9, 6 April 1953.
[26]*Ibid.*
[27]*Ibid.*
[28]*Ibid.* See also Laws Concerning Nationality, U.N. Doc. ST/LEG/SER. B/4 (1954).
[29]Ames, *Proposed Amendments to the Constitution,* 2 Rep. Am. Hist. Assn. 187 (1896).

30 20 Annals of Cong. 549 (1810).

31 Ames, *supra* note 29, at 187.

32 25 Rev. Stat. § 1996 (1875).

33 43 Stat. 1940 (1924). For what it may be worth, Coolidge referred to those in this category as "fellow citizens." See, generally, Gathings, *Loss of Citizenship and Civil Rights for Conviction of Crime*, 43 Am. Pol. Sci. Rev. 1228 (1949).

34 2 Hearings before Committee on Immigration and Naturalization on H.R. 6127, 76th Cong., 1st Sess. 38 (1940). *But see* In the Matter of P——, 1 Bd. Imm. App. 127 (1941).

35 MacKenzie v. Hare, 239 U.S. 299 (1915).

36 307 U.S. 325 (1939).

37 *Id.* at 334.

38 *Id.* at 329.

39 15 Stat. 615 (1868). See Roche, *Loss of American Nationality: The Years of Confusion*, 4 West, Pol. Q. 268, 274–77, at 285–86.

40 31 Annals of Cong. 1050 (1818).

41 Mandoli v. Acheson, 344 U.S. 135 (1952).

42 356 U.S. 129 (1958).

43 *Id.* at 138–39.

44 *Id.* at 139.

45 *Id.* at 142.

46 356 U.S. 44 (1958).

47 356 U.S. at 60–61. (Emphasis added.)

48 *Id.* at 76.

49 *Id.* at 79–84.

50 *Id.* at 84–85.

51 356 U.S. 86 (1958).

52 356 U.S. at 83.

53 6 Richardson, Messages and Papers of the Presidents 223–25 (1899).

54 144 U.S. 323, 337 (1892).

55 356 U.S. at 99.

56 *Id.* at 105–14.

57 *Id.* at 114.

58 *Id.* at 114–28.

59 *Id.* at 124.

60 288 F. 2d 239 (9th Cir. 1957).

61 Mendoza-Martinez v. Mackey, 356 U.S. 258 (1958).

62 Mackey v. Mendoza-Martinez, 362 U.S. 384 (1960).

63 Record, p. 139.

64 *Id.* at 115.

65 *Id.* at 141.

66 *Id.* at 94 (affidavit by Cort).

67 *Id.* at 77.

68 *Id.* at 93.

69 66 Stat. 267 (1952), 8 U.S.C. § 1481 (10) (1958).

70 54 Stat. 1171 (1940).

71 66 Stat. 273–74 (1952), 8 U.S.C. § 1503 (1958).

72 *Ibid.*

73 *Ibid.*

74 Rusk v. Cort, 369 U.S. 367 (1962). Justice Brennan, perhaps a bit leary of Justice Stewart's remarkable feat of converting Senator McCarran and Congressman Walter into liberals, concurred separately, suggesting that had the authors of the statute intended so to limit review, it would have grievous constitutional defects. *Id.* at 380–83.

75 *Id.* at 383–99.

76 Kennedy v. Mendoza-Martinez, 372 U.S. 144 (1963).

77 Tot v. United States, 319 U.S. 463, 467 (1943).

78 372 U.S. at 217.

79 *Id.* at 220.

80 344 U.S. at 135.

81 Luria v. United States, 231 U.S. 9 (1913).

82 Mahler v. Eby, 264 U.S. 32 (1924); Fong Yue Ting v. United States, 149 U.S. 698 (1893).

83 Flemming v. Nestor, 363 U.S. 603 (1960).

84 Johannessen v. United States, 225 U.S. 227, 237–38 (1912).

85 Tutun v. United States, 270 U.S. 568, 576 (1926).

Chapter VI

THE RIGHTS OF ACCUSED PERSONS

The Fourth, Fifth, and Sixth Amendments, and such portions thereof as are applicable to the states through the due process and equal protection clauses of the Fourteenth Amendment, create a number of complex and interrelated protections for persons caught in the toils of criminal law. This whole area, at the levels of case law, public opinion, technological and institutional innovation, police practice, and legislation, is currently in a state of flux. Moreover, changes in any part of this body of law have subtle and far-reaching effects on the rest of it. Therefore, the best introduction to the material that follows is a kind of simple outline or box score of the issues and outcomes involved.

The Fourth Amendment guarantees "The right of the people to be secure in their persons, houses, papers and effects against unreasonable searches and seizures...." The first question is, therefore, "What is an 'unreasonable' search?" Normally, the police may not search a premises without a search warrant, which is issued by a judge or other official only upon probable cause that a person subject to arrest or contraband materials, such as the loot from a robbery, are present. Note that a warrant will not be issued simply so that the police may search for evidence—although, of course, contraband items may themselves be crucial pieces of evidence at a subsequent trial.

There are three circumstances in which a search *without* a warrant may be justified. When a policeman has reasonable cause to believe that a crime is actually in the process of being committed on the premises, he may enter and in doing so, of course, come upon incriminating evidence. The crucial question is whether he really had such a cause or is simply claiming that he did in order to excuse his entry without a warrant.*

Let us say, for instance, that two policemen hear the clicking of an adding machine from an apartment window at 2:00 A.M. They conclude, or so they will claim afterwards, that at that hour of the morning, in that particular neighborhood, the only person who would be running an adding machine would be the operator of an illegal gambling operation adding up his daily take. Do they have sufficient cause to believe that a crime is being committed to legitimate a subsequent entry and search of the premises? It should be remembered that

---

*On the general doctrine of reasonableness of search see *Trupiano* v. *United States,* 334 U.S. 699 (1948); *United States* v. *Rabinowitz,* 339 U.S. 56 (1950); *Chapman* v. *United States,* 365 U.S. 610 (1961).

this question usually arises at a trial that would not have occurred if the police-men had not found incriminating evidence once they entered. At first glance it is likely to seem highly improbable that the mere clicking of an adding machine really gave the policemen sufficient reason to believe that a gambling operation was going on, but when it turns out that the adding machine really is being used to add up the day's take, a judge is likely to think twice before saying that the policemen had no cause to believe that was what the clicking was about.

A policeman may also conduct a search in conjunction with serving an arrest (as opposed to a search) warrant. A rationale for this ruling is that he must be allowed to search arrested persons for weapons in order to insure his own safety. But the area of search incident to arrest has long been extended beyond the person of the accused.† The question is, how far? The police may search the room in which the arrested person resides, but may they search the entire basement of the twelve-story apartment house in which he resides or the automobile parked in the garage behind his house?

The Supreme Court has further held that the police may reasonably con-duct a search without a search warrant in the course of a lawful arrest accom-plished without an arrest warrant. Here, the question of whether the search was reasonable becomes the question of whether the arrest without a warrant was valid. An officer may arrest without a warrant if he has "probable cause" to believe that the person has committed a crime. Thus, the ultimate issue becomes whether the Court is convinced that the facts in the possession of the police would have been sufficient to cause a reasonable man to conclude that a crime had been committed and the person arrested had committed it. For instance, if the police observe a person they know has twice been convicted of dope addiction heading down a dark alley, and one of their informants whispers to them, "He's about to make a buy," can they arrest him as he comes out the other end of the alley, search him, and then use the heroin found in his pockets after the arrest as the evidence necessary to prove the crime of possession of narcotics?‡

Obviously, all these questions must be answered on a case-by-case exami-nation of the facts surrounding each arrest or search, but just as obviously the state of our constitutional rights depends upon whether the courts, led by the Supreme Court, take a narrow or broad view of such slippery words as *reasonable* and *probable*. The courts, for example, have recognized that the search warrant procedures which evolved in the days before automobiles are difficult to apply today. The automobile, unlike the house, may not wait rooted to the spot while the policeman rushes off after a warrant. As a result, the courts have greatly relaxed the standards of probable cause in connection with automobiles, and while presumably the Constitution reigns over every inch of the fifty states, it protects the citizen far less in his car than in his house.§

Two special areas in which the Fourth Amendment's prohibition of search and seizure and the Fifth Amendment's due process protections seem to over-lap and reinforce each other should also be noted.‖ If a man need not testify

---

†See *Weeks* v. *United States*, 232 U.S. 383 (1914); *Marron* v. *United States*, 275 U.S. 192 (1927); *Harris* v. *United States*, 311 U.S. 145 (1947).
‡See *Ker* v. *California*, 374 U.S. 23 (1963).
§See *Carroll* v. *United States*, 267 U.S. 132 (1925).
‖See *Frank* v. *Maryland*, 359 U. S. 360 (1959). It is frequently argued that reading the Fourth and Fifth Amendments together constitutes an error in constitutional interpretation.

against himself, can he be forced to take a blood test, and can the evidence thus seized be used against him [*Breithaupt* v. *Abram*, 352 U.S. 432 (1957)]? In a now famous decision [*Rochin* v. *California*, 342 U.S. 165 (1952)], the Supreme Court held that evidence obtained by pumping a suspect's stomach was unreasonably seized.

The other special problem area is wiretapping and other electronic eavesdropping. The Court long ago refused to forbid the tapping of telephone lines, largely on the grounds that the seizure of evidence did not occur on the premises of the accused.¶ Later, confronted with more advanced electronic techniques, it stuck to the rule that if the listening was done without trespass, it was reasonable, just as it would be reasonable for a policeman to listen from the street at an open window. Such horse-and-buggy analogies have led the Court into an increasingly unrealistic position in this age of electronic wizardry when it makes little difference whether a listening device is in a hall closet or six blocks away.‡‡ The growing concern for a "right of privacy," which the reader has encountered in various portions of this book, promises some changes in the Court's approach in the future.

Once it has been determined that a given search is unreasonable, the next important question is what to do when the police seek to use evidence gained in such a search. The Supreme Court has now held that such illegally obtained evidence shall not be admissable in criminal trials.** This may seem a self-evident conclusion; but for many years it was a bitterly fought issue, and the reader should be aware that the Supreme Court has read the rule of excluding illegally obtained evidence into the Fourth Amendment. The rule will not be found in the actual wording. The question of exclusion is quite separable from the question of what is or is not an unreasonable search. On the other hand, the more liberal the courts are in finding searches reasonable, the less evidence will be excluded. Those who do not like the exclusionary rule are now likely to bend their efforts to convincing courts that almost any search is reasonable.

The Supreme Court has held inadmissable not only illegally seized evidence but also the fruits of such evidence—that is, the later evidence obtained by legal methods as a result of the leads developed from the initial, illegal seizure. Just how closely connected one piece of evidence has to be to another to fall under this ban is also, of course, subject to case-by-case determination. Here again narrow or broad interpretation of the "fruits" doctrine will obviously have considerable effect on the scope of the exclusion rule.

The Fifth Amendment provision against self-incrimination actually involves several distinct problems. The first is coerced confession.†† When is a confession voluntary, and when is it forced? As soon as the Court admitted that a confession might be forced by psychological pressure, it lost the relatively neat line between physical torture and verbal persuasion. Devotees of the cops-and-robbers tradition of movies and television may amuse themselves by

---

¶See *Olmstead* v. *United States*, 277 U.S. 438 (1928). Such evidence is now banned from the federal courts because wiretapping is prohibited by federal statute.
‡‡See *Goldman* v. *United States*, 316 U.S. 129 (1942); *Silverman* v. *United States*, 365 U.S. 505 (1961).
**Mapp* v. *Ohio*, 367 U.S. 643 (1961).
††The state coerced-confession cases technically fall entirely under the due process clause of the Fourteenth Amendment which binds the states, rather than under the self-incrimination clause of the Fifth, because the Supreme Court has generally held that the Fifth Amendment is not applicable to the states. Nevertheless, the Court is still concerned basically with the ban on self-incrimination expressed in the Fifth Amendment, even if it chooses to say that it is deciding such state cases solely under the Fourteenth. See *Malloy* v. *Hogan*, 378 U.S. 1 (1964).

deciding when and if the alternately snarling and sympathetic cop of any given episode ceased to be a persuader and became a coercer. It is not likely to be such an amusing task for the courts. Incidentally, it had always been ruled that forced confessions would not be admitted as evidence, and this custom did much to foster the growth of the exclusionary rule under the Fourth Amendment, although many question whether forced confessions and other illegally obtained evidence are analogous. Evidence is not more or less likely to be true depending on whether it was obtained legally or not, but confessions are much less likely to be true if physically or psychologically coerced than if voluntary.

A second series of questions, this time closely connected with the Sixth Amendment, is also raised by the conjunction of the self-incrimination with the due process clauses of the Fifth Amendment. How long may a prisoner be held before arraignment, or without bail or legal counsel, or without the advice of friends, before a confession obtained during such a period is held invalid? This question leads immediately to the right to counsel under the Sixth Amendment.

The Constitution and the Court have always held that the accused is entitled to counsel in criminal cases. Two questions, however, arise. When does the right begin, and to what extent does the Constitution require the state to provide free legal aid to persons who cannot afford to provide their own? Does the right to counsel begin with the trial, or with arraignment before trial, or at the time of arrest, or at the time the policeman forms the intention to arrest a certain individual but has not yet formally done so? Of course, the earlier the lawyer can appear on the scene, the more difficult it is for the police to pursue their investigation; the later he appears, the more likely is the accused to have been deprived or talked out of some of the rights the law and Constitution allow him. The Supreme Court has held that the indigent defendant must be provided by the government with the protection of counsel. Here again, questions overlap. Imagine the cost of providing every poor drunk a lawyer at the moment of arrest, and you discover one reason why some judges are reluctant to speak of a right to counsel at the time of arrest.

Two other closely interrelated factors weave their way through most of the Fourth, Fifth, and Sixth Amendment cases. One is federalism. The Supreme Court exercises extraordinary administrative powers over the federal courts and police because it is the highest federal court. It has, of course, no such powers over state courts. The Fourth, Fifth, and Sixth Amendments are binding directly on the federal government and on the federal courts as part of the federal government. But they apply to the states only insofar as they are incorporated in the Fourteenth Amendment, and an old constitutional theory is that, as a result, the states are not so strictly bound by the Bill of Rights as is the federal government. Moreover, the police power has always been considered the core of the states' power within our federal system. An agency of the national government, like the Supreme Court, ought to tamper as little as possible in state criminal justice.

For the reasons mentioned above, the Supreme Court for many years has held federal courts and federal police to much higher standards of criminal justice than state courts and local police. As the Supreme Court has moved in recent years to hold state courts and police to more nearly the same levels of performance as federal authorities, all of these arguments have had to be cut through—but wisps of them still float around here and there. A recurrent theme in the materials that follow is the extent to which state courts ought to be bound by precisely the same strict standards that bind the federal courts, even when the Supreme Court is applying similar constitutional restrictions to each.

Closely connected with issues of federalism is the "fair trial rule." For many years the Supreme Court, while imposing many specific limitations on federal courts and officers, imposed the Bill of Rights on the states only to the extent of requiring that, on balance and considered as a whole, the trial be fair. Thus, while the admission of illegally obtained evidence generally would have automatically voided a federal trial, it would not have caused reversal of a state conviction unless it could be said that the admission of the evidence had somehow made the whole trial unfair. The fair trial rule has now largely disappeared in the illegal evidence and right to counsel areas. It never really existed for coerced confession. Nevertheless, the reader will find echoes of it here and there in the discussions that follow.

Selection 15

A Survey of the Expanded Exclusionary Rule

Peter H. Wolf

In the essay that follows, Peter Wolf is principally concerned with one of the search and seizure issues—the exclusionary rule. Wolf refers to the questions of reasonableness of search and probable cause for entry or arrest, and the reader should constantly remind himself that actual constitutional protection does not depend entirely on the exclusion rule itself. The crucial factor may be how much leeway the courts are willing to give the police on questions of probable cause and reasonableness. In this area, what the courts *do* matters much more than what they *say*. For instance, in the case of *Beck* v. *Ohio* [379 U.S. 89 (1964)], the Supreme Court of Ohio and the Supreme Court of the United States used almost identical language to define the probable cause rule, but the state court found the arrest justified and the U.S. Supreme Court did not.

Wolf refers to the "silver platter doctrine" several times, without explaining it fully. At one time, although federal officers might not introduce into federal courts evidence they had themselves obtained illegally, they could introduce evidence obtained illegally by their state colleagues and handed to them "on a silver platter." Wolf tells of the demise of this doctrine.

On June 19, 1961, the federal exclusionary rule, whereby evidence obtained by an unlawful search and seizure must be excluded from a criminal prosecution in a federal court upon due motion by the defendant, was vastly enlarged. *Mapp v. Ohio*[1] made the exclusionary rule more than "federal." By overruling *Wolf v. Colorado*,[2] the Supreme Court imposed that rule of evidence upon the states which may affect a trial so fundamentally that it shades into the realm of a substantive right of an accused.

The breadth and importance of the *Mapp* decision makes a review and prognosis of the law of the exclusionary rule very much in order. It is not this writer's purpose to discuss the "mechanics" of the exclusionary rule, by which is meant those questions which determine whether or not the rule

"A Survey of the Expanded Exclusionary Rule" by Peter H. Wolf, 32 *George Washington Law Review* 193 (1963). Reprinted by permission. Some footnote material has been omitted.

is brought into play in a given factual situation. It is rather intended to examine the consequences of the application of the rule in terms of its now broader significance in our federal system.

THE LAW BEFORE MAPP

Prior to 1886, when *Boyd v. United States*[3] was decided, there was no policy in the federal courts, indeed in any court in the Anglo-American legal system, to exclude evidence illegally obtained if it was otherwise admissible according to the common law rules of evidence. One of the premises upon which this attitude was based was that "the judicial rules of evidence were never meant to be used as an indirect method of punishment." *Boyd* muddied these settled waters by implying that inspection by the federal prosecuting attorney and admission in evidence of an invoice ordered produced by the court resulted in "erroneous and unconstitutional proceedings"[4] violative of the fourth[5] and fifth[6] amendments. Thus were the beginnings of the exclusionary rule launched. *Boyd* also introduced into constitutional law a confusion which persists: "the intimate relation between" the fourth and fifth amendments.[7]

The *Boyd* dicta regarding the unconstitutionality of admitting evidence obtained in violation of the fourth amendment was largely repudiated in *Adams v. New York*.[8] And *ICC v. Baird*[9] retracted that much of the *Boyd* dicta which applied the fourth amendment to an order to produce a document. However, in 1914, the exclusionary rule was removed from drydock and relaunched in its modern form by *Weeks v. United States*.[10]

The *Weeks* opinion deserves careful analysis. It had its faulty conclusions, but it presaged some Court decisions which have come full circle to the intimations in Justice Day's opinion in that case. Unlike *Boyd*, *Weeks* involved a fourth amendment violation in its pure form. A search of the defendant's room was conducted without a warrant and much of his personal property was seized, including some which was not relevant to the charges made against him. Weeks' conviction in a federal court for fraudulent use of the mails, based on this evidence, was reversed by the Supreme Court.

The opinion indicated a somewhat inexplicit constitutional basis for finding exclusion implicit in the right of privacy created by the language of the fourth amendment: "[T]here was involved in the order refusing the application [for return of letters illegally seized by the United States Marshal] a denial of the constitutional rights of the accused."[11] Later cases, particularly *Wolf*, indicated that the exclusionary rule was a judicially

made rule of evidence not required by the Constitution.

The *Weeks* opinion can be criticized for its too hasty dismissal of alternative means of enforcement of the fourth amendment. The Court seemed to assume that exclusion of evidence from the trial of the accused was the proper solution, saying simply, "What [other] remedies the defendant may have...we need not inquire."[12] One could have hoped for a more detailed canvassing of alternatives and explanation of the Court's resort to a means of enforcement whereby the accused might go free. On the other hand, one may find it difficult to quarrel with the Court's statement:

"If letters and private documents can thus be seized and held and used in evidence against a citizen accused of an offense, the protection of the Fourth Amendment declaring his right to be secure against such searches and seizures is of no value, and, so far as those thus placed are concerned, might as well be stricken from the Constitution."[13]

In short, other methods of enforcement were totally ineffective. Subsequent developments suggest the veracity of this statement in the *Weeks* opinion.[14]

Justice Day's opinion made no mention of fifth amendment grounds for violation of the defendant's rights. This exclusive reliance on the fourth amendment persisted, with some digressions, in most of the search and seizure cases in the Supreme Court until *Mapp*. And in the *Weeks* decision were the beginnings of the constellation of refinements surrounding the exclusionary rule: the right "to search the person accused when legally arrested to discover and seize the fruits or evidences of crime" and "other proofs of guilt...within the control of the accused" was recognized,[15] and seizure of articles incidental to the lawful execution of a valid search warrant was held not unreasonable under the fourth amendment.[16]

Whether or not well reasoned and properly decided, the Weeks decision held firm in the federal courts and its influence expanded beyond the federal sphere. Subsequent cases tended to elaborate on or qualify the exclusionary rule set forth in *Weeks*.[17]

In 1948, the Supreme Court granted certiorari in two cases from the Supreme Court of Colorado. Dr. Julius A. Wolf had been convicted in both cases of conspiracy to commit abortion. He had been arrested in his office by the district attorney without a warrant and records of his patients had been seized illegally. These were introduced at his trial. The Supreme Court of Colorado affirmed his conviction, holding that the admission of the evidence did not violate the fourteenth amendment.[18] The United States Supreme Court was confronted with the problem of whether or not the fourteenth amendment due process clause made it unlawful for state authorities to violate an individual's fourth amendment right against unreasonable search and seizure. In *Wolf*, the Court *did* add the fourth amendment protection to those freedoms of the Bill of Rights which were "of the very essence of ordered liberty"[19] and had been held protected against state incursion through the fourteenth amendment.[20] This substantial step forward in the Supreme Court's zealous guarding of the freedoms of the individual, however, could not help but evoke the question of enforcement of the right: was the federal exclusionary rule, without which the Court had said "the protection of the Fourth Amendment...might as well be stricken from the Constitution,"[21] to be imposed upon the states? Here was an issue fraught with competing considerations of law enforcement, civil rights, and federalism.

Justice Frankfurter, speaking for a majority of five, observed at the outset that "the Fourteenth Amendment did not subject criminal justice in the States to specific limitations."[22] He noted this as a prelude to his reiteration of the recent "rejection"[23] of the notion that the due process clause of the fourteenth amendment incorporated the entire first eight amendments to the Constitution. Only those freedoms "implicit in the concept of ordered liberty" were exacted from the states by a "gradual and empiric process of 'inclusion and exclusion.' "[24] He concluded that security against arbitrary intrusion by the police was the "core" of the fourth amendment protection which was basic to a free society and thus enforceable against the states through the due process clause.[25]

Justice Frankfurter described the barring from a *federal* prosecution of illegally obtained evidence in *Weeks* as "a matter of judicial implication."[26] This statement seems inconsistent with Justice Frankfurter's own statement of the holding of *Weeks:* "that in a federal prosecution the Fourth Amendment barred the use of evidence secured through an illegal search and seizure."[27] If the fourth amendment barred such evidence in a federal prosecution—a constitutional basis for exclusion—and if the guarantee of the fourth amendment were applicable to the states through the due process clause of the fourteenth—as already held by the Court—why was exclusion not a constitutional requirement in state prosecutions? Justice Frankfurter stated the question: "the immediate question is whether the basic right to protection against arbitrary intrusion by the police de-

mands the exclusion of logically relevant evidence obtained by an unreasonable search and seizure *because,* in a federal prosecution for a federal crime, it would be excluded."[28] The statement of the question ignored the reason for exclusion in federal prosecutions: *because* there seemed to be no other means of giving substance to the fourth amendment guarantee. Justice Frankfurter attempted to extricate the Court from this predicament with a concept of "the core of the Fourth Amendment."[29] This much was extended to the states under the fourteenth amendment: the *right* of the people to be free from unwarranted incursions by authorities into "their persons, houses, papers, and effects"—in short, their privacy. The coterminous *remedy*[30] for infringement of the right was excluded from this "core," since it could not be "derived from the explicit requirements of the Fourth Amendment."[31] As "a matter of judicial implication"[32] not compelled by the Constitution, the remedy of exclusion became a matter about which reasonable men could differ. Justice Frankfurter then enumerated the attitudes of the states toward the exclusionary rule before and after the *Weeks* decision, apparently to demonstrate that reasonable men *could* differ with respect to its adoption. But if one presumed that the fourth amendment guarantee became efficacious only with the remedy of exclusion, the adoption or nonadoption by a state of the exclusionary rule was no more than a yea or a nay for the fourth amendment protection itself. This was not for the states to decide since the fourteenth amendment imposed the obligations of the fourth amendment upon them whether they liked it or not. Hence the Court's "nose-counting" missed the point. It was the ineffectiveness of the fourth amendment without the exclusionary rule which the Court was compelled to attack to sustain the position elaborated.

The majority opinion in *Wolf* noted that states which had not adopted the exclusionary rule did provide other remedies, both by statute and common law. The effectiveness of these correctives was not contended and was disputed poignantly by Justice Murphy.[33] But the Court did go on to say "that in practice the exclusion of evidence may be an effective way of deterring unreasonable searches, [but] it is not for this Court to condemn as falling below the minimal standards assured by the Due Process Clause a State's reliance upon other methods which, *if consistently enforced,* would be equally effective."[34] The opinion earlier stated that for a state "affirmatively to sanction"[35] police incursion into privacy ran counter to the guarantee of the fourth amendment. These two statements could be said to have implied a tentative approval of experimental freedom by the states within the federal system. This freedom would cease if time proved the state remedies short of exclusion to be ineffective or unenforced to the point where state action or inaction became equivalent to affirmative sanction of illegal searches and seizures.

Justice Frankfurter pointed up the difficult choice involved by alluding to Judge Cardozo's opinion in *People v. Defore:*[36] "On the one side is the social need that crime shall be repressed. On the other, the social need that law shall not be flouted by the insolence of office."[37] Judge Cardozo had noted that the rule embodied in the fourth amendment resulted from prosecutions for damages by Wilkes and Entick *circa* 1765,[38] remedies not unlike many of those provided by the states at the time of the *Wolf* decision.

Justice Frankfurter's final makeweight was that there were better reasons for requiring exclusion on a federal level than on a local level where a more proximate community opinion could be brought to bear on oppressive conduct by local police. This observation did not go to the basic issue of whether or not a rule deemed constitutionally necessary in the federal courts for the enforcement of a pre-existing constitutional guarantee was necessary also in state prosecutions. The last paragraph of the opinion left open the related questions of whether or not Congress could negate the *Weeks* doctrine and, conversely, whether or not it could enforce it against the states under its power "to enforce, by appropriate legislation, the provisions of [the fourteenth amendment]."[39] This treatment was consistent with Justice Frankfurter's already strong intimation that the exclusionary rule was a matter of judicial implication only and not a requirement of the fourth amendment itself.

Justice Black's concurring position deserves mention because of his shift in *Mapp*. He agreed with the Court's decision that the fourth amendment's prohibition was enforceable against the states by the fourteenth amendment, and he agreed "with what appears to be a plain implication of the Court's opinion that the federal exclusionary rule is a judicially created rule of evidence which Congress might negate."[40]

Justices Douglas, Murphy, and Rutledge dissented, all of them feeling that without the exclusionary rule the fourth amendment lacked effective sanction. Justice Murphy and Justice Rutledge believed that exclusion was a constitutional requirement of the fourth amendment not subject to congressional negation, while Justice Douglas termed it a "rule of evidence."[41]

In view of its importance, *Wolf* deserves a look in retrospect. The significance of carrying the fourth amendment's basic command to the states through the due process clause cannot be overemphasized, yet the Court's hesitancy in requiring that the states adopt the exclusionary rule could be said to show a traditional sense of judicial conservatism and a respect for the role of the states in our federal system. But this respect must give way to the mandates of the Constitution. If the fourth amendment is interpreted as requiring not only that the right of freedom from state incursion into privacy be proclaimed but also that its enforcement be effective, the Constitution may require displacement of state remedies deemed inadequate and the imposition of others. *Wolf* left open the possibility that imposition of a more effective remedy was within the power of the Court, yet it avoided an appraisal of the constitutional necessity of imposing it. Twelve years later the Court deemed that appraisal overdue.[42]

A few cases subsequent to *Wolf* affected the degree to which the federal exclusionary rule was intertwined with the non-exclusionary-but-obey-the-fourth-amendment rule for the states. *Lustig v. United States,*[43] decided the same day as *Wolf,* held, in a mild extension of *Byars v. United States,*[44] that a search and seizure by state officials became subject to the federal exclusionary rule if a federal official "had a hand in it."[45] This participation consisted of a sorting on the premises of evidence already seized by state officers to select that evidence usable in a federal prosecution for counterfeiting. But, the Court noted, "it is not a search by a federal official [and thus subject to the exclusionary rule] if evidence secured by state authorities is turned over to the federal authorities on a silver platter"[46] The "silver platter doctrine" produced a gaping hole in the logic of *Wolf*. If the Constitution prohibited unreasonable searches and seizures by state or federal authorities, was it not totally inconsistent for the Supreme Court to allow evasion of the federal rule by activities it had held were unconstitutional for states to sanction? Did this not thoroughly emasculate the enforcement of the fourth amendment?[47]

In *Stefanelli v. Minard,*[48] it was held that a federal court could not issue an injunction under the Civil Rights Act[49] to compel the exclusion from a state criminal proceeding of evidence seized in an unlawful search by state officials. The Court disclaimed the necessity of deciding whether the complaint stated a cause of action under the act, and held instead that "federal courts should refuse to intervene in State criminal proceedings,"[50] for this would tend to upset the delicate balance of federal-state relations, particularly when the interference would occur in state proceedings already begun.[51] These statements in Justice Frankfurter's opinion in *Stefanelli* undoubtedly were correct and the case did not raise the considerations relevant in *Wolf*, since an exclusionary rule compelled by the fourteenth amendment would be one imposed by state tribunals in the midst of their own proceedings and subject to review only by the Supreme Court.[52] But *Stefanelli* closed the door to the only method available after *Wolf* for imposing a form of exclusion of illegally obtained evidence upon state courts. The Civil Rights Act approach was made possible by the *Wolf* decision, which held the fourth amendment enforceable against the states, but when combined with *Wolf's* second holding the low point in the federal enforcement of the exclusionary rule against the states was reached.[53] Only Justice Douglas dissented in *Stefanelli*.[54]

The first case to foreshadow an upward trend, curiously, was one which never mentioned the exclusionary rule. One month after *Stefanelli* came *Rochin v. California*.[55] This case involved the brutal stomach pumping of Rochin to obtain two morphine capsules he had swallowed when police, suspecting Rochin of selling narcotics, broke into the bedroom occupied by him and his wife. Rochin was convicted on this evidence, and the conviction was affirmed in the California courts. The Supreme Court reversed. Justice Frankfurter, again writing for the Court, spoke in broad constitutional terms of the "vague contours"[56] of the due process clause of the fourteenth amendment. The conduct by the officers in this case was brought within these contours by phrases such as "shocks the conscience," "offend[s] even hardened sensibilities," "methods too close to the rack and the screw to permit of constitutional differentiation," and "offend[s] 'a sense of justice.' "[57] Thus was the conviction, "obtained by methods that offend the Due Process Clause,"[58] reversed. The Court alluded to the problem of coerced confessions only to say they were inadmissible under the due process clause because they "offend the community's sense of fair play and decency"[59] and not because of the fifth amendment privilege against self incrimination.[60] The fourth amendment and the exclusionary rule were noticeably avoided.

The significance of the *Rochin* decision for the exclusionary rule as applied to the states lay in the vagueness of the standards by which Rochin's conviction was reversed. That the Court could not long remain content with that decision was a foregone conclusion. "Due process" was a term too fraught with subjective implications to remain unsupported by a more sharply defined elaboration, such as that in the Bill of Rights. The fourth amendment exclusionary rule would have worked in *Rochin*, and far more precisely, but *Wolf* had said "no" a scant two and a half years earlier. Perhaps the coerced confession cases could have been commandeered for the reversal suggested by *Rochin's* appealing fact situation, but the difficult hurdle of extending those cases to "real evidence" in addition to "verbal evidence" blocked the way. The *Rochin* decision was the beginning of a short line of cases which seemed to be based on an *ad hoc* examination of the facts to discern a violation of due process.

The weakness of *Rochin* and the pernicious character of *Wolf* began to appear in *Irvine v. California*[61] where five separate opinions emerged. Irvine was suspected of illegal bookmaking. Police entered his home unlawfully by means of a key made for the purpose, and a microphone was planted. It was twice moved and officers listened in a nearby garage for over a month until incriminating statements sufficient to sustain a conviction were obtained. *Wolf* and *Rochin* did battle with each other over these facts and when the smoke cleared four Justices were of the opinion that *Wolf* governed the circumstances of the case and *Rochin* did not because no physical brutality was involved, though all four adhered to both cases in principle.[62] Justice Clark reluctantly followed *Wolf* on stare decisis grounds but rejected *Rochin* entirely. Thus was the majority gathered to uphold Irvine's conviction. Justices Frankfurter and Burton adhered to both *Wolf* and *Rochin* in principle but thought *Rochin* applied to the facts at hand. Justice Black adhered to neither decision but thought the case should be reversed on fifth amendment grounds as expressed in his opinion in *Adamson v. California*[63] and Justice Douglas maintained his steady position that *Wolf's* refusal to apply the exclusionary rule to the states was error. Whatever *Irvine* decided, *Rochin* was limited to its own facts —where physical brutality was present. *Wolf* was severely weakened, for that decision prevented the Court from providing a remedy to a defendant who had been the object of police activity so flagrantly violative of his rights as to have been termed "incredible" by the Court. As a result of *Irvine*, neither the exclusionary rule nor the *Rochin* ad hoc due process approach could prevent such abusive state action. Eventually, something had to give.[64]

In *Rea v. United States*,[65] the Supreme Court reversed the denial of a motion by a district court to enjoin a federal narcotics agent from testifying in a state trial as to evidence he had seized in violation of petitioner's fourth amendment rights.[66] The evidence had been excluded from an earlier federal criminal proceeding. The Court brushed aside any contrary implications of *Stefanelli*[67] and, putting all constitutional questions to one side, decided the case on the basis of the Supreme

Court's supervisory powers over federal law enforcement officers and agencies.

Elkins v. United States[68] took another big step by overruling the "silver platter doctrine." The case held that evidence obtained by state officers during a search, which would have been unlawful if conducted by federal officers, was inadmissible in a federal prosecution even if federal officers took no part in the search.[69] Justice Stewart's opinion partially relied on a pragmatic evaluation of the exclusionary rule, and stated a rationale in terms of the rule's deterrent effect of removing the incentive to disregard the constitutional guarantee of privacy.[70] He noted, in addition, the trend of the states toward adoption of the exclusionary rule;[71] notable among them was California's adoption in 1955 in *People v. Cahan*.[72] Justice Stewart's opinion contained some language which appeared to foreshadow overruling *Wolf*:

"For surely no distinction can logically be drawn between evidence obtained in violation of the Fourth Amendment and that obtained in violation of the Fourteenth. The Constitution is flouted equally in either case. To the victim it matters not whether his constitutional right has been invaded by a federal agent or by a state officer. [Footnote omitted.] It would be a curiously ambivalent rule that would require the courts of the United States to differentiate between unconstitutionally seized evidence upon so arbitrary a basis. Such a distinction indeed would appear to reflect an indefensibly selective evaluation of the provisions of the Constitution."[73]

Justice Stewart was speaking of the incongruity of admitting one kind of evidence in a *federal trial* and excluding another, but his language applies to the exclusion of *all* illegally obtained evidence whether in a federal *or* state proceeding. Justice Frankfurter dissented in an opinion concurred in by Justices Clark, Harlan, and Whittaker.

The discussion to this point indicates that the federal exclusionary rule stems initially from the fourth amendment, yet it follows not explicitly from that amendment, but by judicial implication. To what extent, however, was exclusion an implicit constitutional requirement of the fourth amendment? Or was it merely an exercise of the Supreme Court's supervisory power over federal law enforcement agencies? Could Congress negate the rule? These questions were unanswered in early 1961. The explicit prohibition of the fourth amendment against unreasonable searches, applied to the states through the due process clause of the fourteenth amendment, imposed a constitutional requirement upon the states not to sanction such searches. But the exclusionary rule itself was held not to be constitutionally required of them, though the loopholes for shuttling illegally obtained evidence between federal and state jurisdictions had steadily been closed. Indeed, *Wolf* had provided incentive for the states to re-examine their policies of protection against illegal police activity. Throughout the entire history of the exclusionary rule ran the controversial policy implications of the rule and the need felt by the courts to somehow prevent official invasion of a citizen's constitutional right of privacy. *Mapp v. Ohio* was to superimpose a number of contributions upon these historical developments.

THE MAPP CASE

The facts

When Dolly Mapp heard her doorbell ring at about 1:30 in the afternoon of May 23, 1957, in Cleveland, Ohio, it was the beginning of a siege of her house and her person by the police which was to last for three hours. Though permitted to call her attorney,[74] who was, however, not allowed to assist her, Mrs. Mapp suffered, among other things, the indignity of a scuffle to retrieve a pretended search warrant which, when displayed to her after the officers had broken into the entrance to her second floor apartment, she had lunged for and shoved down her bosom. She was handcuffed and forced into her bedroom where a search ensued through every room in her apartment and through the basement of the two-family brick dwelling. The officers had received information "from a confidential source"[75] that someone wanted for questioning in connection with a recent bombing was hiding in the home and that there was a large amount of policy paraphernalia[76] hidden there either in the basement or in the second floor suite. The extensive search eventually did turn up some policy material in the basement,[77] but, in addition, the police found some obscene books and pictures which Mrs. Mapp claimed belonged to the occupant of a room she had rented. She had placed some similar material in a suitcase found under her bed when she had cleaned up the roomer's belongings after his unexpected departure. The searching officers took much additional property ranging from Mrs. Mapp's daughter's crayons to souvenir pictures Mrs. Mapp had in her living room.

Mrs. Mapp was indicted for violation of section 2905.34 of Ohio's Revised Code[78]—that she "unlawfully and knowingly had in her possession and under her control, certain lewd and lascivious Books, Pictures and Photographs." A pre-trial motion for suppression of the evidence was denied. Mrs. Mapp was convicted and sentenced to from one to seven years in the Ohio Reformatory for Women.

Appeal was taken to the Supreme Court of Ohio and Mrs. Mapp's conviction was affirmed.[79] The opinion by Justice Taft stated that, assuming the statute under which Mrs. Mapp was convicted was constitutional, her offense clearly fell within the statutory language. Even if her story about the roomer was believed, the books and pictures were nevertheless within her possession and control. The court next noted that an unlawful search had been carried out in this case but that Ohio had held that evidence obtained by an unlawful search and seizure was admissible in a criminal prosecution[80] and *Wolf* permitted this result under the fourteenth amendment. Furthermore, the instant case did not come within the rule of *Rochin v. California*,[81] as that case had subsequently been limited by the Supreme Court,[82] because no brutal or offensive physical force had been used against the defendant.

Four of the justices of the Supreme Court of Ohio went on to hold that the Ohio statute involved was invalid under the federal constitution, relying heavily on *Smith v. California*.[83] However, section two of article IV of the Constitution of Ohio declares that, in order for a law to be held unconstitutional, no more than one judge may dissent from that holding.[84] With only four of the seven justices of the supreme court of that state holding the statute under which Mrs. Mapp was convicted unconstitutional, the judgment had to be affirmed.

At this point, the lawyers for Mrs. Mapp must have thought they had an excellent chance for reversal in the Supreme Court of the United States. Jurisdiction was readily attainable under 28 U.S.C. § 1257(2) (1958);[85] a majority of the Supreme Court of Ohio had declared the Ohio statute unconstitutional on federal grounds; and the federal cases supported the claim of unconstitutionality because the statute imposed strict liability on a defendant in such a way as seriously to impede the circulation of literature protected by the first and fourteenth amendments, in addition to its intended purpose of eliminating circulation of obscene matter. A careful lawyer never puts all his eggs in one basket, however. On appeal to the Supreme Court the argument of Mrs. Mapp's attorneys asserting the unconstitutionality of the Ohio Revised Code § 2905.34, which occupied ten pages of their brief, was balanced by an equal number of pages asserting four additional grounds

for reversal of Dolly Mapp's conviction. Included was a contention that the conduct of the police in searching Mrs. Mapp's suite violated the fourth, fifth, and fourteenth amendments, relying mostly on *Rochin*. The briefs filed with the Supreme Court by appellant and appellee would not be classified as inspiring, though the Brief Amici Curiae on behalf of the American Civil Liberties Union and the Ohio Civil Liberties Union very capably laid the issues regarding the first amendment constitutionality of the Ohio statute before the Court. But the facts of the case and the very terms of Ohio's statute would have led any lawyer confidently to assess the appellant's case as "clearcut." The oral argument on March 29, 1961, reflected this same emphasis and confidence on the issue of constitutionality of the statute.

The Supreme Court's decision

The surprise of the lawyers involved when, on the last day of the term, June 19, 1961, the Supreme Court's opinion came down must have been considerable. *Wolf*—a case not even cited in appellant's brief—was *overruled*. Their surprise was equaled by that of most of the lawyers in the country, a surprise engendered, if not by the short reign of *Wolf*, at least by the completely unheralded advent of such a momentous decision.

Justice Clark wrote a five-part Opinion of the Court in which he discussed the origin of the exclusionary rule, the basis for decision in *Wolf*, the inconsistencies which the *Wolf* doctrine produced, and the "very good sense" of constitutionally making the exclusionary rule a part of the fourth amendment binding upon the states as well as the federal government.[86] Justice Black concurred specially, noting that he concurred in *Wolf* but now found it possible to agree with the present holding when the fourth amendment was supplemented by the fifth.[87] Justice Douglas also concurred specially and reiterated his original dissatisfaction with *Wolf* as one of the three dissenters in that decision.[88]

Justice Harlan, joined by Justices Frankfurter and Whittaker, dissented. The first part of his opinion expressed exasperation at the Court's reaching out to overrule *Wolf* in this particular case as presented—where the jurisdictional statement, briefs, and oral argument were not in the least directed toward that issue.[89] The second part of the dissenting opinion supported the *Wolf* doctrine and criticized the majority's opinion. Justice Stewart agreed in a memorandum with the first part of Justice Harlan's dissent, that *Wolf* should not have been overruled in this particular case, and he expressed no views on that constitutional issue. However, he did agree with the reversal of the case because he felt the Ohio statute was inconsistent with the rights of free thought and expression guaranteed by the fourteenth amendment.[90]

Though the overruling of *Wolf* was unmistakable, there were, and to a lesser extent still are, many questions left unanswered by the decision in *Mapp*. One of the most important of those questions, which has been answered partially by the Supreme Court two years after *Mapp*, was the degree to which the states were free to adopt their own ramifications of a basic policy of exclusion. What policy rationale behind the exclusionary rule was to guide the state courts in their application of it? Did the fifth amendment have a role in the exclusionary rule? Was the fourth amendment now carried *in toto* to the states through the fourteenth including the clauses governing search warrants? Furthermore, what was the status of prisoners already serving time under sentences imposed for convictions based on illegally seized evidence in states which, prior to *Mapp*, did not exclude such evidence? What of the areas not immediately concerned with the fourth amendment, such as the exclusion of wiretap evidence, upon which *Wolf's* dichotomous state-federal approach had left its imprint? And what of other areas which the *Mapp* opinion might affect—particularly that of involuntary confessions?

Many of these questions have yet to be answered definitively by the Supreme Court. An attempt to anticipate the various outcomes, and hopefully the developments themselves, should be guided by a full appreciation of the effects of the exclusionary rule in our federal system and of its limitations.

THE UNCERTAIN STATE OF THE EXCLUSIONARY RULE AFTER MAPP

The policy bases of the exclusionary rule

It is not the purpose of this article to discuss fully the multitude of *pros* and *cons* regarding the exclusionary rule. Nor was it Justice Clark's purpose to do so in his *Mapp* opinion, but at the same time he could not escape the necessity of enumerating some of the "factual considerations"[91] leading toward the wider adoption of the exclusionary rule undertaken by the Court. He did this in spite of his own admonition, in a not-too-subtle jab at Justice Frankfurter's *Wolf* opinion, that such considerations "are not basically relevant to a decision that the exclusionary rule is an essential ingredient

of the Fourth Amendment as the right it embodies is vouchsafed against the States by the Due Process Clause...."[92] Why is a factual analysis of the rationale of the exclusionary rule inescapable? If one assumes that exclusion is the only means of effectively vindicating the fourth amendment right of every citizen to be free from official invasion of privacy in search for evidence of crime, it follows that exclusion must accompany that right; it is this assumption which requires dissection. Any "factual considerations" which validate this assumption are highly relevant and it is *this* type of consideration which Justice Frankfurter ignored in his *Wolf* opinion.

Justice Clark did not make as searching an examination of the exclusionary rule's factual underpinning as might have seemed indicated under the circumstances, though earlier decisions of the Court had gone over this ground thoroughly before.[93] Nevertheless, there was implicit throughout the *Mapp* opinion the belief of the majority in the utter emptiness of the right assimilated by due process in *Wolf* without the remedy of exclusion. That the right against unconstitutional searches and seizures is given substance only by the exclusionary rule is not capable of "proof positive." One may not be able to show empirically, because of the diverse factors involved, that there have been fewer invasions of privacy in states which have heretofore adhered to a policy of exclusion.[94] But at the same time those critics of the rule who say law enforcement suffers in an exclusion state cannot show that there are proportionately more unapprehended criminals in such a state.[95] In addition, one cannot say with certainty that because illegal searches and seizures continue in an exclusionary state, the rule is ineffective. No enactment of a prohibition with its concomitant penalty completely eliminates the objectionable activity in and of itself.

The one observation which can be made with a degree of certainty is that supposed remedies other than exclusion have been almost totally ineffective. Not even the staunchest critics of the exclusionary rule claim that other remedies, whether they be civil actions for damages or criminal prosecutions for overzealous searches and seizures, offer a significant corrective for the undeniable problem of fourth amendment protection.[96] Law enforcement agencies have shown little interest in reducing violations or in devising alternative remedies. It is this inadequacy of means other than the exclusionary rule which has been articulated most by the Supreme Court and other courts adopting the rule, and it is this same inadequacy which is most readily ignored by the courts which have not adopted it.[97]

These arguments cannot be resolved affirmatively on the basis of presently non-existing empirical knowledge about the exclusionary rule. *Mapp*, it seems, almost can be explained by an allocation of the "burden of proof;" whoever bears that burden loses. In *Wolf*, the Court put the burden of showing ineffectiveness of the right of privacy guarantee without exclusion on the advocates of exclusion; in *Mapp*, the burden of showing effectiveness of the guarantee without exclusion fell on the advocates of non-imposition of the exclusionary rule upon the states. Once the Court had unanimously held the right of privacy "vouchsafed against the States by the Due Process Clause,"[98] it gave fair warning to the states that they would bear the burden the next time. Justice Clark relied heavily on this implication of *Wolf*.[99] In the light of the sometimes barbaric violations of individual rights to privacy by state officials which reach the Supreme Court year after year,[100] who can quarrel with Justice Clark's assertion, "our holding that the exclusionary rule is an essential part of both the Fourth and Fourteenth Amendments is not only the logical dictate of prior cases, but it also makes very good sense"?[101]

These "factual considerations" are buttressed by other considerations to which the majority in *Mapp* alluded. Foremost is the concern for judicial integrity. Participation by the courts of the nation in lawless police activities, to the extent of permitting law enforcement agencies' aims of conviction at whatever cost to individual rights to be achieved by admitting illegally obtained evidence, is a self-defeating sacrifice of one legal aim (protection of every individual's constitutional right to privacy) for another (conviction of a criminal). "The criminal goes free, if he must, but it is the law that sets him free," as Justice Clark phrased it.[102] "Nothing can destroy a government more quickly than its failure to observe its own laws, or worse, its disregard of the charter of its own existence."[103] That our courts maintain such an attitude is perhaps of more lasting importance than the conviction of criminals by evidence unlawfully obtained. It is submitted that the Supreme Court is properly a pacesetter in this area of constitutional rights.[104] It is here that a "nose-counting" of the states as to their adoption or non-adoption of the exclusionary rule is noticeably irrelevant.[105]

Closely related to the Court's concern for judicial integrity in *Mapp* was its desire to eliminate the "needless conflict" between state and federal courts and the "double standard," "inducement to evasion," and "working arrangements"[106] produced by the *Wolf* decision. The process of closing the loopholes in the federal exclusionary rule open in non-exclusionary states had, of course, begun before *Mapp*,[107] but that decision now makes some basic form of exclusion applicable throughout the country, thus greatly reducing, if not eliminating, the kind of state-federal "cooperation" which has existed.[108] One could point out that under the decision of *Burdeau v. McDowell*[109] there is still an opportunity for subtle collusion between officials and private persons to avoid the restrictions of the exclusionary rule, but this would seem to account for a relatively insignificant proportion of the violations, and a recent lower court decision shows the far-reaching effect *Mapp* may have had on eliminating this exception to exclusion.[110]

The Court in *Mapp* twice referred to the deterrent value of the exclusionary rule[111]—that it removes the incentive to disregard the constitutional guarantee. While this is an undoubted effect of exclusion, and a desirable one, a more distinct indication of the relative importance the Court placed on this attribute would have been helpful. The exclusionary rule presumably deters unlawful police conduct by bringing such officials to the realization that they'll not be able to obtain the *next* conviction either if they're not more respectful of defendants' constitutional privileges. In this way it is hoped that the rights of *all* individuals who might be the object of a police search will benefit by the generally raised level of police caution and prudence.[112] In this sense the deterrent aspect of the exclusionary rule emphasizes its indirect remedial character as applied to all those who have the fourth amendment privilege. But the Court seems equally, if not more, concerned with the particular individual about to be convicted by illegally seized evidence—that he not be deprived of his liberty without due process of law. Deterrence is relegated to a minor role. The Court was never compelled to consider this distinction in the purely federal sphere of the exclusionary rule where it had supervisory power over the federal courts. A more precise articulation of this dual concern would give an indication of the degree of uniformity to the federal rule required in state courts. Emphasis on a defendant's constitutional rights would indicate a tendency toward uniformity in the treatment of all such defendants since every citizen would be entitled to the same measure of due process of law with minimum variation from state to state. Emphasis on deterrence of unconstitutional searches by police, on the other hand, would seem to allow for variation in means of effecting that deterrence as long as a minimum standard of constitutional protection of the particular citizen, which standard a state could exceed by as much or as little as it chose, was fulfilled in each individual case.

The major shortcomings of the exclusionary rule

must be borne in mind. To name the obvious, the criminal *does* often go free as a result of application of the rule. This disadvantage need not be labored. It may be the necessary cost for a society which regards highly individual rights and freedoms. At the same time, however, one should not be deceived by the Cardozian phrase, "the criminal is to go free because the constable has blundered."[113] The reader of but a few cases in this field will soon realize that many of them involve anything but a "blundering constable"; just as likely, it is a carefully planned, painstaking police operation with full knowledge of violation of the law and sometimes even with permission of superior officers.[114]

The rule is a procedural device rather than a substantive protection. Thus it is subject to all the technicalities and abuse of any procedural matter, and often the question of guilt or innocence of an accused can be obscured by argument over the rule's application. Evidence of the utmost reliability must often be excluded. An offending officer or police force, furthermore, is punished only indirectly by the exclusionary rule. Since it is the rare police force in the United States which so much as reprimands an officer who has violated the laws and Constitution, the officer and the police force usually go completely unpunished by society. The most that can happen is the possible loss of conviction of a criminal.[115] Few other legal prohibitions are so distinctly indirect in their sanction against the offender.

The shortcoming of the exclusionary rule which, pending completion of current studies,[116] may prove most substantial is the fact that even the indirect sanction the rule does apply may be applicable in a far smaller percentage of police activities than formerly has been realized. The sanction of the rule, it can be seen, applies only in those situations where the end result sought by the police is the trial and conviction of the individual whose rights of privacy are violated by unconstitutional search and seizure. But a significant part of the activity of the police, especially in larger cities, is directed at prevention and harassment, typically of those crimes—such as gambling, prostitution and liquor violations—toward which the public expresses a rather ambivalent attitude. These crimes are commonly ones without victims willing to complain and the police are really called upon to regulate crime. They may be left with no recourse from such harassment in light of the indignation expressed in the mass media toward such crime even though there is little public cooperation to fight it. In addition, the punishment for such offenses may amount to mere "overhead" for the offender, thus providing little incentive for the police to seek convictions. Similarly, the exclusionary rule may be of positive assistance to the maintenance of corruption in those police forces already suffering from it. Periodic raids on gambling houses, for example, followed by the granting of a motion to suppress, may become routine enough to give the appearance of vigorous law enforcement when in reality such episodes amount to little more than a minor inconvenience for the offender.

In short, therefore:

"[T]he main thrust of the exclusionary rule is against the police department which is trying to do its job of crime control but is overzealous in its methods. The principal long-run benefit to be expected from the rule is that it will force the administrators of such departments to discipline their forces to be more careful to abide by the rules."[117]

Mapp's implications in a framework of federalism

Wolf, which *Mapp* overruled, showed deep concern for the dictates of federalism. *Mapp*, on the other hand, reached a conclusion opposite to that of *Wolf*, primarily due to regard for individual constitutional rights and the maintenance of an effective fourth amendment prohibition upon the states. Yet the *Mapp* decision had implications of vast proportions with respect to the relationship between federal and state governments.

At the outset it must be noted that when *Wolf* extended the prohibitions of the fourth amendment to the states, the Court entered a vast field of state criminal procedure, yet left behind the sole means of federal enforcement of the prohibition thus created. The implication of *Wolf* that the exclusionary rule was a "judicially created rule of evidence which Congress might negate"[118] could not support the imposition of the exclusionary rule upon the states once the Court came to the conclusion in *Mapp* that this fourth amendment privilege was impotent without the sole means of enforcement by exclusion. The Court had no power to impose a rule of evidence upon state courts or to exercise "supervisory power" over them as it could over federal courts. Unless the Court was willing to adopt the *Rochin* approach, exclusion hardly could be a constitutional requirement of the fourteenth amendment and not of the fourth. Therefore it was necessary in *Mapp* to elevate the exclusionary rule to a constitutional level. This the Court did: "We hold that all evidence obtained by searches and seizures in violation of the Constitution is, by that same authority, inadmissible in a state court."[119]

The significance of this holding can be stated simply: Every time the matter of an illegal search and seizure is raised in a state court, a federal question is now presented. This proliferation of federal questions in state criminal law has occurred before, but there are important differences in the realm of search and seizure after *Mapp*. First, unlike the law of coerced confessions for example, which from its inception imposed a due process restriction upon the states, the law of search and seizure has had an entirely independent development in the federal courts over a period of slightly less than fifty years. *Mapp* thus confronted states without any form of exclusion with one of two possible alternatives: to adopt the federal law of search and seizure suddenly and more or less *in toto,* or to face a substantial handicap in the late-starting development of a state law of search and seizure. The former might have appeared to be a far more attractive choice in light of the doubt engendered by *Mapp* as to whether or not state standards of exclusion would meet the Supreme Court's requirements in any event. Consequently, the unique circumstance of the abrupt imposition of a vast body of well-developed federal decisional law upon the states was a distinct prospect in the wake of *Mapp.*

Secondly, *Wolf* had engenderd a considerable amount of state reliance upon its own devices. This was no less true for those states which, much to their credit in the Supreme Court's view, had adopted some form of exclusion after *Wolf* than for those states which had done little or nothing to correct the abuses of their citizens' fourth amendment rights as required of them by the warning in the *Wolf* opinion.[120] Consider California which had adopted the exclusionary rule decisively in 1955.[121] It filed an amicus curiae petition and brief in support of rehearing of *Mapp.*[122] Its exclusionary rule differs from the federal rule in several respects,[123] and Justice Traynor, in the *Cahan* decision, alluded to these differences as being of beneficial effect.[124] Other states which have adopted the exclusionary rule have similarly not felt bound by the federal decisions; their plight is best summed up in the State of California's Argument Heading *I* in its petition for rehearing of *Mapp:*

"Clarification of the opinion in this case would save years of litigation and confusion. This court upon rejection of *Wolf v. Colorado* has a duty to set out a path through the innumerable conflicts between the decisions of the various state courts and the decisions of the federal courts."

Which kind of development of the exclusionary rule applied to the states was to be permitted? If the states were compelled to adhere to the federal rule, it would seem to penalize those states which had followed the federal lead since *Weeks,* but had built up their own individualized standards of exclusion, more than those states which, by their inaction, continued "affirmatively to sanction" police invasion of privacy.[125] On the other hand, it would be more commensurate with a federalist idea of maximum state authority and minimum centralized control for the Supreme Court to allow the states to develop their own forms of exclusion provided they were consistent with a basic constitutional concern for the efficacy of the fourth amendment and with some minimum standard of protection of the individual victim of an illegal search and seizure. Individual state adaptations to special localized problems of exclusion would thereby be permitted. The reliance on *Wolf* by those states which permitted convictions on evidence obtained by their police in violation of the fourth amendment, though less justified than those states which had adopted the exclusionary rule, was of course obvious.

The third difference raised by *Mapp's* proliferation of federal questions in state proceedings is that the guidance thereby imposed upon state criminal justice will be of a far broader everyday influence than heretofore experienced. It will be more ambitious than that in the area of coerced confessions;[126] real evidence gained illegally undoubtedly is of higher incidence than evidence by coerced verbal confessions; the unconstitutional search itself is what may lead to the suspect being questioned and it is only upon questioning that the coerced confession prohibitions come into play.

Lastly, the law of search and seizure is complicated and technical. Many subquestions inevitably intrude into the mechanics of the operation of the exclusionary rule. There are problems of standing, consent, the reasonableness and extent of the search permitted, search incident to arrest, probable cause for arrest and for search, and validity of a search warrant, to name a few.[127] That state decisions, state statutes, and state constitutions are intimately involved in these questions is apparent. How much will have to give way to the federal exclusionary rule? Furthermore, the federal exclusionary rule is anything but a fixed and precise rule of law.[128] What degree of uniformity would the Supreme Court require?

The basic question raised by the unsettling situation created by *Mapp*—by what standard were state searches and seizures, and therefore exclusion of evidence unlawfully obtained thereby, to be evaluated?—was faced by the Supreme Court in *Ker v. California.*[129] Some tenuous guidelines do emerge from the Court's opinion.

Through a series of events which both the majority and minority of the Court agree gave probable cause for arrest of the petitioner Ker, Los Angeles County Sheriff's Officers were led without a search warrant to his apartment on suspicion that he had just bought a large supply of marijuana. Ascertaining that the apartment was occupied, the officers obtained a pass key from the building manager. While one officer stayed outside to intercept any evidence which might be thrown out a window, three others went to Ker's apartment, unlocked and opened the door, and, proceeding quietly to prevent destruction of the evidence, entered and found Ker in the living room reading a newspaper. A two-pound "brick" of marijuana was then found in the kitchen. It was introduced at the trial of Ker and his wife and resulted in their conviction for illegal possession of narcotics under state law. The California District Court of Appeals affirmed their convictions and the California Supreme Court denied a petition for hearing.

Acknowledging that Ker was "the first case arriving here since our opinion in Mapp which would afford suitable opportunity for further explication of that holding in the light of intervening experience,"[130] Justice Clark wrote a five-part opinion, Part I of which was joined in by all but Justice Harlan. Here the Court said that the fourth amendment was enforceable against the states " 'by the same sanction of exclusion as is used against the Federal Government,' by the application of the same constitutional standard prohibiting 'unreasonable searches and seizures.' "[131] The near-unanimity on this elaboration of Mapp was short-lived, however, for then the eight Justices split down the middle. Justices Clark, Black, Stewart, and White, in applying this "standard," felt that Mapp did not require the exclusion of the marijuana found in the Ker apartment while the Chief Justice, and Justices Douglas and Goldberg, speaking through Justice Brennan, felt that the unannounced intrusion of the arresting officers into the Kers' apartment violated the fourth amendment. Justice Harlan concurred only in the result upholding the Kers' convictions. He adhered to the view that state searches and seizures should be judged, and had been judged, "by the more flexible concept of 'fundamental' fairness" under the due process clause of the fourteenth amendment. He dissented from the standard of "reasonableness" of searches and seizures as applied in federal courts and now applied to the states in the Ker decision.

That states were obliged unequivocally to follow federal standards of search and seizure would seem certain were it not for the nature of the disagreement separating the eight Justices. Justice

Clark, and those who joined him, showed a marked deference to state decisional law engrafting a judicial exception to the California Penal Code, section 844, which permitted unannounced entry when the arrest would have been frustrated if the officer had demanded entrance and stated his purpose.[132] The officers' method of entry to the Ker apartment, "sanctioned by the law of California, was not unreasonable under the standards of the Fourth Amendment as applied to the States through the Fourteenth Amendment."[133] Justice Brennan argued by way of an historical analysis that such an entry was contrary to the fourth amendment notwithstanding Miller v. United States[134] which did not face the constitutional necessity of announcing authority and purpose but relied instead on local law requiring such announcement.[135]

The apparent equivocation underlying Ker's seemingly firm requirement of adherence by the states to federal standards of exclusion was evident also from further statements in Part I of Justice Clark's opinion. He noted that Mapp did not mark any assumption of Supreme Court supervisory authority over state courts and "consequently, it implied no total obliteration of state laws relating to arrests and searches in favor of federal law."[136] Further, Mapp "did not attempt the impossible task of laying down a 'fixed formula' for the application in specific cases of the constitutional prohibition against unreasonable searches and seizures."[137] Justice Clark concluded:

"[T]he demands of our federal system compel us to distinguish between evidence held inadmissible because of our supervisory powers over federal courts and that held inadmissible because prohibited by the United States Constitution....The States are not thereby precluded from developing workable rules governing arrests, searches and seizures to meet 'the practical demands of effective criminal investigation and law enforcement' in the States, provided that those rules do not violate the constitutional proscription of unreasonable searches and seizures and the concomitant command that evidence so seized is inadmissible against one who has standing to complain....Such a standard implies no derogation of uniformity in applying federal constitutional guarantees but is only a recognition that conditions and circumstances vary just as do investigative and enforcement techniques."[138]

That these statements seem confusing and contradictory is perhaps an understatement, but the light may dawn when one emphasizes "by application of the same constitutional standards pro-

hibiting *'unreasonable* searches and seizures.' "
Mapp did little more than overrule *Wolf* and require exclusion of state evidence obtained in violation of the fourth amendment. *Ker* adds to this
only by indicating that the fundamental criterion
for determining when evidence should be excluded
from state trials is now governed by the federal "reasonableness" standard under the fourth
amendment rather than "fundamental fairness"
under the due process clause of the fourteenth
as in *Rochin*. The difference from pre-*Mapp* days
appears to be an opportunity to rely more heavily
on federal search and seizure law and to review
state searches and seizures more often and in cases
less flagrantly violative of fourth amendment rights
than in the pre-*Mapp Rochin* prototype. State law
affecting the validity of a particular search will be
deferred to when federal decisional law, though
declaring such a search invalid, is determined by
an ofttimes thin and wavering majority of the
Supreme Court to be based upon that Court's supervisory power over federal courts and federal
officers. This appears to be what was in fact done
in *Ker*. A more explicit statement of when state
law will govern would not only have been impossible but also would have amounted to judicial legislation without benefit of the vitality
achieved by concrete cases.

The problem for subsequent state search and
seizure cases thus emerges: to determine which
parts of the already established federal law of
search and seizure are constitutionally founded
and which parts are based on the Supreme Court's
supervisory power. Such distinctions have not had
to be made heretofore. A case by case reappraisal
of the federal fourth amendment law will be required, and one may be assured of the continuing
existence of a virulent exclusion controversy in a
new and vibrant context. It will be a lengthy and
difficult process and whatever uniformity eventually is required of the states will be imposed upon
them slowly. In addition, the necessary determination of the constitutional "core" of the fourth
amendment applied to the states will produce
unique problems of its own. For example, if a
difference is allowed to persist between a state's
exclusionary rule and the federal rule, will evidence unlawfully seized by federal officials under
federal standards but lawfully seized under a
state's standards be constitutionally admissible in
that state's courts?[139] A disallowance of such a
silver platter in reverse could mushroom into other
areas of state-federal relations.[140] In the realm of
search and seizure it may become desirable to distinguish "unconstitutional" searches and seizures—
those in violation of the fourth amendment as interpreted by the federal courts—from "illegal" or

"unlawful" searches and seizures—those in violation of state standards grounded upon the fourth
amendment only by their variegated passage
through the fourteenth.

The Supreme Court's "policing" of the states,
depending on the degree of uniformity which becomes required with subsequent cases, should turn
out to be a formidable and docket-enlarging task.
One wonders how far it can go. Is it possible that
such a vast regulation of state criminal procedure
might prove to be as impossible of realization as
the dream of *Swift v. Tyson?*[141] Does not a line
somewhere exist beyond which the tenth amendment[142] will not permit the Supreme Court to
govern state criminal procedures in the name of
due process?

Mapp, and *Ker* after it, has had a tremendous
effect on the balance between the states and the
federal government; the balance scale has not yet
reached an equilibrium and changing effects will
be felt for some time to come. In anticipating the
continuing developments, it will pay to bear in
mind one of the stated objectives of the *Mapp*
decision: "the avoidance of needless conflict between state and federal courts."[143] This objective,
combined with *Mapp's* concern that a citizen not
be convicted by unconstitutional evidence in addition to providing a deterrent remedy against police
misconduct, and *Ker's* indication of a case by case
approach, augur an increasingly uniform exclusionary rule throughout the country.

Constitutional rights under the Fourth Amendment

It seems clear from the *Mapp* opinion that, in
addition to whatever the individual citizen had in
the way of a right of privacy before the decision,
he now has a right or a privilege against conviction by unconstitutionally obtained evidence. This
inheres in the nature of the rule which is uplifted
to a constitutional level[144] and it makes little difference how one terms the effect of the decision.
The fact is apparent from the language used by
Justice Clark:

"[T]he admission of the new constitutional right
by *Wolf* could not consistently tolerate denial of
its most important constitutional privilege, namely,
the exclusion of the evidence which an accused
had been forced to give by reason of the unlawful
seizure. To hold otherwise is to grant the right but
in reality to withhold its privilege and enjoyment."[145]

The fifth amendment was interjected into this concept of privilege by Part *IV* of Justice Clark's opinion in *Mapp*.[146] The manner in which that amendment comes upon the scene can very easily lead to confusion. First it must be said that the fourth amendment is cited traditionally as a protection from official invasion of privacy. But within this delimitation lies that official invasion of privacy whose object is the acquisition of evidence of crime. Such a search involves more than the invasion of privacy itself, for it may lead to the additional consequence of a "deprivation of life, liberty, or property," namely, conviction and imprisonment. Where this greater threat is involved, the effectiveness of the fourth amendment looms of correspondingly greater importance.[147] If prosecution for a crime ensues, the courts are given an opportunity to put teeth into the fourth amendment by excluding evidence obtained in violation of it. The analogy to the fifth amendment is obvious since that amendment *explicitly* excludes compulsory evidence from the accused himself. That the fourth amendment does not say "no evidence obtained by unreasonable search and seizure...shall be used against the victim in any criminal case" is merely evidence of that amendment's greater concern for *all* official invasions of privacy *including* those in search of evidence of crime. The two amendments therefore strive toward the same substantive goal—prevention of governmental intrusion upon the individual—but when the added element of use of evidence in a "criminal case" develops, the Supreme Court has seen fit to make the two amendments analogous procedurally as well, by exclusion of the evidence from the trial. This is the extent of the "intimate relation" between the fourth and fifth amendments and no more. It is submitted that the exclusionary rule may constitutionally stand on the fourth amendment alone. There need be no dependency on the fifth; it merely provides a convenient judicial analogy.

The existence of the privilege against conviction by unconstitutionally obtained evidence is indicated also by the probable retroactive effect of *Mapp* discussed below. As has been stated, the stress the Court has placed or will place on this concept of privilege in relation to its concern about deterrence of police conduct is difficult to determine and may affect the degree of uniformity which will be required of state exclusionary rules. Regardless of other effects, a new privilege, universally applied to all citizens no matter what the forum, has been added to the law of evidence, but the judicial reasoning by which it arises is as yet not clearly articulated by the Supreme Court....

EXTENDED APPLICATION OF EXCLUSION OUTSIDE THE REALM OF SEARCH AND SEIZURE

Coerced confessions

The coerced confession cases, as applied to the states through the fourteenth amendment, show a curious relationship to the search and seizure cases. *Mapp* may well have had the effect of drawing these separate lines of decision very close together.

One of the earliest entries of the Supreme Court into the constitutional supervision of state criminal procedure was in this area of coerced confessions.[148] These cases, like *Rochin* in the search and seizure field, were based solely on the due process clause of the fourteenth amendment. The early decisions were founded on a rationale of the untrustworthiness of such confessions.[149] But gradually they shifted toward an independent examination of the facts by the Supreme Court in an effort to determine the inherent coerciveness of the circumstances undisputed in the particular case—the mere involuntariness of the confession regardless of its extrinsic verification being sufficient to violate concepts of a fair accusatorial criminal procedure under due process of law.[150] If such a confession was admitted into evidence the conviction in the state court was reversed.

In the federal sphere a still more stringent approach was developed. Under the *McNabb* rule, a confession obtained during an illegal detention was inadmissible in a federal court.[151] The rule seemed to depend largely on the existence of a federal prompt-arraignment statute[152] and on the Court's supervisory power over federal law enforcement officials. It has not been required of the states on due process grounds.[153]

Justice Clark drew support from the coerced confession cases for the imposition of the exclusionary rule upon the states in *Mapp*,[154] but Justice Harlan protested that the coerced confession rule "is certainly not a rule that any illegally obtained statements may not be used in evidence."[155] He cited the fact that the *McNabb* rule had not been applied to the states to require reversal of convictions relying on the use of confessions obtained during a period of illegal detention and concluded that "in requiring exclusion of an involuntary statement of an accused, we are concerned not with an appropriate remedy for what the police have done, but with something which is regarded as going to the heart of our concepts of fairness in judicial procedure."[156] The pressures which result in an involuntary confession do not involve independent constitutional violations apart from use at trial of such a confession, hence the accused has a procedural right not to have that confession used. "This, and not the disciplining of the police, as with illegally seized evidence," said Justice Harlan, "is surely the true basis for excluding a statement of the accused which was unconstitutionally obtained."[157]

The first implication which may be drawn from the majority's reliance on the confession cases, based as they have been on a primary concern with procedural fairness to the individual, is that the exclusionary rule, as enlarged by *Mapp*, now has or will have a similar basis. Undoubtedly this due process regard for a trial unmarred by the introduction of unconstitutionally seized evidence will coexist with the deterrent foundation of the rule.[158] Such a coexistent emphasis on procedural fairness is now possible under *Mapp* where it was not possible before: There is now a consistent treatment of a constitutional right which is no longer dependent solely on the forum in which the accused happens to be on trial. The reliance on the confession cases thus gives a clue to the probable trend of future decisions by the Court with regard to exclusion—toward an exclusionary procedure which ensures protection of an individual's right to a fair trial and thus possibly toward a higher degree of uniformity required of the states to secure this protection.[159]

Conversely, it is possible that the confession cases will be moved closer to the search and seizure cases by an increased emphasis on deterrence of police misconduct. *McNabb* articulated what amounted to a factual presumption that a confession obtained during an illegal detention was coerced.[160] Though most states have statutes requiring prompt arraignment of a criminal defendant, the Court has not applied the *McNabb* rule to the states.[161] However, with a realization by the Court that, contrary to Justice Harlan's assertion, "the pressures brought to bear against an accused leading to a confession" often *do* involve "independent constitutional violations" prior to trial,[162] it should not be difficult to apply reasoning similar to *Mapp*—that exclusion of a confession obtained during an illegal detention, state or federal, is necessary to deter police conduct which tends to produce such unconstitutionally obtained confessions. *Mapp* may therefore assist the Court in extending the *McNabb* rule, or a modification of it, to the states in addition to bringing a deterrent element of the confession cases distinctly into the open.[163]

The closer relationship and similarity between the confession rule and the exclusionary rule implied in *Mapp* may indicate also the promulgation of the "fruit of the poisonous tree" doctrine[164] to

the states. This would be another large step in the regulation of state criminal procedure.

The chief distinction between a state coerced confession under present law and the seizing of evidence illegally is that the former is almost always a serious constitutional violation of due process. A mere technical violation is unlikely. On the other hand, the law of search and seizure is full of technicality and comparatively trivial violations can result in exclusion. To the extent seriousness of the constitutional violation is a criterion, therefore, it is understandable that the Supreme Court was more reluctant, and took longer, to require exclusion of unconstitutionally obtained evidence from state courts than to require exclusion of coerced confessions. Now that both types of exclusion are applicable, however, it may be expected that they will become more, not less, similar both in their effects and their rationales.

Wiretap evidence

The exclusion of wiretap evidence from federal or state courts under section 605 of the Federal Communications Act[165] has shown a striking parallel to the development of the exclusionary rule in search and seizure cases prior to *Mapp*.[166] Though the subject of wiretapping is fraught with peripheral problems of what constitutes "interception" and "divulgence," and though the wiretapping prohibitions are based on interpretation of a federal statute rather than on the Constitution, the basic decisions affecting use of wiretap evidence in court have followed the basic decisions affecting use of evidence seized in contravention of the fourth amendment. Both kinds of evidence are inadmissible in a federal court;[167] leads obtained by the acquisition of both kinds of evidence are likewise inadmissible—the "fruit of the poisonous tree" doctrine obtains;[168] the exclusionary rule applicable to both kinds of evidence does not apply to the state courts;[169] only the victim of the illegality can claim exclusion;[170] and federal courts will receive neither kind of evidence if obtained by federal *or state* officials—no "silver platter" will be permitted.[171]

Mapp obviously disturbs the settled terrain. *Schwartz v. Texas*[172] held that:

"Although the intercepted calls [by which Schwartz was convicted in the Texas courts] would be inadmissible in a federal court, it does not follow that such evidence is inadmissible in a state court. Indeed, evidence obtained by a state officer by means which would constitute an unlawful search and seizure under the Fourth Amendment to the Federal Constitution is nonetheless admissible in a state court. *Wolf v. Colorado,* 338 U.S. 25, while such evidence, if obtained by a federal officer, would be clearly inadmissible in a federal court. *Weeks v. United States,* 232 U.S. 383."[173]

Thus under the statute, the Court held, an express intention of Congress was necessary in order to require state criminal procedures to exclude wiretap evidence. In *Benanti v. United States,*[174] however, the Court stated what it had failed to say in *Schwartz,* that section 605 *did* prohibit wiretaps by state officials, quite apart from divulgence in court, even when permitted under state law. The analogy to *Wolf* was complete. Four months before *Mapp,* in *Pugach v. Dollinger,*[175] the Court reaffirmed *Schwartz* by denying injunctive relief against the use of wiretap evidence in the state courts of New York. The evidence had been obtained by state officials pursuant to a state court warrant as permitted by the constitution and statutes of New York.[176] The three-line per curiam opinion also relied on *Stefanelli v. Minard.*[177]

The overruling of *Wolf* by *Mapp,* drastically affecting the law of search and seizure, obviously will require a reappraisal of the use of wiretap evidence in state courts as presently permitted under the authority of *Schwartz.* With exclusion of evidence seized in violation of the fourth amendment now constitutionally required in all courts, state and federal, under a constitutional provision which makes no mention of exclusion, it would be anomalous if wiretap evidence, whose divulgence is *expressly* prohibited under the statute, were still permitted to be used in state courts. Moreover, now that *Mapp* has obviated appellant's quest for equitable relief in *Stefanelli* by providing an adequate remedy at law, there is less excuse for maintaining in the wiretap field the same hiatus which existed under *Wolf* and *Stefanelli* in the search and seizure area—the anomaly whereby the victim has neither a legal nor an equitable remedy against the use of the unlawful evidence.[178] Of course the state official who divulges wiretap evidence is subject to prosecution by federal authorities, but it is just as illusory to expect such prosecution between cooperating arms of our federal system engaged in a continual fight against crime as it is to expect the district attorney to prosecute the police authorities, on whom he depends in his jurisdiction, for violations of individuals' fourth amendment rights? In short, with *Mapp* on the record, either *Pugach* or *Schwartz* will have to give way. *Schwartz's* reliance upon *Wolf* has left it well nigh unsupportable.

CONCLUSION

The applicability of the exclusionary rule has been greatly broadened after a late start and a cautious expansion. Throughout its history it has been caught in the dialogue between advocates of effective but obtrusive police methods and those willing to let the guilty individual go free to ensure protection of the rights of all citizens, innocent or guilty. The sharp disagreement between reasonable men over this inevitable choice of the lesser of two evils has been manifest in the essentially judgmatical decisions which have had to be made. However, it is submitted that the controversy over the exclusionary rule does not present choices as disagreeable as its critics and advocates would have us accept. Not *all* criminals who are victims of an unconstitutional search go free. And police methods, to be effective, need not violate citizens' constitutional rights. If police administrators, and the public behind them, fully comprehended the role of police in our society as enforcers of justice under the Constitution and not mere apprehenders of presumed criminals, police methods less prone to shortcuts undoubtedly would result. Nevertheless, that comprehension is apparently not yet present. Just as apparently, such comprehension had abided in the Supreme Court and other high courts in the land. While the expanded exclusionary rule will not cure unconstitutional police conduct in and of itself it can promote more effective channelling of police energies toward the scientific and ratiocinative solution of crimes for which law enforcement agencies have received an increased and justly deserved reputation. It is perhaps significant that Washington, D.C., whose police force operates under federal legal strictures in respect to all criminal law enforcement, has a clearance rate of major crimes which is about double the national average.[179]

For the courts, the problems created by the expansion of the exclusionary rule are two-fold. First it will be necessary for many judges to become imbued with the "broad view." There are times when a judge is faced with the prospect of excluding vital evidence from the trial of a man he "knows" is guilty, though the jury does not. It is perhaps his hardest task to remember that his decision is broader than the conviction of the defendant before him. The "rule" is really a line drawn to delineate permissible police conduct. That line must exist for all factual variations even if drawn by judicial decision after the fact of particular police conduct. Though such "line drawing" produces technicality, its application must be consistent to produce results. It is only by excluding unconstitutionally obtained evidence in the case before him that the judge can curb police conduct which may affect many more individuals who are searched in violation of the fourth amendment without results compelling prosecution. Furthermore, for the judge to know that the defendant before him is "guilty," in the sense that he committed the act charged, is not to say, under present court decisions, that the man should be convicted when that conviction can be obtained only by evidence obtained in violation of his constitutional rights. The temptation to ignore technicalities in order to convict the "guilty" is very real, but that "crime wave around the corner" will not be precipitated by judicious application of the exclusionary rule any more than police methods will become upright without it.

Secondly, what may at first glance appear to have been the culmination of the constitutional doctrine of exclusion by its expansion to the states in *Mapp*, on further examination may be seen to have created as many, if not more, problems than it solved. The Supreme Court in particular has taken unto itself a substantial measure of intervention in the affairs of the states. This is a one-way road—the first step down it was taken in the area of search and seizure by the very decision *Mapp* overruled. At the same time, it is perhaps a poignant example of an influx of federal power following upon an all too characteristic default of state responsibility—poignant because the states were given all due warning in *Wolf* itself. The many questions remaining after *Mapp* eventually will have to be acknowledged by the Court. . . . *Ker* has invited a substantial revaluation of the federal law of search and seizure in light of the necessity for determining what parts of that law are constitutionally founded. One can hope also for a clarification of the role of the fifth amendment within the judicial rationale of exclusion.

At the very least, the debate of exclusion vel non in state courts is now at an end. The controversy must now settle around a logical and workable evolution of the mandates of exclusion directed toward enhancing respect for the constitutional rights of all citizens by all officials within our federal system. The public and private respect for such rights in this country is presently a long way from the high regard set apart for the protection of civil liberties in England. This respect is reflected in the behavior of the police, where the unarmed British bobby is the symbol of the admiration the police have won for themselves. While such public conscience in the United States cannot be legislated overnight, and certainly not by the courts, the expansion of the exclusionary rule may mark the inception of a needed self-imposed

effort by local police, and citizens generally, inclining toward a greater veneration of the liberties embodied in our Constitution.

Footnotes

[1]367 U.S. 643 (1961).
[2]338 U.S. 25 (1949).
[3]116 U.S. 616.
[4]Boyd v. United States, supra note 3, at 638. The case involved statutory authority granted to the court in revenue cases on the government attorney's motion to require the defendant to produce his private books, invoices, or papers or else "the allegations stated in the said motion shall be taken as confessed." Act of June 22, 1874, § 5, 18 Stat. 187. Although no search and seizure was even remotely involved, the Court said—unnecessarily—that "a compulsory production of ...private books and papers...is the equivalent of a search and seizure—and an unreasonable search and seizure—within the meaning of the Fourth Amendment." Boyd v. United States, supra note 3, at 634-35.
[5]"The right of the people to be secure in their persons, houses, papers, and effects, against unreasonable searches and seizures, shall not be violated, and no Warrants shall issue, but upon probable cause, supported by Oath or affirmation, and particularly describing the place to be searched, and the person or things to be seized."
[6]"[N]or shall [any person] be compelled in any criminal case to be a witness against himself, nor be deprived of life, liberty, or property, without due process of law."
[7]Boyd v. United States, supra note 3, at 633. See Justice Black's concurring opinion in *Mapp* in which he states his inability to overrule *Wolf* on fourth amendment grounds alone, but when "considered together with the Fifth Amendment's ban against compelled self-incrimination, a constitutional basis emerges which not only justifies but actually requires the exclusionary rule." Supra note 1, at 661-62. See also the opinion of the Court in *Mapp*, id. at 656-57. See infra, part III, subsection C.
[8]192 U.S. 585, 598 (1904).
[9]194 U.S. 25, 45-46 (1904).
[10]232 U.S. 383.
[11]Id. at 398.
[12]Ibid.
[13]Id. at 393; quoted in Mapp v. Ohio, supra note 1, at 648.
[14]See, e.g., People v. Cahan, 44 Cal. 2d 434, 445, 447, 282 P.2d 905, 911, 913 (1955) (Traynor, J.); Wolf v. Colorado, supra note 2, at 41-47 (Murphy, J., dissenting); Mapp v. Ohio, supra note 1, at 651-52. For an excellent article, see Allen, The Wolf Case: Search and Seizure, Federalism and the Civil Liberties, 45 Ill. L. Rev. 1, 17-18 (1950).
[15]Weeks v. United States, supra note 10, at 392.
[16]Id. at 395. As mentioned above, *Adams* had repudiated much of the dicta in *Boyd* regarding the unconstitutionality of admitting evidence obtained in violation of the fourth amendment. It was thus necessary for the Court in *Weeks* to overcome the holding of *Adams* that admitting into evidence private papers seized incidental to the execution of a valid search warrant did not violate the constitutional rights of the accused. This the Court did by making the *Adams*

holding essentially an exception to the exclusionary rule, although the case by no means so restricted itself. The Court also dismissed *Adams* on the ground that that case had affirmed the principle that "a court will not...permit a collateral issue to be raised as to the source of competent testimony." Id. at 396. This attempt at overcoming *Adams* left something to be desired.

17E.g., Trupiano v. United States, 334 U.S. 699 (1948) (defendant can compel exclusion of evidence seized in violation of his fourth amendment rights even though the goods are contraband and he has no right to their return); United States v. Lefkowitz, 285 U.S. 452 (1932) (a search for and seizure of an individual's private papers solely to obtain evidence to convict him of crime is unconstitutional even with a search warrant); Marron v. United States, 275 U.S. 192 (1927) (search and seizure incident to a valid arrest is lawful); Byars v. United States, 273 U.S. 28 (1927) (illegal search conducted by a state officer aided by a federal officer; evidence excluded); Carroll v. United States, 267 U.S. 132 (1925) (only unreasonable searches and seizures are prohibited; an automobile may be searched without a warrant when there is "reasonable or probable cause"); Hester v. United States, 265 U.S. 57 (1924) (the area of the search protected must be a "private" one; it "is not extended to the open fields"); Burdeau v. McDowell, 256 U.S. 465 (1921) (evidence obtained by a search and seizure by a private person without a warrant and not in collusion with federal authorities is not excludable); Gouled v. United States, 255 U.S. 298 (1921) (defendant need not move for exclusion before he learns of the illegality of the seizure); Silverthorne Lumber Co. v. United States, 251 U.S. 385 (1920) (evidence obtained indirectly from an unlawful search is excludable also—"fruit of the poisonous tree" doctrine; a corporation may invoke the exclusionary rule); Schenck v. United States, 249 U.S. 47 (1919) (the right to have evidence excluded applies only when it is defendant's right of privacy which has been violated).

18"[N]or shall any State deprive any person of life, liberty, or property without due process of law."

19Palko v. Connecticut, 302 U.S. 319, 325 (1937).

20Wolf v. Colorado, supra note 2, at 27-28.

21Weeks v. United States, supra note 10, at 393.

22Wolf v. Colorado, supra note 2, at 26.

23Adamson v. California, 332 U.S. 46 (1947).

24Davidson v. New Orleans, 96 U.S. 97, 104 (1877), as quoted in Wolf v. Colorado, supra note 2, at 27.

25Wolf v. Colorado, supra note 2, at 27.

26Id. at 28.

27Ibid.

28Ibid. (emphasis supplied).

29Id. at 27.

30The word "remedy" is used here only in a partial sense of redress for a legal wrong. The remedy referred to, of course, is the exclusionary rule but that particular remedy is a strange animal: it is not available to every person who has been wronged by an illegal search and seizure, but only to the accused who happens to have been caught with incriminating evidence. It is not directed against the person who committed a wrong, or his superior, in the sense of compelling a cessation of the wrong or retribution for having committed it; instead, its effect upon the wrongdoer is *strictly* a deterrent.

31Wolf v. Colorado, supra note 2, at 28.

32Ibid. See text following note 26 supra.

33Id. at 41-47 (dissenting opinion). This opinion by Justice Murphy is especially noteworthy both for its cogency in the statement of the position that the exclusion of unlawfully seized evidence is the only way to prevent the fourth amendment from becoming a dead letter and for the fact that he disclosed, id. at 44 n.5, perhaps the only real effort made by anyone to actually gauge the effect on police operations of the limitations imposed by the exclusionary rule. But see, note 116 infra.

34Id. at 31 (emphasis supplied).

35Id. at 28.

36242 N.Y. 13, 150 N.E. 585 (1926).

37Id. at 24-25, 150 N.E. at 589.

38Id. at 24, 150 N.E. at 589. See Boyd v. United States, supra note 3, at 625-27.

39U.S. Const. Amend. XIV, § 5.

40Wolf v. Colorado, supra note 2, at 39-40. See also note 7 supra regarding Justice Black's change of opinion.

41Id. at 40.

42Mapp v. Ohio, 367 U.S. 643 (1961).

43338 U.S. 74 (1949).

44Supra note 17.

45Lustig v. United States, supra note 43, at 78.

46Id. at 79.

47See Kamisar, Wolf and Lustig Ten Years Later: Illegal State Evidence in State and Federal Courts, 43 Minn. L. Rev. 1083 (1959); Allen, The Wolf Case, supra note 14.

48342 U.S. 117 (1951).

49Rev. Stat. § 1979 (1875), 42 U.S.C. § 1983 (1958).

50Stefanelli v. Minard, supra note 48, at 120.

51Compare this holding with the recent case of Monroe v. Pape, 365 U.S. 167 (1961), where it was held that damages could be recovered under the same statute for a fourth amendment violation.

52This view of *Stefanelli* recently has been upheld in Cleary v. Bolger, 371 U.S. 392 (1963). There the Supreme Court again refused to enjoin the use of illegally seized evidence in a state criminal trial or administrative proceeding. However, as the Court pointed out, the petitioner in the lower court was this time not without remedy, as had been the case in *Stefanelli*. "To the extent that such rights have been violated, cf., e.g., Mapp v. Ohio,...he may raise the objection in the state courts and then seek review in this Court of an adverse determination by the New York Court of Appeals. To permit such claims to be litigated collaterally, as is sought here, would in effect frustrate the deep-seated federal policy against piecemeal review." Id. at 400-01.

53It is interesting to contemplate what the historical course of the exclusionary rule might have been had the relief sought in *Stefanelli*, only two years after *Wolf*, been couched in the terms later advocated—successfully—in *Monroe*. The approach via injunctive relief in the midst of state proceedings, as in *Stefanelli*, would have been merely a form of exclusion by another name with all the concomitant features whereby "the criminal is to go free because the constable has blundered." People v. Defore, 242 N.Y. 13, 21, 150 N.E. 585, 587 (1926) (Cardozo, J.). On the other hand, a right of action for damages under the Civil Rights Act, as in *Monroe*, might have qualified as one of the "other methods, which, if consistently enforced, would be equally effective," Wolf v. Colorado, 338 U.S. 25, 31 (1949), on which a state might have relied properly for remedial action even though a remedy in a federal forum. The necessity of applying the exclusionary rule to the states might never have occurred. This speculation breaks down, however, when the more immediate emphasis on the rights of the accused in his criminal trial is brought to bear on the situation. It is then that the more peculiarly defined "remedy" of exclusion, id. at 30-31, is required, and indeed resulted in the elevation of the exclusionary rule to a constitutional level in *Mapp*.

[54]Justices Murphy and Rutledge, who dissented with Justice Douglas in *Wolf*, had been succeeded by Justices Clark and Minton.

[55]342 U.S. 165 (1952).

[56]Id. at 170.

[57]Id. at 172-73.

[58]Id. at 174.

[59]Id. at 173.

[60]Justices Black and Douglas, though concurring in the Court's reversal in *Rochin*, thought the decision required that the fifth amendment be held applicable to the states through the fourteenth.

[61]347 U.S. 128 (1954).

[62]The four were Chief Justice Warren and Justices Jackson, Minton, and Reed.

[63]332 U.S. 46, 68 (1947).

[64]Breithaupt v. Abram, 352 U.S. 432 (1957), was perhaps the last gasp of the *Rochin* approach to search and seizure before *Mapp*. In *Breithaupt*, *Rochin* was rejected as a ground for holding an alcohol blood test of the unconscious defendant unlawful as a means of convicting him for involuntary manslaughter. *Wolf* was followed, and it was held immaterial that evidence of the percentage of alcohol thus found in the defendant's blood was admitted in a state trial.

[65]350 U.S. 214 (1956).

[66]But compare this holding with Wilson v. Schnettler, 365 U.S. 381, 386 (1961), where *Rea* was distinguished.

[67]See notes 48-54 and related text supra.

[68]364 U.S. 206 (1960).

[69]This closed the gap in the enforcement of the federal exclusionary rule left by Lustig v. United States, see notes 43-47 and related text supra.

[70]Elkins v. United States, supra note 68, at 217.

[71]Id. at 219, 224-32. But see Note, The Supreme Court, 1960 Term, 75 Harv. L. Rev. 40, 154 n.398, regarding exaggeration of that trend.

[72]44 Cal. 2d 434, 282 P.2d 905 (1955).

[73]Elkins v. United States, supra note 68, at 215.

[74]Mrs. Mapp previously had engaged attorneys for a civil suit against the prize fighter, Archie Moore. Record, pp. 34-35.

[75]Id. at 4.

[76]"Policy" is a species of lottery whereby the chance is determined by numbers—"the numbers game."

[77]Mrs. Mapp was tried for possession of the policy material and discharged.

[78]"No person shall knowingly . . . have in his possession or under his control an obscene, lewd, or lascivious book [or]...picture....

Whoever violates this section shall be fined not less than two hundred nor more than two thousand dollars or imprisoned not less than one nor more than seven years, or both."

[79]Ohio v. Mapp, 170 Ohio St. 427, 166 N.E.2d 387 (1960).

[80]Ohio v. Lindway, 131 Ohio St. 166, 2 N.E.2d 490, cert. denied, 299 U.S. 506 (1936).

[81]Supra note 55. See notes 55-64 and related text, supra.

[82]Breithaupt v. Abram, supra note 64; Irvine v. California, supra note 61.

[83]361 U.S. 147 (1959). The majority of the Supreme Court of Ohio said:

"Under our statute as now worded, mere possession is forbidden where the possessor does not have a purpose of again looking at the books or pictures; and, in the instant case, the jury could have found the defendant guilty and she could have been (as she was) sentenced as a felon, even though it believed her evidence that she had innocently acquired possession of these articles, had no intention of ever looking at them again and was merely keeping them pending instructions for their disposition from their owner. Cf., Lambert v. California, 355 U.S. 255 [1957]....

[I]f anyone looks at a book and finds it lewd, he is forthwith, under this legislation, guilty of a serious crime, which may involve a sentence to the penitentiary similar to the one given to this defendant." Ohio v. Mapp, supra note 79, at 432-33, 166 N.E.2d at 390-91.

[84]The constitutionality of this provision of the Ohio constitution was at no time challenged in the *Mapp* litigation. Although no case is squarely in point, a strong argument can be made that this provision is an unreasonable impediment to the protection of federal constitutional rights which state courts are bound to uphold. U.S. Const. art. VI, § 2. See People v. Western Union Tel. Co., 70 Colo. 90, 198 P.146 (1921).

[85]Final judgments or decrees rendered by the highest court of a State in which a decision could be had, may be reviewed by the Supreme Court as follows:

* * *

(2) By appeal, where is drawn in question the validity of a statute of any state on the ground of its being repugnant to the Constitution, treaties or laws of the United States, and the decision is in favor of its validity.

[86]Mapp v. Ohio, supra note 42, 646-51, 657-58.

[87]Id. at 661-62.

[88]Id. at 666, 669-70.

[89]Id. at 672, 674, 676-77. At the very least, setting the case down for reargument would not have left such a vacuum in place of *Wolf*. Preconceptions of the Justices, even in this conceptual and somewhat subjective area of constitutional law, and the arguable inevitability of the demise of *Wolf*, could not take the place of informed argument directed to the issues ruled upon.

[90]Id. at 672.

[91]367 U.S. at 651, 653.

[92]Id. at 651.

[93]See Elkins v. United States, supra note 68, at 216-23, for the most recent examination of the bases for the exclusionary rule before *Mapp*.

[94]For example, the training and attitude of the police are relevant. (Indeed one might hope that the imposition of the exclusionary rule would necessitate an improvement in these very factors.) The general public morality also would influence the effectiveness of the rule of exclusion.

[95]In Justice Clark's words in *Mapp*, supra note 42, at 659, "Nor can it lightly be assumed that, as practical matter, adoption of the exclusionary rule fetters law enforcement. Only last year this Court expressly considered that contention and found that 'pragmatic evidence of a sort' to the contrary was not wanting. Elkins v. United States. . . ."

[96]See Justice Murphy's dissent in Wolf v. Colorado, 388 U.S. 25 (1949): "Alternatives are deceptive. Their very statement conveys the impression that one possibility is as effective as the next. In this case their statement is blinding. For there is but one alternative to the rule of exclusion. That is no sanction at all." Id. at 41.

"Self-scrutiny is a lofty ideal, but its exaltation reaches new heights if we expect a District Attorney to prosecute himself or his associates for well-meaning violations of the search and seizure clause during a raid the District Attorney or his associates have ordered." Id. at 42.

Justice Murphy showed the hopelessness of relying on the trespass action for damages. Id. at 42-44.

See also Kamisar, supra note 47, at 1150 n.238.

Monroe v. Pape, 365 U.S. 167 (1961), supra notes 51, 53, provides no practical exception to the statement in the text. The Supreme Court in that case, while holding a cause of action for damages to exist under the Civil Rights Act for violation of fourth amendment rights, also held that no action lay against the city government which sanctioned the abuse of those rights. Id. at 191. The petitioners, provided they could meet their burden of proof, would be left only with a judgment for money damages against the individual police officers who had abused their rights. Relieving those to whom the officers are responsible of liability thus has a much lessened deterrent effect. Such a right of action, however, unlike the exclusionary rule, provides a remedy, meager though it might be, for those for whom the unconstitutional search does not result in criminal prosecution. See Cohen v. Norris. 300 F.2d 24 (9th Cir. 1962); United States v. Cooney, 217 F. Supp. 417 (D. Colo. 1963). See also Monroe v. Pape, 221 F. Supp. 635 (N.D. Ill. 1963), where the jury returned a not-so-meager verdict of $13,000 in favor of James & Flossie Monroe in their suit against the five remaining police officer defendants.

[97]Justice Harlan, dissenting in Mapp v. Ohio, 367 U.S. 643 (1961), similarly gives no answer to the fact that the fourth amendment protection, left with these inadequate remedies and without exclusion, becomes merely an abstraction, when he asserts that the federal remedy of exclusion is not a part of the core of the fourth amendment extended to the states in *Wolf*. Id. at 678-79.

[98]Id. at 651.

[99]See notes 33-35 and related text supra.

[100]See Justice Harlan's recital of the fact that the issue of inadmissibility of illegally state-obtained evidence "appears on an average of about fifteen times per Term just in the *in forma pauperis* cases summarily disposed of by us." Mapp v. Ohio, supra note 97, at 676.

[101]Id. at 657. This incessant press of cases before the Court also seems to have convinced Justice Black of the necessity of exclusion. "[W]ith the more thorough understanding of the problem brought on by recent cases," id. at 622, and in combination "with the Fifth Amendment's ban against compelled self-incrimination, a constitutional basis emerges which not only justifies but actually requires the exclusionary rule." Ibid.

[102]Id. at 659.

[103]Ibid.

[104]This is not to say, however, that the Court should disregard the question of administrability of its rulings, as that factor might affect a decision in a particular case. This question is critically important in *Mapp*. See the discussion in subsections B and D of this section.

[105]Happily, both the majority and the dissenting opinions recognized this truth and the *Mapp* decision has put an end to this practice by putting an end to the debate. The majority: ". . . not basically relevant to the constitutional consideration...." Mapp v. Ohio, supra note 97, at 653. The dissent: "But in any case surely all this is beside the point. . . ." Id. at 680. Justice Harlan still seems to miss the point, however, when he notes, "the relevance of the disparity of views among the States . . . lies simply in the fact that the judgment involved is a debatable one." Ibid. The fact is that the "disparity of views" may reflect on the part of those states rejecting the exclusionary rule a preoccupation with convicting criminals to the detriment of constitutional rights, and not necessarily a belief that exclusion is not required to maintain judicial integrity or to make the constitutional right more than "an empty promise."

[106]Id. at 657, 658.

[107]Rea v. United States, 350 U.S. 214 (1956) (But cf., Wilson v. Schnettler, 365 U.S. 381 (1961)); Elkins v. United States, supra note 68.

[108]For examples of this type of cooperation see Kamisar, Wolf and Lustig Ten Years Later: Illegal State Evidence in State and Federal Courts, 43 Minn. L. Rev. 1083, 1165-90 (1959). Prof. Kamisar's enumeration of the collaborative efforts of state and federal officials in his article are, of course, directed toward his plea for an elimination of the silver platter doctrine, finally overruled by *Elkins*, but it takes only the smallest leap of the imagination to contemplate the cooperation which must also exist in the other direction—toward conviction in state courts for federal crimes. See, particularly, id. at 1188-90.

[109]256 U.S. 465 (1921). See note 17 supra.

[110]Sackler v. Sackler, 224 N.Y.S.2d 790 (N.Y. Sup. Ct., Kings County, 1962) (husband seeking divorce in the New York courts cannot establish his wife's adultery by evidence he procured through unreasonable search and seizure).

"While *Mapp* is no authority for the proposition that the State and Federal Constitutions offer safeguards against actions of private individuals, it surely does point the way to a re-examination of those very same rights protected by the statutory law of this state.... For, it seems to me, *Mapp* does give rise to the reasonable inference that if states may no longer accept evidence which tends to 'flout the insolence of office'... despite the salutary need to protect society against crime, that evidence of invasion of privacy by nonofficials should also be rejected even in private litigation."

Id. at 792. This case has been reversed, however. See 229 N.Y.S.2d 61 (2d Dept. 1962), criticized, 48 Cornell L.Q. 345 (1963).

[111]Supra note 97, at 648, 656.

[112]Indeed this has been the result in some jurisdictions which have adopted the exclusionary rule. See Prof. Kamisar's excellent discussion of the history after the rule's adoption in California. Supra note 108, at 1145-58, particularly at 1158.

[113]People v. Defore, 242 N.Y. 13, 21, 150 N.E. 585, 587 (1926).

[114]See, e.g., People v. Cahan, 44 Cal. 2d 434, 282 P.2d 905 (1955) (microphones installed, forcible entries made, with permission first being obtained from the Los Angeles Chief of Police); Irvine v. California, 347 U.S. 128 (1954) supra notes 61-64 and related text.

[115]But cf., Monroe v. Pape, supra notes 51, 53, 97.

[116]Pilot Studies of the American Bar Foundation's Survey of the Administration of Criminal Justice in the United States; noted in Allen, Federalism and the Fourth Amendment: A Requiem For Wolf, 1961 Sup. Ct. Rev. 1, 32 n.169 (U. of Chi.). Much of what is lightly sketched in this paragraph is reported in greater detail by Prof. Allen, id. at 38-39, and by Kamisar, supra note 108, at 1155 n.250.

[117]Barrett, Exclusion of Evidence Obtained by Illegal Searches—A Comment on *People v. Cahan*, 43 Cal. L. Rev. 565, 586 (1955). For an excellent presentation of all shades of opinion on the policy considerations with regard to the exclusionary rule, see the collection of articles edited by Sowle, Police Power and Individual Freedom 75-128 (1962).

[118]Wolf v. Colorado, supra note 96, at 40 (Black, J., concurring).

[119]Mapp v. Ohio, supra note 97, at 655. In further illustration of the constitutional character of the exclusionary rule, Justice Clark noted that "it was logically and *constitutionally* necessary that the exclusion doctrine—an essential part of the right to privacy—be also insisted upon as an essential ingredient of the right newly recognized by the Wolf case." Id. at 655-56 (emphasis added).

[120]See supra notes 33-35 and related text.

[121]People v. Cahan, supra note 114.

[122]Rehearing denied, 368 U.S. 871 (1961).

[123]E.g., compare People v. Bock Leung Chew. 142 Cal. App. 2d 400, 298 P.2d 118 (1956), with Johnson v. United States, 333 U.S. 10 (1948), where the California court expressly refused to follow the federal standard for probable cause for arrest and search. See also People v. Berger, 44 Cal. 2d 459, 462-64, 282 P.2d 509, 511-12 (1955), 44 Cal. L. Rev. 164 (1956), where the pre-trial motion to suppress was discouraged. This procedure was required by Weeks v. United States, 232 U.S. 383, 396 (1914), and the requirement is mitigated only slightly in rule 41(e) of the Federal Rules of Criminal Procedure. See also note 132 infra and accompanying text.

[124]"In developing a rule of evidence applicable in the state courts, this court is not bound by the decisions that have applied the federal rule, and if it appears that those decisions have developed needless refinements and distinctions, this court need not follow them....Under these circumstances the adoption of the exclusionary rule need not introduce confusion into the law of criminal procedure. Instead it opens the door to the development of workable rules governing searches and seizures and the issuance of warrants that will protect both the rights guaranteed by the constitutional provisions and the interest of society in the suppression of crime."
People v. Cahan, supra note 114 at 450-51, 282 P.2d at 915 (1955).

[125]See People v. DuBois, 221 N.Y.S.2d, 21 (Queens County Ct. Oct. 24, 1961) and related text infra.

[126]Brown v. Mississippi, 297 U.S. 278 (1936).

[127]See note 17 supra.

[128]Justice Frankfurter's comments, dissenting in Elkins v. United States, 364 U.S. 206 (1960), are applicable if one assumes that it is the federal rule that *Mapp* imposes on the states:
"What the Court now decides is that these variegated judgments, these fluctuating and uncertain views of what constitutes an "unreasonable search" under the Fourth Amendment in conduct by federal officials, are to determine whether what is done by state police . . . violates the Due Process Clause."
Id. at 239. The Justice backed up his assertion of the "fluctuating and uncertain views" of the Supreme Court with a string of contradicting citations. Ibid.

[129]374 U.S. 23 (1963).

[130]Id. at 25.

[131]Id. at 30-31.

[132]See People v. Maddox, 46 Cal. 2d 301, 294 P.2d 6, cert. denied, 352 U.S. 858 (1956). Quoted in Ker v. California, supra note 129, at 39-40.

[133]Id. at 40.

[134]357 U.S. 301 (1958).

[135]The eight Justices might have been able to agree on the requirement of announcement of authority and purpose by the arresting officer as exemplified in Masiello v. United States, 317 F.2d 121 (D.C. Cir. 1963) (Arresting officers with experience in the numbers racket were justified in breaking through a door to execute a search warrant after a delay of only twenty to fifty seconds after knocking, under 18 U.S.C. § 3109 (1958)). The same statute was involved in *Miller*, and a holding similar to *Masiello* would have required reversal in *Ker*. But a procedure such as in *Masiello* would seem to have had more constitutional validity than the surreptitious use of a pass key.

[136]Ker v. California, supra note 129, at 31.

[137]Id. at 31-32.

[138]Id. at 33-34.

[139]This question is not foreclosed by *Elkins*, see supra notes 68-73 and related text, since there the Court seemed to base its decision primarily on "the Court's supervisory power over the administration of criminal justice in the federal courts." Id. at 216. See Ralph v. Peppersack, 218 F. Supp. 932, 937-38 (D. Md. 1963).

[140]E.g., for the recent holding that states must now provide counsel for indigents in all cases and not just those for capital offenses, a state of affairs which has been long true in the federal sphere—Johnson v. Zerbst, 304 U.S. 458 (1938)—see, Gideon v. Wainwright, 372 U.S. 335 (1963).

[141]41 U.S. (16 Pet.) 1 (1842).

[142]"The powers not delegated to the United States by the Constitution, nor prohibited by it to the States, are reserved to the States respectively or to the people."

[143]Mapp v. Ohio, supra note 97, at 657-58, quoting Elkins v. United States, supra note 128, at 221.

[144]See text preceding note 119 supra.

[145]Mapp v. Ohio, supra note 97, at 656.

[146]Id. at 657. . . .

[147]This distinction with respect to the invasion of privacy without threat of criminal prosecution and that invasion of privacy for the express purpose of obtaining incriminating evidence, though perhaps not fully realized by the Supreme Court, is evident from three recent cases: Ohio ex rel. Eaton v. Price, 364 U.S. 263 (1960); Abel v. United States, 362 U.S. 217 (1960); Frank v. Maryland, 359 U.S. 360 (1959). The searches (or attempted searches) in each of these cases were conducted with a view to civil or quasi-civil proceedings rather than criminal—the interest sought to be protected, as presented to the Court, was the pure right of privacy and not criminal consequences which might result from evidence found by the invasion thereof. In each case, the search was not

held unconstitutional. See Note, 28 U. of Chi. L. Rev. 664, 667-74 (1961).

148Brown v. Mississippi, 297 U.S. 278 (1936).

149Ward v. Texas, 316 U.S. 547 (1942); Lisenba v. California, 314 U.S. 219 (1941); Chambers v. Florida, 309 U.S. 227 (1940).

150Brown v. Allen, 344 U.S. 443 (1953); Watts v. Indiana, 338 U.S. 49 (1949); Ashcraft v. Tennessee, 322 U.S. 143 (1944).

151McNabb v. United States, 318 U.S. 332 (1943). See also Mallory v. United States, 354 U.S. 449 (1957); Upshaw v. United States, 335 U.S. 410 (1948); United States v. Mitchell, 322 U.S. 65 (1944).

152Fed. R. Crim. P. 5(a).

153Brown v. Allen, supra note 151; Gallegos v. Nebraska, 342 U.S. 55 (1951).

154Mapp v. Ohio, 367 U.S. 643, 656-57 (1961).

155Id. at 683 (dissenting opinion).

156Id. at 684.

157Id. at 685.

158See notes 91-101 and related text supra.

159See notes 111, 112 and related text supra.

160McNabb v. United States, supra note 151, at 343-44.

161Cases cited note 153 supra.

162See Williams v. United States, 341 U.S. 97 (1951) (conviction under § 20 of the Civil Rights Act, 18 U.S.C. § 242 (1958), affirmed where defendant subjected a person suspected of crime "to force and violence in order to obtain a confession").

163This deterrent element has not been totally absent from the confession cases even before *Mapp.* Ashcraft v. Tennessee, supra note 150; Malinski v. New York, 324 U.S. 401 (1945). See United States ex rel. Clinton v. Denno, 309 F.2d 543 (2d Cir. Nov. 1, 1962). "Perhaps Mapp v. Ohio . . . may suggest a trend in the Court toward an extension of the federal [McNabb-Mallory] rule to state proceedings. . . . If the principle is thus to be extended it is more seemly that it be done by the Supreme Court than attempted by us." d. at 545.

164Silverthorne Lumber Co. v. United States, 251 U.S. 385, 391-92 (1920); Wong Sun v. United States, 371 U.S. 471 (Jan. 14, 1963) (both verbal and tangible evidence must be excluded if either is the "fruit" of an unauthorized arrest or search, see Note, 31 GEO. WASH. L. REV. 851 (1963)).

Such an extention of the "poisonous tree" doctrine to a post-arraignment confession excluded from the trial as the "fruit" of a prior illegal confession obtained in violation of Fed. R. Crim. P. 5(a) has been made by the Court of Appeals for the District of Columbia Circuit. Killough v. United States, 315 F.2d 241 (D.C. Cir. Oct. 4, 1962). See Note, 31 GEO. WASH. L. REV. 855 (1963). But this same court has refused to exclude the testimony of a *witness* whose identity was learned during a period of illegal detention. Smith v. United States, 32 U.S.L. Week 2147 (D.C. Cir. Sept. 26, 1963).

16548 Stat. 1103 (1934), 47 U.S.C. § 605 (1958): "[N]o person not being authorized by the sender shall intercept any communication and divulge or publish the existence, contents, substance, purport, effect or meaning of such intercepted communication to any person...."

166See Bradley & Hogan, Wiretapping: From Nardone to Benanti and Rathbun, 46 Geo.L.J. 418, 425-34 (1958) (see particularly the comparison at 430-31).

167Compare Nardone (I) v. United States, 302 U.S. 379 (1937), with Weeks v. United States, 232 U.S. 383 (1914). See notes 10-17 and related text supra.

168Compare Nardone (II) v. United States, 308 U.S. 338 (1939), with Silverthorne Lumber Co. v. United States, 251 U.S. 385 (1920). See note 17 supra.

169Compare Schwartz v. Texas, 344 U.S. 199 (1952), with Wolf v. Colorado, 338 U.S. 25 (1949). See notes 17-47 and related text supra.

170Compare Goldstein v. United States, 316 U.S. 114 (1942), with Schenck v. United States, 249 U.S. 47 (1919). See note 17 supra.

171Compare Benanti v. United States, 355 U.S. 96 (1957), with Elkins v. United States, 364 U.S. 206 (1960). See notes 68-73 and related text supra. Note that this is the only rule of evidence with respect to wiretapping which antedated the corresponding rule in the search and seizure area.

172Supra note 169.

173Id. at 201.

174Supra note 171.

175365 U.S. 458 (1961).

176N.Y. Const. art. I, § 12; N.Y. Code Crim. Proc. § 813(a) (1942).

177342 U.S. 117 (1951). See notes 48-54 and related text supra.

178See notes 52-54 and related text supra.

179Kamisar, Book Review, 76 HARV. L. REV. 1502, 1508 n.22 (1962). The disclosures reported by Prof. Kamisar concerning "arrests for investigation" in the District of Columbia may well be indicative of the invalidity of the claimed necessity of state law enforcement officials to continue the use of unconstitutionally seized evidence.

Selection *16*

The Sixth Amendment and the Law of the Land

Justice Tom C. Clark

Justice Clark offered this concise survey of the then current state of "right to counsel" to the faculty and students of the Saint Louis University School of Law. As a Justice of the Supreme Court, he occasionally avoided the specific commitment that academic commentators could afford, because some of the points he raised would still be coming before the Court for decision in future cases. Since Justice Clark wrote his survey, the Supreme Court has handed down two decisions that seem to extend the right to counsel to an extremely early point in the police investigation—well before an arrest is actually made—and to render inadmissible into evidence the confessions of those taken into custody who have not been informed of their right to be advised by a lawyer and to remain silent.*

The underlying problem of right to counsel is worth consideration. In some ways an accused person needs counsel most while in the state of panic or uncertainty he experiences at the time of arrest. The first thing nearly every lawyer tells an arrested person is not to answer any questions; but since criminals rarely choose to commit their crimes in front of an audience, information and/or confessions gained in early interrogation often seem essential to the efficient apprehension of criminals. The security of our person and property depends on this efficiency. An exchange of slogans about fundamental freedoms and the rising crime rate will not solve this dilemma. We are just now beginning to gather evidence on whether the rate of convictions and the efficiency of the police more generally is increased or reduced by the new decisions. The reader should be cautioned that purely speculative statements by police officials and prosecutors are not evidence. What we know so far suggests that the criminal has no particular cause to rejoice.

"Ye shall have one manner of law, as well for the stranger as for one of your own country."[1]

Evolving "one manner of law" from the Sixth Amendment's "assistance of counsel" clause has been as slow as Job's Tortoise and twice as tough. This article deals with the historical basis of "right to counsel" in our law, the development of the cases, and the future outlook since *Douglas v. California*,[2] and *Gideon v. Wainwright*.[3]

EARLY HISTORY

The recognition of the right to counsel cannot be predicated upon the common law. In England one charged with a felony was originally denied the aid of counsel. Not until 1836 did Parliament grant the full right of counsel in felony cases, although such right had existed in treason cases for almost 150 years.[4] As early as 1769 Blackstone assailed the practice of denial of counsel, declaring in his First Edition, "upon what face of reason can that assistance be denied to save the life of a man, which yet is allowed him in prosecutions for every petty trespass [a civil action]."[5] The

"The Sixth Amendment and the Law of the Land" by Justice Tom C. Clark, 8 *St. Louis University Law Journal* 1 (1963). Reprinted by permission.
*See *Massiah* v. *United States*, 377 U.S. 201 (1964), *Escobedo* v. *Illinois*, 378 U.S. 478 (1964); *Miranda* v. *Arizona*, 86 S. Ct. 1602 (1966).

theory behind denial of counsel was that the court itself would defend the accused. But this made an advocate of the court, depriving it of objectivity and often reducing it to an object of derision. It reminds me of the retort of counsel to an activist judge who insisted on examining witnesses with vigor. As the judge continued the interruption, counsel objected and upon being overruled said, "All right, your honor, but I hope that you don't lose the case for me."

The American Colonies took a more enlightened view of right to counsel than the Mother Country, guaranteeing this right at an earlier date. Maryland, Massachusetts, Delaware, Connecticut, Georgia, New Hampshire, New York and Pennsylvania did so by specific constitutional provision. (The Pennsylvania Colonial Charter of 1701 had a like provision.) North Carolina, South Carolina, Virginia and Rhode Island specifically permitted the assistance of counsel in criminal cases by comprehensive statutory enactments.

THE DEVELOPMENT UP TO BETTS V. BRADY

The Federal Courts have always recognized the right of a litigant to the assistance of counsel. They, of course, have been bound by the provision of the Sixth Amendment requiring that "[i]n all criminal prosecutions, the accused shall enjoy the right...to have the Assistance of Counsel for his defense."[6] The Supreme Court has enforced the Sixth Amendment requirement rigidly. *Johnson v. Zerbst*,[7] orders the appointment of counsel for indigents in all criminal cases. The command of the Sixth Amendment is further implemented by Rule 44 of the Federal Rules of Criminal Procedure, adopted in 1946. It provides:

"If the defendant appears in court without counsel, the court shall advise him of his right to counsel and assign counsel to represent him at every stage of the proceeding unless he elects to proceed without counsel or is able to obtain counsel."[8]

On the other hand, prior to *Gideon*, hereafter considered, no provision of the Federal Constitution had been held by the Court to specifically guarantee an accused the right to counsel in a state prosecution. The bare fact is that although the right of an accused to counsel was but a logical corollary of his constitutional right to a hearing, the contrary practice was common, partly because of the broad language of *Hurtado v. California*.[9] There, in denying the claim that state prosecutions must begin by indictment, the Court

said that the due process clause of the Fourteenth Amendment referred to the "law of the land in each state,"[10] while the Fifth Amendment's due process clause referred to the "law of the land which derives its authority from the legislative powers conferred upon Congress by the Constitution of the United States, exercised within the limits therein prescribed, and interpreted according to the principles of the common law."[11] The Court reasoned that since the Fourteenth Amendment, as contrasted with the Fifth, does not embody a declaration requiring a grand jury, it was not a purpose of the Fourteenth to perpetuate the institution of grand jury in the states. This result remains the law today. But, as the sole dissenter, Mr. Justice Harlan, indicated, this imparted one manner of law for the federal courts and another one for the states because it provided "one thing with reference to the powers of the States, and another with reference to the powers of the general government."[12] A number of states, sensing this anomalous situation as to the right to counsel, had by constitutional provision or statute, required the appointment of counsel in felony cases. Indiana had done so over thirty years before, as evidenced by this language of its Supreme Court in *Webb v. Baird*:[13]

"It is not to be thought of, in a civilized community, for a moment, that any citizen put in jeopardy of life or liberty, should be debarred of counsel because he was too poor to employ such aid. No Court could be respected, or respect itself, to sit and hear such a trial."

But it was little more than a dozen years later that the same dissenter, Justice Harlan, wrote for the Court the opinion in *Chicago, Burlington & Quincy R.R. v. Chicago*.[14] The irony of it was that, through this case he began the undermining of the holding in *Hurtado*. The railroad case concerned the Fifth Amendment's command that private property should not be taken without just compensation. This requirement was held applicable to states in an opinion that enlarged the holding of *Scott v. McNeal*.[15] It completely undermined *Hurtado*, but without overruling it, and was followed by *Smyth v. Ames*,[16] *Norwood v. Baker*,[17] and *San Diego Land & Town Co. v. National City*.[18] These cases laid the basis for the free speech and press decisions that began with *Gitlow v. New York*.[19] The amazing thing to many people was that the First Amendment language "Congress shall make no law" was held by the Court to have been embraced by the due process clause of the Fourteenth Amendment as a prohibition against the states. Seven years later the Court specifically took notice of the broad language of the *Hurtado* decision in the landmark case of *Powell v. Alabama*.[20] It held that the right to counsel was of such fundamental character that it too was "embraced" in the due process clause. The Court said that:

"[t]he rule laid down [in *Hurtado*] is not without exceptions. The rule is an aid to construction, and in some instances may be conclusive; but it must yield to more compelling considerations whenever such considerations exist. The fact that the right involved is of such a character that it cannot be denied without violating those "fundamental principles of liberty and justice which lie at the base of all our civil and political institutions" (*Herbert v. Louisiana*, 272 U.S. 312, 316), is obviously one of those compelling considerations which must prevail in determining whether it is embraced within the due process clause of the Fourteenth Amendment, although it be specifically dealt with in another part of the federal Constitution."[21]

But the Court was not ready to say that even as to capital cases the Sixth Amendment's right to counsel provision was "absorbed" by the Fourteenth Amendment. This is clearly pointed out by the Court's reference to and quotation of the following passage of Mr. Justice Moody in his opinion for the Court in *Twining v. New Jersey*:[22]

"[i]t is possible that some of the personal rights safeguarded by the first eight Amendments against National action may also be safeguarded against state action, because a denial of them would be a denial of due process of law. *Chicago, Burlington & Quincy Railroad v. Chicago*, 166 U.S. 266. If this is so, it is not because those rights are enumerated in the first eight Amendments, but because they are of such a nature that they are included in the conception of due process of law."

This language is, of course, contrary to the theory of some [notably Mr. Justice Black] that the due process clause of the Fourteenth Amendment "absorbed" the Bill of Rights against state action. However, only five years later the absorption doctrine was applied to the free speech, press, assembly and right to counsel (in capital cases) provisions of the Bill of Rights. *Palko v. Connecticut*,[23] specifically provided that:

"In these and other situations immunities that are valid as against the federal government by force of the specific pledge of particular amendments have been found to be implicit in the concept of ordered liberty, and thus through the Fourteenth

Amendment, become valid as against the states ...[as having] been taken over from the earlier articles of the federal bill of rights and brought within the Fourteenth Amendment by a process or absorption."[24]

In *Betts v. Brady*,[25] the Court made certain that the *Powell* rule only applied to capital cases, saying that in other cases the "appoint of counsel is not a fundamental right, essential to a fair trial."[26]

THE 1963 REVOLUTION

Again and again thereafter the Court refused to alter the rule. Only where it found "special circumstances" did it undercut it and then only on an *ad hoc* basis, indicating "the factors which may render state criminal proceedings without counsel so apt to result in injustice as to violate the Fourteenth Amendment."[27] A long line of "special exceptions"[28] covered twenty-one years, and consequently *Betts v. Brady* was not overruled until *Gideon v. Wainwright*,[29] 109 years after Indiana had adopted its constitutional rule and seventy-nine years after *Hurtado*. Gideon, an indigent charged with a felony, appeared for trial in a Florida court and asked that counsel be appointed to represent him. The court answered:

"Mr. Gideon, I am sorry, but I cannot appoint Counsel to represent you in this case. Under the laws of the State of Florida, the only time the Court can appoint Counsel to represent a Defendant is when that person is charged with a capital offense. I am sorry, but I will have to deny your request to appoint Counsel to defend you in this case."[30]

On petition for habeas corpus to the Supreme Court of Florida, Gideon attacked his conviction on the ground that the trial court's refusal to appoint counsel denied him "rights guaranteed by the Constitution and the Bill of Rights of the United States Government." That court "upon consideration thereof" denied him relief.

This is not to say the Florida courts were insensible to the safeguards of due process or that their judges were more casehardened than were their Indiana brethren. Florida was but following the cases of this Court since *Betts v. Brady*. But the ruling in *Gideon* unanimously reversed this former thinking. The Court held that a "provision of the Bill of Rights which is fundamental and essential to a fair trial is made obligatory upon the states by the Fourteenth Amendment."[31] It concluded that the Sixth Amendment's guarantee of counsel was one of these fundamental rights. It has now joined "the First Amendment's freedoms of speech, press, religion, assembly, association, and petition for redress of grievances..., the Fifth Amendment's command that private property shall not be taken for public use without just compensation, the Fourth Amendment's prohibition of unreasonable searches and seizures, and the Eighth's ban on cruel and unusual punishment"[32] as being obligatory upon and enforceable against the states by the Fourteenth Amendment.

There is much speculation on the extent of the coverage of the *Gideon* ruling. Since last March I have attended several state judicial conferences and seminars and *Gideon* was always one of the topics for discussion. It is an important case, but its impact on the states should not cause too heavy a burden. Thirty-five states had already provided for the appointment of counsel in felony cases. The remainder either led the matter within the discretion of the trial court, required counsel only in capital cases, or made no express provision. Some statements in *Gideon* might give pause to courts in these states, viz.:

"[R]eason and reflection require us to recognize that in our adversary system of criminal justice, *any person haled into court,* who is too poor to hire a lawyer, cannot be assured a fair trial unless counsel is provided for him. This seems to us to be an obvious truth."[33] [Emphasis supplied.]

And note the reference of Mr. Justice Harlan in his concurrence:

"The special circumstances rule has been formally abandoned in capital cases, and the time has now come when it should be similarly *abandoned in non-capital cases,* [emphasis supplied] at least as to offenses which, as the one involved here, carry the possibility of a substantial prison sentence. (Whether the rule should extend to *all* criminal cases need not now be decided.)"[34]

There is one other area in which the Court has said that counsel is required. In the case of *Douglas v. California,*[35] decided the same day as *Gideon,* the Court held that in the *"first appeal,* granted as a matter of right to rich and poor alike," an indigent is entitled to a review "at which the claims have once been presented by a lawyer and passed upon by an appellate court."[36] To hold otherwise would be an "invidious discrimination" the Court said. However, pains were taken to point out that the rule as announced covered *"the one and only appeal* an indigent has as of right."[37] Whether counsel must be provided

where an indigent seeks a discretionary hearing after disposition of his first appeal of right, the Court said "[w]e need not now decide."[38] This brought state procedure in line with that of the federal system as required by *Johnson v. United States,*[39] and *Ellis v. United States,*[40] *i.e.,* "The federal courts must honor his (the indigent's) request for counsel regardless of what they think the merits of the case may be."[41] This holding may place, as I said in my dissent in the *Douglas* case, "an intolerable burden on the State's judicial machinery."[42] Few of the states have required counsel in frivolous appeals. In California the intermediate appellate court was required to make "an independent investigation of the record and determine whether it would be of advantage to the defendant or helpful to the appellate court to have counsel appointed."[43] Despite this requirement the Court held that counsel must be appointed. And since *Douglas* the Court has handed down another case which not only appears to be an extension of *Douglas,* but also of *Griffin v. Illinois.*[44] In the case of *Draper v. Washington* the Court's conclusion was:

"We hold today that the conclusion of the trial judge that an indigent's appeal is frivolous [despite a hearing and detail findings to this effect] is a similarly inadequate substitute for the full appellate review available to nonindigents in Washington, when the effect of that finding is to prevent an appellate examination based upon a sufficiently complete record of the trial proceedings themselves."[45]

The Court has gone no further in elaborating upon the scope and coverage of the right to counsel. However, we shall now consider some of the other possible areas and reaches of *Gideon.*

ASSIGNED COUNSEL AND THE INDIGENT

The constitutional right of an indigent to the assistance of counsel includes the right to be informed by the court of the existence of such right; to be offered the assignment of counsel or, if he wishes to be afforded ample opportunity to secure his own counsel. The Sixth Amendment cannot be satisfied by the mere formal assignment of counsel. *Powell v. Alabama* requires the assignment of counsel *at such time* as will afford a defendant *"effective aid* in the *preparation* and trial of the case."[46] [Emphasis supplied.] This includes a reasonable opportunity for the accused and his counsel to confer and prepare their defense.[47] The requirement as to "preparation" is highlighted in a recent case of the Court of Appeals of the District of Columbia, *Greenwell v. United States.*[48] Greenwell's court-appointed counsel wished to conduct certain investigation in Dallas as to the arrest of the defendant, the search of certain premises there and the recovery of the stolen money allegedly taken from a District of Columbia bank. The court refused this request which was made under Rule 17 of the Federal Rules of Criminal Procedure. It also denied an application to take depositions (Rule 15) and to subpoena certain individuals (a cell mate who could testify to the facial appearance of defendant after being questioned by the police; some newspaper reporters who could testify as to the voluntariness of a confession and the jail records of a photograph taken of the defendant at the time he was booked). While none of these situations would occur in the typical state case, it does show the extent to which the "preparation" requirement may be taken.

The paramount question disturbing the state courts is whether the *Gideon* and *Douglas* rulings are retrospective. The Court has not expressed itself on this specific point. However, since the rule is a constitutional one, it may be that the question would be governed by our opinions holding that the right of an indigent to a sufficiently full record of the proceedings is retrospective.[49] Whether the accused must raise the point at trial is moot but indications in *Norvell v. Illinois*[50] support a conclusion that it must be raised. There the Court took pains to point out: "We do not say that petitioner, having had a lawyer, could be found to have waived his rights on appeal. We only hold that a State...may without violation of the Due Process or Equal Protection Clause deny relief to those who, at the time of the trial, had a lawyer and who presumedly had his continuing services for purposes of appeal and yet failed to pursue an appeal."[51] The Court has also denied petitions for certiorari in search and seizure cases where the unreasonableness of the search was not raised at the trial or pursued on appeal.

A litigant may, of course, waive the appointment of counsel, and in such a case, the Sixth and Fourteenth Amendments neither justify nor require appointment of unwanted counsel.[52] However, to be effective, waiver must be made understandingly, intelligently, competently, voluntarily and with the considered approval of the court.[53] The court should make certain that the defendant understands the nature of the charges, the range of allowable punishment, possible defenses or circumstances in mitigation and other facets necessary for a complete understanding of what might result from a refusal to accept the assistance of counsel. In *Von Moltke v. Gillies*[54] the Court

struck down a waiver that is typical of many courtroom scenes. The judge called on a lawyer present in the courtroom to represent the defendant; upon the lawyer's reluctance to do so, the court assured him it would only take two or three minutes; the lawyer then asked the defendant if she understood the nature of the charge and upon receiving an affirmative reply suggested that she stand mute. The Michigan courts held that the plea of guilty that resulted was with the assistance of counsel. The U.S. Supreme Court, in reversing, pointed up the fact that the lawyer did not even read the indictment, inform the accused of the nature of the charges or possible defenses, or advise her of the possible punishment, all of which deprived the defendant of effective counsel. Even prior to *Von Moltke* the Court held in *Johnson v. Zerbst*[55] that an intelligent waiver also depends upon the particular facts and circumstances of the case and includes the background, experience and conduct of the defendant. Finally, the judge should remember this *caveat* from our cases: The primary duty to protect the accused in counsel cases rests on the trial judge.

Another question disturbing the state courts is what precedents control questions arising under these rights to counsel problems. From the rule laid down in *Ker v. California*[56] it appears logical to assume that the federal cases would govern. Let me emphasize that the Court has not passed on this question in the counsel cases; however, given the constitutional rule, *i.e.*, the Sixth Amendment, it is hard to arrive at any other conclusion.

The sixty-four dollar question is at what point in the procedure is an indigent entitled to the assignment of counsel? This difficulty plagues state judges all over the country. We do not have the space to devote more than a casual reference to it here. *Hamilton v. Alabama*[57] seems to point the way, holding that an accused is entitled to counsel at every "critical stage" of the proceeding. In concluding that arraignment in Maryland was "critical" the Court said: "What happens there may affect the whole trial. Available defenses may be as irretrievably lost, if not then and there asserted, as they are when an accused represented by counsel waives a right for strategic purposes....We do not stop to determine whether prejudice resulted."[58] The latest case on the point is *White v. Maryland.*[59] At the preliminary hearing in that case the accused pleaded guilty without the assistance of counsel. At arraignment, with counsel, he entered pleas of "not guilty" and "not guilty by reason of insanity." At trial the guilty plea made at the preliminary hearing was introduced into evidence, without objection. Maryland held the preliminary hearing not a critical stage of the proceeding. The Court reversed:

"Whatever may be the normal function of the 'preliminary hearing' under Maryland law, it was in *this case* [emphasis supplied] as 'critical' a stage as arraignment under Alabama law [*Hamilton v. Alabama, supra*]. For petitioner entered a plea before the magistrate and that plea was taken at a time when he had no counsel.

"We repeat what we said in *Hamilton v. Alabama, supra* at 55, that we do not stop to determine whether prejudice resulted: 'Only the presence of counsel could have enabled this accused to know all the defenses available to him and to plead intelligently.' "[60]

The reader can read this *per curiam* as intelligently as can I. However, what it says to my mind is that the "critical stage" is to be determined on a case by case basis. For example, in *Crooker v. California*[61] we made reference to the fact that coercion seems more likely to result from the state's denial of a specific request for opportunity to engage counsel than it does from the state's failure to appoint counsel immediately upon arrest. That greater possibility, however, is not decisive. It may be negated by the defendant's age, intelligence, experience and education. Crooker's one year of law study, which included a criminal law course, and other circumstances led the lower court to conclude that the failure of the police to honor his request for counsel was not an infringement of any constitutional right. But the Court warned:

"[S]tate refusal of a request to engage counsel violates due process not only if the accused is deprived of counsel at trial on the merits, *Chandler v. Fretag, supra*, [348 U.S. 3] but also if he is deprived of counsel for any part of the pretrial proceedings, provided that he is so prejudiced thereby as to infect his subsequent trial with an absence of "that fundamental fairness essential to the very concept of justice".... The latter determination necessarily depends upon all the circumstances of the case."[62]

It should be noted, however, that the Court overruled the contention that every state failure to honor a request for counsel would be a *per se* infringement of due process. It used these words: "Due process, a concept less rigid and more fluid than those envisaged in other specific and particular provisions of the Bill of Rights; *Betts v. Brady*, 316 U.S. 455, 462 (1942), demands no such rule."[63] However, since *Betts* has been overruled, who knows but that *Crooker* is also on the brink?[64]

CONCLUSION AND RECOMMENDATIONS

These new conditions impose new requirements on the courts—and likewise on the Bar and the law schools. It is to be hoped that the Bar and the law schools will assist state courts in the performance of them. As I pointed out in my Law Day speech at St. Louis University of April 20, 1963, the responsibility lies as much with the Bar and the law schools as it does with the courts. For the present the burden of assigned counsel will have to be shouldered by voluntary counsel. I suggest that the law schools install a legal internship program to assist the Bar and the courts. This could be done under the supervision of a professor and a committee of the local bar. Whenever an indigent is entitled to counsel the court would appoint the professor or a local practitioner to represent him. This assigned counsel would then use the law school internees to do the investigative work, briefing, etc. The student would appear in court with the assigned counsel and assist in defense to such degree as the court would permit. In addition, I have proposed that the law schools upgrade the teaching of the criminal law.[65] I am pleased to know that St. Louis University is now in the process of doing just this. The criminal law is our most important branch of practice because it deals with the life and liberties of the people. Still, very few lawyers are willing to try a criminal case, not wishing to get mixed up in that "dirty business." As a result, the Supreme Court itself is faced with a most serious problem. Over 1500 *in forma pauperis* cases are filed at the Court each year with only about 5% having counsel. In fact, quite a large percentage had no counsel at their trial, and those that did have representation often claim that it was not effective. The answer, I believe, lies with the law schools. They are able to instill in the student a sense of responsibility to the public, a desire to engage in the practice of the criminal law and a determination to assist their more unfortunate fellow citizens. This can be accomplished through emphasizing the importance of the study of criminal law and procedure and by exposing the student to some of its practice during law school as an intern.

The Ford Foundation, I understand, has made grants totalling over two and one-half million dollars for the extension and improvement of the legal defense of indigents, thus giving much needed emphasis to the legal aid effort which I feel is the most important in the history of our profession. Over two and a quarter million dollars of the money is going to the National Legal Aid and Defender Association to establish model defender services. "Matching fund" programs are also in the offing. It is to be hoped that in these model programs the law schools and the local bar associations will take a leading role. The project also will seek to promote the study and practice of the criminal law which today is the graveyard of the profession. As the announcement of Orrison S. Marden, Chairman of the Ford Foundation Advisory Committee, stated, "The participation of the law schools will be encouraged through fellowships, law student internships and faculty research. The aim is to attract better talent to the defense of the indigent and encourage law schools to strengthen curricula and research in criminal law." To this I say, "Amen," adding a fervent prayer of "more power" to Mr. Marden and his Committee.

I close with the hope that this short article has left the reader with a sparkened concern for the plight of the indigent defendant. May this concern lead to a greater interest in the administration of criminal justice and, in the end, light the way for future graduates to devote their careers to its modernization and improvement. This is imperative for the effective protection of our system of government. Moreover, an attorney owes his profession no less. Only then will people agree "that justice is the same whether due from one man to a million, or from a million to one man."[66]

Footnotes

[1]*Leviticus* 24:22, circa 700 B.C.
[2]372 U.S. 353 (1963).
[3]372 U.S. 335 (1963).
[4]1 COOLEY 8 ED. 698.
[5]4 BLACKSTONE 355.
[6]U.S. CONST. amend. VI.
[7]304 U.S. 458 (1938).
[8]FED. R. CRIM. P. 44.
[9]110 U.S. 516 (1884).
[10]*Id.* at 535.
[11]*Ibid.*
[12]*Id.* at 541.
[13]6 Ind. 13, 18 (1854).
[14]166 U.S. 226 (1897).
[15]154 U.S. 34 (1894).
[16]169 U.S. 466 (1898).
[17]172 U.S. 269 (1898).
[18]174 U.S. 739 (1899).
[19]268 U.S. 652 (1925).
[20]287 U.S. 45 (1932).
[21]*Id.* at 67.
[22]211 U.S. 78, 99 (1908).
[23]302 U.S. 319 (1937).
[24]*Id.* at 324-26.
[25]316 U.S. 455 (1942).

[26]*Id.* at 471.
[27]Cash v. Culver, 358 U.S. 633, 636 (1959).
[28]For examples of situations which can be labeled "special exceptions" to the *Powell* rule, see *Rice v. Olson,* 324 U.S. 786 (1945); *De Meerleek v. Michigan,* 329 U.S. 663 (1947); *Foster v. Illinois,* 332 U.S. 134 (1947); *Gayes v. New York,* 332 U.S. 145 (1947); *Bute v. Illinois,* 333 U.S. 640 (1948); *Wade v. Mayo,* 334 U.S. 672 (1948); *Gryger v. Burke,* 334 U.S. 728 (1948); *Townsend v. Burke,* 334 U.S. 736 (1948); *Uveges v. Pennsylvania,* 335 U.S. 437 (1948); *Gibbs v. Burke,* 337 U.S. 773 (1949); *Quicksall v. Michigan,* 339 U.S. 660 (1950); *Palmer v. Ashe,* 342 U.S. 134 (1951); *Massey v. Moore,* 348 U.S. 105 (1954); *Herman v. Claudy,* 350 U.S. 116 (1956); *Moore v. Michigan,* 355 U.S. 155 (1957); *McNeal v. Culver,* 365 U.S. 109 (1961); *Chewning v. Cunningham,* 368 U.S. 443 (1962); *Carnley v. Cochran,* 369 U.S. 506 (1962).
[29]372 U.S. 335 (1963).
[30]*Id.* at 337.
[31]*Id.* at 341.
[32]*Id.* at 341-42.
[33]*Id.* at 344.
[34]*Id.* at 351.
[35]*Id.* at 353.
[36]*Id.* at 356.
[37]*Id.* at 357.
[38]*Id.* at 358.
[39]352 U.S. 565 (1957).
[40]356 U.S. 674 (1958).
[41]Douglas v. California, 372 U.S. 353, 357 (1963).
[42]*Id.* at 359.
[43]People v. Hyde, 51 Cal. 2d 152, 154, 331 P.2d 42, 43 (1958).
[44]351 U.S. 12 (1956).
[45]372 U.S. 487, 499-500 (1963).
[46]287 U.S. 45, 71 (1932).
[47]Avery v. Alabama, 308 U.S. 444 (1940).
[48]317 F.2d 108 (D.C. Cir. 1963).
[49]See *Nowell v. Illinois,* 373 U.S. 420 (1963) which is buttressed by the holding of *Ker v. California,* 374 U.S. 23 (1963), involving the Fourth Amendment's prohibition against "unreasonable" search and seizure.
[50]373 U.S. 420 (1963).
[51]*Id.* at 423.
[52]Carter v. Illinois, 329 U.S. 173 (1946).
[53]Uveges v. Pennsylvania, 335 U.S. 437 (1948); Bute v. Illinois, 333 U.S. 640 (1948); Von Moltke v. Gillies, 332 U.S. 708 (1948).
[54]332 U.S. 708 (1948).
[55]304 U.S. 458 (1938).
[56]374 U.S. 23 (1963).
[57]368 U.S. 52 (1961).
[58]*Id.* at 54-55.
[59]373 U.S. 59 (1963).
[60]*Id.* at 60.
[61]357 U.S. 433 (1958).
[62]*Id.* at 439-440.
[63]357 U.S. 433, 441 (1958).
[64]See also Cicenia v. Lagay, 357 U.S. 504 (1958).
[65]See *The Student Lawyer,* June 1963, p. 5.
[66]Chisholm v. Georgia, 2 U.S. (2 Dall.) 419, 479 (1793).

Selection *17*

Equal Protection and the Indigent Defendant: Griffin and Its Progeny

Philip Fahringer

Many of the selections in this book seek to convince the reader and the courts that some specific policy, doctrine, or rule of decision should be adopted. A favorite tactic of lawyers in this respect is to confuse "is" with "ought." They choose the doctrine they think the court *ought* to use and then seek to show that it *is* the one the courts have been using all along and, therefore, ought to use in the future as well. The reader should pay particular attention to footnote 55 of this essay, where the cat begins to peek out of the bag. It is possible to read the cases as showing the Court to be not so much concerned with balancing the rights of the accused against the demands of efficient law enforcement; instead, the Court might be moving closer to a position of insisting on the absolute right for the accused to have all possible aid at every stage of the legal process.

Why not? Why should we balance a poor man's rights instead of giving him everything a rich man gets? We often complain that the poor man goes to jail and the rich man gets off in the end. Out of our great regard for human rights, our legal system contains nearly endless opportunities for delays and appeals. Much of our dissatisfaction with the differing treatment of rich and poor undoubtedly is caused by the specter of the rich gangster who, with endless sums for lawyers and litigation, manages to escape or at least delay his punishment, while the poor man goes directly to jail. This situation will not be cured by giving the poor man the same chance as the rich one to buy delay and evasion—this time with the taxpayers' money. Our legal system is really designed to work on the basis of the defendant of moderate means. He only makes appeals or adopts other legal tactics to the extent that the strength of his case warrants the expenditure. The system does not work well when dealing with the very rich, who can afford any maneuver so long as it has an infinitesimal chance of succeeding, or the very poor, who either cannot afford legal services even when they would be worth while or are given such services free by the state and so will want to use them to the full whether they are warranted or not. The notion of balancing is designed to say in legal language that we would like to treat the poor man as we treat the man of moderate means—not the rich man—giving him the legal services that are worth while—not every one he can possibly think of.

Few of our ideals are more venerable than is equal justice for rich and poor. The Old Testament exhorts us to espouse this ideal,[1] and it was codified in England during the Anglo-Saxon period. Magna Charta proclaimed that "to no one will we sell...right or justice." In the seventeenth century Locke argued that government must be "by promulgated established laws, not to be varied in particular cases, but to have one rule for rich and poor, for the favourite at court and the countryman at plough."[2] In America Benjamin Franklin pleaded for equal rights of men, "whatever Difference Time, Chance, or Industry may occasion in

"Equal Protection and the Indigent Defendant: Griffin and Its Progeny" by Philip Fahringer, 16 *Stanford Law Review* 394 (1964). Copyright 1964 by the Board of Trustees of the Leland Stanford Junior University. Reprinted by permission.

their circumstances."[3] The vast majority of our states included in their constitutions provisions adopting the ideal of equal justice for all, and United States Supreme Court Justices swear to "administer justice without respect to persons, and do equal right to the poor and to the rich...." Despite this heritage our law in many ways treats the poor man unfavorably,[4] and until fairly recent cases, notably *Griffin v. Illinois*,[5] the Supreme Court had given only hesitant relief in special circumstances to the state court indigent[6] criminal defendant.

In *Griffin*, where it had been conceded that a trial transcript was needed for adequate appellate review,[7] the Court held that a state could not deprive indigent defendants of adequate review of alleged trial errors solely because of their inability to pay the cost of a necessary transcript. An affirmative constitutional obligation to provide a transcript was thus placed upon the state whenever other means, such as a bystander's bill of exceptions, would not afford effective appellate review. Mr. Justice Black, writing for the prevailing four Justices,[8] stated that no "rational relationship" exists between ability to pay costs and the defendant's guilt or innocence and found that both the due process clause and the equal protection clause of the fourteenth amendment forbid such "invidious discriminations."[9] His opinion contained the broad assertion, fraught with implications for other situations in which wealthy criminal defendants are favored over indigents, that "there can be no equal justice where the kind of trial a man gets depends on the amount of money he has."[10]

Griffin immediately evoked a spate of commentary. While it was common sentiment that *Griffin's* implications were indefinite,[11] there were frequent comments[12] that the case represented a change in the law with great potential effect. Consideration was given to whether the rationale of *Griffin* rendered unconstitutional the application to indigents of practices like the imposition of "ten dollars or ten days" alternative sentences,[13] the setting of monetary bail,[14] or the requirement of filing fees and appellate bonds.[15] The decision's implications on state appointment of counsel for the indigent were also considered,[16] and the issue was raised whether *Griffin* required providing the indigent with means to obtain expert witnesses and investigation.[17] One writer, foreseeing such sweeping contentions based on *Griffin*, asked, "if future litigants permit their imaginations to fly this high, is there any reason to believe they will stop half-way to the moon?"[18] and suggested that wealthy litigants might invoke *Griffin* to argue that equal protection would be denied unless the affluent, like the indigent, were granted free access to courts.

Some of these questions have been answered, but the outer limits of *Griffin's* implications remain undefined. This Note attempts to measure the ultimate reach of the equal protection rationale of *Griffin* through an analysis of prior and subsequent cases. In particular, *Griffin's* effect on monetary bail, alternative sentencing, and the practice of trying indigent defendants without providing funds to aid presentation of their cases is evaluated.

THE EQUAL PROTECTION CLAUSE

The function of the Supreme Court and the judiciary in general in review of state action under the equal protection clause has traditionally been characterized as (1) ascertaining the purpose of the law under review and determining whether the purpose constitutes a legitimate governmental objective and (2) determining whether the classification objected to bears a reasonable relationship to the attainment of the purpose of the statute. This is the role the Court has in fact performed in reviewing state action involving classifications not considered hostile to the fundamental ideals of the equal protection clause. In this role once the Court has determined that the legislative objective is legitimate, it has been more permissive in upholding legislative classification in the area of regulation and control of economic activity than in instances of invasion of basic civil rights.

Characteristic of the Court's permissiveness in review of classifications employed in governmental regulation of economic activity are the following: "[A] statute aimed at what is deemed an evil, and hitting it presumably where experience shows it to be most felt, is not to be upset...."[19] A legislature may select for separate treatment "conspicuous examples" of an evil even though, except for their conspicuousness, they are "otherwise and merely logically not distinguishable" from other instances of the evil.[20] Perhaps the broadest statement of judicial tolerance is that in *McGowan v. Maryland*, indicating that "only if the classification rests on grounds wholly irrelevant to the achievement of the State's objectives" would the statute be unconstitutional.[21]

Where state action has invaded basic civil rights, more careful scrutiny has been given to the classification. Thus, in *Skinner v. Oklahoma*[22] the Court overturned a statute which provided for the sterilization of three-time felons, with the exception of embezzlers, because there was no eugenic significance to the distinction thus drawn between embezzlement and the similar crime of larceny. Stating that "we are dealing here with...one of the basic civil rights of man,"[23] the Court emphasized that "scrutiny of the classification...is essential"[24] and invalidated the under-inclusive classification.

Distinct from classifications normally involved in economic legislation and from classifications like that involved in *Skinner* are classifications inherently hostile to fundamental American ideals. The notion of human equality which is the source of the demand that no state shall "deny to any person within its jurisdiction the equal protection of the laws"[25] denies that differences in race, color, or alienage, in religious belief, political belief, or creed, or in wealth—at least in the area of the administration of criminal justice[26]—are normally relevant to the manner in which men should be treated by their government. Classifications based upon such distinctions have accordingly been regarded as suspect by the Court.

Where these classifications have been challenged, the Court, following custom, has both examined the governmental objective and required that the classification be reasonably related to the attainment of the legislative purpose. But the Court appears to have made a further inquiry in such situations. Although it has not carefully articulated the rationale of its decisions in cases involving suspect classifications, the Court has in fact found state action to violate the equal protection clause where, upon balance, the good or benefit reasonably to be accomplished for society by the state action fails to outweigh the harm or deprivation imposed upon those individuals unfavorably classified.

The assumption by the Court, where a suspect classification has been used, of a role essentially different from that accorded to it under the traditional formulation of equal protection review was perhaps explicitly recognized for the first time in *Griffin v. Illinois*.[27] Mr. Justice Harlan in a dissenting opinion properly suggested that the Court could not be deciding that the governmental objective was not legitimate or that the classification selected was not appropriate to the attainment of that objective.[28] That *Griffin* was in fact decided upon the basis of the balancing approach suggested is evidenced by the emphasis placed on the severity of the harm to the indigent defendant from depriving him of appellate review:

"Statistics show that a substantial proportion of criminal convictions are reversed by state appellate courts. Thus to deny adequate review to the poor means that many of them may lose their life, liberty or property because of unjust convictions which appellate courts would set aside."[29]

The opposing consideration of economy to the state pervades the dissenters' assertion that Illinois should not have to equalize the financial position of all criminal defendants. Moreover, Mr. Justice Frankfurter qualified his concurring opinion so as not to require provision of transcripts for taking frivolous appeals, necessarily cases in which the monetary benefit to the state of not having to provide a transcript should prevail since no harm could be done by refusing a transcript.[30]...

A more careful articulation than that given by the Court of its role in equal protection review of state action using suspect classifications therefore appears to be that, while the Court must be satisfied, first, that the legislation has a legitimate governmental objective and, secondly, that the classification involved is reasonably related to the attainment of the legislative purpose, it must also be satisfied that the benefit to society from the state action outweighs the harm caused to those unfavorably classified. Some of the pre-*Griffin* suspect classification cases, most notably *Oyama*[31] and *Takahashi*,[32] seem capable of explanation only as a Court determination of the weight of competing interests under this final inquiry. Even in those suspect-classification cases which can perhaps be explained on the basis of the two traditional inquiries, such as *Yick Wo*[33] and *Kotch*,[34] the Court has given important consideration to the question of the harm caused to those unfavorably classified. Such an inquiry would seem irrelevant under the traditional formulation of the Court's role in equal protection review.

The use of this approach in suspect-classification cases is a proper role for the Court. Justification for unequal treatment of persons on the basis of race, creed, color, blood, wealth, or the like is peculiarly a matter with which the equal protection clause requires the Court to be concerned. The Supreme Court is perhaps in the best position of all our governmental institutions to preserve equality in a state's treatment of minority groups, which are apt to be the objects of local prejudice. Moreover, when a state chooses to act on the basis of classifications repugnant to fundamental American ideals, it is appropriate that the state should have the burden of justifying its action.[35] Since the task of the Court is to determine in particular cases the relative importance of interests of an individual or a minority group and interests of society as a whole, the merit of inquiring whether the benefit to society from the state action outweighs the harm to those unfavorably classified is that it focuses the Court's attention on the precise issue to be decided.

EQUAL PROTECTION AND THE INDIGENT CRIMINAL DEFENDANT

Griffin and its progeny have been concerned with state treatment of the indigent criminal defendant. It is commonly accepted that states "are prohibited by the Equal Protection Clause from discriminating between 'rich' and 'poor' *as such* in the formulation and application of their laws."[36] A more difficult question arises where financial inequality produces consequences of state action which differ for rich and poor although the action of the state itself is neutral. This situation occurs most clearly where access to an appellate court is conditioned upon payment of a fee, where monetary bail is set, or where an alternative sentence of fine or imprisonment is decreed. It occurs no less certainly when an indigent defendant who is found guilty would have been found innocent if he had had funds for expert witnesses, investigation, or other preparation of his case and when an indigent defendant who is unsuccessful on appeal would have been successful were he furnished the assistance of counsel. Although Mr. Justice Harlan has argued that the equal protection clause is inapposite where the action of the state is neutral,[37] the Supreme Court has found the clause applicable where the consequences of neutral state action differ for rich and poor. Thus, in *Griffin* the issue was formulated by Mr. Justice Black to be "whether Illinois may, consistent with the Due Process and Equal Protection Clauses of the Fourteenth Amendment, administer this statute [establishing appeal as of right] so as to deny adequate appellate review to the poor while granting such review to all others."[38] And in *Douglas v. California,*[39] although the Constitution does not guarantee the right to appeal[40] and although the defendant was not precluded by lack of counsel from prosecuting his appeal, the Court held, "[T]here is lacking that equality demanded by the Fourteenth Amendment where the rich man, who appeals as of right, enjoys the benefit of counsel's examination into the record, research of the law, and marshalling of arguments on his behalf, while the indigent...is forced to shift for himself."[41]

If equal justice for rich and poor is properly regarded as one of the objectives of the equal protection clause, the Supreme Court is surely correct in considering the provision applicable where the administration of criminal justice may achieve one result for the rich and another result for the poor. Classification between rich and poor can be reasonably related to the achievement of legitimate governmental objectives.[42] Under the standard of equal protection review which has been suggested, the appropriate inquiry then becomes whether the benefit to society from the state action outweighs the harm caused to the indigent defendant. In cases decided subsequent to *Griffin,* the Court has struggled with this question.

In two of the cases the Court has been concerned with discrimination against those unable to pay prerequisite fees in litigation involving personal liberty. *Burns v. Ohio*[43] invalidated the practice of requiring a twenty-dollar filing fee before the Ohio Supreme Court would consider motions to hear appeals from felony convictions affirmed by an intermediate appellate court. The Court relied upon the magnitude of the harm done, stating:

"The State's action in this case in some ways is more final and disastrous from the defendant's point of view than was the *Griffin* situation. At least in *Griffin,* the defendant might have raised in the Supreme Court any claims that he had that were apparent on the bare record, though trial errors could not be raised. Here, the action of the State has completely barred the petitioner from obtaining any review at all in the Supreme Court of Ohio"[44]

In *Smith v. Bennett,*[45] which held violative of the equal protection clause Iowa's requirement that a four-dollar filing fee accompany petitions for state writs of habeas corpus, the Court declared that one deprived of habeas corpus was deprived of "the highest remedy in law, for any man that is imprisoned."[46] Answering the state's contention that habeas corpus petitions were procedurally civil actions and that therefore application of *Griffin* to them would dictate that indigents could never be required to pay fees in any civil actions, the Court explicitly stated that it was not passing on all civil cases, in which presumably the harm of financial preclusion from the courts varies and may be slight, but rather was restricting its holding to cases involving indigent convicted prisoners,[47] for whom inability to petition for habeas corpus is invariably a substantial harm.

A state's refusal to appoint counsel to argue an indigent's first appeal granted to all as a matter of right, where the appellate court had determined that "no good" would be accomplished by the appointment was challenged in *Douglas v. California.*[48] This refusal was held to be a denial of equal protection, "a discrimination at least as invidious as that condemned in *Griffin v. Illinois,*"[49] since failure to appoint counsel afforded an indigent appellant only a "meaningless ritual"[50] undertaken without legal research and the marshalling of effective arguments by counsel. That the Court was concerned with the magnitude of the deprivation is confirmed by the conspicuous limitation of the holding so as not to require appointment of counsel in presumably less meritorious subsequent appeals or collateral attacks, where less harm would consequently result from denial of counsel. Mr.

Justice Clark's dissent in *Douglas* constitutes merely a different subjective judgment concerning the relative weight of the competing interests. Believing that the overwhelming percentage of *in forma pauperis* appeals are frivolous, he considered the majority decision to be an "extravagance and a waste of the State funds" and felt that "with this new fetish for indigency the Court piles an intolerable burden on the State's judicial machinery."[51] The suggestion in *Douglas* that appointment of counsel, a relatively costly undertaking, may not be required for all phases and types of judicial review gains significance when compared with the holdings of *Burns v. Ohio* and *Smith v. Bennett* that states must forego the relatively slight benefits of charging filing fees in criminal cases for all subsequent appeals and collateral attacks.

A final example of a case explicable by a balancing analysis is *Norvell v. Illinois*.[52] Petitioner, who had counsel at trial, had been convicted of murder in 1941. He had been denied a transcript because of his indigence and did not take an appeal. In 1956, after *Griffin*, he again moved for a transcript,[53] but none could then be provided because the trial reporter had died and his shorthand notes could not be translated. The United States Supreme Court affirmed Illinois's refusal to grant Norvell a new trial, stating that where transcripts are no longer available through no fault of the state "some practical accomodation [*sic*] must be made."[54] The prevention of the expense and inconvenience of new trials at dates remote from conviction with great difficulties of proof and therefore with frequent liberation of presumably guilty defendants was apparently believed to outweigh the harm of continued incarceration to the few whose convictions would have been reversed.

Without defending the subjective value judgment made by the Court as to the weight of the competing interests in each of these cases, one may say that the approach apparently followed by the Court[55] has succeeded in focusing attention upon the appropriate considerations.

THE PROBLEMS OF BAIL, ALTERNATIVE SENTENCES, AND AID FOR INVESTIGATION AND EXPERT WITNESSES

The constitutionality of bail and alternative sentencing and the scope of a state's constitutional duty to furnish the indigent defendant with funds for expert witnesses and for investigation are as yet undecided by the Supreme Court. By pursuing the inquiry which it appears the Court is making where classification on the basis of indigency is involved, one can suggest possible resolutions of the undecided issues. Initially the balancing process must extend beyond an analysis of the relative weights of the interests in the particular case. Thus, for example, the scope of a state's duty to furnish a particular defendant with funds for his defense can only be determined after considering the total cost to society of providing funds for all indigent defendants and the magnitude of harm to all indigent defendants from lack of funds. In this evaluation, the need to maintain an effective adversary system is also relevant. Since justice cannot result from a determination of guilt under an adversary system if one party is financially unable to compete with his opponent, innocent and productive men may be convicted and withdrawn from society, and community respect for the administration of criminal justice may be reduced. Also relevant are the appropriateness of federal intervention into these local concerns, necessarily inherent in application of federal constitutional standards, and the appropriateness of judicial, rather than legislative, solution of these problems. The balancing process may thereafter be useful in determining the extent of a state's constitutional duty in particular cases.

Bail

If classification by ability to pay judicial costs were an absolutely forbidden classification,[56] the setting of monetary bail would be unconstitutional discrimination between indigent and wealthy. If, however, *People v. Norvell* demonstrates that classification by ability to pay is valid in some contexts, it must be asked whether the benefit from permitting the state to incarcerate the indigent defendant prior to trial outweighs the harm caused to the defendant.

It is indisputable that imprisonment because of inability to make monetary bail frequently[57] imposes a grave handicap upon the indigent in his struggle to secure personal liberty and to avoid stigmatization as a criminal. Imprisonment prevents the defendant from earning money to use for his defense. He is also unable to seek out friendly witnesses, an undertaking in which perhaps the defendant alone can be successful, and communication with his attorney is rendered more burdensome and possibly less effective.[58] Furthermore, loss of desired employment and family strife are undoubtedly often caused by imprisonment before trial. If the defendant is ultimately acquitted, poverty alone has in a sense been made a crime punished by an irretrievable loss of liberty, often for a substantial period,[59] in the company of convicted criminals. Some of these considerations have prompted Mr. Justice Douglas to ask, "[C]an an indigent be denied freedom, where a wealthy man would not, because he does not happen to have enough property to pledge for his freedom?"[60]

Despite the grave harm imposed upon the indigent, monetary bail tends to assure the presence of the defendant at trial.[61] However, the extent to which this function is served in a particular case is questionable, for there are numerous "natural" deterrents to flight. A bail jumper "must leave his job, his friends, often his family, and may also be forced to leave some wealth behind,"[62] and he is undoubtedly aware that modern techniques of investigation and communication make the possibility of ultimate detection substantial.

In many cases the good accomplished by monetary bail is slight.[63] Absolute prohibition of detention under monetary bail is unnecessary. Since the accused is presumably innocent, the state should have the burden of justifying the serious impositions that accompany requiring an indigent to make monetary bail. Therefore, whenever the state is unable to show that increased likelihood of the defendant's presence at trial outweighs the harm done by pretrial imprisonment, it seems that, unless the prisoner is released until trial, the law has been administered to deprive him of equal protection of the laws.[64] In measuring the increased likelihood of appearance, the pertinent considerations include the presence of natural deterrents to flight, the severity of the crime, and the likelihood of the defendant's guilt; this should be balanced against the harm done by incarceration before trial in the particular case.[65]

Alternative sentences

The practice of sentencing alternatively to a fine or imprisonment also constitutes a discrimination against indigents, for while they suffer the indignity and stigma of "doing time," their wealthy counterparts are able to buy their freedom. This practice was held constitutional at an early date by the Supreme Court,[66] but since *Griffin* at least two judges[67] have agreed that it seems clearly unconstitutional.

Possible remedies for an equal protection objection to alternative sentencing are an absolute prohibition of alternative sentences or a requirement that when an indigent is so sentenced the state provide money to secure his release. Forbidding alternative sentencing is not justified. Indigent defendants would invariably still remain in jail, and the mere satisfaction of knowing that wealthy defendants are also in jail should not prevail over the harm done to society by imprisoning the defendant with funds: the payment of a fine when an alternative sentence is imposed is presumably an effective criminal penalty for the defendant with funds and is financially advantageous for the state.

The second possible remedy, gratis relief for the indigent from alternative sentences, would totally enervate the deterrent effect of the criminal sentence. A requirement that the state furnish the indigent defendant with funds to secure his release is tenable, then, only if the funds are provided on loan. The inconvenience and expense to the state of establishing and administering a full-blown criminal credit administration for the benefit of those who, rather than being presumably innocent, are convicted criminals may, under a balancing approach, preclude the placing of such an obligation upon the states. Assuming that such a criminal credit administration were required and established, the burden might be placed upon the convicted defendant to show that in his particular case the deterrent and rehabilitative objectives of the criminal law would be effectuated if he purchased his freedom with borrowed funds and to demonstrate a substantial likelihood that he would repay the state. This would be proper because the state would be discriminating, no longer between the rich and the poor, but among indigents.

State aid to the indigent defendant

Little could be more repugnant to our ideal of equal justice for rich and poor than the specter of innocent men convicted because of financial inability to show their innocence. Even if *Gideon v. Wainwright*[68] established an unqualified right to representation by counsel at trial, unavailability of funds to pay for costs of investigation and for the services of expert witnesses still frequently frustrates the efforts of assigned counsel, of public defenders,[69] and of judges to achieve justice.

The magnitude of our indigency problem is great—studies have indicated that over fifty percent of those accused are unable to afford even counsel fees,[70] to say nothing of the other fees necessary for an effective defense. Yet we have fallen sadly behind other countries in meeting this problem. The constitutional provision that "all Swiss are equal before the law" has made representation of the indigent a constitutional mandate in that country and as early as 1837 was interpreted to forbid the requiring of court costs for an indigent's criminal appeal.[71] The English Legal Aid and Advice Act[72] makes possible governmental payment of expenses for expert witnesses and investigation. In the Scandinavian countries every criminal defendant, rich or poor, is entitled to counsel, expert testimony, investigation at government expense, and the use of state laboratories.[73]

It can scarcely be doubted that improvement in the functioning of our guilt determining process when trying an indigent is desirable. The equal protection clause provides a practicable remedy by dictating that a state may not convict an indigent defendant after refusing his request for funds for his defense unless the benefit of economy to the state because of the refusal outweighs the harm to the defendant. This is but to say that the Constitution requires a state to do what is reasonable under all the circumstances to minimize those inequalities in the assistance available to indigent and wealthy defendants which may significantly affect the reliability of the guilt-determining process.

As the amount requested by an indigent increases, the economic good accomplished by refusal likewise increases, and for a large request to prevail there must be an appropriately great harm worked by denial. There are of course numerous considerations pertinent to evaluating the magnitude of the harm caused by a refusal of funds in any particular case. The severity of the official sanction and the opprobrium attached to the particular offense will be important, as will be the complexity of the issues in the case, the necessity for investigation and expert witnesses, and the likelihood that the funds will help the defendant's case. The range of expenditures made by defendants of means for like purposes in similar cases should be relevant although not determinative. Because the adversary system presupposes that the parties are roughly comparable in legal, investigative, and expert resources, regard should also be given to the prosecution's expenditures.

Under the analysis suggested, it might well be constitutional for a state to refuse to provide a large sum in hope of locating a witness to aid the defense against a charge of common drunkenness but unconstitutional for a state to refuse to provide a smaller amount for expert ballistic testimony in a murder case. Different judges might arrive at different results in a single case under this approach because no exact line can be drawn. But the indigent's rights would to some extent be protected by appropriate elaboration of the standard on review.[74]

Mr. Justice Harlan has intimated that in his view the equal protection clause offers no ascertainable, logical standard for limiting the duty of a state to minimize inequities in the assistance available to the affluent and to the indigent de-

fendant, that it can only require that the state "furnish...[the indigent defendant] with legal services...equivalent to those that the affluent defendant can obtain."[75] But the equal protection clause does offer a rational standard for reaching results that comport with our ideals. The Supreme Court has stated in *Douglas* that "absolute equality is not required; lines can be and are drawn and we often sustain them."[76]

CONCLUSION

Whenever a classification between indigent and wealthy is made in the area of criminal law, the equal protection clause demands that the state justify its use of the classification. Use of this classification, and of other classifications which are contrary to fundamental ideals embodied in the equal protection clause, can be justified only by showing that the good accomplished by its use outweighs the harm caused to those unfavorably classified. The equal protection clause, in short, demands nothing but a sensible solution to problems created by indigency in the areas of bail, alternative sentencing, and the conduct of criminal trials.

Footnotes

[1]"Ye shall do no unrighteousness in judgment: Thou shalt not respect the person of the poor, nor honour the person of the mighty: *but* in righteousness shalt thou judge thy neighbour." *Leviticus* 19:15.

[2]LOCKE, TWO TREATISES ON CIVIL GOVERNMENT 266 (Routledge ed. 1884).

[3]ROSSITER, SEEDTIME OF THE REPUBLIC 292 (1953).

[4]Anatole France has made the relevant criticism that "the law, in its majestic equality, forbids the rich as well as the poor to sleep under bridges, to beg in the streets and to steal bread." FRANCE, JOHN COURNOS, A MODERN PLUTARCH 27, quoted in Griffin v. Illinois, 351 U.S. 12, 23 (1956) (Frankfurter, J., concurring). Even if one were to assume that the ideal of equality has been realized to a large extent in the substantive law, it would still be true that the indigent is greatly handicapped by court costs and by the costs of establishing the facts of his case....

Marx and Engels have made more vitriolic criticisms. "But don't wrangle with us so long as you apply, to our intended abolition of your bourgeois property, the standard of your bourgeois notions of freedom, culture, law, etc. Your very ideas are but the outgrowth of the conditions of your bourgeois production and bourgeois property, just as your jurisprudence is but the will of your class made into a law for all, a will whose essential character and direction are determined by the economic conditions of existence of your class. . . . The bourgeoisie has stripped of its halo every occupation hitherto honoured and looked up to with reverent awe. It has converted...the lawyer...into its paid wage-labourers." MARX & ENGELS, THE COMMUNIST MANIFESTO 11, 26 (Engels ed. 1932).

[5]351 U.S. 12 (1956)....

[6]In this Note the term indigent has been used to signify not one who is absolutely destitute but one who is financially unable to employ to his advantage the institution or service under consideration. For lack of better words, those who are not indigent are described by terms like wealthy and affluent. For discussions of the problem of what constitutes indigency, see REPORT OF THE ATTORNEY GENERAL'S COMMITTEE ON POVERTY AND THE ADMINISTRATION OF FEDERAL CRIMINAL JUSTICE 7–8, 40–41 (1963) [hereinafter cited as POVERTY]; Kamiser & Choper, *The Right to Counsel in Minnesota: Some Field Findings and Legal-Policy Observations*, 48 MINN. L. REV. 1, 17–33 (1963); Note, 47 MINN. L. REV. 1054, 1073–74 (1963).

The question of what constitutes indigency has arisen in State v. Vallejos, 87 Ariz. 119, 348 P.2d 554 (1960); In re Patterson, 136 Colo. 401, 317 P.2d 1041 (1957); Pearlman v. State, 226 Md. 67, 172 A.2d 395 (1961); Lloyd v. Warden, 217 Md. 667, 143 A.2d 483 (1958).

[7]351 U.S. at 16.

[8]Chief Justice Warren and Justices Douglas and Clark joined in this opinion.

[9]351 U.S. at 17.

[10]*Id.* at 19.

[11]"When nine men split four ways and no opinion has the complete support of any five, I humbly submit that the implications are a matter for a Delphic oracle...." Qua, *Griffin v. Illinois*, 25 U. CHI. L. REV. 143, 147 (1957).

[12]See, *e.g.*, Willcox & Bloustein, *The Griffin Case—Poverty and the Fourteenth Amendment*, 43 CORNELL L.Q. 1 (1957); 18 MONT. L. REV. 103, 107 (1956); 10 VAND. L. REV. 141, 144 (1956).

[13]See Wildeblood v. United States, 284 F.2d 592, 594 (D.C. Cir. 1960) (dissenting opinion).

[14]See Hamley, *The Impact of Griffin v. Illinois on State Court–Federal Court Relationships*, 24 F.R.D. 75, 78 (1960).

[15]See *ibid.*; U.C.L.A.L. REV. 274, 279 (1957).

[16]See Hamley, *supra* note 14, at 79; Willcox & Bloustein, *supra* note 12, at 23; 17 OHIO ST. L.J. 553, 555 (1956).

[17]See Allen, *Griffin v. Illinois: Antecedents and Aftermaths*, 25 U. CHI. L. REV. 151, 157 (1957).

[18]Hamley, *supra* note 14, at 80.

[19]Keokee Coke Co. v. Taylor, 234 U.S. 224, 227 (1914).

[20]Central Lumber Co. v. South Dakota, 226 U.S. 157, 161 (1912).

[21]366 U.S. 420, 425 (1961). The sole recent instance of a strict application of the equal protection clause to economic regulation is found in Morey v. Doud, 354 U.S. 457 (1947), which invalidated an Illinois statute exempting the American Express Company alone, because of its prosperity, from state regulation of the selling of money orders. The majority emphasized that the "singling out" of American Express would yield competitive advantages, and this anticompetitive effect of the statute perhaps explains the anomalous use of the equal protection clause. Even Morey v. Doud, *id.* at 463–64, however, contained language deferring to the permissive function of equal protection review adopted in *McGowan v. Maryland*, and it is established that the equal protection clause will rarely invalidate economic legislation....

[22]316 U.S. 535 (1942).

[23]*Id.* at 541.

[24]*Ibid.*

[25]U.S. CONST. amend. XIV, § 1.

[26]"Providing equal justice for poor and rich, weak and powerful alike is an age old problem. People have never ceased to hope and strive to move closer to that goal. This hope, at least in part, brought about in 1215 the royal concessions of Magna Charta: 'To no one will we sell, to no one will we refuse, or delay, right or justice....No free man shall be taken or imprisoned, or disseised, or outlawed, or exiled, or anywise destroyed; nor shall we go upon him nor send upon him, but by the lawful judgment of his peers or by the law of the land.' These pledges were unquestionably steps toward a fairer and more nearly equal application of criminal justice. In this tradition, our own constitutional guaranties of due process and equal protection both call for procedures in criminal trials which allow no invidious discriminations between persons and different groups of persons. Both equal protection and due process emphasize the central aim of our entire judicial system—all people charged with crime must, so far as the law is concerned 'stand on an equality before the bar of justice in every American court.' " Griffin v. Illinois, 351 U.S. 12, 16–17 (1956).

Mr. Justice Jackson was perhaps articulating this notion when he said, "the mere state of being without funds is a neutral fact—constitutionally an irrelevance, like race, creed, or color." Edwards v. California, 314 U.S. 160, 184–85 (1941).

Difference in wealth can be a valid and proper classification in some areas of the law, as in taxation. It is, however, difficult to think of an area in which this classification would be more contrary to our ideals than the administration of criminal justice, and here the Court has accordingly treated it as suspect.

[27]351 U.S. 12 (1956).

[28]"Trial errors cannot be reviewed without an appropriate record of the proceedings below; if a transcript is used it is surely not unreasonable to require the appellant to bear its cost....I do not understand the Court to dispute either the necessity for a bill of exceptions or the reasonableness of the general requirement that the trial transcript, if used in its preparation, be paid for by the appealing party." *Id.* at 34–35.

[29]*Id.* at 18–19. The proposition that *Griffin* was decided by balancing the competing interests has perhaps been noted by only one commentator. "[I]t seems more likely that the Court's conclusion was based upon a weighing of the seriousness of precluding certain defendants in criminal cases from obtaining appellate review against the value to Illinois of its practice of requiring payment for a record on appeal." Note, *The Supreme Court, 1955 Term*, 70 HARV. L. REV. 95, 128 (1956).

[30]In Draper v. Washington, 372 U.S. 487 (1963), the Court required that transcripts be furnished despite a finding of frivolousness by the trial court because of the need for a transcript in determining whether an appeal is in fact frivolous.

[31]332 U.S. 633 (1948).

[32]334 U.S. 410 (1948).

[33]118 U.S. 356 (1886).

[34]330 U.S. 552 (1947).

[35]See Pollack, *Racial Discrimination and Judicial Integrity: A Reply to Professor Wechsler*, 108 U. PA. L. REV. 1, 24–31 (1959).

[36]Douglas v. California, 372 U.S. 353, 361 (1963) (Mr. Justice Harlan dissenting). This statement seems

indisputable in the context of the administration of criminal justice. State action in other contexts, such as welfare legislation, however, might properly use this classification. If a balancing approach were used, society's interest in the health and welfare of its citizens might outweigh the harm done to the affluent who received no benefits. Progressive income taxation may be another example of valid discrimination.

37Mr. Justice Harlan has consistently dissented from recent decisions aiding indigents on the basis that, while it may be unconstitutional to discriminate between rich and poor as such, "it is a far different thing to suggest that this provision [the equal protection clause] prevents the State from adopting a law of general applicability that may affect the poor more harshly than it does the rich...." *Id.* at 361 (dissenting opinion).

38351 U.S. at 13.

39372 U.S. 353 (1963).

40Mr. Justice Black stated in *Griffin*, 351 U.S. at 18, that due process does not require states to grant appellate review, citing, *e.g.*, McKane v. Durston, 153 U.S. 684 (1894).

41372 U.S. at 357–58. The equal protection clause might also be the basis of a request for counsel of the same quality as that enjoyed by the wealthy defendant. Although Gideon v. Wainwright, 372 U.S. 353 (1963), resolved the question of appointment of counsel for trial under the due process clause, *Douglas v. California* has required appointment of counsel for a first appeal on the basis of the *Griffin*-type violation of both equal protection and due process that results from an "invidious discrimination" between rich and poor. Assuming that the equal protection clause is applicable to such requests, the balancing approach suggested indicates they may well not prevail.

42If the purpose of bail is to ensure the defendant's presence at trial, the differing consequences produced for rich and poor may well be related to the achievement of this purpose. While the nonindigent's monetary interest in appearing at trial may be a sufficient deterrent to flight, imprisonment is perhaps the only deterrent available for the indigent.

Similarly, the differing results to rich and poor under an alternative sentencing provision may be related to the purpose of such sentences, which is to allow the convicted defendant to choose between imprisonment and fine in situations where both penalties are considered effective to serve the purposes of the criminal law. Since the indigent defendant is unable to pay the fine, imprisonment may be regarded as the only penalty which is effective as to him.

43360 U.S. 252 (1959).

44*Id.* at 258.

45365 U.S. 708 (1961).

46*Id.* at 712.

47*Id.* at 713. In McCrary v. Indiana, 364 U.S. 277 (1960) (per curiam), the indigent defendant alleged that his appeal from denial of coram nobis had been dismissed solely because he was unable to provide a transcript of the trial proceedings. The Supreme Court remanded so that this allegation could be passed on in light of *Griffin*. In Lane v. Brown, 372 U.S. 477 (1963), the Supreme Court held unconstitutional the operation of Indiana law which precluded state review of a denial of coram nobis unless the public defender exercised his discretion to secure a transcript of the hearing for the indigent.

48372 U.S. 353 (1963).

49*Id.* at 355.

50*Id.* at 358.

51*Id.* at 359.

52373 U.S. 420 (1963).

53Upon remand in *Griffin* the Illinois Supreme Court had promulgated rules providing for furnishing a transcript to the indigent defendant whether his conviction had occurred before or after *Griffin*. ILL. ANN. STAT. ch. 110, §101.65–1 (Smith-Hurd Supp. 1963). Such petition was to be denied, however, if for any reason it was impossible to provide the transcript.

Two years after *Griffin*, in Eskridge v. Washington, 357 U.S. 214 (1958) (per curiam), the Supreme Court made *Griffin* retroactively applicable by requiring the provision of an available transcript of a 1935 murder trial. In *Eskridge*, unlike *Norvell*, the petitioner had appealed his conviction and had also sought a writ of mandate to compel production of the transcript.

54373 U.S. at 424.

55In some cases a balancing approach arguably was not used. In Eskridge v. Washington, 357 U.S. 214 (1958), the petitioner's appeal had been dismissed for failure to file a transcript which the trial judge, in accordance with Washington law, had refused to provide since "justice would not be promoted." The Supreme Court, holding such exercise of discretion unconstitutional, stated in absolute terms that "destitute defendants must be afforded as adequate appellate review as defendants who have enough money to buy transcripts." *Id.* at 216 (quoting from *Griffin*). Similarly in Lane v. Brown, 372 U.S. 477 (1963), a public defender's discretionary refusal to secure a transcript and thus enable the petitioner to appeal a denial of coram nobis relief was overturned, the court again demanding that indigents have as adequate appellate review as those able to purchase transcripts. In another case involving a request for transcript, Draper v. Washington, 372 U.S. 487 (1963), the trial court's denial was based on the ground that the assignments of error were frivolous and that furnishing the transcript would be a waste of state funds. The Court overturned the Washington Supreme Court's affirmance of the denial as not constituting adequate appellate review since it had not been made with consideration of relevant portions of the trial transcript.

However, it is improper to read these cases as establishing a rigid proposition that in all situations the state must establish absolute economic equality of all criminal defendants. Norvell v. Illinois, 373 U.S. 420 (1963), undermines such a reading, as does the language of Douglas v. California, 372 U.S. 353, 357 (1963), that "absolute equality is not required; lines can be and are drawn and we will often sustain them." Instead, *Eskridge, Lane*, and *Draper* seem more properly understood to establish as a matter of law that one cannot be effectively deprived of an entire phase of appellate review because of the economy to the state of not having to provide a transcript.

The Court has also been liberal in requiring transcripts for in forma pauperis appeals from federal convictions. See Coppedge v. United States, 369 U.S. 438 (1962); Johnson v. United States, 352 U.S. 565 (1957).

56The Supreme Court understandably has never adopted the "forbidden classification" doctrine. Regardless of how ostensibly odious a classification is, a situation might arise which would justify its use. Classification by membership in the Negro race, similar to the racial classifications of *Hirabayashi* and *Korematsu*, might be justified in the event of a Black Muslim uprising or a war with a united African state if it were proved that many Negroes had engaged in effective sabotage. Classification by blood has been sustained in Kotch v. Board of River Port Pilot Comm'rs, 330 U.S. 552 (1947); *Korematsu* and *Hirabayashi* sustained classification by race.

[57]A 1958 study of New York City showed that 28% of all defendants could not make $500 bail; 45% could not make $1,500 bail; 63% could not make $2,500 bail and 81% could not make $7,500 bail. See POVERTY 66, 135.

[58]See generally POVERTY 68–72.

[59]Statistics published by the Federal Bureau of Prisons show that during the year ending June 30, 1960, the average pretrial detention period was 25.3 days. FEDERAL PRISONS, 1960, 60–61; see POVERTY 65 (time before disposition).

[60]Bandy v. United States, 81 S. Ct. 197, 198 (1960) (opinion in chambers). Less than a year later in Bandy v. Chambers, 82 S. Ct. 11, 13 (1961) (opinion in chambers), Mr. Justice Douglas said, "[F]urther reflection has led me to believe that no man should be denied release because of indigence. Instead…a man is to be released on 'personal recognizance' where other relevant factors make it reasonable to believe that he will comply with the orders of the Court."

[61]The effectiveness of placing primary reliance on financial loss to prevent flight from justice has been incisively criticized. Financial loss would not deter the flight of the wealthy defendant hoping to purchase his freedom. See POVERTY 68; Note, *Bail: An Ancient Practice Reexamined*, 70 YALE L.J. 966, 970–71 (1961). Proposals to place less reliance on financial security have been made, POVERTY 73–82; Note, *supra* at 973–77, but present administrative difficulties and as yet have not been adopted.

[62]*Id.* at 973.

[63]Pretrial imprisonment may accomplish good other than appearance at trial, such as preventing spoliation of evidence and the commission of other crimes, although the consensus appears to be that such considerations are irrelevant in the setting of bail. See POVERTY 60; Note, *supra* note 62, at 969 n.26 (1961).

[64]The eighth amendment provision that demands that "excessive bail shall not be required" has not been incorporated by the fourteenth amendment. No federal case has been found interpreting it as applicable simply because the bail set was more than the defendant could provide.

[65]The setting of bail on an individual case basis after

evaluation of such factors is advocated in Note, *supra* note 62.

[66]See *Ex parte* Jackson, 96 U.S. 727, 737 (1877); Hill v. Wampler, 298 U.S. 460, 463 (1936) (dictum).

[67]Wildeblood v. United States, 284 F.2d 592, 596 (D.C. Cir. 1960) (Bastian and Burger, JJ., dissenting).

[68]372 U.S. 335 (1963).

[69]See N.Y. BAR ASS'N & NAT'L LEGAL AID & DEFENDERS' ASS'N, EQUAL JUSTICE FOR THE ACCUSED 66, 70 (1959). In many cases public defender systems do not exist and therefore cannot provide even a part of the funds necessary for the preparation of a defense. Only 51% of the counties with populations of more than 400,000 have defender systems, and only 39% with populations of more than 100,000 do. Gossert, *Making Paper Rights Worth Something*, 49 A.B.A.J. 641–42 (1963).

[70]See BROWNELL, LEGAL AID IN THE UNITED STATES 83–84 (1951); Kadish & Kimball, *Legal Representation of the Indigent in Criminal Cases in Utah*, 4 UTAH L. REV. 198, 214 (1954).

[71]See Jacoby, *Legal Aid to the Poor*, 53 HARV. L. REV. 940, 942–44 (1940).

[72]12 & 13 Geo. 6, c. 51 (1949).

[73]See Judge Frank's dissenting opinion in United States v. Johnson, 238 F.2d 565, 573 (2d Cir. 1956). See also FRANK & FRANK, NOT GUILTY 87 (1957). A brief summary of the treatment of the indigent defendant in Europe is contained in POVERTY 31–32. See also Schweinburg, *Legal Assistance Abroad*, 17 U. CHI. L. REV. 270 (1950).

[74]Requests by indigents for expert witnesses have been made in Smith v. Baldi, 344 U.S. 561 (1953); United States v. Brodson, 241 F.2d 107 (7th Cir. 1957); United States v. Hines, 148 F. Supp. 73 (E.D.N.Y. 1957). A balancing approach also seems appropriate in cases like United States v. Coson, 286 F.2d 453 (9th Cir. 1961) (inability to use remedy available to wealthy); Pacheco v. People, 146 Colo. 200, 360 P.2d 975 (1961) (state must provide court reporter in nonsupport action so that transcript will be available for possible appeal); and in cases involving requests for transcripts such as Jackson v. Steiner, 261 F.2d 447 (4th Cir. 1958) (request for trial transcript on motion for new trial heard in banc), Eddy v. United States, 256 F.2d 78 (9th Cir. 1958) (request for transcript of proceedings at arraignment and plea); Banks v. United States, 249 F.2d 672 (9th Cir. 1957) (request for trial transcript to use in federal habeas corpus proceeding).

[75]Douglas v. California, 372 U.S. 353, 363 (1963) (dissenting opinion).

[76]*Id.* at 357.

Selection *18*

Federalism v. Individual Rights: The Legal Squeeze on Self-Incrimination

Richard A. Watson

This article deals with immunity statutes and self-incrimination in the matrix of federalism. Many of the arguments made here also apply to the problem of double jeopardy. Because of the judicial view of separate sovereignties in the state and nation, the same man has often been tried for the same criminal action in both a federal and state court if the action, such as bank robbery, happens to violate both a state and a federal statute. The Supreme Court has now accepted much of the position argued here. A brief note at the end of the article describes the Court's new position.

Two key problems of self-incrimination are not discussed at length in this book. The first concerns a waiver of Fifth Amendment rights. The reason that witnesses before congressional and other inquiries often refuse to answer even a question about their names and addresses is that if they answer some questions, they sometimes "waive" their right to take the Fifth on others. The waiver doctrine as enunciated by the courts is now so confused that no one knows just how much an individual can say before he unintentionally waives his right to refuse to answer other questions. Many lawyers, therefore, advise their clients to answer *no* questions.

The other issue is whether the requirement that such groups as the Communist party must register their membership violates the self-incrimination clause.*

This study deals with one reputed value of federalism, its service in the cause of freedom or liberty (both terms are used interchangeably here to mean an immunity from arbitrary governmental action). In particular, I shall examine one aspect of that sort of freedom in our federal system, namely, the right against self-incrimination. The general case for the peculiar virtue of our constitutional system as a means of assuring such a right was summarized by Madison:

"In the compound republic of America the power surrendered by the people is first divided between two distinct governments, and then the portion allotted to each subdivided among distinct and separate departments. Hence a double security arises to the rights of the people. The different governments will control each other at the same time that each will be controlled by itself."[1]

Passing over argument about the contribution of the separation of powers and judicial review,

our attention will center on the complexities introduced by the federal division of powers. William Anderson posed the broad question some years ago: "Does federalism imply not only a division of powers between national and state government, but also a subtraction of powers from both in favor of the individual? Will there be less government in a federal than in a unitary state, or possibly even more?"[2] And we might add—what his formulation leaves partly open—if more government, then necessarily less freedom? More explicitly, Franz Neumann has suggested recently that "whether the federal state does increase freedom

"Federalism v. Individual Rights: The Legal Squeeze on Self-Incrimination" by Richard A. Watson, 54 *American Political Science Review* 887 (1960). Reprinted by permission.
*Those interested in this question should see *Communist Party* v. *Subversive Activities Control Board* [367 U.S. 1 (1961)]; *Albertson* v. *Subversive Activities Control Board* [86 S.Ct. 194 (1965)]; and Rich, "Communist Registration and the Fifth Amendment" [15 University of Florida Law Review 435 (1962)].

cannot be abstractly determined. We have some evidence that the federal state as such (that is regardless of the form of government) has not fulfilled this role."[3]

Neumann proposed as one of the possible tests the extent to which federalism promotes civil liberties. He thought that "on the whole, one may perhaps say that the federal system may have speeded up inroads into the civil liberties rather than protecting them," and he considered a study of that topic to be one of "real importance."[4] My purpose in this discussion is to contribute to such a study. What has been the impact of federalism upon the right against self-incrimination? Other specific rights might have been selected, but probably few would quarrel with Justice Frankfurter's view that "the history of liberty has largely been the history of the observance of procedural safeguards."[5] And, as events of the 1950s attest, none of these safeguards puts the larger issue of freedom from governmental constraint more sharply than this one.

The discussion which follows delineates the effect of judicial concepts of federalism on the rights of individuals under this constitutional guaranty, and seeks a reconciliation of policy dilemmas in current doctrines. The dilemmas arise because the principles of federalism necessarily affect the right against self-incrimination in two distinct situations: one when the right is first asserted in national proceedings and its effect on a later state prosecution must be considered; and the other the obverse case, when the right is first claimed in state proceedings and its consequence for a federal prosecution is in issue. These cases will be treated separately, in order.

1

The immediate source of the right against self-incrimination in national proceedings is the Fifth Amendment of the federal Constitution: "nor shall [any person] be compelled in any criminal case to be a witness against himself..." Over the years this right has been construed liberally by the courts, and it now may be invoked not only in actual criminal trials, but also before administrative agencies, Congressional committees, and federal grand juries. Moreover, a witness may plead the right even when his answer to the immediate question is not itself incriminating; it is enough if the answer might furnish a link in a chain of evidence that will ultimately result in establishing his guilt. But it must be claimed at an early stage in a line of questioning, lest it be deemed to have been waived.

Does the possibility of incrimination under a state criminal statute constitute a valid excuse for a refusal to answer a question in a federal proceeding where the Fifth Amendment is clearly applicable? For many years the judicial answer to this question was uncertain. One line of cases upheld the witness' right not to answer if there was any real danger of state prosecution.[6] Diametrically opposed to this judicial position was another, indicating that the fate of the witness before the state courts was no concern of federal officials. The courts reaching this latter result based it on the argument that two separate sovereignties were involved, borrowing by way of analogy from certain English decisions which supposedly refused to take judicial notice of the possibility of a defendant's incriminating himself under the laws of another country.[7]

The persisting uncertainty between these positions was settled in 1931 in the now-famous decision, *United States v. Murdock*.[8] The defendant refused to answer certain questions put to him by federal tax officials concerning protection money he allegedly paid in connection with gambling operations—and claimed as a deductible business expense—on the ground that the answers to these questions might incriminate him under state law. The Supreme Court held that since the investigation was under federal law in respect of federal matters, namely, his tax liability, and not for the purpose of discovering evidence of violations of state laws, he must answer. In so holding, the Court reasoned that the Supremacy Clause of the national Constitution (Art VI, sec. 2) gives inquiries duly authorized for national purposes an overriding legality that may not be hindered by obstacles that depend upon state law.

The *Murdock* principle, that the investigation must be for a *bona fide* national purpose in order to compel the witness to answer, was underscored in a case decided some twenty years later. In *United States v. DiCarlo*,[9] a federal District Court ruled that a witness who appeared before the Kefauver Crime Investigating Committee need not answer questions that might incriminate him under state law since one of the major purposes of the investigation by the Congressional committee was to ascertain violations of state criminal laws.[10] The case could accordingly be distinguished from *Murdock* in which the investigation was for a national purpose alone, and any information obtained from the witness was only incidentally revealed for possible use by state officials.

With judicial doctrine in this posture, a related question vital to a federal system of law enforcement immediately arises: can the national government, if it so desires, protect the witness legally from state prosecution? To answer this question, and understand the essential issues it raises, the effect of the immunity statutes must be considered.

Federal immunity statutes

Immunity laws hurdle the constitutional guaranty against self-incrimination: they protect a witness from prosecution in exchange for compulsion on him to disclose information the investigating officials consider to be worth the exchange; the witness may or may not think so. The philosophy behind their passage is that in some circumstances it is more beneficial to gain facts that will ultimately result in better law enforcement, or better laws, than it is to prosecute the offender immediately in hand.

Immunity statutes are of two major types: "partial" ones which merely forbid the use of the witness' actual testimony, and "complete" ones which shield him from prosecution for any matters that relate to his compelled testimony.[11] Both types of statutes usually make an exception for perjury charges growing out of statements made in such testimony. The "partial" type has gradually been abandoned as ineffective since the decision in *Counselman v. Hitchcock*.[12] Over the years the national government has utilized immunity statutes in seeking information from witnesses appearing before Congressional committees, courts, grand juries, and administrative agencies where the constitutional right against self-incrimination is applicable. At the present time, their application is restricted to the fields of subversion, narcotics, and certain regulatory activities of the national government.[13] All the statutes currently in force are "complete."

Effect of federal immunity statutes on state prosecution

With this general background in mind, let us return to the previous question: does the national government have the power to immunize witnesses testifying before federal bodies from potential prosecutions by state authorities if these prosecutions are based upon information compulsorily disclosed to federal officials? If such a power exists, may the national government merely forbid the use of the compelled testimony itself as evidence in state courts—a partial immunity—or may it also give the witness complete immunity from state prosecution for all matters growing out of his statements before federal authorities?

Although the Supreme Court did suggest many years ago that a complete federal immunity statute protected the witness against state as well as federal prosecution,[14] it was not squarely faced with the issue until the 1954 case of *Adams v. Maryland*.[15] Adams had appeared before the Kefauver Committee and answered questions put to him by the Congressmen; largely on the basis of this testimony, he was convicted of violating Maryland's anti-lottery laws. He appealed his conviction to the Supreme Court, contending that the "partial" immunity statute then applicable to Congressional investigations[16] prevented the use of his compelled testimony as evidence in both state and federal courts.

The Supreme Court upheld Adams' contention, interpreting the words of the national statute— "any criminal proceeding in *any court*" (emphasis added)—to include a state court. As constitutional justification for such a statute, the Court pointed to the Necessary and Proper Clause of the Constitution, saying that the power to compel testimony through immunity statutes is a necessary part of Congress' power to investigate. On this premise the Supremacy Clause of the Constitution binds state courts to obey the federal statute even though it affects their rules of evidence.

Only two years later, the 1954 "complete" immunity statute dealing with testimony concerning national security and defense was presented to the Supreme Court for interpretation in *Ullman v. U.S.*[17] Ullman refused to answer questions relating to his alleged Communist associations put to him by a federal grand jury, contending, among other reasons, that the immunity statute was unconstitutional since it did not afford him protection against state prosecution.

The court refused to uphold Ullman's contention, ruling that the statute did protect him from prosecution by state authorities for any matters arising from his compelled testimony. The authority of the Congress to so affect state enforcement activities was traced to its power over national defense; the right to compel testimony from witnesses on matters relating to the nation's security was considered to be complementary to, or necessary and proper for, the exercise of this specific enumerated power. The Court pointed to Congress' "paramount concern" in safeguarding national security and held that the statute's contribution to the more effective exercise of this conceded federal power justifies the restriction placed on the exercise of state powers.

The *Adams* and *Ullman* decisions carry important implications for the principles of federalism as applied in the field of law enforcement. Under the reasoning of *Adams*, the national government can forbid states from utilizing actual testimony elicited by Congress in the course of its investigations into any substantive area. Given the expansive authority of Congress under the interstate commerce, taxing and spending powers, the scope of this area is virtually unlimited. Moreover, the Court's rationale in *Ullman* indicates that in fields of its "paramount concern" the national government can completely bar state prosecutions for all matters arising from the compelled testimony. A crucial question left as yet unanswered by the Courts is whether the national government has constitutional authority to enact a "complete" immunity statute precluding state prosecutions when the statute is designed to aid inquiries by the national government in a substantive area where it enjoys only a concurrency of powers with the state governments.[18] Of course, if this open question should be answered in the negative, the important issue would then shift to the determination of the specific fields of governmental activity where the national concern is paramount over that of the states.

The *power* of the national government to preclude state prosecutions is important to a witness appearing before a national agency for questioning. Equally important is the *policy* of Congress toward immunity against state prosecution. For example, the *Murdock* ruling allows federal inquiries for national purposes notwithstanding possible incrimination under state law. Yet in *Ullman* the Supreme Court construed the federal immunity statute of 1954 as granting witnesses complete protection from state prosecution, even though, in a national inquiry for an admittedly national purpose, they could have been legally required to answer regardless of the consequences for state criminal action.

Some of the immunity statutes, that is to say, embody a policy determination by Congress that national investigative purposes warrant the offering of immunity against state prosecutions in selected cases. For despite a legal compulsion to answer, a witness may prefer to risk national perjury or even contempt charges rather than divulge matters that will subject him to the more severe risk of state prosecution for a felony. A federal immunity statute is thus designed to insure that his answers will be forthcoming and honest; to the extent that this occurs, the national purpose of gaining reliable, factual information on matters under investigation will be served. The Supreme Court's validation of statutes of this type indicates judicial agreement with the view that the national purpose underlying their passage in certain substantive areas has sufficient constitutional priority to justify their consequent effect on state prosecutions.

Use of federally compelled evidence in state courts

If national officials do compel testimony, and federal courts determine that no immunity statute prohibits its use by state authorities, one further question remains to be considered: will state courts either admit this testimony as evidence itself, or allow it to be used as a source for gathering other information on criminal activities of the witness? As might be expected, most state tribunals have little compunction about accepting this windfall evidence. However, the courts of one or two states have proved to be exceptions to this general rule. The Florida Supreme Court in a 1914 case, *Clark v. State*,[19] and the Michigan Supreme Court in a 1916 decision, *People v. Lay*,[20] both refused to allow information gathered in national bankruptcy proceedings to be used in state embezzlement actions. More recently in *Boynton v. State*,[21] the Florida Supreme Court, citing *Clark* as precedent, refused to allow information on gambling activities, gathered by federal revenue officials, to be used in a state legal action against the individuals involved.[22]

This review of what the witness faces when he is brought before national officials for questioning leads naturally to a comparison with the position of a witness in the obverse situation. What happens if one refuses to answer questions put to him by state authorities on the ground that his answers will tend to incriminate him under national laws?

II

The right of an individual to plead self-incrimination before state agencies arises from the state and not from the federal Constitution. In *Twining v. New Jersey*,[23] decided over fifty years ago, the Supreme Court refused to read the Fifth Amendment privilege against self-incrimination over into either the privileges and immunities or the due process clause of the Fourteenth Amendment as applicable to state authorities. However, forty-eight of the fifty state constitutions have clauses granting this privilege, and the other two jurisdictions have recognized it in judicial decisions.[24]

Like the Congress, state legislatures have passed immunity statutes. They are of the two general types discussed previously; that is, some grant complete immunity from prosecution, while others offer only partial immunity.[25] However, unlike federal legislation with respect to state proceedings, state immunity statutes cannot prevent federal prosecution, for that would constitute a direct violation of the Supremacy Clause of the federal Constitution. The majority of the state courts, nevertheless, do not excuse a witness from testifying because the state cannot give him either complete or partial immunity from federal prosecution. The leading case on the question, *Jack v. Kansas*,[26] was decided in 1905. Although it is difficult to determine the precise basis of the decision, the end result of compelling the witness to answer continues to be the action taken by the majority of state courts.[27]

The Michigan Supreme Court is primarily responsible for the development of the minority position that the witness need not answer questions that will lead straight to federal prosecution. The leading case to this effect is *People v. Den Uyl*,[28] in which the Court excused a witness from testifying who was under a federal indictment at the time for matters relating to those about which he was being questioned. The opinion emphasized the very real probability of dangerous incrimination under federal law, in light of the pending indictment, and held that compelling the witness to testify under the circumstances would violate the provisions against self-incrimination in the Michigan constitution. The Michigan rule has been adopted by the courts of Louisiana, Kentucky, and Florida[29]

It is difficult to determine just how far apart the majority and minority positions are. Conceivably some state courts, now supposedly lined up on the majority side, might excuse witnesses from testifying if it were clearly demonstrated that the danger of aiding federal prosecutions in particular instances was as real as it obviously was in *Den Uyl*. Others, however, might expound the separate sovereignties theory or, as one writer suggests, indulge in the legal fiction that no danger exists regardless of the actual circumstances surrounding the case.[30]

Use of state-compelled evidence in federal courts

The federal courts were not faced with the constitutional question about using state-compelled information until some sixteen years ago when evidence elicited in a state creditors' proceeding was sought to be introduced in a federal mail-fraud suit in the leading case of *Feldman v. United States*.[31] Justice Frankfurter, speaking for the majority of the Court, used several arguments to buttress his decision that the testimony was admissible. He pointed to the historical background of the Bill of Rights and to Chief Justice Marshall's famous opinion in *Barron v. Baltimore* to show that the Fifth Amendment pertains to the national government only and does not restrain the action of state authorities. Frankfurter also declared that "the distinctive operation of the two governments

(national and state) is basic to our federal constitutional system, however complicated and difficult the practical accommodation to it may be," and cautioned that to give effect to the New York State "complete" immunity statute would be to place "the criminal law of the United States at the hazard of the carelessness or connivance in some petty civil litigation in any state court, quite beyond the reach of even the most alert watchfulness of law officers of the Government." He did concede that if federal officials participated in the gathering of the evidence by state authorities, it would be inadmissible in federal courts, but found no suggestion of complicity between the persons involved in the state proceeding and the federal officers concerned.

Justice Black wrote a powerful dissent. In it he emphasized the fact that, in the long period since the Bill of Rights was adopted, no federal court had ever before sustained a conviction for a federal offense based on self-incriminating testimony forced from the accused. He reasoned that "testimony is no less compelled because a state rather than a federal officer compels it, or because the state officer appears to be primarily interested at the moment in enforcing a state rather than a federal law," and pointed out that the defendant did not question the power of the national court to prosecute him on the mail-fraud charge on other evidence, but only claimed that the Fifth Amendment prevented the testimony elicited by state authorities from being introduced in the federal proceeding. Finally, Black attacked the majority rationale with vigor:

"The Court's holding that a defendant can be so convicted [that is, with the use of state-compelled evidence] cuts into the very substance of the Fifth Amendment, and it justifies this result not by the language or history of the Constitution, but by a process of syllogistic reasoning based upon broad premises of 'dual sovereignty' stated in previous opinions of the court relating to immunity statutes...Constitutional interpretations should involve more than dialectics. The great principles of liberty written in the Bill of Rights cannot be treated as imprisoned in a wall of formal logic built upon vague abstractions found in the United States Reports."[32]

Thus generally the witness who appears before a state governmental body for interrogation finds himself, if anything, in a more vulnerable position than one who is faced with questions from federal officials; the former does not even have the possible shield of an immunity statute to protect him against prosecution at the hands of the other jurisdiction. The only safeguard which operates in his favor is the exception allowed by Justice Frankfurter in *Feldman,* namely, the bar against the introduction in federal proceedings of evidence which has been collected through complicity between national and state officials. However, even this protection is meaningful only in terms of the specific kind of joint activities necessary to bring the proscription into play. This brings us to the issue of collaboration between national and state authorities in compelling testimony from witnesses, leading to the most extreme form of what might be termed the "legal squeeze" on self-incrimination.

III

"Cooperative federalism" (sometimes referred to as the "new" federalism) is the recent term applied to the trend of federal-state relations in which, as William Anderson suggests, the two governments operate more as partners than as rivals.[33] Generally this trend has been hailed as a favorable development, as indeed it is; however, from the viewpoint of a witness subject to interrogation it is not an altogether unmixed blessing and it can lead to serious inroads on individual liberties.

A recent case underscoring the possibilities of collaboration between federal and state law enforcement officials to the detriment of the accused is *Knapp v. Schweitzer.*[34] A witness subpoenaed by a New York State grand jury to answer questions concerning the possible bribery of labor representatives was cited for contempt because he refused to answer inquiries put to him, citing the possible incriminatory effects of his testimony under federal labor-management legislation. In so refusing, the defendant alleged that the United States Attorney for the area made a public announcement of his intention to cooperate with the local District Attorney in the prosecution of criminal cases growing out of the subject matter under investigation.

On appeal the majority of the Supreme Court upheld the contempt citation. Justice Frankfurter, speaking for the majority, reiterated his language in *Feldman* that if a federal officer should be a party to the compulsion of testimony by state agencies the Fifth Amendment would bar its introduction in a federal prosecution. However, he pointed out that the question in this case was a different one, namely whether as a result of such collaboration, a defendant could successfully assert his Fifth Amendment privilege in a state proceeding, and he saw no necessity of deciding this latter issue in the case at hand:

"...The record before us is barren of evidence that the State was used as an instrument of federal prosecution or investigation. Petitioner's assertion that a federal prosecuting attorney announced his intention of cooperating with State officials in the prosecution of cases in a general field of criminal law presents a situation devoid of legal significance as a joint state-federal endeavor."[35]

Chief Justice Warren and Justice Black both dissented. Warren stressed the fact that the New York Court had ordered the witness to answer under the misconception that the alleged cooperation between the federal and state officials would bar the use of the compelled testimony in federal courts. Under the circumstances, the Chief Justice felt that the case should be remanded so that the state court could reconsider the state law in light of the majority's conclusion that the role of the federal prosecutor was not such as to prevent federal use of the state-elicited information. Justice Black concurred with Warren's reasoning and also attacked the majority's reasoning on broader grounds:

"*Feldman* places a witness who is called before a state agency and ordered to testify in a desperate position; he must either remain silent and risk state imprisonment for contempt or confess himself into a federal penitentiary."[36]

The collaboration between federal and state officials alleged in *Knapp* was minor compared to that involved in *Mills v. Louisiana* decided by the Supreme Court last year.[37] Here the parties—the state of Louisiana and the defendants who refused to answer questions of a state grand jury on the ground that their testimony would place them in danger of federal prosecution—stipulated that during the pendency of the state investigation into alleged bribery of New Orleans police officials, the Intelligence Division of the Internal Revenue Service, the United States Attorney concerned, and a federal grand jury were also investigating some members of the police department for income tax evasion. Moreover, it was agreed in the record that there was cooperation and collaboration between state and federal officials, and that conferences had been held between the local District Attorney and the United States Attorney.

Despite this showing of specific cooperative activities, the majority of the Supreme Court affirmed without opinion the contempt conviction entered by the state court, and simply cited the *Knapp* case. Chief Justice Warren dissented again, commenting that "all facts point to the conclusion that the State was used as an instrument of federal investigation." Moreover, he announced his dissatisfaction with the adequacy of the remedy proposed in *Feldman*—the bar to the introduction of such state-elicited evidence in federal courts—and asked instead that the self-incrimination clause of the Fifth Amendment be construed more liberally so as to protect a witness against any federal prosecution that might relate to his state-compelled testimony.

The joint dissent of Justices Black and Douglas also stated that it was the duty of the state court to protect the federal right. However, they laid this duty to the consequences of *Feldman* in permitting the introduction of state-compelled evidence in federal proceedings; if such evidence had been barred there, then the two Justices indicated that they would be willing to leave the protection of the federal right to federal courts. This suggests that Black and Douglas are not willing to grant the witness the complete protection against federal prosecution which Chief Justice Warren advocates.

Collaboration between the national and state governments whereby one jurisdiction compels the testimony which the other uses has not been restricted to *ad hoc* relationships between law enforcement officers alone; Congress has made it a matter of national policy to aid states actively in enforcing their anti-gambling laws. Largely as a result of the Kefauver Committee hearings, a 1951 federal statute taxes certain gambling activities; under this law gamblers by occupation must register, disclosing their names and places of business, as well as similar information about all persons with whom they conduct gambling operations. Moreover, federal tax officials are required to keep for public inspection detailed information on persons paying the gambling taxes and, upon application, must furnish certified copies thereof to prosecuting officers of states, counties or municipalities.[38]

The validity of this statute was upheld two years after its passage in *U. S. v. Kahriger*.[39] The majority of the Supreme Court answered the charge of its incriminating effect by reasoning that registration under the Act is indicative of a possible future intent to gamble, not such an admission of guilt for past acts as is proscribed by the Fifth Amendment. Justice Black dissented, arguing that the statute creates a squeezing device contrived to put a man in prison as a violator of state gambling laws. An unexpected judicial bedfellow, Justice Frankfurter, joined Black in a separate dissenting opinion, objecting not only that the statute makes a specious use of the taxing power to reach activities beyond the authority of the federal government, but also that it is designed for the systematic confession of crimes under state law.

The purpose of the Congress in enacting this tax revenue measure was realized in the circumstances leading up to *Irvine v. California*.[40] Part of the State's case against the defendant for violation of anti-gambling laws was based upon information filed with federal tax officials. In affirming the defendant's conviction by the state, the majority of the Supreme Court saw no constitutional issue at stake; the judges dealt only in statutory interpretation. Since the federal statute specifically says that the payment of the federal tax does not exempt any person from possible penalties or punishments under state law—the gambler's federal license is not a license to violate state law—the Court could see no barrier to California's prosecution of Irvine even though the state officials reaped the benefits of the information exacted by the federal revenue measure.

Justice Black, writing for himself and Justice Douglas, dissented, contending that the Fifth Amendment's guarantee against self-incrimination cannot be "spirited away by the ingenious contrivance of using federally-extorted confessions to convict of state crimes and vice versa." They would interpret the Fifth Amendment so as to prevent state courts from convicting a person of a crime on the basis of testimony compelled by federal officers; they also thought that the Fourteenth Amendment could be construed to accomplish that purpose.

As a practical matter, then, "cooperative federalism" means among other things an arrangement whereby one jurisdiction compels testimony in return for immunity from prosecution, only to see to it that the testimony winds up in the hands of the other jurisdiction which is free to use it against the victim of the squeeze.[41] But lest we lose perspective in thinking too rigidly in terms of legal rights and duties, let it be borne in mind that the compulsion that the Fifth Amendment may or may not bar in the cases so far discussed is only the *legal* sanction of a penalty for refusal to testify; the squeeze may take subtler forms. Suppose, for instance, a felon convicted in a federal court and awaiting sentence is approached with a suggestion that, if he gives information about his accomplices that will enable state authorities to convict them of state crimes, the federal authorities will recommend leniency on the judge in sentencing him. He must weigh a light sentence against the likelihood of private vengeance later, and no Fifth Amendment can save him the choice. Is the squeeze in this sort of "cooperative federalism" any easier for being wholly constitutional? The point in this example is not so much the contribution of a prospective state prosecution to the squeeze—for the source of the duress is private and would exist equally if two federal prosecutions were in view —as it is a reminder that the intensity and hardship of the squeeze, as it is actually felt, depends on more factors than the legal penalties and protections involved.

It is time now to turn from the web of intergovernmental relationships in which witnesses appear to be legally ensnared, to some concluding comments concerning federalism and self-incrimination.

IV

I referred earlier to Anderson's provocative query whether the division of powers between two levels of government means a subtraction of powers from both in favor of the individual, or the contrary. The evidence examined above invites some conclusions on this issue as it applies to the right against self-incrimination. The remainder of this study attempts to draw such conclusions and to consider various tests and means for reconciling the interests of the national and state governments in effective law enforcement with the right of the accused not to be forced to be a witness against himself. Let us start with a summary.

Although some early cases took account of the danger of state prosecution, federal agencies today can legally compel a witness to answer questions even though his testimony will expose him to the danger of criminal action by state authorities; and they may coach the latter. The only present qualification of this rule is that the national officials must be pursuing a genuine national purpose in making their inquiries; they may not compel information from the witness if their primary aim is to aid in investigating violations of state laws.

The national government may, however, pass immunity statutes that grant witnesses more or less protection from state action. Decisions upholding such statutes indicate that the courts are willing to defer to the judgment of the Congress that in some areas, although a witness has no constitutional grounds for refusing to testify, it may be advisable to give him protection against state prosecution in order to obtain truthful testimony from him. But the extent to which the Congress can go in offering such protection has not been fully determined: apparently "partial" immunity can be granted in connection with any investigation in which the national government has a legitimate interest, but to date the Supreme Court has chosen to limit its validation of "complete" immunity to fields in which the national government has a "paramount" interest.

Whatever the legal potentialities of federal immunity statutes, in most instances none is applicable: presently the only complete immunity laws are restricted to matters of national defense and security, and narcotics; and most federal regulatory agencies which benefit from special legislation containing immunity authorizations are concerned more with economic rights of corporations than civil liberties of individuals. Thus the potential use of federally compelled testimony by state courts is virtually unlimited, and generally they have no judicial qualms about accepting this windfall evidence.

The witness before a state agency similarly finds his state-granted right against self-incrimination of little value as protection against federal prosecution. No state immunity statute, whether "partial" or "complete," can bar federal criminal proceedings; such a result would be out of keeping with national supremacy. The witness, therefore, must depend either upon the state agency seeking information, or the federal agency which stands to gain by it, for relief from his predicament. In general, neither has been willing to give up the advantages it gains from present arrangements. It is true that the courts of some states will not compel testimony that will aid a federal prosecution; however, not only are they in the minority, but they usually demand fairly clear evidence—such as a pending indictment—that federal action is actually probable. Moreover, federal courts, like most of their state counterparts, will gladly accept the windfall evidence gathered in the other jurisdiction unless evidence of cooperation between federal and state officers goes so far as to establish that the one set has become merely the agent of the other. One man's complicity is another man's cooperation.

For even this latter qualification—the inadmissibility in federal courts of evidence tainted by collusion between officials of the two jurisdictions— has not served as a real source of protection for the witnesses involved. Recent cases indicate that a majority of the Supreme Court is willing to condone a considerable degree of collaboration between federal and state officers, including joint investigations and conferences. Moreover, the Supreme Court has upheld the registration provision of the federal gambling tax statute, even though it is quite clear that the law is designed to aid states in enforcing their own laws; and the Court has not even found a constitutional issue at stake when it sustained a state conviction obtained largely upon information filed with the federal tax authorities.

Viewing this record as a whole, one must conclude that the concepts of federalism applied by the courts over the years have operated to the detriment of the individual's right against self-incrimination: the existence of two governments has produced rather less than more of this particular freedom. Madison's logical argument that the division of political powers between two distinct governments serves as a security to the liberties of the people has accordingly not proved to be true for this civil right. Madison's premise was that the two governments will control each other. The litigation of self-incrimination cases indicates, on the contrary, that the national and state governments not only fail to control each other, but that in some instances they collaborate at the expense of the witness.

Significantly, it is by a similar resort to abstract logical principles of federalism that judicial rulings operating to limit the right against self-incrimination have been justified. One such principle is the historical argument utilized by Justice Frankfurter —that the Fifth Amendment applies only to the federal government and not to the states. On that principle compulsion of testimony by state tribunals for use in federal courts does not violate the witness' federal right. But when both governments are committed in their constitutions to outlaw self-incrimination, such a rationale seems essentially unsound. To read the Fifth Amendment, as Justice Frankfurter does, to forbid the national government to compel testimony itself, but to allow it to make good use of that elicited by state officials, is to give the clause an unduly restrictive interpretation. The Fifth Amendment was designed to protect the individual against arbitrary treatment at the hands of the national government; it should be broadly construed to serve that purpose. Justice Black's comment that testimony used in a federal court against an individual is no less compelled because a state rather than a federal government officer compels it, hits the judicial issue with a bullseye shot.

The two-sovereignties theory borrowed from English decisions is also patently unsuitable for dealing with the issues of federalism and self-incrimination. J. A. C. Grant, after a careful examination of pertinent English and Empire cases, concludes that as applied to the issue of self-incrimination, it is erroneous to view these cases as standing for the idea that at common law one sovereign had no interest in the law enforcement activities of another sovereign. Moreover, he reasons that even if this were not so the analogy is a poor one, since a defendant violating the laws of two countries would only place himself in danger by leaving one land voluntarily and going to another, whereas a defendant in the United States is simultaneously subject to the two jurisdictions.[42]

Both the historical and two-sovereignties theories posit an abstract concept of two entities going their separate ways in enforcing laws, each with little concern for what the other does. Such a conceptual scheme, however, flies in the face of present reality; as a practical matter the broadening scope of federal activities means that, to an ever-increasing extent, both the national and state governments are policing and regulating the same activities as well as the same people. A witness' testimony before one government is often likely to be of great aid to enforcement officials of the other. The process whereby the governmental right hand takes a positive interest in what the governmental left hand is doing makes a mockery of the separate sovereignties model. If cooperation in law enforcement is desirable—as it is—then cooperation in observance of the right it endangers is equally needed.

For no amount of logic or verbal skill can erase the obvious fact that the interests of the national and state governments in effective law enforcement are opposed to the individual's right against self-incrimination. If the opportunities of both these governments, either to compel testimony, or to benefit from that elicited by the other, are maximized, the result inevitably redounds to the detriment of the witness concerned. Resolving the problem of federalism and self-incrimination therefore means weighing conflicting interests and seeking an appropriate balance of values in our constitutional system.

In the present disagreement between the majority of the Court, represented by Justice Frankfurter, and the minority, of which Black is the major spokesman, this conflict of values has sharply emerged. The most succinct statement of Frankfurter's position was enunciated in *Knapp:*

"If a person may, through immunized self-disclosure before a law enforcing agency of the State, facilitate to some extent his amenability to federal process or vice versa, this is a price to be paid for our federalism. Against it must be put what would be a greater price, that of sterilizing the powers of both governments by not recognizing the autonomy of each within its proper sphere."[43]

Over against this attitude stands Black's, expressed most cogently in the dissent to that same decision:

..."Things have now reached the point where a person can be whipsawed into incriminating himself under both state and federal law even though there is a privilege against self-incrimination in the constitution of each...I cannot agree that we must accept this intolerable state of affairs as part of our federal system of government."[44]

As a matter of public policy, the law enforcement powers of neither government should be sterilized, as Justice Frankfurter fears; nor should the witness be whipsawed into incriminating himself under both state and federal law as Justice Black decries. If it is possible to work out such an accommodation what kinds of judicial tests and rulings offer most promise for serving this purpose?

It is submitted here that the practice of collaborative investigations and prosecutions by national and state officials is not a price we have to pay for our federal system, if it means compelling a witness to testify in exchange for immunity and then seeing to it that this testimony is made available to another jurisdiction. Denying these governments the fruits of such an admittedly expeditious arrangement cannot fairly be said to sterilize their enforcement powers.

An alternative approach is to let the issue of compelling evidence turn on whether or not the testimony is likely to expose the witness to danger of prosecution by the other jurisdiction. This test was utilized at one time by some federal courts, and several states have followed the leadership of the Michigan Supreme Court in applying it to state investigations. At first blush it is a solution that appears to have merit, but there is some question as to how well it would actually serve to protect the witness involved. The jurisdiction engaged in the interrogating may have little or no knowledge of the probability of prosecution by another government. Moreover, it has a vested interest in seeking information and hence, regardless of the circumstances, may be tempted to find no danger to the witness so that testimony can be compelled. For these reasons, this judicial test seems inadequate.

From the defendant's point of view, of course, the most favorable approach would be to grant the witness who is compelled to testify complete immunity from prosecution by any level of government. This must be rejected, however, for it would interfere seriously with the enforcement activities of the government that did not have the fortune to be first in gaining jurisdiction over the witness: conceivably this government might have the more serious charge to bring against him. A case in point is *Feldman,* in which the New York creditors' proceeding was a civil action, whereas the federal case against the witness was criminal. Such a rule would open the door to the danger of "immunity baths," whereby witnesses could confess their venial sins to one jurisdiction and so save their cardinal offenses from prosecution in another.

Perhaps the most satisfactory solution is a compromise, namely, to say that testimony compelled by one jurisdiction should not be admissible as evidence in the courts of another, but that the second sovereignty should not be barred from prosecuting the witness on other evidence for matters related to those about which he was previously interrogated. This approach would certainly offer the witness more protection than the present rule affords, although it would still enable one jurisdiction to secure leads which another could follow in developing the other evidence. This risk seems preferable to that of foreclosing any action against the witness by the second jurisdiction, as a grant of complete immunity would do.

This suggestion can most conveniently be implemented through a Supreme Court ruling broadening the interpretation of constitutional safeguards to prohibit the use of a nationally coerced confession in state courts; and following Justice Black's suggestion, either the Fifth or the Fourteenth Amendment could serve as the vehicle to accomplish this purpose. Such a ruling would obviate the necessity of depending upon state courts not to use such testimony: to date, only the courts of Michigan and Florida have been able to resist the lure of windfall evidence. In addition, *Feldman* should be overruled so as to construe the Fifth Amendment to forbid all federal courts from using confessions elicited by state courts. Such an interpretation should work little hardship on federal authorities since the same result was obtained by means of Congressional legislation in effect from 1868 until 1910.

At the same time, and for the reasons already suggested, the Fifth Amendment should not be interpreted to grant the witness complete immunity against prosecution by another level of government than the one which is interrogating him. However, if the Congress determines that in particular fields such a result is needed in order to secure reliable testimony, and passes laws, restricted in coverage to those fields, which specifically provide for complete immunity, the Supreme Court should continue to validate them. But it should be necessary to make a showing of paramount national interest in the areas so marked out, because of the rather serious consequences such statutes might have on state law enforcement operations. The "paramount interest" test is sufficiently broad to give the courts some leeway in judgment, where "partial" immunity is the normal rule.

In *The Federalist,* No. 51, Madison stated succinctly the general problem, of which we have been considering a special case: "In forming a government which is to be administered by men over men, the great difficulty lies in this: you must first enable the government to control the governed and in the next place oblige it to control itself." The course of action I have urged is designed to help meet this eternal dilemma as it applies to the issue of federalism and self-incrimination. It aims to enable us to slip between Frankfurter's horn of sterilizing the powers of the national and state governments, and Black's, of whipsawing an unfortunate witness into incriminating himself under the laws of each.

Editor's note: In *Murphy* v. *Waterfront Commission* [378 U.S. 52 (1964)], the Supreme Court rejected the earlier decisions in *United States* v. *Murdock, Knapp* v. *Schweitzer,* and *Feldman* v. *United States.* The Court held that a witness can refuse to answer questions put by the state, the answers to which would incriminate him under federal law, and that if the state compelled testimony under an immunity act, the testimony and its fruits would be inadmissible in federal courts. Also implied in the Court's decision was that a witness could invoke the self-incrimination privilege before a federal tribunal when asked about matters that would incriminate him under state law.

Footnotes

[1]*The Federalist,* No. 51.
[2]William Anderson, *Federalism and Intergovernmental Relations* (Chicago: Public Administration Service, 1946), p. 33.
[3]Franz L. Neumann, "Federalism and Freedom: A Critique," in A. W. Macmahon (ed.), *Federalism Mature and Emergent* (Garden City, N.Y., 1955), p. 47.
[4]*Ibid.,* p. 48. His argument ran counter to the tenor of other essays in the symposium.
[5]McNabb v. United States, 318 U.S. 332, 347 (1943).
[6]The leading cases are United States v. Saline Bank of Virginia, 1 Pet. (U.S.) 100 (1828) and Ballmann v. Fagin, 200 U.S. 186 (1905). For an excellent historical analysis see J. A. C. Grant, "Federalism and Self-Incrimination," U.C.L.A. LAW REV., Vol. 4 (June, 1957), pp. 550 ff.
[7]The American decisions taking this viewpoint include Brown v. Walker, 161 U.S. 591 (1896) and Hale v. Henkel, 201 U.S. 43 (1905). The English decisions most often cited are King of the Two Sicilies v. Willcox, 61 Eng. Rep. 116 (1851) and Crown v. Boyes, 121 Eng. Rep. 730 (1861). Actually the latter decision did not even involve a second sovereignty: the issue in the case was whether the testimony of a witness implicated in alleged vote-buying in a Parliamentary election could legally be compelled to answer when a Crown Pardon could not protect him against the highly remote possibility of an impeachment action by the House of Commons. Yet once the case was incorrectly cited, it continued to be considered as authority for the two sovereignties rule. See *infra,* note 42, for a further criticism of the use of English and Empire cases as precedents for the self-incrimination issue faced by American courts.
[8]284 U.S. 141.
[9]102 Fed. Supp. 597 (N.D. Ohio, 1952). Two companion cases, United States v. Licavoli and United States v. Aiuppa, *ibid.,* 607 and 609, also applied the same reasoning to similar fact situations.
[10]The Committee was investigating local crime conditions in order to determine whether the facilities of interstate commerce were being used to aid local violations.
[11]The usual wording is that "no witness shall be prosecuted or be subjected to any penalty or forfeiture on account of any transaction, matter or thing concerning which he is so compelled." See 18 *U.S.C.* (1958) sec. 3486 for a recent example. The first immunity statute was passed in 1857, 11 *U.S. Stat.* 155. For an excellent summary of their evolution see H. Rept. No. 2606 on S. 16, in *U.S. Code Congressional and Administrative News,* 83d Cong., 2d sess., 1954, pt. 2, pp. 3062 ff.
[12]142 U.S. 547 (1892). The Supreme Court there ruled that a witness need not testify even though he is offered the protection of a "partial" immunity statute because the compelled information, while not itself admissible as evidence against him, may be utilized to gain other incriminating facts. The Court reasoned that in such a situation a "partial" immunity is not an adequate substitute for the constitutional privilege. In a subsequent decision, Brown v. Walker, cited *supra,* the Court upheld the testimony-compelling features of a "complete" immunity statute on the ground that the protection it affords the witness is coextensive with his constitutional right.
[13]In the course of legislative investigations into subversive and treasonous activities which endanger national security and defense, Congress, or any of its committees, may petition the United States District Court for an order compelling the witness to answer; the United States District Attorney is given similar authority in judicial inquiries into these matters before both grand and petit juries. 18 *U.S.C.* (1958), sec. 3486. A similar statute applies to judicial proceedings pertaining to narcotics violations. 18 *U.S.C.* (1958), sec. 1406. The authority of certain regulatory agencies —the ICC, FPC, etc.—to compel testimony by the use of "complete" immunity statutes has been granted on a statute-by-statute basis. For a list of such statutes see Shapiro v. United States, 335 U.S. 1, 6, n. 4 (1948).
[14]Brown v. Walker, cited *supra.* However, the language on this point must be considered as *dictum* only since there was nothing in the facts surrounding that case to indicate that any real question of state prosecution was present, and the Court indicated that it considered the danger of any such future prosecution as exceedingly remote. Moreover, the Court also seemed to adopt the position that in any event such an eventuality was irrelevant under the "separate sovereignties" rationale. See note 7 *supra.*
[15]347 U.S. 179 (1954).
[16]12 *Stat.* 333 (1862). This statute was repealed in 1954 when the present complete immunity law dealing with testimony affecting the national security and defense was enacted. See note 13, *supra.*
[17]350 U.S. 422 (1956).
[18]In Tedesco v. United States, 255 F. (2d) 35 (6th Cir., 1958), a federal Circuit Court sidestepped the issue by holding that the portion of the federal narcotics statute which purported to give this "complete" protection from state prosecution was separable from its remaining provisions, and only the latter had to be validated in order to deal with the essential questions

raised by the case. However, the Court expressed its doubts that this power exists in a field, such as narcotics, of concurrent governmental powers.

[19]68 Fla. 433, 67 So. 135 (1914).

[20]193 Mich. 17, 1959 N.W. 299 (1916). Both courts interpreted provisions of the national bankruptcy act stipulating that elicited testimony could not be used in "any criminal proceeding" as applying to state, as well as federal courts. But the Florida Court also held that the use of such evidence would violate provisions of the State Constitution pertaining to self-incrimination.

[21]75 So. (2d) 211 (Sup. Ct. Fla., 1954).

[22]See *infra*, p. 896 ff, for a further discussion on this matter.

[23]211 U.S. 78 (1908). This doctrine was affirmed more recently in Adamson v. California, 332 U.S. 46 (1947).

[24]See John Wigmore, *A Treatise on the Anglo-American System of Evidence in Trials at Common Law* (3d ed., Boston, 1945), VIII, sec. 2252, for a list of the pertinent constitutional provisions and cases.

[25]For a list of these immunity statutes, see Wigmore, *ibid.*, sec. 2281.

[26]199 U.S. 372 (1905). The Court emphasized the remoteness of the danger of federal prosecution; however, it also indicated that the legal immunity granted the witness need only apply to a prosecution in the same jurisdiction. *Ibid.*, p. 382.

[27]For examples of recent decisions taking this line see Cabot v. Corcoran, 332 Mass. 44, 123 N.E.(2d) 221 (1954); State v. Arnold, 124 N.E.(2d) 473 (Sup. Ct. Ohio, 1954), and Wyman v. DeGregory 101 N.H. 171, 137 At(2d) 512 (1957).

[28]318 Mich. 645, 29 N.W.(2d) 284 (1947). Actually the test had been formulated in earlier decisions, but did not apply to the defendants concerned. See In re Watson, 293 Mich. 263, 291 N.W. 562 (1940); In re Schnitzer, 295 Mich. 736, 295 N.W. 478 (1940); In re Ward, 295 Mich. 742, 295 N.W. 483 (1940); and In re Cohen, 295 Mich. 748, 295 N.W. 481 (1940).

[29]Louisiana v. Dominguez, 228 La. 284, 82 So.(2d) 12 (1955); Kentucky v. Rhine, 303 So.(2d) 301 (Sup. Ct., Ky., 1957); State v. Kelly, 71 So. (2d) 887 (Sup. Ct., Fla., 1954); and Lorenzo v. Blackburn, 74 So.

(2d) 289 (Sup. Ct., Fla., 1954). The rule was cited in the latter two decisions, even though the Court could find no likelihood of the witness' testimony aiding federal prosecution.

[30]Case Comment, *U. of Pa. L. Rev.*, Vol. 96 (Feb. 1948), 416.

[31]322 U.S. 487 (1944). A law passed in 1868 made information compelled by both national and state officials inadmissible in federal courts. See 15 *Stat.* 37 (1868), *Rev. Stat.* (1875) sec. 860. However, the statute was repealed in 1910, 36 *Stat.* 352 (1910).

[32]*Ibid.*, pp. 498 ff.

[33]See William Anderson, *The Nation and The States, Rivals or Partners?* (Minneapolis: The University of Minnesota Press, 1955); Jane Perry Clark; *The Rise of a New Federalism* (New York: Columbia University Press, 1938).

[34]357 U.S. 371 (1958).

[35]*Ibid.*, p. 380.

[36]*Ibid.*, p. 384.

[37]360 U.S. 230 (1959).

[38]26 *U.S.C.* (1958) secs. 4401–4422. Two separate taxes are involved: one (sec. 4401) is a 10 per cent tax on the amount of wagers placed with the gambling operator; the other (sec. 4411) is an occupational tax of fifty dollars for the privilege of engaging in the business of wagering. Sec. 4412 prescribes the registration requirements; sec. 6107, *ibid.*, covers public inspection and certification.

[39]345 U.S. 22 (1953).

[40]347 U.S. 128 (1954).

[41]It will be recalled, however, that the Florida Supreme Court in Boynton v. State refused to uphold the results of a forfeiture proceeding, pertaining to gambling operations, based at least in part upon information filed with federal tax authorities. See note 21 above.

[42]J. A. C. Grant, *op. cit.* note 6 above, Vol. 5 (January, 1958), 23 f. Professor Grant also points out that in some circumstances a person fleeing the jurisdiction of a state can be brought back by federal officials under the provisions of the Fugitive Felon Act, 18 *U.S.C.* (1958) sec. 1073.

[43]Cited *supra* note 34, pp. 380 f.

[44]*Ibid.*, p. 385.

Further Research

Obviously the principal problem confronting the student of the Supreme Court and civil rights is keeping up to date. Many of the areas of law with which this book is concerned are developing rapidly. One way of keeping abreast is to read the Supreme Court opinions themselves as they appear in *United States Reports, The Supreme Court Reporter*, or the *Lawyers Edition of the Supreme Court Reporter*, one of which should be available in nearly any library. Most of the references in this book are to the official publication, *United States Reports* (*U.S.*), but the two commercially published reporters have extensive headnotes, annotations and digests that often make them more useful than *United States Reports*. Each year the November issue of the *Harvard Law Review* contains an excellent survey of the previous term's Supreme Court cases. This survey is the quickest and easiest method of following the Court's progress and provides the leads necessary for further investigation of any given problem. *The Supreme Court Review*, from which several of the pieces in this book are taken, also provides a kind of annual running commentary on the work of the Court.

The nation's lawyers are constantly trying to keep one another informed and up to date on all legal problems through the very large number of law reviews. All this material is indexed in the *Index to Legal Periodicals*, which operates much like the *Readers Guide to Periodical Literature*. If the student should want extra background or commentary on any given case, the *Index* not only lists articles by subject and author but contains a special section which lists many of the commentaries on a given case under the name of the case. There is now also an *Index to Periodical Articles Related to Law*, which will lead the student to legal discussions in scholarly publications other than law reviews.

Often the student will wish to trace the history of a given case. Has it been overruled? Has it subsequently been cited or used as the basis for later decisions? *Sheppard's Citations* will provide this information through an elaborate system of listing citations, which is explained in the front of each volume.

Particularly in the area of the rights of the accused, lower federal court and state court opinions may be just as important as—and even more important than—those of the Supreme Court. If a law library is available, the reader will find not only the opinions of these courts, which run to hundreds of volumes, but various systems of digests which pull together summaries of all the cases on a given topic so that he need not hunt through many volumes. The *Federal Digest* and the *Modern Federal Practice Digest* do this for the federal courts, and the *Decennial Digest*, together with its annual supplements, does it for all important American courts.

In a book of this sort, many problems are touched on only briefly or not at all. For instance, little is said of freedom of association, particularly the right of anonymity—that is, the right not to have your membership in any given group publicized. Either a standard text like C. Herman Pritchett, *The American Constitution* (1958), or the two-volume casebook by Thomas I. Emerson and David Haber, *Political and Civil Rights in the United States* (3rd ed., 1967) will provide a checklist of all the civil rights problems confronting the Court. William

Lockhart, Yale Kamisar, and Jesse H. Choper, *Constitutional Law: Cases, Comments and Questions* (1964), is also extremely useful. In general there is nothing very esoteric about research on civil rights. It requires careful reading of the arguments of others and the opinions of the courts, followed by an attempt to construct a coherent position of one's own. Perhaps the most important thing is to occasionally pull oneself out of the welter of competing doctrines and formulae and ask: What is the real-life problem involved, what is the best solution for it, and should the Supreme Court or someone else provide that solution? These questions sometimes tend to get lost in the welter of deductive reasoning and verbal manipulation that is an inevitable part of legal discussion.

As was noted in the preface, this book is largely devoted to substantive questions of civil rights. In recent years there has been a growing concern with developing alternative methods to traditional case analysis for studying the Supreme Court and particularly with fitting the courts into the general context of the American political process rather than treating them as an entirely separate, legal institution. The early efforts in this direction are summarized, from somewhat differing points of view, in Glendon Schubert, "Bibliographical Essay Behavioral Research in Public Law," 57 *American Political Science Review* 433 (1963), and Martin Shapiro, "Political Jurisprudence," 52 *Kentucky Law Journal* 294 (1964). Several good collections of materials seeking to give a better picture of the courts in politics are available. Among these are Walter Murphy and C. Herman Pritchett, ed., *Courts, Judges and Politics* (1961); Carl Auerbach, Charles Garrison, Willard Hurst, and Samuel Mermin, *The Legal Process* (1961); Glendon Schubert, ed., *Judicial Behavior* (1964); and John R. Schmidhauser, ed., *Constitutional Law in the Political Process* (1963). Two works that remain in the traditional constitutional law channels but develop strong viewpoints on the political role of the Court are Charles Black, *The People and the Court* (1960), and Alexander Bickel, *The Least Dangerous Branch* (1962).

While the study of the Supreme Court's constitutional, civil rights business is of great intrinsic interest and its decisions in this area sometimes have tremendous political impact, this author personally believes that any attempt to understand the basic nature and functions of the Supreme Court by exclusive attention to constitutional law and civil rights is rather like the old story of the blind man trying to describe the elephant by feeling its trunk. [See Martin Shapiro, *Law and Politics in the Supreme Court* (1964)]. While the Court in recent years has exerted enormous influence over the states, in its relations with other agencies of the national government, it is rarely the giant champion of civil rights waving the club of judicial review that one is likely to picture after long preoccupation with freedom of speech and due process of law. As far as national politics go, the Court is largely concerned not with constitutional review but with statutory interpretation. When the Taft-Hartley Act says that an employer must bargain "in good faith," does that mean that he must show his books to the union? If a retiring minister gets a Cadillac from his congregation, is that a gift or income under the language of the Internal Revenue Code? It is in this kind of decision that the Court picks out its daily relationships with the half a hundred other agencies in Washington which also deal in making, changing, and administering laws. To understand the role of the Supreme Court in American national politics, it would be necessary to understand all these nonconstitutional problems as well as the great issues of *Baker* v. *Carr* or *Brown* v. *Board*. These problems are not easy to understand because there are few great cases on which to focus. The Court makes policy in the tax or labor field not by ringing opinions in leading cases but often by a number of "little" decisions whose overall pattern shapes the development of law.

For those readers who are primarily concerned with civil rights or constitutional law, the footnotes in this book and the great stream of new materials constantly appearing in the law reviews will provide huge amounts of material for future study and reflection. For those whose central concern is the Supreme Court, it will be necessary to go far beyond such materials and follow the Court down the winding paths of patent law and utilities regulation, antitrust and income tax. This is not an easy task, because most past students of the Court have themselves stuck pretty much to constitutional law. Yet it will be the business of the next generation of scholars to look at the whole of the Supreme Court and not just at its constitutional trunk. In the meantime, we are lucky to have a body of materials of the highest scholarly quality on one aspect of the Court's work, civil rights, and for the moment that must remain the jumping-off point for most work on the Supreme Court.

Today the Court is undoubtedly more active than ever before in the civil rights area, and far more active than many observers of the 1940's and 1950's ever expected. Each term seems to bring important new decisions on some of the most controversial issues of American life, from school prayers to miscegenation. The Supreme Court is far from being coequal with Congress or the President, but it is an important agency of the national government that is continuing to make important policy decisions, particularly in relation to the states. Moreover, the decisions it reaches on civil rights tend to strike at many of the basic moral and political questions of American society. In the final analysis, therefore, the study of the Supreme Court and civil rights becomes the study of many of the crucial issues of public policy and political procedures facing the American people.

1 2 3 4 5 6 7 8 9 10 11 12 13 14 15 16 17 18 19 20 21 22 23 24 25 SH 74 73 72 71 70 69 68 67